MIKE JANES/FOUR SEAM IMAGES

TRIPLE-A

Affiliation Relocation: New Orleans (Marlins) moves to Wichita, renames as Wind Surge.

DOUBLE-A

Affiliation Relocation: Mobile (Angels) moves to Madison, Ala. and renames as Rocket City Trash Pandas

HIGH CLASS A

Affiliation Relocation: Potomac (Nationals) moves to Fredericksburg, Va.
Affiliate Rename: Fort Myers (Twins) changes from Miracle to Mighty Mussels

LOW CLASS A

Affiliate Rename: Kannapolis (White Sox) changes from Intimidators to Cannon Ballers

SHORT-SEASON

Affiliate Rename: Connecticut (Tigers) changes from Tigers to Sea Unicorns

ROOKIE

Affiliate Rename: Missoula (D-backs) changes from Osprey to Paddleheads

INDEPENDENT

League Merger: Canadian-American merges with Frontier League. New Jersey, Quebec, Sussex, Trois-Rivieres, Rockland move from Can-Am to Frontier; Rockland changes name to New York Boulders.
Team Deletions: New Britain Bees (Atlantic), Ottawa (Can-Am), River City (Frontier), California City (Pecos), High Desert (Pecos) fold.
Team Additions: Martinez Mackerel, Pittsburg Anchors join Pecos League.

Map illustrations by Paul Trap

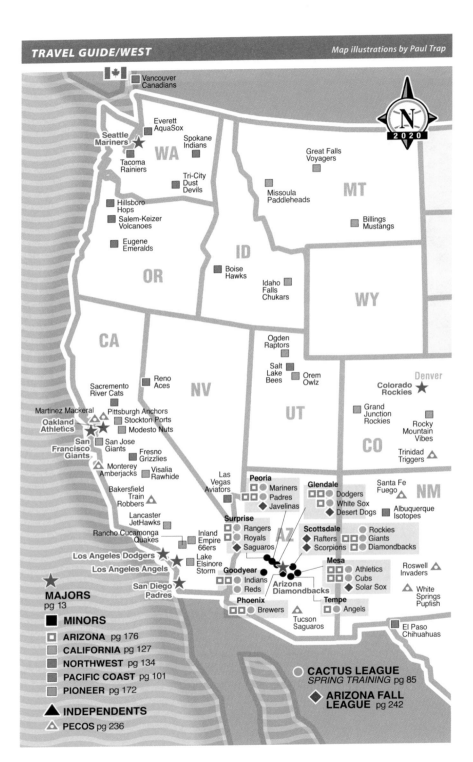

Vancouver Canadians

Everett AquaSox

Spokane Indians

Seattle Mariners

Tacoma Rainiers

WA

Great Falls Voyagers

Tri-City Dust Devils

Missoula Paddleheads

MT

Hillsboro Hops

Salem-Keizer Volcanoes

Billings Mustangs

Eugene Emeralds

Boise Hawks

ID

Idaho Falls Chukars

OR

WY

Ogden Raptors

CA

Salt Lake Bees

Orem Owlz

Denver

Colorado Rockies

Reno Aces

Sacramento River Cats

NV

UT

Grand Junction Rockies

Rocky Mountain Vibes

Martinez Mackeral

Pittsburgh Anchors

Stockton Ports

Oakland Athletics

Modesto Nuts

CO

San Jose Giants

San Francisco Giants

Fresno Grizzlies

Trinidad Triggers

Monterey Amberjacks

Visalia Rawhide

Las Vegas Aviators

Santa Fe Fuego

NM

Bakersfield Train Robbers

Peoria
- Mariners
- Padres
- ◆ Javelinas

Glendale
- Dodgers
- White Sox
- ◆ Desert Dogs

Albuquerque Isotopes

Lancaster JetHawks

Rancho Cucamonga Quakes

Inland Empire 66ers

Surprise
- Rangers
- Royals
- ◆ Saguaros

AZ

Scottsdale
- Rockies
- ◆ Rafters
- Giants
- Scorpions
- Diamondbacks

Los Angeles Dodgers

Los Angeles Angels

Lake Elsinore Storm

Goodyear
- Indians
- Reds

Arizona Diamondbacks

Mesa
- Athletics
- Cubs
- ◆ Solar Sox

Roswell Invaders

San Diego Padres

Phoenix
- Brewers

Tempe
- Angels

White Springs Pupfish

Tucson Saguaros

El Paso Chihuahuas

MAJORS
pg 13

■ **MINORS**

□ **ARIZONA** pg 176

■ **CALIFORNIA** pg 127

■ **NORTHWEST** pg 134

■ **PACIFIC COAST** pg 101

■ **PIONEER** pg 172

▲ **INDEPENDENTS**

△ **PECOS** pg 236

○ **CACTUS LEAGUE**
SPRING TRAINING pg 85

◆ **ARIZONA FALL LEAGUE** pg 242

Baseball America
DIRECTORY

American	National

Baseball America
DIRECTORY

Editors
Josh Norris, Chris Hilburn-Trenkle

Assistant Editors
Justin Coleman, Carlos Collazo,
J.J. Cooper, Teddy Cahill,
Kyle Glaser, Ben Badler

Contributing
Paul Trap

**Database & Application
Development**
Brent Lewis

Photo Editor
Brendan Nolan

Design & Production
James Alworth,
Leah Tyner

**Programming & Technical
Development**
Brent Lewis

Cover Photo
Dilip Vishwanat/Getty Images

Baseball America

EDITOR AND PUBLISHER B.J. Schecter @bjschecter
EXECUTIVE EDITORS J.J. Cooper @jjcoop36, Matt Eddy @MattEddyBA
CHIEF REVENUE OFFICER Don Hintze
DIRECTOR OF BUSINESS DEVELOPMENT Ben Leigh
DIRECTOR OF DIGITAL STRATEGY Mike Salerno

EDITORIAL
ASSOCIATE EDITORS Justin Coleman, Josh Norris @jnorris427
SENIOR WRITER Ben Badler @benbadler
NATIONAL WRITERS Teddy Cahill @tedcahill, Carlos Collazo @CarlosACollazo, Kyle Glaser @KyleAGlaser
COLLEGE BASEBALL ANALYST Dave Serrano @DaveSerrano11
DIRECTOR EDITORIAL PRODUCTION/AUDIENCE DEVELOPMENT Mark Chiarelli @Mark_Chiarelli
SPECIAL CONTRIBUTOR Tim Newcomb @tdnewcomb, Joe Healy @joe_on_sports

PRODUCTION
CREATIVE DIRECTOR James Alworth
GRAPHIC DESIGNER Leah Tyner

BUSINESS
TECHNOLOGY MANAGER Brent Lewis
ACCOUNT EXECUTIVE Kellen Coleman
MARKETING/OPERATIONS COORDINATOR Angela Lewis
CUSTOMER SERVICE Melissa Sunderman

STATISTICAL SERVICE
Major League Baseball Advanced Media

Alliance
>>> BASEBALL <<<

BASEBALL AMERICA ENTERPRISES
CHAIRMAN & CEO Gary Green
PRESIDENT Larry Botel
GENERAL COUNSEL Matthew Pace
DIRECTOR OF MARKETING Amy Heart
INVESTOR RELATIONS Michele Balfour
DIRECTOR OF OPERATIONS Joan Disalvo
PARTNERS Jon Ashley, Stephen Alepa, Martie Cordaro, Brian
Rothschild, Andrew Fox, Maurice Haroche, Dan Waldman, Sonny Kalsi,
Glenn Isaacson, Robert Hernreich, Craig Amazeen, Peter Ruprecht, Beryl
Snyder, Tom Steiglehner

3 STEP

MANAGING PARTNER David Geaslen
CHIEF CONTENT OFFICER Jonathan Segal
CHIEF FINANCIAL OFFICER Sue Murphy

TABLE OF CONTENTS

JAY ZYNISM VIA GETTY IMAGES

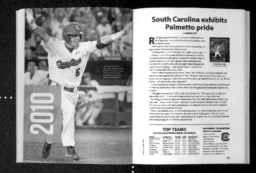
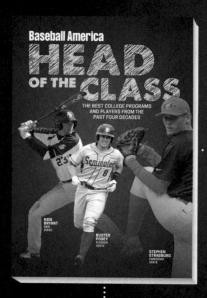

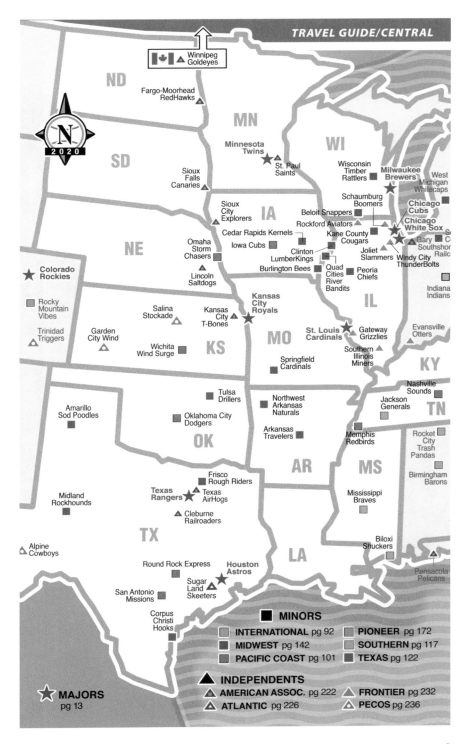

Winnipeg Goldeyes

Fargo-Moorhead RedHawks

ND

N 2020

SD

MN

WI

Minnesota Twins

St. Paul Saints

Wisconsin Timber Rattlers

Milwaukee Brewers

West Michigan Whitecaps

Sioux Falls Canaries

Schaumburg Boomers

Chicago Cubs

Sioux City Explorers

Beloit Snappers

Rockford Aviators

Chicago White Sox

IA

Cedar Rapids Kernels

Kane County Cougars

Gary

S

Southshor

Omaha Storm Chasers

Iowa Cubs

Clinton LumberKings

Joliet Slammers

Windy City ThunderBolts

Railc

NE

Burlington Bees

Quad Cities River Bandits

Peoria Chiefs

Colorado Rockies

Lincoln Saltdogs

Kansas City Royals

IL

Indiana Indians

Rocky Mountain Vibes

Salina Stockade

Kansas City T-Bones

St. Louis Cardinals

Gateway Grizzlies

Evansville Otters

Trinidad Triggers

Garden City Wind

Wichita Wind Surge

KS

MO

Southern Illinois Miners

KY

Springfield Cardinals

Nashville Sounds

Amarillo Sod Poodles

Tulsa Drillers

Northwest Arkansas Naturals

Jackson Generals

TN

Oklahoma City Dodgers

Arkansas Travelers

Memphis Redbirds

Rocket City Trash Pandas

OK

AR

MS

Midland Rockhounds

Frisco Rough Riders

Texas Rangers

Texas AirHogs

Mississippi Braves

Birmingham Barons

Cleburne Railroaders

TX

Biloxi Shuckers

Alpine Cowboys

LA

Pensacola Pelicans

Round Rock Express

Houston Astros

San Antonio Missions

Sugar Land Skeeters

Corpus Christi Hooks

■ MINORS

■ INTERNATIONAL pg 92   ■ PIONEER pg 172

■ MIDWEST pg 142   ■ SOUTHERN pg 117

■ PACIFIC COAST pg 101   ■ TEXAS pg 122

▲ INDEPENDENTS

☆ MAJORS
pg 13

△ AMERICAN ASSOC. pg 222   △ FRONTIER pg 232

△ ATLANTIC pg 226   △ PECOS pg 236

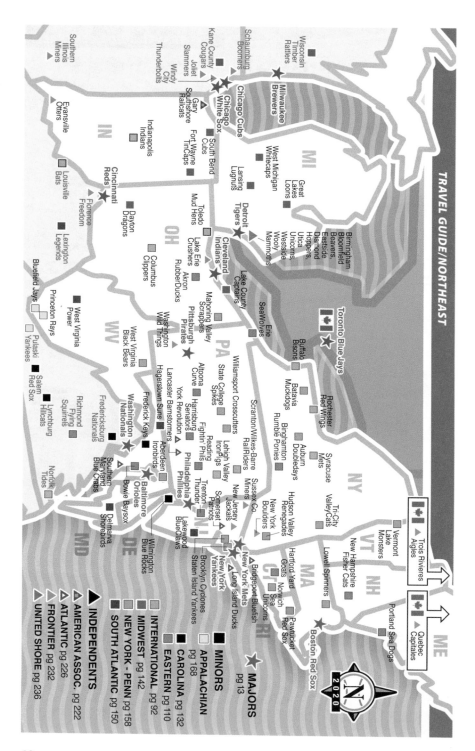

Southern Illinois Miners
Wisconsin Timber Rattlers
Schaumburg Boomers
Kane County Cougars
Joliet Slammers
Windy City Thunderbolts
Gary SouthShore Railcats
Chicago White Sox
Chicago Cubs
Milwaukee Brewers
Evansville Otters
Indianapolis Indians
South Bend Cubs
Fort Wayne TinCaps
West Michigan Whitecaps
Great Lakes Loons
Lansing Lugnuts
Detroit Tigers
MI
Louisville Bats
Cincinnati Reds
Florence Freedom
Dayton Dragons
Toledo Mud Hens
Lake Erie Crushers
Akron RubberDucks
Cleveland Indians
Lake County Captains
OH
Lexington Legends
Bluefield Jays
Princeton Rays
West Virginia Power
Columbus Clippers
Mahoning Valley Scrappers
Erie SeaWolves
Buffalo Bisons
Birmingham Bloomfield Beavers, Diamond Hoppers, Utica Unicorns, Eastside Westside Wooly Mammoths
IN
Pulaski Yankees
Salem Red Sox
Richmond Flying Squirrels
Fredericksburg Nationals
West Virginia Black Bears
Washington Wild Things
Pittsburgh Pirates
Altoona Curve
Williamsport Crosscutters
State College Spikes
Scranton/Wilkes-Barre RailRiders
Batavia Muckdogs
Rochester Red Wings
Toronto Blue Jays
WV
Lynchburg Hillcats
Norfolk Tides
Southern Maryland Blue Crabs
Delmarva Shorebirds
Baltimore Orioles
Washington Nationals
Frederick Keys
Hagerstown Suns
Lancaster Barnstormers
York Revolution
Harrisburg Senators
Reading Fightin' Phils
Lehigh Valley IronPigs
PA
Auburn Doubledays
Syracuse Mets
Binghamton Rumble Ponies
New Jersey Jackals
Sussex Co. Miners
Hudson Valley Renegades
Tri-City ValleyCats
NY
Bowie Baysox
Wilmington Blue Rocks
Aberdeen Ironbirds
Philadelphia Phillies
Trenton Thunder
Lakewood BlueClaws
Somerset Patriots
New York Yankees
New York Mets
Long Island Ducks
Brooklyn Cyclones
Staten Island Yankees
Bridgeport Bluefish
Norwich Sea Unicorns
Hartford Yard Goats
Pawtucket Red Sox
New Hampshire Fisher Cats
Lowell Spinners
Vermont Lake Monsters
Portland Sea Dogs
Boston Red Sox
MD
DE
NJ
CT
RI
MA
VT
NH
ME

Trois Rivières Aigles
Quebec Capitales

INDEPENDENTS
▲ AMERICAN ASSOC. pg 226
△ ATLANTIC pg 222
▷ FRONTIER pg 232
◁ UNITED SHORE pg 236

MINORS
◼ INTERNATIONAL pg 142
◻ MIDWEST pg 142
▢ NEW YORK - PENN pg 158
◼ SOUTH ATLANTIC pg 150
▢ EASTERN pg 92
◻ CAROLINA pg 132
▲ APPALACHIAN pg 168
pg 13

★ MAJORS
pg 13

Dayton Dragons

Washington Nationals

Southern Maryland Blue Crabs

Cincinnati Reds

Fredericksburg Nationals

Delmarva Shorebirds

Florence Freedom

West Virginia Power

Richmond Flying Squirrels

Evansville Otters

Louisville Bats

Lexington Legends

KY

Norfolk Tides

Princeton Rays

Salem Red Sox

Lynchburg Hillcats

VA

Bluefield Jays

Bowling Green Hot Rods

Bristol Pirates

Pulaski Yankees

Danville Braves

Burlington Royals

Durham Bulls

Kingsport Mets

Winston-Salem Dash

Elizabethton Twins

Carolina Mudcats

Greeneville Reds

High Point Rockers

Greensboro Grasshoppers

Nashville Sounds

Johnson City Cardinals

Kannapolis Cannon Ballers

Down East Wood Ducks

Tennessee Smokies

Hickory Crawdads

NC

Asheville Tourists

Charlotte Knights

TN

Chattanooga Lookouts

Rocket City Trash Pandas

Rome Braves

Greenville Drive

SC

Myrtle Beach Pelicans

Atlanta Braves

Gwinnett Stripers

Columbia Fireflies

Birmingham Barons

Augusta GreenJackets

Charleston River Dogs

AL

Montgomery Biscuits

GA

★ MAJORS pg 13

▲ INDEPENDENTS

△ ATLANTIC pg 226

△ FRONTIER pg 232

Pensacola Blue Wahoos

oxi rs

Jacksonville Jumbo Shrimp

FL

GRAPEFRUIT LEAGUE
SPRING TRAINING
pg 87

Daytona Tortugas

Daytona Beach

Flying Tigers

Braves

Tigers

Lake Buena Vista

Blue Jays

Fire Frogs

Kissimmee

MINORS

Phillies

Threshers

Dunedin

Lakeland

APPALACHIAN pg 168

Yankees

Clearwater

CAROLINA pg 132

Tampa

Mets

Hammerheads

EASTERN pg 110

Tarpons

Tampa Bay Rays

Palm Beach Cardinals

FLORIDA STATE pg 136

St. Petersburg

Port St. Lucie

Cardinals

GULF COAST pg 176

Pirates

Bradenton

Jupiter

Marlins

INTERNATIONAL pg 92

Marauders

Sarasota

Port Charlotte

MIDWEST pg 142

Orioles

Ft. Myers

Astros

PACIFIC COAST pg 101

West Palm Beach

Nationals

SOUTH ATLANTIC pg 150

Rays

Miami Marlins

SOUTHERN pg 117

Stone Crabs

Twins

Red Sox

Mighty Mussels

Miami

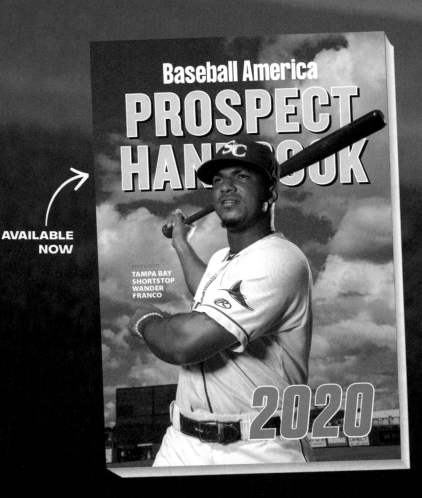

MAJOR LEAGUES

MAJOR LEAGUE BASEBALL

Mailing Address: 1271 Avenue of the Americas, New York, NY 10020.
Telephone: (212) 931-7800. **Website:** www.mlb.com.
Commissioner of Baseball: Rob Manfred.
Deputy Commissioner, Baseball Administration and Chief Legal Officer: Dan Halem.
Deputy Commissioner, Business & Media: Tony Petitti. **Chief Communications Officer:** Pat
Courtney. **Chief Baseball Officer:** Joe Torre. **Chief Financial Officer/Sr. Advisor:** Bob Starkey.
Executive Vice President, Strategy, Technology & Innovation: Chris Marinak. **Executive
Vice President, Business & Sales:** Noah Garden. **Chief Technology Officer:** Jason Gaedtke.

Rob Manfred

ON-FIELD OPERATIONS

Senior VP, On-Field Operations & Umpiring: Peter Woodfork. **VP, On-Field Operations,
Initiatives & Strategy:** Chris Young. **Senior Director, Umpire Operations:** Matt McKendry.
Senior Director, Instant Replay: Justin Klemm. **Director, Minor League Operations:**
Fred Seymour. **Director, Major League Umpiring:** Randy Marsh. **Director, Umpiring
Development:** Rich Rieker. **Director, Umpire Medical and Performance:** Scott Sheridan.
Senior Video Coordinator: Freddie Hernandez. **Manager, Instant Replay:** Jeffrey Moody. **Manager, Umpire
Operations:** Raquel Wagner. **Senior Coordinator, On-Field Operations:** Michael Sansarran. **Coordinator, Umpire
Operations:** Alejandro Bermudez. **Analyst, Baseball Operations:** Josh Keen. **Executive Assistant, Baseball
Operations:** Chris Romanello. **Umpiring Supervisors:** Cris Jones, Tom Lepperd, Ed Montague, Ed Rapuano, Charlie
Reliford, Larry Young. **Consultant, Umpire Medical Services:** Mark Letendre.

LABOR RELATIONS

Senior Vice President, Deputy General Counsel, Labor Relations: Patrick Houlihan. **Vice President, Deputy
General Counsel, Labor Relations & Player Programs:** Paul Mifsud. **Vice President, Drug, Health & Safety
Programs:** Jon Coyles. **Director, Labor Relations & Player Programs:** Yenifer Fauche. **Senior Manager, Labor
Relations & Player Programs:** Ricardhy Grandoit. **Senior Manager, MLB Drug, Health & Safety Program:** Lindsey
Ingraham. **Senior Counsel:** Kasey Sanossian. **Counsel:** Vanish Grover. **Counsel:** Justin Wiley. **Coordinator, Drug Health
& Safety Programs:** Isabel Caro.

LEAGUE ECONOMICS & OPERATIONS

Senior Vice President, League Economics & Operations: Morgan Sword. **Vice President, League Economics:**
John D'Angelo. **Vice President, League Economics:** Reed MacPhail. **Senior Director, League Operations:** Jeff
Pfeifer. **Director, International Operations:** Rebecca Seesel. **Manager, League Operations:** Garrett Horan. **Manager,
League Economics:** Cameron Barwick. **Senior Coordinator, League Operations:** Gina Liento. **Senior Coordinator,
League Economics:** Travis Buck. **Senior Coordinator, League Economics:** Kyle Krueger. **Senior Coordinator,
International Operations:** Patrick Nathanson. **Senior Coordinator, Medical Administration:** Kevin Ma. **Coordinator,
League Economics:** Jalen Phillips. **Coordinator, Amateur Administration:** Diego Delgado. **Coordinator, Amateur
Administration:** Ariel Kenney. **Coordinator, International Operations:** Maritza Grillo. **Coordinator, Medical
Administration:** Dana Rowe.

BASEBALL & SOFTBALL DEVELOPMENT

Executive Vice President, Baseball & Softball Development: Tony Reagins. **Senior Vice President, Baseball
Operations & International Development:** Kim Ng. **Vice President, Baseball & Softball Development:** David
James. **Vice President, Youth & Facility Development:** Darrell Miller. **Vice President, Baseball Development:** Del
Matthews. **Senior Director, Baseball & Softball Development:** Chris Haydock. **Senior Director, Baseball & Softball
Development:** Bill Bavasi. **Senior Director, Compliance:** Katherine Anderson.
Director, Baseball Development: Bob Fontaine. **Senior Manager, Baseball & Softball Development:** Chuck Fox.
Senior Manager, Play Ball & RBI: Bennett Shields. **Senior Coordinator, International Baseball Operations:** Max
Thomas. **Manager, Baseball & Softball Development:** Henry Gonzalez. **Senior Coordinator, Baseball Development:**
Kindu Jones. **Senior Coordinator, Softball Development and Legal:** Sarah Padove. **Senior Coordinator, Baseball
Development, RBI:** Steven Smiegocki. **Coordinator, Softball Development:** Koely Kempisty. **Coordinator, MLB
Compton Youth Academy:** Kenneth Landreaux. **Coordinator, Softball:** Eliza Crawford. **Senior Administrative
Assistant:** Grace Carrasco.

COMMUNICATIONS

Telephone: (212) 931-7878. **Fax:** (212) 949-5654.
Chief Communications Officer: Pat Courtney. **Senior Vice President, Communications:** Matt Bourne. **Vice
President, Communications:** John Blundell, Mike Teevan. **Senior Director, Business Communications & Youth
Engagement:** Steve Arocho. **Senior Director, Business Communications:** Ileana Peña. **Director, Communications:**
Donald Muller. **Manager, Communications:** Lydia Devlin. **Manager, Business Communications:** David Hochman.
Senior Coordinator, Communications & Scheduling: Paul Koehler. **Senior Coordinator, Communications:**
Yolayna Alvarez. **Coordinator, Business Communications:** Kerline Batista, Troy Watson. **Executive Assistant,
Communications:** Ginger Dillon. **Senior Administrative Assistant, Communications:** Lisa Teitelbaum. **Official
Historian:** John Thorn.

AMERICAN LEAGUE

Year League Founded: 1901.
2019 Opening Date: March 26. **Closing Date:** Sept. 27.
Regular Season: 162 games.
Division Structure: East—Baltimore, Boston, New York, Tampa Bay, Toronto.
Central—Chicago, Cleveland, Detroit, Kansas City, Minnesota. **West**—Houston, Los Angeles, Oakland, Seattle, Texas.
Playoff Format: Two non-division winners with best records meet in one-game wild card. Wild card winner and three division champions meet in two best-of-five Division Series. Winners meet in best-of-seven Championship Series.
All-Star Game: July 14, Dodger Stadium, Los Angeles (American League vs. National League).
Roster Limit: 26, through Sept. 1, when rosters expand to 28. **Brand of Baseball:** Rawlings.
Statistician: MLB Advanced Media, 75 Ninth Ave., 5th Floor, New York, NY 10011.

STADIUM INFORMATION

Team	Stadium	Dimensions			Capacity	2019 Att.
		LF	CF	RF		
Baltimore	Oriole Park at Camden Yards	333	410	318	45,971	1,307,807
Boston	Fenway Park	310	390	302	37,673	2,924,627
Chicago	Guaranteed Rate Field	330	400	335	40,615	1,649,775
Cleveland	Progressive Field	325	405	325	37,675	1,738,642
Detroit	Comerica Park	345	420	330	41,782	1,501,430
Houston	Minute Maid Park	315	435	326	40,976	2,857,367
Kansas City	Kauffman Stadium	330	410	330	37,903	1,479,659
Los Angeles	Angel Stadium	333	404	333	45,050	3,019,012
Minnesota	Target Field	339	404	328	39,504	2,294,152
New York	Yankee Stadium	318	408	314	50,291	3,304,404
Oakland	Oakland Coliseum	330	400	367	35,067	1,662,211
Seattle	T-Mobile Park	331	401	326	47,447	1,791,863
Tampa Bay	Tropicana Field	315	404	322	41,315	1,178,735
Texas	Globe Life Park in Arlington	332	400	325	48,114	2,132,994
Toronto	Rogers Centre	328	400	328	50,598	1,750,144

NATIONAL LEAGUE

Year League Founded: 1876.
2019 Opening Date: March 26. **Closing Date:** Sept. 27.
Regular Season: 162 games.
Division Structure: East—Atlanta, Miami, New York, Philadelphia, Washington.
Central—Chicago, Cincinnati, Milwaukee, Pittsburgh, St. Louis. **West**—Arizona, Colorado, Los Angeles, San Diego, San Francisco.
Playoff Format: Two non-division winners with best records meet in one-game wild card. Wild card winner and three division champions meet in two best-of-five Division Series. Winners meet in best-of-seven Championship Series.
All-Star Game: July 14, Dodger Stadium, Los Angeles (American League vs. National League).
Roster Limit: 26, through Sept. 1 when rosters expand to 28. **Brand of Baseball:** Rawlings.
Statistician: MLB Advanced Media, 75 Ninth Ave., 5th Floor, New York, NY 10011.

STADIUM INFORMATION

Team	Stadium	Dimensions			Capacity	2018 Att.
		LF	CF	RF		
Arizona	Chase Field	330	407	334	49,033	2,135,510
Atlanta	SunTrust Park	335	400	325	41,500	2,655,100
Chicago	Wrigley Field	355	400	353	41,160	3,094,865
Cincinnati	Great American Ball Park	328	404	325	42,319	1,808,685
Colorado	Coors Field	347	415	350	50,499	2,993,244
Los Angeles	Dodger Stadium	330	395	330	56,000	3,974,309
Miami	Marlins Park	344	407	335	36,742	811,302
Milwaukee	Miller Park	344	400	345	41,900	2,923,333
New York	Citi Field	335	408	330	42,200	2,442,532
Philadelphia	Citizens Bank Park	329	401	330	43,647	2,727,421
Pittsburgh	PNC Park	325	399	320	38,496	1,491,439
St. Louis	Busch Stadium	336	400	335	46,681	3,480,393
San Diego	Petco Park	336	396	322	42,685	2,396,399
San Francisco	Oracle Park	339	399	309	41,503	2,707,760
Washington	Nationals Park	336	402	335	41,888	2,259,781

ARIZONA DIAMONDBACKS

Office Address: Chase Field, 401 E. Jefferson St, Phoenix, AZ 85004.
Mailing Address: P.O. Box 2095, Phoenix, AZ 85001.
Telephone: (602) 462-6500. **Fax:** (602) 462-6599. **Website:** www.dbacks.com

OWNERSHIP
Managing General Partner: Ken Kendrick. **General Partners:** Mike Chipman, Jeff Royer.

BUSINESS OPERATIONS
President/CEO: Derrick Hall. **Executive Vice President, Business Operations/Chief
Revenue Officer:** Cullen Maxey. **Executive Vice President/Chief Financial Officer:** Tom
Harris. **Executive Vice President, Chief Legal Officer:** Nona Lee. **Senior Advisor, President/
CEO:** Luis Gonzalez.

BROADCASTING
VP, Broadcasting: Scott Geyer. **VP, Game Operations/DBTV Productions:** Rob
Weinheimer.

CORPORATE PARTNERSHIPS/MARKETING
VP, Corporate Partnerships: Judd Norris. **Senior Director, Corporate Partnership Services:**
Kerri White. **VP, Marketing/Analytics:** Kenny Farrell. **Director, Marketing:** Rayme Lofgren. **Senior
Manager, Hispanic Marketing:** Jerry Romo.

Ken Kendrick

FINANCE/LEGAL
VP, Finance: Craig Bradley. **Director, Financial Management and Purchasing:** Jeff Jacobs. **Director, Accounting:**
Jeffrey Barnes. **General Counsel:** Caleb Jay. **Associate General Counsel:** Maacah Scott.

COMMUNITY AFFAIRS
Senior VP, Corporate/Community Impact: Debbie Castaldo. **Director, Community Events:** Robert Itzkowitz.
Senior Manager, Community/Foundation Operations: Tara Trzinski. **Senior Manager, Community Initiatives/
Partner Programs:** Dustin Payne.

COMMUNICATIONS/MEDIA RELATIONS
Senior VP, Content/Communications: Josh Rawitch. **Senior Director, Player/Media Relations:** Casey Wilcox.
Director, Player/Media Relations: Patrick O'Connell. **Manager, Player/Media Relations:** Patrick Kurish. **Senior
Manager, Corporate Communications:** Katie Krause.

SPECIAL PROJECTS/FAN EXPERIENCE
VP, Special Projects: Graham Rossini. **Director, Special Projects/Fan Experience:** Matt Helmeid. **Director, Baseball
Outreach/Development:** Jeff Rodin. **General Manager, Salt River Fields:** David Dunne.

TICKET SALES
Telephone: (602) 514-8400. **Fax:** (602) 462-4141. **Senior VP, Ticket Sales/Marketing:** John Fisher. **VP, Ticket Sales/**

2020 SCHEDULE
Standard Game Times: 6:40 p.m.; Sun. 1:10.

MARCH		
26-29 . . . . Atlanta	9-10 . . . . . . at Milwaukee	**JULY**
30-31 . . . . . San Francisco	11-13 . . . . . New York (NL)	1 . . . . at Kansas City
	14-17 . . . . . . Washington	3-5 . . . . Cincinnati
APRIL	19-21 . . . at New York (NL)	7-8 . . . . at Colorado
1 . . . . San Francisco	23-24 . . . . . . .at St. Louis	11-12 . . . .at Chicago (AL)
3-5 . . . . .at Chicago (NL)	27-29 . . . . . at San Diego	17-19 . . . . Miami
7-9 . . . . . at San Francisco	29-31 . . . . Detroit	20-22 . . . . . . Minnesota
10-12 . . . . .Colorado		25-26 . . . at San Francisco
14-16 . . . . . . Pittsburgh	**JUNE**	27-29 . . . . . .Philadelphia
18-19 . . . . . . San Diego	1-3 . . . . Colorado	30-31 . . . Los Angeles (NL)
21-23 . . . . . . at Atlanta	5-7 . . . . San Diego	
24-26 . . . . .at Cincinnati	10-11 . . . . . at Colorado	**AUGUST**
28-29 . . . . Houston	13-14 . . . . . at San Diego	1-2 . . . . Los Angeles (NL)
30 . . . . . . Chicago (NL)	16-19 . at Los Angeles (NL)	4-5 . . . . . . .at Houston
	19-21 . . . . Milwaukee	6-9 . . . . at Pittsburgh
MAY	22-24 . . . Los Angeles (NL)	10-13 . . . . .Colorado
1-3 . . . . . . Chicago (NL)	26-29 . . . . at Philadelphia	15-16 . at Los Angeles (NL)
5-7 . . . . . at Washington	30 . . . . . . .at Kansas City	17-18 . . . . . . Kansas City
		20-23 . . . . . San Francisco

25-27 . . . . . .at Cleveland		
28-31 . . . . at Miami		
SEPTEMBER		
1-2 . . . . Los Angeles (NL)		
4-6 . . . . St. Louis		
7-10 . . . . . . at San Diego		
2-13 . . at Los Angeles (NL)		
14-16 . . . . . San Francisco		
17-20 . . . . . . San Diego		
23-24 . . at San Francisco		
26-27 . . . . . at Colorado		
16-18 . . . . Miami		
20-22 . . . . at San Diego		
23-25 . . . . St. Louis		
27-29 . . . . . . San Diego		

GENERAL INFORMATION
Stadium (year opened): Chase Field (1998). **Home Dugout:** Third Base.
Team Colors: Sedona Red, Sonoran Sand **Playing Surface:** Grass.
and Black.

Events: Ryan Holmstedt.

BASEBALL OPERATIONS

Executive Vice President/General Manager: Mike Hazen. **Senior VP/Assistant GMs:** Jared Porter, Amiel Sawdaye. **VP, Latin Operations:** Junior Noboa. **Special Assistants to GM:** Burke Badenhop, Craig Shipley. **Director, Baseball Operations:** Sam Eaton. **VP, Research & Development:** Michael Fitzgerald. **Assistant Director, Amateur Scouting & Baseball Administration:** Kristyn Pierce. **Assistant, Baseball Operations:** Connor Shannon. **Assistant, International Scouting:** Alex Lorenzo. **Baseball Operations Fellow:** Carl Gonzalez. **Manager, Baseball Systems:** John Krazit. **Baseball Systems Developer:** Thomas Johnson.**Developer, Baseball Systems:** Gavin Sweeny. **Analysts, R&D:** Cody Callahan, Max Glick, Taylor Chloe, Micah Daley-Harris. **Coordinator, Baseball Operations:** Max Phillips. **Analyst, Player Personnel:** Matt Roffe. **Specialist Assistant to GM/Pitching Strategist:** Dan Haren. **Assistant Pitching Coordinator/Pitching Analyst:** Ross Seaton. **Coordinator, Run Production:** Drew Hedman. **Coordinator, Run Prevention:** Alex Cultice. **Coordinator, Major League Video:** Allen Campbell. **Coordinator, Mental Skills:** Zach Brandon.

Mike Hazen

MAJOR LEAGUE STAFF

Manager: Torey Lovullo. **Coaches: Bench**—Luis Urueta, **Pitching**—Matt Herges, **Hitting**—Darnell Coles, **First Base**—Dave McKay, **Third Base**—Tony Perezchica, **Bullpen**—Mike Fetters, **Assistant Hitting Coach**—Eric Hinske, **Quality Control/Catching**—Robby Hammock, **Bullpen Catcher**—Dan Butler, Humberto Quintero.

MEDICAL/TRAINING

Club Physician: Dr. Gary Waslewski. **Director, Sports Medicine & Performance:** Ken Crenshaw. **Head Trainer:** Ryan DiPanfilo. **Assistant Trainer:** Ryne Eubanks. **Strength & Conditioning Coordinator:** Nate Shaw. **Assistant Strength & Conditioning Coordinator:** Matt Tenney. **Physical Therapist:** Ben Hagar. **Physical Therapist:** Junko Yazawa. **Analyst, Sports Medicine:** Patrick Sellas. **Team Performance Dietitian:** Michelle Riccardi.

PLAYER DEVELOPMENT

Director, Player Development: Josh Barfield. **Assistant Director, Player Development:** Matt Grabowski. **Assistant Director, Minor League Administration:** Shawn Marette. **Assistant, Player Development:** Peter Bransfield. **Assistant, Latin American Baseball Operations:** Mariana Patraca. **Coordinators:** Blake Lalli (field), Dan Carlson (pitching), Jonny Gomes (outfield/baserunning), Gil Velazquez (infield), Mark Reed (catching), Ross Seaton (assistant pitching/pitching analyst), Brad Arnsberg (rehab pitching), Orlando Hudson (assistant), Gil Heredia (short-season pitching), Casey Chenoweth (short-season hitting), Jaime Del Valle (DSL field), Max Esposito (medical), Vaughn Robinson (strength). **Medical Administrator:** Jon Herzner. **Hillsboro Consultant:** Ben Petrick.

FARM SYSTEM

Class	Club (League)	Manager	Hitting Coach	Pitching Coach
Triple-A	Reno (PCL)	Chris Cron	Jason Camilli	Jeff Bajenaru
Double-A	Jackson (SL)	Blake Lalli	Rick Short	Doug Drabek
High A	Visalia (CAL)	Shawn Roof	Travis Denker	Shane Loux
Low A	Kane County (MWL)	Vince Harrison	KC Judge	Barry Enright
Short-season	Hillsboro (NWL)	Javier Colina	Franklin Stubbs	Mike Parrott
Rookie	Missoula (PIO)	Darrin Garner	Jose Amado	Manny Garcia
Rookie	Diamondbacks (AZL)	Nick Evans	Micah Franklin	Hatuey Mendoza

SCOUTING

Telephone: (602) 462-6500. **Fax:** (602) 462-6425.

Director, Amateur Scouting: Deric Ladnier. **Coordinator, Amateur Scouting:** Ian Rebhan. **Director, Pro Scouting:** Jason Parks. **Coordinator, Pro Scouting:** Cory Hahn. **Vice President, Latin American Scouting & Player Development:** Cesar Geronimo. **Assistant Director, International Scouting:** Peter Wardell. **Director, Pacific Rim Operations:** Mack Hayashi. **Senior Advisor, Pacific Rim Operations:** Jim Marshall. **National Crosscheckers:** Greg Lonigro (Connellsville, PA), James Merriweather III (Glendale, AZ). **National Pitching Supervisor:** Jeff Mousser (Gilbert, AZ). **National Junior College Supervisor:** Clark Crist (Phoenix, AZ). **Regional Supervisors:** Steve Connelly (Emerald Isle, NC), Frank Damas (Miami Lakes, FL), Steve McAllister (Chillicothe, IL), Doyle Wilson (Queen Creek, AZ). **Area Scouts:** Hudson Belinsky (Smyrna, GA), Nathan Birtwell (St. Louis, MO), Eric Cruz (Pembroke Pines, FL), Kerry Jenkins (Nashville, TN), Jeremy Kehrt (Avon, IN), Gil Kubski, Jeremiah Luster (Oceanside, CA), Rick Matsko (Davidsville, PA), Mike Meyer, Rusty Pendergrass (Missouri City, MO), Mark Ross (Tucson, AZ), JR Salinas (Roanoke, TX), Dennis Sheehan (Glasco, NY), George Swain (Wilmington, NC), Garry Templeton (San Marcos, CA), Jake Williams (Kansas City, MO), Luke Wrenn. **Part-Time Scouts:** Hal Kurtzman (Lake Balboa, CA), Doug Mathieson (Aldergrove, BC), Homer Newlin, Jerry Nyman (Stevensville, MT). **Special Assignment Scouts:** Todd Greene (Alpharetta, GA), Danny Haas (Madeira, OH), Alex Jacobs (Lakeland, FL), Tim Wilken (Dunedin, FL). **Major League Scouts:** Bill Bryk (Schererville, IN), Bill Gayton (San Diego, CA), Mike Piatnik (Winter Haven, FL). **Major League Advance Scout:** Jeff Gardner (Costa Mesa, CA). **Professional Scouts:** Tucker Blair (Estero, FL), Mike Brown (Naples, FL), Chris Carminucci (Scottsdale, AZ), Jacob Frisaro (Scottsdale, AZ), Jack Goin (Eagan, MN), Matt Hahn (Tampa, FL), Drew Hedman, Brad Kelley (Scottsdale, AZ), Rob Leary (Melbourne, FL), T.R. Lewis, Matt Mercurio (Indialantic, FL), Dan Ramsay (Spokane, WA), Tom Romenesko (Santee, CA), Brett West (Palm Harbor, FL). **Crosschecker, Latin America:** Francisco Cartaya (Collierville, TN). **Crosschecker, Dominican Republic:** Mark Snipp. **Coordinator, Dominican Republic:** Omar Rogers. **International Scouts:** Jose Ortiz, Ronald Rivas, Diego Bordas (Dominican Republic); Alfonso Mora, Didimo Bracho, Kristians Pereira, David Chicarelli, Gregory Blanco (Venezuela); Luis Gonzalez Arteaga (Colombia); Julio Sanchez (Nicaragua); Bradley Stuart (Curacao); Kyle Lee (Korea); TY Wei (Taiwan).

ATLANTA BRAVES

Office Address: 755 Battery Avenue, SE Atlanta, GA 30339-3017.
Mailing Address: PO Box 723009, Atlanta, GA 31139-2704.
Telephone: (404) 522-7630. **Website:** www.braves.com.

OWNERSHIP
Operated/Owned By: Liberty Media. **Chairman:** Terry McGuirk. **Chairman Emeritus:** Bill Bartholomay. **Vice Chairman Emeritus:** John Schuerholz. **Senior Vice President:** Henry Aaron.

BUSINESS OPERATIONS
President/CEO: Derek Schiller. **Executive VP/Chief Legal Officer:** Greg Heller.

MARKETING/SALES
Senior VP, Marketing: Adam Zimmerman. **Senior VP, Ticket Sales:** Paul Adams. **Senior VP, Corporate & Premium Partnerships:** Jim Allen. **Senior VP, Human Resources:** DeRetta Rhodes.

FINANCE
Executive VP, Chief Financial Officer: Jill Robinson.

COMMUNICATIONS
Telephone: (404) 522-7630.
Vice President, Communications: Beth Marshall. **Director, Baseball Communications:** Jonathan Kerber. **Manager, Baseball Communications:** Jared Burleyson. **Bilingual Coordinator, Baseball Communications:** Franco García. **Coordinator, Baseball Communications:** Matt Grilli. **Coordinator, Corporate Communications:** Kara Zoellner.

Terry McGuirk

STADIUM OPERATIONS
Senior Vice President, Facility Operations: Eric Perestuk. **Field Director:** Ed Mangan. **VP, Fan Experience:** Scott Cunningham. **PA Announcer:** Casey Motter. **Official Scorers:** Richard Musterer, Mike Stamus.

TICKETING
Telephone: (404) 577-9100. **Email:** ticketsales@braves.com.
VP, Ticket Operations: Anthony Esposito.

TRAVEL/CLUBHOUSE
Director of Team Travel: Jim Lovell. **Director, Equipment & Clubhouse Service:** John Holland.
Visiting Clubhouse Manager: Fred Stone.

BASEBALL OPERATIONS
Telephone: (404) 522-7630. **Fax:** (404) 614-3308.
Executive Vice President/General Manager: Alex Anthopoulos. **Sr. Vice President of Baseball Operations/**

2020 SCHEDULE
Standard Game Times: 7:35; Sat. 4:10; Sun. 1:35.

MARCH		
26-29 . . . . . . at Arizona	8-10 . . . . Miami	JULY
31 . . . . at San Diego	12-13 . . . . Boston	1 . . . . .at Texas
	16-17 . . . at San Francisco	3-5. . . . . Los Angeles (AL)
APRIL	19-21 . . . . . . .at St. Louis	6-9. . . . . Pittsburgh
1 . . . . at San Diego	22-24 . . . .New York (NL)	10-12 . . . . Chicago (NL)
3-5 . . . . .Miami	25-27 . . . . St. Louis	18-19 . . . . . . at Colorado
6-8. . . . . San Diego	30-31 . . . . . .at Seattle	22 . . . . .at Oakland
9-12 . . . . at Miami		24-26 . . . . at Washington
13-16 . . . at New York (NL)	JUNE	27-30 . . . . Cincinnati
17-19 . . . . . San Francisco	2-4. . . at Los Angeles (NL)	31 . . . . Washington
21-23 . . . . Arizona	5-7. . . . . . . .Philadelphia	
24-26 . . . . .New York (NL)	9-11 . . . . Washington	AUGUST
27-29 . . . . . .at Cincinnati	12-14 . . . Los Angeles (NL)	1-2. . . . . Washington
	16-17 . . . . .at Boston	4-6. . . . . .at Chicago (NL)
MAY	19-21 . . . at Washington	7-9 . . . . at Miami
1-3 . . . . at New York (NL)	22-25 . . . . . Philadelphia	11-13 . . . at New York (NL)
4-6. . . . . at Philadelphia	26-28 . . . . at Miami	14-16 . . . . Miami
	29-30 . . . . .at Texas	

17-19 . . . . . .Milwaukee		
21-23 . . . . at Philadelphia		
25-26 . . . . Oakland		
27-30 . . . . .Colorado		
SEPTEMBER		
1-3 . . . . . . at Washington		
4-6. . . . . . . at Pittsburgh		
7-9. . . . . .New York (NL)		
11-13 . . . . . .Philadelphia		
15-17 . . . . . at Milwaukee		
18-20 . . . at Philadelphia		
21-24 . . . . . . Washington		
25-27 . . . . Houston		
27-29 . . . at New York (NL)		

GENERAL INFORMATION
Stadium (year opened):
SunTrust Park (2017).
Team Colors: Red, white and blue.

Home Dugout: First Base.
Playing Surface: Grass.

Assistant GM: Perry Minasian. **Assistant GM/Research & Development:** Jason Paré. **Assistant GM/Major League Operations:** Alex Tamin. **VP, Scouting:** Dana Brown. **Special Assistant to the GM:** Mike Fast. **Special Assistants:** Dom Chiti, Andruw Jones, Chipper Jones, & Dave Wallace. **Director, Baseball Administration:** Dixie Keller. **Manager, Baseball Video Operations:** Rob Smith. **Executive Assistant:** Elizabeth Terán. **Manager, Major League Operations:** Doug Wachter. **Analysts, Major League Operations:** Caelan Collins, Nick Coppola, Dylan Mortimer, Tom O'Donnell, & Adam Sonabend. **Manager, Baseball Systems:** Garrett Wilson. **Data Architect & Systems Developer:** Mike Copeland. **Developer, Baseball Systems:** Dana Bennett. **Coordinators, Research & Development:** Michael Lord & Josh Malek. **Analysts, Research & Development:** Scott Rapponotti, Kyle Sargent, & Kevin Song, PhD. **Data Scientist:** Evan Tucker, PhD. **Manager, Family Relations:** Rafael Becerra. **Assistant, Family Relations:** Seth Heizer, Bill Lucas. **Apprentice:** Jeremy Dorsey.

Alex Anthopoulos

MAJOR LEAGUE STAFF

Manager: Brian Snitker. **Coaches: Bench**—Walt Weiss, **Pitching**—Rick Kranitz, **Hitting**—Kevin Seitzer, **Assistant Hitting Coach**—Jose Castro, **First Base**—Eric Young, **Third Base**—Ron Washington. **Catching Coach:** Sal Fasano. **Bullpen Coach:** Marty Reed. **Bullpen Catchers:** Jimmy Leo & Jose Yepez. **Batting Practice Pitcher:** Tomas Perez.

MEDICAL/TRAINING

Director, Player Health/Head Athletic Trainer: George C. Poulis. **Head Team Physician:** Dr. Gary M. Lourie. **Senior Advisor, Athletic Training:** Jeff Porter. **Assistant Athletic Trainer:** Mike Frostad. **Head Strength & Conditioning Coach:** Bradford Scott. **Assistant Strength & Conditioning Coach:** Jordan Wolf. **Head Physical Therapist:** Pete Cicinelli. **Assistant Physical Therapist:** Nick Valencia. **Massage Therapist:** Yoshi Nishio.

PLAYER DEVELOPMENT

Telephone: (404) 522-7630.

Assistant GM/Player Development: Ben Sestanovich. **Special Assistants to Player Development:** Demarlo Hale, Terry Pendleton & Eddie Perez. **Assistant Director of Player Development—Operations:** Ron Knight. **Manager, PD Analytics:** Colin Wyers. **Assistant, Player Development:** Dylan Quantz. **Field Coordinator:** Doug Mansolino. **Pitching Coordinator:** Paul Davis. **Hitting Coordinator:** Mike Brumley. **Roving Coordinators:** Bobby Magallanes (assistant hitting), JD Closser (catching), Nick Flynn (medical), Jeff Stevenson (assistant medical), Mike Schofield (strength & conditioning), Ryan Driscoll (assistant strength & conditioning), Kyle Clements (video), Fernando Pineres (cultural development). **Coordinator, Florida Operations:** Jeff Pink. **Physical Therapist:** Ben Cuddy. **Player Development Trainee:** Tucker Meredith.

FARM SYSTEM

Class	Club (League)	Manager	Hitting Coach	Pitching Coach
Triple-A	Gwinnett (IL)	Damon Berryhill	Carlos Mendez	Mike Maroth
Double-A	Mississippi (SL)	Chris Maloney	Einar Diaz	David Chavarria
High A	Florida (FSL)	Barrett Kleinknecht	Danny Santiesteban	Dan Meyer
Low A	Rome (SAL)	Matt Tuiasosopo	Michael Bard	Kanekoa Teixeira
Rookie	Danville (APP)	Michael Saunders	Connor Narron	TBD
Rookie	Braves (GCL)	Anthony Nunez	B. Moore/O. Rosario	Elvin Nina
Rookie	Braves (DSL)	TBD	TBD	H. Astacio/J.
Rodriguez				

SCOUTING

Telephone: (404) 522-7630. **Fax:** (404) 614-1350.

Special Assistants to Baseball Operations: Fred McGriff, Greg Walker. **Assistant Director, Pro Scouting:** Jonathan Schuerholz. **Professional Scouts:** Alan Butts, Jason Dunn, Dave Holliday, Matt Kinzer, Devlin McConnell, Trenton Moses, Rick Ragazzo, Paul Runge, Billy Ryan, Ted Simmons, Terry R. Tripp, Rick Williams. **Pro Scouting Trainee:** Peyton Skinner (Sharpsburg, GA). **Assistant, Amateur Scouting Operations:** Ronit Shah. **Special Assistants to Amateur Scouting:** Ralph Garr, John Gibbons, Fred McGriff, Greg Walker. **Ambassador to Amateur Scouting:** Smoke Laval (Reserve, LA). **National Cross Checkers:** Joe Jordan, Ron Marigny, Gary Rajsich, Deron Rombach. **Regional Cross Checkers: West/Southwest**—Joey Davis, **Southeast**—Reed Dunn, **West/Pacific Northwest**—Alan Hull, **Northeast**—Brian Sankey, **Midwest**—Terry C Tripp. **Deep South Scout:** Mac Seibert. **Area Scouting Supervisors:** Kevin Barry (Alma, IL), Billy Best (Holly Springs, NC), Jim Blueberg (Carson City, NV), Jon Bunnell (Tampa, FL), Travis Coleman (Trail Hoover, AL), Dan Cox (Huntington Beach, CA), JD French (Kennett, MO), Jeremy Gordon (Clinton Township, MI), Ted Lekas (Brewster, MA), Chris Lionetti (Rome, GA), Cody Martin (Vancouver, WA), Kevin Martin (Los Angeles, CA), Trey McNickle (Olive Branch, MS), Freddy Perez (Nashville, TN), Lou Sanchez (Miami, FL), Alan Sandberg (Hopatcong, NJ), Darin Vaughan (Kingwood, TX), Ricky Wilson (Buckeye, AZ). **Scouts:** Hank Aaron Jr. (Austell, GA), Darin Blair (Lawrenceville, IL), Hugh Buchanan (Snellville, GA), Stu Cann (Bradley, IL), Tom Davis (Ripon, CA), Dewayne Kitts (Moncks Corner, NC), Abraham Martinez (Santa Isabel, PR). **Video Coordinators:** Alex Burritt (St. Petersburg, FL), Anthony Flora (Katy, TX), Daniel Sabatino (Katy, TX). **Amateur Scouting Trainee:** Will Rich (Savannah, TN). **Coordinator, Latin American Operations:** Jonathan Cruz. **Manager, International Scouting Administration:** Gerald Milanes. **Manager, Dominican Republic Administration & Operations:** Lothar Schott. **Administrative Assistant:** Ruth Peguero. **Scouting Supervisors:** Orlando Covo (South America), Chris Roque (Central America), Carlos Sequera (Venezuela). **International Scouts: Dominican Republic**—Reymond Nunez, Miguel Prestol, Luis Santos, Victor Torres. **Venezuela** — Richard Castillo, Raphachel Colatosti, Winder Leon, Rafael Marcano, Edison Sanchez. **Video Coordinators**: Jaime Gil (Dominican Republic), Jesus Simancas (Venezuela).

BALTIMORE ORIOLES

Office Address: 333 W Camden St., Baltimore, MD 21201.
Telephone: (888) 848-BIRD. **Fax:** (410) 547-6272.
E-mail Address: birdmail@orioles.com. **Website:** www.orioles.com.

OWNERSHIP
Operated By: The Baltimore Orioles Limited Partnership Inc.
Chairman/CEO: Peter Angelos. **Executive Vice President:** John Angelos. **Ownership Representative:** Louis Angelos.

BUSINESS OPERATIONS

Peter Angelos

SENIOR LEADERSHIP TEAM
Executive Vice President and General Manager: Mike Elias
Senior Vice President, Administration & Experience: Greg Bader. **Senior Vice President, Chief Revenue Officer:** T.J. Brightman. **Senior Vice President, Community Development & Communications:** Jennifer Grondahl. **Senior Vice President, Human Resources:** Lisa Tolson.

EXECUTIVE BUSINESS ADMINISTRATION
Vice President, Ticket Partnerships: Neil Aloise. **Vice President, Corporate Partnerships:** Marco Gentile. **Vice President, Digital Marketing & Content Creation:** Tyler Hoffberger. **Vice President, Finance:** Michael D. Hoppes, CPA. **Senior Vice President, Business Development:** Lou Kousouris. **Vice President, Strategy & Analytics:** Scott Lewis. **Vice President, Ballpark Experience & Operations:** Troy Scott. **Executive Vice President, Planning & Development:** Michael Shapiro.

BALLPARK OPERATIONS & EXPERIENCE
Director, Ballpark Operations: Kevin Cummings. **Director, Ballpark Experience:** Kristen Schultz. **Director, Field Operations:** Nicole Sherry. **Director, Hospitality:** Tom Orszulak.

COMMUNICATIONS/ALUMNI
Telephone: (410) 547-6150. **Fax:** (410) 547-6272.
Director, Public Relations: Kristen Hudak. **Senior Manager, Baseball Communications:** Jim Misudek. **Senior Coordinator, Public Relations & Publications:** Kailey Adams. **Senior Coordinator, Baseball Communications:** Adam Esselman. **Senior Coordinator, Player & Family Relations:** Jackie Harig. **Public Relations Assistant:** Liam Davis. **Director, Orioles Alumni:** Bill Stetka. **Official Scorers:** Jim Henneman, Marc Jacobson, Ryan Eigenbrode.

CORPORATE PARTNERSHIPS
Director, Strategy & Corporate Partner Relations: Cory Daniele. **Director, Suite Sales:** Matt Dryer.

INFORMATION TECHNOLOGY
Director, Information Technology: James L. Kline. **Director, Business Intelligence:** Doug Nickerson.

2020 SCHEDULE
Standard Game Times: 7:05 p.m; Sun. 1:35

MARCH
26-29 . . . . . New York (AL)
30-31 . . . . Boston

APRIL
1 . . . . Boston
2-5 . . . . at St. Louis
6-9 . . . . at New York (AL)
10-12 . . . . Pittsburgh
14-15 . . . . . Chicago (NL)
17-19 . . . . at Kansas City
21-22 . at Los Angeles (AL)
24-26 . . . . .Toronto
27-30 . . . . . Kansas City

MAY
2-3 . . . . . at Chicago (AL)
4-6 . . . . at Toronto
8-10 . . . . Los Angeles (AL)

11-13 . . . . . . Cleveland
15-17 . . . . at Tampa Bay
18-20 . . . . at Minnesota
21-24 . . . . at Toronto
25-28 . . . . Chicago (AL)
29-31 . . . . .Toronto

JUNE
2-3 . . . .at Chicago (NL)
5-7 . . . . Houston
9-11 . . . . Minnesota
12-14 . . . at Tampa Bay
15-18 . . . .at Cleveland
19-21 . . . . . . .Tampa Bay
22-24 . . at New York (AL)
26-28 . . . . Detroit
29-30 . . . .New York (AL)

JULY
1 . . . . New York (AL)
3-5 . . . . .at Oakland
7-8 . . . . .at Seattle
10-12 . . . . . . .at Boston
17-19 . . . . . .Tampa Bay
20-22 . . . . Seattle
24-26 . . . . Oakland
27-29 . . . . . . .at Boston
31 . . . . at Toronto

AUGUST
1-2 . . . . at Toronto
4-6 . . . . Boston
8-9 . . . . Washington
11-13 . . . . . . .at Detroit
14-16 . . . at Tampa Bay
17-19 . . . . Texas
20-23 . . . . Boston

25-26 . . . at New York (AL)
27-30 . . . . .at Texas
31 . . . . .at Cincinnati

SEPTEMBER
1-2 . . . . .at Cincinnati
4-7 . . . . . .New York (AL)
8-10 . . . . .Toronto
11-13 . . . . . .Milwaukee
15 - 16 . . . at Washington
18 - 20 . . . .at Houston
21 - 24 . . . .Tampa Bay
25 - 27 . . . . . .at Boston
13-16 . . . . . . .at Detroit
17-19 . . . . .Toronto
20-22 . . . . Seattle
23-25 . . . . . . .at Toronto
27-29 . . . . . . .at Boston

GENERAL INFORMATION
Stadium (year opened): Oriole Park at Camden Yards (1992).
Team Colors: Orange, black and white.

Home Dugout: First Base.
Playing Surface: Grass.

MARKETING/PRODUCTIONS

Senior Director, Marketing & Product Development: Jason Snapkoski. **Director, Orioles Productions:** Mike Stashik. **PA Announcer:** Ryan Wagner.

TICKET OPERATIONS, FAN SERVICES & PARTNERSHIPS

Telephone: (888) 848-BIRD. **Fax:** (410) 547-6270. **Director, Ticket Operations & Fan Services:** Scott Rosier. Director, **Birdland Memberships:** Zach Brown. **Director, Group Events & Hospitality:** Mark Hromalik. **Director, Ticket Partnerships:** Ryan Kreissig.

BASEBALL OPERATIONS

Mike Elias

Telephone: (410) 547-6107. **Fax:** (410) 547-6271.
Executive Vice President and General Manager: Mike Elias.
Director, Baseball Development: Eve Rosenbaum. **Director, Baseball Administration:** Kevin Buck. **Manager, Team Travel:** Jeff Gillis. **Manager, Advance Scouting Operations:** Bill Wilkes. **Coordinator, Major League Video/Advance Scouting:** Ben Sussman-Hyde. **Coordinator, Major League Scouting:** Ryan Klimek. **Equipment Manager (Home):** Christopher Guth. **Equipment Manager (Road):** Frederick Tyler. **Umpire Room Manager:** James W. Tyler. **Assistant Equipment Manager:** Irving "Bunny" German. **Asst. Equipment Manager:** Charles Allen.

BASEBALL ANALYTICS

Vice President and Assistant General Manager, Analytics: Sig Mejdal.
Manager, Baseball Systems: Di Zou. **Analysts, Baseball Analytics:** Ryan Hardin, James Martin III, Michael Weis. **Full-Stack Developers:** Peter Ash, James Daniels.

MAJOR LEAGUE STAFF

Manager: Brandon Hyde.
Coaches: Major League Field Coordinator/Catching Instructor—Tim Cossins. **Pitching**—Doug Brocail. **Hitting**—Don Long. **Assistant Hitting**— José Hernández. **First Base**—Anthony Sanders. **Third Base**—José Flores. **Bullpen**—Darren Holmes. **Coach**— Fredi González.

MEDICAL/TRAINING

Team Physician: Dr. Sean Curtin. **Orthopedists:** Dr. Michael Jacobs, Dr. Christopher Looze, Dr. Leigh Ann Curl, Dr. Derek Papp. **Primary Care:** Dr. Meyer Heyman, Dr. Jeff Mayer. **Dentist:** Dr. Gus Livaditis. **Optometrist:** Dr. Elliott Myrowitz. **Head Athletic Trainer:** Brian Ebel. **Assistant Athletic Trainer:** Mark Shires, Pat Wesley. **Strength and Conditioning Coaches:** Joseph Hogarty, Ryosuke Naito. **Team Masseuse:** Adrian Pettaway. **Rehab Coordinator:** Kyle Corrick. **Mental Skills Coordinator:** Kathryn Rowe.

PLAYER DEVELOPMENT

Fax: (410) 547-6298.
Director, Player Development: Matt Blood. **Director, Minor League Operations:** Kent Qualls. **Director, Pitching:** Chris Holt. **Director, Dominican Republic Academy:** Felipe Rojas. **Senior Manager, Minor League and International Administration:** J. Maria Arellano. **Coordinator, Florida and Latin America Pitching:** Dave Schmidt. **Dominican Republic Field Coordinator:** Miguel Jabalera. **Coordinator, Pitching Rehabilitation:** Mike Griffin. **Minor League Medical Coordinator:** Dave Walker. **Latin American Medical Coordinator:** Manny Lopez. **Minor League Strength and Conditioning Coordinator:** Nick White. **Administrator, Dominican Republic Academy:** Rancel Rosado. **Minor League Equipment Manager:** Jake Parker. **Dominican Republic Equipment Manager:** Franklin Fajardo. **Spanish Translator and Coordinator, Latin American Operations:** Ramón Alarcón.

FARM SYSTEM

Class	Club (League)	Manager	Hitting Coach	Pitching Coach
Triple-A	Norfolk (IL)	Gary Kendall	Sean Berry	Kennie Steenstra
Double-A	Bowie (EL)	Buck Britton	Tim Gibbons	Justin Ramsey
High A	Frederick (CL)	Kyle Moore	Tom Eller	Josh Conway
Low A	Delmarva (SAL)	Dave Anderson	Ryan Fuller	Robbie Aviles
Short-season	Aberdeen (NYP)	Kevin Bradshaw	Anthony Villa	Joe Haumacher
Rookie	Orioles (GCL)	Alan Mills	Patrick Jones	Adam Bleday
Rookie	Orioles (DSL)	Elvis Morel	Ramon Caballo	Dionis Pascual

SCOUTING

Telephone: 410-547-6107. **Fax:** 410-547-6928.
Senior Director, International Scouting: Koby Perez. **Director, Pro Scouting:** Mike Snyder. **Supervisor, Domestic Scouting Operations:** Brad Ciolek. **Analysts, Scouting:** Hendrik Herz, Chad Tatum, Alex Tarandek, Kevin Carter, Ryan Carlson. **Scouting Analyst Consultant:** Luke Siler. **Area Scouts:** Rich Amaral (Huntington Beach, CA), David Blume (Elk Grove, CA), Thom Dreier (The Woodlands, TX), Trent Friedrich (Louisville, KY), Ken Guthrie (Sanger, TX), David Jennings (Spanish Fort, AL), Arthur McConnehead (Atlanta, GA), Rich Morales (Blacksburg, VA), Donovan O'Dowd (Arnold, MD), Jim Richardson (Marlow, OK), Logan Schuemann (Scottsdale, AZ), Scott Thomas (St. Louis, MO), Brandon Verley (Stuart, FL), Scott Walter (Manhattan Beach, CA), Doug Witt (Euless, TX). **Scouting Consultant:** Steven DiPuglia (Bradenton, FL). **Scouting Consultant, Puerto Rico:** Anibal Zayas. **Dominican Republic Scouting Supervisor (Santo Domingo):** Geraldo Cabrera. **Dominican Republic Scouting Assistant (Santo Domingo):** Michael Cruz. **Area Scouts:** Luis Noel (San Pedro de Macorís), Francisco Rosario (Santiago), Rafael Belen (Santo Domingo). **Area Scout, Venezuela:** Adel Granadillo (Barquisimeto). **Administrative Consultant:** Scarlett Blanco (Caracas). **Scouting Consultant, Japan:** Naohiko Ihara (Tokyo). **Scouting Consultants, Australia:** Grant Weir (Melbourne), Jason Pospishil (Sydney).

BOSTON RED SOX

Office Address: Fenway Park, 4 Yawkey Way, Boston, MA 02215.
Telephone: (617) 226-6000. **Fax:** (617) 226-6416. **Website:** www.redsox.com

OWNERSHIP
Principal Owner: John Henry. **Chairman:** Thomas C. Werner. **President/CEO:** Sam Kennedy. **President/CEO Emeritus:** Larry Lucchino.

BUSINESS OPERATIONS

EVP/COO: Jonathan Gilula. **SVP/Ballpark Operations:** Peter Nesbit. **SVP/Fan Services & Entertainment:** Sarah McKenna. **VP/Fan Services & Entertainment:** Stephanie Maneikis. **VP/Red Sox Productions:** John Carter. **VP/Fenway Park Tours:** Marcita Thompson. **VP/Facilities Management:** Jonathan Lister.

STRATEGY & BUSINESS DEVELOPMENT / FINANCE & ANALYTICS
EVP/Chief Strategy Officer: Dave Beeston. **EVP/Chief Financial Officer:** Tim Zue. **SVP/Finance:** Ryan Oremus. **VP/Financial Planning & Operations:** Ryan Scafidi. **VP/Business Analytics:** Jonathan Hay. **Financial Advisor to the President:** Jeff White.

HUMAN RESOURCES / INFORMATION TECHNOLOGY
EVP/Chief Human Resources Officer: Amy Waryas. **VP/Human Resources:** Mike Danubio. **VP/Information Technology:** Brian Shield. **VP/IT Operations:** Randy George.

Sam Kennedy

LEGAL
EVP/FSG Corporate Strategy & General Counsel: Ed Weiss. **SVP/ Legal & Gov. Affairs & Special Counsel/FSG:** David Friedman. **VP/ Senior Club Counsel:** Elaine Weddington Steward.

MARKETING / COMMUNICATIONS
EVP/Chief Marketing Officer: Adam Grossman. **VP/Corporate Communications:** Zineb Curran. **SVP/Marketing & Broadcasting:** Colin Burch. **VP/Media Relations:** Kevin Gregg.

PARTNERSHIPS / CLIENT SERVICES
EVP/Partnerships: Troup Parkinson. **SVP/Client and Sponsor Services:** Marcell Bhangoo. **SVP/Community, Alumni & Player Relations:** Pam Kenn.

TICKETING / SALES / EVENTS
EVP/Ticketing, Concerts, & Events: Ron Bumgarner. **SVP/Fenway Concerts & Entertainment:** Larry Cancro. **SVP/Ticketing:** Richard Beaton. **SVP/Ticketing Services & Operations:** Naomi Calder. **SVP/Ticket Sales:** William Droste. **SVP/Fenway Park Events:** Carrie Campbell.

RED SOX FOUNDATION
Honorary Chairman: Tim Wakefield. **Executive Director:** Rebekah Salwasser.

2020 SCHEDULE
Standard Game Times: 7:10 p.m.; Sun. 1:35

MARCH	8 - 10 . . . at New York (AL)	**JULY**	18 - 19 . . . . . Cincinnati
26 - 29 . . . . . . at Toronto	12 - 13 . . . . . . at Atlanta	1 . . . . Seattle	20 - 23 . . . . . at Baltimore
30 - 31 . . . . . at Baltimore	14 - 17 . . . . .at Texas	3 - 5 . . . . . at Pittsburgh	26 - 28 . . . at Chicago (AL)
APRIL	19 - 21 . . . . . .Tampa Bay	6 - 8 . . . . .Toronto	28 - 30 . . . . . . .at Detroit
1 . . . . .at Baltimore	22 - 24 . . . . . . Houston	10 - 12 . . . . . Baltimore	31 . . . . . . .New York (AL)
2 - 5 . . . . . Chicago (AL)	25 - 28 . . . . Kansas City	17 - 19 . . .at Kansas City	**SEPTEMBER**
6 - 8 . . . . . . .Tampa Bay	30 - 31 . . . . .at Houston	20 - 22 . . . . . at Toronto	1 - 2 . . . . . .New York (AL)
10 - 12 . . . .at Seattle	**JUNE**	24 - 26 . . at New York (AL)	4 - 7 . . . . .Detroit
14 - 15 . . . .at Oakland	1 - 3 . . . . . .at Cleveland	27 - 29 . . . . . Baltimore	8 - 10 . . . at New York (AL)
17 - 20 . . . . . Cleveland	5 - 7 . . . . . . .Milwaukee	30 - 31 . . . .New York (AL)	11 - 13 . . . . . .Tampa Bay
21 - 23 . . . . . .Toronto	9 - 11 . . . . at Tampa Bay		15 - 16 . . . .at Cincinnati
25 - 26 . . . at Minnesota	12 - 14 . . . .New York (AL)	**AUGUST**	17 - 20 . . . at Tampa Bay
27 - 29 . . . . . at Toronto	16 - 17 . . . . Atlanta	1 - 2 . . . . . .New York (AL)	22 - 24 . . . . .Toronto
MAY	19 - 21 . . .at Chicago (NL)	4 - 6 . . . . . . .at Baltimore	25 - 27 . . . . . Baltimore
1 - 3 . . . . Texas	23 - 24 at Los Angeles (AL)	7 - 9 . . . . . at Tampa Bay	
5 - 7 . . . Los Angeles (AL)	26 - 28 . . . . . . St. Louis	10 - 13 . . . . . .Minnesota	
	29 - 30 . . . . Seattle	14 - 16 . . . . Oakland	

GENERAL INFORMATION
Stadium (year opened):
Fenway Park (1912).
Team Colors: Navy blue, red and white.

Home Dugout: First Base.
Playing Surface: Grass.

BASEBALL OPERATIONS

Chief Baseball Officer: Chaim Bloom
General Manager: Brian O'Halloran
EVP/Assistant GM: Raquel Ferreira, Eddie Romero, Zack Scott. **Senior Advisor:** Jack McCormick. **Director, Team Travel:** Mark Cacciatore. **Director, Major League Operations:** Mike Regan. **Coordinator, Major League Operations:** Alex Gimenez. **Executive Assistant:** Erin Cox. **Director, Baseball Analytics:** Joe McDonald. **Director, Education and Process Analysis:** Greg Rybarczyk. **Analyst, Baseball Analytics:** Brad Alberts, Spencer Bingol, Dan Meyer, Dave Miller. **Analyst, Major League Clubhouse:** Jeb Clarke. **Assistant, Baseball Analytics:** Kayla Mei, Jimmy O'Donnell **Director, Baseball Systems:** Mike Ganley. **Sr. Developer, Baseball Systems:** Eric Edvalson, Fred Hubert. **Data Architect, Baseball Systems:** Bill Letson **Developer, Baseball Systems:** Connor McCann. **Special Assistants to GM:** Pedro Martinez, Jason Varitek.

Dave Dombrowski

MAJOR LEAGUE STAFF

Manager: TBD. **Coaches: Bench**—Ron Roenicke; **Pitching**—David Bush; **Assistant Pitching**—Kevin Walker; **Bullpen**—Craig Bjornson; **Hitting**—Tim Hyers; **Assistant Hitting**—Peter Fatse; **First Base**—Tom Goodwin; **Third Base**—Carlos Febles; **Major League Coach**—Ramon Vazquez; **Bullpen Catchers:** Mani Martinez, Michael Brenly. **BP Thrower:** Matt Noone.

SPORTS MEDICINE SERVICE

Director, Sports Medicine Service/Head Athletic Trainer: Brad Pearson. **Medical Director:** Dr. Larry Ronan. **Head Team Orthopedist:** Dr. Peter Asnis. **Senior Physical Therapist/Clinical Specialist:** Jamie Creps. **Assistant Athletic Trainers:** Masai Takahashi, Jon Jochim, Brandon Henry. **Head Strength/Conditioning Coach:** Kiyoshi Momose. **Coordinator of Athletic Performance/Major League Strength/Conditioning Coach:** Mike Roose. **Assistant Strength/Conditioning Coach:** Edgar Barreto.

PLAYER DEVELOPMENT

Vice President, Player Development: Ben Crockett. **Director, Minor League Operations:** Brian Abraham. **Coordinator, Minor League Operations:** Patrick McLaughlin. **Assistant, Florida Baseball Operations:** Stephen Aluko. **Minor League Field Coordinator:** Ryan Jackson. **Assistant Field Coordinator/Infield Coordinator:** Andy Fox. **Hitting Coordinator:** Greg Norton. **Catching Coordinator:** Chad Epperson. **Outfield/Baserunning Coordinator:** Darren Fenster. **Pitching Coordinator, Logistics:** Ralph Treuel. **Pitching Coordinator, Performance:** Shawn Haviland, Chris Mears. **Assistant Hitting Coordinator:** Reed Gragnani. **Latin American Pitching Coordinator/Rehab Coordinator:** Walter Miranda. **Latin American Field Coordinator:** Jose Zapata. **Latin American Pitching Advisor:** Goose Gregson. **Assistant Coordinator, Baseball Development:** Chris Stasio. **Assistant, Baseball Development:** Jordan Elkary. **Coach/Interpreter:** Mickey Jiang. **ATC Coordinator:** Eric Velazquez. **GCL ATC/Assistant ATC Coordinator:** Joel Harris. **Minor League Physical Therapist:** Kevin Avilla. **Minor League Equipment Manager:** Mike Stelmach. **Minor League Clubhouse Assistant:** RJ Warner.

FARM SYSTEM

Class	Club (League)	Manager	Hitting Coach	Pitching Coach	Position Coach
Triple-A	Pawtucket (IL)	Billy McMillon	Rich Gedman	Paul Abbott	Bruce Crabbe
Double-A	Portland (EL)	Joseph Oliver	Lance Zawadzki	Lance Carter	Frankie Rios
High A	Salem (CAR)	Corey Wimberly	Nelson Paulino	Brett Merritt	Matt O'Neil
Low A	Greenville (SAL)	Iggy Suarez	Josh Prince	Bob Kipper	John Shelby
Short-season	Lowell (NYP)	Luke Montz	Nate Spears	Nick Green	Aly Gonzalez
Rookie	Red Sox (GCL)	Tom Kotchman	Junior Zamora	Miguel Bonilla	Angel Berroa
Rookie	Red Sox (DSL)	Ozzie Chavez	Carlos Adolfo	Oscar Lira	Leonel Vasquez
Rookie	Red Sox (DSL)	Sandy Madera	Eider Torres	H. Sanchez	C. Sanchez

SCOUTING

VP/ Professional Scouting: Gus Quattlebaum. **VP/ Scouting:** Mike Rikard. **Director, Professional Scouting:** Harrison Slutsky. **Director, Amateur Scouting:** Paul Toboni. **Assistant Director, Amateur Scouting:** Devin Pearson. **Coordinator, Player Personnel:** Marcus Cuellar. **Advance Scouting Assistant:** JT Watkins. **Assistant, Amateur and Pro Scouting:** Jake Bruml. **Special Assignment Scouts:** Steve Peck, Brad Sloan. **Special Assistant, Player Personnel:** Mark Wasinger. **Global Crosschecker:** Paul Fryer. **Professional Scouts:** Nate Field, Bob Hamelin, Blair Henry, Tim Huff, Steve Langone, Dana Levangie, John Lombardo, Matt Mahoney, Anthony Turco, Kyri Washington. **Crosscheckers:** John Booher, Quincy Boyd, Dan Madsen, Fred Petersen, Jim Robinson, Tom Kotchman, Justin Horowitz, Stephen Hargett. **Area Scouts:** Brandon Agamennone (Frisco, TX), JJ Altobelli (Costa Mesa, CA), Lee Bryant (Katy, TX), Matt Davis (Mechanicsburg, OH), Lane Decker (Piedmont, OK), Raymond Fagnant (East Granby, CT), Kirk Fredriksson (Mid Atlantic), Todd Gold (Chicago, IL), Josh Labandeira, (Fresno, CA), Brian Moehler (Marietta, GA), Carl Moesche (Gresham, OR), Edgar Perez (Vega Baja, PR), Dante Ricciardi (North Florida), Willie Romay (Miami Springs, FL), Danny Watkins (Daphne, AL), Vaughn Williams (Gilbert, AZ), Jim Woodward (Claremont, CA). **Part Time Scouts:** Rob English, Tim Martin, Greg Morhardt, David Scrivines, Dick Sorkin, Terry Sullivan. **Co-Director, International Scouting:** Todd Claus, Ronaldo Pino. **Special Assistant, International Scouting:** Chris Becerra. **Coordinator, Pacific Rim Operations:** Brett Ward. **Ambassador to the Red Sox in the DR:** Jesus Alou. **Assistant Director, DR Academy:** Javier Hernandez. **Assistant, DR Academy:** Martin Rodriguez. **Assistant, Latin American Operations:** Alberto Mejia. **Supervisor, Dominican Republic:** Manny Nanita. **Assistant Supervisor, Dominican Republic:** Jonathan Cruz. **International Scouts:** Domingo Brito (Dominican Republic), Juan Carlos Calderon (Dominican Republic), Alfredo Castellon (Colombia), Angel Escobar (Venezuela), Aneko Knowles (Bahamas), Steve Fish (Australia), Cris Garibaldo (Panama), Ernesto Gomez (Venezuela), John Kim (Korea), Matias Laureano (Dominican Republic), Louie Lin (Taiwan), Wilder Lobo (Venezuela), Esau Medina (Dominican Republic), Rafael Mendoza (Nicaragua), Ramon Mora (Venezuela), Cesar Morillo (Venezuela), Rafael Motooka (Brazil), Dennis Neuman (Aruba/Curacao), Alex Requena (Venezuela), Hector Rincones (Venezuela), Lenin Rodriguez (Venezuela), Rene Saggiadi (Europe), Sotero Torres (Mexico). **International Pro Scouts:** Won Lee (Korea).

CHICAGO CUBS

Office Address: Wrigley Field, 1060 W. Addison St., Chicago, IL 60613.
Telephone: (773) 404-2827. **Website:** www.cubs.com.

OWNERSHIP

Chairman: Tom Ricketts. **Board of Directors:** Laura Ricketts, Pete Ricketts and Todd Ricketts. **Executive Assistant, Executive Chairman:** Lorraine Swiatly.

BUSINESS OPERATIONS

President, Business Operations: Crane Kenney. **Executive Vice President:** Alex Sugarman. **Executive Vice President, Chief Financial Officer:** Jon Greifenkamp. **Executive Assistant, President Business Operations:** Michele Dietz.

BALLPARK/EVENT OPERATIONS

Senior Vice President, Operations: David Cromwell. **Director, Event Operations & Security:** Morgan Bucciferro. **Director, Guest Services:** Vanessa Ward. **Vice President, Facility & Supply Chain Operations:** Patrick Meenan. **Vice President, Wrigley Field Events:** Carl Rice. **Director, Facilities:** Ryan Egan.

LEGAL

EVP, Community & Gov't Affairs, Chief Legal Officer: Michael Lufrano. **Vice President, General Counsel:** Brett Scharback. **Counsel:** Amy Timm. **Counsel:** Shameeka Quallo. **Executive Director, Cubs Charities:** Alicia Gonzalez.

TICKET SALES/SALES & PARTNERSHIPS

Executive Vice President, Sales & Marketing: Colin Faulkner. **Senior Vice President, Marquee 360:** Cale Vennum. **Vice President, Partnerships, Marquee 360:** Alex Seyferth.

MEDIA RELATIONS

Director, Media Relations: Peter Chase.

Tom Ricketts

BASEBALL OPERATIONS

Telephone: (773) 404-2827. **Fax:** (773) 404-4147.
President, Baseball Operations: Theo Epstein. **Executive VP/General Manager:** Jed Hoyer. **Assistant GM:** Randy Bush. **Senior Vice President, Player Personnel:** Jason McLeod. **Senior Director, Major League Data & Development:** Kyle Evans. **Director, Pro Scouting & Baseball Operations:** Jeff Greenberg. **Director, Research & Development:** Chris Moore. **Director, Baseball Systems Development:** Ryan Kruse. **Director, High Performance:** Adam Beard. **Director, Team Travel:** Vijay Tekchandani. **Assistant Director, Baseball Operations:** Greg Davey. **Assistant Directors, Research & Development:** Jeremy Greenhouse, Chris Jones. **Manager, Baseball Operations Administration and Executive Assistant to the President/GM:** Meghan Jones. **Special Assistants, President/GM:** Ryan Dempster, Ted Lilly, Jaron Madison, Kerry Wood. **Senior Biomechanist:** John Dewitt. **Analysts, Research & Development:** Garrett Chiado, Bryan

2020 SCHEDULE

Standard Game Times: Mon.-Sat., 7:05 pm; Sun. 1:20 pm.

MARCH			
26-29 . . . . . at Milwaukee	5-7. . . at Los Angeles (NL)	26-28 . . . at New York (AL)	10-12 . . . . . .at Cincinnati
30-31 . . . . . . .Pittsburgh	8-10 . . . . . .Washington	30 . . . . .Milwaukee	14-16 . . . . . . at Toronto
	11-13 . . . . . .Milwaukee		18-20 . . . Los Angeles (NL)
APRIL	15-17 . . . . . at San Diego	**JULY**	21-23 . . . . St. Louis
1 . . . . Pittsburgh	19-21 . . . . at Pittsburgh	1-2. . . . . .Milwaukee	25-27 . . . . at Miami
3-5 . . . . Arizona	23-24 . . . . . at Milwaukee	3-5. . . . . .Tampa Bay	28-30 . . . at New York (NL)
6-9. . . . . . at Pittsburgh	27-28 . . . . .Miami	8-9. . . . . at Chicago (AL)	
10-12 . . . . St. Louis	29-31 . . . . Cincinnati	10-12 . . . . . . at Atlanta	**SEPTEMBER**
13-15 . . . . . at Baltimore		17-19 . . . . Cincinnati	1-2. . . . . . San Francisco
16-19 . . at Washington	**JUNE**	21-22 . . . . Chicago (AL)	4-6. . . . . Cincinnati
21-23 . . . . . . San Diego	2 . . . . Cincinnati	24-26 . . . . . .at St. Louis	7-10 . . . . . . at Colorado
24-26 . . . . . .Philadelphia	3-4. . . . . Baltimore	28-30 . . . at San Francisco	11-13 . . . . . . .at St. Louis
27-29 . . . . . . Pittsburgh	4-7. . . . . . .at Cincinnati	31 . . . . .Milwaukee	14-17 . . . . . . Pittsburgh
30 . . . . at Arizona	8-10 . . . . at Philadelphia		18-20 . . . . . . .Colorado
	13-14 . . . . . . .at St. Louis	**AUGUST**	22-23 . . . . . at Pittsburgh
MAY	17-18 . . .New York (NL)	1-2. . . . . .Milwaukee	25-27 . . . . St. Louis
1-3. . . . . at Arizona	19-21 . . . . Boston	4-6. . . . . Atlanta	
	23-25 . . . . . .at Cincinnati	8-9. . . . . . at Milwaukee	

GENERAL INFORMATION

Stadium (year opened):
Wrigley Field (1914).
Team Colors: Royal blue, red and white.

Home Dugout: Third Base.
Playing Surface: Grass.

Cole, Jacob Eisenberg, Jennifer Gossels, Troy Mulholland, Eli Shayer. **Coordinator, Research & Development:** Ryan Otero. **Developers, Baseball Systems:** Zack Brusso, Kyle Chin, Dan Codos, Jonathan Robins. **Coordinator, Baseball Operations:** Alex Smith. **Assistant, Baseball Operations:** Sam Abrams. **Assistant, Research & Development:** Garrett Chiado. **Assistant Director, Baseball Operations:** Greg Davey.

Theo Epstein

MAJOR LEAGUE STAFF
Manager: David Ross. **Coaches: Bench**—Andy Green, **Pitching**—Tommy Hottovy, **Hitting**—Anthony Iapoce, **Assistant Hitting**—Terrmel Sledge, **Third Base**—Will Venable, **First Base**—Craig Driver, **Associate Pitching, Catching and Strategy**—Mike Borzello, **Bullpen**—Chris Young. **Quality Assurance Coach:** Mike Napoli. **Staff Assistants:** Juan Cabreja, Franklin Font. **Bullpen Catcher:** Chad Noble. **Assistant Director, Run Production:** Nate Halm. **Assistant Director, Run Prevention:** Brad Mills. **Coordinator, Major League Video/Pacific Rim Liaison:** Nao Masamoto.

MEDICAL/TRAINING
Team Physician: Dr. Stephen Adams. **Team Orthopedist:** Dr. Stephen Gryzlo. **Orthopedic Consultant:** Dr. Michael Schafer. **Major League Athletic Trainer:** P.J. Mainville. **Assistant Athletic Trainers:** Nick Frangella, Chuck Baughman. **Head Major League S&C Coach:** Shane Wallen. **Assistant Major League S&C Coach:** Austin Smith. **MLB Head Applied Mental Skills Coach:** John Baker. **Coordinator, Mental Skills:** Bob Tewksbury. **Head of Sports Nutrition & Dietitian Services:** Julia Long. **Major League Sports Dietitian:** Jordan Brown.

PLAYER DEVELOPMENT
Telephone: (773) 404-2827. **Fax:** (773) 404-4147.
Senior Director, Player Development: Matt Dorey. **Director, Player Development:** Bobby Basham. **Director, Pitching/Special Assistant to the President/GM:** Craig Breslow. **Director, Hitting:** Justin Stone. **Assistant Director, Baseball Development:** Jeremy Farrell. **Coordinator, Minor League Operations:** Allyson Darragh. **Assistant, Player Development:** Ella Cahill. **Manager, Mesa Administration:** Gil Passarella. **Equipment Manager:** Dana Noeltner. **Minor League Coordinators:** Chris Valaika (hitting), Casey Jacobson (pitching development), James Ogden (pitching performance), Mark Johnson (catching), Doug Dascenzo (outfield & baserunning), Jonathan Mota (infield), Dave Keller (Latin America field), Tom Beyers (asst. hitting development), Steven Pollakov (D.R. hitting analytics), Mike Mason (asst. pitching performance), Carlos Chantres (asst. pitching development), Josh Zeid (rehab pitching), Tyler Pearson (rehab hitting). **Head S&C and Performance Science:** Cory Kennedy. **Rehab S&C Coordinator:** Doug Jarrow. **Minor League Training Coordinator:** Mike McNulty. **Assistant Training Coordinator:** Jonathan Fierro. **Mental Skills Coordinators:** Dave DaSilva, Javier Guerrero. **Coordinator, Player Development Video & Operations:** Sam Hunter. **Assistant, Player Development/Research & Development:** Ryan Reinsel. **Assistant, Player Development Technology:** Ryan West. **Special Assignment Scout/Advisor to Baseball Development:** David Howard. **Advisor, Baseball Development:** Mike Roberts.

FARM SYSTEM
Class	Club (League)	Manager	Hitting Coach	Pitching Coach
Triple-A	Iowa (PCL)	Marty Pevey	D. Wilson/Will Remillard	Ron Villone
Double-A	Tennessee (SL)	Michael Ryan	Chad Allen/Chase Spivey	Charlie Haeger
High A	Myrtle Beach (CL)	Steven Lerud	Paul McAnulty/Will Skett	Anderson Tavarez
Low A	South Bend (MWL)	Buddy Bailey	D. Puente/R. Medina	Jamie Vermilyea
Short-season	Eugene (NWL)	Lance Rymel	O. Melendez/T. Fitta	Armando Gabino
Rookie	Cubs 1 (AZL)	Carmelo Martinez	J. Rogers/R. Folden	Doug Willey
Rookie	Cubs 2 (AZL)	Jimmy Gonzalez	E. Patterson/C. Rojas	Tony Cougoule
Rookie	Cubs 1 (DSL)	Carlos Ramirez	D. Jimenez/C. Pieters	Jose Zapata
Rookie	Cubs 2 (DSL)	Leo Perez	E. Wilson/J. Rosario	Luis Hernandez

SCOUTING
Director, Pro Scouting & Baseball Operations: Jeff Greenberg. **Assistant Director, Pro Scouting:** Andrew Bassett. **Special Assignment Scouts:** Jason Cooper, Dave Klipstein, Spike Lundberg. **Major League Scouts:** Jake Ciarrachi, Joe Nelson, Steve Boros. **Pro Scouts:** Billy Blitzer, Willie Fraser, Nic Jackson, Terry Kennedy, Mark Kiefer, Kyle Phillips, Aaron Sele, Thad Weber, Adam Wogan. **Advisor to Pro Scouting:** Jim Benedict. **Baseball Operations Assistant:** Matt Murton. **Part-Time Pro Scouts:** Robert Lofrano, Mark Servais. **Vice President, Scouting:** Dan Kantrovitz. **Assistant Director, Amateur Scouting:** Lukas McKnight. **Assistant, Amateur Scouting:** Adam Unes. **Analyst, Amateur Scouting:** Jasmine Horan. **National Supervisor:** Ron Tostenson. **Crosscheckers: Midwest/Northeast**—Tim Adkins (Huntington, WV), **Central**—Daniel Carte (McKinney, TX), **Southeast**—Bobby Filotei (Mobile, AL), **Canada**—Gabe Sandy (Gresham, OR). **Area Scouts:** Tom Clark (Lake City, FL), Trey Forkerway (Houston, TX), Todd George (Temple, TX), Edwards Guzman (Toa Baja, PR), Evan Kauffman (Irvine, CA), John Koronka (Clermont, FL), Keith Lockhart (Dacula, GA), Alex Lontayo (Murrieta, CA), Alex McClure (Memphis, TN), Steve McFarland (Scottsdale, AZ), Tom Myers (Santa Barbara, CA), Ty Nichols (Broken Arrow, OK), John Pedrotty (Chicago, IL), Gabe Sandy (Gresham, OR), Matt Sherman (Kingston, MA), Billy Swoope (Norfolk, VA), Jacob Williams (Lexington, KY), Gabe Zappin (Walnut Creek, CA). **Coordinator, Scouting Video:** Mitch Duggins. **Amateur Video Scouts:** Zach Zielinski, Garrett Tolivar. **Part-Time Area Scouts:** Keronn Walker (Chicago, IL), Korey Kier (Vancouver, WA). **Director, International Scouting:** Louie Eljaua. **Director, International Pro Scouting:** Alex Suarez. **Coordinator, International Scouting:** Kenny Socorro. **Latin America Crosschecker/Venezuela Scouting Supervisor:** Hector Ortega. **International Crosschecker:** Gian Guzman. **Coordinator, Dominican Republic Scouting:** Miguel Diaz. **Scouting Supervisor, Central and South America:** Cirilo Cumberbatch, **Mexico:** Sergio Hernandez. **Coordinator, Colombian Operations:** Manny Esquivia. **International Scouts:** Hansel Izquierdo, Jamie McFarland, Brent Phelan. **Latin America Scouts: Dominican Republic**—Alejandro Pena, Marino Encarnacion, Carlos Pellerano, Valerio Heredia, **Venezuela**—Julio Figueroa, Manuel Pestana, Rafael Jimenez, Carlos Figueroa, **Mexico**—Salvador Hernandez, **Colombia**—Dalmiro Alvarez.

CHICAGO WHITE SOX

Office Address: Guaranteed Rate Field, 333 W. 35th St., Chicago, IL 60616.
Telephone: (312) 674-1000. **Fax:** (312) 674-5116.
Website: whitesox.com, loswhitesox.com.

OWNERSHIP
Chairman: Jerry Reinsdorf.
Board of Directors: Robert Judelson, Judd Malkin, Allan Muchin, Jay Pinsky, Lee Stern, Burton Ury, Charles Walsh.
Special Assistant to Chairman: Dennis Gilbert. **Assistant to Chairman:** Katie Hermle. **Coordinator, Administration/Investor Relations:** Elizabeth Anderson.

BUSINESS OPERATIONS
Senior Executive Vice President: Howard Pizer. **Senior Systems Analyst:** Stan Czyzewski. Vice President, **Human Resources:** Moira Foy. Senior Coordinator, **Human Resources:** Leslie Gaggiano.

FINANCE
Senior VP, Administration/Finance: Tim Buzard. **VP, Finance:** Bill Waters. **Director of Accounting:** Mallory Penn.

MARKETING/SALES
Senior VP, Sales/Marketing: Brooks Boyer. **Senior Director, Business Development/Broadcasting:** Bob Grim. **Director, Game Presentation:** Cris Quintana. **Sr. Manager, Scoreboard Operations/Production:** Jeff Szynal. **Sr. Manager, Game Operations:** Dan Mielke. **Sr. Director, Corporate Partnerships Sales Development:** George McDoniel. **Sr. Director, Corporate Partnerships Activation:** Gail Tucker. **Sr. Manager, Corporate Partnerships Development:** Jeff Floerke. **Coordinators/Managers, Corporate Partnership:** Adam Delgado, Ashley Sorenson, Kat Claeys, Drew Fischer, Krista Pulcini. **VP of Sales and Service:** Jim Willits. **Sr. Manager, Ticket Sales:** Rich Kuchar.

Jerry Reinsdorf

MEDIA RELATIONS/PUBLIC RELATIONS
Telephone: (312) 674-5300. **Fax:** (312) 674-5116.
Senior VP, Communications: Scott Reifert. **Senior Director, Media Relations:** Bob Beghtol. **Director, Public Relations:** Sheena Quinn. **Assistant Director, Media Relations:** Ray Garcia. **Coordinator, Public Relations:** Colin McGauley. **Coordinators, Media Relations/Services:** Joe Roti, Hannah Sundwall. **VP, Community Relations/Executive Director/CWS Charities:** Christine O'Reilly. **Director, Community Relations:** Sarah Marten, Lindsey Jordan. **Manager, Youth Baseball Initiatives:** Anthony Olivo. **Director, Digital Communications:** Brad Boron. **Director, Design Services:** Matt Peterson. **Manager, Online Communications:** Dakin Dugaw.

STADIUM OPERATIONS
Senior VP, Stadium Operations: Terry Savarise. **Senior Director, Park Operations:** Jonathan Vasquez.
Senior Director, Guest Services/Diamond Suite Operations: Julie Taylor. **Head Groundskeeper:** Roger Bossard.

2020 SCHEDULE
Standard Game Times: Mon.-Sat., 7:15 p.m.; Sun. 1:10 pm.

MARCH	9 - 10 . . . at San Francisco	30 . . . . at Toronto	13 - 16 . . . .New York (AL)
26 - 29 . . . . . Kansas City	12 - 13 . . . . at San Diego	**JULY**	19 . . . . . . at Minnesota
30 - 31 . . . . .at Cleveland	15 - 17 . . . . . . .Toronto	1 - 2 . . . . at Toronto	21 - 23 . . . . . .at Seattle
	20 . . . . .Colorado	3 - 5 . . . . .at Texas	26 - 28 . . . . Boston
APRIL	21 - 24 . . . . at Minnesota	8 - 9 . . . . . Chicago (NL)	29 - 30 . . . . . . Houston
1 . . . . .at Cleveland	25 - 28 . . . .at Baltimore	11 - 12 . . . . Arizona	31 . . . . . . at Tampa Bay
2 - 5 . . . . .at Boston	30 - 31 . . . . .Minnesota	17 - 19 . . . . . .at Detroit	
6 - 8 . . . . Seattle		21 - 22 . . .at Chicago (NL)	**SEPTEMBER**
11 - 12 . . . . .Minnesota	**JUNE**	24 - 26 . . . . . .Minnesota	1 - 3 . . . . . . at Tampa Bay
13 - 15 . . .at Kansas City	2 - 4 . . . . . .at Kansas City	28 - 30 . . . . Detroit	5 - 6 . . . . . . at Minnesota
17 - 19 . . . . Texas	6 - 7 . . . . Detroit	30 - 31 . . . at Cleveland	9 - 10 . . . Los Angeles (NL)
21 - 22 . . . . Kansas City	10 - 11 . . . . . Cleveland		11 - 13 . . . .at Kansas City
24 - 26 . at Los Angeles (AL)	13 - 14 . . . . .at Houston	**AUGUST**	15 - 16 . . . . .at Oakland
29 . . . . at Colorado	16 - 18 . . . . . .at Detroit	1 - 2 . . . . . . .at Cleveland	18 - 20 . . . . Kansas City
	19 - 21 . . . . . .at Cleveland	3 - 5 . . . at New York (AL)	22 - 23 . . . . . . Cleveland
MAY	23 - 26 . . . . . . Detroit	8 - 9 . . . . Cleveland	25 - 27 . . . . . .at Detroit
2 - 3 . . . . Baltimore	27 - 28 . . . . . . Oakland	11 - 12 . . Los Angeles (AL)	
6 - 7 . . . . . . .Tampa Bay			

GENERAL INFORMATION
Stadium (year opened):
Guaranteed Rate Field (1991).
Team Colors: Black, white and silver.

Home Dugout: Third Base.
Playing Surface: Grass.

PA Announcer: Gene Honda. **Official Scorers:** Don Friske, Allan Spear, Bill Sieple.

TICKETING

Senior Director, Ticket Operations: Mike Mazza. **Manager, Ticket Operations:** Pete Catizone.

TRAVEL/CLUBHOUSE

Director, Team Travel: Ed Cassin. **Manager, White Sox Clubhouse:** Rob Warren. **Manager,Visiting Clubhouse:** Jason Gilliam. **Manager, Umpires Clubhouse:** Joe McNamara Jr.

BASEBALL OPERATIONS

JON DURR/GETTY IMAGES

Rick Hahn

Executive Vice President: Ken Williams.
Senior VP/General Manager: Rick Hahn. **Assistant GM:** Jeremy Haber. **Special Assistants:** Bill Scherrer, Dave Yoakum, Marco Paddy, Jim Thome, Nick Hostetler, Jose Contreras. **Major League Advance Scout:** Bryan Little. **Executive Assistant to GM:** Nancy Nesnidal. **Senior Director, Baseball Operations:** Dan Fabian. **Director, Baseball Operations:** Daniel Zien. **Special Assignment, Baseball Operations:** Kenny Williams, Jr. **Manager Baseball Operations:** Jeff Lachman. **Director Baseball Analytics:** Matt Koenig. **Analyst, Baseball Operations:** Emily Blady.

MAJOR LEAGUE STAFF

Manager: Rick Renteria. **Coaches—Bench:** Joe McEwing. **Pitching:** Don Cooper. **Hitting:** Frank Menechino. **First Base:** Daryl Boston. **Third Base:** Nick Capra. **Bullpen:** Curt Hasler. **Assistant Hitting Coach:** Scott Coolbaugh. **Bullpen Catcher:** Miguel Gonzalez. **Mgr. of Cultural Development/ Bullpen Catcher:** Luis Sierra.

MEDICAL/TRAINING

Senior Team Physician: Dr. Nikhil Verma. **Head Athletic Trainer Emeritus:** Herm Schneider. **Head Athletic Trainer:** Brian Ball. **Assistant Athletic Trainer/Physical Therapist:** Brett Walker. **Assistant Athletic Trainer:** James Kruk, Josh Fallin. **Director, Strength & Conditioning:** Allen Thomas.

PLAYER DEVELOPMENT

Director, Player Development: Chris Getz.
Senior Director, Minor League Operations: Grace Guerrero-Zwit. **Senior Coordinator, Minor League Administration:** Kathy Potoski. **Senior Coordinator, Latin American and Minor League Operations:** Arturo Perez. **Field Coordinator:** Doug Sisson. **Pitching Coordinator:** Everett Teaford. **Assistant Pitching Coordinator:** J.R. Perdew. **Hitting Coordinator:** Ben Broussard. **Assistant Hitting Coordinator:** Ryan Johansen. **Catching Coordinator:** John Orton. **Performance Coordinator:** Goldy Simmons. **Senior Biomechanical Engineer:** Ben Hansen. **Managers, Player Development:** Rod Larson, Graham Harboe. **Assistants, Player Development:** Rafael Santana, Tommy Thompson, Diego Francisco. **Rehab Pitching Coach:** Steve McCatty. **Education Coordinator:** Erin Santana. **Latin/Cultural Development Coordinator:** Anthony Santiago. **Quality Control:** Zach Jones, Nate Pearson, Devin Pickett. **Medical Coordinator:** Scott Takao. **Physical Therapist/Rehab Coordinator:** Derek Garris. **Physical Therapist:** Brooks Klein. **Strength and Conditioning Advisor:** Dale Torborg. **Arizona Operations—Facility Manager:** Joe Lachcik, **Minor League Clubhouse and Equipment Manager:** Dan Flood. **Assistant Minor League Clubhouse Manager:** Bryant Biasotti. **Assistant, Player Development/Latin Education Assistant:** Grant Flick. **D.R. Academy Field Coordinator:** Guillermo Reyes.

FARM SYSTEM

Class	Club (League)	Manager	Hitting Coach	Pitching Coach
Triple-A	Charlotte (IL)	Wes Helms	Howie Clark	Matt Zaleski
Double-A	Birmingham (SL)	Justin Jirschele	Charlie Romero	Richard Dotson
High A	Winston-Salem (CL)	Ryan Newman	Charlie Poe	Danny Farquhar
Low A	Kannapolis (SAL)	Guillermo Quiroz	Cole Armstrong	Jose Bautista
Rookie	Great Falls (PIO)	Mike Gellinger	Cam Seitzer	John Ely
Rookie	White Sox (AZL)	Ever Magallanes	Drew Hasler	Felipe Lira
Rookie	White Sox (DSL)	Angel Rosario	Angel Gonzalez	Leo Hernandez

SCOUTING

Telephone: (312) 674-1000. **Fax:** (312) 674-5105.
Pro Scouts: Bruce Benedict (Atlanta, GA), Joe Butler (Long Beach, CA), Toney Howell (Darien, IL), Alan Regier (Gilbert, AZ), Daraka Shaheed (Vallejo, CA), Joe Siers (Wesley Chapel, FL), Keith Staab (College Station, TX), Chris Walker (Katy, TX), Bill Young (Scottsdale, AZ). **Director, Amateur Scouting:** Mike Shirley. **Senior Advisor, Scouting Operations:** Doug Laumann. **Assistant Director, Amateur Scouting:** Garrett Guest. **National Crosschecker:** Nathan Durst (Sycamore, IL), **National Pitching Crosschecker:** Kirk Champion. **Regional Crosscheckers—East:** Tim Bittner (Mechanicsville, PA), **West**—Derek Valenzuela (Temecula, CA), **Southeast**—Juan Alvarez (Miami, FL), **Midwest**— Rob Cummings (Kansas City, MO). **Advisor to Baseball Department:** Larry Monroe (Schaumburg, IL). **Area Scouts:** Mike Baker (Santa Ana, CA), Kevin Burrell (Sharpsburg, GA), Ryan Dorsey (Dallas, TX), Abe Fernandez (Miami, FL), Mike Gange (Portland, OR), Phil Gulley (Morehead, KY), Jason Howell (Atlanta, GA), Warren Hughes (Mobile, AL), JJ Lally (Denison, IA), George Kachigian (Coronado, CA), John Kazanas (Phoenix, AZ), Steve Payne (Barrington, RI), Steffan Segui (St. Petersburg, FL), Noah St. Urbain (Stockton, CA), Adam Virchis (Modesto, CA), Justin Wechsler (Niles, MI), Tyler Wilt (Wilus, TX), Torreon Woods (Overland Park, KS). **International Scouts:** Amador Arias (Maracay, Venezuela), Marino DeLeon (Yamasa, D.R.), Robinson Garces (Maracaibo, VZ), Tomas Herrera (Saltillo, Mexico), Reydel Hernandez (Puerto La Cruz, VZ), **Supervisor Latin America:** Ruddy Moreta (Santo Domingo, D.R.). Miguel Peguero (Santo Domingo, D.R.), Guillermo Peralta (Santiago, D.R.), Omar Sanchez (Valencia, VZ), Fermin Ubri (Bani, D.R.), Ricardo Ortiz (Colon, Panama).

CINCINNATI REDS

Office Address: 100 Joe Nuxhall Way, Cincinnati, OH 45202.
Telephone: (513) 765-7000. **Fax:** (513) 765-7342. **Website:** www.reds.com.

OWNERSHIP
Operated by: The Cincinnati Reds LLC. **Chief Executive Officer:** Robert H. Castellini. **Chairman:** W. Joseph Williams Jr. **Vice Chairman:** Thomas L. Williams. **President & Chief Operating Officer:** Phillip J. Castellini. **Executive Operations Manager:** Shellie Petrey. **Executive Advisor to the CEO:** Walt Jocketty. **Secretary & Treasurer:** Christopher L. Fister. **Senior Vice President, Finance & CFO:** Doug Healy.

BUSINESS OPERATIONS
Senior Vice President, Business Operations: Karen Forgus. **Business Operations Assistant:** Theodora Siegel. **Business Operations, Assistant/Speakers Bureau:** Emily Mahle.

FINANCE/ADMINISTRATION
Sr. Vice President of Finance and CFO: Doug Healy. **Chief Legal Counsel:** James A. Marx. **Assistant to CFO/CLO:** Teena Schweier. **Vice President of Finance, Controller:** Bentley Viator. **Accounting Manager:** Jill Niemeyer. **Sr. Accountant:** Cathy Brakers.

TICKETING/BUSINESS DEVELOPMENT
VP, Ticketing & Business Development: Aaron Eisel. **Sr. Director, Ticket Sales & Service:** Mark Schueler. **Director, Ticketing New Business:** Patrick Motague.

Bob Castellini

MEDIA RELATIONS
Vice President, Media Relations: Rob Butcher. **Director, Media Relations:** Larry Herms. **Director, Media Relations/Digital Content:** Jamie Ramsey.

COMMUNICATIONS/MARKETING
Vice President of Communications & Marketing: Ralph Mitchell. **Director of Digitial Media:** Lisa Braun. **Director of Marketing:** Audra Sordyl. **Director of Communications & Web Content:** Jarrod Rollins. **Public Relations Manager:** Michael Anderson.

COMMUNITY RELATIONS
Director, Community Relations: Lindsey Dingeldein. **Diversity Relations Coordinator:** Natalya Herndon. **Executive Director, Community Fund:** Charley Frank. **Assistant Director, Community Fund:** Matthew Wagner.

BALLPARK OPERATIONS
Vice President, Ballpark Operations: Tim O'Connell. **Senior Director, Ballpark Operations:** Sean Brown.

BASEBALL OPERATIONS
President of Baseball Operations: Dick Williams. **Vice President & General Manager:** Nick Krall. **Executive Assistant to Pres. of Baseball Ops/GM:** Sarah Vedder. **Vice President, Assistant General Manager:** Sam Grossman.

2020 SCHEDULE
Standard Game Times: 7:10 p.m.; Sun. 1:10

MARCH	8-10 . . . . at Colorado	30 . . . at Los Angeles (NL)
26-29 . . . . St. Louis	11-13 . . . . Miami	
30-31 . . . . at Toronto	14-17 . . . . Milwaukee	**JULY**
	19-20 . . . . at Cleveland	1-2 . . . at Los Angeles (NL)
APRIL	22-25 . . . . . San Diego	3-5 . . . . at Arizona
1 . . . . at Toronto	26-28 . . . . . . Pittsburgh	7-8 . . . . Cleveland
2-5 . . . . . . at Pittsburgh	29-31 . . . . at Chicago (NL)	10-12 . . . . . . Pittsburgh
6-7 . . . . Milwaukee		17-19 . . . . at Chicago (NL)
9-12 . . . . . . Philadelphia	**JUNE**	21-23 . . . . . New York (NL)
14-16 . . . . San Francisco	1 . . . . . . at Chicago (NL)	24-26 . . . . Colorado
17-19 . . at New York (AL)	2-3 . . . . . . at Pittsburgh	27-30 . . . . . . at Atlanta
20-22 . . . . . . at St. Louis	4-7 . . . . . . Chicago (NL)	31 . . . . Tampa Bay
24-26 . . . . Arizona	9-11 . . . Los Angeles (NL)	
27-29 . . . . Atlanta	13-14 . . . . at Milwaukee	**AUGUST**
	17-18 . . . at San Diego	1-2 . . . . Tampa Bay
MAY	20-21 . . . . . . at St. Louis	4-6 . . . . . at Philadelphia
1-3 . . . . at Washington	23-25 . . . . Chicago (NL)	8-9 . . . . at St. Louis
4-6 . . . . at New York (NL)	26-28 . . . . . . Washington	11-12 . . . . . Chicago (NL)

13-16 . . . . Pittsburgh
18-19 . . . . at Boston
21-23 . . . . at Milwaukee
24-26 . . . . St. Louis
27-30 . . . . . . Milwaukee
31 . . . . Baltimore
SEPTEMBER
1-2 . . . . Baltimore
4-6 . . . . at Chicago (NL)
8-9 . . . . . at Milwaukee
11-13 . . . at San Francisco
15-16 . . . . Boston
17-20 . . . . St. Louis
21-23 . . . . at Miami
24-27 . . . . . at Pittsburgh

GENERAL INFORMATION
Stadium (year opened): Great American Ball Park (2003). **Team Colors:** Red, white and black.
Home Dugout: First Base.
Playing Surface: Grass.

Vice President, Senior Advisor to Pres. of Baseball Ops/GM: Buddy Bell. **Vice President, Player Personnel:** Chris Buckley. **Senior Director, Player Personnel:** Jeff Graupe. **Senior Advisor to Baseball Operations:** Joe Morgan. **Coordinator, Baseball Operations:** Mark Edwards. **Director, Sports Science Initiatives:** Charles Leddon. **Manager, Baseball Systems:** Brett Elkins. **Applications Specialist, Baseball Systems:** Ryan Barger. **Manager, Baseball Analytics:** Michael Schatz. **Coordinator, Baseball Analytics:** Melissa Booker. **Senior Data Scientist:** Kevin Corby. **Data Scientist:** Chris Jackson, Stuart Wallace, Nick Wan. **Major League Analyst:** James Brand. **Baseball Analytics Developer:** Samantha Rack. **Baseball Systems Developer:** Joe Delia. **Data Engineer, Baseball Systems:** Bryce Dugar. **DevOps Engineer:** Christina Harlow. **Manager, Advance Scouting:** Bo Thompson. **Coordinator, Major League Video & Technology:** Gary Hall. **Advance Scouting Coach:** Cristian Perez. **Baseball Operations Analyst:** Katie Krall. **Senior Director, Team Travel:** Gary Wahoff. **Sports Science Assistant:** Jesus Ramos. **Senior Director, Clubhouse Operations:** Rick Stowe. **Visiting Clubhouse Manager:** Josh Stewart. **Clubhouse Assistant:** Mark Stowe.

Dick Williams

MEDICAL/TRAINING

Senior Director, Health & Performance: Geoff Head. **Head Trainer:** Steve Baumann. **Assistant Trainer:** Jimmy Mattocks, Tomas Vera. **Director, Strength & Conditioning:** Sean Marohn. **Assistant Director, Strength & Conditioning:** Zach Gjestvang. **Director, Athletic Training:** Patrick Serbus. **Manager, Athletic Training:** Clete Sigwart. **Director of Physical Therapy/Rehab:** Brad Epstein. **Rehabilitation Coach:** Casey Weathers. **Physical Therapist:** Marcus Ahrens, Josh Bickel. **Coordinator, Strength & Conditioning:** Morgan Gregory. **Assistant Strength & Conditioning Coordinator:** Alex Puskarich. **Rehab Strength & Conditioning Coordinator:** Will Gilmore. **Major League Sports Dietitian:** Ashley Meuser. **Coordinator, Minor League Nutrition:** Leah Reitmayer. **Coordinator, Minor League Wellness:** Becky Schnakenberg. **Wellness Coach (DR Academy):** Rafael Castillo.

MAJOR LEAGUE STAFF

Manager: David Bell. **Coaches: Bench**—Freddie Benavides, **Hitting**—Alan Zinter, **Pitching**— Derek Johnson, **First Base**—Delino DeShields, **Third Base/Catching**—J.R. House, **Bullpen**—Lee Tunnell, **Game Planning/Outfield**—Jeff Pickler, **Assistant Hitting**—Joe Mather, **Assistant Pitching/Director of Pitching:** Caleb Cotham, **Associate Coach:** Rolando Valles, **Bullpen Catcher:** Jose Duarte, Nate Irving.

PLAYER DEVELOPMENT

Vice President, Player Development: Shawn Pender. **Senior Director, Player Development:** Eric Lee. **Special Assistant, Player Performance:** Eric Davis, Bill Doran, Barry Larkin, Mario Soto. **Coordinator, Player Development:** Mark Heil. **Coordinator, Baseball Administration:** Melissa Hill. **Coordinator, Minor League Video & Technology:** Mitchell Bonds. **Player Development Analyst:** Harris Kingsley. **Player Development Assistant:** Charlie Rodriguez. **Manager, Arizona Operations:** Mike Saverino. **Arizona Operations Assistant:** Branden Croteau. **Manager, Minor League Equipment:** Jon Snyder. **Minor League Clubhouse Assistant:** John Bryk, Ryan Dammeyer. **Field Coordinator:** Chris Tremie. **Director of Pitching Initiatives/Pitching Coordinator:** Kyle Boddy. **Outfield/Baserunning Coordinator:** Willie Harris. **Catching Coordinator:** Corky Miller. **Hitting Coordinator:** C.J. Gillman. **Academies Coordinator:** Luis Bolivar. **Latin American Field Coordinator:** Joel Noboa. **Infield Coordinator:** Jose Nieves. **Assistant Pitching Coordinator:** Eric Jagers. **Pitching Roving Instructor:** Tony Fossas. **Mental Skills Coach:** Frank Pfister. **Minor League Video and Technology Specialist:** Kyle Arnsberg. **Data Collection Specialist:** Tim Rosenbaum.

FARM SYSTEM

Class	Club (League)	Manager	Hitting Coach	Pitching Coach
Triple-A	Louisville (IL)	Pat Kelly	Leon Durham	James Baldwin
Double-A	Chattanooga (SL)	Ricky Gutierrez	Daryle Ward	Seth Etherton
High A	Daytona (FSL)	Dick Schofield	Alex Pelaez	Tom Brown
Low A	Dayton (MWL)	Gookie Dawkins	Darryl Brinkley	Brian Garman
Rookie	Greeneville (APP)	Derrin Ebert	Luis Terrero	Chris Booker
Rookie	Billings (PIO)	Bryan LaHair	Jordan Stouffer	Forrest Herrmann
Rookie	Reds (AZL)	Jose Moreno	Todd Takayoshi	Elmer Dessens
Rookie	Reds (DSL)	Luis Saturria	Wilton Veras	L. Andujar/L. Montano

SCOUTING

Director, Professional Scouting: Rob Coughlin. **Special Assistant to GM, Player Personnel:** Cam Bonifay. **Special Assistants to the General Manager:** "J" Harrison, Marty Maier, John Morris, Jeff Schugel. **Pro Scouts:** Gary Glover, Joe Jocketty, Ben Jones, Bruce Manno, Mick Mattaliano, Jeff Morris, Steve Roadcap. **Director, Amateur Scouting:** Brad Meador. **Assistant Director, Amateur Scouting:** Paul Pierson. **Assistant Director, National Crosschecker:** Joe Katuska. **National Crosschecker:** Jerry Flowers, Mark McKnight. **Regional Crosscheckers:** Bill Byckowski, Rex De La Nuez, Will Harford, Greg Zunino. **Scouting Supervisors:** Charlie Aliano, Rich Bordi, Jeff Brookens, Sean Buckley, John Ceprini, Dan Cholowsky, Andrew Fabian, Tyler Gibbons, Jerel Johnson, Mike Keenan, Brandon Marr, Mike Misuraca, Jim Moran, Mike Partida, Jonathan Reynolds, Paul Scott, Lee Seras, Andy Stack. **Scouts:** Larry Barton, Jamie Bodaly, Ed Daub, Rob Gorrell, Jim Grief, Bill Killian, Denny Nagel, Juan Silva, Lou Snipp, Marlon Styles, Mike Wallace. **Director, International Scouting:** Trey Hendricks. **Assistant Director, International Scouting:** Greg McMillin. **Director, Latin America Scouting:** Richard Jimenez. **Assistant Director, Latin American Scouting:** Richard Castro. **Crosschecker, International Scouting:** David Espinosa, Matt Gaski, Boomer Prinstein. **Supervisor, South American Scouting:** Herman Albornoz. **Supervisor, Dominican Republic:** Enmanuel Cartagena. **Coordinator, Venezuela:** Richard Quintero. **Manager, Pacific Rim Scouting:** Rob Fidler. **Scout, Pacific Rim:** Jamey Storvick. **Video Scout, D.R:** Jenfry Del Rosario. **International Scouts:** Jose Valdelamar, Mafel Brito, Jose Diaz, Edgar Melo, Victor Nova, Samuel Pimentel, Alex Ahumada, Gustavo Martinez, Concepcion Rodriguez, Dan Kim, Sal Varriale, Ryan Schuman, Wayne Durbridge, Matt Everingham, Brian Ambrister, Jean Paul Conde, Aguido Gonzalez, Victor Oramas, Ricardo Quintero, Evert-Jan't Hoen.

CLEVELAND INDIANS

Office Address: Progressive Field, 2401 Ontario St., Cleveland, OH 44115.
Telephone: (216) 420-4200. **Fax:** (216) 420-4396.
Website: www.indians.com.

OWNERSHIP
Owner: Larry Dolan. **Chairman/Chief Executive Officer:** Paul Dolan.

BUSINESS OPERATIONS
President, Business Operations: Brian Barren. **Senior Vice President, Marketing/
Strategy:** Alex King. **Executive Administrative Assistant:** Dru Kosik.

CORPORATE PARTNERSHIPS/FINANCE
Vice President, Corporate Partnership: Ted Baugh. **Senior Director, Corporate
Partnership & Premium Hospitality:** Dom Polito. **Director, Corporate Partnership &
Premium Hospitality:** Kevin Murphy. **Senior Sales Manager, Corporate Partnerships:**
Bryan Hoffart. **Administrative Assistant:** Kim Scott. **VP/General Counsel:** Joe Znidarsic. **Vice
President, Finance:** Rich Dorffer. **Controller:** Erica Chambers. **Manager, Accounting:** Karen
Menzing. **Manager, Payroll Accounting/Services:** Mary Forkapa. **Concessions Accounting
Manager:** Diane Turner.

Larry Dolan

HUMAN RESOURCES
VP, Human Resources/Chief Diversity Officer: Sara Lehrke. **Director, Human Resources
Operations:** Jennifer Gibson. **Director, Talent Acquisition:** Mailynh Vu. **Manager, Talent Acquisition:** Valencia
Kimbrough. **Manager, Talent Development:** Nate Daymut. **Coordinator, Talent Development:** Colleen Lynch.

MARKETING
VP, Marketing/Brand Management: Nicole Schmidt. **Director, Brand Management:** Jason Wiedemann. **Manager,
Advertising/Promotions:** Anne Madzelan.

COMMUNICATIONS/BASEBALL INFORMATION
Telephone: (216) 420-4380. **Fax:** (216) 420-4430.
Senior VP, Public Affairs: Bob DiBiasio. **Vice President, Communications and Community Impact:** Curtis
Danburg. **Director, Baseball Information & Player Relations:** Bart Swain. **Director, Communications & Player
Relations:** Court Berry-Tripp. **Manager, Communications:** Austin Controulis. **Coordinator, Player Engagement
& Family Relations:** Megan Ganser. **Team Photographer:** Dan Mendlik. **Coordinator, Communications & Team
Historian:** Jeremy Feador.

BALLPARK OPERATIONS
VP, Ballpark Operations: Jim Folk. **Senior Director, Ballpark Operations:** Jerry Crabb. **Senior Director, Facility
Operations:** Seth Cooper. **Senior Director, Security:** Jonathan Wilham. **Head Groundskeeper:** Brandon Koehnke.
Director, Facility Maintenance: Ron Miller. **Manager, Event Security:** Andy Finn. **Manager, Ballpark Operations:**

2020 SCHEDULE
Standard Game Times: Mon.-Sat., 7:10 pm; Sun. 1:10 pm.

MARCH		
26 - 29 . . . . Detroit	4 - 7 . . . . Texas	26 - 28 . . . .at Kansas City	11 - 12 . . . . . . San Diego
30 - 31 . . . . Chicago (AL)	8 - 10 . . . . . . .at Detroit	29 - 30 . . . . Houston	14 - 16 . . . . Seattle
	11 - 13 . . . . .at Baltimore		18 - 19 . . . . .at Oakland
APRIL	15 - 17 . . . . . Minnesota	**JULY**	20 - 23 . . . .at Kansas City
	19 - 20 . . . . . Cincinnati	1 - 2 . . . . Houston	25 - 27 . . . . Arizona
1 . . . . Chicago (AL)	23 - 24 .at Los Angeles (NL)	3 - 5 . . . . Minnesota	28 - 30 . . . .New York (AL)
2 - 5 . . . . .at Detroit	26 - 27 .at Los Angeles (AL)	7 - 8 . . . . . .at Cincinnati	
6 - 8 . . . . . at Minnesota	29 - 31 . . . . . Kansas City	9 - 12 . . . . . Kansas City	**SEPTEMBER**
9 - 12 . . . . . .Tampa Bay		17 - 19 . . . . . at Toronto	1 - 3 . . . . . at Minnesota
14 - 16 . . . . Detroit	**JUNE**	21 - 23 . . . . . .at Detroit	5 - 6 . . . . . . at Colorado
17 - 20 . . . . . .at Boston	1 - 3 . . . . Boston	25 - 26 . . . . .at Houston	8 - 10 . . . . . . Minnesota
21 - 23 . . . . . . Oakland	5 - 7 . . . .at Kansas City	28 - 29 . . . . . Kansas City	11 - 13 . . Los Angeles (AL)
24 - 26 . . at New York (AL)	10 - 11 . . .at Chicago (AL)	30 - 31 . . . . Chicago (AL)	14 - 16 . . . . Detroit
27 - 29 . . . . at Tampa Bay	12 - 14 . . . . . . .at Texas		18 - 20 . . . . . .at Seattle
	15 - 18 . . . . . . Baltimore	**AUGUST**	22 - 23 . . .at Chicago (AL)
MAY	19 - 21 . . . . Chicago (AL)	1 - 2 . . . . . . Chicago (AL)	25 - 27 . . . . .Toronto
1 - 3 . . . . . . San Francisco	24 . . . . at San Diego	4 - 5 . . . . . . at Minnesota	
		8 - 9 . . . . .at Chicago (AL)	

GENERAL INFORMATION
Stadium (year opened):
Progressive Field (1994).
Team Colors: Navy blue, red and silver.

Home Dugout: Third Base.
Playing Surface: Grass.

Steve Walters. **Manager, Ballpark Operations:** Tyler Cochran. **Manager, Safety Policy and Training:** David Bonacci.

TICKETING
Telephone: (216) 420-4487. **Fax:** (216) 420-4481.
Director, Ticket Services: Matt Coppo. **Ticket Services Manager:** Eric Fronczek. **Manager, Ticket Operations:** Seth Fuller. **Ticket Services Coordinator:** Paige Selle.

TEAM OPERATIONS/CLUBHOUSE
Director, Team Travel: Mike Seghi. **Home Clubhouse Manager:** Tony Amato. Asst. **Home Clubhouse Manager:** Brandon Biller. **Director, Video Operations:** Bob Chester.

BASEBALL OPERATIONS

President, Baseball Operations: Chris Antonetti. **General Manager:** Mike Chernoff.
Assistant GMs: Matt Forman, Carter Hawkins, Sky Andrecheck. **Vice President, Baseball Operations—Strategy/Administration:** Brad Grant. **Vice President, Baseball Operations:** Eric Binder. **Director, Baseball Operations:** Alex Merberg. **Assistant Director, Baseball Research/Development:** Kevin Tenenbaum. **Principal Data Scientist:** Keith Woolner. **Baseball Analyst:** Max Marchi. **Director, Baseball Administration:** Wendy Hoppel. **Executive Administrative Assistant:** Marlene Lehky. **Assistant Director, Baseball Operations:** Sam Giller. **Assistant, Baseball Operations:** Zach Morton.

MAJOR LEAGUE STAFF
Manager: Terry Francona. **Coaches: Bench**—Brad Mills. **Pitching**—Carl Willis. **Hitting**—Ty Van Burkleo. **First Base**—Sandy Alomar Jr. **Third Base**—Mike Sarbaugh. **Bullpen**—Brian Sweeney. **Assistant Hitting Coach**—Victor Rodriguez. **Assistant Pitching Coach**—Ruben Niebla. **Assistants, Major League Staff:** Mike Barnett, Armando Camacaro, Ricky Pacione.

Chris Antonetti

MEDICAL/TRAINING
Vice President, Medical Services: Lonnie Soloff. **Head Team Physician:** Dr. Mark Schickendantz. **Head Athletic Trainer:** James Quinlan. **Assistant Athletic Trainers:** Jeff Desjardins, Chad Wolfe. **Sports Psychologist & Director of Psychological Services:** Dr. Charles Maher. **Performance Coach (Triple-A/Major League):** Brian Miles.

PLAYER DEVELOPMENT
Vice President, Player Development: James Harris. **Special Assistants:** Travis Fryman, Dave Wallace, Travis Hafner, Tim Belcher, Tom Wiedenbauer. **Assistant Directors, Player Development:** Matt Cody Buckel, Rob Cerfolio, Andrew Bahnert. **Assistant, Player Development:** Rob Cerfolio. **Director, Administration:** Wendy Hoppel. **Advisor, Player Development:** Minnie Mendoza, Tim Tolman, Johnny Goryl. **Administrative Assistant:** Nilda Taffanelli. **Field Coordinator:** John McDonald. **Assistant Field Coordinator:** Anthony Medrano. **Coordinators:** Kevin Howard (hitting), Pete Lauritson (short-season hitting), Joe Torres (pitching), Joel Mangrum (pitching), Stephen Osterer (pitching resource), Tony Mansolino (infield defense). **Player Programs Coordinator:** Larry Day. **Medical Coordinator:** Andrew Pipkin. **Performance Analyst, Player Development:** Todd Kubacki, Todd Tubbs, Josh Morrison. **Education & Language Coordinator:** Anna Bolton. **Mental Performance Coach:** Oscar Gutierrez. **Performance Coordinator:** Ryan Faer (Arizona), Hasani Torres (Dominican Republic).

FARM SYSTEM

Class	Club	Manager	Hitting Coach	Pitching Coach
Triple-A	Columbus (IL)	Andy Tracy	Jason Esposito	Rigo Beltran
Double-A	Akron (EL)	Rouglas Odor	Junior Betances	Tony Arnold
High A	Lynchburg (CL)	Dennis Malave	Grant Fink	Owen Dew
Low A	Lake County (MWL)	Greg DiCenzo	Mike Mergenthaier	Jason Blanton
Short-season	Mahoning Valley (NYP)	Luke Carlin	Craig Massoni	Kevin Erminio
Rookie	Indians Red (AZL)	Ken Knutson	Chris Smith	TBD
Rookie	Indians Blue (AZL)	Jerry Owens	Jordan Becker	Mike Steele
Rookie	Indians 1/2 (DSL)	Mejia/Tavares	Forster/Valdez	Sanchez/Polanco

SCOUTING
Senior Director, Scouting Operations: John Mirabelli. **Special Assistants to the GM:** Steve Lubratich, Dave Malpass, Don Poplin. **Director, Amateur Scouting:** Scott Barnsby. **Assistant Director, Amateur Scouting:** Clint Longenecker. **Assistants, Amateur Scouting:** Will Clements, Matt Czechanski. **Coordinators, Amateur Scouting:** David Compton (Newport Beach, CA), Jon Heuerman (Chandler, AZ), Ethan Purser (Dallas, GA). **Underclass Coordinator:** Brad Tyler (Bishop, GA). **Area Scouts:** Kyle Bamberger (Kansas City, MO), CT Bradford (Pensacola, FL), Mike Bradford (Nashville, TN), Garrick Chaffee (Dallas, TX), Aaron Etchison (Dexter, MI), Conor Glassey (Bothell, WA), Mike Kanen (Hoboken, NJ), Andrew Krause (Jacksonville, FL), Jhonatan Leyba (Seminole, FL), Pete Loizzo (Durham, NC), Don Lyle (Sacramento, CA), Bob Mayer (Somerset, PA), Carlos Muniz (San Pedro, CA), Ryan Perry (Phoenix, AZ), Kyle Van Hook (Brenham, TX). **Part-Time Scouts:** Bob Malkmus, Jose Trujillo. **Amateur Scouting Fellows:** Matt Linder, Jake Vollen.
Vice President, Player Acquisitions: Victor Wang. **Special Assistant to President of Baseball Operations/GM:** Steve Lubratich (Lee, NH) , Dave Malpass (Huntington Beach, CA), Don Poplin (Norwood, NC). **Assistant Director, Pro Scouting:** Dan Budreika. **Special Assistant to Baseball Operations:** Tim Belcher (Marengo, OH). **Special Assignment Scout:** Scott Meaney (Holly Springs, NC), Doug Carpenter (North Palm Beach, FL) , Dave Miller (Wilmington, NC), Bo Hughes (Sherman Oaks, CA). **Senior Player Acquisitions Scout:** Chris Calciano (Milton, DE), Kevin Cullen (Frisco, TX). **Professional Scout**—Jim Rickon (Seven Hills, OH). **Vice President, International Scouting:** Paul Gillispie. **Assistant Directors, International Scouting:** Richard Conway, Chris Gale. **Coordinator, International Scouting:** Junie Melendez (Avon, OH).

COLORADO ROCKIES

Office Address: 2001 Blake St., Denver, CO 80205.
Telephone: (303) 292-0200. **Fax:** (303) 312-2116.
Website: www.Rockies.com.

OWNERSHIP

Operated by: Colorado Rockies Baseball Club Ltd.
Owner/Chairman & Chief Executive Officer: Richard L. Monfort. **Executive Assistant to the Owner/Chairman & Chief Executive Officer:** Terry Douglass. **Owner/General Partner:** Charles K. Monfort.

BUSINESS OPERATIONS

Executive Vice President/Chief Operating Officer: Greg Feasel. **Assistant to Executive VP/Chief Operating Officer:** Kim Olson. **VP, Human Resources:** Elizabeth Stecklein.

FINANCE

Executive VP: Hal Roth. **Assistant to the Executive Vice President:** Tammy Vergara. **VP/CFO:** Michael Kent. **VP/General Counsel:** Brian Gaffney. **Senior Director, Procurement:** Gary Lawrence. **Coordinator, Purchasing:** Robert Wilkinson. **Senior Director, Accounting:** Phil Emerson. **Accountants:** Joel Binfet, Laine Campbell.

Richard Monfort

MICHAEL MARTIN/GETTY IMAGES

CORPORATE PARTNERSHIPS

VP, Corporate Partnerships: Walker Monfort. **Assistant to VP, Corporate Partnerships:** Nicole Ortiz. **Senior Director, Client Services & Events:** Kari Anderson. **Assistant Director:** Nate VanderWal. **Account Executives:** Sam Porter, Chris Zumbrennen. **Senior Director, In-Game Entertainment & Broadcasting:** Kent Krosbakken. **Public Address Announcer:** Reed Saunders.

COMMUNITY/RETAIL OPERATIONS

VP, Community & Retail Operations: James P. Kellogg. **Assistant to the VP, Community & Retail Operations:** Kelly Hall. **Senior Director, Retail Operations:** Aaron Heinrich. **Director, Community Affairs:** Dallas Davis.

MARKETING/COMMUNICATIONS

VP, Communications & Marketing: Jill Campbell. **Senior Director, Communications:** Warren Miller. **Supervisor, Communications:** Cory Little. **Coordinator, Communications:** Nick Parson. **Coordinator, Spanish Translator/Communications:** Abby Sanders. **Director, Brand Management & Social Media:** Julian Valentin. **Coordinator, Marketing:** Lauren Jacaruso. **Assistant, Social Media:** Nicole Morris. **Editor/Designer, Communications & Marketing:** Sarah Topf. **Graphic Designer & Marketing Assistant:** Justin Cox. **Team Photographer:** Matt Dirksen.

BALLPARK OPERATIONS

VP/Chief Customer Officer, Ballpark Operations: Kevin Kahn. **Assistant to the VP/Chief Customer Officer, Ballpark Operations:** Lenus Lucero. **Senior Director, Food Service Operations/Development:** Albert Valdes. **Senior**

2020 SCHEDULE

Standard Game Times: Mon.-Fri., 6:40 pm; Sat., 6:10 pm; Sun., 1:10 pm.

MARCH
26-29 . . . . . at San Diego
31 . . . at Los Angeles (NL)

APRIL
1 . . . . at Los Angeles (NL)
3-5 . . . . San Diego
6-8 . . . . Texas
10-12 . . . . . at Arizona
15-16 . . . . . at San Diego
18-19 . . . . St. Louis
22-23 . . at San Francisco
25-26 . . . . . . .Milwaukee
29 . . . . Chicago (AL)

MAY
1-3 . . . . . at Philadelphia
4-6 . . . . .at Detroit
8-10 . . . . Cincinnati

12-14 . . . . . San Francisco
15-17 . . . . at Miami
20 . . . . . .at Chicago (AL)
23-24 . . . . . .Philadelphia
25-28 . . . Los Angeles (NL)
30-31 . . . at San Francisco

JUNE
1-3 . . . . at Arizona
5-7 . . . at Los Angeles (NL)
10-11 . . . . .Arizona
13-14 . . . . Pittsburgh
17-18 . . . . .at St. Louis
20-21 . . . . San Diego
23-24 . . . . . . Kansas City
27-28 . . . . . at Minnesota
29-30 . . . . . at Pittsburgh

JULY
1 . . . . at Pittsburgh
4-5 . . . . . . San Francisco
7-8 . . . . .Arizona
10-12 . . . . . at Milwaukee
18-19 . . . . Atlanta
21-23 . . . . .Miami
24-26 . . . . . .at Cincinnati
27-29 . . . . at Washington

AUGUST
1-2 . . . . . . San Francisco
4-5 . . . . . .New York (NL)
8-9 . . . . . . at San Diego
10-13 . . . . . . at Arizona
15-16 . . . at San Francisco
18-20 . . . . . .Washington
22-23 . . Los Angeles (NL)

24-25 . . . . .at Texas
27-30 . . . . at Atlanta
31 . . . . . at New York (NL)

SEPTEMBER
1-3 . . . at New York (NL)
5-6 . . . . Cleveland
7-10 . . . . . . Chicago (NL)
12-13 . . . . San Diego
16-17 . at Los Angeles (NL)
18-20 . . . .at Chicago (NL)
23-25 . . .Los Angeles (NL)
26-27 . . . . .Arizona
27-29 . . . . . .Milwaukee

GENERAL INFORMATION

Stadium (year opened): Coors Field (1995). **Playing Surface:** Grass.
Team Colors: Purple, black and silver.
Home Dugout: First Base.

Director, Guest Services: Steven Burke. **Head Groundskeeper:** Mark Razum. **Assistant Head Groundskeeper:** Doug Zabinsky. **Senior Director, Engineering & Facilities:** Allyson Gutierrez.

TICKETING
Telephone: (303) 762-5437, (800) 388-7625. **Fax:** (303) 312-2115.
VP, Ticket Operations, Sales & Services: Sue Ann McClaren.

TRAVEL/CLUBHOUSE
Senior Director, Major League Operations: Paul Egins. **Manager, Major League Clubhouse:** Mike Pontarelli. **Coordinator, Major League Clubhouse:** Tyler Sanders.

BASEBALL OPERATIONS
Executive VP/General Manager: Jeff Bridich. **Assistant to Executive VP/GM:** Irma Castañeda. **Assistant GM, Baseball Operations/Assistant General Counsel:** Zack Rosenthal. **Assistant GM/Player Personnel:** Jon Weil. **Assistant GM/Player Development:** Zach Wilson. **Director, Baseball Operations:** Domenic Di Ricco. **Coordinator, Baseball Operations/ Staff Counsel:** Matt Obernauer. **Director, Baseball Research & Development:** Trevor Patch. **Manager, Baseball Research & Development:** Jamie Hollowell. **Analyst, Baseball Research & Development:** Evan Eshleman. **Full Stack Developer, Baseball Research & Development:** Bryce Leonard. **Baseball Operations Fellow:** Brittany Haby. **Data Engineer, Baseball Research and Development:** Abi Sislo. **Special Assistant to the GM:** Danny Montgomery.

Jeff Bridich

MAJOR LEAGUE STAFF
Manager: Bud Black. **Coaches: Bench**—Mike Redmond, **Pitching**—Steve Foster, **Hitting**— Dave Magadan, **Assistant Hitting Coach**—Jeff Salazar, **Third Base**—Stu Cole, **First Base**— Ron Gideon, **Bullpen**—Darryl Scott, **Bullpen Catcher**—Aaron Munoz, Director, **Physical Performance**—Gabe Bauer, **Video**—Brian Jones. **ML Data & Game Planning Coordinator**—Doug Bernier.

MEDICAL/TRAINING
Senior Director, Medical Operations/Special Projects: Tom Probst. **Medical Director:** Dr. Thomas Noonan. **Club Physicians:** Dr. Allen Schreiber, Dr. Douglas Wyland. **Head Trainer:** Keith Dugger. **Assistant Athletic Trainer:** Scott Gehret.

PLAYER DEVELOPMENT
Assistant Director: Chris Forbes. **Manager:** Jesse Stender. **Camps and Fundamentals Coordinator:** Andy Gonzalez. **Director, Pitching Operations:** Mark Wiley. **Pitching Coordinator:** Doug Linton, Steve Merriman. **Catching Coordinator:** Mark Strittmatter. **Hitting Coordinator:** Darin Everson. **Rehab Coordinator:** Scott Murayama. **Assistant Rehab Coordinator/Manager, Scottsdale Operations, Scottsdale:** Andy Stover. **Physical Performance Coordinator:** Trevor Swartz. **Director, Mental Skills Development:** Doug Chadwick. **Assistant Mental Skills Coordinator:** Jerry Amador. **Minor League Video Coordinator:** Jeff Nelson. **Coordinator, Cultural Education:** Angel Amparo. **Latin America Field & Pitching Coordinator:** Edison Lora. **Minor League Clubhouse and Equipment Manager:** Daniel Kleinholz. **Special Assistant, Player Development:** Bob Apodaca. **Special Assistant, Player Development & Scouting:** Jerry Weinstein. **Latin America Field & Pitching Coordinator:** Edison Lora.

FARM SYSTEM

Class	Club (League)	Manager	Hitting Coach	Pitching Coach
Triple-A	Albuquerque (PCL)	Warren Schaeffer	Tim Doherty	Blaine Beatty
Double-A	Hartford (EL)	Chris Denorfia	Tom Sutaris	Frank Gonzales
High A	Lancaster (CAL)	Scott Little	Michael Ramirez	Ryan Kibler
Low A	Asheville (SAL)	Robinson Cancel	Zach Osborne	Mark Brewer
Short-season	Boise (NWL)	Cesar Galvez	Nic Wilson	Dave Burba
Rookie	Grand Junction (PIO)	Jake Opitz	Trevor Burmeister	Helmis Rodriguez
Rookie	Rockies 1 (DSL)	Mauricio Gonzalez	Eugenio Jose	Florentino Nunez
Rookie	Rockies 2 (DSL)	Julio Campos	Jorge Oviedo	TBA

SCOUTING
VP, Scouting: Bill Schmidt. **Special Assistant to the GM, Scouting:** Danny Montgomery. **Sr. Director, Scouting Operations:** Marc Gustafson. **Assistant Scouting Director:** Damon Iannelli. **Special Assistant, Scouting:** Rick Mathews. **Assistant Director, Scouting Operations:** Sterling Monfort. **Advance Scouts:** Chris Warren (Denver, CO), Peter Bourjos (Scottsdale, AZ). **Special Assistant, Player Personnel:** Ty Coslow (Louisville, KY). **Major League Scouts:** Kevin Bootay (Elk Grove, CA), Steve Fleming (Louisa, VA), Will George (Milford, DE), Jack Gillis (Sarasota, FL), Mark Germann (Denver, CO), Joe Housey (Hollywood, FL), John Corbin (Savannah, GA). **Professional Scout:** Joe Little (Arvada, CO). **National Crosscheckers:** Mike Ericson (Phoenix, AZ), Jay Matthews (Concord, NC). **Area Scouts:** Scott Alves (Phoenix, AZ), Brett Baldwin (Kansas City, MO), Julio Campos (Guaynabo, PR) John Cedarburg (Fort Myers, FL), Jermaine Clark (Fresno, CA) Scott Corman (Lexington, KY), Jordan Czarniecki (Greenville, SC), Jeff Edwards (Fresno, TX), Sean Gamble (Atlanta, GA), Mike Garlatti (Edison, NJ), Matt Hattabaugh (Westminster, CA), Matt Pignataro (Seattle, WA), Jesse Retzlaff (Dallas, TX), Rafael Reyes (Miami, FL), Ed Santa (Powell, OH), Zack Zulli (Hammond, LA). **Part-Time Scouts:** Norm DeBriyn (Fayetteville, AR), Dave McQueen (Bossier City, LA), Greg Pullia (Plymouth, MA). **VP, International Scouting/Player Development:** Rolando Fernandez. **Dominican Scouting/Development Coordinator:** Arnaldo Gomez. **Dominican Scouting/Development Assistant:** Enmanuel Frias. **International Crosschecker:** Marc Russo. **Supervisor, Latin America Scouting:** Orlando Medina. **International Scouting:** Martin Cabrera (Dominican Republic), Carlos Gomez (Venezuela), Raul Gomez (Cuba), Alving Mejias (Mexico), Frank Roa (Dominican Republic), Josher Suarez (Venezuela) Rogers Figueroa (Colombia).

DETROIT TIGERS

Office Address: 2100 Woodward Ave, Detroit, MI 48201.
Telephone: (313) 471-2000. **Fax:** (313) 471-2138. **Website:** www.tigers.com

OWNERSHIP
Operated By: Detroit Tigers Inc. **Chairman & CEO, Detroit Tigers:** Christopher Ilitch. **Group President, Sports & Entertainment, Ilitch Holdings, Inc.:** Chris Granger

BUSINESS OPERATIONS
Executive Vice President, Business Operations: Duane McLean. **Executive Assistant to Executive VP, Business Operations:** Peggy Thompson.

Chris Ilitch

FINANCE/ADMINISTRATION
VP, Finance/Administration/CFO: Stephen Quinn. **Senior Director, Finance:** Kelli Kollman. **Director, Purchasing/Supplier Diversity:** DeAndre Berry. **Accounting Manager/Treasury Analyst:** Sheila Robine. **Financial Analyst:** Kristin Jorgensen. **Accounts Payable Coordinator:** Debra Sword. **Accounts Receivable Coordinator:** Monica Basil. **Senior Director, Human Resources:** Karen Gruca. **Human Resources Coordinator:** Kelsey Shuck. **Internal Audit Manager:** Candice Lentz. **Payroll Administrator:** Mark Cebelak. **Payroll Coordinator:** Stephanie Jenkins. Director, **Authentics:** Marc Himelstein. **Authentics Coordinator:** Ashley Baughman. **Administrative/Accounting Assistant:** Tina Sidney.

PUBLIC/COMMUNITY AFFAIRS
VP, Community/Public Affairs: Elaine Lewis. **Director, Player Relations & Detroit Tigers Foundation:** Jordan Field. **Manager, Community Affairs:** Courtney Kaplan. **Detroit Tigers Foundation Coordinator:** Ashley Robinson.

SALES/MARKETING
VP, Corporate Partnerships: Steve Harms. **Corporate Partnership Sales Directors:** Kurt Tiesman, John Wolski. **Corporate Partnership Sales Managers:** Soula Burns, Matt Stepnes. **Corporate Partnerships Account Executive:** Corey Thomas. **Partnership Services Manager:** Kaitlin Knutson. **Partnership Services Coordinators:** Jessica Langolf, Ellyn Yurgalite. **VP, Ticket/Suite Sales:** Scot Pett. **Director, Ticket Sales:** Steve Fox. **Director, Group Sales:** Dwain Lewis. **Assistant Director, Ticket Sales:** Jeff Lutz. **Manager, Suite Sales/Service:** Dan Griesbaum. **Suite Sales/Services Account Manager:** Jeff Sanders. **Suite Sales/Services Coordinator:** Kelsey Decker. **VP, Marketing:** Ellen Hill Zeringue. **Director, Marketing:** Ron Wade.

MEDIA RELATIONS/COMMUNICATIONS
Telephone: (313) 471-21092. **Fax:** (313) 471-2138.
VP, Communications: Ron Colangelo. Director, **Baseball Media Relations:** Chad Crunk. Coordinators, **Media Relations:** Ben Fidelman, Bryan Loor-Almonte, Michele Wysocki. **Director, Broadcasting/In-Game Entertainment:** Stan Fracker. **VP, Communications:** Ron Colangelo. **Director, Baseball Media Relations:** Chad Crunk. **Coordinators, Media Relations:** Ben Fidelman, Michele Wysocki. **Director, Broadcasting/In-Game Entertainment:** Stan Fracker.

2020 SCHEDULE
Standard Game Times: Mon-Sat., 7:10 pm; Sun.,1:10 pm.

MARCH
26 - 29 . . . . .at Cleveland
30 . . . . Kansas City

APRIL
1 . . . . Kansas City
2 - 5 . . . . Cleveland
6 - 8 . . . . . .at Kansas City
10 - 12 . . Los Angeles (AL)
14 - 16 . . . . .at Cleveland
18 - 19 . . . at Minnesota
20 - 23 . . . .New York (AL)
24 - 26 . . . . . San Diego
28 - 30 . . at New York (AL)

MAY
1 - 3 . . . . . .at Kansas City

4 - 6 . . . . Colorado
8 - 10 . . . . . . Cleveland
11 - 14 . . . . . Minnesota
16 - 17 . . . . . .at Seattle
20 . . . . at San Francisco
22 - 25 . . . . .Tampa Bay
26 - 28 . . . . Seattle
29 - 31 . . . . . at Arizona

JUNE
3 - 4 . . . . .at Oakland
6 - 7 . . . . .at Chicago (AL)
9 - 11 . . . . Oakland
12 - 14 . . . . . . .Toronto
16 - 18 . . . . Chicago (AL)
20 - 21 .at Los Angeles (NL)
23 - 26 . . .at Chicago (AL)

26 - 28 . . . . .at Baltimore
30 . . . . Minnesota

JULY
1 - 2 . . . . Minnesota
3 - 5 . . . . . . Kansas City
7 - 10 . at Los Angeles (AL)
11 - 12 . . . . . .at Houston
17 - 19 . . . . Chicago (AL)
21 - 23 . . . . . . Cleveland
24 - 26 . . . . at Tampa Bay
28 - 30 . . .at Chicago (AL)
30 - 31 . . . . . Kansas City

AUGUST
1 - 2 . . . . Kansas City
4 - 5 . . . . . .San Francisco

6 - 9 . . . . .at Texas
11 - 13 . . . . . Baltimore
14 - 16 . . . . Texas
18 - 19 . . at Pittsburgh
22 - 23 . . . . at Minnesota
24 - 27 . . . . . . Houston
28 - 30 . . . . Boston

SEPTEMBER
1 - 3 . . . . at Toronto
4 - 7 . . . . .at Boston
8 - 9 . . . . Pittsburgh
11 - 13 . . . . . Minnesota
14 - 16 . . . .at Cleveland
19 - 20 . . . . at Minnesota
21 - 24 . . . .at Kansas City
25 - 27 . . . Chicago (AL)

GENERAL INFORMATION
Stadium (year opened):
Comerica Park (2000).
Team Colors: Navy blue, orange and white.

Home Dugout: Third Base.
Playing Surface: Grass.

BASEBALL OPERATIONS

Telephone: (313) 471-2000. **Fax:** (313) 471-2099.

Executive Vice President, Baseball Operations/General Manager: Al Avila. **Special Assistants to the GM:** Willie Horton, Al Kaline, Jim Leyland, Alan Trammell, Dick Egan, Mike Russell. **VP/Assistant GM:** David Chadd **VP/Assistant GM/General Counsel:** John Westhoff. **VP, Player Personnel:** Scott Bream. **VP/Player Development:** Dave Littlefield. **Senior Director, Baseball Analytics/Operations:** Jay Sartori. **Director, Baseball Operations/ Professional Scouting:** Sam Menzin. **Manager, Baseball Analytics:** Jim Logue. **Assistant Counsel, Baseball Operations:** Alan Avila. **Executive Assistant to the Executive Vice President, Baseball Operations/General Manager:** Marty Lyon.

Al Avila

MAJOR LEAGUE STAFF

Manager: Ron Gardenhire. **Coaches: Pitching**—Chris Bosio, **Hitting** —Lloyd McClendon, **First Base**—Ramon Santiago, **Third Base**—Dave Clark, **Bullpen**—Rick Anderson, **Bench**— Steve Liddle, **Assistant Hitting**—Phil Clark, **Quality Control**—Joe Vavra.

MEDICAL/TRAINING

Senior Director, Medical Services: Kevin Rand. **Head Athletic Trainer:** Doug Teter. **Assistant Athletic Trainer:** Matt Rankin. **Physical Therapist:** Robbie Williams. **Strength/Conditioning Coach:** Chris Walter. **Assistant Strength/Conditioning Coach:** Yousef Zamat. **Team Physicians:** Dr. Michael Workings, Dr. Stephen Lemos, Dr. Louis Saco (Florida). **Coordinator, Medical Services:** Gwen Keating.

PLAYER DEVELOPMENT

VP, Player Development: Dave Littlefield. **Director, Minor League Operations:** Dan Lunetta. **Director, Player Development:** Dave Owen. **Director, Minor League/Scouting Administration:** Cheryl Evans. **Director, International Operations:** Tom Moore. **Director, Latin American Player Development:** Manny Crespo. **Director, Latin American Operations:** Miguel Garcia. **Director, Dominican Republic Operations:** Ramon Perez. **Director, Dominican Academy/ Cuban Specialist:** Oliver Arias. **Coordinator, Minor League Operations:** Avi Becher. **Coordinator, International Operations:** Rafael Gonzalez. **Coordinator, International Player Programs:** Sharon Lockwood. **Administrative Assistant, Minor League Operations:** Marilyn Acevedo. **Minor League Field Coordinator:** Bill Dancy. **Minor League Medical Coordinator:** Corey Tremble. **Minor League Strength/Conditioning Coordinator:** Steve Chase. **Assistant Medical Coordinator—International:** Manny Pena. **Lakeland Clubhouse Manager:** Patrick Saenz. **Minor League Trackman & Analytics Coordinator:** Adam Daily. **Minor League Video Coordinator:** Jim McKew. **Assistant Minor League Video Coordinator:** Kan Ikeda. **Minor League Operations Intern:** Alex Gonzalez. **Roving Instructors:** Bruce Fields (hitting), Scott Fletcher (hitting), A.J. Sager (pitching), Joe DePastino (catching), Jose Valentin (Infield), Gene Roof (outfield/baserunning), Jaime Garcia (assistant pitching), Brian Peterson (mental skills instructor), Josman Robles (Latin American performance coach).

FARM SYSTEM

Class	Club	Manager	Hitting Coach	Pitching Coach
Triple-A	Toledo (IL)	Doug Mientkiewicz	Brian Harper	Jeff Pico
Double-A	Erie(EL)	Andrew Graham	Mike Hessman	Willie Blair
High A	Lakeland (FSL)	Mike Rabelo	Tim Garland	Mark Johnson
Low A	West Michigan (MWL)	Lance Parrish	Mariano Duncan	Jorge Cordova
Short-season	Norwich (NYP)	Gerald Laird	Rafael Martinez	Ace Adams
Rookie	Tigers West (GCL)	Gary Cathcart	Bill Springman	Mike Alvarez
Rookie	Tigers East (GCL)	Luis Lopez	Rafael Gil	Carlos Bohorquez
Rookie	DSL Tigers (DSL)	Ramon Zapata	Jose Ovalles	Jose Parra
Rookie	DSL Tigers 2 (DSL)	Jesus Garces	Marcos Yepez	Luis Marte

SCOUTING

VP, Assistant General Manager: David Chadd. **VP, Player Personnel:** Scott Bream. **Director, Amateur Scouting:** Scott Pleis. **Assistant Director, Amateur/International Scouting:** Eric Nieto. **Amateur Scouting Video Coordinator:** Sam Nasci. **Amateur Scouting Interns:** Alex Tarandek, Joey Lothrop. **Amateur Scouting Video Intern:** Matt Zmuda. **Major League Scouts:** Ray Crone, Jim Elliott, Kevin Ellis, Joe Ferrone, Randy Johnson, Don Kelly, Paul Mirocke, Yadalla Mufdi, Jim Olander Gary Pellant, Jim Rough, Bruce Tanner, **Senior Advisors:** Scott Reid, Murray Cook. **Special Assistants to the GM:** Dick Egan, Mike Russell. **National Crosscheckers:** Tim Hallgren, Steve Hinton. **Regional Crosscheckers: East**—James Orr, **Central**—Tim Grieve, **Midwest**—Mike Hankins, **West**—Marti Wolever. **Area Scouts:** Nick Avila, Bryson Barber, Taylor Black, Jim Bretz, RJ Burgess, Scott Cerny, Dave Dangler, Brad Fidler, Justin Henry, Ryan Johnson, Jeff Kunkel, Matt Lea, Dave Lottsfeldt, Tim McWilliam, Steve Pack, Mike Smith, Harold Zonder. **Part-Time Scouts:** German Geigel (PR), Deryl Horton (MI), Mark Monahan (MI), Clyde Weir (MI). **Director, International Operations:** Tom Moore. **Director, Latin American Scouting:** Miguel Garcia. **Director, Latin American Player Development:** Manny Crespo. **International Operations Coordinator:** Rafael Gonzalez. **International Crosschecker:** Jeff Wetherby. **International Crosschecker:** Alejandro Rodriguez. **Coordinator, Pacific Rim:** Kevin Hooker. **Director, Dominican Republic Operations:** Ramon Perez. **Director, Dominican Academy/Cuban Specialist:** Oliver Arias. **Dominican Scouting Supervisor:** Aldo Perez. **Administrative Asst., Dominican Academy:** Jimmy Ortiz. **Administrative Assistant, Dominican Academy:** Wilfredo Crespo. **Asst., Dominican Academy:** Pablo Rodriguez. **Venezuelan Scouting Supervisor:** Jesus Mendoza. **Venezuelan Academy Administrator/Area Scout:** Oscar Garcia. **International Operations Interns:** Marcelo Parker, Cristian Crespo. **International Area Scouts:** Michael Hsieh (Taiwan), Ho-Kyun Im (Korea), Raul Leiva (Venezuela), Luis Molina (Panama), Delvis Pacheco (Venezuela), Rodolfo Penalo (Dominican Republic), Miguel Rodriguez (Dominican Republic), Carlos Santana (Dominican Republic), Yas Sato (Japan), Glenn Williams (Australia)

HOUSTON ASTROS

Office Address: Minute Maid Park, Union Station, 501 Crawford, Suite 400, Houston, TX 77002.
Mailing Address: PO Box 288, Houston, TX 77001. **Telephone:** (713) 259-8000. **Fax:** (713) 259-8981.
Email Address: fanfeedback@astros.mlb.com. **Website:** www.astros.com.

OWNERSHIP
Owner/Chairman: Jim Crane.

BUSINESS OPERATIONS

Jim Crane

Executive Assistant: Eileen Colgin. **Executive Assistant:** Adriana Moya. **Senior VP, Business Operations:** Marcel Braithwaite. **Senior VP, Corporate Partnerships:** Matt Brand. **Senior VP, Community Relations/Executive Director, Astros Foundation:** Twila Carter. **Senior VP/ General Counsel:** Giles Kibbe. **Senior VP, Marketing/Communications:** Anita Sehgal. **Chief Financial Officer:** Michael Slaughter. **VP, Tax:** Vito Ciminello. **VP, Communications:** Gene Dias. **VP, Strategy/Analytics:** Michael Dillon. **VP, Stadium Operations:** Bobby Forrest. **VP, Information Technology:** Chris Hanz. **VP, Foundation Development:** Marian Harper. **VP, Merchandising/Retail Operations:** Tom Jennings. **VP, Human Resources:** Vivian Mora. **VP, Finance:** Doug Seckel. **VP, Event Sales/Operations:** Stephanie Stegall. **VP, Marketing:** Jason Wooden. **VP, Ticket Sales and Service:** Creighton Kahoalii. **VP, Corporate Partnerships:** Jeff Stewart. **Senior Director, Business Operations:** Dan O'Neill.

COMMUNICATIONS/COMMUNITY RELATIONS
Senior Manager, Communications: Steve Grande. **Manager, Communications:** Chris Peixoto. **Coordinator, Communications:** Meshach Sullivan. **Manager, Broadcasting:** Ginny Gotcher Grande. **Director, Astros Youth Academy:** Daryl Wade. **Manager, Astros Youth Academy:** Duane Stelly. **Coordinators, Community Relations/Astros Foundation:** Rachel Bubier, Andrew Remson. **Coordinator, Astros Youth Academy:** Megan Hays.

MARKETING/ANALYTICS
Senior Director, Marketing Operations and Insights: Craig Swaisgood. **Senior Director, Ballpark Entertainment:** Chris E. Garcia. **Senior Director, Business Strategy/Analytics:** Jay Verrill. **Director, Content:** Brianna Hughes. **Senior Managers, Marketing Entertainment:** Kyle Hamsher, Richard Tapia. **Coordinator, Social Media:** Ryan Lasneske.

CORPORATE PARTNERSHIPS
Director, Corporate Partnerships: Melissa Hahn. **Director, Sales/Corporate Sponsorships:** Keshia Henderson. **Sales Managers, Corporate Partnerships:** Enrique Cruz, Jimmy Comerota. **Account Managers, Corporate Partnerships:** Lauren Hill, Haleigh Sanders.

STADIUM OPERATIONS
Senior Director, Stadium Operations: Thomas Bell. **Director, Audio/Visual:** Lowell Matheny. **Director, Security/**

2020 SCHEDULE
Standard Game Times: Mon.-Sat., 7:10 pm; Sun. 1:10 pm.

MARCH	4 - 6 . . . . . .at Kansas City	27 - 28 . . . . Texas	14 - 16 . at Los Angeles (AL)
26 - 29 . . Los Angeles (AL)	8 - 10 . . . . Seattle	29 - 30 . . . .at Cleveland	18 - 19 . . . . Seattle
31 . . . . .at Oakland	12 - 14 . . . . Kansas City	**JULY**	22 - 23 . . . . Texas
	16 - 17 . . .New York (AL)	1 - 2 . . . . . .at Cleveland	24 - 27 . . . . . .at Detroit
APRIL	18 - 20 . . . . . at Toronto	3 - 5 . . . . at Washington	29 - 30 . . .at Chicago (AL)
1 . . . . .at Oakland	22 - 24 . . . . . .at Boston	8 - 9 . . . . . .Philadelphia	
4 - 5 . . at Los Angeles (AL)	25 - 28 . . . . Oakland	11 - 12 . . . . Detroit	**SEPTEMBER**
8 - 9 . . . . .New York (NL)	30 - 31 . . . . Boston	18 - 19 . . . .at Oakland	2 - 3 . . . . .Miami
10 - 12 . . . . . .at Texas		20 - 23 . . . . . . .at Texas	5 - 6 . . . . Seattle
13 - 15 . . . . at Tampa Bay	**JUNE**	25 - 26 . . . . . Cleveland	8 - 10 . at Los Angeles (AL)
18 - 19 . . Los Angeles (AL)	2 - 3 . . . at New York (NL)	28 - 29 . . . . . . Oakland	11 - 13 . . . . .at Texas
20 - 23 . . . .Tampa Bay	5 - 7 . . . . . . .at Baltimore		15 - 16 . . Los Angeles (AL)
25 - 26 . . . . . . Oakland	10 - 12 . . . . Texas	**AUGUST**	18 - 20 . . . . . Baltimore
28 - 29 . . . . . . at Arizona	13 - 14 . . . . Chicago (AL)	1 - 2 . . . . . at Minnesota	21 - 24 . . at New York (AL)
	17 - 18 . . . . . .at Seattle	5 . . . . Arizona	25 - 27 . . . . . . at Atlanta
MAY	20 - 21 . . . . . .at Oakland	6 - 9 . . . . .Toronto	
1 - 3 . . . . .at Seattle	23 - 25 . . . . . . Minnesota	11 - 12 . . . . . .at Seattle	

GENERAL INFORMATION
Stadium (year opened): Minute Maid Park (2000).
Team Colors: Navy and orange.
Home Dugout: First Base.
Playing Surface: Grass.

Parking: Ben Williams. **Manager, Parking:** Gary Rowberry. **Manager, Engineering:** Michael Seighman. **Head Groundskeeper:** Izzy Hinojosa. **First Assistant Groundskeeper:** Chris Wolfe.

TICKETING

Senior Director, Ticket Sales: P.J. Keene. **Director, Box Office Operations:** Bill Cannon. **Director, Season Ticket Service:** Jeff Close. **Director, Ticket Operations:** Mark Cole.

BASEBALL OPERATIONS

Assistant GM, Player Development: Pete Putila. **Special Assistant to the GM, Player Personnel:** Kevin Goldstein. **Special Assistants:** Craig Biggio, Jeff Bagwell, Roger Clemens, Enos Cabell. **Sr. Director, Player Evaluation:** Ehsan Bokhari. **Sr. Director, Baseball Strategy:** Bill Firkus. **Sr. Director, Baseball Operations:** Armando Velasco. **Director, Minor League Operations:** Derrick Fong. **Director, Research/ Development:** Sarah Gelles. **Director, Player Evaluation:** Charles Cook. **Director, Latin American Operations:** Caridad Cabrera. **Director, Advance Information:** Tom Koch-Weser.

MAJOR LEAGUE STAFF

Manager: Dusty Baker. **Coaches: Bench**—Joe Espada, **Pitching**—Brent Strom, **Hitting**— Alex Cintron. **Second Hitting**—Troy Snitker. **First Base**—Omar Lopez. **Third Base**—Gary Pettis, **Bullpen**—Josh Miller.

TEAM OPERATIONS/CLUBHOUSE

Senior Manager, Team Operations: Derek Vigoa. **Coordinator, Major League Advance Information:** Tommy Kawamura. **Manager, MLB Video and Technologies:** Antonio Padilla. **Clubhouse Manager:** Carl Schneider. **Visiting Clubhouse Manager:** Steve Perry.

MEDICAL/TRAINING

Head Team Physician: Dr. David Lintner. **Team Physicians:** Dr. Thomas Mehlhoff, Dr. James Muntz, Dr. Pat McCulloch, Dr. Vijay Jotwani. **Head Athletic Trainer and Head Physical Therapist:** Jeremiah Randall. **Team Physical Therapist:** Sam Bell. **Massage Therapist:** Katsumi Oka. **Major League Strength/Conditioning Coach:** Brendan Verner.

PLAYER DEVELOPMENT

Assistant GM, Player Development: Pete Putila. **Director, Minor League Operations:** Derrick Fong. **Minor League Coordinators:** Bill Murphy (pitching), Jeremy Barnes (hitting), Jason Bell (fundamentals), Mark Bailey (catching).

FARM SYSTEM

Class	Club	Manager	Hitting Coach	Pitching Coach
Triple-A	Round Rock (PCL)	Mickey Storey	Ben Rosenthal	Drew French
Double-A	Corpus Christi (TL)	Gregorio Petit	Jason Kanzler	Graham Johnson
High A	Fayetteville (CAR)	Nate Shaver	Rafael Pena	Thomas Whitsett
Low A	Quad Cities (SAL)	Ray Hernandez	Sean Godfrey	Erick Abreu
Short-season	Tri-City (NYP)	Wladimir Sutil	Ernesto Irizarry	John Kovalik
Rookie	Astros (GCL)	Ricardo Rivera	Rene Rojas	Jose Rada
Rookie	Astros 1 (DSL)	Carlos Lugo	Luis Reynoso	Rick Aponte

SCOUTING

Senior Scouting Advisor: Charlie Gonzalez. **National Scouting Supervisor:** Kris Gross. **Supervisor, Area Scouting:** Landon Townsley, Andrew Johnson. **Domestic Crosscheckers:** Evan Brannon (St. Petersburg, FL), Gavin Dickey (Atlanta, GA). **Domestic Scouts:** Travis Coleman (Birmingham, AL), Tim Costic (Los Angeles, CA), Ryan Courville (Scottsdale, AZ), Ryan Leake (San Diego, CA), Bobby St. Pierre (Atlanta, GA), Jim Stevenson (Tulsa, OK), Joey Sola (San Juan, PR). **Manager, Pro Scouting Analysis:** Matt Hogan. **Scouting Analysts:** Aaron DelGiudice, Will Sharp, Cam Pendino. **Assistant Director, International Scouting:** Roman Ocumarez. **Supervisors:** Alfredo Ulloa, Jose Palacios. **Dominican Republic:** Leocadio Guevara. **Dominican Republic:** Jose Lima. **Mexico:** Miguel Pintor. **Venezuela:** Enrique Brito.

VIDEO & TECHNOLOGY

Coordinator, Minor League Technology: Sam Visser. **Coordinator, International TechnologyAssistant, Dominican Scouting:** Francisco Navarro. **Assistant, Dominican Scouting:** Carlos Vasquez. **Assistant, Venezuela Scouting:** Carlos Freites. **Amateur Video Technicians:** Aaron DelGuidice, Cam Pendino.

KANSAS CITY ROYALS

Office Address: One Royal Way, Kansas City, MO 64129.
Mailing Address: PO Box 419969, Kansas City, MO 64141.
Telephone: (816) 921-8000. **Fax:** (816) 924-0347. **Website:** www.royals.com.

OWNERSHIP
Operated By: Kansas City Royals Baseball Club, LLC. **Chairman & CEO:** John Sherman.

ADVISORS TO THE CHAIRMAN
Sr. Advisor, Business Processes: Brooks Sherman. **Sr. Advisor, Business Strategy:** Sarah Tourville.

BUSINESS OPERATIONS

GITTINGS PHOTOGRAPHY

John Sherman

Sr. Vice President, Business Operations: Kevin Uhlich. **Executive Administrative Assistant:** Cindy Hamilton. **Director, Royals Hall of Fame:** Curt Nelson. **Manager, Authentic Merchandise Sales:** Ashley Ficken.

FINANCE/ADMINISTRATION
VP, Finance/Administration: David Laverentz. **Director, Finance:** Whitney Beaver. **Director, Human Resources:** Miriam Maiden. **Director, Accounting/Risk Management:** Patrick Fleischmann. **Director, Payroll:** Jodi Parsons. **Sr. Director, Information Systems:** Brian Himstedt. **Director, Information Systems:** Neil Sell. **Sr. Director, Ticket Operations:** Anthony Blue. **Director, Ticket Ops:** Chris Darr.

COMMUNICATIONS/BROADCASTING
VP, Communications/Broadcasting: Mike Swanson. **Assistant Director, Media Relations:** Mike Cummings. **Manager, Media Relations/Alumni:** Dina Blevins. **Manager, Communications/Broadcasting:** Nick Kappel.

PUBLICITY/COMMUNITY RELATIONS
VP, Publicity: Toby Cook. **Director, Publicity:** Amanda Turk. **VP, Community Relations:** Ben Aken. **Director, Charities:** Amanda Grosdidier. **Director, Community Outreach:** Betty Kaegel. **Director, Community Relations:** Katie McMullen.

BALLPARK OPERATIONS
Sr. Director, Ballpark Operations: Isaac Riffel. **Sr. Director, Landscaping:** Trevor Vance. **Sr. Director, Stadium Engineering:** Todd Burrow. **Director, Ballpark Services:** Johnny Williams. **Director, Guest Services:** Travis Bryant.

MARKETING/BUSINESS DEVELOPMENT
VP, Marketing/Business Development: Michael Bucek. **Sr. Director, Event Presentation/Production:** Don Costante. **Director, Event Presentation/Production:** Steven Funke. **Director, Event Presentation:** Nicole Averso. **Sr. Director, Marketing/Advertising:** Brad Zollars. **Sr. Director, Digital/Social Media:** Erin Sleddens. **Sr. Director, Corporate Partnerships/Broadcast Sales:** Jason Booker.

2020 SCHEDULE
Standard Game Times: Mon.-Sat., 7:15 pm; Sun., 1:15 pm.

MARCH
26 - 29 . . . at Chicago (AL)
30 . . . . at Detroit

APRIL
1 . . . . .at Detroit
2 - 5 . . . . Seattle
6 - 8 . . . . Detroit
9 - 12 . . . . . . at Toronto
13 - 15 . . . . Chicago (AL)
17 - 19 . . . . . Baltimore
21 - 22 . . at Chicago (AL)
24 - 26 . . . . at Tampa Bay
27 - 30 . . . . . at Baltimore

MAY
1 - 3 . . . . Detroit

4 - 6 . . . . Houston
9 - 10 . . . . at Minnesota
12 - 14 . . . . .at Houston
15 - 17 . . Los Angeles (NL)
18 - 21 . . Los Angeles (AL)
22 - 24 . . . . Texas
25 - 28 . . . . .at Boston
29 - 31 . . . .at Cleveland

JUNE
2 - 4 . . . . . Chicago (AL)
5 - 7 . . . . Cleveland
9 - 11 . . at New York (AL)
12 - 14 . . . . . Minnesota
15 - 17 . . . . . . .at Texas
19 - 21 . . . . . .at Seattle
23 - 24 . . . . at Colorado

26 - 28 . . . . . Cleveland
30 . . . . Arizona

JULY
1 . . . . Arizona
3 - 5 . . . . .at Detroit
7 - 8 . . . . . . at Minnesota
9 - 12 . . . . .at Cleveland
17 - 19 . . . . Boston
20 - 22 . . . . . Tampa Bay
24 - 26 . . . . . San Diego
28 - 29 . . . .at Cleveland
30 - 31 . . . . . .at Detroit

AUGUST
1 - 2 . . . . .at Detroit
4 - 5 . . . . St. Louis
6 - 9 . . . . Minnesota

10 - 12 . . . .New York (AL)
15 - 16 . . . . at Minnesota
17 - 18 . . . . . . at Arizona
20 - 23 . . . . . . Cleveland
24 - 26 . . . . .Toronto
29 - 30 . . at San Francisco

SEPTEMBER
1 - 2 . . . . .at Oakland
5 - 6 . . at Los Angeles (AL)
7 - 10 . . . . Oakland
11 - 13 . . . . Chicago (AL)
15 - 16 . . . . .at St. Louis
18 - 20 . . at Chicago (AL)
21 - 24 . . . . Detroit
25 - 27 . . . . . . Minnesota

GENERAL INFORMATION
Stadium (year opened):
Ewing M. Kauffman Stadium (1973).
Team Colors: Royal blue and white.

Home Dugout: First Base.
Playing Surface: Grass.

BASEBALL OPERATIONS

Dayton Moore

Telephone: (816) 921-8000. **Fax:** (816) 924-0347.
Sr. VP, Baseball Operations/General Manager: Dayton Moore. **Executive Asst. to the GM:** Emily Penning. **VP/Asst. GMs: Major League/International Operations:** Rene Francisco. **Player Personnel:** J.J. Picollo, **Baseball Operations:** Scott Sharp. **Asst. GM: Baseball Administration:** Jin Wong. **Research & Development:** Dr. Daniel Mack. **Special Asst. to the GM/Player Development:** Chino Cadahia. **Special Asst. to Baseball Ops:** Blaine Boyer, Reggie Sanders, Mike Sweeney. **Sr. Directors—Baseball Ops/Admin:** Kyle Vena. **Research & Development:** Guy Stevens. **Performance Science:** Austin Driggers. **Directors, Behavioral Science:** Dr. Ryan Maid. **Leadership Development:** Matt Marasco. **Pro Development:** Jeff Diskin. **Baseball Ops:** Mitch Maier. **Asst. Director, Behavioral Science:** Melissa Lambert. **Manager: Arizona Ops:** Nick Leto. **Sr. Developer:** Paul Turner. **Developers:** Joseph San Diego, Jenny Segelke. **Analysts:** Pravin Santhanam, Daniel Schoenfeld.

TRAVEL/CLUBHOUSE

Sr. Directors: Clubhouse Operations/Team Travel: Jeff Davenport. **Clubhouse Operations:** Chuck Hawke. Sr. **Manager, Clubhouse Operations/Team Travel:** Nick Richie. **Managers: Equipment:** Patrick Gorman.

MAJOR LEAGUE STAFF

Manager: Mike Matheny. **Coaches: Bench**—Pedro Grifol, **Pitching**—Cal Eldred, **Hitting**—Terry Bradshaw, **First Base**—Rusty Kuntz, **Third Base**—Vance Wilson, **Bullpen**—Larry Carter. **Special Assistant to the GM/Infield Coach:** Rafael Belliard. **Major League Coach:** John Mabry. **Replay/Advance Scouting Coordinator:** Bill Duplissea. **Bullpen Catchers:** Ryan Eigsti, Parker Morin.

MEDICAL/TRAINING

Team Physician: Dr. Vincent Key. **Head Athletic Trainer:** Nick Kenney. **Asst. Athletic Trainers:** Kyle Turner, Chris Delucia. **Strength & Conditioning:** Ryan Stoneberg. **Asst. Strength & Conditioning:** Luis Perez. **Physical Therapist:** Jeff Blum. **Registered Sports Dietitian:** Erika Sharp.

PLAYER DEVELOPMENT

Directors: Hitting Performance/Player Development: Alec Zumwalt. **Pitching Performance:** Paul Gibson, **Performance Science:** John Wagle. **Manager: Minor League Ops:** Nick Relic. **Pitching Performance:** Mitch Stetter. **Field Coordinator:** Victor Baez (DSL). **Special Asst., Player Development:** John Wathan, Harry Spilman. **Special Assignment Hitting Coach:** Mike Tosar. **Coordinators:** Jason Simontacchi (pitching), Drew Saylor (hitting), Keoni DeRenne (asst. hitting), Eddie Rodriguez (infield), J.C. Boscan (catching), Justin Hahn (rehab), Carlos Reyes (pitching rehab), Damon Hollins (outfield, bunting, baserunning), David Iannicca, Tony Medina (medical), Jarret Abell (strength/conditioning), Phil Falco (Asst. strength/conditioning), Will Simon (equipment), Monica Ramirez (Ed/ESL & Latin American Initiatives), Rustin Sveum (Video). **Assistant:** Malcom Culver. **Roving Pitching Coach:** Jeff Suppan, **Assistant Pitching Coach:** Derrick Lewis, **Bench Coaches:** Willie Aikens (AZ), Glenn Hubbard (LEX), Nelson Liriano (IF). **Development Coaches:** Tony Medina, Brandon Nelson, Jason Goldstein, Matt Malott.

FARM SYSTEM

Class	Club (League)	Manager	Hitting Coach	Pitching Coach
Triple-A	Omaha (PCL)	Brian Poldberg	Brian Buchanan	Dane Johnson
Double-A	Northwest Arkansas (TL)	Scott Thorman	Abraham Nunez	Doug Henry
High A	Wilmington (CL)	Chris Widger	Andy LaRoche	Steve Luebber
Low A	Lexington (SAL)	Brooks Conrad	Jesus Azuaje	Carlos Martinez
Rookie	Idaho Falls (PIO)	Omar Ramirez	Chris Nelson	C. Mortensen
Rookie	Burlington (APP)	Tony Pena, Jr.	Ramon Castro	John Habyan
Rookie	Royals (AZL)	M. Bernard	A. David	Davis/Pimentel
Rookie	Royals (DSL1)	Ramon Martinez	Wilson Betemit	Rafael Feliz
Rookie	Royals (DSL2)	Sergio de Luna	Evaristo Lantigua	Jose Veras

SCOUTING

Telephone: (816) 921-8000. **Fax:** (816) 924-0347. **Assistant GM/Amateur Scouting:** Lonnie Goldberg. **Sr. Director, Pro Scouting/Assistant to the GM:** Gene Watson. **Director, Pro Scouting:** Michael Cifuentes. **Assistant Director, Amateur Scouting:** Danny Ontiveros. **Coordinators: Scouting Operations:** Jack Monahan. **Amateur Video/Underclass Scout:** Tim Bavester. **Sr. Advisors:** Mike Arbuckle, Art Stewart, Donnie Williams, Gene Lamont. **Special Assistants to the GM:** Tim Conroy, Jim Fregosi, Jr., Mike Jirschele, Louie Medina. **Special Assignment Scouts:** Mitch Webster, Dale Sveum. **Pro Scouts:** Nate Adcock, Dennis Cardoza, Gregg Kilby, Dave Oliver, Mike Pazik, Jon Williams. **Part-Time Pro Scout:** Rene Lachemann. **Advance Scouts:** Cody Clark, Tony Tijerina. **Regional Supervisors: Midwest**—Gregg Miller, **Northeast**—Keith Connolly, **Southeast**—Sean Gibbs, **Southwest**—Colin Gonzales, **West**—Gary Wilson. **Pitching Assignment Scout:** Chris Reitsma. **Area Supervisors:** Joe Barbera, Travis Ezi, Casey Fahy, Abe Flores, Jim Farr, Mike Farrell, Buddy Gouldsmith, Josh Hallgren, Will Howard, Mark Leavitt, Chad Lee, Scott Melvin, Alex Mesa (Miami, FL), Ken Munoz, Matt Price, Joe Ross, Bobby Shore. **Underclass Scout:** Daniel Guerrero. **Part-Time Scouts:** Kirk Barclay, Eric Briggs, Rick Clendenin, Louis Collier, Corey Eckstein, Jeremy Jones, Jerry Lafferty, Brittan Motley, Chad Raley, Johnny Ramos, Lloyd Simmons, Adam Stern. **Asst. GM/Int'l Operations:** Albert Gonzalez. **Coordinators: Latin America:** Orlando Estevez. **Pacific Rim:** Phil Dale. **Manager, International Ops:** Fabio Herrera. **International Scouts:** Nicolas Bautista (D.R.), Neil Burke (Australia), Elias Despardel (D.R.), Fernando Encarnacion (D.R.), Jose Figuera (VZ), Edgarluis Fuentes (VZ), Alberto Garcia (VZ), Joelvis Gonzalez (VZ), Jose Gualdron (VZ), Djionny Joubert (Curacao), Edson Kelly (Aruba), Hyunsung Kim (S. Korea). Manabu Kuramochi (Tokyo), Juan Lopez (Nicaragua), Nathan Miller (Taiwan), Rafael Miranda (Colombia), Fausto Morel (Dominican Republic), Luis Ortiz (Texas), Hiroyuki Oya (Japan), Edis Perez (D.R), Manuel Samaniego (Mexico), Rafael Vasquez (D.R.),

LOS ANGELES ANGELS

Office Address: 2000 Gene Autry Way, Anaheim, CA 92806.
Mailing Address: 2000 Gene Autry Way, Anaheim, CA 92803.
Telephone: (714) 940-2000. **Fax:** (714) 940-2205. **Website:** www.angels.com.

OWNERSHIP
Owner: Arte Moreno. **Chairman:** Dennis Kuhl. **President:** John Carpino.

BUSINESS OPERATIONS
Executive Vice President: Dana Wells. **Senior Vice President, Finance/Administration:** Molly Jolly. **Director, Legal Affairs/Risk Management:** Alex Winsberg. **Associate Legal Counsel:** Jen Tedmori. **Director, Finance:** Doug Mylowe. **Controller:** Sue Bassett. **Assistant Controller:** Jennifer Whynott. **Financial Operations Manager:** Jennifer Jeanblanc. **Payroll Manager:** Lorelei Schlitz. **Payroll Coordinator:** Katrina Ceballos. **Accountants:** Kylie McManus, Matt Asato. **Payroll Assistant:** Alison Kelso. **Accounts Payable Specialist:** Sarah Talamonte Director, **Human Resources:** Deborah Johnston. **Benefits Manager:** Cecilia Schneider. **Human Resources Manager:** Mayra Castro. **Human Resources Coordinator:** Reyna Mancilla. **Director, Information Services:** Al Castro. **Senior Manager Network Infrastructure:** Neil Fariss. **Senior Customer Support Analyst:** David Yun. **Technical Services Manager:** Aron Linville. **Network Administrator:** James Sheu. **Helpdesk Support Assistant:** Michael Gallant.

Arte Moreno

CORPORATE SALES
Vice President, Sales: Neil Viserto. **Senior Director, Business Development:** Mike Fach. **Senior Account Executive, National Accounts:** Rick Turner. **Senior Corporate Account Executive:** Drew Zinser. **Account Executive:** Ashley Fleck. **Director, Partner Services:** Bobby Kowan. **Senior Account Manager:** Adam Overgaard. **Manager Partner Services:** Andie Mitsuda. **Account Manager:** Alli Serrano, Maddy Stover, Ryan Vitelli.

MARKETING/ENTERTAINMENT
Director, Ticket Marketing and Business Analytics: Ryan Vance. **Senior Marketing Managers:** Alex Tinyo, Vanessa Vega. **Graphic Designers:** Tricia Kami, Dominic Mitrano. **Junior Graphic Designer:** Arianne Tano. **Digital and Promotions Coordinator:** Hannah Stange. **Manager, Business Analytics:** Julius Evans. **Business Analyst:** Hayden Keown, Nicole Yamasaki. **Director, Entertainment/Production:** Peter Bull. **Manager, Video Production:** Jordan Esswein. **Production Coordinator:** Cole Dragon. **Engineer:** Zac Applegate. **Marketing and Entertainment Coordinator:** Mandi Ortiz.

PUBLIC/MEDIA RELATIONS/COMMUNICATIONS
Telephone: (714) 940-2014. **Fax:** (714) 940-2205.
Director, Communications: Adam Chodzko. **Managers, Communications:** Matt Birch, Grace McNamee. **Manager, Social Media/Digital Marketing:** Danny Farris. **Team Photographer:** Blaine Ohigashi. **Photography Assistant:** Ricardo Zapata.

COMMUNITY RELATIONS
Director, Corporate & Community Partnerships: Nicole Provansal. **Manager, Foundation and Community Initiatives:** Adam Cali. **Coordinator, Community Relations:** Nnedy Obiwuru. **Scholarship Programs and Marketing Coordinator:** Lillea Acasio.

2020 SCHEDULE
Standard Game Times: Mon.-Sat., 7:07 pm; Sun., 12:37 pm.

MARCH
26 - 29 . . . . . .at Houston
31 . . . . .at Texas

APRIL
1 - 2 . . . . .at Texas
4 - 5 . . . . Houston
7 - 9 . . . . Oakland
10 - 12 . . . . . . .at Detroit
14 - 15 . . . . . at Miami
18 - 19 . . . . .at Houston
21 - 22 . . . . Baltimore
24 - 26 . . . . Chicago (AL)
29 - 30 . . . . . . .at Seattle

MAY
2 - 3 . . . . . . .Minnesota

5 - 7 . . . . .at Boston
8 - 10 . . . . .at Baltimore
12 - 14 . . . . . Washington
16 - 17 . . . . Oakland
18 - 21 . . .at Kansas City
23 - 24 . . . . .at Oakland
26 - 27 . . . . . Cleveland
30 - 31 . . .New York (AL)

JUNE
1 - 3 . . . . .at Texas
5 - 7 . . . . . at Minnesota
10 - 11 . . . . .Miami
13 - 14 . . . . Seattle
16 - 17 . . . . .at Oakland
19 - 21 . . . . Texas
23 - 24 . . . . Boston

26 - 28 . . . . . . at Toronto
29 - 30 . . . . at Tampa Bay

JULY
1 - 2 . . . . . . at Tampa Bay
3 - 5 . . . . at Atlanta
7 - 10 . . . . Detroit
11 . . . . . Los Angeles (NL)
17 - 19 . . . at Philadelphia
20 - 23 . . at New York (AL)
24 - 26 . . . . . . .at Texas
28 - 30 . . . . .Toronto
31 . . . . Seattle

AUGUST
1 - 2 . . . . Seattle
4 . . . . Texas

7 - 9 . . . . .at Seattle
11 - 12 . . .at Chicago (AL)
14 - 16 . . . . Houston
19 - 21 . . . .New York (AL)
22 - 23 . . . . . . .Tampa Bay
26 - 27 .at Los Angeles (NL)
29 - 30 . . . . . . .at Seattle

SEPTEMBER
1 - 4 . . . . Texas
5 - 6 . . . . . . Kansas City
8 - 10 . . . . Houston
11 - 13 . . . . .at Cleveland
15 - 16 . . . . .at Houston
18 - 20 . . . . .at Oakland
23 - 25 . . . . Seattle
26 - 27 . . . . Oakland

GENERAL INFORMATION
Stadium (year opened): Angel Stadium of Anaheim (1966). **Playing Surface:** Grass.
Team Colors: Red, dark red, blue and silver.
Home Dugout: Third Base.

BALLPARK OPERATIONS/FACILITIES

Senior Director, Ballpark Operations: Brian Sanders. **Director, Ballpark Operations:** Sam Maida. **Director, Stadium Operations:** Calvin Ching. **Director, Special Events:** Courtney Wallace. **Senior Manager, Stadium Operations:** Nathan Bautista.

TICKETING

Senior Director, Ticket Sales: Jim Panetta. **Senior Director, Ticket Operations/Service:** Tom DeTemple. **Senior Manager, Ticket Operations:** Sheila Brazelton. **Manager, Ticket Operations:** Armando Reyna. **Manager, Ticket Services:** Brandon Cosio.

TRAVEL/CLUBHOUSE

Traveling Secretary: Tom Taylor. **Clubhouse Manager:** Keith Tarter. **Assistant Clubhouse Manager:** Shane Demmitt. **Visiting Clubhouse Manager:** Brian "Bubba" Harkins. **Manager, Major League Video:** Adam Hunt. **Video Coordinator:** Ruben Montano.

Billy Eppler

BASEBALL OPERATIONS

General Manager: Billy Eppler.
Assistant GMs: Jonathan Strangio, Steve Martone. **Senior Advisors, Baseball Operations:** Tony LaRussa, Bill Stoneman. **Assistants to GM:** Eric Chavez, Ben Francisco, Marcel Lachemann. **Director, Baseball Operations:** Andrew Ball. **Director, Quantitative Analysis:** Kevin Ferris. **Coordinator, Baseball Administration:** Peggy Berroa-Morales. **Assistant Director, Quantitative Analysis:** Richard Anderson. **Assistant Director, Baseball Operations:** Andrew Mack. **Analyst, Baseball Operations:** Kevin Brice. **Assistant, Baseball Operations:** Nick Spar. **Assistant, Baseball Operations Video:** Brooke Wakenhut. **Assistant, Quantitative Analysis:** Bryce Rogan, Matt Johnson, Jonah Krop, Connor Moffatt.

MAJOR LEAGUE STAFF

Manager: Joe Maddon. **Coaches: Bench** — Mike Gallego, **Pitching** — Mickey Callaway, **Hitting** — Jeremy Reed, **First Base**— Jesus Feliciano, **Third Base** — Brian Butterfield, **Bullpen** — Matt Wise, **Assistant Hitting** — John Mallee, **Hitting Instructor**— Paul Sorrento, **Catching** — Jose Molina. **Replay** — Ryan Garko. **Manager, Video Operations**— Adam Hunt. **Director, Mental Conditioning** — Will Lenzner.

MEDICAL/TRAINING

Team Physician: Dr. Craig Milhouse. **Team Orthopedist:** Dr. Brian Schulz, Dr. Steve Yoon, Dr. John Itamura, Dr. Carlos Uquillas. **Director, Sport Science/Performance:** Bernard Li. **Director of Performance Integration:** Ryan Crotin. **Assistant Director, Performance Integration:** Kenneth Smale. **Head Athletic Trainer:** Adam Nevala. **Assistant Athletic Trainer:** Eric Munson. **Athletic Training Services Coordinator:** Rick Smith. **Strength/Conditioning Coach:** Lee Fiocchi. **Physical Therapist/Assistant Strength/Conditioning:** Sean Johnson. **Assistant Strength and Conditioning:** Adam Auer. **Quality Assurance:** Tim Buss. **Massage Therapist:** Yoichi Terada. **Registered Dietician:** Rebecca Twombley.

PLAYER DEVELOPMENT

Director, Minor League Operations: Mike LaCassa. **Coordinator, Minor League Operations:** Chris Mosch. **Assistant, Minor League Operations:** Andrea LaPointe. **Field Coordinator:** Chad Tracy. **Manager, Minor League Equipment & AZ Operations:** Brett Crane. **Video Coordinator:** Ryan Dundee. **Assistant, AZ Operations & Clubhouse:** Louie Raya. **Asst Clubhouse:** Aaron Wiedeman. **Roving Instructors:** Damon Mashore (hitting), Ryan Parker (coordinator hitting analysis), Buddy Carlyle (pitching), Dylan Axelrod (assistant pitching), Jordan Oseguera (pitching analyst), Bill Lachemann (catching/special assignment), Ryan Barba (assistant field coordinator), Chris Constantine (outfield/baserunning), Hainley Statia (infield), Kernan Ronan (rehab coach), Andrew Hawkins (rehab coordinator), Geoff Hostetter (medical coordinator), Danny Escobar (strength/conditioning), Dylan Cintula (rehab strength & conditioning), Humberto Miranda (Latin America field coordinator), Glen Steele (medical cross checker), Michael Noboa (Latin America Operations Coordinator), Fausto Betances (Coordinator, DR Academy Administration), and Fabio Fermin (Asst., DR Academy Administration).

FARM SYSTEM

Class	Club	Manager	Hitting Coach	Pitching Coach
Triple-A	Salt Lake (PCL)	Lou Marson	Brian Betancourth	Jairo Cuevas
Double-A	Rocket City (SL)	Jay Bell	Matt Spring	Tim Norton
High A	Inland Empire (CAL)	Jack Santora	Kenny Hook	Michael Wuertz
Low A	Burlington (MWL)	Jack Howell	Will Bradley	Tyler Anderson
Rookie	Orem (PIO)	Andy Schatzley	R.Sebra/D.Ortega	J.Fort/B.Martino
Rookie	Angels (AZL)	David Stapleton	T. Jeske/C.Shaw	T.Reklaitis/B.Baumann
Rookie	Angels (DSL)	Hector De La Cruz	R. Gomez/A. De Los Santos	J.Marte/E.Gonzalez

SCOUTING

Director, Pro Scouting: Nate Horowitz. **Coordinator, Pro and International Scouting:** Nick Lampe. **Major League/Special Assignment Scout:** Ric Wilson. **Professional Scouts:** Jeff Cirillo, Buck Coats, Phil Geisler, Nick McCoy, Jim Miller, Jayson Nix, Roman Rodriguez, Travis Ice, Tim McIntosh, Andrew Schmidt, Ken Stauffer, Bobby Williams. **Director, Amateur Scouting:** Matt Swanson. **Coordinator, Amateur Scouting:** Aidan Donovan. **National Crosscheckers:** Jeremy Schied, Jason Smith, Steffan Wilson. **Regional Supervisors: East**—Jason Baker. **South**—Brandon McArthur. **Southeast**—Nick Gorneault. **Northwest**—Scott Richardson. **Southwest**—Jayson Durocher. **Hitting Crosschecker:** Jason Ellison. **Area Scouts:** Brett Bittiger, John Burden, Tim Corcoran, Christopher Cruz, Ben Diggins, Drew Dominguez, Brian Gordon, Chad Hermansen, Todd Hogan, Kennard Jones, Ryan Leahy, Billy Lipari, Chris McAlpin, Joel Murrie, Ralph Reyes, Brett Smith, Brian Tripp. **Director, International Scouting:** Carlos Gomez. **Asst. Director, International Scouting:** Giovanni Hernandez. **Administrator, International Scouting:** Grace Mercedes. **International Scouting Supervisor:** Marlon Urdaneta. **International Regional Crosscheckers:** Andres Garcia, Francisco Tejeda. **International Scouts:** Jochy Cabrera, Rusbell Cabrera, Joel Chicarelli, Domingo Garcia, Ender Gonzalez, Raul Gonzalez, Aneudi Mercado, Rubylin Nicasia.

LOS ANGELES DODGERS

Office Address: 1000 Vin Scully Ave., Los Angeles, CA 90012.
Telephone: (323) 224-1500. Fax: (323) 224-1269. **Website:** www.dodgers.com.

OWNERSHIP/EXECUTIVE OFFICE
Chairman: Mark Walter. **Partners:** Earvin 'Magic' Johnson, Peter Guber, Todd Boehly, Robert 'Bobby' Patton, Jr, Billie Jean King, Ilana Kloss, Robert L. Plummer, Alan Smolinisky. **President/CEO:** Stan Kasten. **Special Advisor to Chairman:** Tommy Lasorda.

BUSINESS OPERATIONS

Executive Vice President/COO: Bob Wolfe. **Executive VP/Chief Marketing Officer:** Lon Rosen. **President, Dodgers Business Enterprise/Managing Director, Guggenheim Baseball Management:** Tucker Kain. **Executive VP/General Counsel:** Sam Fernandez. **Senior VP, Marketing, Communications and Broadcaster:** Erik Braverman. **Senior VP, Stadium Operations:** Joe Crowley. **Senior VP, Ticket and Premium Sales & Service:** Antonio Morici. **Senior VP, Planning/ Development:** Janet Marie Smith. **Senior VP, Global Partnerships:** Michael Wandell.

FINANCE AND BUSINESS ANALYTICS
VP, Finance: Eric Hernandez. **Sr. Director, Financial Planning/Analysis:** Gregory Buonaccorsi. **Director, Purchasing:** Lisa McShane. **Controller:** Sara Curran. **VP, Business Development & Analytics:** Royce Cohen. **Director, Business Development & Analytics:** Gabe Gershenfeld. **Director, Business Analytics:** Michael Spetner.

Mark Walter

EMMA MCINTYRE/GETTY IMAGES

GLOBAL PARTNERSHIPS
VP, Global Partnerships: Corey Norkin. **Sr. Director, Global Partnership Administration & Services:** Jenny Oh. **Sr. Director, Marketing Solutions:** Matt Grable. **Director, Global Partnership Services:** Corey Schimmel.

MARKETING/BROADCASTING AND COMMUNICATIONS
Sr. VP, Marketing/Broadcasting Communications: Erik Braverman. **Vice President, Digital Strategy:** Caroline Morgan. **Sr. Director, Public Relations:** Joe Jareck. **Sr. Director, Marketing/Advertising/Promotions:** Shelley Wagner. **Executive Producer, Production:** Greg Taylor. **Sr. Director, Graphic Design:** Ross Yoshida. **Sr. Director, Broadcast Engineering:** Tom Darin.

HUMAN RESOURCES/LEGAL
VP, Human Resources: Marilyn Davis. **Sr. Director, Human Resources:** Leonor Romero. **Associate General Counsel:** Chad Gunderson. **Associate General Counsel:** Daniel Martens.

LOS ANGELES DODGERS FOUNDATION AND COMMUNITY AFFAIRS
Chief Executive Officer, Los Angeles Dodgers Foundation: Nichol Whiteman. **VP, External Affairs/Community Relations:** Naomi Rodriguez. **COO, Los Angeles Dodgers Foundation:** Chaitali Gala Mehta.

TICKETING
Telephone: (323) 224-1471. **Fax:** (323) 224-2609.
VP, Ticket Operations: Seth Bluman. **VP, Premium Sales & Services:** Craig Sindici. **Director, Premium Sales & Services:** Bobby Mayorga. **Executive Director, Sales & Service:** Wade Graf.

2020 SCHEDULE
Standard Game Times: 7:10 p.m.; Sun. 1:10

MARCH	4 - 6 . . . . . San Francisco	27 - 28 . . . . . . Colorado
26 - 29 . . . . .at Oakland	9 - 10 . . . . . Kansas City	30 . . . . .at Detroit
31 . . . . .at Seattle	11 - 14 . . . . . .at Detroit	**JULY**
	15 - 17 . . .at Cleveland	1 - 2 . . . . .at Detroit
APRIL	18 - 20 . . . . . Baltimore	3 - 5 . . . . . .at Cleveland
1 . . . . .at Seattle	21 - 24 . . . . Chicago (AL)	7 - 8 . . . . . . Kansas City
2 - 5 . . . . Oakland	26 - 28 . . at New York (AL)	9 - 12 . . . . .Toronto
6 - 8 . . . . Cleveland	30 - 31 . . .at Chicago (AL)	17 - 19 . . . . . . .at Texas
11 - 12 . . .at Chicago (AL)		20 - 22 . . . . . at Arizona
13 - 15 . . . . . at Toronto	**JUNE**	24 - 26 . . .at Chicago (AL)
18 - 19 . . . . Detroit	2 - 4 . . . . .Tampa Bay	29 . . . . . Los Angeles (NL)
20 - 23 . . . . Seattle	5 - 7 . . . . Los Angeles (AL)	
25 - 26 . . . . Boston	9 - 11 . . . . . .at Baltimore	**AUGUST**
29 - 30 . .at Los Angeles (NL)	12 - 14 . . .at Kansas City	1 - 2 . . . . Houston
	17 . . . . .Milwaukee	4 - 5 . . . . Cleveland
MAY	19 - 21 . . . .New York (AL)	6 - 9 . . . . . .at Kansas City
2 - 3 . . at Los Angeles (AL)	23 - 25 . . . . . .at Houston	10 - 13 . . . . . . .at Boston

15 - 16 . . . . . Kansas City	
19 . . . . . . Chicago (AL)	
22 - 23 . . . . Detroit	
26 . . . . . . at Milwaukee	
28 - 30 . . . .at Tampa Bay	
SEPTEMBER	
1 - 3 . . . . Cleveland	
5 - 6 . . . . . Chicago (AL)	
8 - 10 . . . . .at Cleveland	
11 - 13 . . . . . . .at Detroit	
15 - 17 . . . . Texas	
19 - 20 . . . . Detroit	
23 - 24 . . . . at San Diego	
25 - 27 . . . .at Kansas City	

GENERAL INFORMATION
Stadium (year opened): Dodger Stadium (1962).
Team Colors: Dodger blue and white.
Home Dugout: Third Base.
Playing Surface: Grass

BASEBALL OPERATIONS

Telephone: (323) 224-1500. **Fax:** (323) 224-1463.
President: Andrew Friedman. **Assistant General Managers:** Jeff Kingston & Brandon Gomes.
Senior Vice President: Josh Byrnes. **Vice Presidents:** Dave Finley (Amateur & International Scouting), Galen Carr (Player Personnel), Ismael Cruz (International Scouting), Billy Gasparino (Amateur Scouting). **Senior Directors:** Ellen Harrigan (Baseball Administration); Scott Akasaki (Team Travel). **Directors:** Alex Slater (Baseball Operations); Duncan Webb (Baseball Resources); Scott Powers (Quantitative Analysis); Megan Schroeder (Performance Science); John Focht & Brian McBurney (Baseball Systems). **Senior Advisors & Special Assistants:** Gerry Hunsicker, Pat Corrales, Raul Ibañez, Rick Honeycutt, Jose Vizcaino.

Andrew Friedman

MAJOR LEAGUE STAFF

Manager: Dave Roberts. **Coaches:** Bob Geren (Bench); Mark Prior (Pitching); Robert Van Scoyoc & Brant Brown (Hitting); George Lombard (First Base); Dino Ebel (Third Base); Josh Bard (Bullpen); Aaron Bates (Assistant Hitting); Connor McGuiness (Assistant Pitching). **Coordinator, Game Planning/Run Prevention:** Danny Lehmann. **Bullpen Catchers:** Steve Cilladi & Jonathan Langley. **Director, Player Health:** Ron Porterfield. **Head Athletic Trainer:** Neil Rampe. **Director, Performance Rehab:** Andrew Hauser. **Director, Player Performance:** Brandon McDaniel. **Director, Clubhouse Operations:** Alex Torres. **Strength & Conditioning Coach:** Travis Smith. **Sports Scientist:** Kate Weiss. **Physical Therapist:** Johnathan Erb. **Assistant Athletic Trainers:** Yosuke Nakajima, Thomas Albert.

PLAYER DEVELOPMENT

Telephone: (323) 224-1500. **Fax:** (323) 224-1359.
Director: Will Rhymes. **Assistant Director:** Matt McGrath. **Assistant Director, Minor League Operations:** Joe Harrington. **Manager, Minor League Administration:** Adriana Urzua. **Field Coordinator:** Clayton McCullough. **Assistant Field Coordinator:** Shaun Larkin. **Coordinators:** Don Alexander (pitching), Gabe Ribas (Pitching), Rob Hill (Pitching), Ryan Sienko (Catching), Chris Antariksa (Hitting), Bill Haselman (Managers), Chris Gimenez (Game Planning), AJ LaLonde (Strong Mind), Leo Ruiz (Strong Mind), Charles Wagner (Video), Kevin Orloski (Medical), Brian Stoneberg (Performance), Colt Hynes (Rehab Pitching), Lou Iannotti (Hitting Analytics), Brent Minta (Pitching Analytics), Cathy Lara (Education). **Special Assistants:** Charlie Hough, Joel Peralta, Placido Polanco, Jamey Wright, Bobby Cuellar, Brandon Erbe.

CAMPO LOS PALMAS

Sr. Facility Manager: Jesus Negrette. **Latin American Field Coordinator:** Keyter Collado. **Latin American Pitching Coordinator:** Luis Meza. **Latin American Defensive Coordinator:** Pedro Mega. **Latin American Medical Coordinator:** Jorge Gonzalez. **Latin American S&C Coordinator:** Carl Kochan.

CAMELBACK RANCH

Manager, Arizona Operations: Matt Peabody. **Minor League Equipment Manager:** Troy Timney.

FARM SYSTEM

Class	Club (League)	Manager	Hitting Coach	Pitching Coach
Triple-A	Oklahoma City (PCL)	Travis Barbary	Manny Burriss	Bill Simas
Double-A	Tulsa (TL)	Scott Hennessey	Brett Pill	Dave Borkowski
High A	Rancho Cucamonga (CAL)	Austin Chubb	Dustin Kelly	Ryan Dennick
Low A	Great Lakes (MWL)	John Shoemaker	Seth Connor	Stephanos Stroop
Rookie	Ogden (PIO)	Tony Cappuccilli	Dylan Nasiatka	Dean Stiles
Rookie	Dodgers (AZL)	Jair Fernandez	Jarek Cunningham	Rob Ellis
Rookie	Dodgers (DSL)	Danny Dorn	Keith Beauregard	Ramon Troncoso

SCOUTING

VP, Amateur/International Scouting: David Finley. **Director, Amateur Scouting:** Billy Gasparino. **Assistant Director, Amateur Scouting:** Zach Fitzpatrick. **Coordinator, Amateur Scouting:** Greg Bekiaris. **Video Coordinator, Amateur Scouting:** Trey Magnuson. **Athleticism Development Coordinator:** Eric Yavarone. **Global Crosschecker:** John Green. **National Crosscheckers:** Brian Stephenson, Rob St. Julien. **Pitching Crosschecker, Amateur Scouting:** Jack Cressend. **Advisor, Amateur Scouting:** Gary Nickels. **Crosscheckers: Midwest**—Stephen Head, **Northeast**—Jon Adkins, **Southeast**—Alan Matthews, **West Coast**—Paul Cogan. **Area Scouts:** John Pyle, Paul Murphy, Jonah Rosenthal, Garrett Ball, Wes Sargent, Kelvin Colon, Luis Faccio, Benny Latino, Marty Lamb, Clint Bowers, Heath Holliday, Mitch Schulewitz, Brian Compton, Brent Mayne, Dennis Moeller, Jeff Stevens, Tom Kunis. **Director of Player Personnel, Pro Scouting:** Galen Carr. **Coordinator, Professional Scouting:** Lucas Geoghegan. **Director of Baseball Operations:** Alex Slater. **Pro Scouts:** Peter Bergeron, Franco Frias, Scott Groot, Bill Latham, Jason Lynn, Tydus Meadows, Steve Pope, Tim Schmidt, Chris Smith, Philip Stringer, Lee Tacket, Yogo Suzuki (Japan), Les Walrond. **Special Assignment Scouts:** Vance Lovelace, Jeff McAvoy, Matt Smith. **VP, International Scouting:** Ismael Cruz. **Latin American Scouting Supervisor:** Roman Barinas. **Manager, International Scouting:** Javier Camps. **Advisor:** Ralph Avila. **Coach, International Scouting:** Alejandro Bautista. **Video Scout, Venezuela:** Rafael Arcila. **Coordinators: Venezuela**—Leon Jackson Canelon, **D.R.**—Jesus Lantigua, **Crosscheckers: Venezuela**—Jose Briceno, **Latin America**—Jairo Castillo, **International**—Brian Parker, James Kang, **D.R.**—Manelik Pimentel. **Director, Pacific Rim:** Jon Deeble. **Assistant Director, Pacific Rim:** San-Tai 'Allen' Lin. **Associate Video/Analytics:** Alant Moncion. **Coordinator, Analytics:** Matthew Doppelt. **Supervisor, D.R.:** Laiky Uribe. **Video Scout, D.R.:** Jonathan Genao. **International Scouts: D.R.**—Moises Alou, Dawlyn Lantigua, Domingo Toribio, Felvin Veloz, **Venezuela**—Paul Brazon, Cristian Guzman, Jean Castro, Andres Simancas, Oswaldo Villalobos, **Mexico**—Mike Brito, Juvenal Soto, **Panama**—Carlos Gonzalez, **Curacao & Aruba:** Rolando Chirino, **Korea**—Seungyun 'Simon' Kim, **Colombia**—Miguel Orozco, **Europe**—Nestor Perez.

MIAMI MARLINS

Office Address: Marlins Park, 501 Marlins Way, Miami, FL 33125
Telephone: (305) 480-1300. **Fax:** (305) 480-3012.
Website: www.marlins.com.

OWNERSHIP

Chairman & Principal Owner: Bruce Sherman.

BUSINESS OPERATIONS

Chief Executive Officer: Derek Jeter. **Chief Revenue Officer:** Adam Jones. **Chief
Operating Officer:** Caroline O'Connor.

ADMINISTRATIVE SERVICES

Executive Assistant to CEO: Nicolette Lawrence. **Executive Assistant, Business Operations:**
Kristen Keane. **Manager, Investor Relations & Special Projects:** Karen De Leon. **Executive
Assistant to EVP, Special Projects & VP, Head of Experience & Innovation:** Teresita Garcia.

FINANCE

Executive Vice President & Chief Financial Officer: Michel Bussiere. **Vice President,
Accounting & Financial Planning:** Fred Koczwara. **Manager, Accounting:** Richard Williams.
Administrator, Payroll: Carolina Calderon. **Assistant Payroll Administrator:** Edgar
Perez. **Supervisor, Accounts Payable:** Anthony Paneque. **Staff Accountant:** David Villa.
Coordinator, Finance: Felix Anderson.

Derek Jeter

MARKETING

Director, Events/Promotions: Juan Martinez. **Director, Event Presentation & Entertainment:** Matthew Mendez.
Director, Digital Marketing: Paulo O'Swath. **Supervisor, Promotions:** Rafael Capdevila. **Manager, Digital Marketing:**
Karry Pomes. **Manager, Marketing:** Mariah Monahan. **Coordinator, Marketing:** Karen Castellon.

LEGAL & RISK MANAGEMENT

Vice President and General Counsel: Ashwin Krishnan. **Associate General Counsel:** Stephanie Galvin. **Director,
Risk Management:** Fred Espinosa. **Coordinator, Risk Management:** Claudia Avila.

SALES/TICKETING

Vice President, Sales & Service: Andre Luck. **Director, Membership Sales:** Evans Adonis. **Director, Inside Sales:**
David Campbell. **Director, Premium Sales & Service:** Ryan Sember. **Senior Premium Sales Executive:** Chema
Sanchez. **Senior Event Planning Executive:** Patty Lora. **Director, Membership Experience:** Brian Jemison. **Manager,
Membership Experience:** Jason Liss. **Coordinator, Member Experience:** Jessica Lee. **Coordinator, Membership Sales
& Service:** Kassandra Webb. **Membership Experience Executive:** Samantha MacIntosh, Eric Sutcliffe. **Membership Sales
Executive:** Isaac Paladino, Ryan Plasencia, Christian Capozzi, Jennifer Owston. **Director, Group Sales & Service:** Kyle
Brant. **Senior Group Sales & Service Executive:** Shoshana Baker-Bradley. **Group Sales & Service Executive:** Antonio Diz,
Ernesto Penton, Brad Johnson. **Director, Ticket Operations:** Mardi Dilger.

2020 SCHEDULE

Standard Game Times: Mon.-Sat., 7:10 pm; Sun., 1:10 pm.

MARCH		
26-29 . . . . . .Philadelphia	8-10 . . . . at Atlanta	30 . . . . .at Oakland
30-31 . . . . Washington	11-13 . . . . .at Cincinnati	
APRIL	15-17 . . . . .Colorado	**JULY**
1 . . . . Washington	19-21 . . . . . San Diego	1 . . . . .at Oakland
3-5. . . . . . . at Atlanta	22-25 . . . . at Washington	4-5. . . at Los Angeles (NL)
6-8. . . . . . at Washington	27-28 . . . .at Chicago (NL)	7-9. . . . . Texas
9-12 . . . . Atlanta	30-31 . . . . . at San Diego	10-12 . . . . .New York (NL)
14-15 . . . Los Angeles (AL)	**JUNE**	17-19 . . . . . . at Arizona
17-19 . . . . at Philadelphia	2-4. . . . . .Philadelphia	21-23 . . . . . at Colorado
21-23 . . at New York (NL)	5-7. . . . . Seattle	24-27 . . .Los Angeles (NL)
25-26 . . . . . . .at St. Louis	10-11 . at Los Angeles (AL)	28-29 . . . . at Tampa Bay
28-30 . . . . .New York (NL)	13-14 . . . at San Francisco	30-31 . . at New York (NL)
MAY	16-18 . . . . at Philadelphia	**AUGUST**
1-3. . . . . .Pittsburgh	19-21 . . . . .San Francisco	1-2. . . . at New York (NL)
4-7. . . . . .Milwaukee	22-25 . . . . St. Louis	4-6. . . . . .Washington
	26-28 . . . . Atlanta	7-9. . . . . Atlanta
		12-13 . . . . . at Milwaukee

14-16 . . . . at Atlanta
18-19 . . . . . .Philadelphia
20-23 . . . . . at Pittsburgh
25-27 . . . . . Chicago (NL)
28-31 . . . . .Arizona
SEPTEMBER
2-3. . . . . .at Houston
4-7. . . . . . at Philadelphia
8-9. . . . . .Tampa Bay
11-13 . . . . . . Washington
15-17 . . at New York (NL)
18-20 . . . . at Washington
21-23 . . . . Cincinnati
25-27 . . . . .New York (NL)

GENERAL INFORMATION

Stadium (year opened): Marlins Park (2012). **Playing Surface:** Grass.
Team Colors: Caliente Red, Miami Blue, Midnight Black and Slate Grey
Home Dugout: Third Base.

COMMUNICATIONS/MEDIA RELATIONS

Senior VP, Communications & Broadcasting: Jason Latimer. **Manager, Baseball Communications & Publications:** Joe Vieira. **Manager, Business Communications & Spanish Media:** Jon Erik Alvarez. **Coordinator, Communications:** Maria Armella. **Player Relations & Spanish Media Liaison:** Luis Dorante. **Manager, Broadcasting:** Kyle Sielaff. **Coordinator, Social Media:** Sarah Penalver.

TRAVEL/CLUBHOUSE

Director, Team Travel: Manny Colon. **Equipment Manager:** John Silverman. **Visiting Clubhouse Manager:** Rock Hughes. **Assistant Clubhouse Manager:** Michael Diaz.

BASEBALL OPERATIONS

Telephone: (305) 480-1300. **Fax:** (305) 480-3032.
President, Baseball Operations: Michael Hill. **Assistant General Manager:** Brian Chattin. **Director, Team Travel:** Manny Colon. **Major League Video Coordinator:** Joseph Nero. **Executive Assistant, Baseball Operations:** Amanda Guevara. **Special Advisor, Pres. of Baseball Operations:** Stan Meek. **Advisor to Baseball Operations:** Jorge Posada. **Director, Player Personnel:** Dan Greenlee. **Special Assistant, Scouting/BBOPS:** Adrian Lorenzo. **Director, International Operations:** Fernando Seguignol. **Director, Amateur Scouting:** DJ Svihlik.

Michael Hill

MAJOR LEAGUE STAFF

Manager: Don Mattingly. **Pitching Coach:** Mel Stottlemyre Jr. **Hitting Coach:** Eric Duncan. **Assistant Hitting Coach:** Robert Rodriguez. **Bench Coach:** James Rowson. **First Base Coach:** Billy Hatcher. **Third Base Coach:** Trey Hillman. **Bullpen Coordinator:** Robert Flippo. **Bullpen Coach:** Wellington Cepeda. **Catching Coach:** Eddy Rodriguez. **Bullpen Catcher:** Koji Tanaka. **Pitching Analyst:** Justin Pope.

MEDICAL/TRAINING

Medical Director: Dr. Lee Kaplan. **Head Athletic Trainer:** Kevin Barr. **Strength & Conditioning Coach:** Gene Basham. **Athletic Trainers:** Bradley LaRosa, Chris Mudd. **Rehab Coordinator:** Steve Carlin. **Equipment Managers, Home Clubhouse:** John Silverman, Mike Diaz. **Visiting Clubhouse Manager:** Michael Rock Hughes.

PLAYER DEVELOPMENT

VP, Player Development & Scouting: Gary Denbo. **Director, Player Development:** Dick Scott. **Director, Sports Development:** Derick Anderson. **Special Assistant, Player Development & Scouting:** Geoff Degroot. **Assistant Director, Player Development:** Hector Crespo. **Director, Sports Performance:** Derick Anderson. **Analyst, Player Development:** Danny Henriquez, David Beayne-Hernandez. **Pitching Coordinator:** Scott Aldred, Gabriel Luckert. **Hitting Coordinator:** Edwar Gonzalez, Jeff Livsey. **Hitting Consultant:** Greg Colbrunn. **Infield/Baserunning Coordinator:** Gene Glynn. **Catching Coordinator:** Jamie Quirk. **Catching Analyst:** Sharif Othman. **Strength & Conditioning Coordinator:** Spencer Clevenger. **Rehab Strength & Conditioning Coordinator:** Lee Tressel. **Athletic Training Coordinator:** Eric Reigelsberger. **Rehab Pitching Coach:** Chris Michalak. **Rehab Coordinator:** Andrew Turpin. **Rehab Position Player Coach:** Ty Hawkins. **Video Coordinator:** Austin Lamkey. **Assistant Video Coordinator:** Tim Sylvester. **MiLBClubhouse/Equipment Coordinator:** Mark Brown. **Coordinator, Player Development & International Operations:** Jake Jola.

FARM SYSTEM

Class	Club (League)	Manager	Hitting Coach	Pitching Coach
Triple-A	Wichita (PCL)	Keith Johnson	Justin Mashore	Jeremy Powell
Double-A	Jacksonville (SL)	Kevin Randel	Scott Seabol	Bruce Walton
High A	Jupiter (FSL)	Mike Jacobs	TBD	Reid Cornelius
Low A	Clinton (MWL)	Tom Lawless	Matt Snyder	Mark DiFelice
Short-season	Batavia (NYP)	Jorge Hernandez	Nathan Mikolas	Gabe Luckert
Rookie	Marlins (GCL)	John Pachot	Jesus Merchan	Jason Erickson
Rookie	Marlins (DSL)	TBD	R. Silverio/E. Linares	Freddery Arias

SCOUTING

Director, Amateur Scouting: DJ Svihlik. **Coordinator, Amateur Scouting:** Josh Kapiloff. **Senior Advisor, Amateur Scouting:** Marti Wolever. **Special Assistant to President of Baseball Operations:** Stan Meek. **National Crosschecker:** Eric Valent. **Special Assignment Scout:** T.R. Lewis. **West Supervisor:** Scott Goldby. **Central Supervisor:** Ryan Wardinsky. **South Supervisor:** Carmen Carcone. **East Supervisor:** Mike Soper. **Area Scouts:** Eric Brock, Tim McDonnell, Scott Stanley, Scott Fairbanks, Joe Dunigan, Chris Joblin, Shaeffer Hall, James Vilade, Christian Castorri, JT Zink, Blake Newsome, Hank LaRue, Alex Smith, Dana Duquette. **Intern, Amateur Scouting:** Spencer Brown. **Director, International Scouting:** Fernando Seguignol. **Coordinator, Player Development & International Operations:** Jacob Jola. **Special Assignment Scout, International Operations:** Rich Arena. **International Crosschecker:** Carlos Herazo. **Coordinator, Pacific Rim:** Jalal Leach. **Supervisor, Dominican Republic:** Rigoberto De Los Santos. **Administrator, Venezuela:** Clifford Nuitter. **Scouts, Dominican Republic:** Domingo Ortega, Angel Izquierdo, Sahir Fersobe, Carlos Vasquez. **Scouts, Venezuela:** Robin Ordonez, Tibaldo Hernandez, Nestor Moreno. **Scout, Panama:** Luis Cordoba. **Scout, Colombia:** Alvaro Julio. **Scout, Mexico:** Andres Guzman. **Manager, Dominican Operations:** Ismael Granadillo.

Video Coordinator, Dominican Republic: Shamir Arias. **Special Assistant, Baseball Operations & Scouting:** Adrian Lorenzo. **Director, Professional Scouting:** Hadi Raad. **Professional Scouting Analyst:** Alexandria Rigoli. **Professional Scouts:** Jose Almonte, Pierre Arsenault, Jared Barnes, Joe Caro, John Eshleman, Jim Howard, Joe Lisewski, Carlos Lugo, Bill Masse, Alexander Noel, Patrick Osborn, Adrian Puig, Paul Ricciarini, Clint Robinson, Phil Rossi, Tony Russo, Brian Sikorski. **Intern, Professional Scouting:** Jordan Jackson.

MILWAUKEE BREWERS

Office Address: Miller Park, One Brewers Way, Milwaukee, WI 53214.
Telephone: (414) 902-4400. **Fax:** (414) 902-4053. **Website:** www.brewers.com.

OWNERSHIP
Operated By: Milwaukee Brewers Baseball Club.
Chairman/Principal Owner: Mark Attanasio.

BUSINESS OPERATIONS
President, Business Operations: Rick Schlesinger. **Senior Vice President, Communications & Affiliate Operations:** Tyler Barnes. **Senior Vice President, Stadium Operations:** Steve Ethier. **Chief Financial Officer:** Daniel Fumai. **Chief Revenue Officer:** Jason Hartlund. **Senior Vice President, Marketing & Fan Experience:** Teddy Werner. **General Counsel & Senior Vice President, Administration:** Marti Wronski. **Executive Assistant, Ownership Group:** Samantha Ernest. **Executive Assistant, General Manager:** Nichole Kinateder. **Executive Assistant, Paralegal:** Kate Rock. **Executive Assistant:** Adela Reeve. **Executive Assistant:** Kate Stempski. **Executive Assistant:** Sonya Martinez.

Mark Attanasio

FINANCE/ACCOUNTING
VP, Finance/Accounting: Jamie Norton. **Accounting Director:** Vicki Wise. **Disbursements Director:** Erica Umbach. **Senior Payroll Administrator:** Corrine Wolff. **Senior Financial Analyst:** Cory Loppnow. **Financial Analysts:** Mike Anheuser, Kristin Hahn, Pat Fennell. **Staff Accountant:** Samantha Berg. **Senior Accounts Payable Specialist:** Taikana Bentley. **VP, Human Resources:** Cas Castro. **Director, Human Resources:** Brenda Best.

MARKETING
VP, Marketing: Sharon McNally. **Senior Manager, Marketing:** Kelley Sibley. **Art Director:** Jeff Harding. **Director, Audio/Video Production:** Deron Anderson. **Director, New Media:** Caitlin Moyer. **Executive Assistant, Marketing:** Brittany Luznicky. **Coordinator, New Media:** Aaron Oberley.

BUSINESS STRATEGY
VP, Business Analytics & Strategic Support: Sam Mahjub. **Director, Consumer Insights & Strategy:** Marla Grossberg. **Senior Manager, Data Science:** Michael Dairyko. **Data Scientist:** Sara Halloran. **Senior Coordinator, Business Intelligence Systems:** Danny Henken.

MEDIA RELATIONS/PUBLICATIONS
Senior Director, Media Relations: Mike Vassallo. **Director, Broadcasting & Publications:** Ken Spindler. **Senior Coordinator, Media Relations:** Matt Stein. **Director, Business Communications:** Leslie Stachowiak.

MILLER PARK OPERATIONS
Senior Director, Security: Randy Olewinski. **Senior Director, Event Services:** Matt Lehmann. **Senior Director, Facility Services:** Mike Brockman. **Director, Grounds:** Ryan Woodley. **Senior Manager, Event**

2020 SCHEDULE
Standard Game Times: Mon.-Sat., 7:10 pm; Sun., 1:10 pm.

MARCH		
26-29 . . . . . Chicago (NL)		
30-31 . . . . St. Louis		
APRIL		
1 . . . . St. Louis		
2-5 . . . . . at Philadelphia		
6-7 . . . . .at Cincinnati		
10-12 . . . . .New York (NL)		
13-16 . . . . . .Philadelphia		
17-19 . . at New York (NL)		
21-23 . . . . at Pittsburgh		
25-26 . . . . . at Colorado		
28-30 . . . . . .Washington		
MAY		
2-3 . . . . St. Louis		
4-7 . . . . at Miami		

9-10 . . . . .Arizona
11-13 . . . .at Chicago (NL)
14-17 . . . . .at Cincinnati
19-21 . . . . .New York (AL)
23-24 . . . . . Chicago (NL)
26-28 . . . . . San Francisco
30-31 . . . . . at Tampa Bay
JUNE
1-3 . . . . . . at Washington
5-7 . . . . .at Boston
9-11 . . . . San Diego
13-14 . . . . Cincinnati
17 . . . . at Minnesota
19-21 . . . . . . at Arizona
23-24 . . . . .Toronto
27-28 . . . . Pittsburgh

30 . . . . . at Chicago (NL)
JULY
1-2 . . . . . .at Chicago (NL)
4-5 . . . . .at St. Louis
8 . . . . .Tampa Bay
10-12 . . . . .Colorado
18-19 . . . . . at San Diego
21-22 . . at Los Angeles (NL)
25-26 . . . . . . Pittsburgh
28-30 . . . . St. Louis
31 . . . . . .at Chicago (NL)
AUGUST
1-2 . . . . . .at Chicago (NL)
3-5 . . . . . . at Pittsburgh
8-9 . . . . . . Chicago (NL)
12-13 . . . . .Miami

15-16 . . . . . . .at St. Louis
17-19 . . . . at Atlanta
21-23 . . . . Cincinnati
26 . . . . Minnesota
27-30 . . . . . .at Cincinnati
31 . . . . at Pittsburgh
SEPTEMBER
1-3 . . . . at Pittsburgh
5-7 . . . Los Angeles (NL)
8-9 . . . . Cincinnati
11-13 . . . . . .at Baltimore
15-17 . . . . Atlanta
19-20 . . . . . . Pittsburgh
21-23 . . . . . . .at St. Louis
25-27 . . . at San Francisco

GENERAL INFORMATION
Stadium (year opened):
Miller Park (2001).
Team Colors: Navy blue, gold and white.

Home Dugout: First Base.
Playing Surface: Grass.

Services: Scott Quade. **Manager, Guest Services:** Kari Dawson. **Manager, Grounds:** Zak Peterson. **Manager, Landscape:** Josh Ruplinger. **Manager, Fields:** Tom Henke. **Manager, Warehouse:** John Weyer.

TICKET SALES
Telephone: (414) 902-4000. **Fax:** (414) 902-4056.
VP, Ticket Sales: Jim Bathey. **Sr. Director, Ticket Sales:** Billy Friess. **Sr. Director, Ticket Services & Technology:** Jessica Brown. **Director, Group Sales:** Chris Kimball. **Director, Suite Sales:** Chris Rothwell. **Director, Suite Services:** Kristin Miller.

BASEBALL OPERATIONS
Telephone: (414) 902-4400. **Fax:** (414) 902-4515.
President, Baseball Operations & General Manager: David Stearns. **Senior VP/Assistant GM:** Matt Arnold. **Senior Advisor:** Doug Melvin. **VP, Baseball Projects:** Gord Ash. **Senior Vice President, Player Personnel:** Karl Mueller. **Special Assistant to GM, Player Development:** Carlos Villanueva. **Special Assistant, General Manager/Pro Scouting/Player Personnel:** Dick Groch. **Special Assistant, Baseball Strategy:** Shawn Hoffman. **VP, Baseball Operations:** Matt Kleine. **Director, Baseball Systems:** Will Hudgins. **Director, Baseball Research & Development:** Dan Turkenkopf. **Assistant, Baseball Operations/Spanish Translator:** Carlos Brizuela. **Special Assistant, Baseball Research and Development:** Nick Davis. **Manager, Video Operations:** Matt Kerls. **Senior Analyst, Baseball Research & Development:** Ethan Bein. **Analysts, Baseball Research & Development:** Austin Harcarik, Dan Kutner.

David Stearns

MAJOR LEAGUE STAFF
Manager: Craig Counsell. **Coaches: Bench**—Pat Murphy, **Pitching**—Chris Hook, **Hitting**—Andy Haines, **First Base**—Jason Lane, **Third Base**—Ed Sedar, **Bullpen**—Steve Karsay. **Assistant Coach:** Jacob Cruz. **Bullpen Catchers:** Marcus Hanel, Robinson Diaz.

MEDICAL/TRAINING
Senior Director, Medical Operations: Roger Caplinger. **Head Team Physician:** Dr. William Raasch. **Team Physicians:** Dr. Mark Niedfeldt, Dr. Craig Young. **Director, Psychological Services:** Matt Krug. **Head Athletic Trainer:** Scott Barringer. **Asst. Athletic Trainers:** Rafael Freitas, Dave Yeager. **Director, Integrative Sports Performance:** Bryson Nakamura. **Strength & Conditioning Specialists:** Josh Seligman, Jason Meredith. **Rehab Coordinator:** Blair Bundy. **Coordinator, Integrative Sports Performance:** Sara Goodrum. **Assistant Director, Psychological Services:** Blake Pindyck. **Consulting Orthopedic Physician, Phoenix:** Dr. Evan Lederman. **Consulting Team Physician, Phoenix:** Dr. Cartlon Richie.

PLAYER DEVELOPMENT
Farm Director: Tom Flanagan. **Asst. Farm Director:** Eduardo Brizuela. **Roving Outfield/Baserunning Coordinator:** Quintin Berry. **Sr. Manager, Baseball Administration:** Mark Mueller. **Hitting Coordinator:** Kenny Graham. **Field Coordinator & Catching Instructor:** Charlie Greene. **Roving Infield Coordinator:** Bob Miscik. **Director, Player Development Initiatives:** Jake McKinley. **Phoenix Clubhouse Manager:** Travis Voss.

FARM SYSTEM
Class	Club (League)	Manager	Hitting Coach	Pitching Coach
Triple-A	San Antonio (PCL)	Rick Sweet	Al LeBoeuf	Jim Henderson
Double-A	Biloxi (SL)	Mike Guerrero	Chuckie Caufield	Fred Dabney
High A	Carolina (CAR)	Joe Ayrault	Bobby Spain	Nick Childs
Low A	Wisconsin (MWL)	Matt Erickson	Dave Joppie	Carson Cross
Rookie	Rocky Mountain (PIO)	Liu Rodriguez	TBA	Kevin Walsh
Rookie	Brewers Blue (AZL)	Rafael Neda	Brenton Del Chiaro	Hiram Burgos
Rookie	Brewers Gold (AZL)	Nick Stanley	Brandon Macias	Michael Schlact
Rookie	Brewers (DSL)	Victor Estevez	Luis De Los Santos	Jesus Hernandez
Rookie	Brewers/Indians (DSL)	Fidel Pena	Mike Habas	Victor Moreno

SCOUTING
Telephone: (414) 902-4400. **Fax:** (414) 902-4059.
VP, Scouting: Ray Montgomery. **Senior Advisor, Scouting:** Marv Thompson. **Special Assignment Scout:** Scott Campbell. **Director, Amateur Scouting:** Tod Johnson. **Director, International Scouting:** Mike Groopman. **Assistant Director, Amateur Scouting:** Tim McIlvaine. **Manager, Advance Scouting:** Brian Powalish. **Coordinator, Advance Scouting:** Walker McKinven. **Coordinator, Scouting Operations:** Oscar Garcia, Adam Hayes. **Assistant Director, Scouting:** Bryan Gale. **Assistant Director, International Scouting:** Luis Pérez. **Assistant Director, Scouting/International Player Development:** Taylor Green. **Pro Scouting Crosschecker:** Mike Berger. **Pro Scouts:** Lary Aaron, Bryan Bullington. **National Supervisor, Amateur Scouting:** Doug Reynolds. **Supervisor, Scout Teams/West Coast Special Assignment Scout:** Corey Rodriguez. **Regional Supervisors:** Josh Belovsky, Dan Nellum, Mike Serbalik. **Regional Supervisor, Scouting:** Drew Anderson. **Area Scouts:** Ty Blankmeyer, Jeff Bianchi, Mike Burns, Pete Orr, James Fisher, Taylor Frederick, Joe Graham, KJ Hendricks, Harvey Kuenn, Jr., Lazaro Llanes, Mark Muzzi, Scott Nichols, Wynn Pelzer, Jeff Scholzen, Jeff Simpson, Craig Smajstrla, Riley Bandelow, Steve Smith, Pete Vuckovich Jr., Shawn Whalen. **Regional Crosschecker:** Esteban Castillo. **Scouting Coordinator, Dominican Republic:** Fernando Veracierto. **Scouting Coordinator, Dominican Republic:** Gary Peralta. **Scouts, Latin America:** Rodolfo Rosario, Trino Aguilar Navarro. **Scouts, Colombia:** Jose Barraza, Teofilo Gutierrez. **Scouts, Dominican Republic:** Julio De La Cruz, José Morales, Jean Carlos Reynoso, Jonas Lantigua. **Scout, Nicaragua:** Salvador Ayestas. **Scouts, Venezuela:** Diego Flores, Kenji Galavis, Reinaldo Hidalgo, Javier Meza, José Rodriguez. **Latin American Video Scout:** Luis Eduardo Rosario.

MINNESOTA TWINS

Office Address: Target Field, 1 Twins Way, Minneapolis, MN 55403.
Telephone: (612) 659-3400. **Fax:** 612-659-4025. **Website:** www. twinsbaseball.com.

OWNERSHIP

Operated By: The Minnesota Twins. **Executive Chair:** Jim Pohlad. **Executive Board:** Jim Pohlad, Bob Pohlad, Bill Pohlad, Dave St. Peter.

BUSINESS OPERATIONS

Jim Pohlad

President/Chief Executive Officer, Minnesota Twins: Dave St. Peter. **Executive Vice President/Chief Business Officer, Business Development:** Laura Day. **Executive VP/Chief Administrative Officer/CFO:** Kip Elliott. **Senior Director, Ballpark Development/Planning:** Dan Starkey.

HUMAN RESOURCES/FINANCE/TECHNOLOGY

Vice President, Human Resources: Leticia Silva. **Director, Payroll:** Lori Beasley. **Human Resources Generalist:** Holly Corbin. **Administrator, Payroll/HRIS:** Molly Partyka. **Coordinator, Human Resources:** Maria Salazar.

MARKETING

Senior Director, Brand Experience and Innovation: Chris Iles. **Senior Director, Brand Strategy:** Heather Hinkel. **Creative Director:** Kevin Hughes. **Director, Game Day Experience:** Sam Henschen. **Manager, Digital Content:** Brea Hinegardner. **Manager,Video:** Jim Diehl. **Manager, Marketing/Promotions:** Mitch Retelny. **Manager, Marketing/Communications:** Beth Vail Palm.

CORPORATE PARTNERSHIPS

Senior Director, Corporate Partnerships: Ryan Gorman. **Managers, Corporate Partnerships:** Doug Beck, Karen Cleary, Chad Jackson. **Director, Partnership Strategy/Development**: Jordan Woodcroft. **Director, Partnership Activation**: Amy Johnson. **Project Manager and Special Projects:** Joe Morin

COMMUNICATIONS

Telephone: (612) 659-3471. **Fax:** (612) 659-4029.
Senior Director, Communications: Dustin Morse. **Senior Manager, Communications:** Mitch Hestad. **Manager, Communications:** Matt Hodson. **Coordinator, Communications:** Cori Frankenberg. **Coordinator, Team Photographer and Publications:** Brace Hemmelgarn. **Communications Assistant/Translator:** Elvis Martinez.

COMMUNITY RELATIONS

Vice President, Community Engagement: Nancy O'Brien. **Director, Community Relations:** Kristen Rortvedt. **Executive Director, Twins Community Fund:** Stephanie Johnson. **Senior Manager, Community Engagement/Events:** Julie Vavsuska. **Manager, Community Programs:** Josh Ortiz. **Senior Coordinator, Community Relations:** Sondra Ciesielski.

2020 SCHEDULE

Standard Game Times: Mon.-Sat., 7:10 pm; Sun., 1:10 pm.

MARCH
26 - 29 . . . . . .at Oakland
31 . . . . .at Seattle

APRIL
1 . . . . .at Seattle
2 - 5 . . . . Oakland
6 - 8 . . . . Cleveland
11 - 12 . . .at Chicago (AL)
13 - 15 . . . . . . at Toronto
18 - 19 . . . . . . Detroit
20 - 23 . . . . Seattle
25 - 26 . . . . Boston
29 - 30 .at Los Angeles (NL)

MAY
2 - 3 . . at Los Angeles (AL)

4 - 6 . . . . . .San Francisco
9 - 10 . . . . . . Kansas City
11 - 14 . . . . . .at Detroit
15 - 17 . . . . .at Cleveland
18 - 20 . . . . . Baltimore
21 - 24 . . . Chicago (AL)
26 - 28 . . at New York (AL)
30 - 31 . . .at Chicago (AL)

JUNE
2 - 4 . . . . .Tampa Bay
5 - 7 . . . Los Angeles (AL)
9 - 11 . . . . . .at Baltimore
12 - 14 . . . .at Kansas City
17 . . . . .Milwaukee
19 - 21 . . .New York (AL)
23 - 25 . . . . . .at Houston

27 - 28 . . . . . . .Colorado
30 . . . . .at Detroit

JULY
1 - 2 . . . . .at Detroit
3 - 5 . . . . . .at Cleveland
7 - 8 . . . . . . Kansas City
9 - 12 . . . . .Toronto
17 - 19 . . . . . .at Texas
20 - 22 . . . . . at Arizona
24 - 26 . . .at Chicago (AL)
29 . . . . Los Angeles (NL)

AUGUST
1 - 2 . . . . Houston
4 - 5 . . . . Cleveland
6 - 9 . . . . . .at Kansas City
10 - 13 . . . . . . .at Boston

15 - 16 . . . . . Kansas City
19 . . . . Chicago (AL)
22 - 23 . . . . Detroit
26 . . . . at Milwaukee
28 - 30 . . . . at Tampa Bay

SEPTEMBER
1 - 3 . . . . Cleveland
5 - 6 . . . . . . Chicago (AL)
8 - 10 . . . . .at Cleveland
11 - 13 . . . . . . .at Detroit
15 - 17 . . . . Texas
19 - 20 . . . . Detroit
23 - 24 . . . . at San Diego
25 - 27 . . . .at Kansas City

GENERAL INFORMATION

Stadium (year opened): Target Field (2010). **Playing Surface:** Grass.
Team Colors: Red, navy blue and white.
Home Dugout: First Base.

TICKETING/EVENTS
   Telephone: 1-800-33-TWINS. **Fax:** (612) 659-4030. **Vice President, Ticket Operations:** Paul Froehle. **Senior Director, Box Office:** Mike Stiles. **Manager, Box Office:** Ashley Geldert.

BALLPARK OPERATIONS
   Senior Vice President, Operations: Matt Hoy. **Vice President, Ballpark Operations:** Dave Horsman. **Senior Director, Facilities:** Gary Glawe. **Senior Director, Guest Experience:** Patrick Forsland. **Security Director:** Jeff Beahen. **Sr. Manager, Guest Services:** Katie Rock. **Head Groundskeeper:** Larry DiVito.

BASEBALL OPERATIONS
   Executive VP/President of Baseball Operations: Derek Falvey. **Senior VP/General Manager:** Thad Levine. **VP, Player Personnel:** Mike Radcliff. **VP/Assistant GM:** Rob Antony. **Director, Baseball Administration:** Kate Townley. **Assistant GM:** Daniel Adler. **Assistant GM:** Jeremy Zoll. **Assistant Director, Baseball Operations:** Nick Beauchamp. **Director, Pro Scouting:** Brad Steil. **Special Assistants:** Michael Cuddyer, LaTroy Hawkins, Torii Hunter, Justin Morneau. **Coordinator, Pro Scouting R&D:** Zane MacPhee. **Analyst, R&D:** Andrew Ettel. **Analyst, Player Development:** Rachel Heacock. **Coordinator, Amateur Scouting R&D:** Ezra Wise. **Director, Team Travel:** Mike Herman. **Senior Data Engineer:** Jerad Parish. **Developer, Baseball Systems:** Hans Van Slooten. **Director, Baseball Systems:** Jeremy Raadt. **Director, R&D:** Karim Kassam. **Data Quality Engineer:** John Edman. **Developer, Business Systems:** Nick Winegar. **Motion Data Analyst:** Colin Robertson. **Motion Performance Coach:** Martijn VerHoeven. **Analyst, Advance Scouting:** Josh Ruffin. **Analyst, Baseball Research:** Sam Isenberg and Kevin Wright. **Junior Developer, Baseball Systems:** Anthony Metcalfe. **Administrative Assistant, Baseball Operations:** Shelly Brandt.

Derek Falvey

MAJOR LEAGUE STAFF
   Manager: Rocco Baldelli. **Coaches: Bench**—Mike Bell, **Pitching**—Wes Johnson, **Hitting**—Edgar Varela, **Catching**—Bill Evers, **First Base**—Tommy Watkins, **Third Base**—Tony Diaz, **Assistant Pitching**—Bob McClure, **Hitting Coach**—Rudy Hernandez. **Equipment Manager:** Rod McCormick. **Assistant Home Clubhouse Manager:** Tim Burke. **Assistant, Home Clubhouse:** Frank Hanzlik. **Visitors Clubhouse Manager:** Marcus McKenzie. **Coordinator, Major League Video:** David Jeffrey.

MEDICAL/TRAINING
   Director, Medical Services: Dr. Christopher Camp. **Club Physicians:** Dr. John Steubs. Dr. Rahul Kapur, Dr. David Olson, Dr. Corey Wulf, Dr. Amy Beacom. **Head Trainer:** Michael Salazar. **Assistant Trainers:** Masamichi Abe, Matt Biancuzzo. **Physical Therapist:** Jeff Lahti. **Head Dietician:** Rasa Troup. **Strength & Conditioning Coach:** Ian Kadish. **Assistant Strength & Conditioning coach:** Andrea Hayden.

PLAYER DEVELOPMENT
   Telephone: (612) 659-3480. **Fax:** (612) 659-4026.
   Director, Minor League Operations: Alex Hassan. Assistant Director, **Minor League Operations:** Drew MacPhail. Senior Advisor, **Player Development:** Sam Perlozzo. Senior Manager, **Minor League Administration:** Brian Maloney. Manager, **Florida Operations:** Victor Gonzalez. Assistant, **Florida Operations:** Jason Davila. **Minor League Coordinators:** Kevin Morgan (field), Donegal Fergus (hitting), Billy Boyer (infield/baserunning), Mike Quade (outfield), Micheal Thomas (catching), Pete Maki (pitching), JP Martinez (assistant pitching), Justin Willard (assistant pitching), Zach Bove (special projects), Tommy Bergjans (player development), David Rak (strength & conditioning), Chad Jackson (rehab), Tyler Schmitz (video).

FARM SYSTEM

Class	Club (League)	Manager	Hitting Coach	Pitching Coach
Triple-A	Rochester (IL)	Toby Gardenhire	M. Borgschulte / R. Robinson	M. McCarthy / C. Bello
Double-A	Pensacola (SL)	Ramon Borrego	R. Smith/J. Mangiameli	Ramirez/Ballenberg
High A	Fort Myers (FSL)	Aaron Sutton	Rasmussen / Meyer	Vasquez / Hernandez
Low A	Cedar Rapids (MWL)	Brian Dinkelman	B. Berg / L. Rodriguez	P. Larson / C. Maduro
Rookie	Elizabethton (APP)	Ray Smith	J.Reed / J. Alvarez	Richard Salazar
Rookie	Twins (GCL)	T. Miyoshi	S. Schlecter/Rodriguez	T. Smarlok/McKenney
Rookie	Twins (DSL)	Seth Feldman	Perez /Nanita /Rosen	Gaynor/K. Rodriguez

SCOUTING
   Director, Amateur Scouting: Sean Johnson. **Coordinator, Pro Scouting:** Vern Followell. **Director, Latin American Scouting & US Integration Assistant Scouting Director:** Tim O'Neil. **Senior Advisor, Scouting:** Deron Johnson. **National Crosschecker:** Billy Corrigan. **Amateur Crosschecker:** Freddie Thon. **Senior Manager, International Administration and Education:** Amanda Daley. **Coordinator, Amateur Scouting:** Brit Minder. **Scouting Supervisors: East**—Mark Quimuyog, **Mideast**—Derrick Dunbar, **Midwest**—Mike Ruth, **West**—Elliott Strankman. **Area Scouts:** Andrew Ayers, Joe Bisenius, Kyle Blackwell, Trevor Brown, Walt Burrows, Ty Dawson, J.R. DiMercurio, Brett Dowdy, John Leavitt, Seth Moir, Mitch Morales, Jeff Pohl, Jack Powell, Michael Quesada, Nick Venuto, Matt Williams, Gre, John Wilson. **Professional Scouts:** Ken Compton, Earl Frishman, Bob Hegman, John Manuel, Jose Marzan, Billy Milos, Jason Pennini, Keith Stohr, Earl Winn, Wesley Wright, Rafael Yanez. Coordinator, **Dominican Republic Scouting:** Eduardo Soriano. **Dominican Republic:** Luis Lajara, Manuel Luciano, Eury Luis, Daniel Sanchez. **Coordinator, Venezuela Scouting:** Jose Leon. **Venezuela:** Marlon Nava, Oswaldo Troconis. **Pacific Rim:** David Kim. **Part-Time Scouts:** Hector Barrios (Panama), John Cortese (Italy), Kenny Su (Taiwan), Koji Takahashi (Japan), Lester Victoria (Curacao) Juan Padilla, Franklin Parra, Pablo Torres (Venezuela).

NEW YORK METS

Office Address: Citi Field, 126th Street, Flushing, NY 11368.
Telephone: (718) 507-6387. **Fax:** (718) 507-6395.
Website: www.mets.com. **Twitter:** @mets.

OWNERSHIP

Operated By: Sterling Mets LP. **Chairman/Chief Executive Officer:** Fred Wilpon. **President:** Saul B. Katz. **Chief Operating Officer:** Jeff Wilpon.

BUSINESS OPERATIONS

Executive VP/Chief Revenue Officer: Lou DePaoli. **Senior VP, Senior Strategy Officer:** John Ricco. **Executive Director, Business Intelligence/Analytics:** John Morris.

LEGAL/HUMAN RESOURCES

Executive VP/Chief Legal Officer: David Cohen. **VP/Deputy General Counsel:** Neal Kaplan. **Senior Counsel:** James Denniston. **Senior Counsel:** Jessica Villanella. **Senior VP, Human Resources & Diversity:** Holly Lindvall.

FINANCE

CFO: Mark Peskin. **VP, Controller:** Len Labita. **VP, Financial Planning & Analysis:** Peter Woll. **Senior Director, Assistant Controller:** John Ventimiglia.

MARKETING/COMMUNICATIONS/SALES

Fred Wilpon

Executive Producer, Entertainment, Marketing & Productions: Joe DeVito. **Executive Director, Broadcasting/Special Events:** Lorraine Hamilton. **VP, Alumni Public Relations & Team Historian:** Jay Horwitz. **Senior Director, Social Media:** Will Carafello. **Senior Director, Entertainment Marketing & Productions:** Vito Vitiello. **Vice President, External Affairs & Community Engagement:** Haeda Mihaltses. **Executive Director, External Affairs & Community Engagement:** Danielle Parillo. **Director, Player Relations & Community Engagement:** Donovan Mitchell.

MEDIA RELATIONS

Telephone: (718) 565-4330. **Fax:** (718) 639-3619.
VP, Communications: Harold Kaufman. **Senior Director, Communications:** Ethan Wilson. **Manager, Communications:** Zach Weber. **Coordinator, Communications:** Kristin Wojcik. **Bilingual Media Coordinator:** Alan Suriel. **Assistant, Communications:** Zack Becker.

TRAVEL/CLUBHOUSE

Equipment Manager: Kevin Kierst. **Assistant Clubhouse Manager:** Jimmy Voigt. **Visiting Clubhouse Manager:** Dave Berni. **Director, Team Travel:** Brian Small.

2020 SCHEDULE

Standard Game Times: 7:10 p.m.; Sun. 1:10.

MARCH
26-29 . . . . . Washington
30-31 . . . . . Philadelphia

APRIL
1 . . . . Philadelphia
2-5 . . . . . at Washington
8-9 . . . . at Houston
10-12 . . . at Milwaukee
13-16 . . . . Atlanta
17-19 . . . . . Milwaukee
21-23 . . . . Miami
24-26 . . . . . . at Atlanta
28-30 . . . . at Miami

MAY
1-3 . . . . Atlanta
4-6 . . . . Cincinnati

9-10 . . . . . . at St. Louis
11-13 . . . . . . at Arizona
15-18 . . . . . . Pittsburgh
19-21 . . . . Arizona
22-24 . . . . . . at Atlanta
26-28 . . . at Philadelphia
29-31 . . . Los Angeles (NL)

JUNE
2-3 . . . . Houston
4-7 . . . . . at Washington
8-10 . . . . St. Louis
12-14 . . . . . Washington
17-18 . . . . at Chicago (NL)
19-21 . . . . . Philadelphia
23-25 . . at San Francisco
27-28 . . . . . at San Diego

30 . . . . . . San Francisco

JULY
1-2 . . . . . . San Francisco
3-6 . . . . San Diego
7-8 . . . . at New York (AL)
10-12 . . . . at Miami
17-19 . . . . Seattle
21-23 . . . . . at Cincinnati
24-26 . . . . at Philadelphia
28-29 . . . . New York (AL)
30-31 . . . . Miami

AUGUST
1-2 . . . . Miami
4-5 . . . . . . at Colorado
7-9 . . at Los Angeles (NL)
11-13 . . . . Atlanta

14-16 . . . . . Philadelphia
19-21 . at Los Angeles (AL)
22-23 . . . . . . at Oakland
25-27 . . . . at Washington
28-30 . . . . . Chicago (NL)
31 . . . . Colorado

SEPTEMBER
1-3 . . . . Colorado
4-6 . . . . Washington
7-9 . . . . at Atlanta
11-13 . . . . at Pittsburgh
15-17 . . . . Miami
18-20 . . . . Texas
21-24 . . . at Philadelphia
25-27 . . . . at Miami

GENERAL INFORMATION

Stadium (year opened): Citi Field (2009).
Team Colors: Blue and orange.
Home Dugout: First Base.
Playing Surface: Grass.

BASEBALL OPERATIONS

Telephone: (718) 803-4013, (718) 565-4339. **Fax:** (718) 507-6391.

Executive Vice President & General Manager: Brodie Van Wagenen. **Vice President, Assistant General Manager, Scouting & Player Development:** Allard Baird. **Special Assistant to the General Manager:** Omar Minaya. **Assistant General Manager, Systematic Development:** Adam Guttridge. **Senior Advisor, Amateur Scouting:** Tommy Tanous. **Senior Director, Baseball Operations:** Ian Levin. **Special Assistant to the General Manager:** Terry Collins. **Special Advisor to Mets COO & General Manager:** David Wright. **Special Advisors, Baseball Operations:** Al Leiter & Jessica Mendoza. **Manager, Baseball Systems & Development:** Joe Lefkowitz. **Manager, Video Operations:** Joe Scarola. **Senior Coordinator, Video Operations:** Sean Haggans. **Director, Professional Scouting:** Bryn Alderson. **Assistant Director, Professional Scouting:** Jeff Lebow. **Coordinator Coordinator, Pitching Research & Development:** David Lang. **Administrative Assistant, Baseball Operations:** Janine Laboy-Gonzalez.

Brodie Van Wagenen

MAJOR LEAGUE STAFF

Manager: Luis Rojas. **Coaches: Bench**—Hensley Meulens. **Hitting**—Chili Davis. **Assistant Hitting**—Tom Slater. **Pitching**—Jeremy Hefner. **First Base**—Tony DeFrancesco. **Third Base**—Gary DiSarcina. **Bullpen**—Ricky Bones. **Pitching Strategist**—Jeremy Accardo. **Bullpen Catchers**—Dave Racaniello, Eric Langill.

MEDICAL/TRAINING

Medical Coordinator: Matt Hunter. **Strength and Conditioning Coordinator:** Dustin Clarke. **Rehabilitation & Physical Therapy Coordinator:** David Pearson. **Mental Skills Coach, Gulf Coast League Mets:** Cristian Guzman. **Minor League Education Coordinator:** Neskys Liriano. **Minor League Physical Therapist:** Jhomelger Garcia. **Dominican Republic Strength & Conditioning Coordinator:** Angel Ponce. **Latin American Performance Coaching Coordinator Coach:** Alex Tavarez.

PLAYER DEVELOPMENT

Telephone: (718) 565-4302. **Fax:** (718) 205-7920.

Executive Director, Player Development: Jared Banner. **Minor League Field Coordinator:** Kevin Boles. **Director, Minor League Operations:** Ronny Reyes. **Director, Latin American Operations:** Juan Henderson. **Player Development Manager:** Kevin Walsh. **Minor League Information Coordinator:** Colin Schwarz. **Assistant, Minor League Operations:** Amy Ross. **Pitching Coordinator:** Ricky Meinhold. **Outfield/Baserunning Coordinator:** Marlon Anderson. **Rehabilitation Pitching Coordinator:** Jon Debus. **Hitting Coordinator:** Ryan Ellis. **International Field Coordinator:** Rafael Landestoy. **Catching Coordinator:** Bob Natal. **Assistant Pitching Coordinator:** Mike Cather. **Infield Coordinator:** Tim Teufel. **Equipment/Operations Manager:** John Mullin. **Assistant Clubhouse Manager:** Drew Dunton. **Senior Advisors:** Guy Conti, Bobby Floyd, Ozzie Virgil, Sr.

FARM SYSTEM

Class	Club	Manager	Hitting Coach	Pitching Coach
Triple-A	Las Vegas (PCL)	Brain Schneider	Joel Chimelis	DJ Carrasco
Double-A	Binghamton (EL)	Lorenzo Bundy	Tony Jaramillo	Jonathan Hurst
High A	St. Lucie (FSL)	Chad Kreuter	Bruce Fields	Royce Ring
Low A	Columbia (SAL)	Reid Brignac	Mariano Duncan	Jerome Williams
Short-season	Brooklyn (NYP)	Ed Blankmeyer	Rafael Fernandez	Josh Towers
Rookie	Kingsport (APP)	Chris Newell	Trey Hannam	Glenn Abbott
Rookie	Mets (GCL)	David Davalillo	Joel Fuentes	Josue Matos
Rookie	Mets 1 (DSL)	Manny Martinez	Leo Hernandez	Christian Martinez
Rookie	Mets 2 (DSL)	Yucarybert De La Cruz	Richie Benes	Victor Ramos

SCOUTING

Telephone: (718) 565-4311. **Fax:** (718) 205-7920.

Vice President, Amateur Scouting: Thomas Tanous. **Director, Amateur Scouting:** Marc Tramuta. **Assistant Director, Amateur Scouting & International Scouting:** Bryan Hayes. **Coordinator, Amateur & International Scouting:** Andrew Christie. **Assistant, Amateur & International Scouting:** Tom Fleischman. **National Crosschecker:** Doug Thurman. **Special Assignment Scouts:** Steve Barningham, Rudy Terrasas. **Pitching Crosschecker:** Chris Hervey. **East Coast Supervisor/National Crosschecker:** Mike Ledna. **Regional Supervisor, Midwest:** Nathan Beuster. **Regional Supervisor, West:** Drew Toussaint. **Area Scouts:** Cesar Aranguren, (So. FL), Gary Brown, (No. TX), Jet Butler, (LA, MS, AR, AL), Daniel Coles, (No. NC, Va, Md, Pa), Jarrett England, (KY, So. OH, TN), Chris Heidt, (IL, IA, IN, MN, WI, MI, No.OH), Tyler Holmes, (No. CA, No. NV, HI), John Kosciak, (MA, CT, ME, RI, NH, VT, NY, NJ), Jim Reeves, (Az, Co, Nm, UT, Las Vegas), Brian Reid, (AZ, CO, NM, UT, Las Vegas), Harry Shelton, (So. TX), Rusty Mcnamara (Southern Ca), Marlin Mcphaillrmo, (Southern Nc, Sc, Ga), Claude Pelletier, (Canada), Harry Shelton (South Tx), Taylor Terrasas (Ks, Ok, Ne, Mo, Nd, Sd, Ia), Adam Weisenburger (North/Central Fl), Glenn Walker (So. CA). **Director, Professional Scouting:** Bryn Alderson. **Assistant Director, Professional Scouting:** Jeff Lebow. **Assistant, Pro Scouting:** Jason Stein. **Pro Scouts:** Jaymie Bane, Conor Brooks, Tom Clark, Jason Davis, Pat Jones, David Keller, Bon Kim, Joseph Kowal, Ash Lawson, Chad Macdonald, Shaun Mcnamara, Andy Pratt, Roy Smith. **Director, International Scouting & Player Development:** Rafael Perez. **Director, Latin American Scouting:** Luis Marquez. **Supervisor, Latin American Scouting:** Moises de la Mota. **Supervisor, Latin America & Puerto Rico Scouting:** Manny Batista. **Coordinator, Mexico:** Martin Arvuiz. **Coordinator, Latin American Scouting:** Harold Herrera. **Supervisor, Dominican Scouting & Administration:** Martin Valerio. **Coordinators, D.R.:** Felix Romero, Oliver Dominguez. **Scouts, Dominican Republic:** Kelvin Dominguez, Wilson Peralta. **Scout, Mexico:** Fred Mazuca, Henry Sandoval. **Scouts, Venezuela:** Robert Espejo, Carlos Perez, Andres Nunez. **Scout, Panama:** Elvis Rios. **Tryout Coach, Dominican Republic:** Rolando Martinez. **Venezuelan Video Coordinator:** Manuel Lopez.

NEW YORK YANKEES

Office Address: Yankee Stadium, One East 161st St., Bronx, NY 10451.
Telephone: (718) 293-4300.
Website: www.yankees.com, www.yankeesbeisbol.com.
Twitter: @Yankees, @YankeesPR, @LosYankees, @LosYankeesPR.

OWNERSHIP

Managing General Partner/Co-Chairperson: Harold Z. (Hal) Steinbrenner. **General Partner/Co-Chairperson:** Hank Steinbrenner. **General Partner/Vice Chairperson:** Jennifer Steinbrenner Swindal. **General Partner/Vice Chairperson:** Jessica Steinbrenner.

BUSINESS OPERATIONS

President: Randy Levine, Esq.
Chief Operating Officer/General Counsel: Lonn A. Trost, Esq.
Senior VP, Strategic Ventures: Marty Greenspun. **Senior VP, Chief Security Officer:** Sonny Hight. **Senior VP, Yankee Global Enterprises/Chief Financial Officer:** Anthony Bruno. **Chief Financial Officer/Senior VP, Financial Operations:** Scott M. Krug. **Senior VP, Corporate/Community Relations:** Brian E. Smith. **Senior VP, Partnerships:** Michael J. Tusiani. **Senior VP, Marketing:** Deborah A. Tymon. **Senior VP, Stadium Operations:** Doug Behar. **VP/Chief Financial Officer, Accounting:** Robert B. Brown. **Deputy General Counsel/VP, Legal Affairs:** Alan Chang. **VP, Chief Information Officer:** Mike Lane.

Harold Z.
Steinbrenner

COMMUNICATIONS/MEDIA RELATIONS

Telephone: (718) 579-4460. **Email:** media@yankees.com.
Vice President, Communications/Media Relations: Jason Zillo. **Director, Baseball Information/Public Communications:** Michael Margolis. **Assistant Director, Baseball Information:** Lauren Moran. **Manager, Media Services:** Alexandra Trochanowski. **Sr. Coordinator, Communications/Media Relations:** Rob Morse. **Coordinator, Communications/Media Relations:** Kaitlyn Brennan. **Assistant, Communications/Media Relations:** Andrew Kivette. **Administrative Assistant, Communications/Media Relations:** Germania-Dolores Hernandez. **Bilingual Media Relations Coodinator:** Marlon Abreu. **Japanese Media Advisor:** Yoshiki Sato.

TICKET OPERATIONS

Telephone: (718) 293-6000.
VP, Ticket Sales/Service/Operations: Kevin Dart.

BASEBALL OPERATIONS

Senior VP/General Manager: Brian Cashman.
Senior VP/Assistant GM: Jean Afterman, Esq. **VP/Assistant GM:** Michael Fishman. **VP, Baseball Operations:** Tim

2020 SCHEDULE

Standard Game Times: Mon.-Fri., 7:05 pm; Sat.-Sun., 1:05 pm.

MARCH
26 - 29 . . . . . at Baltimore
30 - 31 . . . . at Tampa Bay

APRIL
1 . . . . at Tampa Bay
2 - 5 . . . . .Toronto
6 - 9 . . . . Baltimore
11 - 12 . . . . . .at Oakland
13 - 15 . . . . . . .at Texas
17 - 19 . . . . . Cincinnati
20 - 23 . . . . . .at Detroit
24 - 26 . . . . . . Cleveland
28 - 30 . . . . Detroit

MAY
1 - 3 . . . . . . at Toronto
5 - 6 . . . . Pittsburgh

8 - 10 . . . . Boston
11 - 14 . . . . at Tampa Bay
16 - 17 . . . . . .at Houston
19 - 21 . . . . at Milwaukee
22 - 25 . . . . Seattle
26 - 28 . . . . . . Minnesota
30 - 31 . at Los Angeles (AL)

JUNE
2 - 3 . . . . .at Seattle
5 - 7 . . . . . . .Tampa Bay
9 - 11 . . . . . Kansas City
12 - 14 . . . . . . .at Boston
16 - 17 . . . . at Pittsburgh
19 - 21 . . . . at Minnesota
22 - 24 . . . . . Baltimore
26 - 28 . . . . Chicago (NL)

29 - 30 . . . . .at Baltimore

JULY
1 . . . . .at Baltimore
3 - 5 . . . . .at Toronto
7 - 8 . . . . .New York (NL)
10 - 12 . . . . Texas
18 - 19 . . . . .at St. Louis
20 - 23 . . Los Angeles (AL)
24 - 26 . . . . Boston
28 - 29 . . at New York (NL)
30 - 31 . . . . . . .at Boston

AUGUST
1 - 2 . . . . .at Boston
3 - 5 . . . . . . Chicago (AL)
6 - 9 . . . . Oakland
10 - 12 . . . .at Kansas City

13 - 16 . . .at Chicago (AL)
17 - 19 . . . . . .Tampa Bay
20 - 23 . . . . . . .Toronto
25 - 26 . . . . . . Baltimore
28 - 30 . . . . .at Cleveland
31 . . . . .at Boston

SEPTEMBER
1 - 2 . . . . .at Boston
4 - 7 . . . . . .at Baltimore
8 - 10 . . . . Boston
11 - 13 . . . . .Toronto
14 - 16 . . . at Tampa Bay
18 - 20 . . . . . at Toronto
21 - 24 . . . . . . Houston
25 - 27 . . . . .Tampa Bay

GENERAL INFORMATION

Stadium (year opened):
Yankee Stadium (2009).
Team Colors: Navy blue and white.

Home Dugout: First Base.
Playing Surface: Grass.

Naehring. **Special Advisors:** Carlos Beltran, Reggie Jackson, Hideki Matsui, Andy Pettitte, Alex Rodriguez, Nick Swisher.
Director, Team Travel & Player Services: Ben Tuliebitz. **Director, Quantitative Analysis:** David Grabiner. **Director, Baseball Operations:** Matt Ferry. **Director, Mental Conditioning:** Chad Bohling. **Director, Advance Scouting:** Brett Weber. **Director, Baseball Systems:** Brian Nicosia. **Senior Web Developer:** Nick Eby. **Senior iOS Developer:** Michael Traverso. **Senior Analyst, Quantitative Analysis:** Christopher Fonnesbeck. **Analysts, Quantitative Analysis:** Theodore Feder, John Morris, Christopher Pang, Justin Sims, Sam Waters. **Database Engineer, Baseball Operations:** Jesse Bradford. **Nutritional Consultant:** Cynthia Sass.

Brian Cashman

MAJOR LEAGUE STAFF
Manager: Aaron Boone.
Coaches: Bench—Josh Bard, **Pitching**—Matt Blake, **Hitting**—Marcus Thames, **Assistant Hitting**—P.J. Pilittere, **First Base**—Reggie Willits, **Third Base**—Phil Nevin, **Catching**— Jason Brown, **Infield/Quality Control**— Carlos Mendoza, **Bullpen**—Mike Harkey, **Bullpen Catcher**—Radley Haddad.

MEDICAL/TRAINING
Team Physician, New York: Dr. Christopher Ahmad. **Head Team Internist:** Paul Lee, M.D., M.P.H. **Team Internist:** William Turner, M.D. **Senior Advisor, Orthopedics:** Stuart Hershon, M.D. **Head Athletic Trainer:** Steve Donohue. **Physical Therapist/Assistant Athletic Trainer:** Michael Schuk. **Assistant Athletic Trainer:** Tim Lentych. **Massage Therapist:** Doug Cecil. **Director, Strength/Conditioning:** Matthew Krause.

PLAYER DEVELOPMENT
Senior Director, Player Development: Kevin Reese.
Director, Player Development: Eric Schmitt. **Pitching Coordinator/ Performance Science Consultant:** John Kremer. **Assistant Director, Player Development:** Stephen Swindal Jr. **Enterprise Solutions Engineer:** Rob Owens. **Complex Coordinator/Minor League Manager:** David Adams. **Coordinator, Instruction/Outfield Coordinator:** Pat McMahon. **Hitting Coordinator:** Dillon Lawson, Edwar Gonzalez. **Director, Pitching:** Sam Briend. **Catching Coordinator:** Aaron Gershenfeld. **Infield Coordinator:** Miguel Cairo. **Assistant Infield Coordinator/Minor League Manager:** Travis Chapman. **Baserunning Coordinator/Roving Hitting Coach:** Matt Talarico. **Rehab Pitching Instructor:** Greg Pavlick. **Player Development Analysts:** Brad Smith, Dan Walco. **Player Development Consultants:** Marc Bombard, Tino Martinez. **Manager, Pitch Development:** Desi Druschel. **Manager, International Operations:** Vic Roldan. Assistant, **International Operations:** Giuliano Montanez. **Manager, Minor League Operations:** Nick Avanzato. Assistant, **Minor League Operations:** Nick Leon. Medical Coordinator, **Preventative and Performance Programs:** Mike Wickland. **Medical Coordinator:** Mark Littlefield. **Assistant Strength & Conditioning Coordinator:** Rigo Febles. **Strength & Rehab Coordinator:** Mike Kicia.

FARM SYSTEM

Class	Club (League)	Manager	Hitting Coach	Pitching Coach
Triple-A	Scranton/WB (IL)	Doug Davis	Phil Plantier	Tommy Phelps
Double-A	Trenton (EL)	Julio Mosquera	Ken Joyce	Travis Phelps
High A	Tampa (FSL)	David Adams	Joe Migliaccio	Jose Rosado
Low A	Charleston (SAL)	Luis Dorante	Casey Dykes	Daniel Moskos
Short-season	Staten Island (NYP)	Dan Fiorito	Ryan Chipka	Dustin Glant
Rookie	Pulaski (APP)	TBD	Kevin Martir	Gerardo Casadiego
Rookie	Yankees West (GCL)	TBD	Jake Hirst	Preston Claiborne
Rookie	Yankees East (GCL)	Travis Chapman	Aaron Leanhardt	Ben Buck
Rookie	Yankees (DSL)	TBA	TBA	TBA

SCOUTING
Telephone: (813) 875-7569. **Fax:** (813) 873-2302.
VP, Domestic Scouting: Damon Oppenheimer. **Asst. Director, Domestic Scouting:** Ben McIntyre. **Director, Professional Scouting:** Dan Giese. **Asst. Director, Amateur Scouting—Analytics:** Scott Benecke. **Assistant Director, Pro Scouting:** Matt Daley. **National Crosscheckers:** Brian Barber, Tim Kelly, Steve Kmetko, Jeff Patterson, Mike Wagner. **Pitching Analyst, Amateur Scouting:** Scott Lovekamp. **Draft Medical Coordinator:** Justin Sharpe. **Pro Scouts:** Kendall Carter, Jay Darnell, Brad Del Barba, Marc DelPiano, Jonathan Diaz, Brandon Duckworth, Bill Emslie, Tyler Greene, Kevin Hart, Shawn Hill, Cory Melvin, Pat Murtaugh, James Stokes, JT Stotts, Alex Sunderland, Dennis Twombley, Donnie Veal, Aron Weston, Tom Wilson. **Special Assignment Scout:** Jim Hendry. **Area Scouts:** Troy Afenir, Tim Alexander, Chuck Bartlett, Denis Boucher, Andy Campbell, Jeff Deardorff, Bobby DeJardin, Mike Gibbons, Billy Godwin, Matt Hyde, David Keith, Steve Lemke, Mike Leuzinger, Ronnie Merrill, Darryl Monroe, Nick Ortiz, Bill Pintard, Cesar Presbott, Matt Ranson, Brian Rhees, Tyler Robertson, Kelly Rodman, Mike Thurman. **Director, International Scouting:** Donny Rowland. **Asst. Director, International Scouting:** Brady LaRuffa. **Asst. to Director, Latin America:** Edgar Mateo. **Crosscheckers, International Scouting:** Steve Wilson, Dennis Woody, Ricardo Finol. **Supervisor, Dominican Republic:** Juan Rosario. **Crosscheckers, Latin America:** Miguel Benitez, Victor Mata. **Supervisor, Venezuela:** Jose Gavidia. **Coordinator, Latin America:** Raymon Sanchez. **Video Coordinator, International Scouting:** Ethan Sander. **Video Assistant, Dominican Republic:** Luis Rodriguez. **Technology/Data Analyst:** Vianco Martinez. **Technology/Data Analyst, Venezuela:** Victor Deyan. **Amateur Research, Data Analysis:** Cary Broder. **International Scouts:** Doug Skiles, John Wadsworth, Borman Landaeta, Luis Sierra, Esdras Abreu, Luis Brito, R. Arturo Pena, Juan Piron, Jose Ravelo, Jose Sabino, Troy Williams, Rudy Gomez, Lee Sigman, Raul Gonzalez, Edgar Rodriguez, Carlos Levy, Chi Lee, Peng Pu Lee, Alan Atacho, Darwin Bracho, Roney Calderon, Cesar Suarez, Jesus Taico, Luis Tinoco.

OAKLAND ATHLETICS

Office Address: 7000 Coliseum Way, Oakland, CA 94621.
Telephone: (510) 638-4900. **Fax:** (510) 562-1633. **Website:** www.oaklandathletics.com.

OWNERSHIP
Managing Partner: John Fisher. **Chairman Emeritus:** Lew Wolff. **Board Members:** Sandy Dean, Bill Gurtin, Keith Wolff.

BUSINESS OPERATIONS
President: David Kaval. **Chief of Staff:** Miguel Duarte. **VP, Government Affairs:** Taj Tashombe. **VP, General Counsel:** D'Lonra Ellis.

FINANCE/ADMINISTRATION
VP, Finance: Adam Buckfielder. **Senior Director, Finance:** Kasey Jarcik. **Director, Accounting:** John Anki. **Senior Payroll Manager:** Rose Dancil. **Senior Accountant, Accounts Payable:** Isabelle Mahaffey. **Financial Analysts:** Alex Wong, Ryan De Vera. **Senior Accountants:** Danna Mouat, Paul Basillo. **GL Accountant:** Stephen Curry. **Vice President, People Operations:** Andre Chambers. **Director, People Operations:** Tina Buss. **People Operations Coordinator:** Katie Strehlow, Mari Rodriguez. **Vice President, Technology:** Vince Vengapally. **Senior Manager, IT:** David Frieberg. **Manager, Technology Innovation:** Dylan Webster.

MARKETING
VP, Marketing: Tonya Antonucci. **Creative Director:** Ben Mayberry. **Creative Services Manager:** Mike Ono. **Graphic Designers:** Rhonda Romero, Garrett Lyons. **Project Manager:** Nicole Alvarez. **Photography Manager:** Michelle Minahen. **Marketing Coordinator:** Elizabeth Staub. **Senior Marketing Manager:** Charlie Hunts. **Senior Social Media Coordinator:** Kyle Skinner. **Promotions Coordinator:** Tavis McDowell. **Team Photographer:** Michael Zagaris. **Director, Performance Marketing & Broadcasting:** Matthew Perl. **Broadcasting & Media Content Coordinator:** Joey Liberatore.

David Kaval

PUBLIC RELATIONS/COMMUNICATIONS
VP, Communications/Community: Catherine Aker. **Baseball Communications Director:** Fernando Alcalá. **Corporate Communications Director:** Erica George. **Baseball Information Manager:** Mike Selleck. **Baseball Communications Manager:** Mark Ling. **Baseball Communications Coordinator:** Olivia Hummer.

STADIUM OPERATIONS
VP, Stadium Operations: David Rinetti. **Senior Director, Stadium Operations:** Paul La Veau. **Senior Manager, Stadium Operations Events:** Kristy Ledbetter. **Senior Stadium Services Manager:** Randy Duran. **Senior Guest Services Manager:** Elisabeth Aydelotte. **Senior Stadium Operations Manager:** Matt Van Norton. **Stadium Operations Systems Manager:** Jason Silva. **Head Groundskeeper:** Clay Wood.

TICKET SALES/OPERATIONS/SERVICES
Director, Ticket Operations: David Adame. **Senior Director, Service/Retention:** Josh Ziegenbusch. **Senior Ticket**

2020 SCHEDULE
Standard Game Times: Mon.-Sat., 7:05 pm; Sun. 1:05 pm.

MARCH		
26 - 29 . . . . . Minnesota		
31 . . . . Houston		

APRIL
1 . . . . Houston
2 - 5 . . . . . at Minnesota
7 - 9 . . at Los Angeles (AL)
11 - 12 . . . .New York (AL)
14 - 15 . . . . Boston
17 - 19 . . . . Seattle
21 - 23 . . . . .at Cleveland
25 - 26 . . . . . .at Houston
27 - 29 . . . . . . .at Texas

MAY
1 - 3 . . . . .Tampa Bay
5 - 6 . . . . Seattle

8 - 10 . . . . .Toronto
13 - 15 . . . . . .at Seattle
16 - 17 . at Los Angeles (AL)
20 - 21 . . . . Texas
23 - 24 . . Los Angeles (AL)
25 - 28 . . . . . .at Houston
29 - 31 . . . . . . .at Texas

JUNE
3 - 4 . . . . Detroit
7 . . . . San Francisco
9 - 11 . . . . .at Detroit
12 - 14 . . . at Philadelphia
16 - 17 . . Los Angeles (AL)
20 - 21 . . . . Houston
23 - 25 . . . at Tampa Bay
27 - 28 . . at Chicago (AL)
30 . . . . .Miami

JULY
1 . . . . .Miami
3 - 5 . . . . Baltimore
8 - 9 . . . at San Francisco
10 - 12 . . . . . .at Seattle
18 - 19 . . . . . . Houston
22 . . . . Atlanta
24 - 26 . . . . .at Baltimore
28 - 29 . . . .at Houston
31 . . . . Texas

AUGUST
1 - 2 . . . . Texas
4 . . . . Seattle
6 - 9 . . . at New York (AL)
10 - 12 . . at Washington
14 - 16 . . . . . .at Boston

18 - 19 . . . . . Cleveland
22 - 23 . . . .New York (NL)
25 - 26 . . . . at Atlanta
27 - 30 . . . . at Toronto

SEPTEMBER
1 - 2 . . . . . . Kansas City
5 - 6 . . . . Texas
7 - 10 . . . .at Kansas City
12 - 13 . . . . . .at Seattle
15 - 16 . . . . Chicago (AL)
18 - 20 . . Los Angeles (AL)
22 - 24 . . . . .at Texas
26 - 27 . at Los Angeles (AL)

GENERAL INFORMATION
Stadium (year opened): Oakland Coliseum (1968). **Team Colors:** Kelly green and gold.

Home Dugout: Third Base.
Playing Surface: Grass.

Operations Manager: Austin Redman. Box Office Coordinator: Patricia Heagy.

TRAVEL/CLUBHOUSE
Director, Team Travel: Mickey Morabito. Equipment Manager: Steve Vucinich. Visiting Clubhouse Manager: Mike Thalblum. Assistant Equipment Manager: Brian Davis. Umpire/Clubhouse Assistant: Matt Weiss. Arizona Senior Facility Manager: James Gibson. Arizona Clubhouse Manager: Chad Yaconetti.

BASEBALL OPERATIONS

Billy Beane

Executive VP, Baseball Operations: Billy Beane.
General Manager: David Forst. Assistant GM, Major League & International Operations: Dan Feinstein. Assistant GM/Director, Player Personnel: Billy Owens. Sr. Advisor to Baseball Operations: Sandy Alderson. Sr. Director, Baseball Development & Technology: Rob Naberhaus. Special Assistants to GM: Grady Fuson, Chris Pittaro. Director, Baseball Administration: Pamela Pitts. Video Coordinator: Adam Rhoden. Special Assistant to Baseball Operations: Scott Hatteberg. Research Scientist: David Jackson-Hanen. Asst. Director, Research and Analytics: Pike Goldschmidt. Asst. Director, Research and Analytics: Ben Lowry. Analyst, Baseball Operations, Samantha Schultz.

MAJOR LEAGUE STAFF
Manager: Bob Melvin.
Coaches: Bench—Ryan Christenson. Pitching— Scott Emerson. Batting—Darren Bush. First Base—Mike Aldrete. Third Base—Al Pedrique. Bullpen—Marcus Jensen. Assistant Hitting Coach—Eric Martins. Quality Control Coach— Mark Kotsay. Bullpen Catcher—Phil Pohl. Bullpen Catcher—Dustin Hughes.

MEDICAL/TRAINING
Head Athletic Trainer: Nick Paparesta. Assistant Athletic Trainers: Jeff Collins, Brian Schulman. Strength/Conditioning Coach: Josh Cuffe. Asst. Strength/Conditioning Coach: Terence Brannic. Major League Massage Therapist: Ozzie Lyles. Team Physicians: Dr. Allan Pont, Dr. Elliott Schwartz. Team Orthopedist: Dr. Jon Dickinson. Associate Team Orthopedist: Dr. Will Workman. Arizona Team Physicians: Dr. Fred Dicke, Dr. Doug Freedberg.

PLAYER DEVELOPMENT
Telephone: (510) 638-4900. Fax: (510) 563-2376.
Director, Player Development: Ed Sprague. Sr. Advisor to Player Development: Keith Lieppman. Director, Minor League Operations: Zak Basch. Manager, Minor League Operations: Nancy Moriuchi. Manager, Minor League Equipment: Thomas Miller. AZ Field Coordinator: Aaron Nieckula. Minor League Infield Coordinator: Juan Navarrete. Minor League Outfield/Base Running Coordinator: Steve Scarsone. Minor League Roving Pitching Coordinator: Gil Patterson. Minor League Hitting Coordinator: Jim Eppard. Minor League Catching Coordinator: Gabriel Ortiz. Minor League Performance Throwing Coach: Casey Upperman. Minor League Medical Coordinator: Nate Brooks. Coordinator, Medical Services: Larry Davis. Latin American Medical Coordinator: Javier Alvidrez. Minor League Strength/Conditioning Coordinator: A.J. Seeliger. Minor League Assistant Strength/Conditioning Coordinator: Matt Rutledge. Latin America Strength/Conditioning Coordinator: J.D. Howell. Special Instructor, Pitching/Rehabilitation: Craig Lefferts. Minor League Rehabilitation Coordinator: Travis Tims. Manager, Minor League Technology & Development: Ed Gitlitz. Jr. Baseball Systems Developer: Ben Lewis.

FARM SYSTEM

Class	Club (League)	Manager	Hitting Coach	Pitching Coach
Triple-A	Las Vegas (PCL)	Fran Riordan	Todd Steverson	Rick Rodriguez
Double-A	Midland (TL)	Scott Steinmann	Tommy Everidge	Steve Connelly
High A	Stockton (CAL)	Bobby Crosby	Brian McArn	Chris Smith
Low A	Beloit (MWL)	Lloyd Turner	Javier Godard	Don Schulze
Short-season	Vermont (NYP)	Rick Magnante	Francisco Santana	Carlos Chavez
Rookie	Athletics Grn (AZL)	Eddie Menchaca	Ruben Escalera	Gabriel Ozuna
Rookie	Athletics Gld (AZL)	Webster Garrison	Kevin Kouzmanoff	Bryan Corey
Rookie	Athletics (DSL)	Luis Baez	Rahdames Mota	David Brito

SCOUTING
Director, Scouting: Eric Kubota. Assistant Director, Scouting: Sean Rooney. Assistant Director, Scouting and Baseball Operations: Haley Alvarez. Coordinator, Scouting and Baseball Operations: Greg Ledford (San Francisco, CA). Master Pitching Scout: John Hughes. West Coast Supervisor: Scott Kidd. Midwest Supervisor: Mark Adair. Midwest Supervisor: Armann Brown. East Coast Supervisor: Marc Sauer. Pro Scouts: Shooty Babitt, Jeff Bittiger, Grant Brittain, Dan Freed, Trevor Ryan, Will Schock, Tom Thomas, Mike Ziegler. Area Scouts: Steve Abney (Lawrence, KS), Anthony Aliotti (Lake Forest, CA), Anthony Aloisi (Nashville, TN), Neil Avent (Charlotte, NC), Jim Coffman (Portland, OR), Steve Cohen (Spring, TX), Ruben Escalera (Carolina, PR), Tripp Faulk (Richmond, VA), Julio Franco, (Weston, FL), Matt Higginson (Grimsby, ON), Derek Lee (Frankfort, IL), Kevin Mello (El Cerrito, CA), Kelcey Mucker (Denham Springs, LA), Chris Reilly (Rockwall, TX), Trevor Schaffer (Belleair, FL), Rich Sparks (Macomb, MI), Jemel Spearman (Cumming, GA), Dillon Tung (Los Angeles, CA), Jeff Urlaub (Phoenix, AZ), Ron Vaughn (Windsor, CT). Special Assistant, Scouting and International Operations: Steve Sharpe. Director, Latin American Operations: Raymond Abreu (Santo Domingo, D.R.). Scouting Supervisor, Latin America: Juan Mosquera (Panama). Coordinator, Pacific Rim: Adam Hislop. International Scouts: Javier Agelvis (Mexico), Yendri Bachelor (VZ), Ruben Barradas (VZ), Jose Barradas (VZ), Dan Betreen (Australia), Juan Carlos De La Cruz (D.R.), Angel Eusebio (D.R.), Andri Garcia (VZ), Oswaldo Garcia (Colombia), Lewis Kim (South Korea), Wilfredo Magallanes (D.R.), Argenis Paez (Venezuela), Tito Quintero (Colombia), Amaurys Reyes (D.R.), Toshiyuki Tomizuka (Japan), Oswaldo Troconis (VZ), Juan Carlos Villanueva (VZ).

PHILADELPHIA PHILLIES

Office Address: Citizens Bank Park, One Citizens Bank Way, Philadelphia, PA 19148.
Telephone: (215) 463-6000. **Website:** www.phillies.com.

OWNERSHIP

Operated By: The Phillies. **Managing Partner:** John Middleton. **President:** Andy MacPhail. **Chairman Emeritus:** Bill Giles.

BUSINESS OPERATIONS

EXECUTIVE MANAGEMENT

Executive VP: David Buck. **VP/General Counsel:** Rick Strouse. **VP, Administration:** Kathy Killian. **VP, Chief Technology Officer:** Sean Walker. **Director, Human Resources/Benefits:** JoAnn Marano. **Director, Human Resources:** Marie Hanley.

BUSINESS AFFAIRS

VP, Business Affairs: Howard Smith. **Director, Ballpark Enterprises & Business Development:** Joe Giles. **Director, Operations/Facility:** Mike DiMuzio. **Director, Operations/Events:** Eric Tobin. **Director, Operations/Security:** Sal DeAngelis. **Director, Field Operations:** Mike Boekholder.

David Montgomery

COMMUNICATIONS

Telephone: (215) 463-6000. **Fax:** (215) 389-3050
VP, Communications: Bonnie Clark. **Director, Communications:** Greg Casterioto. **PA Announcer:** Dan Baker. **Official Scorers:** Mark Gola, Mike Maconi, Dick Shute.

FINANCE

Sr. VP/CFO: John Nickolas. **Director, Business Analytics:** Josh Barbieri. **Director, Finance:** John Fetsick. **Director, Finance:** Shannon Snellman. **Director, Payroll:** Bryan Humphreys.

BROADCAST/VIDEO SERVICES

Director, Broadcasting/Video Services: Mark DiNardo. **Director, Video Production:** Dan Stephenson. **Director, Video Coaching Services:** Kevin Camiscioli. **Director, Video Engineering:** Martin Otremsky.

MARKETING/PROMOTIONS

VP, Partnership Sales and Corporate Marketing: Jacqueline Cuddeback. **VP, Marketing Programs & Events:** Kurt Funk. **VP, Marketing & New Media:** Michael Harris. **Director, Partnership Sales & Corporate Marketing:** Rob MacPherson. **Director, Advertising Sales:** Brian Mahoney. **Director, Corporate Sales:** Scott Nickle. **Director, Marketing Events & Special Projects:** James Trout.

SALES/TICKETS

Telephone: (215) 463-1000. **Fax:** (215) 463-9878.

2020 SCHEDULE

Standard Game Times: Mon.-Sat., 7:05 pm; Sun. 1:35 pm.

MARCH
26-29 . . . . at Miami
30-31 . . . at New York (NL)

APRIL
1 . . . . . . at New York (NL)
2-5 . . . . Milwaukee
6-7 . . . . Toronto
9-12 . . . . . . at Cincinnati
13-16 . . . . . at Milwaukee
17-19 . . . . Miami
21-22 . . . . Texas
24-26 . . . at Chicago (NL)
28-29 . . . at San Francisco

MAY
1-3 . . . . Colorado
4-6 . . . . Atlanta

8-10 . . . . . . at Pittsburgh
12-14 . . . Los Angeles (NL)
15-17 . . . . St. Louis
19-21 . at Los Angeles (NL)
23-24 . . . . . at Colorado
26-28 . . . . . New York (NL)
29-31 . . . . . . Washington

JUNE
2-4 . . . . at Miami
5-7 . . . . at Atlanta
8-10 . . . . . Chicago (NL)
12-14 . . . . Oakland
16-18 . . . . Miami
19-21 . . at New York (NL)
22-25 . . . . . at Atlanta
26-29 . . . . Arizona

30 . . . . San Diego

JULY
1-2 . . . . San Diego
4-5 . . . . at Seattle
8-9 . . . . at Houston
10-12 . . . at Washington
17-19 . . Los Angeles (AL)
20-23 . . . . . Washington
24-26 . . . . New York (NL)
27-29 . . . . . . at Arizona
31 . . . . . . at San Diego

AUGUST
1-2 . . . . . . at San Diego
4-6 . . . . Cincinnati
7-10 . . . . . San Francisco
11-12 . . . . at Texas

14-16 . . . at New York (NL)
18-19 . . . . at Miami
21-23 . . . . Atlanta
24-26 . . . . . . Pittsburgh
28-30 . . . at Washington
31 . . . . at St. Louis

SEPTEMBER
1-3 . . . . at St. Louis
4-7 . . . . Miami
8-10 . . . . . Washington
11-13 . . . . . . at Atlanta
15-16 . . . . . . at Toronto
18-20 . . . . Atlanta
21-24 . . . New York (NL)
25-27 . . . at Washington

GENERAL INFORMATION

Stadium (year opened):
Citizens Bank Park (2004).
Team Colors: Red, white and blue.

Home Dugout: First Base.
Playing Surface: Natural Grass.

Sr. VP, Ticket Operations & Projects: John Weber. **Director, Ticket Technology & Development:** Chris Pohl. **Director, Sales:** Derek Schuster. **Director, Suite Sales & Business Ventures:** Kevin Beale. **Director, Group Sales:** Vanessa Mapson. **Director, Ticket Services & Intern Program:** Phil Feather. **Director, Season Ticket Services:** Mike Holdren. **Director, Premium Sales & Services:** Matt Kessler. **Director, Ticket Operations:** Ken Duffy.

TRAVEL/CLUBHOUSE

Coordinator, Team Travel: Jameson Hall. **Manager, Clubhouse Services:** Phil Sheridan. **Manager, Equipment/ Umpire Services:** Dan O'Rourke. **Manager, Visiting Clubhouse:** Kevin Steinhour.

BASEBALL OPERATIONS

VP/General Manager: Matt Klentak. **Assistant GM:** Bryan Minniti. **Assistant GM:** Scott Proefrock. **Assistant GM:** Ned Rice. **Senior Advisor:** Pat Gillick. **Senior Advisors, GM:** Larry Bowa, Charlie Manuel. **Special Assistants, GM:** Bart Braun, Pete Mackanin, Jorge Velandia. **Director, Player Development:** Josh Bonifay. **Director, International Scouting:** Sal Agostinelli. **Director, Amateur Scouting:** Brian Barber. **Director, Professional Scouting:** Mike Ondo. **Director, Strategic Initiatives:** Andy Galdi. **Director, Integrative Baseball Performance:** Sam Fuld. **Director, Amateur Scouting Administration:** Rob Holiday. **Director, Minor League Operations:** Lee McDaniel.

MAJOR LEAGUE STAFF

Matt Klentak

Manager: Joe Girardi. **Coaches: Bench**—Rob Thomson, **Pitching**—Bryan Price, **Hitting**—Joe Dillon, **First Base**—Paco Figueroa, **Third Base**—Dusty Wathan, **Assistant Pitching**—Dave Lundquist, **Infield**—Juan Castro, **Bullpen**—Jim Gott, **Coaching Assistant**— Bobby Meacham, **Bullpen Catcher/Catching**—Greg Brodzinski, Bob Stumpo. **Manager, Advance Scouting:** Mike Calitri. **Major League Player Information Coordinator:** Cesar Ramos.

MEDICAL/TRAINING

Director, Medical Services: Dr. Michael Ciccotti. **Head Athletic Trainer:** Paul Buchheit. **Assistant Athletic Trainers:** Shawn Fcasni, Aaron Hoback. **Major League Strength & Conditioning Coach:** Paul Fournier. **Assistant Strength & Conditioning Coach:** Dong Lien. **Major League Physical Therapist:** Joe Rauch.

PLAYER DEVELOPMENT

Director, Player Development: Josh Bonifay. **Director, Minor League Operations:** Lee McDaniel. **Director, Florida Operations/GM, Clearwater Threshers:** John Timberlake. **Assistant Director, Minor League Operations/ Florida:** Joe Cynar. **Assistant Director, International Operations:** Ray Robles. **Field Coordinator:** Chris Truby. **Hitting Coordinator:** Jason Ochart. **Assistant Hitting Coordinator:** Rob Segedin. **Director, Pitching Development:** Rafael Chaves. **Assistant Pitching Coordinator:** Travis Hergert. **Infield Coordinator:** Marty Malloy. **Outfield Coordinator:** Andy Abad. **Catching Coordinator:** Ernie Whitt. **Baserunning and Bunting Coordinator:** Kimera Bartee. **Coordinator, Dominican Academy:** Manny Amador. **Roving Pitching Coach:** Carlos Arroyo. **Rehab Pitching Coach:** Ray Burris. **Minor League Player Information Coordinator:** Ben Werthan.

FARM SYSTEM

Class	Club (League)	Manager	Hitting Coach	Pitching Coach
Triple-A	Lehigh Valley (IL)	Gary Jones	Darryl Robinson	Aaron Fultz
Double-A	Reading (EL)	Shawn Williams	Tyler Henson	Brad Bergesen
High A	Clearwater (FSL)	Pat Borders	Chris Heintz	Hector Mercado
Low A	Lakewood (SAL)	Chris Adamson	Christian Marrero	Matt Hockenberry
Short-season	Williamsport (NYP)	Milver Reyes	Joel McKeithan	Hector Berrios
Rookie	Phillies West (GCL)	Bobby Wernes	Zack Jones	Bruce Billings
Rookie	Phillies East (GCL)	Roly deArmas	Rafael DeLima	Pat Robles
Rookie	Phillies-1 (DSL)	Waner Santana	Samuel Hiciano	Alex Concepcion
Rookie	Phillies-2 (DSL)	Orlando Munoz	Homy Ovalles	Les Straker

SCOUTING

Director, Amateur Scouting: Brian Barber. **Director, Amateur Scouting Administration:** Rob Holiday. **Assistant Director, Scouting:** Greg Schilz. **National Scouting Coordinators:** David Crowson, Darrell Conner. **Regional Supervisors:** Alex Agostino, Shane Bowers, Buddy Hernandez, Brad Holland, Brian Kohlscheen. **Area Scouts:** Chris Duffy, Tommy Field, Zach Friedman, Mike Garcia, Ralph Garr Jr., Victor Gomez, Bryce Harman, Aaron Jersild, Tim Kissner, Chris Knabenshue, Kellan McKeon, Timi Moni, Justin Morgenstern, Justin Munson, Demerius Pittman, Mike Stauffer, Jason Waugh, Jeff Zona Jr. **Director, International Scouting:** Sal Agostinelli. **International Scouting Coordinator:** Derrick Chung. **Latin America Coordinator:** Jesús Méndez. **Latin America Supervisor:** Carlos Salas. **Venezuela Supervisor:** Rafael Alvarez. **Mexico Supervisor:** Oneri Fleita. **International Cross-checkers, Dominican Republic:** Robert Aquino and Andres Hiraldo. **International Cross-checker, Pacific Rim:** Howard Norsetter. **International Scouts:** Alvaro Blanco (Colombia), Jesus Blanco (Venezuela), Alex Choi (South Korea), Juan Feliciano de Castro (Dominican Republic) Elvis García (Venezuela), Luis García (Dominican Republic), Charlie Gastelum (Mexico), Gene Grimaldi (Antilles), Jose Guzman (Dominican Republic), Jonatan Hernandez (Venezuela), Dargello Lodowica (Curacao), William Mota (Venezuela), Romulo Oliveros (Venezuela), Bernardo Pérez (Dominican Republic), Abdiel Ramos (Panama), Philip Riccobono (Japan), Franklin Rojas (Venezuela), Claudio Scerrato (Europe), Ebert Velásquez (Venezuela), Youngster Wang (Taiwan) **Special Assignment Scouts:** Dean Albany, Craig Colbert, Howie Freiling, Dave Hollins, Charley Kerfeld, Mike Koplove, Terry Ryan, Dan Wright. **Director, Professional Scouting:** Mike Ondo. **Professional Scouts:** Erick Dalton, Todd Donovan, Jeff Harris, Jesse Levis, Jon Mercurio.

PITTSBURGH PIRATES

Office Address: PNC Park at North Shore, 115 Federal St., Pittsburgh, PA, 15212.
Mailing Address: PO Box 7000, Pittsburgh, PA 15212.
Telephone: (412) 323-5000. **Fax:** (412) 325-4412.
Website: www.pirates.com. **Twitter:** @Pirates.

BUSINESS OPERATIONS

OWNERSHIP
Chairman of the Board: Bob Nutting.
President: Travis Williams. **Senior Vice President, Business Affairs & General Counsel:** Bryan Stroh. **Assistant General Counsel:** Frankie Garland. **Executive Assistant:** Monica Robinson.

COMMUNICATIONS
VP, Communications/Broadcasting: Brian Warecki. **Director, Baseball Communications:** Jim Trdinich. **Director, Broadcasting:** Marc Garda. **Director, Media Relations:** Dan Hart. **Manager, Business Communications/Social Media:** Terry Rodgers.

COMMUNITY RELATIONS
Senior VP, Community/Public Affairs: Patty Salerno. **Director, Pirates Charities:** Jackie Hunter. **Manager, Youth Baseball Initiatives:** Chris Ganter.

MARKETING/CORPORATE SPONSORSHIPS
Senior Vice President, Revenue: Brian Colbert. **Senior Director, Marketing/Advertising:** Brian Chiera. **Director, Alumni Affairs/Promotions/Licensing:** Joe Billetdeaux. **Director, Advertising/Creative Services:** Kiley Cauvel. **Director, Special Events:** Christine Serkoch. **Director, PNC Park Events:** Ann Regan. **Manager, Advertising/Digital Marketing:** Haley Artayet. **Manager, Special Events:** Jason Koval. **Manager, Promotions/Licensing/Authentics:** Megan Vizzini. **Manager, Entertainment Media:** Paul Denillo. **Manager, Game Day Presentation:** Jon Cofer. **Manager, Corporate Partnerships:** Chris Stevens. **Director, Corporate Partnership Activation:** Brittany Hudzik. **Senior Account Manager, Corporate Partnerships:** Dave Shinsky.

STADIUM OPERATIONS
Executive VP/General Manager, PNC Park: Dennis DaPra. **Vice President, Ballpark Operations:** Chris Hunter. **Senior VP, Florida and Dominican Operations:** Jeff Podobnik. **Director, Field Operations:** Matt Brown. **Manager, Guest Experience:** Danny Garcia. **Manager, Cleaning Operations:** Sissy Burkhart. **Director, PNC Park Operations:** J.J. McGraw.

TRAVEL/CLUBHOUSE
Home Clubhouse Manager: Scott Bonnett. **Visiting Clubhouse Manager:** Kevin Conrad. **Assistant Equipment Manager:** Kiere Bulls. **Traveling Secretary:** Greg Johnson.

2020 SCHEDULE

Standard Game Times: Mon.-Sat., 7:05 pm; Sun.,1:35 pm.

MARCH		
26-29 . . . . . at Tampa Bay		
30-31 . . . .at Chicago (NL)		

APRIL		
1 . . . . . . .at Chicago (NL)		
2-5. . . . . Cincinnati		
6-9. . . . . . . Chicago (NL)		
10-12 . . . . . at Baltimore		
14-16 . . . . at Arizona		
18-19 . at Los Angeles (NL)		
21-23 . . . . . . .Milwaukee		
24-26 . . .Los Angeles (NL)		
27-29 . . .at Chicago (NL)		

MAY		
1-3. . . . . at Miami		
5-6. . . . . at New York (AL)		

8-10 . . . . Philadelphia		
11-13 . . . . St. Louis		
15-18 . . . at New York (NL)		
19-21 . . . . . Chicago (NL)		
22-25 . . . . .San Francisco		
26-28 . . . . .at Cincinnati		
30-31 . . . . . .at St. Louis		

JUNE		
2-3. . . . . Cincinnati		
4-7. . . . . St. Louis		
10-11 . . at San Francisco		
13-14 . . . . . at Colorado		
16-17 . . .New York (AL)		
19-21 . . . . .Toronto		
22-25 . . . at Washington		
27-28 . . . at Milwaukee		
29-30 . . . . . . .Colorado		

JULY		
1 . . . . .Colorado		
3-5. . . . . Boston		
6-9. . . . . at Atlanta		
10-12 . . . .at Cincinnati		
17-19 . . . .Washington		
21-23 . . . . . . San Diego		
25-26 . . . . at Milwaukee		
28-29 . . . . at San Diego		
31 . . . . St. Louis		

AUGUST		
1-2. . . . . St. Louis		
3-5. . . . . .Milwaukee		
6-9. . . . . Arizona		
10-12 . . . . . .at St. Louis		
13-16 . . . .at Cincinnati		
18-19 . . . . Detroit		

20-23 . . . . .Miami		
24-26 . . . . at Philadelphia		
29-30 . . . . . .at St. Louis		
31 . . . . .Milwaukee		

SEPTEMBER		
1-3. . . . . .Milwaukee		
4-6. . . . . Atlanta		
8-9. . . . . .at Detroit		
11-13 . . . .New York (NL)		
14-17 . . .at Chicago (NL)		
19-20 . . . . at Milwaukee		
22-23 . . . . . Chicago (NL)		
24-27 . . . . Cincinnati		

GENERAL INFORMATION

Stadium (year opened): PNC Park (2001).
Team Colors: Black and gold.
Home Dugout: Third Base.
Playing Surface: Grass.

BASEBALL OPERATIONS

Executive Vice President, General Manager: Ben Cherington. **Assistant General Manager:** Kevan Graves. **Assistant General Manager:** Steve Sanders. **Special Assistants to the General Manager:** Ron Hopkins, Sean McNally, Jax Robertson, Matt Ruebel, Greg Smith, Doug Strange. **Special Assistant, Offensive Coordinator:** Kevin Young. **Special Assistant, Defensive Coordinator:** Jamey Carroll. **Special Assistant, Pitching:** Scott Elarton. **Special Assistant to the GM, Player Personnel:** Oz Ocampo. **Special Assistant to GM, Cultural Initiatives:** Mike Gonzalez. **Director, Personnel:** Chris Johnson. **Director, Baseball Operations:** Will Lawton. **Assistant, Baseball Operations:** Trey Rose. **Fellow, Baseball Operations:** Zach Aldrich.

MAJOR LEAGUE STAFF

Manager: Derek Shelton. **Bench Coach:** Don Kelly. **Hitting Coach:** Rick Eckstein. **Assistant Hitting Coach:** Mike Rabelo. **Pitching Coach:** Oscar Marin. **First Base Coach:** Tarrik Brock. **Third Base Coach:** Joey Cora. **Bullpen Coach:** Justin Meccage. **Coach:** Glenn Sherlock. **Coaching Assistant:** Heberto Andrade. **Bullpen Catcher:** Jordan Comadena.

MEDICAL/TRAINING

Director, Sports Medicine: Todd Tomczyk. **Director, Performance Science:** Brendon Huttmann. **Head Major League Athletic Trainer:** Bryan Housand. **Assistant Major League Athletic Trainer:** Ben Potenziano. **Physical Therapist:** Kevin "Otis" Fitzgerald. **Medical Director:** Dr. Patrick DeMeo. **Team Physicians:** Dr. Darren Frank, Dr. Dennis Phillips, Dr. Michael Scarpone, Dr. Robert Schilken, Dr. Edward Snell. **Senior Coordinator, Prevention, Rehab & Athlete Development:** A.J. Patrick. **Coordinator, Team Video:** Kevin V. Roach.

INFORMATICS

Senior Director, Baseball Informatics: Dan Fox. **Assistant Director, Baseball Informatics:** Andrew Gibson. **Senior Quantitative Analyst:** Joe Douglas. **Senior Quantitative Analyst:** Sean Ahmed. **Senior Quantitative Analyst:** Justin Newman. **Major League Advance Coordinator:** Aaron Razum. **Quantitative Analyst:** Grant Jones. **Quantitative Analyst:** Justin Perline. **Quantitative Analyst:** Matt Kane. **Assistant, Major League:** Tim McKeithan. **Senior Developer, Baseball Informatics:** Brian Hulick. **Data Architect, Baseball Systems:** Matthew Reiersgaard. **Developer, Baseball Informatics:** Frank Wolverton.

PLAYER DEVELOPMENT

Senior Director, Minor League Operations: Larry Broadway. **Assistant Director, Minor League Operations:** Brian Selman. **Senior Coordinator, Minor League Pitching Operations:** Scott Mitchell. **Coordinator, Minor League Pitching Operations:** T.J. Large. **Coordinator, Minor League Hitting Operations:** Shawn Johnston. **Administrator, Minor League Operations:** Michael Chernow. **Field Coordinator:** Bobby Scales. **Assistant Field Coordinator:** Shawn Bowman. **Roving Infield Instructor:** Gary Green. **Senior Advisor, Latin American Operations:** Luis Silverio. **Senior Advisors, Player Development:** Woody Huyke, Mike Lum, Brad Fischer. **Latin American Field Coordinator:** Mendy Lopez. **Latin American Pitching Coordinator:** Amaury Telemaco. **Senior Advisor, DSL:** Cecilio Beltre. **Education Coordinator:** Mayu Fielding. **Director, Mental Strength:** Bernie Holliday. **Director, Cultural Readiness & Peak Performance Coach:** Hector Morales. **Director, Sports Nutrition & Fueling:** Allison Maurer. **Coordinator, Mental Strength:** Tyson Holt. **Coordinator, Mental Strength:** Andy Bass. **Coordinator, Athletic Development:** Joe Hughes. **Coordinator, Medical Services:** Carl Randolph. **Strength & Conditioning Coach:** Jim Malone.

FARM SYSTEM

Class	Club (League)	Manager	Hitting Coach	Pitching Coach
Triple-A	Indianapolis (IL)	Brian Esposito	Jon Nunnally	Joel Hanrahan
Double-A	Altoona (EL)	Dave Turgeon	David Newhan	Tom Filer
High A	Bradenton (FSL)	Miguel Perez	Chris Peterson	Drew Benes
Low A	Greensboro (SAL)	Kieran Mattison	Jonny Tucker	Stan Kyles
Short-season	West Virginia (NYP)	TBA	TBA	TBA
Rookie	Bristol (APP)	TBA	TBA	TBA
Rookie	Pirates (GCL)	TBA	TBA	TBA
Rookie	Pirates 1 (DSL)	TBA	TBA	TBA
Rookie	Pirates 2 (DSL)	TBA	TBA	TBA

SCOUTING

Fax: (412) 325-4414. **Senior Director, Amateur Scouting:** Joe DelliCarri. **Assistant Director, Amateur Scouting:** Mike Mangan. **Coordinator, Amateur Scouting:** Matt Skirving. **National Supervisors:** Jack Bowen (Bethel Park, PA), Jimmy Lester (Columbus, GA). **Regional Supervisors:** Jesse Flores (Sacramento, CA), Trevor Haley (Temperance, MI), Sean Heffernan (Lexington, SC). **Area Supervisors:** Rick Allen (Moorpark, CA), Matt Bimeal (Olathe, KS), Adam Bourassa (Cincinnati, OH), Eddie Charles (Auburn, NY), Phil Huttmann, (McKinney, TX), Jerry Jordan (Kingsport, TN), Wayne Mathis (Cuero, TX), Darren Mazeroski (Panama City Beach, FL), Cam Murphy (Atlanta, GA), Nick Presto (Palm Beach Gardens, FL), Dan Radcliff (Palmyra, VA), Mike Sansoe (Clayton, CA), Brian Tracy (Yorba Linda, CA), Derrick Van Dusen (Phoenix, AZ), Anthony Wycklendt (Oak Creek, WI). **Director, Pro Scouting:** Steve Williams. **Major League Scouts:** Mike Basso, Ricky Bennett, Jim Dedrick, Bob Minor. **Pro Scouts:** Carlos Berroa, John Birkbeck, Rodney Henderson, Andrew Lorraine, Alvin Rittman, Everett Russell, Gary Varsho. **Scouting Assistants:** Kinza Baad, Joe Hutlzen, Michael Landestoy. **Director, International Scouting:** Junior Vizcaino. **Assistant Director, International Scouting:** Max Kwan. **Coordinator of International Operations:** Matt Benedict. **International Supervisors:** Saul Torres (Venezuela); Emmanuel Gomez (Dominican Republic); Raul Lopez (Mexico); Tony Harris (International/Australia); Fu-Chun Chiang (Far East); Tom Gillespie (Europe/Africa). **International Scouts:** Esteban Alvarez, Daurys Nin, Victor Santana, Cristino Valdez, Omelbis Corporan (Dominican Republic); Victor Alvarez (Colombia), Pedro Avila, Omar Gonzalez, Jesus Morelli, Jessie Nava, Jose Partidas Dirimo Chavez (Venezuela); Roberto Saucedo (Mexico); Marcos Guimaraes (Brasil); Eugene Helder (Aruba); Mark Van Zanten (Curacao); Jose Pineda (Panama).

ST. LOUIS CARDINALS

Office Address: 700 Clark Street, St. Louis MO 63102.
Telephone: (314) 345-9600. **Fax:** (314) 345-9523. **Website:** www.cardinals.com.

OWNERSHIP
Operated By: St. Louis Cardinals, LLC. **Chairman/Chief Executive Officer:** William DeWitt, Jr. **President:** Bill DeWitt III. **Senior Administrative Assistant to Chairman:** Grace Pak. **Senior Administrative Assistant to President:** Julie Laningham. **Sr. VP & General Counsel:** Mike Whittle. **Associate Counsel:** Nick Garzia.

BUSINESS OPERATIONS

FINANCE
Fax: (314) 345-9520.
Senior VP/Chief Financial Officer: Brad Wood. **Director, Risk Management:** Rex Carter. **Director, Human Resources:** Ann Seeney. **VP, Event Services/Merchandising:** Vicki Bryant.

MARKETING/SALES/COMMUNITY RELATIONS
Fax: (314) 345-9529.
Senior VP, Sales & Marketing: Dan Farrell. **Administrative Assistant, VP, Sales & Marketing:** Gail Ruhling. **VP, Corporate Sales, Marketing & Stadium Entertainment:** Thane Van Breusegen.

COMMUNICATIONS
Fax: (314) 345-9530.
Director, Communications: Brian Bartow. **Director, Multimedia Communications:** Jill Falk. **Manager, Baseball Communications:** Michael Whitty. **Administrator, Baseball Information & Media Services:** Chris Tunno. **Spanish Interpreter:** Carlos Villoria. **PA Announcer:** John Ulett. **Official Scorers:** Gary Muller, Jeff Durbin, Mike Smith.

Bill DeWitt III

STADIUM OPERATIONS
Fax: (314) 345-9535.
VP, Stadium Operations: Matt Gifford. **VP, Facility Planning & Engineering:** Joe Abernathy.

TICKETING
Fax: (314) 345-9522.
VP, Ticket Sales/Service: Joe Strohm. **Director, Ticket Sales & Marketing:** Martin Coco. **Director, Ticket Sales & Retention:** Rob Fasoldt. **Director, Ticket Operations:** Kerry Emerson.

TRAVEL/CLUBHOUSE
Fax: (314) 345-9523.
Team Travel Director: Ernie Moore. **Equipment Manager:** Mark Walsh. **Visiting Clubhouse Manager:** Rip Rowan. **Video Coordinator:** Chad Blair.

2020 SCHEDULE
Standard Game Times: Mon.-Sat., 7:15 pm; Sun., 1:15 pm.

MARCH
26-29 . . . . . .at Cincinnati
30-31 . . . . . at Milwaukee

APRIL
1-3 . . . . . . at Pittsburgh
4-7 . . . . San Diego
8-11 . . Los Angeles (NL)
13-14 . . . .at Cincinnati
15-17 . . . . . at Milwaukee
19-21 . . .New York (NL)
22-24 . . . . . . .Milwaukee
26-28 . . . . Cincinnati
29-30 . . . . at Washington

MAY
2-3 . . . . . . at Milwaukee
4-6 . . . . San Diego

9-10 . . . . .New York (NL)
11-13 . . . . . at Pittsburgh
15-17 . . . at Philadelphia
19-21 . . . . Atlanta
23-24 . . . . Arizona
25-27 . . . . . . at Atlanta
30-31 . . . . . Pittsburgh

JUNE
2-3 . . . . .Toronto
4-7 . . . .. at Pittsburgh
8-10 . .. at New York (NL)
13-14 . . . . Chicago (NL)
16-18 . . . . .Colorado
19-21 . . . . . . Cincinnati
22-25 . . . . . at Miami
26-28 . . . . .at Boston

30 . . . . Washington

JULY
1-2 . . . . Washington
3-5 . . . . Milwaukee
7-9 . . . . . at Washington
10-12 . . . . . at Tampa Bay
18-19 . . . . . New York (AL)
20-22 . . . . . San Francisco
24-26 . . . ... Chicago (NL)
28-30 . . . . . at Milwaukee
31 . . . . at Pittsburgh

AUGUST
1-2 . . . . at Pittsburgh
4-5 . . . . at Kansas City
7-9 . . . . Cincinnati
10-12 . . . . Pittsburgh

14-16 . . . . Milwaukee
18-19 . . . . at Toronto
21-23 . . . .at Chicago (NL)
24-26 . . . . at Cincinnati
28-30 . . . . . . Pittsburgh
31 . . . . . . .Philadelphia

SEPTEMBER
1-3 . . . . .Philadelphia
4-6 . . . . at Arizona
7-9 . . . . at San Francisco
10-13 . . . . . Chicago (NL)
15-16 . . . . . Kansas City
17-20 . . . . .at Cincinnati
21-23 . . . . . . .Milwaukee
25-27 . . at Chicago (NL)

GENERAL INFORMATION
Stadium (year opened):
Busch Stadium (2006).
Team Colors: Red and white.

Home Dugout: First Base.
Playing Surface: Grass.

BASEBALL OPERATIONS

President of Baseball Operations: John Mozeliak. **Vice President & General Manager:** Michael Girsch. **Senior Executive Assistant to the President of Baseball Operations:** Linda Brauer. **Assistant GM:** Moises Rodriguez. **Assistant GM & Director of Scouting:** Randy Flores. **Senior Special Assistant to GM:** Bob Gebhard. **Special Assistant to GM:** Ryan Franklin. **Special Assistant to GM, Player Procurement:** Matt Slater. **Director, Baseball Administration:** John Vuch. **Director, Analytics:** Kevin Seats. **Director, Baseball Analytics & Systems:** Jeremy Cohen. **Director, Baseball Systems:** Patrick Casanta. **Project Dir./Baseball Systems:** Matt Bayer. **Manager, Player Communications:** Melody Yount. **Manager, Senior Developer:** Brian Seyfert. **Sr. Analytics Engineer:** Todd Heitmann. **Analytics Engineer:** Jack Hanley. **Baseball Operations Analyst:** Javier Duren. **Baseball Development Analysts:** Julia Prusaczyk. **Baseball Analyst:** Garrett Greenwood. **Senior Data Scientist:** Alan Kessler. **Data Engineer:** Isaiah Berg. **Application Developer:** Austin Lukaschewski.

John Mozeliak

MAJOR LEAGUE STAFF

Telephone: (314) 345-9600.
Manager: Mike Shildt. **Coaches: Bench**—Oliver Marmol. **Pitching**—Mike Maddux. **Hitting**—Jeff Albert. **Assistant Hitting Coach**—Jobel Jimenez. **First Base**—Richard "Stubby" Clapp. **Third Base**—Ron "Pop" Warner. **Bullpen**—Bryan Eversgerd. **Assistant Coach:** Willie McGee. **Pitching Specialist:** Chris Carpenter. **Internal Player Strategist:** Patrick Elkins. **Bullpen Catchers**—Jamie Pogue, Kleininger Teran.

MEDICAL/TRAINING

Head Orthopedist Surgeon: Dr. George Paletta. **Coordinator of Medical Services & Team Physician:** Brian Mahaffey. **Director of Medical Operations:** Adam Olsen. **Director of Performance:** Robert Butler. **Assistant Athletic Trainers:** Jeremy Clipperton, Chris Conroy. **Assistant Director, Performance:** Thomas Knox. **Performance Specialist & Physical Therapist:** Jason Shutt. **Strength & Conditioning Coach:** Lance Thomason.

PLAYER DEVELOPMENT

Director, Player Development: Gary LaRocque. **Manager, Player Development:** Tony Ferreira. **Manager, Player Dev & Performance:** Emily Wiebe. **Minor League Equipment Manager:** Dave Vondarhaar. **Field Coordinator:** Chris Swauger. **Minor League Hitting Coordinator:** Russ Steinhorn. **Minor League Hitting Instructor/Analyst:** Daniel Nicolaisen. **Coordinator:** Jose Leger (Latin America Field & Academy Development), Tim Leveque (senior pitching), **Pitching Strategist:** Cale Johnson. **Minor League Roving Instructors:** Randy Niemann (pitching), Jose Oquendo (roving), Johnny Rodriguez (infield), Ryan Ludwick (hitting), Jason Isringhausen (pitching), Barry Weinberg (medical advisor), Keith Joynt (medical coordinator, player development), Matt Leonard (rehab coordinator), Aaron Rhodes (strength & conditioning), DC MacLea (performance speacialist), Victor Kuri (assistant rehab coordinator).

FARM SYSTEM

Class	Club (League)	Manager	Hitting Coach	Pitching Coach
Triple-A	Memphis (PCL)	Ben Johnson	Brandon Allen	Dernier Orozco
Double-A	Springfield (TL)	Joe Kruzel	Tyger Pederson	Darwin Marrero
High A	Palm Beach (FSL)	Dann Bilardello	Brian Burgamy	Rick Harig
Low A	Peoria (MWL)	Erick Almonte	Cody Gabella	Adrian Martin
Short-season	State College (NYP)	Jose Leon	Jason Broussard	Dean Kiekhefer
Rookie	Johnson City (APP)	Roberto Espinoza	Daniel Nicolaisen	Renee Cortez
Rookie	Cardinals (GCL)	Joe Hawkins	T. Wolfe/B. Gilkey	Giovanni Carrara
Rookie	Cardinals 1 (DSL)	Frey Peniche	BJ Roper-Hubbert	Bill Villallanueva
Rookie	Cardinals 2 (DSL)	Estuar Ruiz	I. Castro/L. Cruz	TBD

SCOUTING

Fax: (314) 345-9519.
Assistant General Manager & Director of Scouting: Randy Flores. **Assistant Director, Scouting:** Tyler Hadzinsky. **Manager, Pro Scouting:** Jared Odom. **Special Assistant to Amateur Scouting:** Mike Roberts. **Special Advisor to the Scouting Director:** Jamal Strong. **Professional Scouts:** Chris Bourjos (Scottsdale, AZ), Brian Hopkins (Holly Springs, NC), Jeff Ishii (Chino, CA), Aaron Klinic (Baltimore, MD), Deric McKamey (Cincinnati, OH), Craig Richmond (Tampa, FL) Joe Rigoli (Parsippany, NJ), Kerry Robinson (Ballwin, MO). **National Crosscheckers:** Aaron Looper (Shawnee, OK), Zachary Mortimer (Pilesgrove, NJ), Jamal Strong (Surpirse, AZ). **Regional Crosscheckers:** Dominic "Ty" Boyles (Dallas, TX), Aaron Krawiec (Gilbert, AZ), Clint Brown (Braselton, GA), Sean Moran (Furlong, PA) **Area Scouts:** Jabari Barnett (Humble, TX), Nick Longmire (Alpharetta, GA), Jason Bryans (Tecumseh, ON), TC Calhoun (Abingdon, VA), Josh Lopez (West Palm Beach, FL), Mike Garciaparra (Manhattan Beach, CA), Dirk Kinney (Lenexa, KS), Tom Lipari (Aubrey, TX), Jim Negrych (Phoenixville, PA), Charles Peterson (Columbia, SC), Stacey Pettis (Brentwood, CA), Chris Rodriguez (Vancouver, WA), Mauricio Rubio (Tempe, AZ), Nathan Sopena (Cary, IL), Eli Tupuola (San Diego, CA). **Part-Time Scouts:** Jim Foster (St. Louis, MO), Juan C Ramos (Caguas, PR). **Director, International Operations & Administration:** Luis Morales. **Manager, International Operations:** Joseph Quezada. **Senior International Crosschecker:** Joe Almaraz. **International & Domestic Crosschecker:** Damaso Espino. **Senior Latin American Crosschecker/DR Scouting Supervisor:** Angel Ovalles. **Latin American Crosschecker/DR Crosschecker:** Alix Martinez. **International Scouts:** Braly Guzman, Raymi Dicent, Filiberto Fernandez, Darluimis Almonte (Dominican Republic); Jhohan Acevedo, Jesus Perez, Neriel Morillo, Wilmer Castillo (Venezuela); Ramon Garcia (Mexico); Carlos Balcazar (Colombia); Nahim Attaf (Curacao).

SAN DIEGO PADRES

Office and Mailing Address: Petco Park, 100 Park Blvd., San Diego, CA 92101.
Telephone: (619) 795-5000.
E-mail address: comments@padres.com. **Website:** www.padres.com. **Twitter:** @padres.
Facebook: www.facebook.com/padres. **Instagram:** www.instagram.com/padres

OWNERSHIP
Operated By: Padres LP. **Executive Chairman:** Ron Fowler. **General Partner:** Peter Seidler.

BUSINESS OPERATIONS
President, Business Operations: Erik Greupner. **Senior VP, Chief Financial Officer:** Ronda Sedillo. **Vice President, Information Technology:** Ray Chan. **Sr. Director, Human Resources:** Sara Greenspan. **Director, Accounting:** Chris James. **VP, Sports Programs:** Bill Johnston.

LEGAL
Senior Vice President/General Counsel: Caroline Perry. **Associate General Counsel/ Baseball Operations Compliance Officer:** Stephanie Wilka.

COMMUNITY RELATIONS/MILITARY AFFAIRS
Telephone: (619) 795-5265. **Fax:** (619) 795-5266. **Senior VP, Community/Military Affairs:** Tom Seidler. **Senior Manager, Community Outreach:** Connor Novak. **Military Affairs Advisor:** J.J. Quinn. **Director, Public Affairs:** Diana Puetz.

ENTERTAINMENT/MARKETING/COMMUNICATIONS/CREATIVE SERVICES
Sr. VP/Chief Marketing Officer: Wayne Partello. **Director, Communications:** Craig Hughner. **Director, Content:** Nicky Patriarca. **Sr. Director, Entertainment/Broadcasting/Archives:** Erik Meyer. **VP, Marketing:** Katie Jackson. **Director, Creative Services**: Brendan Nieto.

Ron Fowler

BALLPARK OPERATIONS/HOSPITALITY
VP, Ballpark Operations/GM, Petco Park: Mark Guglielmo. **Senior Director, Security/Transportation:** Kevin Dooley. **Senior Director, Event Operations:** Ken Kawachi. **Director, Field Operations:** Matt Balough. **Director, Guest Experience:** Erin Sheehan. **Official Scorers:** Jack Murray, Bill Zavestoski, Dave Matheson and Nick Canepa.

TICKETING
Telephone: (619) 795-5500. **Fax:** (619) 795-5034. **Senior VP, Corporate Partnerships:** Sergio Del Prado. **VP, Ticket Sales and Service:** Curt Waugh. **Director, Membership Services:** Sindi Edelstein. **Director, Partnership Services:** Eddie Quinn. **Senior Director, Ticket Operations:** Jim Kiersnowski. **VP, Special Events:** Jaclyn Lash.

TRAVEL/CLUBHOUSE
Director, Player & Staff Services: T.J. Lasita. **Manager, Equipment & Clubhouse:** Spencer Dallin. **Assistant Equipment Manager/Umpire Room Attendant:** Tony Petricca. **Visiting Clubhouse Manager:** TJ Laidlaw.

2020 SCHEDULE
Standard Game Times: Mon.-Fri., 7:10 pm; Sat., 5:40 pm; Sun,. 1:40 pm.

MARCH
26-29 . . . . .Colorado
31 . . . . Atlanta

APRIL
1 . . . . Atlanta
3-5 . . . . at Colorado
6-8 . . . . at Atlanta
11-12 . . . . . San Francisco
15-16 . . . . .Colorado
18-19 . . . . . at Arizona
21-23 . . .at Chicago (NL)
24-26 . . . . .at Detroit
28-30 . . . . St. Louis

MAY
2-3 . . . . . Los Angeles (NL)

4-6 . . . . .at St. Louis
9-10 . . at Los Angeles (NL)
12-13 . . . . . Chicago (AL)
15-17 . . . . . Chicago (NL)
19-21 . . . . at Miami
22-25 . . . .at Cincinnati
27-29 . . . . Arizona
30-31 . . . . .Miami

JUNE
2-4 . . . . . at San Francisco
5-7 . . . . at Arizona
9-11 . . . at Milwaukee
13-14 . . . . . . .Arizona
17-18 . . . . . . Cincinnati
20-21 . . . . . at Colorado
23-24 . . . . . . Cleveland

27-28 . . . . .New York (NL)
30 . . . . . . at Philadelphia

JULY
1-2 . . . . . . at Philadelphia
3-6 . . . . . at New York (NL)
8-10 . . . Los Angeles (NL)
11-12 . . . at San Francisco
18-19 . . . . . . .Milwaukee
21-23 . . . . . at Pittsburgh
24-26 . . . .at Kansas City
28-29 . . . . Pittsburgh
31 . . . . . . .Philadelphia

AUGUST
1-2 . . . . .Philadelphia
4-6 . . . at Los Angeles (NL)

8-9 . . . . .Colorado
11-12 . . . . .at Cleveland
13-16 . . . . at Washington
19-20 . . . . San Francisco
22-23 . . . . . Washington
25-27 . . at San Francisco
28-30. . .at Los Angeles (NL)

SEPTEMBER
2-3 . . . . Seattle
4-6 . . . . . . San Francisco
7-10 . . . . .Arizona
12-13 . . . . . at Colorado
15-16 . . . . . . .at Seattle
17-20 . . . . . . at Arizona
23-24 . . . . . .Minnesota
26-27 . . . Los Angeles (NL)

GENERAL INFORMATION
Stadium (year opened):
Petco Park (2004).
Team Colors: Padres Blue and White

Home Dugout: First Base.
Playing Surface: Grass.

BASEBALL OPERATIONS

Telephone: (619) 795-5077. **Fax:** (619) 795-5361.
Executive VP, General Manager: A.J. Preller. **VP/Assistant GM:** Fred Uhlman Jr. **Assistant GM:** Josh Stein. **Senior Advisor, Baseball Operations:** Trevor Hoffman. **Senior Advisor/ Director, Player Personnel:** Logan White. **Special Assistants to the GM:** Moises Alou, James Keller, David Post. **Special Assistant to the GM, Research & Development:** Dave Cameron. **Advisor to Baseball Operations:** Darren Balsley, Allen Craig, A.J. Ellis, Ian Kinsler. **Director, Baseball Operations:** Nick Ennis. **Director, Baseball Information Services:** Matt Klotsche. **Director, Player & Staff Services:** TJ Lasita. **Director, Baseball Systems:** Wells Oliver. **Director, Baseball Research & Development:** Adam Esquer. **Developers, Baseball Systems:** Garret Doe, Michael Vanger. **Assistant Director, Baseball Operations:** David Longley. **Manager, Baseball Administration & Special Assistant to the GM:** Michaelene Courtis. **Senior Analyst, Baseball Research & Development:** Cody Zupnick. **Coordinator, Baseball Operations:** Brett Becker. **Analysts, Baseball Research & Development:** Jeremy Muesing, Mario Paciuc.

A.J. Preller

MAJOR LEAGUE STAFF

Manager: Jayce Tingler. **Associate Manager:** Skip Schumaker. **Bench Coach:** Bobby Dickerson. **Pitching Coach:** Larry Rothschild. **Hitting Coach:** Damion Easley. **First Base Coach:** Wayne Kirby. **Third Base Coach:** Glenn Hoffman. **Bullpen Coach:** Ben Fritz. **Catching & Quality Control Coach:** Rod Barajas. **Advance Scout/Development Coach:** Ryan Flaherty. **Bullpen Catchers:** Griffin Benedict, Peter Summerville. **Development Coordinator:** Keith Werman. **Video Coordinator:** Joe McAlpin. **Home Clubhouse Manager:** Spencer Dallin. **Visiting Clubhouse Manager:** TJ Laidlaw.

MEDICAL/TRAINING

Club Physician: UC San Diego Health—Dr. Catherine Robertson, Dr. Kenneth Taylor. **Director, Player Health and Performance:** Don Tricker. **Head Athletic Trainer:** Mark Rogow. **Physical Therapist:** Scott Hacker. **Assistant Athletic Trainers:** Ben Fraser, Ricky Huerta, Kevin Pillifant. **Director, Strength & Conditioning:** Dan Byrne. **Strength & Conditioning Coaches:** Scott Cline, Jay Young. **Massage Therapist:** Atsushi Nakasone. **Baseball Performance Dietician:** Whitney Miliano.

PLAYER DEVELOPMENT

Telephone: (619) 795-5392. **Fax:** (619) 795-5036.
Senior Director, Player Development: Sam Geaney. **Director, Player Development:** Ryley Westman. **Special Assistant, Player Development:** Steve Finley. **Manager, Minor Leagues/Peoria Operations:** Todd Stephenson. **Coordinators:** Steve Lyons & Eric Junge (pitching), Johnny Washington & Oscar Bernard (hitting), Kevin Hooper (infield), Paul Porter (minor league ATC), JoJo Tarantino (minor league medical administration), Eric Wood & Drew Heithoff (strength & conditioning). **Physical Therapists:** Tanner Fields & Aaron Wengertsmen. **Rehab Pitching Coach:** Curt Young. **Player Development Instructor:** Dave Bingham. **Manager, Minor League Equipment & Clubhouse:** Zach Nelson. **Coordinator, Player Development:** Rohanna Pacheco. **Coordinator, Scouting/Player Development Video Ops:** Ethan Dixon. **Analyst, Player Development:** Nathan Landau. **Director, International Operations:** Cesar Rizik. **Director, Professional Development:** Jason Amoroso. **Coordinator, Latin American Player Development:** Vicente Cafaro. **Coordinator, Mental Skills:** Rosa Pou. **Coordinator, English Instruction:** Kaitlyn Teske. **Assistant, Player Development Technology and Video:** Clint Sewell.

FARM SYSTEM

Class	Farm Club (League)	Manager	Hitting Coach	Pitching Coach
Triple-A	El Paso (PCL)	Edwin Rodriguez	Morgan Burkhart	Pete Zamora
Double-A	Amarillo (TL)	Philip Wellman	Raul Padron	Jimmy Jones
High A	Lake Elsinore (CAL)	Mike McCoy	Pat O'Sullivan	TBD
Low A	Fort Wayne (MWL)	Anthony Contreras	Jonathan Mathews	Leo Rosales
Short-season	Tri-City (NWL)	Vinny Lopez	Raul Gonzalez	Gorman Heimueller
Rookie	Padres 1 (AZL)	Aaron Levin	Doug Banks	Christian Wonders
Rookie	Padres 2 (AZL)	Oscar Salazar	Jed Morris	John Halama
Rookie	Padres (DSL)	Miguel Del Castillo	Yunir Garcia	N. Cruz/J. Quezada

SCOUTING

Director, Amateur Scouting: Mark Conner. **Director, Professional Scouting:** Pete DeYoung. **Director, International Scouting/Field Coordinator:** Chris Kemp. **Director, Pacific Rim Operations:** Acey Kohrogi. **Assistant Scouting Director:** Kurt Kemp. **National Crosschecker:** Chip Lawrence. **Scouting Crosschecker:** Luke Murton. **Manager, Amateur Scouting:** Sam Ray. **Manager, Professional Scouting:** Preston Mattingly. **Coordinator, Amateur Scouting:** Layne Gross. **Coordinator, Arizona Video Operations:** Max Kraust. **Amateur Scouting Supervisors:** Yancy Ayres, Nick Brannon, Josh Emmerick, Matt Haas, Chris Kelly, Andrew Salvo. **Analyst, Amateur Scouting:** Tristan Sandler. **Area & Amateur Scouts:** Stephen Baker, Justin Baughman, Brian Cruz, Carlos Fisher, Kevin Ham, Clint Harrison, Troy Hoerner, Chris Kemlo, Nick Long, Matt Maloney, John Martin, John McNamara, Stephen Moritz, James Parker, Tim Reynolds, Danny Sader, Matt Schaffner, Tyler Stubblefield. **Special Assistant, Professional Scouting:** Spencer Graham. **Professional Scouting Crosscheckers:** Mike Juhl, Chuck LaMar, Dominic Viola. **Professional Scouts:** Keith Boeck, Patrick Coghlan, Kimball Crossley, Tim Holt, Chris Kusiolek, Mark Merila, Dominic Scavone, Duane Shaffer, Matt Simonetti, Tyler Tufts, Mike Venafro, Cory Wade. **International Scouting Supervisors:** Trevor Schumm, Bill McLaughlin. **Area Scout/International Crosschecker:** Jake Koenig. **Coordinator, Latin American Scouting:** Felix Feliz. **Supervisor, Dominican Republic:** Alvin Duran. **Supervisor, Venezuela:** Luis Prieto. **International Scouts:** Antonio Alejos (Venezuela), Andres Cabadias (Colombia), Emenejildo Diaz (Dominican Republic), Jhonathan Feliz (Dominican Republic), Po-Hsuan Keng (Taiwan), Sherman Lacrus (Curacao), Victor Magdaleno (Venezuela), Richard Montenegro (Panama), Hoon Namgung (Korea/Taiwan), Ysrael Rojas (Dominican Republic), Keiji Uezono (Japan), Jose Salado (Dominican Republic), Damian Shanahan (Australia).

SAN FRANCISCO GIANTS

Office Address: Oracle Park, 24 Willie Mays Plaza, San Francisco, CA 94107.
Telephone: (415) 972-2000. **Fax:** (415) 947-2800. **Website:** sfgiants.com, sfgigantes.com.

OWNERSHIP

Operated By: San Francisco Baseball Associates L.P.

BUSINESS OPERATIONS

Laurence M. Baer

President/Chief Executive Officer: Laurence M. Baer. **Executive VP:** Brian R. Sabean.
Special Assistants: Will Clark, Willie Mays. **Special Advisor:** Barry Bonds.

FINANCE/LEGAL/INFORMATION TECHNOLOGY

Executive VP/General Counsel: Jack F. Bair. **VP/General Counsel:** Amy Tovar. **Senior VP/Chief Financial Officer:** Lisa Pantages. **Senior VP/CIO/Chairman, San Jose Giants:** Bill Schlough. **VP, Information Technology:** Ken Logan. **VP, Finance:** Matt Causey.

ADMINISTRATION

Executive VP, Administration: Alfonso Felder. **Chief Venue Officer:** Jorge Costa. **VP, Ballpark Operations:** Gene Telucci. **Senior Director, Guest Services:** Alexis Lustbader. **Chief People Officer:** Jose Martin. **President, Giants Enterprises:** Stephen Revetria. **Senior VP, Event Strategy & Services:** Sara Grauf.

COMMUNICATIONS

Telephone: (415) 972-2445. **Fax:** (415) 947-2800.
Executive VP, Communications/Senior Advisor to the CEO: Staci Slaughter. **VP, Public Affairs/Community Relations:** Shana Daum. **Executive Director, Giants Community Fund:** Sue Petersen. **Senior Director, Broadcast Communications & Media Operations:** Maria Jacinto. **Senior Director, Media Relations:** Matt Chisholm. **Senior Manager, Hispanic Communications & Marketing:** Erwin Higueros. **Media Relations Manager:** Megan Brown. **Baseball Information Manager:** Mike Passanisi.

BUSINESS OPERATIONS

Executive VP, Business Operations: Mario Alioto. **VP, Business Operations:** Jason Pearl. **VP, Partnership Sales & Business Development:** Brenden Mallette. **VP, Marketing/Advertising:** Danny Dann. **VP, SFG Productions:** Paul Hodges. **VP, Brand Development/Digital Media:** Bryan Srabian. **VP, Creative Services/Visual Identity:** Nancy Donati. **PA Announcer:** Renel Brooks-Moon.

TICKETING

Telephone: (415) 972-2000. **Fax:** (415) 972-2500.
Senior VP, Ticket Sales/Services: Russ Stanley. **VP, Ticket Sales/Premium Seating:** Jeff Tucker. **VP, Ticket Operations & Services:** Steve Fanelli. **VP, Strategic Revenue Services:** Jerry Drobny. **VP, Business Analytics:** Rocky Koplik.

2020 SCHEDULE

Standard Game Times: Mon.-Sat., 7:15 pm; Sun., 1:05 pm.

MARCH
26-29 . at Los Angeles (NL)
30-31 . . . . at Arizona

APRIL
1 . . . . at Arizona
3-6 . . . . . Los Angeles (NL)
7-9 . . . . Arizona
11-12 . . . . . at San Diego
14-16 . . . . . at Cincinnati
17-19 . . . . at Atlanta
22-23 . . . . Colorado
25-26 . . . . . . Washington
28-29 . . . . . Philadelphia

MAY
1-3 . . . . at Cleveland
4-6 . . . . at Minnesota

9-10 . . . . . . Chicago (AL)
12-14 . . . . . . at Colorado
16-17 . . . . Atlanta
19-20 . . . . Detroit
22-25 . . . . . at Pittsburgh
26-28 . . . . . at Milwaukee
30-31 . . . . Colorado

JUNE
2-4 . . . . San Diego
6-7 . . . . at Oakland
10-11 . . . . Pittsburgh
13-14 . . . . Miami
16-18 . . . at Washington
19-21 . . . . at Miami
23-25 . . . . New York (NL)
27-28 . . . Los Angeles (NL)

30 . . . . . at New York (NL)

JULY
1-2 . . . . at New York (NL)
4-5 . . . . at Colorado
8-9 . . . . Oakland
11-12 . . . . San Diego
17-19 . at Los Angeles (NL)
21-22 . . . . . . at St. Louis
25-26 . . . . Arizona
28-30 . . . . . Chicago (NL)

AUGUST
1-2 . . . . at Colorado
4-5 . . . . at Detroit
7-10 . . . . at Philadelphia
12-13 . . . Los Angeles (NL)
15-16 . . . . Colorado

19-20 . . . . . at San Diego
20-23 . . . . at Arizona
25-27 . . . . San Diego
29-30 . . . . . . Kansas City

SEPTEMBER
1-2 . . . . . at Chicago (NL)
4-6 . . . . at San Diego
7-9 . . . . St. Louis
11-13 . . . . Cincinnati
14-16 . . . . at Arizona
19-20 . at Los Angeles (NL)
23-24 . . . . Arizona
25-27 . . . . . . Milwaukee

GENERAL INFORMATION

Stadium (year opened): Oracle Park (2000). **Playing Surface:** Grass.
Team Colors: Black, orange and cream.
Home Dugout: Third Base.

BASEBALL OPERATIONS

Farhan Zaidi

Telephone: (415) 972-1922. **Fax:** (415) 947-2929.
President of Baseball Ops.: Farhan Zaidi. **General Manager:** Scott Harris. **Senior Advisor to President of Baseball Ops:** JP Ricciardi, Dick Tidrow, John Barr. **VP/Assistant GM:** Jeremy Shelley. **VP, Baseball Resources and Development:** Yeshayah Goldfarb. VP, **Player Performance and Wellness:** Colin Cahill. **Special Assistant, Scouting:** Craig Weissmann. **Special Assist. to Baseball Ops:** Felipe Alou. **Executive Assist. to Baseball Ops/Admin.:** Karen Sweeney. **Director of Baseball Analytics:** Paul Bien. **Director of Baseball Personnel Admin:** Clara Ho. **Baseball Ops Analyst:** Michael Schwartze, Jack McGeary, Brian Huey. **Sports Science Analyst:** Matt Chan. **Data Scientist:** Greg Starek. **Coord. of Org Travel:** Mike Scardino. **Assistant, Baseball Ops:** Josh Zimmerman.

MAJOR LEAGUE STAFF

Manager: Gabe Kapler. **Coaches: Bench**—Kai Correa. **Director of Pitching**—Brian Bannister. **Pitching Coach**—Andrew Bailey. **Asst Pitching Coach**—Ethan Katz. **Hitting Coach**—Donnie Ecker/Justin Viele. **Director of Hitting/Assistant ML Hitting:** Dustin Lind. **Third Base**—Ron Wotus. **First Base**—Antoan Richardson. **Bullpen**—Craig Albernaz. **Quality Assurance Coach:** Nick Ortiz. **Assistant Coaches:** Alyssa Nakken/Mark Hallberg. **Bullpen Catchers:** Taira Uematsu, Brant Whiting. **Manager, Baseball Video Systems:** Yo Miyamoto. **Coordinator, Baseball Video Systems:** Patrick Yount.

MEDICAL/TRAINING

Team Physicians: Dr. Anthony Saglimbeni, Dr. Ken Akizuki, Dr. Robert Murray, Dr. Chris Chung, Dr. Ben Ma. **Senior Dir. of Athletic Training:** Dave Groeschner. **Head Athletic Trainer:** Anthony Reyes. **Asst. Athletic Trainer:** James Petra. **Physical Therapist:** Tony Reale. **Strength & Conditioning Coach:** Brad Lawson. **Asst. Strength & Conditioning Coach/Sports Science Specialist:** Saul Martinez. **Massage Therapist:** Haro Ogawa. **Coordinator, Medical Admin.:** Chrissy Yuen. **Director of Mental Skill:** Derin McMains. **Employee Assistance Program:** Shana Alexander. **Director of Performance Nutrition:** Leron Sarig. **Medical Review Analyst:** Eric Ortega.

PLAYER DEVELOPMENT

Director, Player Development: Kyle Haines. **Asst. Director Player Development (Administration):** Eric Flemming. **Director of Minor League Medical:** Dustin Luepker. **Coordinator, Minor League Pitching:** Justin Lehr. **Coordinator, Minor League Hitting:** David Hansen. **Coordinator of Pitching Sciences:** Matt Daniels. **Assistant Pitching Coordinator:** Clayton Rapada. **Assistant Hitting Coordinator/SK Hitting Coach:** Michael Brdar. **Rehab Pitching Coordinator:** Matt Yourkin. **Sr. Analyst, Player Development:** Michael Gries. **Coordinator, Fundamentals:** Tom Trebelhorn. **Outfield and Baserunning Coordinator:** Tim Leiper. **Infield Coordinator:** Jason Wood. **Coordinator of Latin American Development:** Hector Borg. **Director, AZ Operations:** Alan Lee. **Manager, Arizona Baseball Ops.:** Gabe Alvarez. **Manager, Education/Cultural Development:** Laura Nunez. **Special Assistants, Player Development:** Joe Amalfitano, Gene Clines, Shawon Dunston, Dave Righetti. **Director, Arizona Field Operations:** Josh Warstler. **Manager of Minor League Field Operations:** Jeff Winsor.

FARM SYSTEM

Class	Farm Club (League)	Manager	Hitting Coach	Pitching Coach
Triple-A	Sacramento (PCL)	Dave Brundage	Damon Minor	Glenn Dishman
Double-A	Richmond (EL)	Jose Alguacil	Doug Clark	Steve Kline
High A	San Jose (CAL)	Dennis Pelfrey	Pat Burrell	TBD
Low A	Augusta (SAL)	Carlos Valderrama	Jake Fox	Alain Quijano
Short-season	Salem-Keizer (NWL)	Lenn Sakata	Michael Brdar	Paul Oseguera
Rookie	Giants Orange (AZL)	Tony Diggs	TBD	Mike Couchee
Rookie	Giants Black (AZL)	Jose Montilla	Juan Parra	O. Matos
Rookie	Giants (DSL)	Juan Ciriaco	TBD	TBD

SCOUTING

Telephone: (415) 972-2360. **Fax:** (415) 947-2929.
Director of Pro Scouting: Zack Minasian. **Director of Amateur Scouting:** Michael Holmes. **International Scouting, Director of Scouting:** Joe Salermo. **Director of International Operations/Baseball Administration:** Jose Bonilla. **Amateur Scouting Coordinator:** Mike Navolio. **Baseball Operations Assistant:** Josh Zimmerman. **Pro Scouts:** Ellis Burks (Moreland Hills, OH), Keith Champion (Ballwin, MO), Jim D'Aloia, Steve Decker, Lee Elder, Paul Gale, Michael Kendall, Joe Lefebvre, Ben McDonough, Ross Pruitt, Steve Riha, Ryan Thompson, Paul Turco Jr., Shane Turner, Derek Watson, Tom Zimmer. **Senior Advisors to President:** JP Ricciardi, John Barr. **Special Assistant, Scouting:** Craig Weissmann. **Senior Advisor, Scouting (Part-Time):** Ed Creech. **National Cross Checkers:** Brian Bridges, John Castleberry. **National Pitching Coordinator:** Dan Murray. **Special Assignment Scout:** Bert Bradley. **Scouting Supervisors: Northeast**—Arnold Brathwaite, **Southeast**—Jim Buckley, **Midwest** —Andrew Jefferson, **West**—Matt Woodward. **Area Scouts:** Jose Alou, Ray Callari, Brad Cameron, Larry Casian, Todd Coryell, John DiCarlo, Chuck Fick, Jim Gabella, Chuck Hensley Jr., DJ Jauss, James Mouton, Tim Osborne, Mark O'Sullivan, Junior Roman, Jared Schlehuber, Keith Snider, Todd Thomas, Jeff Wood. **International Crosscheckers:** Jose Alou, Michael Silvestri, Charlie Sullivan. **Director, Dominican Republic Operations:** Pablo Peguero. **Assistant Director, DR Operations/Latin America Crosschecker:** Felix Peguero. **Scouting Supervisors, Venezuela:** Ciro Villalobos, Edgar Fernandez. **Dominican Republic Crosschecker:** Jesus Stephens. **International Scouts (Dominican Republic):** Abner Abreu, Jonathan Bautista, Gabriel Elias, Luis Polonia Jr. **International Scouts (Venezuela):** Jonathan Arraiz, Jose Beyronti, Carlos Leon, Juan Marquez, Oscar Montero, Robert Moron, Ciro Villalobos Jr. **International Scouts:** Daniel Mavarez (Colombia), Quincy Martina (Curacao/Bonaire/Aruba), Luis Pena (México), Ernesto Cantu (México), Sandy Moreno (Nicaragua), Rogelio Castillo (Panamá), Evan Hsueh (Pacific Rim), Koo Ji-Young (Pacific Rim).

SEATTLE MARINERS

Office Address: 1250 First Ave. South, Seattle, WA 98134.
Mailing Address: PO Box 4100, Seattle, WA 98194.
Telephone: (206) 346-4000. **Fax:** (206) 346-4400. **Website:** www.mariners.com.

OWNERSHIP

Board of Directors: John Stanton (Chairman), John Ellis, Buck Ferguson, Chris Larson, Howard Lincoln, Jeff Raikes, Frank Shrontz. **President/CEO:** Kevin Mather. **Senior VP/Special Advisor to the Chairman and CEO:** Randy Adamack.

BUSINESS OPERATIONS

John Stanton

FINANCE

Executive Vice President and CFO: Tim Kornegay. **VP, Finance:** Greg Massey. **Director, Internal Audit Operations:** Connie McKay. **Senior VP, People and Culture:** Lisa Winsby.

LEGAL & GOVERNMENTAL AFFAIRS/ COMMUNITY RELATIONS

Executive Vice President and General Counsel: Fred Rivera. **VP, Deputy General Counsel:** Melissa Robertson. **VP, Partnerships & Community Relations:** Joe Chard. **Senior Director, Community Relations:** Gina Hasson.

SALES

Senior VP, Sales: Frances Traisman. **Senior Director, Partnerships:** Ingrid Russell-Narcisse. **VP, Ticket Sales & Service:** Cory Carbary. **Director, Group Business Development:** Bob Hellinger.

MARKETING/COMMUNICATIONS

Telephone: (206) 346-4000. **Fax:** (206) 346-4400.
Senior VP, Marketing/Communications: Kevin Martinez. **VP, Communications:** Tim Hevly. **VP, Marketing:** Gregg Greene. **Senior Director, Public Information:** Rebecca Hale. **Senior Manager, Baseball Information:** Kelly Munro. **Manager, Baseball Information:** Ryan Hueter. **Coordinator, Baseball Information:** Adam Gresch. **Coordinator Baseball Information:** Ian Kraft. **Senior Director, Productions:** Ben Mertens. **Director, Marketing:** Mandy Lincoln. **Director, Graphic Design:** Carl Morton.

TICKETING

Telephone: (206) 346-4001. **Fax:** (206) 346-4100.
VP, Ticket Operations and Event Services: Malcolm Rogel. **Senior Director, Ticket Services:** Jennifer Sweigert.

STADIUM OPERATIONS

Senior VP, Ballpark Events & Operations: Trevor Gooby. **Senior Director, Construction and Planning:** Ryan van Maarth. **Senior Director, Event Sales:** Alisia Anderson. **Director, Ballpark Services:** Juan Rodriguez-Velez. **Director, Security:** Jessica Reid-Bateman. **Director, Facilities:** Dave Wilke. **VP, Information Services:** Dave Curry. **Director, Information Systems:** Oliver Roy. **Director, Database/Applications:** Justin Stolmeier.

2020 SCHEDULE

Standard Game Times: Mon.-Sat., 7:10 pm; Sun., 1:10 pm.

MARCH
26 - 29 . . . . Texas
31 . . . . Minnesota

APRIL
1 . . . . Minnesota
2 - 5 . . . . . at Kansas City
6 - 8 . . . . at Chicago (AL)
10 - 12 . . . . Boston
14 . . . . Washington
17 - 19 . . . . . at Oakland
20 - 23 . . . . at Minnesota
24 - 26 . . . . . . .at Texas
29 - 30 . . Los Angeles (AL)

MAY
1 - 3 . . . . Houston
5 - 6 . . . . . . .at Oakland

8 - 10 . . . . . .at Houston
13 - 15 . . . . . . Oakland
16 - 17 . . . . . . Detroit
19 - 20 . . . at Washington
22 - 25 . . at New York (AL)
26 - 28 . . . . . .at Detroit
30 - 31 . . . . . . Atlanta

JUNE
2 - 3 . . . . . New York (AL)
5 - 7 . . . . at Miami
9 - 11 . . . . . at Toronto
13 - 14 . at Los Angeles (AL)
17 - 18 . . . . . . Houston
19 - 21 . . . . . Kansas City
23 - 24 . . . . Texas
26 - 28 . . . . at Tampa Bay
29 - 30 . . . . . .at Boston

JULY
1 . . . . .at Boston
4 - 5 . . . . . . Philadelphia
7 - 8 . . . . Baltimore
10 - 12 . . . . . . Oakland
17 - 19 . . at New York (NL)
20 - 22 . . . .at Baltimore
25 - 26 . . . . . . .Toronto
29 . . . . Texas
31 . . . at Los Angeles (AL)

AUGUST
1 - 2 . . at Los Angeles (AL)
4 . . . . .at Oakland
7 - 9 . . . . Los Angeles (AL)
11 - 12 . . . . . . Houston
14 - 16 . . . . .at Cleveland
18 - 19 . . . . . .at Houston

21 - 23 . . . . Chicago (AL)
25 - 26 . . . . . .Tampa Bay
29 - 30 . . Los Angeles (AL)

SEPTEMBER
2 - 3 . . . . . . at San Diego
5 - 6 . . . . .at Houston
7 - 10 . . . . .at Texas
12 - 13 . . . . . . Oakland
15 - 16 . . . . . San Diego
18 - 20 . . . . . . Cleveland
23 - 25 . at Los Angeles (AL)
25 - 27 . . . . .at Texas

GENERAL INFORMATION

Stadium (year opened): T-Mobile Park (1999). **Home Dugout:** First Base.
Team Colors: Northwest green, silver and navy blue. **Playing Surface:** Grass.

Senior Director, Procurement: Norma Cantu. Head Groundskeeper: Bob Christofferson. Assistant Head Groundskeepers: Tim Wilson. PA Announcer: Tom Hutyler. Official Scorer: Eric Radovich. Senior Director, Procurement: Norma Cantu. Head Groundskeeper: Bob Christofferson. Assistant Head Groundskeepers: Tim Wilson, Leo Liebert. PA Announcer: Tom Hutyler. Official Scorer: Eric Radovich.

MERCHANDISING

Sr. Director, Retail Operations: Julie McGillivray. Director, Retail Merchandising: Renee Steyh. Director, Retail Stores: Mary Beeman.

TRAVEL/CLUBHOUSE

Director, Major League Operations: Jack Mosimann. Clubhouse Manager: Ryan Stiles. Visiting Clubhouse Manager: Jeff Bopp. Video Coordinator: Patrick Hafner.

BASEBALL OPERATIONS

Executive VP/General Manager: Jerry Dipoto.
Assistant GMs: Justin Hollander, Joe Bohringer. Special Assistants to the GM: Roger Hansen, Tom McNamara. Director, Major League Operations: Jack Mosimann. Manager, Baseball Operations: Tim Stanton. Project Manager, Baseball Operations: David Hesslink. Coordinator, Advance Scouting: Frankie Piliere. Data Strategist, Baseball Operations: Skylar Shibayama. Director, Analytics: Jesse Smith. Manager, Analytics: Joel Firman.

Jerry Dipoto

MAJOR LEAGUE STAFF

Manager: Scott Servais. Bench—Jared Sandberg. Pitching—Pete Woodworth. Hitting—Tim Laker. Asst. Hitting: Jarret DeHart. First Base—Perry Hill. Third Base—Manny Acta. Bullpen—Brian DeLunas. Bullpen Catcher — Fleming Baez. Field Coordinator—Carson Vitale. Video Coordinator: Patrick Hafner.

MEDICAL/TRAINING

Medical Director: Dr. Ed Khalfayan. Team Doctor: Dr. Tim Johnson. Senior Athletic Trainer: Rob Nodine. Head Athletic Trainer: Kyle Torgerson. Asst. Athletic Trainer: Matt Toth. Physical Therapist: Ryan Bitzel. Director, Performance Training: James Clifford. Assistant Performance Specialist: Derek Cantieni.

PLAYER DEVELOPMENT

Telephone: (206) 346-4316. Fax: (206) 346-4300.
Director, Player Development: Andy McKay. Coordinator, Player Development: Mat Snider. Administrator, Player Development: Jan Plein. Special Assistant, Pitching Coach: Pete Harnisch. Special Assistants, Player Development: Alvin Davis, Dan Wilson, Mike Cameron. Coordinator, Medical/Athletic Training: John Walker. Coordinator, Pitching Strategy: Trent Blank. Hitting Strategist: Connor Dawson. Field Coordinator: Tony Arnerich. Hitting Coordinator: Hugh Quattlebaum. Pitching Coordinator: Max Weiner. Coordinator, Minor League Rehab: Michael Feliciano. Latin American Development Coodinator: Cesar Nicolas. Performance Specialist Coordinator: Aaron Reis.

FARM SYSTEM

Class	Club (League)	Manager	Hitting Coach	Pitching Coach
Triple-A	Tacoma (PCL)	Daren Brown	Roy Howell	Rob Marcello
Double-A	Arkansas (TL)	Dave Berg	Joe Thurston	Alon Leichman
High A	Modesto (CAL)	Denny Hocking	Shawn O'Malley	Sean McGrath
Low A	West Virginia (SAL)	Eric Farris	Rob Benjamin	Nathan Bannister
Short-season	Everett (NWL)	Louis Boyd	Mike Fransoso	Ari Ronick
Rookie	Peoria (AZL)	Zac Livingston	Jose Umbria	Yoel Monzon
Rookie	Mariners (DSL)	Austin Knight	B. Schneider/L. Caballero	Jose Amancio

SCOUTING

VP, Scouting: Tom Allison. Director, Amateur Scouting: Scott Hunter. Player Personnel Managers: Brendan Domaracki, Jason Karegeannes, Emanuel Sifuentes. International Scouting Coordinator: Andrew Herrera. Asst. Amateur Scouting Coordinator: Ty Bowman (Phoenix, AZ). Special Assistants to Scouting: Howard McCullough (Greenville, NC), Woody Woodward (Palm Coast, FL). Pro Scouts: Greg Hunter (Seattle, WA), Bobby Korecky (Estero, FL), John McMichen (Cincinnati, OH), Chris Pelekoudas (Mesa, AZ), Chris Rosenbaum (Arlington, VA), Tyler Warmoth (Orlando, FL), Independent League Scout: Ross Vecchio (Canonsburg, PA) Territorial Crosscheckers: West: Taylor Cameron (Long Beach, CA), Central: Mark Lummus (Godley, TX), Midwest: Ben Collman (German Valley, IL), Northeast: Devitt Moore (Bryn Mawr, PA), Southeast: Jesse Kapellusch (Cooper City, FL). Area Scouts: Jordan Bley (Dallas, TX), Preston Higbe (Des Moines, IA), Dan Holcomb (Birmingham, AL), Ryan Holmes (Moorpark, CA), Tyler Holub (Durham, NC), Chris Hom (Benicia, CA), Amanda Hopkins (Phoenix, AZ), Robert Keller (Mobile, AL), Jackson Laumann (Florence, KY), Les McTavish (Lethbridge, Alberta), Derek Miller (Sugar Land, TX), Rob Mummau (Palm Harbor, FL), Patrick O'Grady (Conshohocken, PA), Gary Patchett (Wildomar, CA), David Pepe (Caldwell, NJ), Alex Ross (Kirkland, WA), Dan Rovetto (Davie, FL), Rafael Santo Domingo (San Juan, PR), John Wiedenbauer (Cumming, GA). Director, International Amateur Scouting: Frankie Thon (Doral, FL). International Crosschecker: Kevin Fox (Roseville, CA), Supervisor, Dominican Republic: Audo Vicente (Santo Domingo, DR). Coordinator, Special Projects: Ted Heid (Peoria, AZ). Latin America Supervisor: David Brito (Baranquilla, CO). Venezuela Supervisor: Federico Hernandez (Caracas, VZ) Assistant, International Scouting and Informatics: Frederick Rioux (Tampa, FL) International Scouts: Tim Ballard (Australia), Felipe Burin (Brazil), Alfredo Celestin (D.R.), Rodrigo Cortez (Venezuela) Franklin Diaz (D.R.) Luis Fuenmayor (Venezuela), Sam Kao (Taiwan), Luis Martinez (Venezuela), Rafael Mateo (D.R.) Manabu Noto (Japan), Rigoberto Rangel (Panama), Ismael Rosado (Dominican Republic), Illich Salazar (Venezuela).

TAMPA BAY RAYS

Office Address: Tropicana Field, One Tropicana Drive, St. Petersburg, FL 33705.
Telephone: (727) 825-3137. **Fax:** (727) 825-3111.

OWNERSHIP
Principal Owner: Stuart Sternberg

BUSINESS OPERATIONS

Presidents: Brian Auld, Matt Silverman.
Chief Development Officer: Melanie Lenz. **Senior Vice President, Administration/
General Counsel:** John Higgins. **Senior Vice President, Baseball Operations/General
Manager:** Erik Neander. **VP, Public Affairs & Corporate Communications:** Rafaela A. Amador.
VP, Baseball Development: Peter Bendix. **VP, Baseball Operations:** James Click. **VP/Chief
Financial Officer:** Rob Gagliardi. **VP, Communications:** Dave Haller. **VP, Business Operations
& Analytics:** Barry Newell. **VP, Information Technology:** Juan Ramirez. **VP, Corporate
Partnerships:** Brian Richeson. **VP, Player Development & International Scouting:**
Carlos Rodriguez. **VP, Ticket Sales and Service:** Jeff Tanzer. **VP, Human Resources and
Organizational Engagement:** Jennifer Lyn Tran. **VP, Strategy & Development:** Bill Walsh. **VP,
Marketing & Creative Services:** Eric Weisberg. **VP, Employee & Community Development:**
Bill Wiener, Jr.

Stuart Sternberg

FINANCE
Senior Director, Controller: Patrick Smith. **Director, Financial Planning and Analysis:** Jason Gray.

MARKETING/COMMUNITY RELATIONS
Director, Creative: Warren Hypes. **Director, Marketing & Creative Services:** Emily Miller. **Executive Director, Rays
Baseball Foundation:** Stephen Thomas. **Director, Community Relations:** David Egles.

GAME OPERATIONS
Director, Game Presentation & Production: Mike Weinman. **Director, Guest Services:** Scott Wilson. **Director,
Promotions:** Stephon Thomas.

COMMUNICATIONS/BROADCASTING
Senior Director, Broadcasting: Larry McCabe. **Director, Communications:** Ryan Sheets.

BASEBALL OPERATIONS
Senior VP Baseball Operations/GM: Erik Neander. **VP, Baseball Operations:** James Click. **VP, Baseball
Development:** Peter Bendix. **VP, Player Development/International Operations:** Carlos Rodriguez. **Special Assistant
to the GM:** Bobby Heck. **Director, Development Strategy:** Sandy Sternberg. **Director, Staff Development and
Recruiting:** Chanda Lawdermilk. **Director, Team Travel and Logistics:** Chris Westmoreland. **Director, Baseball
Performance Science:** Joe Myers. **Director, Baseball Systems:** Brian Plexico. **Director, Baseball R&D:** Will Cousins.

2020 SCHEDULE
Standard Game Times: 7:10 p.m.; Sun. 1:10.

MARCH	8 - 10 . . . . Texas	29 - 30 . . Los Angeles (AL)	14 - 16 . . . . . Baltimore
26 - 29 . . . . . Pittsburgh	11 - 14 . . . New York (AL)	**JULY**	17 - 19 . . at New York (AL)
30 - 31 . . . . New York (AL)	15 - 17 . . . . . Baltimore	1 - 2 . . . . Los Angeles (AL)	22 - 23 . at Los Angeles (AL)
APRIL	19 - 21 . . . . . .at Boston	3 - 5 . . . .at Chicago (NL)	25 - 26 . . . . . . .at Seattle
1 . . . . . . New York (AL)	22 - 25 . . . . . .at Detroit	8 . . . . at Milwaukee	28 - 30 . . . . . Minnesota
3 - 5 . . . . .at Texas	26 - 28 . . . . . . .Toronto	10 - 12 . . . . . . St. Louis	31 . . . . Chicago (AL)
6 - 8 . . . . .at Boston	30 - 31 . . . . . .Milwaukee	17 - 19 . . . .at Baltimore	**SEPTEMBER**
9 - 12 . . . . .at Cleveland	**JUNE**	20 - 22 . . .at Kansas City	1 - 3 . . . . . Chicago (AL)
13 - 15 . . . . . . Houston	2 - 4 . . . . . at Minnesota	24 - 26 . . . . Detroit	4 - 6 . . . . at Toronto
17 - 19 . . . . . .Toronto	5 - 7 . . . . at New York (AL)	28 - 29 . . . . .Miami	8 - 9 . . . . at Miami
20 - 23 . . . . .at Houston	9 - 11 . . . . Boston	31 . . . . .at Cincinnati	11 - 13 . . . . . .at Boston
24 - 26 . . . . . Kansas City	12 - 14 . . . . . Baltimore	**AUGUST**	14 - 16 . . . .New York (AL)
27 - 29 . . . . . . Cleveland	16 - 18 . . . . . at Toronto	1 - 2 . . . . . .at Cincinnati	17 - 20 . . . . Boston
MAY	19 - 21 . . . . .at Baltimore	3 - 5 . . . . at Toronto	21 - 24 . . . . .at Baltimore
1 - 3 . . . . .at Oakland	23 - 25 . . . . Oakland	7 - 9 . . . . Boston	25 - 27 . . at New York (AL)
6 - 7 . . . . .at Chicago (AL)	26 - 28 . . . . Seattle	10 - 13 . . . . . . .Toronto	

GENERAL INFORMATION
Stadium (year opened): Tropicana Field (1998).   **Playing Surface:** AstroTurf
Team Colors: Dark blue, light blue, yellow.   Game Day Grass 3D-60 H.
Home Dugout: First Base.

Assistant Director, Baseball R&D: Anirudh Kilambi. **Coordinator, Baseball Development:** Simon Rosenbaum. **Analyst, Baseball Development:** Jeff Sullivan **Assistants, Baseball Development:** Brad Ballew, Danielle Dockx, Mark Watson **Coordinator, Baseball Administration:** Samantha Bireley. **Coordinator, Major League Operations:** Jeremy Sowers. **Coordinator, Baseball Performance Science:** Ryan Pennell. **Assistant, Performance Science:** Vishnu Sarpeshkar. **Lead Sports Dietician:** Ryan Harmon. **Assistant Dietician:** Kate Martinez. **Biomechanist:** Mike McNally. **Developers, Baseball Systems:** Brandon Cordell, Ryan Kelley. Daniel Nolan. **Database Architect:** Clayton Elger. **Product Designers:** Luke Fair, Lauren Griffin. **Data Technician, R&D:** Michael Topol. **Analysts, R&D:** Keegan Henderson, Salem Marrero, Michael McClellan, David Marshall, Jason Pellettiere, Taylor Smith. Jr. **Analyst, R&D:** Josh Arthurs Jr. **Data Technician:** Ben Smith. **Dev Ops Engineer:** Louis Palma. **Assistant, Advance Scouting/Replay:** Robert Kinne. **Interpreter, Spanish:** Manny Navarro.

SKIP MILOS

Erik Neander

MAJOR LEAGUE STAFF

Manager: Kevin Cash. **Coaches: Bench**—Matt Quatraro, **Pitching**—Kyle Snyder, **Hitting**—Chad Mottola, **First Base**—Ozzie Timmons, **Third Base**—Rodney Linares, **Bullpen**—Stan Boroski, **Field Coordinator**—Paul Hoover. **Process /Analytics Coach**—Jonathan Erlichman.

MEDICAL/TRAINING

Medical Director: Dr. James Andrews. **Orthopedic Team Physician:** Dr. Koco Eaton. **Team Chiropractor:** Christopher Williams. **Massage Therapist:** Ray Allen. **ML Medical Coordinator:** Paul Harker. **Head Athletic Trainer:** Joe Benge.

PLAYER DEVELOPMENT

Telephone: (727) 825-3267. **Fax:** (727) 825-3493.

Director, Minor League Operations: Jeff McLerran. **Senior Advisor, Player Development and Baseball Operations:** Mitch Lukevics **Manager, Player Development:** George Pappas. **Administrator, International/Minor League Operations:** Giovanna Rodriguez. **Director, Pitching Development:** Dewey Robinson. **Assistant Director, Pitching Development:** Winston Doom **Assistant Director, Hitting Development:** Cole Figueroa. **Assistant, Minor League Operations:** Wilson Made. **Video Coordinator:** Brett Ebers. **Minor League Equipment Manager:** Tim McKechney. **Assistant Minor League Equipment Manager:** Shane Rossetti. **Florida Education Coordinator:** Lenore Sutton. **Field Coordinators:** Alejandro Freire, Michael Johns. **Minor League Coordinators: Pitching:** Jorge Moncada, Rolando Garza. **Hitting:** Greg Brown, Dan Dement, Steve Livesey. **Catching:** Tomas Francisco. **Infield:** Hector Torres, Ivan Ochoa. **OF/Baserunning:** Christian Prieto. **Medical:** Aaron Scott. **Rehab:** Joel Smith. **Latin America Medical:** Chris Tomashoff. **Latin America Cultural:** Jairo De La Rosa. **S&C:** Patrick Trainor. **Mental Skills:** Josh Kozuch, James Schwabach.

FARM SYSTEM

Class	Club (League)	Manager	Hitting Coach	Pitching Coach
Triple-A	Durham (IL)	Brady Williams	Kyle Wilson	Rick Knapp
Double-A	Montgomery (SL)	Morgan Ensberg	J. Nelson	Brian Reith
High A	Charlotte (FSL)	Jeff Smith	Brady North	Steve Watson
Low A	Bowling Green (MWL)	Blake Butera	W. Rincones	Jim Paduch
Short-season	Hudson Valley (NYP)	Rafael Valenzuela	Joe Szekely	R.C. Lichtenstein
Rookie	Princeton (APP)	Sean Smedley	Manny Castillo	Alberto Bastardo
Rookie Rays	(GCL)	Reinaldo Ruiz	F. Maldonado	M. DeMerritt/ J.Gonzalez
Rookie Rays 1	(DSL)	Julio Zorrilla	Omar Luna	L. Urena/Y. Almonte
Rookie Rays 2	(DSL)	Esteban Gonzalez	Alejandro Segovia	L. Romero/J. Sanchez

SCOUTING

Sr. Director, Pro Personnel & Pro Scouting: Kevin Ibach. **Assistant Director, Pro Personnel & Pro Scouting:** Ryan Bristow. **Analyst, Pro Personnel & Pro Scouting:** Tyler Chamberlain-Simon. **Sr. Director, Amateur Scouting:** Rob Metzler. **Assistant Director, Amateur Scouting:** Hamilton Marx. **Senior Advisor, Scouting/Baseball Operations:** R.J. Harrison. **Coordinator, Amateur Scouting:** Jeff Johnson. **Administrator, Amateur Scouting:** Sydney Malone. **Special Assignment Scout:** Fred Repke. **Pro Personnel Specialists:** Mike Brown, Jason Cole, Jason Grey, Mike Langill, Tyler Stohr. **Pro Scouts:** Ken Califano, Max Cohen, JD Elliby, Jose Gomez, Nate Howard, Brian Keegan, Ken Kravec, Dave Myers, Jaylon Pimentel, Jeff Stewart. **National Crosschecker:** Chuck Ricci. **Midwest Regional Supervisor:** Jeff Cornell. **Northeastern Regional Supervisor:** Brian Hickman. **Southeastern Regional Supervisor:** Kevin Elfering. **Western Regional Supervisor:** Jake Wilson. **Pitching Crosschecker:** Ryan Henderson. **Scout Supervisors:** Matt Alison, Steve Ames, James Bonnici, Zach Clark, Tom Couston, Rickey Drexler, Brett Foley, Tim Fortugno, Luke Harrigan, Landon Lassiter, David Hamlett, Joe Hastings, Milt Hill, Jaime Jones, Paul Kirsch, Reggie Lawson, Pat Murphy, Victor Rodriguez, Greg Whitworth. **Part-Time Area Scouts:** Jose Hernandez, Dave Jorn, Gil Martinez, Casey Onaga, Jack Sharp, Marcos Tovar, Lou Wieben. **Director, International Scouting:** Steve Miller. **Director, International Operations:** Patrick Walters. **Assistant Director, International Operations:** Ronnie Blanco. **International Crosschecker:** Brad Budzinski. **Consultant, International Operations:** John Gilmore. **Scouting Supervisor, Colombia:** Angel Contreras. **Scouting Supervisor, Dominican Republic:** Danny Santana. **Venezuela Crosschecker:** William Bergolla. **International Scouts:** Abraham Despradel, Remmy Hernandez, Marlon Roche, Juan Francisco Castillo, Carlos Leon, Edward Rojas (Venezuela), Tiago Campos (Brazil), Karla Espinoza (Mexico), Keith Hsu (Taiwan), Chairon Isenia (Curacao), Joe Park (Korea), Tateki Uchibori (Japan), Jesus Valdez (Mexico), Gustavo Zapata (Panama).

TEXAS RANGERS

Office Address: 734 Stadium Drive, Arlington, TX 76011.
Telephone: (817) 273-5222. **Website:** www.texasrangers.com. **Twitter:** @Rangers.

OWNERSHIP
Co-Chairman/Managing Partner: Ray C. Davis. **Co-Chairman:** Bob R. Simpson. **Chief Operating Officer:** Neil Leibman.

BUSINESS OPERATIONS
Executive VP, Business Operations: Rob Matwick. **Executive VP, Chief Marketing & Revenue Officer:** Joe Januszewski. **Executive VP/CFO:** Kellie Fischer. **Executive VP/General Counsel:** Katie Pothier. **Executive VP, Communications:** John Blake. **Executive VP, Entertainment/Productions:** Chuck Morgan. **Executive VP, Sports and Entertainment:** Sean Decker. **Sr. VP/Finance:** Starr Gulledge.

HUMAN RESOURCES/LEGAL/INFORMATION TECHNOLOGY
VP, Human Resources: Danita Maxwell. **Corporate Counsels:** Erin Kearney, Ilana Miller. **Director, Human Resources:** Mercedes Riley. **VP, Info Technology:** Mike Bullock. **Asst. VP, Customer Service:** Donnie Pordash. **Asst. VP, Business Operations:** Richard Price.

PROJECT DEVELOPMENT
Senior VP, Project Development: Jack Hill. **Project Accountant:** Kelley Walker.

Ray Davis

COMMUNICATIONS/COMMUNITY RELATIONS
VP, Broadcasting/Communications: Angie Swint. **Asst. VP, Player/Alumni Relations:** Taunee Taylor. **Sr. Director, Communications:** Rich Rice. **Director, Photography:** Kelly Gavin. **Manager, Communications:** Madison Pelletier. **Manager, Baseball Information:** Matt Mallian. **Coordinator, Media Services:** Kate Munson. **Coordinator, Communications:** Tyler Strachan. **Asst. Director, Player Relations:** Monique Corralez. **Coordinator, Player Relations:** Ashley Quintilone. **VP, Community Outreach/Executive Director, Foundation:** Karin Morris. **Director, Youth Baseball and Youth Academy Programs:** Juan Leonel Garciga. **Manager, Development:** Justin Henry. **Manager, Foundation & Community Outreach:** Reynaldo Casas.

FACILITIES/RETAIL/EVENTS
Sr. VP, Ballpark Venue Operations & Guest Experience: Mike Healy. **VP, Security & Parking:** Blake Miller. **Sr. Director, Parking & Security:** Mike Smith. **Sr. Director, Maintenance:** Mike Call. **Sr. Director, Facility Operations:** Duane Arber. **Director, Major League Grounds:** Dennis Klein. **Director, Complex Grounds:** Steve Ballard. **Director, Special Projects & Events:** John Marsh. **Director, Parking, Security & Badges:** Dana Jons. **Director, Tours & Experiences:** Lindsey Hopper. **Director, Sales:** Jared Schrom. **Director, Event Operations:** Pedro Soto, Jr.

TICKET AND SPONSORSHIP SALES
Sr. VP, Ticket Sales & Service: Paige Farragut. **Sr. VP, Partnerships & Client Services:** Jim Cochrane. **Director,**

2020 SCHEDULE
Standard Game Times: 7:05 p.m.; Sun. 2:05.

MARCH		JULY	SEPTEMBER
26 - 29 . . . . . . .at Seattle	8 - 10 . . . . . at Tampa Bay	29 - 30 . . . . Atlanta	14 - 16 . . . . . . .at Detroit
31 . . . . . Los Angeles (AL)	11 - 13 . . . . . . .Toronto	**JULY**	17 - 19 . . . . .at Baltimore
APRIL	14 - 17 . . . . Boston	1 . . . . Atlanta	22 - 23 . . . . . .at Houston
1 - 2 . . . Los Angeles (AL)	20 - 21 . . . . .at Oakland	3 - 5 . . . . . Chicago (AL)	24 - 25 . . . . . .Colorado
3 - 5 . . . . .Tampa Bay	22 - 24 . . .at Kansas City	7 - 9 . . . . at Miami	27 - 30 . . . . . Baltimore
8 . . . . at Colorado	26 - 28 . . . . .Washington	10 - 12 . . at New York (AL)	**SEPTEMBER**
10 - 12 . . . . . . Houston	29 - 31 . . . . Oakland	17 - 19 . . . . . Minnesota	1 - 4 . . at Los Angeles (AL)
13 - 15 . . .New York (AL)	**JUNE**	20 - 23 . . . . . . Houston	5 - 6 . . . . .at Oakland
17 - 19 . . .at Chicago (AL)	1 - 3 . . Los Angeles (AL)	24 - 26 . . Los Angeles (AL)	7 - 10 . . . . Seattle
21 - 22 . . at Philadelphia	4 - 7 . . . . at Toronto	29 . . . . .at Seattle	11 - 13 . . . . . . Houston
24 - 26 . . . . Seattle	10 - 12 . . . . . .at Houston	31 . . . . .at Oakland	15 - 17 . . . . at Minnesota
27 - 29 . . . . Oakland	12 - 14 . . . . . Cleveland	**AUGUST**	18 - 20 . . at New York (NL)
MAY	15 - 17 . . . . . Kansas City	1 - 2 . . . . .at Oakland	22 - 24 . . . . Oakland
1 - 3 . . . . .at Boston	19 - 21 . at Los Angeles (AL)	4 . . . . at Los Angeles (AL)	25 - 27 . . . . Seattle
4 - 7 . . . . . .at Cleveland	23 - 24 . . . . . . .at Seattle	6 - 9 . . . . Detroit	
	27 - 28 . . . . . .at Houston	11 - 12 . . . . .Philadelphia	

GENERAL INFORMATION
Stadium (year opened): Globe Life Park in Arlington (1994). **Team Colors:** Royal blue and red.
Home Dugout: First Base. **Playing Surface:** Grass.

Season Tickets: Dan Hessling. **Director, Inside Sales:** Nick Richardson. **Director, Group Sales:** Jamie Roberts. **Director, Suites & Premium Services:** Delia Wilms. **Director Ticket Services:** Mike Lentz. **Director, Business Analytics:** Katie Morgan. **Director, Corporate Partnerships:** Chad Wynn. **Director, Corporate Sales:** Sean Ferretti. **Director, Business Development:** Devron Jeffers.

MARKETING/GAME PRESENTATION
VP, Marketing: Travis Dillon. **Director, Marketing & Advertising:** Milagros Pacheco. **Creative Director:** Scott Biggers. **Senior Director, Game Entertainment/Productions:** Chris DeRuyscher. **Manager, Social Media:** Kyle Smith.

Jon Daniels

BASEBALL OPERATIONS
Telephone: (817) 273-5222. **Fax:** (817) 273-5285.
President, Baseball Operations/General Manager: Jon Daniels. **Executive Assistant to President, Baseball Operations/GM:** Joda Parent. **Assistant General Managers:** Josh Boyd, Mike Daly, Shiraz Rehman. **Special Assistants to the GM:** Colby Lewis, Brandon McCarthy, Darren Oliver, Ivan Rodriguez, Michael Young. **Senior Director, Baseball Systems:** Todd Slavinsky. **Director, Pitching Analysis:** Todd Walther. **Director, Baseball Analytics:** Ryan Murray. **Director, Peak Performance:** Josiah Igono. **Director, Dominican Republic Operations:** Allen Rowin. **Assistant Director, Baseball Operations:** Ben Baroody. **Assistant Director, Baseball Systems:** Ethan Faggett. **Senior Developers, Baseball Systems:** Bradley Ankrom, Kim Eskew. **Developer, Baseball Systems:** Alexander Booth. **Analysts, Baseball Operations:** Bobby Bandelow, Andrew Koo, R.J. Walsh.

MAJOR LEAGUE STAFF
Manager: Chris Woodward.
Coaches: Bench—Don Wakamatsu. **Pitching**—Julio Rangel. **Hitting**—Luis Ortiz. **First Base**—Héctor Ortiz. **Third Base**—Tony Beasley. **Bullpen**—Doug Mathis. **Assistant Hitting Coach**—Callix Crabbe. **ML Field Coordinator**—Corey Ragsdale.

MEDICAL/TRAINING
Senior Director, Medical Operations: Jamie Reed. **Team Physician:** Dr. Keith Meister. **Head Trainer:** Matt Lucero. **Assistant Trainer:** Jacob Newburn. **Physical Therapist:** Regan Wong. **Director, Strength/Conditioning:** José Vázquez.

PLAYER DEVELOPMENT
Telephone: (817) 436-5999. **Fax:** (817) 273-5285.
Director, Minor League Operations: Paul Kruger. **Field Coordinator:** Matt Hagen. **Coordinators:** Kenny Holmberg (infield), Danny Clark (pitching), Jono Arnold (pitching), Cody Atkinson (hitting), Greg Hibbard (roving pitching), Geno Petralli (roving coach), Turtle Thomas (roving catching coach), Keith Comstock (rehab pitching). **Director, Performance:** Napoleon Pichardo. **Arizona Medical Coordinator:** Sean Fields. **International Medical:** Chris Olson. **Minor League Strength Coordinator:** Logan Frandsen. **Coordinator, Arizona Operations:** Stosh Hoover. **Minor League Equipment Manager:** Chris Ackerman. **Coordinator, Rangers Village:** Lauren Fields. **Assistant, Rangers Village:** Austin Argust.

FARM SYSTEM

Class	Club (League)	Manager	Hitting Coach	Pitching Coach
Triple-A	Nashville (PCL)	Darwin Barney	Chase Lambin	Brendan Sagara
Double-A	Frisco (TL)	Bobby Wilson	Josue Perez	Jeff Andrews
High A	Down East (CL)	Josh Johnson	Jared Goedert	Steve Mintz
Low A	Hickory (SAL)	Carlos Cardoza	Jason Hart	Jose Jaimes
Short-season	Spokane (NWL)	Sean Cashman	Sharnol Adriana	Bryan Conger
Rookie	Rangers (AZL)	TBA	Eric Dorton/Brad Flanders	Jesus Delgado/Jordan Tiegs
Rookie	Rangers (DSL)	Carlos Maldonado	Lance Miles/Luis Sumoza	Pablo Blanco/Ricardo Valencia

SCOUTING
Senior Director, Pro/International Scouting: Ross Fenstermaker. **Assistant, Pro Scouting:** Mike Parnell. **Special Assistants:** Mike Anderson, Scot Engler, Scott Littlefield, Greg Smith. **Pro Scouts:** Russ Ardolina, Elliott Blair, Jay Eddings, Jonathan George, Mike Grouse, Donzell McDonald, Vinny Rottino, Mitchell Webb. **Special Assignment Scout:** Curtis Jung. **Senior Director, Amateur Scouting:** Kip Fagg. **Assistant Director, Amateur Scouting:** Adam Lewkowicz. **National Crosscheckers: Eastern Crosschecker:** Ryan Coe, **Special Assignment Crosschecker:** Bobby Crook, **West Coast Crosschecker:** Casey Harvie, **National Crosschecker:** Jake Krug, **Midwest Crosschecker:** Demond Smith, **Southeast Crosschecker:** Brian Williams. **Area Scouts:** Brett Campbell, Chris Collias, Tommy Duenas, Steve Flores, Todd Guggiana, Jay Heafner, Levi Lacey, Brian Matthews, Gary McGraw, Michael Medici, Brian Morrison, Patrick Perry, Takeshi Sakurayama, Josh Simpson, Dustin Smith, Randy Taylor, Derrick Tucker. **Director, International Scouting:** Rafic Saab. **Assistant Director, International Scouting:** Hamilton Wise. **Asst. International Scouting:** Jonny Clum. Supervisor, **Dominican Republic:** Willy Espinal. **International Scouts:** Jhonny Gomez (Crosschecker, Venezuela). Chu Halabi (Latin America Crosschecker). Jose Fernandez (International Scout). Yfrain Linares (Latin America Crosschecker), Johnny Gomez (Crosschecker, Venezuela), Maikol Rojas (D.R.Video Scout), JC Alvarez (D.R.), Christian Cabral (D.R., Nelson Muniz (D.R.), Carlos Gonzalez (Venezuela), Jose Gabriel Rodriguez (Venezuela), Juan Salazar (Venezuela), Carlos Plaza (Venezuela), Rafael Cedeno (Panama), Hamilton Sarabia (Colombia), Efrain Lara (Mexico). **Manager, Dominican Republic Operations:** Jose Vargas. **Assistant, International Operations:** Angel Jimenez. **Manager, International Player Personnel:** Andre Park. **DR Complex Administrator:** Marlenis Alejo. **Director, Pacific Rim Operations:** Joe Furukawa (Japan). **Manager, Pacific Rim:** Hajime Watabe (Japan). **International Scout:** Daniel Chang (Taiwan).

TORONTO BLUE JAYS

Office/Mailing Address: 1 Blue Jays Way, Suite 3200, Toronto, Ontario M5V 1J1.
Telephone: (416) 341-1000. **Fax:** (416) 341-1245. **Website:** www.bluejays.com.

OWNERSHIP

Operated by: Toronto Blue Jays Baseball Club. **Principal Owner:** Rogers Communications Inc. **Chairman, Toronto Blue Jays:** Edward Rogers. **Vice Chairman, Rogers Communications Inc.:** Phil Lind. **President and CEO, Rogers Communication:** Joe Natale. **President, Media Business Unit:** Rick Brace. **Chief Financial Officer, Rogers Communication:** Tony Staffieri.

BUSINESS OPERATIONS

Mark Shapiro

President and CEO: Mark A. Shapiro. **President Emeritus:** Paul Beeston. **Executive Vice President, Baseball Operations/General Manager:** Ross Atkins. **Senior Vice President, Business Operations:** Bryan Blew. **Executive Assistant to the President/CEO:** Gail Ricci.

FINANCE/ADMINISTRATION

Director, Finance: Janet Chant. **Senior Manager, Blue Jays US Payroll & Benefits:** Sharon Dykstra. **Senior Manager, Finance:** Josh Hoffman. **Manager, Financial Business:** Leslie Galant-Gardiner. **Manager, Finance:** Derek Nicholson. **Manager, Treasury & Vault Operations:** Garrett Mercer. **Payroll Analyst:** Joyce Chan. **Senior Financial Analyst:** Jan Andrejuk, Melissa Patterson. **Financial Analyst:** Troy Mercuri.

MARKETING/COMMUNITY RELATIONS

Senior VP, Marketing & Business Operations: Marnie Starkman. **Director, Creative Services & Marketing Management:** Sherry Oosterhuis. **Director, Promotions & Events:** Michelle Seniuk. **Senior Manager, Game Entertainment & Producer:** Stefanie Wright. **Senior Manager, Player Relations & Community Marketing:** Shannon Curley. **Manager, Events Production:** Carol Balfour. **Program Manager, Amateur Baseball:** T.J. Burton. **Program Manager, MyBlueJays:** Maureen Kinghorn. **Marking Department Marketing & Alumni Relations:** Maria Cresswell.

BASEBALL MEDIA

Director, Baseball Media: Richard Griffin. **Senior Manager, Business Communications:** Jessica Beard. **Manager, Baseball Media:** Ryan Brown. **Manager, Social Media:** Simone Gervais. **Social Content Specialist:** Nico Canavo. **Social Community Manager:** Alykhan Ravjiani. **Business Communications Specialist:** Madeleine Davidson. **Coordinator, Baseball Media:** Adam Felton.

TRAVEL/CLUBHOUSE

Director, Team Travel/Clubhouse Operations: Mike Shaw. **Senior Manger, Visiting Clubhouse:** Kevin Malloy. **Clubhouse Manager, Operations:** Scott Blinn. **Clubhouse Manager, Equipment:** Mustafa Hassan.

2020 SCHEDULE

Standard Game Times: 7:07 p.m.; Sat/Sun: 1:07

MARCH
26 - 29 . . . . Boston
30 - 31 . . . . . Cincinnati

APRIL
1 . . . . Cincinnati
2 - 5 . . . at New York (AL)
6 - 7 . . . . at Philadelphia
9 - 12 . . . . . Kansas City
13 - 15 . . . . . Minnesota
17 - 19 . . . at Tampa Bay
21 - 23 . . . . . at Boston
24 - 26 . . . . at Baltimore
27 - 29 . . . . . . Boston

MAY
1 - 3 . . . . . New York (AL)
4 - 6 . . . . Baltimore

8 - 10 . . . . . .at Oakland
11 - 13 . . . . . . .at Texas
15 - 17 . . .at Chicago (AL)
18 - 20 . . . . . . Houston
21 - 24 . . . . . . Baltimore
26 - 28 . . . at Tampa Bay
29 - 31 . . . .at Baltimore

JUNE
2 - 3 . . . . . . .at St. Louis
4 - 7 . . . . Texas
9 - 11 . . . . Seattle
12 - 14 . . . . . .at Detroit
16 - 18 . . . . .Tampa Bay
19 - 21 . . . at Pittsburgh
23 - 24 . . . . at Milwaukee
26 - 28 . . Los Angeles (AL)
30 . . . . . . Chicago (AL)

JULY
1 - 2 . . . . . Chicago (AL)
3 - 5 . . . . .New York (AL)
6 - 8 . . . . .at Boston
9 - 12 . . . . at Minnesota
17 - 19 . . . . . Cleveland
20 - 22 . . . . Boston
25 - 26 . . . . . .at Seattle
28 - 30 .at Los Angeles (AL)
31 . . . . Baltimore

AUGUST
1 - 2 . . . . . . Baltimore
3 - 5 . . . . . . .Tampa Bay
6 - 9 . . . . . . .at Houston
10 - 13 . . . . at Tampa Bay
14 - 16 . . . . Chicago (NL)
18 - 19 . . . . . . St. Louis

20 - 23 . . at New York (AL)
24 - 26 . . . . .at Kansas City
27 - 30 . . . . Oakland

SEPTEMBER
1 - 3 . . . . Detroit
4 - 6 . . . . .Tampa Bay
8 - 10 . . . . . at Baltimore
11 - 13 . . at New York (AL)
15 - 16 . . . .Philadelphia
18 - 20 . . . .New York (AL)
22 - 24 . . . . . .at Boston
25 - 27 . . . . .at Cleveland

GENERAL INFORMATION

Stadium (year opened): Rogers Centre (1989).
Team Colors: Blue and white.

Home Dugout: Third Base.
Playing Surface: AstroTurf 3D Xtreme.

BASEBALL OPERATIONS

Senior Vice President, Player Personnel: Tony Lacava. **Vice President, Baseball Operations:** Ben Cherington. **VP, International Scouting:** Andrew Tinnish. **Assistant General Manager:** Joe Sheehan. **Director, Baseball Operations:** Michael Murov. **Director, Team Travel & Clubhouse Operations:** Michael Shaw. **Senior Manager, Visiting Clubhouse:** Kevin Malloy. **Senior Manager, Baseball Administration:** Heather Connolly. **Clubhouse Manager, Operations:** Scott Blinn. **Clubhouse Manager, Equipment:** Mustafa Hassan. **Assistant Director, Research & Development:** Sanjay Choudhury. **Assistant Director, Baseball Operations:** Jeremy Reesor. **Coordinator, Baseball Research:** Adam Yudelman. **Assistant, Baseball Research:** Graydon Carruthers, Cal Aldred, Liam Stevenson. **Assistant, Advance Scouting:** John Babocsi. **Fellow:** Ginger Poulson. **Data Architect:** Peter Saunders. **Baseball Systems Developer:** Spencer Estey. **Bullpen Catcher:** Alex Andreopoulos. **Bilingual Player Interpreter:** Hector Lebron. **Major League Video Coordinator:** Eric Slotter. **Executive Assistant to the General Manager:** Anna Coppola.

Ross Atkins

MAJOR LEAGUE STAFF

Manager: Charlie Montoyo. **Coaches: Bench**—Dave Hudgens, **Pitching**—Pete Walker, **Hitting**—Guillermo Martinez, **First Base**—Mark Budzinski, **Third Base**—Luis Rivera, **Bullpen**—Matt Buschmann. **Major League Coach** — John Schneider. **Bullpen Catcher:** Alex Andreopoulos.

HIGH PERFORMANCE/MEDICAL STAFF

VP, High Performance: Angus Mugford. **Assistant Director, High Performance Operations:** Dehra Harris. **Major League Head Athletic Trainer:** Jose Ministral. **Major League Assistant Athletic Trainer:** Voon Chong. **Major League Assistant Physical Therapist:** Scott Peters. **Head of Strength & Conditioning:** Donovan Santas. **Major League Assistant Strength & Conditioning Coach:** Scott Weberg. **Medical Coordinator:** Pat Chasse. **Assistant Medical Coordinator:** Drew MacDonald.

PLAYER DEVELOPMENT

Telephone: (727) 734-8007. **Fax:** (727) 734-8162.

Director, Player Development: Gil Kim. **Director, Minor League Operations:** Charlie Wilson. **Director, Latin America Operations:** Sandy Rosario. **Business Manager, Minor League Operations:** Michelle Rodgers. **Assistant Director, Player Development:** Joe Sclafani. **Assistant, Player Development:** Michael Rivera. **Administrative Assistant:** Dea Jones. **Field Coordinator:** Casey Candaele. **Pitching Coordinator:** Jeff Ware. **Rehab Pitching Coordinator:** Darold Knowles. **Hitting Coordinator:** Hunter Mense. **Infield Coordinator:** Danny Solano. **Special Assistant to Player Development:** Tim Raines. **Short-Season Field Coordinator:** John Tamargo. **Special Assistant, Player Development:** Omar Malave. **Video Coordinator:** Eric Slotter. **Video Advisor:** Robert Baumander. **Minor League Performance and Development Analyst:** Evan Short. **Equipment Coordinator:** Billy Wardlow.

FARM SYSTEM

Class	Club (League)	Manager	Hitting Coach	Pitching Coach	Position Coach
Triple-A	Buffalo (IL)	Ken Huckaby	Corey Hart	Jeff Ware	Devon White
Double-A	New Hampshire (EL)	Cesar Martin	Matt Young	Jim Czajkowski	Chris Schaeffer
High A	Dunedin (FSL)	Donnie Murphy	Matt Hague	Antonio Caceres	George Carroll
Low A	Lansing (MWL)	Luis Hurtado	Ryan Wright	Phil Cundari	Dave Pano
Short-season	Vancouver (NWL)	Brent Lavallee	Andy Fermin	Demetre Kokoris	Danny Canellas
Rookie	Bluefield (APP)	Jose Mayorga	Paul Elliott	Rafael Lazo	Aaron Mathews
Rookie	Blue Jays (GCL)	Dennis Holmberg	Michel Abreu	Cory Popham	Unavailable
Rookie	Blue Jays (DSL)	Dane Fujinaka	Petr Stribrcky	Yoel Hernandez	Jose Mateo

SCOUTING

Director, Pro Scouting: Ryan Mittleman. **Manager, Baseball Operations & Pro Scouting:** David Haynes. **Pro Scouting Analyst:** Tommy Farah. **Special Assignment Scout:** Russ Bove. **Special Assignment Scout:** Dean Decillis. **Major League Scouts:** Sal Butera,, Jim Skaalen. **Professional Scouts:** Matt Anderson, Kevin Briand, Blake Bentley, David May Jr, Marc Lippman, Mitch Leeds, Tim Rooney. **Player Personnel Coordinators:** Carson Cistulli, Jon Lalonde, Nick Manno, Brent Urcheck. **Pro Scouting Fellow:** Stephen Yoo.

Director, Amateur Scouting: Shane Farrell. **Manager, Amateur & International Scouting:** Harry Einbinder. **Coordinator, Amateur Scouting:** Kory Lafreniere. **National Supervisor:** Blake Crosby. **Regional Crosscheckers:** CJ Ebarb, Michael Youngberg, Matt Bishoff, Jamie Lehman. **Crosscheckers:** Brian Johnson, Paul Tinnell. **Area Scouts:** Joey Aversa, Coulson Barbiche Jr., Jason Beverlin., Brandon Bishoff, Dallas Black, Adam Arnold, Ryan Fox, Pete Holmes, Randy Kramer, Jim Lentine, Nate Murrie, Don Norris, Matt O'Brien, Wes Penick, Bud Smith, Mike Tidick, Max Semler, Manny Padron, Tom Burns, Chris Curtis, Matt Huck. **Amateur Scouting Video Coordinators:** Chirag Nanavati, Kyle Fleming. **Canadian Scouting:** Jay Lapp, Rene Tosoni, Jasmin Roy, Pat Griffin. **Director, Latin American Operations:** Sandy Rosario. **Assistant, International Scouting:** Julio Ramirez. **Dominican Scouting Supervisor:** Lorenzo Perez. **Mexican Scouting Supervisor:** Aaron Acosta. **Venezuelan Scouting Supervisor:** Jose Contreras. **International Scouting: Venezuela**—Franklin Briceno, Miguel Leal, **Dominican Republic**—Alexis de la Cruz, Luciano del Rosario, Eric Ramirez, Joan Gomez, Luis Natera, **Colombia**—Enrique Falcon, **Nicaragua**—Daniel Sotolo, **Panama**—Alex Zapata. **Scouting Coordinator, South America:** Francisco Plasencia.

WASHINGTON NATIONALS

Office Address: 1500 South Capitol Street SE, Washington, DC 20003.
Telephone: (202) 640-7000. **Fax:** (202) 547-0025.
Website: www.nationals.com.

OWNERSHIP
Managing Principal Owner: Mark D. Lerner. **Founding Principal Owner:** Theodore N. Lerner.
Principal Owners: Annette M. Lerner, Marla Lerner Tanenbaum, Debra Lerner Cohen, Robert K. Tanenbaum, Edward L. Cohen, Judy Lenkin Lerner.

BUSINESS OPERATIONS

Mark Lerner

Chief Operating Officer, Lerner Sports: Alan H. Gottlieb. **Chief Financial Officer:** Lori Creasy. **Senior Vice President:** Elise Holman.

BALLPARK ENTERPRISES
Vice President, Corporate Strategy: Emily Dunham. **Senior Directors, Ballpark Enterprises:** Lise Sutherland, Derrick Mays.

LEGAL
Senior Vice President & General Counsel, Baseball & Business Operations: Damon Jones. **Deputy General Counsel:** Betsy Philpott.

HUMAN RESOURCES
Vice President, Human Resources: Alexa Herndon. **Senior Director, Human Resources:** Kelvin Scott. **Director, Benefits:** Stephanie Giroux.

COMMUNICATIONS
Vice President, Communications: Jennifer Giglio. **Senior Executive Director, Communications:** Elizabeth Alexander. **Director, Communications:** Kyle Brostowitz. **Manager, Communications:** Melissa Strozza. **Manager, Communications:** Christopher Browne.

COMMUNITY RELATIONS
Vice President, Community Engagement: Gregory McCarthy. **Executive Director, Player & Community Relations:** Shawn Bertani. **Director, Community Relations:** Nicole Murray.

BROADCASTING/GAME PRESENTATION
Senior Vice President, Broadcasting & Game Presentation: Jacqueline Coleman. **Vice President, Production & Broadcasting:** David Lundin. **Director, Game Production:** Mike Masino. **Director, Video & Broadcast Engineering:** Benjamin Smith.

TICKETING/SALES
Vice President, Ticket Sales & Service: Ryan Bringger. **Senior Director, Ticket Sales:** Joseph Dellwo.

2020 SCHEDULE
Standard Game Times: Mon.-Sat., 7:05 pm; Sun., 1:35 pm.

MARCH
26-29 . . . at New York (NL)
30-31 . . . . at Miami

APRIL
1 . . . . at Miami
2-5 . . . . . . New York (NL)
6-8 . . . . Miami
10-12 . at Los Angeles (NL)
13-14 . . . . .at Seattle
16-19 . . . . Chicago (NL)
21-23 . . . Los Angeles (NL)
24-26 . . . at San Francisco
28-30 . . . . . at Milwaukee

MAY
1-3 . . . . Cincinnati

5-7 . . . . Arizona
8-10 . . . . .at Chicago (NL)
12-14 . at Los Angeles (AL)
14-17 . . . . at Arizona
19-20 . . . . Seattle
22-25 . . . . .Miami
26-28 . . . . .at Texas
29-31 . . . . at Philadelphia

JUNE
1-3 . . . . .Milwaukee
4-7 . . . . . .New York (NL)
9-11 . . . . at Atlanta
12-14 . . at New York (NL)
16-18 . . . . San Francisco
19-21 . . . . Atlanta
22-25 . . . . . . Pittsburgh

26-28 . . . .at Cincinnati
30 . . . . .at St. Louis

JULY
1-2 . . . . .at St. Louis
3-5 . . . . Houston
7-9 . . . . St. Louis
10-12 . . . . .Philadelphia
17-19 . . . . at Pittsburgh
20-23 . . . . at Philadelphia
24-26 . . . . Atlanta
27-29 . . . . Colorado
31 . . . . at Atlanta

AUGUST
1-2 . . . . at Atlanta
4-6 . . . . at Miami

8-9 . . . . . . .at Baltimore
10-12 . . . . Oakland
13-16 . . . . . . San Diego
18-20 . . . . . at Colorado
21-23 . . . . at San Diego
25-27 . . . .New York (NL)
28-30 . . . . .Philadelphia

SEPTEMBER
1-3 . . . . Atlanta
4-6 . . . . at New York (NL)
8-10 . . . . at Philadelphia
11-13 . . . . at Miami
15-16 . . . . . Baltimore
18-20 . . . . .Miami
21-24 . . . . . . at Atlanta
25-27 . . . . .Philadelphia

GENERAL INFORMATION
Stadium (year opened):
Nationals Park (2008).
Team Colors: Red, white and blue.

Home Dugout: First Base.
Playing Surface: Grass.

BALLPARK OPERATIONS
Senior Vice President, Ballpark Operations: Frank Gambino. **Vice President, Ballpark Ops:** Jonathan Stahl.

BASEBALL OPERATIONS

President of Baseball Operations and General Manager: Mike Rizzo. **Assistant General Manager & Vice President, Player Personnel:** Doug Harris. **Assistant General Manager & Vice President, Scouting Operations:** Kris Kline. **Assistant General Manager & Vice President, Finance:** Ted Towne. **Assistant General Manager & Vice President, International Operations:** Johnny DiPuglia. **Assistant General Manager, Baseball Operations:** Michael DeBartolo. **Assistant General Manager, Baseball Research & Development:** Sam Mondry-Cohen. **Assistant General Manager, Player Development:** Mark Scialabba. **Senior Advisor to the General Manager:** Jack McKeon, Phillip Rizzo. **Special Assistant, Major League Administration:** Harolyn Cardozo. **Assistant, Major League Administration:** Jordan Missal. **Senior Analyst, Baseball Operations:** James Badas. **Coordinator, Baseball Operations:** John Wulf. **Manager, Advance Scouting:** Jonathan Tosches. **Coordinator, Advance Scouting:** Greg Ferguson. **Advance Scout:** Jim Cuthbert. **Assistant, Major League Video/Technology:** Kenny Diaz.

Mike Rizzo

BASEBALL RESEARCH AND DEVELOPMENT
Director, Baseball Research: Lee Mendelowitz. **Director, Software Development:** Isaac Gerhart-Hines. **Senior Analyst, Baseball R&D:** Max Ehrman, Scott Van Lenten. **Analysts, Baseball R&D:** Saul Forman, David Gagnon, David Higgins, Jordan Rassman. **Data Engineer, Baseball R&D:** Chris Jordan. **Senior Developer, Baseball R&D:** Jay Liu. **Developer, Baseball R&D:** Ted Lopez.

MAJOR LEAGUE OPERATIONS
Vice President, Clubhouse Operations & Team Travel: Rob McDonald. **Clubhouse & Equipment Manager:** Mike Wallace. **Visiting Clubhouse Manager:** Matt Rosenthal. **Equipment Manager:** Dan Wallin. **Major/Minor League Equipment Coordinator:** Calvin Minasian. **Assistant, Clubhouse & Team Travel:** Ryan Wiebe. **Clubhouse Assistants:** Mike Gordon, Andrew Melnick, Gregory Melnick.

MAJOR LEAGUE STAFF
Manager: Dave Martinez. **Coaches: Bench—** Tim Bogar. **Pitching—**Paul Menhart. **Hitting—**Kevin Long. **First Base—** Bob Henley. **Third Base—** Chip Hale. **Bullpen—**Henry Blanco. **Assistant Hitting Coach:** Pat Roessler.

MEDICAL/TRAINING
Executive Director, Medical Services: Harvey Sharman. **Lead Team Physician:** Dr. Robin West. **Director, Mental Conditioning:** Mark Campbell. **Director, Athletic Training:** Paul Lessard. **Head Athletic Trainer:** Dale Gilbert.

PLAYER DEVELOPMENT
Vice President, Senior Advisor to the General Manager: Bob Boone. **Director, Minor League Operations:** Ryan Thomas. **Senior Advisor, Player Development:** Spin Williams. **Manager, Minor League Operations:** JJ Estevez. **Florida Operations Manager:** Dianne Wiebe. **Co-Field Coordinators:** Jeff Garber, Tommy Shields. **Pitching Coordinator:** Brad Holman. **Hitting Coordinator:** Troy Gingrich. **Outfield/Baserunning Coordinator:** Gary Thurman. **Catching Coordinator:** Michael Barrett. **Quality Control Coordinator:** Matt LeCroy. **Medical and Rehab Coordinator:** Jon Kotredes. **Assistant Minor League Medical Coordinator:** Jeff Allred. **Rehab Pitching Coordinator:** Mark Grater. **Strength and Conditioning Coordinator:** Tony Rogowski. **Baseball Operations Video Coordinator:** James Goodwin. **Minor League Clubhouse & Equipment Coordinator:** Carlos Felix. **Player Education and Cultural Development Coordinator:** Andrew Scarlata.

FARM SYSTEM

Class	Club	Manager	Hitting Coach	Pitching Coach
Triple-A	Fresno (PCL)	Randy Knorr	Brian Daubach	Michael Tejera
Double-A	Harrisburg (EL)	Billy Gardner Jr.	Brian Rupp	Sam Narron
High A	Fredericksburg (CL)	Tripp Keister	Luis Ordaz	Justin Lord
Low A	Hagerstown (SAL)	Mario Lisson	Jorge Mejia	Pat Rice
Short-season	Auburn (NYP)	Patrick Anderson	Mark Harris	Franklin Bravo
Rookie	Nationals (GCL)	Rocket Wheeler	Amaury Garcia	Larry Pardo
Rookie	Nationals (DSL)	Sandy Martinez	Freddy Guzman	Edwin Hurtado

SCOUTING
Director, Scouting Operations: Eddie Longosz. **Director, Player Procurement:** Kasey McKeon. **Director, Pitching Evaluation & Special Asst. to the President of Baseball Ops & GM:** Jeff Zona. **Assistant Director, Amateur Scouting:** Mark Baca. **Special Assistants to the President of Baseball Operations & GM:** Steve Arnieri, Chuck Cottier, Mike Cubbage, Mike Daughtry, Dan Jennings, Ron Rizzi, Jay Robertson, Bob Schaefer, Pete Vuckovich, De Jon Watson, Terry Wetzel. **Major League Professional Scout:** Colin Sabean. **East Crosschecker:** Alan Marr. **Midwest Crosschecker:** Jimmy Gonzales. **West Crosschecker:** Fred Costello. **Southeast Crosschecker and Area Supervisor:** Alex Morales. **Area Supervisors:** Justin Bloxom, Bryan Byrne, Brian Cleary, Ben Gallo, Jerad Head, Tommy Jackson, Brandon Larson, Steve Leavitt, John Malzone, Bobby Myrick, Scott Ramsay, Eric Robinson, Mitch Sokol, Cody Staab. **Director, International Operations:** Mike Cadahia. **Director, Latin American Scouting:** Fausto Severino. **Director, Dominican Republic Academy:** Jazhiel Morel. **Assistant, International Scouting:** Taisuke Sato. **Crosscheckers:** Tony Arias, Alex Rodriguez, Modesto Ulloa, Riki Vasquez. **Coordinator, Venezuela:** German Robles. **Colombia:** Eduardo Cabrera. **Curacao and Aruba:** David Leer. **Dominican Republic Supervisor:** Pablo Arias. **Dominican Republic:** Virgilio De Leon, Bolivar Pelletier, Carlos Ulloa. **Panama:** Miguel Ruiz. **Venezuela:** Oscar Alvarado, Salvador Donadelli, Juan Indriago, Ronald Morillo, Juan Munoz.

INFORMATION

LOCAL MEDIA INFORMATION

AMERICAN LEAGUE

BALTIMORE ORIOLES
Radio Announcers: Jim Hunter, Kevin Brown, Ben McDonald, Brian Roberts. **Flagship Station:** WJZ-FM 105.7 The Fan.
TV Announcers: Mike Bordick, Brian Roberts, Tom Davis, Jim Palmer, Gary Thorne. **Flagship Station:** Mid-Atlantic Sports Network.

BOSTON RED SOX
Radio Announcers: Joe Castiglione, Will Flamming, Sean McDonough, Lou Merloni. **Flagship Station:** WEEI (93.7 FM).
TV Announcers: Dave O'Brien, Jerry Remy. **Flagship Station:** New England Sports Network (regional cable).

CHICAGO WHITE SOX
Radio Announcers: Ed Farmer, Darrin Jackson. **Flagship Station:** WLS-AM 720.
TV Announcers: Steve Stone, Jason Benetti. **Flagship Stations:** WGN TV-9, WPWR-TV, NBC Sports Chicago (regional cable).

CLEVELAND INDIANS
Radio Announcers: Tom Hamilton, Jim Rosenhaus. **Flagship Station:** WTAM 1000-AM.
TV Announcers: Rick Manning, Matt Underwood, Al Pawlowski (Pre/post). **Flagship Station:** FOX Sports Ohio.

DETROIT TIGERS
Radio Announcers: Dan Dickerson, Jim Price. **Flagship Station:** WXYT 97.1 FM and AM 1270.
TV Announcers: Jack Morris, Kirk Gibson, Matt Shepherd, Craig Monroe, John Keating. **Flagship Station:** FOX Sports Detroit (regional cable).

HOUSTON ASTROS
Radio Announcers: Steve Sparks, Robert Ford. **Spanish:** Alex Trevino, Francisco Romero, Alex Trevino (Spanish), Francisco Romero (Spanish). **Flagship Stations:** KBME 790-AM, KLAT 1010-AM (Spanish).
TV Announcers: Todd Kalas, Geoff Blum, Julia Morales. **Flagship Station:** AT&T Sports Net Southwest.

KANSAS CITY ROYALS
Radio Announcers: Denny Matthews, Steve Physioc, Steve Stewart. **Kansas City Affiliate:** KCSP 610-AM.
TV Announcers: Ryan Lefebvre, Rex Hudler, Joel Goldberg, Steve Physioc, Jeff Montgomery (pre-game). **Flagship Station:** FOX Sports Kansas City.

LOS ANGELES ANGELS
Radio Announcers: Terry Smith, Mark Langston, Jose Tolentino (Spanish). **Flagship Station:** AM 830, 1330 KWKW (Spanish).
TV Announcers: Victor Rojas, Mark Gubicza, Jose Mota. **Flagship TV Station:** Fox Sports West (regional cable).

MINNESOTA TWINS
Radio Announcers: Cory Provus, Dan Gladden. **Radio Network Studio Host:** Kris Atteberry. **Spanish Radio:** Alfonso Fernandez, Tony Oliva. **Flagship Station:** WCCO-AM 830. **TV Announcers:** Bert Blyleven, Dick Bremer, Roy Smalley, Jack Morris, LaTroy Hawkins, Justin Morneau. **Flagship Station:** Fox Sports North.

NEW YORK YANKEES
Radio Announcers: John Sterling, Suzyn Waldman. **Flagship Station:** WFAN 660-AM, WADO 1280-AM. **Spanish Radio Announcers:** Francisco Rivera, Rickie Ricardo.
TV Announcers: David Cone, Jack Curry, John Flaherty, Michael Kay, Ryan Ruocco, Meredith Marakovits, Paul O'Neill, Ken Singleton. **Flagship Station:** YES Network (Yankees Entertainment & Sports).

OAKLAND ATHLETICS
Radio Announcers: Vince Cotroneo, Ken Korach, Coco Crisp, Ray Fosse. **Flagship Station:** KTRB 860 AM.
TV Announcers: Ray Fosse, Glen Kuiper, Dallas Braden. **Flagship Stations:** NBC Sports California.

SEATTLE MARINERS
Radio Announcers: Rick Rizzs, Aaron Goldsmith. **Flagship Station:** 710 ESPN Seattle (KIRO-AM 710).
TV Announcers: Mike Blowers, Dave Sims, Aaron Goldsmith, Alex Rivera. **Flagship Station:** ROOT Sports Northwest.

TAMPA BAY RAYS
Radio Announcers: Andy Freed, Dave Wills. **Flagship Station:** WDAE 620 AM/95.3 FM Tampa/St. Petersburg **TV Announcers:** Brian Anderson, Dewayne Staats, Tricia Whitaker. **Flagship Station:** FOX Sports Sun.

TEXAS RANGERS
Radio Announcers: Eric Nadel, Matt Hicks. **Spanish:** Eleno Ornelas, Jose Guzman. **Flagship Station:** 105.3 The FAN FM, KFLC 1270 AM (Spanish).
TV Announcers: Dave Raymond, Tom Grieve, C.J. Nitkowski, Emily Jones. **Flagship Station:** FOX Sports Southwest (regional cable).

TORONTO BLUE JAYS
Radio Announcers: Ben Wagner, Mike Wilner. **Flagship Station:** SportsNet Radio Fan 590-AM.
TV Announcers: Buck Martinez, Pat Tabler, Dan Shulman, Hazel Mae. **Flagship Station:** Rogers Sportsnet.

NATIONAL LEAGUE

ARIZONA DIAMONDBACKS
Radio Announcers: Greg Schulte, Tom Candiotti, Mike Ferrin, Rodrigo Lopez (Spanish), Oscar Soria (Spanish), Richard Saenz (Spanish). **Flagship Stations:** Arizona Sports 98.7 FM, TUDN 105.1 (Spanish).
TV Announcers: Steve Berthiaume, Bob Brenly. **Flagship Stations:** FOX Sports Arizona (regional cable).

ATLANTA BRAVES
Radio Announcers: Jim Powell, Don Sutton, Ben Ingram. **Flagship Stations:** WCNN-AM 680 The Fan.
TV Announcers: Chip Caray, Joe Simpson, Tom Glavine, Jeff Francoeur. **Flagship Stations:** FOX Sports South/Southeast (regional cable).

CHICAGO CUBS
Radio Announcers: Pat Hughes, Ron Coomer. **Flagship Station:** WSCR-670 The Score.
TV Announcers: Len Kasper, Jim Deshaies. **Flagship Stations:** Marquee Sports Network.

CINCINNATI REDS
Radio Announcers: Marty Brennaman, Thom Brennaman, Jeff Brantley, Doug Flynn, Tommy Thrall. **Flagship Station:** WLW 700-AM.
TV Announcers: Chris Walsh, Jeff Brantley, Jim Day. **Flagship Station:** Fox Sports Ohio.

COLORADO ROCKIES
Radio Announcers: Jack Corrigan, Jerry Schemmel, Salvador Hernandez (Spanish), Carlos Valdaz (Spanish). **Flagship Station:** KOA 850-AM & 94.1 FM, Rockies Spanish Radio 1150 AM.
TV Announcers: Drew Goodman, Jeff Huson, Ryan Spilborghs. **Flagship Station:** AT&T SportsNet.

LOS ANGELES DODGERS
Radio Announcers: Rick Monday, Charley Steiner, Tim Neverett. **Spanish:** Jaime Jarrín, Jorge Jarrin. **Flagship Stations:** AM570 Fox Sports LA, KTNQ 1020-AM (Spanish).
TV Announcers: Joe Davis, Orel Hershiser, Nomar Garciaparra, Alanna Rizzo, Tim Neverett. **Spanish:** Pepe Yniguez, Fernando Valenzuela. **Flagship Stations:** SportsNet LA (regional cable).

MIAMI MARLINS
Radio Announcers: Dave Van Horne, Glenn Geffner. **Flagship Stations:** WINZ 940-AM.
TV Announcers: Paul Severino, Todd Hollandsworth. **Flagship Stations:** FSN Florida (regional cable).

MILWAUKEE BREWERS
Radio Announcers: Bob Uecker, Jeff Levering, Lane Grindle. **Flagship Station:** WTMJ 620-AM.
TV Announcers: Brian Anderson, Bill Schroeder, Matt Lepay, Sophia Minnaert. **Flagship Station:** Fox Sports Wisconsin.

NEW YORK METS
Radio Announcers: Howie Rose, Josh Lewin and Wayne Randazzo. **Flagship Station:** WCBS 880-AM.
TV Announcers: Gary Cohen, Keith Hernandez, Ron Darling, Steve Gelbs, Todd Zeile. **Flagship Stations:** Sports Net New York (regional cable), PIX11-TV.

PHILADELPHIA PHILLIES
Radio Announcers: Scott Franzke, Larry Andersen, Jim Jackson. **Flagship Station:** SportsRadio 94WIP (94.1 FM).
TV Announcers: Tom McCarthy, Ben Davis, Kevin Frandsen, John Kruk, Gregg Murphy, Mike Schmidt. **Flagship Stations:** NBC 10 (regional cable).

PITTSBURGH PIRATES
Radio Announcers: Joe Block, Matt Capps, Kevin Young, Michael McKenry, Greg Brown, Bob Walk, John Wehner. **Flagship Station:** Sports Radio 93.7 FM The Fan.
TV Announcers: Joe Block, Matt Capps, Kevin Young, Michael McKenry, Greg Brown, Bob Walk, John Wehner. **Flagship Station:** AT&T SportsNet Pittsburgh (regional cable).

ST. LOUIS CARDINALS
Radio Announcers: Mike Shannon, John Rooney, Ricky Horton, Mike Claiborne. **Flagship Station:** KMOX 1120 AM.
Spanish Radio Announcers: Polo Ascencio, Bengie Molina. **Flagship Station:** WJIR 880
TV Announcers: Dan McLaughlin, Ricky Horton, Brad Thompson, Jim Edmonds, Tim McCarver, Rick Ankiel, Jim Hayes, Erica Weston, Scott Warmann. **Flagship Station:** Fox Sports Midwest.

SAN DIEGO PADRES
Radio Announcers: Ted Leitner, Jesse Agler, Tony Gwynn Jr. **Flagship Stations:** 97.3 The Fan.
TV Announcers: Don Orsillo, Mark Grant, Bob Scanlan, Mike Pomeranz, Mark Sweeney. **Flagship Station:** Fox Sports San Diego. **Spanish Announcers:** Eduardo Ortega, Carlos Hernandez on XEMO-860-AM.

SAN FRANCISCO GIANTS
Radio Announcers: Mike Krukow, Duane Kuiper, Jon Miller, Dave Flemming. **Spanish:** Tito Fuentes, Edwin Higueros. **Flagship Station:** KNBR 680-AM (English); ESPN Deportes-860AM (Spanish).
TV Announcers: Mike Krukow, Duane Kuiper, Jon Miller, Mike Krukow. **Flagship Stations:** KNTV-NBC 11, CSN Bay Area (regional cable).

WASHINGTON NATIONALS
Radio Announcers: Charlie Slowes, Dave Jageler. **Flagship Station:** WJFK 106.7 FM.
TV Announcers: Bob Carpenter, FP Santangelo, Alex Chappell. **Flagship Station:** Mid-Atlantic Sports Network.

NATIONAL MEDIA INFORMATION

BASEBALL STATISTICS

ELIAS SPORTS BUREAU INC. NATIONAL MEDIA BASEBALL STATISTICS
Official Major League Statistician Mailing Address: 500 Fifth Ave., Suite 2140, New York, NY 10110.
Telephone: (212) 869-1530. **Fax:** (212) 354-0980. **Website:** esb.com.
President: Joe Gilston.
Vice President: Chris Thorn. **Email Address:** Chris.Thorn@ESB.com
Manager, Baseball Operations: John Labombarda. **Email Address:** John.Labombarda@ESB.com

MLB ADVANCED MEDIA
Official Minor League Statistician Mailing Address: 75 Ninth Ave., New York, NY 10011.
Telephone: (212) 485-3444. **Fax:** (212) 485-3456. **Website:** MiLB.com.
Director, Stats: Chris Lentine. **Senior Manager, Stats:** Shawn Geraghty.
Senior Stats Supervisors: Jason Rigatti, Ian Schwartz. **Stats Supervisors:** Lawrence Fischer, Jake Fox, Dominic French, Kelvin Lee.

MILB.COM OFFICIAL WEBSITE OF MINOR LEAGUE BASEBALL
Mailing Address: 75 Ninth Ave, New York, NY 10011.
Telephone: (212) 485-3444. **Fax:** (212) 485-3456. **Website:** MiLB.com.
Director, Minor League Club Initiatives: Nathan Blackmon. **Sr. Producer, MiLB.com:** Dan Marinis.

STATS PERFORM
Mailing Address: 203 N. LaSalle St. Chicago, IL, 60601.
Telephone: (847) 583-2100. **Fax:** (847) 470-9140. **Website:** statsperform.com.
Email: sales@stats.com. **Twitter:** @STATSBiznews; @STATS_MLB. **CEO:** Carl Mergale. **Chief Operating Officer:** Mike Perez. **Chief Revenue Officer:** Steve Xeller. **Chief Financial Officer:** Ashley Milton. **Chief Technology Officer:** Dr. Helen Sun. **Advanced Analytics Coordinatior:** Micah Parshall.

GENERAL INFORMATION

SCOUTING

PROFESSIONAL BASEBALL SCOUTS FOUNDATION
Mailing Address: 3914 Corte Cancion, Thousand Oaks, CA 91360.
Telephone: (818) 224-3906 / **Fax** (805) 378-7126. **Email:** cindy.pbsf@yahoo.com. **Website:** www.pbsfonline.com
Chairman: Dennis J. Gilbert. **Executive Director:** Cindy Picerni. **Board of Directors:** Billy Eppler, Bill "Chief" Gayton, Pat Gillick, Derrick Hall, Roland Hemond, Gary Hughes, Jeff Idelson, Dan Jennings, JJ Lally, Tommy Lasorda, Frank Marcos, Roberta Mazur, Danny Montgomery, Bob Nightengale, Pat O'Conner, Damon Oppenheimer, Jared Porter, Tracy Ringolsby, John Scotti, Brian Stephenson, Dale Sutherland, Dave Yoakum.

SCOUT OF THE YEAR FOUNDATION
Mailing Address: P.O. Box 211585, West Palm Beach, FL 33421.
Telephone: (561) 798-5897, (561) 818-4329. **E-mail Address:** bertmazur@aol.com.
President: Roberta Mazur. **Vice President:** Tracy Ringolsby. **Treasurer:** Ron Mazur II. **Board of Advisers:** Pat Gillick, Roland Hemond, Gary Hughes, Tommy Lasorda. **Scout of the Year Program Advisory Board:** Grady Fuson, Roland Hemond, Gary Hughes, Dan Jennings, Linda Pereira, Gene Watson.

MUSEUMS

NATIONAL BASEBALL HALL OF FAME AND MUSEUM
Address: 25 Main St., Cooperstown, NY 13326.
Telephone: (888) 425-5633, (607) 547-7200. **Fax:** (607) 547-2044. **E-mail Address:** info@baseballhall.org. **Website:** www.baseballhall.org.
Year Founded: 1939.
Chairman: Jane Forbes Clark. **Vice Chairman:** Joe Morgan. **President:** Jeff Idelson.
Museum Hours: Open daily, year-round, closed only Thanksgiving, Christmas and New Year's Day. 9 a.m.-5 p.m. Summer hours, 9 a.m.-9 p.m. (Memorial Day weekend through the day before Labor Day.)
2020 Hall of Fame Induction Weekend: July 24-27, Cooperstown, N.Y.

NEGRO LEAGUES BASEBALL MUSEUM
Mailing Address: 1616 E. 18th St., Kansas City, MO 64108.
Telephone: (816) 221-1920. **Fax:** (816) 221-8424.
E-mail Address: bkendrick@nlbm.com. **Website:** www.nlbm.com.
Year Founded: 1990.
President: Bob Kendrick.
Museum Hours: Tues.-Sat. 9 a.m.-6 p.m.; Sun. noon-6 p.m.

RESEARCH

SOCIETY FOR AMERICAN BASEBALL RESEARCH

Mailing Address: Cronkite School at ASU, 555 N Central Ave., #416 , Phoenix, AZ 85004.
Website: www.sabr.org.
Year Founded: 1971.
President: Mark Armour. **Vice President:** Leslie Heaphy. **Secretary:** Todd Lebowitz. **Treasurer:** F.X. Flinn. **Directors:** Bill Nowlin, Mark Armour, Allison Levin, Emily Hawks, Tyrone Brooks. **CEO:** Scott Bush. **Director of Editorial Content:** Jacob Pomrenke.

ALUMNI ASSOCIATIONS

MAJOR LEAGUE BASEBALL PLAYERS ALUMNI ASSOCIATION

Mailing Address: 1631 Mesa Ave., Copper Building, Suite D, Colorado Springs, CO 80906.
Telephone: (719) 477-1870. **Fax:** (719) 477-1875.
E-mail Address: postoffice@mlbpaa.com. **Website:** www.baseballalumni.com.
Facebook: facebook.com/majorleaguebaseballplayersalumniassociation. **Twitter:** @MLBPAA.
Chief Executive Officer: Dan Foster (dan@mlbpaa.com). **Chief Operating Officer:** Geoffrey Hixson (geoff@mlbpaa .com). **Vice President, Operations:** Mike Groll (mikeg@mlbpaa.com). **Director, Communications:** Nikki Warner (nikki @mlbpaa.com). **Director, Membership & Development:** Kate Tyo (Kate@mlbpaa.com). **Director, Memorabilia Operations:** Greg Thomas (greg@mlbpaa.com). **Database Manager:** Chris Burkeen (cburkeen@mlbpaa.com).

BASEBALL ASSISTANCE TEAM (B.A.T.)

Mailing Address: 245 Park Ave., 31st Floor, New York, NY 10167.
Telephone: (212) 931-7822, **Fax:** (212) 949-5433.
Website: www.baseballassistanceteam.com.

MINISTRY

BASEBALL CHAPEL

Mailing Address: P.O. Box 10102, Largo FL 33773.
Telephone: (610) 999-3600.
E-mail Address: office@baseballchapel.org. **Website:** www.baseballchapel.org.
Year Founded: 1973.
President: Vince Nauss. **Hispanic Ministry:** Cali Magallanes, Gio Llerena. **Ministry Operations:** Rob Crose, Steve Sisco. **Board of Directors:** Don Christensen, Greg Groh, Dave Howard, Vince Nauss, Walt Wiley.

CATHOLIC ATHLETES FOR CHRIST

Mailing Address: 3703 Cameron Mills Road, Alexandria, VA 22305.
Telephone: (703) 239-3070.
E-mail Address: info@catholicathletesforchrist.org. **Website:** www.catholicathletesforchrist.org.
Year Founded: 2006.
President: Ray McKenna. **MLB Ministry Coordinator:** Kevin O'Malley. **MLB Athlete Advisory Board Members:** Mike Sweeney (Chairman), Jeff Suppan (Vice Chairman), Sal Bando, Lauren Bauer, David Eckstein, Terry Kennedy, Jack McKeon, Darrell Miller, Mike Piazza, Vinny Rottino, Craig Stammen.

TRADE/EMPLOYMENT

BASEBALL WINTER MEETINGS

Mailing Address: P.O. Box A, St. Petersburg, FL 33731.
Telephone: (727) 822-6937. **Fax:** (727) 821-5819.
E-Mail Address: BaseballWinterMeetings@milb.com. **Website:** www.baseballwintermeetings.com.
2019 Convention: Dec. 6-10, Dallas

BASEBALL TRADE SHOW

Mailing Address: P.O. Box A, St. Petersburg, FL 33731-1950.
Telephone: (866) 926-6452. **Fax:** (727) 683-9865.
E-Mail Address: TradeShow@MiLB.com. **Website:** www.BaseballTradeShow.com.
Contact: Noreen Brantner, Sr. Asst. Director, Exhibition Services & Sponsorships.
2019 Convention: Dec. 6-10, Dallas

PROFESSIONAL BASEBALL EMPLOYMENT OPPORTUNITIES

Mailing Address: P.O. Box A, St. Petersburg, FL 33731-1950.
Telephone: 866-WE-R-PBEO. **Fax:** 727-821-5819.
Email: info@PBEO.com. **Website:** www.PBEO.com.

Contact: Paige Hegedus, Manager, Special Events/Affiliate Programming.

REVIVING BASEBALL IN INNER CITIES
Mailing Address: 245 Park Avenue 30th Fl, New York, NY 10167
Telephone: (212) 931-7800. **Fax:** (212) 949-5695
Year Founded: 1989
Executive Vice President, Baseball & Softball Development: Tony Reagins (Tony.Reagins@mlb.com). **Vice President, Baseball & Softball Development:** David James (David.James@mlb.com). **E-mail:** rbi@mlb.com. **Website:** www.mlb.com/rbi

MLB YOUTH ACADEMIES
CINCINNATI REDS YOUTH ACADEMY
Director: Jerome Wright
Asst. Director: Jeremy Hamilton
Mailing Address: 2026 E. Seymour Avenue. Cincinnati , OH 45327
Phone Number: 513-765-5000

COMPTON YOUTH ACADEMY
Vice President: Darrell Miller
Mailing Address: 901 East Artesia Blvd. Compton, CA

HOUSTON ASTROS YOUTH ACADEMY
Director: Daryl Wade
Mailing Address: 2801 South Victory Drive. Houston, TX 77088.
Email: uya@astros.com

KANSAS CITY ROYALS URBAN YOUTH ACADEMY
Executive Director: Darwin Pennye
Email: Darwin.Pennye@royals.com

NEW ORLEANS YOUTH ACADEMY
Director: Eddie Anthony Davis III
Mailing Address: 6403 Press Drive. New Orleans, LA 70126
Phone Number: 504-282-0443

PHILADELPHIA PHILLIES YOUTH ACADEMY
Director: Jon Joaquin
Phone Number: 215-218-5634
Director: Rob Holiday
Phone Number: 215-218-5204

PUERTO RICO BASEBALL ACADEMY AND HIGH SCHOOL
Director: Luis Cintron
Phone Number: 787-712-0700
Lucy Batista: Headmaster
Phone Number: 787-531-1768

TEXAS RANGERS YOUTH ACADEMY
Director: Juan Leonel Garciga
Mailing Address: 1000 Ballpark Way, Arlington, TX 76011
Phone Number: 817-273-5297

WASHINGTON NATIONALS YOUTH ACADEMY
Executive Director: Tal Alter
Mailing Address: 3675 Ely Place SE. Washington, DC 20019
Phone Number: 202-827-8960

SPRING TRAINING

CACTUS LEAGUE

ARIZONA DIAMONDBACKS

MAJOR LEAGUE

Complex Address: Salt River Fields at Talking Stick, 7555 North Pima Road, Scottsdale, AZ 85256. **Telephone:** (480) 270-5000. **Seating Capacity:** 11,000 (7,000 fixed seats, 4,000 lawn seats). **Location:** From Loop-101, use exit 44 (Indian Bend Road) and proceed west for approximately one-half mile; turn right at Pima Road to travel north and proceed one-quarter mile; three entrances to Salt River Fields will be available on the right-hand side.

MINOR LEAGUE

Complex Address: Same as major league club.

CHICAGO CUBS

MAJOR LEAGUE

Complex Address: Sloan Park, 2330 West Rio Salado Parkway, Mesa, AZ 85201. **Telephone:** (480) 668-0500. **Seating Capacity:** 15,000. **Location:** on the land of the former Riverview Golf Course, bordered by the 101 and 202 interchange in Mesa.

MINOR LEAGUE

Complex Address: 2510 W. Rio Salado Parkway, Mesa, AZ 85201. **Telephone:** (480) 668-0500

CHICAGO WHITE SOX

MAJOR LEAGUE

Complex Address: Camelback Ranch-Glendale, 10710 West Camelback Road, Phoenix, AZ 85037. **Telephone:** (623) 302-5000. **Seating Capacity:** 13,000. **Hotel Address:** Residence Inn Phoenix Glendale Sports and Entertainment District, 7350 N Zanjero Blvd, Glendale, AZ 85305, **Telephone:** (623) 772-8900. **Hotel Address:** Renaissance Glendale Hotel & Spa, 9495 W Coyotes Blvd, Glendale, AZ 85305. **Telephone:** 629-937-3700.

MINOR LEAGUE

Complex/Hotel Address: Same as major league club.

CINCINNATI REDS

MAJOR LEAGUE

Complex Address: Cincinnati Reds Player Development Complex, 3125 S Wood Blvd, Goodyear, AZ 85338. **Telephone:** (623) 932-6590. **Ballpark Address:** Goodyear Ballpark, 1933 S Ballpark Way, Goodyear, AZ 85338. **Telephone:** (623) 882-3120. **Hotel Address:** Marriott Residence Inn, 7350 N Zanjero Blvd, Glendale, AZ 85305. **Telephone:** (623) 772-8900. **Fax:** (623) 772-8905.

MINOR LEAGUE

Complex/Hotel Address: Same as major league club.

CLEVELAND INDIANS

MAJOR LEAGUE

Complex Address: Cleveland Indians Player Development Complex 2601 S Wood Blvd, Goodyear, AZ 85338; Goodyear Ballpark 1933 S Ballpark Way, Goodyear, AZ 85338. **Telephone:** (623) 882-3120. **Location: From Downtown Phoenix/East Valley:** West on I-10 to

Exit 127, Bullard Avenue and proceed south (left off exit), Bullard Avenue turns into West Lower Buckeye Road. Turn left onto Wood Blvd. **Hotel Address:** (Media) Hampton Inn and Suites, 2000 N Litchfield Rd, Goodyear, AZ 85395. **Telephone:** (623) 536-1313. **Hotel Address:** Holiday Inn Express, 1313 N Litchfield Rd, Goodyear, AZ 85395. **Telephone:** (623) 535-1313. **Hotel Address:** TownePlace Suites, 13971 West Celebrate Life Way, Goodyear, AZ 85338. **Telephone:** (623) 535-5009. **Hotel Address:** Residence Inn by Marriott, 2020 N Litchfield Rd, Goodyear, AZ 85395. **Telephone:** (623) 866-1313.

MINOR LEAGUE

Complex Address: Same as major league club.

COLORADO ROCKIES

MAJOR LEAGUE

Complex Address: Salt River Fields at Talking Stick, 7555 North Pima Rd, Scottsdale, AZ 85258. **Telephone:** (480) 270-5800. **Seating Capacity:** 11,000 (7,000 fixed seats, 4,000 lawn seats). **Location:** From Loop-101, use exit 44 (Indian Bend Road Talking Stick Way) and proceed west for approximately one-half mile; turn right at Pima Road to travel north and proceed one-quarter mile; three entrances to Salt River Fields will be available on the right-hand side. **Visiting Team Hotel:** The Scottsdale Plaza Resort, 7200 North Scottsdale Road, Scottsdale, AZ 85253. **Telephone:** (480) 948-5000. **Fax:** (480) 951-5100.

MINOR LEAGUE

Complex/Hotel Address: Same as major league club.

KANSAS CITY ROYALS

MAJOR LEAGUE

Complex Address: Surprise Stadium, 15850 North Bullard Ave, Surprise, AZ 85374. **Telephone:** (623) 222-2000. **Seating Capacity:** 10,700. **Location:** I-10 West to Route 101 North, 101 North to Bell Road, left on Bell for five miles, stadium on left. **Hotel Address:** Wigwam Resort, 300 East Wigwam Blvd, Litchfield Park, Arizona 85340. **Telephone:** (623) 935-3811.

MINOR LEAGUE

Complex Address: Same as major league club. **Hotel Address:** Comfort Hotel and Suites, 13337 W Grand Ave, Surprise, AZ 85374. **Telephone:** (623) 583-3500.

LOS ANGELES ANGELS

MAJOR LEAGUE

Complex Address: Tempe Diablo Stadium, 2200 West Alameda Drive, Tempe, AZ 85282. **Telephone:** (480) 858-7500. **Fax:** (480) 438-7583. **Seating Capacity:** 9,558. **Location:** I-10 to exit 153B (48th Street), south one mile on 48th Street to Alameda Drive, left on Alameda.

MINOR LEAGUE

Complex Address: Tempe Diablo Minor League Complex, 2225 W Westcourt Way, Tempe, AZ 85282. **Telephone:** (480) 858-7558.

LOS ANGELES DODGERS

MAJOR LEAGUE
Complex Address: Camelback Ranch, 10710 West Camelback Rd, Phoenix, AZ 85037. **Seating Capacity:** 13,000, plus standing room. **Location:** I-10 or I-17 to Loop 101 West or North, Take Exit 5, Camelback Road West to ballpark. **Telephone:** (623) 302-5000. **Hotel:** Unavailable.

MINOR LEAGUE
Complex/Hotel Address: Same as major league club.

MILWAUKEE BREWERS

MAJOR LEAGUE
Complex Address: Maryvale Baseball Park, 3600 N 51st Ave, Phoenix, AZ 85031. **Telephone:** (623) 245-5555. **Seating Capacity:** 9,000. **Location:** I-10 to 51st Ave, north on 51st Ave. **Hotel Address:** Unavailable.

MINOR LEAGUE
Complex Address: Maryvale Baseball Complex, 3805 N 53rd Ave, Phoenix, AZ 85031. **Telephone:** (623) 245-5600. **Hotel Address:** Unavailable.

OAKLAND ATHLETICS

MAJOR LEAGUE
Complex Address: Hohokam Stadium, 1235 North Center Street, Mesa, AZ 85201. **Telephone:** 480-907-5489. **Seating Capacity:** 10,000.

MINOR LEAGUE
Complex Address: Fitch Park, 160 East 6th Place, Mesa, AZ 85201. **Telephone:** 480-387-5800. **Hotel Address:** Unavailable.

SAN DIEGO PADRES

MAJOR LEAGUE
Complex Address: Peoria Sports Complex, 8131 West Paradise Lane, Peoria, AZ 85382. **Telephone:** (619) 795-5720. **Fax:** (623) 486-7154. **Seating Capacity:** 12,000. **Location:** I-17 to Bell Road exit, west on Bell to 83rd Ave. **Hotel Address:** La Quinta Inn & Suites (623) 487-1900, 16321 N 83rd Avenue, Peoria, AZ 85382.

MINOR LEAGUE
Complex/Hotel: Country Inn and Suites (623) 879-9000, 20221 N 29th Avenue, Phoenix, AZ 85027.

SAN FRANCISCO GIANTS

MAJOR LEAGUE
Complex Address: Scottsdale Stadium, 7408 East Osborn Rd, Scottsdale, AZ 85251. **Telephone:** (480) 990-7972. **Fax:** (480) 990-2643. **Seating Capacity:** 11,500. **Location:** Scottsdale Road to Osborne Road, east on Osborne for a 1/2 mile. **Hotel Address:** Hilton Garden Inn Scottsdale Old Town, 7324 East Indian School Rd, Scottsdale, AZ 85251. **Telephone:** (480) 481-0400.

MINOR LEAGUE
Complex Address: Giants Minor League Complex 8045 E Camelback Road, Scottsdale, AZ 85251. **Telephone:** (480) 990-0052. **Fax:** (480) 990-2349.

SEATTLE MARINERS

MAJOR LEAGUE
Complex Address: Seattle Mariners, 15707 North 83rd Street, Peoria, AZ 85382. **Telephone:** (623) 776-4800. **Fax:** (623) 776-4829. **Seating Capacity:** 12,339. **Location:** Hwy 101 to Bell Road exit, east on Bell to 83rd Ave, south on 83rd Ave. **Hotel Address:** La Quinta Inn & Suites, 16321 N 83rd Ave, Peoria, AZ 85382. **Telephone:** (623) 487-1900.

MINOR LEAGUE
Complex Address: Peoria Sports Complex (1993), 15707 N 83rd Ave, Peoria, AZ 85382. **Telephone:** (623) 776-4800. **Fax:** (623) 776-4828. **Hotel Address:** Hampton Inn, 8408 W Paradise Lane, Peoria, AZ 85382. **Telephone:** (623) 486-9918.

TEXAS RANGERS

MAJOR LEAGUE
Complex Address: Surprise Stadium, 15754 North Bullard Ave, Surprise, AZ 85374. **Telephone:** (623) 266-8100. **Seating Capacity:** 10,714. **Location:** I-10 West to Route 101 North, 101 North to Bell Road, left at Bell for seven miles, stadium on left. **Hotel Address:** Residence Inn Surprise, 16418 N Bullard Ave, Surprise, AZ 85374. **Telephone:** (623) 249-6333.

MINOR LEAGUE
Complex Address: Same as major league club. **Hotel Address:** Holiday Inn Express and Suites Surprise, 16549 North Bullard Ave, Surprise AZ 85374. **Telephone:** (800) 939-4249.

GRAPEFRUIT LEAGUE

ATLANTA BRAVES

MAJOR LEAGUE
Complex Address: Cool Today Park, 18800 South West Villages Pkwy Venice, FL 34293. **Telephone:** (941) 413-5000. **Seating Capacity:** 8,000. **Location:** From I-75S: Take Exit 191 (River Rd Englewood/North Port). Keep Right onto River Road for 3.9 miles. Turn Right onto US 41/Tamiami Trail. In 1.5 miles take a left onto W. Villages Pkwy. Continue on W. Villages Pkwy for .75 miles.
From I-75N: Take Exit 191 (River Rd Englewood/North Port). Turn left onto River Road. Continue for 3.9 miles. Turn Right onto US 41/Tamiami Trail. In 1.5 miles take a left onto W. Villages Pkwy. Continue on W. Villages Pkwy for .75 miles.
Hotel Address: Unavailable.

MINOR LEAGUE
Complex Address: Same as major league club. **Telephone:** (407) 939-2232. **Fax:** (407) 939-2225. **Hotel Address:** Marriot Village at Lake Buena Vista, 8623 Vineland Ave, Orlando, FL 32821. **Telephone:** (407) 938-9001.

BALTIMORE ORIOLES

MAJOR LEAGUE
Complex Address: Ed Smith Stadium, 2700 12th Street, Sarasota, FL 34237. **Telephone:** (941) 893-6300. **Fax:** (941) 893-6377. **Seating Capacity:** 7,500. **Location:** I-75 to exit 210, West on Fruitville Road, right on Tuttle Avenue.

MINOR LEAGUE
Complex Address: Buck O'Neil Baseball Complex at Twin Lakes Park, 6700 Clark Rd, Sarasota, FL 34241. **Telephone:** (941) 923-1996.

BOSTON RED SOX

MAJOR LEAGUE
Complex Address: JetBlue Park at Fenway South, 11500 Fenway South Drive, Fort Myers, FL 33913. **Telephone:** (239) 334-4700. **Directions: From the North:** Take I-75 South to Exit 131 (Daniels Parkway); Make a left off the exit and go east for approximately two miles; JetBlue Park will be on your left. **From the South:** Take I-75 North to Exit 131 (Daniels Parkway); Make a right off exit and go east for approximately two miles; JetBlue Park will be on your left.

MINOR LEAGUE
Complex/Hotel Address: Fenway South, 11500 Fenway South Drive, Fort Myers, FL 33913.

DETROIT TIGERS

MAJOR LEAGUE
Complex Address: Joker Marchant Stadium, 2301 Lakeland Hills Blvd, Lakeland, FL 33805. **Telephone:** (863) 686-8075. **Seating Capacity:** 9,568. **Location:** I-4 to exit 33 (Lakeland Hills Boulevard).

MINOR LEAGUE
Complex Address: Tigertown, 2125 N Lake Ave, Lakeland, FL 33805. **Telephone:** (863) 686-8075.

HOUSTON ASTROS

MAJOR LEAGUE
Complex Address: The Ballpark of the Palm Beaches, 5444 Haverhill Road, West Palm Beach, FL 33407. **Telephone:** (844) 676-2017. **Seating Capacity:** 7,838. **Location:** Exit Florida's Turnpike onto Okeechobee Blvd. Proceed east to Haverhill Road turning left onto Haverhill Road. On game days, all vehicles may park in one of two grass parking areas. Proceed toward the stadium for disabled parking or drop-off. The North entrance on Haverhill Road will be right-out only. **Hotel Address:** Unavailable.

MINOR LEAGUE
Complex Information: Same as major league club. **Hotel Address:** Unavailable.

MIAMI MARLINS

MAJOR LEAGUE
Complex Address: Roger Dean Stadium, 4751 Main Street, Jupiter, FL 33458. **Telephone:** (561) 775-1818. **Telephone:** (561) 799-1346. **Seating Capacity:** 7,000. **Location:** I-95 to exit 83, east on Donald Ross Road for one mile to Central Blvd, left at light, follow Central Boulevard to circle and take Main Street to Roger Dean Stadium. **Hotel Address:** Palm Beach Gardens Marriott, 4000 RCA Boulevard, Palm Beach Gardens, FL 33410. **Telephone:** (561) 622-8888. **Fax:** (561) 622-0052.

MINOR LEAGUE
Complex/Hotel Address: Same as major league club.

MINNESOTA TWINS

MAJOR LEAGUE
Complex Address: Centurylink Sports Complex/Hammond Stadium, 14100 Six Mile Cypress Parkway, Fort Myers, FL 33912. **Telephone:** (239) 533-7610. **Seating Capacity:** 8,100. **Location:** Exit 21 off I-75, west on Daniels Parkway, left on Six Mile Cypress Parkway. **Hotel Address:** Four Points by Sheraton, 13600 Treeline Avenue South, Ft. Myers, FL 33913. **Telephone:** (800) 338-9467.

MINOR LEAGUE
Complex/Hotel Address: Same as major league club.

NEW YORK METS

MAJOR LEAGUE
Complex Address: Tradition Field, 525 NW Peacock Blvd, Port St. Lucie, FL 34986. **Telephone:** (772) 871-2100. **Seating Capacity:** 7,000. **Location:** Exit 121C (St Lucie West Blvd) off I-95, east 1/4 mile, left onto NW Peacock. **Hotel Address:** Hilton Hotel, 8542 Commerce Centre Drive, Port St. Lucie, FL 34986. **Telephone:** (772) 871-6850.

MINOR LEAGUE
Complex Address: Same as major league club. **Hotel Address:** Main Stay Suites, 8501 Champions Way, Port St. Lucie, FL 34986. **Telephone:** (772) 460-8882.

NEW YORK YANKEES

MAJOR LEAGUE
Complex Address: George M. Steinbrenner Field, One Steinbrenner Drive, Tampa, FL 33614. **Telephone:** (813) 875-7753. **Hotel:** Unavailable.

MINOR LEAGUE
Complex Address: Yankees Player Development/ Scouting Complex, 3102 N Himes Ave, Tampa, FL 33607. **Telephone:** (813) 875-7569. **Hotel:** Unavailable.

PHILADELPHIA PHILLIES

MAJOR LEAGUE
Complex Address: Spectrum Field, 601 N Old Coachman Road, Clearwater, FL 33765. **Telephone:** (727) 467-4457. **Fax:** (727) 712-4498. **Seating Capacity:** 8,500. **Location:** Route 60 West, right on Old Coachman Road, ballpark on right after Drew Street. **Hotel Address:** Holiday Inn Express, 2580 Gulf to Bay Blvd, Clearwater, FL 33765. **Telephone:** (727) 797-6300. **Hotel Address:** La Quinta Inn, 21338 US 19 North, Clearwater, FL 33765. **Telephone:** (727) 799-1565.

MINOR LEAGUE
Complex Address: Carpenter Complex, 651 N Old Coachman Rd, Clearwater, FL 33765. **Telephone:** (727) 799-0503. **Fax:** (727) 726-1793. **Hotel Addresses:** Hampton Inn, 21030 US Highway 19 North, Clearwater, FL 34625. **Telephone:** (727) 797-8173. **Hotel Address:** Econolodge, 21252 US Hwy 19, Clearwater, FL 34625. **Telephone:** (727) 799-1569.

PITTSBURGH PIRATES

MAJOR LEAGUE
Stadium Address: 17th Ave West and Ninth Street West, Bradenton, FL 34205. **Seating Capacity:** 8,500. **Location:** US 41 to 17th Ave, west to 9th Street. **Telephone:** (941) 747-3031. **Fax:** (941) 747-9549.

MINOR LEAGUE
Complex: Pirate City, 1701 27th St E, Bradenton, FL 34208.

ST. LOUIS CARDINALS

MAJOR LEAGUE
Complex Address: Roger Dean Stadium, 4751 Main Street, Jupiter, FL 33458. **Telephone:** (561) 775-1818. **Fax:** (561) 799-1380. **Seating Capacity:** 7,000. **Location:** I-95 to exit 58, east on Donald Ross Road for ¼ mile. **Hotel**

Address: Embassy Suites, 4350 PGA Blvd, Palm Beach Gardens, FL 33410. **Telephone:** (561) 622-1000.

MINOR LEAGUE
Complex: Same as major league club. **Hotel:** Double Tree Palm Beach Gardens. **Telephone:** (561) 622-2260.

TAMPA BAY RAYS

MAJOR LEAGUE
Stadium Address: Charlotte Sports Park, 2300 El Jobean Road, Port Charlotte, FL 33948. **Telephone:** (941) 206-4487. **Seating Capacity:** 6,823 (5,028 fixed seats). **Location:** I-75 to US-17 to US-41, turn left onto El Jobean Rd. **Hotel Address:** None.

MINOR LEAGUE
Complex: Same as major league club.

TORONTO BLUE JAYS

MAJOR LEAGUE
Stadium Address: Florida Auto Exchange Stadium, 373 Douglas Ave, Dunedin, FL 34698. **Telephone:** (727) 733-9302. **Seating Capacity:** 5,509. **Location:** US 19 North to Sunset Point; west on Sunset Point to Douglas Avenue; north on Douglas to Stadium; ballpark is on the southeast corner of Douglas and Beltrees.

MINOR LEAGUE
Complex Address: Bobby Mattick Training Center at Englebert Complex, 1700 Solon Ave, Dunedin, FL 34698. **Telephone:** (727) 734-8007. **Hotel Address:** Clarion Inn & Suites, 20967 US Highway 19 North Clearwater, FL 33765. **Telephone:** (727) 799-1181.

WASHINGTON NATIONALS

MAJOR LEAGUE
Stadium Address: The Ballpark of the Palm Beaches, 5444 N. Haverhill Road, West Palm Beach, FL 33407. **Telephone:** (844) 676-2017.

MINOR LEAGUE
Complex: Same as major league club.

MINOR
LEAGUES

MINOR LEAGUE BASEBALL

THE NATIONAL ASSOCIATION OF PROFESSIONAL BASEBALL LEAGUES

Pat O'Conner

Street Address: 9550 16th St. North, St. Petersburg, FL 33716. **Telephone:** (727) 822-6937.

President & CEO: Pat O'Conner. **Vice President:** Stan Brand. **Chief Marketing & Commercial Officer:** David Wright. **Chief Financial Officer:** Sean Brown. **Sr. VP, Legal Affairs & General Counsel:** D. Scott Poley. **Sr. VP, Baseball & Business Operations:** Tim Brunswick. **Sr. VP, Digital Strategy & Business Development:** Katie Davison. **VP, Business Development & Media:** Gerald Jones. **Head of Licensing & Consumer Products:** Brian Earle. **Sr. Executive Advisor to the President:** Dan O'Brien **Jr. Assistant to the President:** Bill Smith. **Sr. Director, Communications:** Jeff Lantz. **Director, Information Technology:** Rob Colamarino. **Director, Special Events:** Stefanie Loncarich. **Director, Partnership Marketing:** Heather Raburn. **Director, Human Resources:** Tara Thornton. **Director, Marketing Strategy & Research:** Cory Bernstine. **Director, Diversity & Inclusion:** Belicia Montgomery. **Director, Community Engagement:** Courtney Nehls. **Deputy General Counsel:** Robert Fountain. **Special Counsel:** George Yund. **Controller:** James Dispanet. **Asst. Director, Licensing:** Carrie Adams. **Asst. Director, Baseball & Business Operations:** Andy Shultz. **Asst. Director, Corporate Communications:** Mary Marandi. **Asst. Director, Special Events & Affiliate Programming:** Mark Labban. **Strategist, Digital Partnerships:** Kristi Albano. **Sr. Manager, Event Partners & Trade Show Services:** Eileen Sahin-Murphy. **Sr. Manager, Digital Marketing & Communications:** Mallory Roberts. **Sr. Manager, Business Development & Media:** Curtis Walker. **Sr. Manager, Partnership Marketing:** Will Kent, **Jr. Associate Counsel:** Shannon Finucane. **Sr. Accountant:** Michelle Heystek. **Manager, Baseball Ops./ Executive Assistant To President:** Mary Wooters. **Manager, Partnership Marketing:** Scott Ester. **Manager, Social Media Marketing:** Brad Friedman. **Manager, Partnership Marketing:** Meghan Madson. **Manager, Brand Development:** Vincent Pettofrezzo. **Manager, Trademarks & Intellectual Properties:** Melissa Giesler-Hassell. **Manager, Digital Activation:** Ryan Rosenberger. **Coordinator, Events & Partnerships:** Jessica Nori. **Coordinator, Ecommerce:** Tajma Brown. **Coordinator, Baseball & Business Ops:** Melanie Pendleton. **Coordinator, Digital Media:** Ishita Tibrewali.

AFFILIATED MEMBERS/COUNCIL OF LEAGUE PRESIDENTS

Triple-A

League	President	Telephone	Fax Number
International	Randy Mobley	(614) 791-9300	(614) 791-9009
Mexican	Horacio De La Vega	011-52-555-557-1007	01152-53952454
Pacific Coast	Branch Rickey	(512) 310-2900	(512) 310-8300

Double-A

League	President	Telephone	Fax Number
Eastern	Joe McEacharn	(207) 761-2700	(207) 761-7064
Southern	Lori Webb	(770) 321-0400	(770) 321-0037
Texas	Tim Purpura	(682) 316-4100	(682) 316-4100

High Class A

League	President	Telephone	Fax Number
California	Charlie Blaney	(805) 985-8585	(805) 985-8580
Carolina	Geoff Lassiter	(336) 691-9030	(336) 464-2737
Florida State	Terry Reynolds	(727) 257-8423	(386) 252-7495

Low Class A

League	President	Telephone	Fax Number
Midwest	Dick Nussbaum	(574) 231-3000	(574) 231-3000
South Atlantic	Eric Krupa	(727) 538-4270	(727) 499-6853

Short-Season

League	President	Telephone	Fax Number
New York-Penn	Ben Hayes	(727) 289-7112	(727) 683-9691
Northwest	North Johnson	(850) 588-6205	(406) 543-9463

Rookie Advanced

League	President	Telephone	Fax Number
Appalachian	Dan Moushon	(919) 656-5357	Unavailable
Pioneer	Jim McCurdy	(509) 456-7615	(509) 456-0136

Rookie

League	President	Telephone	Fax Number
Arizona	Bob Richmond	(208) 429-1511	(208) 429-1525
Dominican Summer	Orlando Diaz	(809) 532-3619	(809) 532-3619
Gulf Coast	Operated by MiLB	(727) 456-1734	(727) 821-5819

NATIONAL ASSOCIATION BOARD OF TRUSTEES

TRIPLE-A

At-large: Ken Young (Norfolk). **International League:** Ken Schnacke, Chairman (Columbus). **Pacific Coast League:** Sam Bernabe (Iowa). **Mexican League:** Gerardo Benavides Pape (Monclova).

DOUBLE-A

Eastern League: Joe Finley (Trenton). **Southern League:** Stan Logan, Secretary (Birmingham). **Texas League:** D.G. Elmore (Amarillo).

CLASS A

California League: Tom Volpe (Stockton). **Carolina League:** Chuck Greenberg (Myrtle Beach). **Florida State League:** Ron Myers (Lakeland). **Midwest League:** Tom Dickson (Lansing). **South Atlantic League:** Chip Moore (Rome).

SHORT-SEASON

New York-Penn League: Marv Goldklang, Vice Chairman (Hudson Valley). **Northwest League:** Jake Kerr (Vancouver).

ROOKIE

Appalachian League: Mitch Lukevics (Princeton). **Pioneer Baseball League:** Dave Heller, (Billings). **Gulf Coast League:** Reid Ryan (Astros).

PROFESSIONAL BASEBALL UMPIRE CORP.

President & CEO: Pat O'Conner.
Secretary/Sr. VP, Legal Affairs & General Counsel: D. Scott Poley.
Senior VP, Baseball/Business Operations: Tim Brunswick. **Director, MiLB Umpire Development:** Dusty Dellinger.
Mgr., Umpire Technology: Tom Honec. **Mgr., Umpire Development:** Jess Schneider. **Chief of Instruction:** Mike Felt.
Field Evaluators/Instructors: Jorge Bauza, Tyler Funneman, Jay Pierce, Brian Sinclair, Darren Spagnardi. **Medical Coordinator:** Mark Stubblefield.

GENERAL INFORMATION

Medical Coordinator: Mark Stubblefield.
VP, Baseball/Business Operations: Tim Brunswick. **Director, MiLB Umpire Development:** Dusty Dellinger. **Chief of Instruction:** Mike Felt. **Field Evaluators/Instructors:** Jorge Bauza, Tyler Funneman, Mark Lollo, Larry Reveal, Brian Sinclair, Darren Spagnardi. **Video Technician:** Tom Honec. **Medical Coordinator:** Mark Stubblefield.

		REGULAR SEASON			ALL-STAR GAMES	
	Teams	Games	Opening Day	Closing Day	Date	Host
International	14	140	April 9	Sept. 7	* July 15	Scranton
Pacific Coast	16	140	April 9	Sept. 7	* July 15	Scranton
Eastern	12	140	April 9	Sept. 7	July 15	Binghamton
Southern	10	140	April 9	Sept. 7	June 23	Jackson
Texas	8	140	April 9	Sept. 7	June 30	Amarillo
California	8	140	April 9	Sept. 7	June 23	Stockton
Carolina	10	140	April 9	Sept. 7	June 23	Lynchburg
Florida State	12	140	April 9	Sept. 6	June 23	Daytona
Midwest	16	140	April 9	Sept. 7	June 23	Bowling Green
South Atlantic	14	140	April 9	Sept. 7	June 23	Rome
New York-Penn	14	76	June 18	Sept. 7	Aug. 18	Mahoning Valley
Northwest	8	76	June 17	Sept. 6	^ Aug. 4	Rocky Mountain
Appalachian	10	68	June 22	Sept. 1	None	
Pioneer	8	76	June 19	Sept. 12	^ Aug. 4	Rocky Mountain
Arizona	15	56	June 22	Aug. 31	None	
Gulf Coast	18	56	June 29	Sept. 5	None	

*Triple-A All-Star Game. ^Northwest League vs. Pioneer Baseball League.

INTERNATIONAL LEAGUE

Address: 55 South High St., Suite 202, Dublin, Ohio 43017.
Telephone: (614) 791-9300. **Fax:** (614) 791-9009.
E-Mail Address: office@ilbaseball.com.
Website: www.ilbaseball.com.
Years League Active: 1884.
President/Treasurer: Randy Mobley.
   Vice President: Ken Young. **League Administrator:** Chris Sprague. **Corporate Secretary:** Max Schumacher.
   Directors: Don Beaver (Charlotte); Jeff Wilpon (Syracuse); Joe Finley (Lehigh Valley); Mike Birling (Durham); Erik Ibsen (Toledo); Chip Moore (Gwinnett); Stuart Katzoff (Louisville); Bob Rich Jr. (Buffalo); Joe Gregory (Norfolk); David Abrams (Scranton/Wilkes-Barre); Ken Schnacke (Columbus); Bruce Schumacher (Indianapolis); Naomi Silver (Rochester); Mike Tamburro (Pawtucket). **Office Manager:** Gretchen Addison.
   Division Structure: North—Buffalo, Lehigh Valley, Pawtucket, Rochester, Scranton/Wilkes-Barre, Syracuse. **West**—Columbus, Indianapolis, Louisville, Toledo. **South**—Charlotte, Durham, Gwinnett, Norfolk.
   Regular Season: 140 games. **2020 Opening Date:** April 9. **Closing Date:** Sept 7.
   All-Star Game: July 15 at Scranton/Wilkes-Barre (PCL vs International League).
   Playoff Format: South winner meets West winner in best of five series; wild card (non-division winner with best winning percentage) meets North winner in best of five series. Winners meet in best-of-five series for Governors' Cup championship.
   Triple-A Championship Game: Sept 22 at Las Vegas (PCL vs International League).
   Roster Limit: 25. **Player Eligibility:** No restrictions.
   Official Baseball: Rawlings ROM-INT.
   Umpires: Ryan Additon (Davie, FL); Erich Bacchus (Germantown, MD); Adam Beck (Winter Springs, FL); John Bacon (Sherrodsville, OH); Sean Barber (Lakeland, FL); Travis Godec (Roanoke, VA); Rich Grassa (Limehurst, NY); Shane Livensparger (Jacksonville Beach, FL); John Mang (Youngstown, OH); Brennan Miller (Woodbridge, VA); Daniel Merzel (Hopkinton, MA); Jose Navas (Barquisimeto, Venezuela); Charlie Ramos (Grand Rapids, MI); Jeremie Rehak (Monroesville, PA); Jeremy Riggs (Suffolk, VA); Richard Riley (Alexandria, VA); Randy Rosenberg (Alexandria, VA); Skyler Shown (Owensboro, KY); Alex Tosi (Lake Villa, IL); Jansen Visconti (Latrobe, PA); Ryan Wills (Williamsburg, VA); Mike Wiseman (White Lake, MI).

RENATA RAMSINI

Randy Mobley

STADIUM INFORMATION

Club	Stadium	Opened	LF	CF	RF	Capacity	2019 Att.
Buffalo	Sahlen Field	1988	325	404	325	18,025	518,741
Charlotte	BB&T Ballpark	2015	325	400	315	10,002	581,006
Columbus	Huntington Park	2009	325	400	318	10,100	590,504
Durham	Durham Bulls Athletic Park	1995	305	400	327	10,000	529,105
Gwinnett	Coolray Field	2009	335	400	335	10,427	212,342
Indianapolis	Victory Field	1996	320	402	320	14,500	586,860
Lehigh Valley	Coca-Cola Park	2008	336	400	325	10,000	585,110
Louisville	Louisville Slugger Field	2000	325	400	340	13,131	485,356
Norfolk	Harbor Park	1993	333	400	318	12,067	350,086
Pawtucket	McCoy Stadium	1946	325	400	325	10,031	331,010
Rochester	Frontier Field	1997	335	402	325	10,840	451,853
Scranton/WB	PNC Field	2013	330	408	330	10,000	414,891
Syracuse	NBT Bank Stadium	1997	330	400	330	11,671	327,478
Toledo	Fifth Third Field	2002	320	408	315	10,300	481,496

Dimensions (columns: LF, CF, RF)

BUFFALO BISONS

Address: Sahlen Field, One James D. Griffin Plaza, Buffalo, NY 14203.
Telephone: (716) 846-2000. **Fax:** (716) 852-6530.
E-Mail Address: info@bisons.com. **Website:** www.bisons.com.
Affiliation (first year): Toronto Blue Jays (2013). **Years in League:** 1886-90, 1912-70, 1998-

OWNERSHIP/MANAGEMENT

   Operated By: Rich Products Corp. **Principal Owner/President:** Robert Rich Jr. **President, Rich Entertainment Group:** Melinda Rich. **Vice President/Chief Operating Officer, Rich Entertainment Group:** Joseph Segarra. **President, Rich Baseball Operations/General Manager:** Mike Buczkowski. **VP/Secretary:** William Gisel. **Corporate Counsel:** Jill Bond, William Grieshober. **VP/Operations & Finance:** Kevin Parkinson. **VP/Food Service Operations:** Robert Free. **Assistant General Manager:** Anthony Sprague. **Director, Stadium Operations:** Brian Phillips. **Senior Accountants:** Chas Fiscella. **Accountants:** Amy Delaney, Tori Dwyer. **Director, Ticket Operations:** Mike Poreda. **Director, Marketing & Public Relations:** Brad Bisbing. **Graphic Design:** Michele Cicatello. **Director, Corporate Sales:** Jim Harrington. **Director, Sales:** Geoff Lundquist. **Entertainment/Promotions Manager:** Mike Simoncelli. **Sales Coordinators:** Rachelle

Szymanski. **Account Executives:** Bryce Adrian, Mark Gordon, Nick Iacona, Kim Milleville, Burt Mirti, Shaun O'Lay. **Manager, Merchandise:** Theresa Cerabone. **Social Media & Sponsorship Coordinator:** Bethany Sickler. **Manager, Office Services:** Margaret Russo. **Executive Assistant:** Tina Lesher. **Community Relations:** Gail Hodges. **Director, Food & Beverage Operations, Food Service Operations:** Sean Regan. **Food Service Operations Supervisor:** Curt Anderson. **Head Groundskeeper:** Danny Keene. **Chief Engineer:** Gerald Hamilton. **Home Clubhouse/Baseball Operations Coordinator:** Scott Lesher. **Visiting Clubhouse Manager:** Steve Morris.

FIELD STAFF
Manager: Ken Huckaby. **Hitting Coach:** Corey Hart. **Pitching Coach:** Jeff Ware. **Position Coach:** Devon White. **Athletic Trainer:** Bob Tarpey. **Strength/Conditioning Coach:** Aaron Spano.

GAME INFORMATION
Radio Announcers: Pat Malacaro, Duke McGuire. **No. of Games Broadcast:** 140. **Flagship Station:** ESPN 1520. **PA Announcer:** Jerry Reo, Tom Burns. **Official Scorers:** Kevin Lester, Jon Dare. **Stadium Name:** Sahlen Field. **Location:** From north, take I-190 to Elm Street exit, left onto Swan Street; From east, take I-190 West to exit 51 (Route 33) to end, exit at Oak Street, right onto Swan Street; From west, take I-190 East, exit 53 to I-90 North, exit at Elm Street, left onto Swan Street. **Standard Game Times:** 7:05 pm, Sun. 1:05. **Ticket Price Range:** $9-17. **Visiting Club Hotel:** Adams Mark, 120 Church St, Buffalo, NY 14202. **Telephone:** (716) 845-5100.

CHARLOTTE KNIGHTS

Address: BB&T Ballpark, 324 S. Mint St., Charlotte, NC 28202.
Telephone: (704) 274-8300. **Fax:** 704-274-8330.
E-Mail Address: knights@charlotteknights.com. **Website:** www.charlotteknights.com.
Affiliation (first year): Chicago White Sox (1999). **Years in League:** 1993-

OWNERSHIP/MANAGEMENT
Operated by: Knights Baseball, LLC. **Principal Owners:** Don Beaver, Bill Allen. **Chief Operating Officer:** Dan Rajkowski. **General Manager:** Rob Egan. **Director, Special Projects:** Julie Clark. **Finance/HR Manager:** Sara Maple. **VP, Communications:** Tommy Viola. **VP, Sales:** Tom Ward. **VP, Entertainment:** David Ruckman. **VP, Stadium Operations:** Tom Gorter. **VP, Marketing:** Matt DuBois. **Director, Field Operations:** Matt Parrott. **Director, Broadcasting/Team Travel:** Matt Swierad. **Director, Community Relations:** Megan Smithers. **Director, Video Production:** Chase Christiansen. **Director, Stadium Operations:** Nick Braun. **Director, Season Membership Sales:** Brett Butler. **Director, Group Sales:** Yogi Brewington. **Director, Ticket Operations:** Jonathan English. **Director, Special Events:** Grace Eng. **Director, Sponsorship:** Rob Keith. **Business Development Executives:** Corey Bass, Jack Noble. **Client Services Manager:** Aida Smailagic. **Inside Sales Manager:** Michael Rapp. **Senior Ticket Sales Account Executive:** Aaron Freeman. **Ticket Sales Account Executives:** Carter Buffkin, Drew Carlson, Holly Foscolos, Taylor Hes, Cooper Kinsey, Will McPherson. **Ticket Sales Service Representative:** Sandy Elliott, Lauren Teer. **Premium Services Manager:** Tanya Stevens. **Merchandise Director:** Elijah Saint Blanchard. **Creative/IT Director:** Bill Walker. **Manager, Hispanic/Latino Marketing:** Rafael Bastidas. **Entertainment Coordinator:** Nick Farmer. **Community Relations Coordinator:** Trevor Fay. **Assistant Groundskeeper:** Joe Miles. **Special Events Coordinator:** Hannah Harris. **Inside Sales:** Brandon Lewis, Nate Tomey. **Front Desk:** Tori Gryglewski.

FIELD STAFF
Manager: Wes Helms. **Pitching Coach:** Matt Zaleski. **Hitting Coach:** Howie Clark. **Coach:** Mike Daniel. **Trainer:** Cory Barton. **Performance Coach:** Shawn Powell.

GAME INFORMATION
Radio Announcers: Matt Swierad, Mike Pacheco. **No. of Games Broadcast:** 140. **Flagship Station:** 730 The Game ESPN Charlotte. **PA Announcer:** Ken Conrad. **Official Scorers:** Jerry Bowers, Jim Morrison, Richard Walker. **Stadium Name:** BB&T Ballpark. **Location:** Exit 10 off Interstate 77. **Ticket Price Range:** $10-$23. **Visiting Club Hotel:** DoubleTree by Hilton Charlotte, 895 W. Trade St., Charlotte, NC 28202.

COLUMBUS CLIPPERS

Address: 330 Huntington Park Lane, Columbus, OH 43215.
Telephone: (614) 462-5250. **Fax:** (614) 462-3271. **Tickets:** (614) 462-2757.
E-Mail Address: info@clippersbaseball.com. **Website:** www.clippersbaseball.com.
Affiliation (first year): Cleveland Indians (2009). **Years in League:** 1955-70, 1977-

OWNERSHIP/MANAGEMENT
General Manager: Ken Schnacke. **Director, Merchandising:** Krista Oberlander. **Director, Marketing/Sales:** Mark Galuska. **Director, Communications/Media:** Joe Santry. **Assistant Director, Sales, Special Events/Birthday Parties:** Travis Allard. **Director, Game Operations/Creative Services:** Yoshi Ando. **Director, Ballpark Operations:** Steve Dalin. **Assistant Director of Ballpark Operations:** Spencer Harrison. **Assistant Director, Ticket Sales:** Kevin Daniels. **Assistant Director of Ticket Sales:** Matthew Harrison. **Ballpark Superintendent:** Gary Delozier. **Support Services:** Marvin Dill. **Assistant Director of Marketing:** Michael Eckstein. **Assistant Director of Group Sales:** Jacob Fleming. **Home Clubhouse Manager:** Tanner Graham. **Assistant Director, Group Sales:** Cedric Hatton. **Director, Corporate Sales:** Jason Hillyer. **Executive Assistant to the President/GM:** Ashley Held. **Director, Promotions/In-Game Entertainment:** Steve Kuilder. **Assistant Director, Ticket Operations:** Eddie Langhenry. **Assistant Director of Broadcasting:** Scott Leo. **Maintenance**

Supervisor: Curt Marcum. **Director, Sponsorship Relations:** Joyce Martin. **Director, Multimedia/Telecast:** Larry Mitchell. **Assistant Office Manager:** Beth Morris. **Assistant Director, Marketing/School Programs/Kids Club:** Emily Poynter. **Director, Finance/Administration:** Ashley Ramirez. **Assistant Director, Ballpark Operations:** Tom Rinto. **Visiting Clubhouse Manager:** Colin Shaub. **Director, Event Planning:** Micki Shier. **Assistant Director, Media Relations/Statistics:** Anthony Slosser. **Assistant Director, Assistant GM:** Mark Warren. **Assistant Director, Multimedia/Telecast:** Pat Welch. **Assistant Director, Business Operations:** Shelby White.

Assistant Director Corporate Sales: Austin Smith. **Assistant Director Group Sales:** Chase Green. **Assistant Director, Merchandising:** Schuyler Wright. **Director, Ticket Operations:** Scott Ziegler. **Head Groundskeeper:** Wes Ganobcik. **Assistant Groundskeeper:** Connor Smith. **Assistant Groundskeeper:** Alex Polnow. **Director, Multimedia:** Ryan Mitchell. **Director, Social Media/Website:** Matt Leininger. **GM, Levy Food/Beverage:** Jeff Roberts.

FIELD STAFF

Field Manager: Andy Tracy. **Pitching Coach:** Rigo Beltran. **Hitting Coach:** Jason Esposito. **Bench Coach:** Kyle Hudson. **Trainer:** Jeremy Heller. **Strength/Conditioning Coach:** Travis Roberson.

GAME INFORMATION

Stadium Name: Huntington Park. **Location: From North:** South on I-71 to I-670 west, exit at Neil Avenue, turn left at intersection onto Neil Avenue. **From South:** North on I-71, exit at Front Street (#100A); turn left at intersection onto Front Street, turn left onto Nationwide Blvd. **From East:** West on I-70, exit at Fourth Street, continue on Fulton Street to Front Street, turn right onto Nationwide Blvd. **From West:** East on I-70, exit at Fourth Street, continue on Fulton Street to Front Street, turn right onto Front Street, turn left onto Nationwide Blvd. **Ticket Price Range:** $5-21. **Visiting Club Hotel:** Crowne Plaza, 33 East Nationwide Blvd, Columbus, OH 43215. **Telephone:** (614) 461-4100. **Visiting Club Hotel:** Drury Hotels Columbus Convention Center, 88 East Nationwide Blvd, Columbus, OH 43215. **Telephone:** (614) 221-7008. **Visiting Club Hotel:** Hyatt Regency Downtown, 350 North High Street, Columbus, OH 43215. **Telephone:** (614) 463-1234. **Visiting Club Hotel:** Red Roof Inn, 111 East Nationwide Blvd., Columbus Ohio 43215. **Telephone:** 614-224-6539.

DURHAM BULLS

Office Address: 409 Blackwell St., Durham, NC 27701. **Mailing Address:** PO Box 507, Durham, NC 27702

Telephone: (919) 687-6500. **Fax:** (919) 687-6560
Website: durhambulls.com. **Twitter:** @DurhamBulls
Affiliation (first year): Tampa Bay Rays (1998). **Years in League:** 1998-

OWNERSHIP/MANAGEMENT

Operated by: Capitol Broadcasting Company, Inc. **President/CEO:** Jimmy Goodmon. **Vice President:** Mike Birling. **Assistant General Manager, Sales:** Chip Allen. **Assistant General Manager, Operations:** Scott Strickland. **Business Manager:** Kristen Maniscalco. **Accounting Supervisor:** Theresa Stocking. **Staff Accountant:** Alicia McMillen. **Receptionist:** Caitlynn Walker. **Director of Corporate Partnerships:** Nick Bavin. **Sponsorship Account Executive:** Ashley Crabtree. **Sponsorship Account Executive:** Andrew Ferrier, Edward Richards. **Head Groundskeeper:** Cameron Brendle. **Senior Operations Manager:** Cortlund Beneke. **Operations Manager:** Cody Grube. **Head Groundskeeper, Durham Athletic Park:** Joe Stumpo. **Director, Special Events:** LaTosha Smith. **Promotions Director:** Faith Inman. **Radio/TV Broadcaster:** Patrick Kinas. **Mascot/Community Relations Coordinator:** Nico Tennant. **Marketing & Fan Engagement Coordinator:** Emily Amond. **Production Designer:** Paxton Rembis. **Video & Digital Production Manager:** Patrick Norwood. **Digital & Social Content Manager:** Andrew Green. **Director of Merchandising/Team Travel:** Bryan Wilson. **Assistant Director of Merchandise/E-commerce:** Ashley Larson. **Director of Ticketing:** Peter Wallace. **Senior Corporate Account Executive:** Chris Jones. **Corporate Account Executive:** Brad Cook. **Season Membership Services Coordinator:** Izzy Piedmonte, Caitlin Wallen. **Senior Account Executive, Group Sales:** Cassie Fowler. **Group Sales Account Executive:** Fulton Beasley, Marcus Carlson. **Ticket Sales Representative:** Callie Horn, Brendan Nash. **Director of Food and Beverage:** Dave Levey. **Executive Chef:** Jason Boone. **Assistant Food and Beverage Director:** Todd Feneley. **Hospitality & Catering Manager:** Matt Messner. **Concessions Manager:** Andrew Houston.

FIELD STAFF

Manager: Brady Williams. **Pitching Coach:** Rick Knapp. **Coach:** Kyle Wilson, Quinton McCracken. **Athletic Trainer:** Scott Thurston. **Strength & Conditioning Coach:** Bryan King.

GAME INFORMATION

Broadcasters: Patrick Kinas, Scott Pose. **No. of Games Broadcast:** 140. **Flagship Station:** 96.5 FM and 99.3 FM. **PA Announcer:** Tony Riggsbee. **Official Scorer:** Brent Belvin. **Stadium Name:** Durham Bulls Athletic Park. **Location:** From Raleigh, I-40 West to Highway 147 North, exit 12B to Willard, two blocks on Willard to stadium; From I-85, Gregson Street exit to downtown, left on Chapel Hill Street, right on Mangum Street. **Standard Game Times:** 7:05 pm, Sat. 6:35 pm, Sun. 5:05 pm. **Ticket Price Range:** $7-14.

Visiting Club Hotel: Hilton Durham. 3800 Hillsborough Road, Durham, NC 27705. **Telephone:** (919) 383-8033.

GWINNETT STRIPERS

Office Address: 2500 Buford Drive, Lawrenceville, GA 30043.
Mailing Address: P.O. Box 490310, Lawrenceville, GA 30049.

MINOR LEAGUES

Telephone: (678) 277-0300. **Fax:** (678) 277-0338.
E-Mail Address: stripersinfo@braves.com. **Website:** www.gostripers.com.
Affiliation (first year): Atlanta Braves (1966). **Years in League:** 1884, 1915-17, 1954-64, 1966-

OWNERSHIP/MANAGEMENT

Vice President & General Manager: Adam English. **Assistant General Manager:** Erin O'Donnell. **Office Manager:** Tyra Williams. **Manager of Corporate Partnerships:** Ryan Kees. **Corporate Partnership Account Executive:** Robbie Burnstein. **Partnership Services Coordinator:** Hannah Craig. **Ticket Sales Manager:** Jerry Pennington. **Account Executives:** Jordan Bradford, Hashim Cole, Zach Mandelblatt, Carlos Ortiz, Dylan Powers, Taylor Roach. **Ticket Operations Coordinator:** Jimmy Pembroke. **Media Relations Manager & Broadcaster:** Dave Lezotte. **Digital Marketing Coordinator:** Morgan Shiver. **Director of Fun:** Nino Dandan. **Promotions Coordinator:** Kyle Kamerbeek. **Creative Services Coordinator:** Nick Gosen. **Graphic Designer:** Hunter Moore. **Merchandise Manager:** Taryn Taylor. **Director, Stadium Operations:** Ryan Stoltenberg. **Stadium Operations Coordinator:** Rick Fultz. **Facilities Engineer:** Gary Hoopaugh. **Sports Turf Manager:** McClain Murphy. **Sports Turf Assistant:** Dylan Cagle. **Home Clubhouse Manager:** Nick Dixon. **Director of Operations, Professional Sports Catering:** Chiara Perkins.

FIELD STAFF

Manager: Damon Berryhill. **Pitching Coach:** Mike Maroth. **Hitting Coach:** Carlos Mendez. **Coach:** Alfredo Amezaga. **Trainer:** T.J. Saunders. **Strength and Conditioning Coach:** Paul Howey.

GAME INFORMATION

Radio Announcer: Dave Lezotte. **No. of Games Broadcast:** 140. **Flagship Station:** TBA. **PA Announcer:** Kevin Kraus **Official Scorers:** Guy Curtright, Jack Woodard, Stan Awtrey, Phil Engel, Paul Melendez. **Stadium Name:** Coolray Field **Location:** I-85 (at Exit 115, State Road 20 West) and I-985 (at Exit 4); follow signs to park. **Ticket Price Range:** $8-45. **Visiting Club Hotels:** Courtyard by Marriott Buford/Mall of Georgia, 1405 Mall of Georgia Boulevard, Buford, GA 30519. **Telephone:** (678) 745-3380. Fairfield Inn & Suites Atlanta Buford/Mall of Georgia, 1355 Mall of Georgia Boulevard, Buford, GA 30519. **Telephone:** (678) 714-0248.

INDIANAPOLIS INDIANS

Address: 501 W. Maryland Street, Indianapolis, IN 46225.
Telephone: (317) 269-3542. **Fax:** (317) 269-3541.
E-Mail Address: Indians@IndyIndians.com. **Website:** www.indyindians.com.
Affiliation (first year): Pittsburgh Pirates (2005). **Years in League:** 1963, 1998-

OWNERSHIP/MANAGEMENT

Operated By: Indians Inc.

Chairman of the Board/Chief Executive Officer: Bruce Schumacher. **President & General Manager:** Randy Lewandowski. **Chairman Emeritus:** Max Schumacher. **Assistant General Manager, Corporate Sales/Marketing:** Joel Zawacki. **Assistant General Manager, Tickets/Operations:** Matt Guay. **Senior Director, Business Operations:** Brad Morris. **Director, Business Systems/Talent:** Bryan Spisak. **Business Intelligence Analyst:** Bill Fulton. **Business Operations Manager:** Sarah Haynes. **Director, Communications:** Cheyne Reiter. **Baseball Communications Coordinator:** Anna Kayser. **Voice of the Indians:** Howard Kellman. **Broadcaster:** Andrew Kappes. **Director, Corporate Sales:** Christina Toler. **Corporate Sales Account Executives:** Erica Otey, Jeremy Smith. **Senior Director, Facilities:** Tim Hughes. **Senior Facilities Manager:** Allan Danehy. **Facilities Maintenance Tech:** Kyle Winters. **Director, Field Operations:** Joey Stevenson. **Field Operations Manager:** Adam Basinger. **Community Outreach Manager:** Jo Garcia. **Director, Marketing/Promotions:** Kim Stoebick. **Game Presentation/Promotions Manager:** Hayden Barnack. **Digital Marketing Manager:** Shayla Smith. **Telecast/Production Coordinator:** Alex Leachman. **Community Relations Coordinator:** Zach McDonald. **Social Media Coordinator:** Casey McGaw. **Motion/Graphic Designer:** Laura Lee. **Graphic Designers:** Jessica Davis, Matthew Lipke. **Director, Merchandise:** Mark Schumacher. **Merchandise Manager:** Patrick Westrick. **Partnership Activation Manager:** Kylie Kinder. **Partnership Activation Coordinator:** Sydney Glover. **Stadium Operations Manager:** Eddie Acheson. **Stadium Operations Coordinator:** Joshua Ball. **Operations Support:** Ricky Floyd, Ki Hubbard, Sandra Reaves. **Home Clubhouse Manager/Operations Support:** Bobby Martin. **Visiting Clubhouse Manager:** Jeremy Martin. **Director, Tickets Sales:** Chad Bohm. **Director of Tickets, Premium Services/Events:** Kerry Vick. **Premium/Ticket Services Manager:** Kathryn Bobel. **Ticket Services Coordinator:** Cara Carrion. **Senior Ticket Sales Account Executives:** Ryan Barrett, Jonathan Howard, Garrett Rosh. **Ticket Sales Account Executives:** Ty Eaton, David Diehl, Matt Marencik. **ARAMARK General Manager:** Chris Scherrer. **Concession Manager:** Jamie Nicholson.

FIELD STAFF

Manager: Brian Esposito. **Pitching Coach:** Joel Hanrahan. **Hitting Coach:** Jon Nunnally. **Coach:** Argenis Diaz. **Athletic Trainer:** Justin Ahrens. **Strength & Conditioning Coach:** Alan Burr.

GAME INFORMATION

Radio Announcers: Howard Kellman, Andrew Kappes. **Flagship Station:** Fox Sports 1260 AM. **PA Announcer:** David Pygman. **Official Scorers:** Ed Holdaway, Bill McAfee, Kim Rogers, Geoff Sherman, Jeff Williams. **Stadium Name:** Victory Field. **Location:** I-70 to West Street exit, north on West Street to ballpark; I-65 to Martin Luther King and West Street exit, south on West Street to ballpark. **Standard Game Times:** 7:05 pm; 1:35 (Wed/Sun.); 7:15 (Fri.). **Ticket Price Range:** $11-17. **Visiting Club Hotel:** Holiday Inn Indy Downtown, 515 S. West Street, Indianapolis, IN 46225. **Telephone:** (317) 631-9000.

LEHIGH VALLEY IRONPIGS

Address: 1050 IronPigs Way, Allentown, PA 18109.
Telephone: (610) 841-7447. **Fax:** (610) 841-1509.
E-Mail Address: info@ironpigsbaseball.com. **Website:** www.ironpigsbaseball.com.
Affiliation (first year): Philadelphia Phillies (2008). **Years in League:** 2008-

OWNERSHIP/MANAGEMENT
Ownership: LV Baseball LP.
President & General Manager: Kurt Landes. **Vice President, Marketing:** Tricia Matsko. **Vice President, Ticket Sales:** Brian DeAngelis. **Manager, Media Relations:** Mike Ventola. **Director, Digital Media & Communications:** Chris Dunham Jr. **Director, Multimedia Design:** Kevin Whitehead. **Manager, Multimedia Design & Entertainment:** Alfred Greenbaum. **Director, Promotions/Entertainment:** Kelly Scott. **Manager, Promotions:** Jessica Morgan. **Executive Director, IronPigs Charities:** Diane Donaher. **Manager, Community Relations:** Kali Grelle. **Senior Director, Food & Beverage:** Alex Rivera. **Director, Food & Beverage:** Brock Hartranft. **Director, Special Events:** Allison Valentine. **Manager, Catering & Hospitality:** Jared Takacs. **Executive Chef:** Heather Williams. **Director, Corporate Partnerships:** Tom Bendetti. **Managers, Sponsorship Services:** Maria Valentyn, Nick Wilder. **Administrative Assistant:** Pat Golden. **Director, Field Operations:** Ryan Hills. **Senior Director, Stadium Operations:** Jason Kiesel. **Managers, Stadium Operations:** Mike Moneta, Tyler Woscek. **Director, Finance:** Denise Ahner. **Director, Administration:** Michelle Perl. **Senior Manager, Corporate Partnerships:** Zach Betkowski. **Managers, Corporate Partnerships:** Andrew Beck, Ray Bleam. **Director, Guest Experience:** Brad Ludwig. **Director, Group Sales:** Ryan Hines. **Senior Manager, Group Sales:** Billy Misiti. **Managers, Group Sales:** Josh Mullin, Daniel Sterenberg, Kelsey Carlon. **Director, Memberships:** Erik Hoffman. **Managers, Memberships:** Cody Hallman. **Director, Ticket Operations:** Brittany Balonis. **Manager, Ticket Operations & Analytics:** Collin DeJong. **Manager, Ticket Coordinator:** Nick DiChristofaro, Erik Kerns. **Manager, Corporate Ticket Sales:** Tanner Case. **Senior Manager, Premium Sales:** Adam Puskar. **Director, Merchandise:** Mike Luciano.

FIELD STAFF
Manager: Gary Jones. **Hitting Coach:** Darryl Robinson. **Pitching Coach:** Aaron Fultz. **Assistant Coach:** Greg Legg. **Trainer:** Mickey Kozack. **Strength/Conditioning:** Mike Lidge.

GAME INFORMATION
Radio Announcers: Pat McCarthy and Mike Ventola. **No. of Games Broadcast:** 140. **Flagship Radio Station:** FOX Sports Radio 1230/1320 AM & 94.7 FM. **Television Station:** TV2. **Television Announcers:** Mike Zambelli, Steve Degler, Doug Heater. **No. of Games Televised:** 70 (all home games). **PA Announcer:** Chris Roman. **Official Scorers:** Mike Falk, Jack Logic, David Sheriff, Dick Shute. **Stadium Name:** Coca-Cola Park. **Location:** Take US 22 to exit for Airport Road South, head south, make right on American Parkway, left into stadium. **Standard Game Times:** 7:05 pm, Sat. 6:35, Sun. 1:35.

LOUISVILLE BATS

Address: 401 E Main St, Louisville, KY 40202.
Telephone: (502) 212-2287. **Fax:** (502) 515-2255.
E-Mail Address: info@batsbaseball.com. **Website:** www.batsbaseball.com.
Affiliation (first year): Cincinnati Reds (2000). **Years in League:** 1998-

OWNERSHIP/MANAGEMENT
Chairman: Stuart and Jerry Katzoff (MC Sports).
Board of Directors: Dan Ulmer Jr., Edward Glasscock, Gary Ulmer, Kenny Huber, Steve Trager, Michael Brown. **President/CEO:** Gary Ulmer. **Senior Vice President:** Greg Galiette. **Vice President, Stadium Operations/Technology:** Scott Shoemaker. **Controller:** Michele Anderson. **Accounting Assistant:** Becky Reeves. **Director, Media/Public Relations:** Alex Mayer. **Director, Broadcasting:** Nick Curran. **Director, Baseball Operations:** Josh Hargreaves. **Director, Online Media/Design:** Tony Brown. **Graphic Designer:** Rachel Suding. **Director of Ticket Sales:** Bryan McBride. **Director, Business Operations:** Kyle Reh. **Director, Corporate Suites:** Malcolm Jollie. **Assistant Director, Ticket Operations:** Andrew Siers. **Corporate Marketing Manager:** Michael Harmon. **Corporate Marketing Manager:** Kristen Stonicher. **Corporate Marketing Manager:** David Barry. **Corporate Marketing Manager:** Peyton Rhea. **Director of Entertainment:** Casey Rusnak. **Manager, Corporate Partnerships:** Shelby Harding. **Manager, Team Store/Merchandise:** Kat Steponovich. **Manager, Corporate Partnerships:** Chip Sobel. **Manager/Coordinator, Stadium Operations:** Nathan Renfrow. **Head Clubhouse Manager:** Derrick Jewell. **Visiting Clubhouse Manager:** Tyler Smith. **Head Groundskeeper:** Tom Nielsen. **Assistant Groundskeeper:** Bobby Estienne. **Club Physicians:** Walter Badenhausen, M.D.; John A. Lach, Jr., M.D. **Club Dentist:** Pat Carroll, D.M.D. **Chaplains:** Bob Bailey, Jose Castillo.

FIELD STAFF
Manager: Jody Davis. **Pitching Coach:** Jeff Fassero. **Hitting Coach:** Leon Durham. **Bench Coach:** Dick Schofield. **Trainer:** Steve Gober. **Strength/Conditioning Coach:** Matt Hall.

GAME INFORMATION
Radio Announcers: Nick Curran. **No. of Games Broadcast:** 140. **Flagship Station:** WKRD 790-AM. **PA Announcer:** Charles Gazaway. **Official Scorer:** Nick Evans, Neil Rohrer. **Organist:** Bob Ramsey. **Stadium Name:** Louisville Slugger Field. **Location:** I-64 and I-71 to I-65 South/North to Brook Street exit, right on Market Street, left on Jackson Street; stadium on Main Street between Jackson and Preston. **Ticket Price Range:** $8-18. **Visiting Club Hotel:** Omni Hotel, 400 South 2nd Street, Louisville, KY 40202. **Telephone:** (502) 313-6664.

NORFOLK TIDES

Address: 150 Park Ave, Norfolk, VA 23510.
Telephone: (757) 622-2222. **Fax:** (757) 624-9090.
E-Mail Address: receptionist@norfolktides.com. **Website:** www.norfolktides.com.
Affiliation (first year): Baltimore Orioles (2007). **Years in League:** 1969-

OWNERSHIP/MANAGEMENT

Operated By: Tides Baseball Club Inc.
President: Ken Young. **General Manager:** Joe Gregory.
Director, Communications: Ian Locke. **Director, Community Relations:** John Rogerson. **Director, Ticket Operations:** Sze Fong. **Director, Ticket Sales:** John Muszkewycz. **Director, Premium Services:** Stephanie Hierstein. **Director, Stadium Operations:** Mike Zeman. **Business Manager:** Dawn Coutts. **Director, Sales and Fan Experience Experience:** Mike Watkins. **Director, Marketing and Promotions:** Jonathan Mensink. **Director, Merchandising:** AnnMarie Piddisi Ambler. **Administrative Assistant:** Lisa Blocker. **Head Groundskeeper:** Kenny Magner. **Assistant Groundskeeper:** Justin Hall. **Visiting Clubhouse Manager:** Jack Brenner. **Media Relations Assistant:** Collin Perry.

FIELD STAFF

Manager: Gary Kendall. **Hitting Coach:** Sean Berry. **Pitching Coach:** Kennie Steenstra. **Fundamentals Coach:** Ramon Sambo. **Development Coach:** Eli Steinfeld. **Athletic Trainer:** Chris Poole. **Strength/Conditioning Coach:** TBA.

GAME INFORMATION

Radio Announcers: Pete Michaud. **No. of Games Broadcast:** 140. **Flagship Station:** ESPN 94.1 FM. **PA Announcer:** Jack Ankerson. **Official Scorers:** Mike Holtzclaw, Jim Hodges. **Stadium Name:** Harbor Park. **Location:** Exit 9, 11A or 11B off I-264, adjacent to the Elizabeth River in downtown Norfolk. **Standard Game Times:** 6:35 pm during weekdays in April & May, 7:05 pm, Sun 1:05 pm (first half of season); 4:05 pm (second half of season). **Ticket Price Range:** $10-15. **Visiting Club Hotel:** Sheraton Waterside, 777 Waterside Dr, Norfolk, VA 23510. **Telephone:** (757) 622-6664.

PAWTUCKET RED SOX

Office Address: One Ben Mondor Way, Pawtucket, RI 02860.
Mailing Address: PO Box 2365, Pawtucket, RI 02861.
Telephone: (401) 724-7300. **Fax:** (401) 724-2140.
E-Mail Address: info@pawsox.com. **Website:** www.pawsox.com.
Affiliation (first year): Boston Red Sox (1973). **Years in League:** 1973-

OWNERSHIP/MANAGEMENT

Principal Owner & Chairman: Larry Lucchino. **Vice Chairman:** Mike Tamburro. **President:** Dr. Charles Steinberg. **Executive Vice President/Real Estate Development & Business Affairs:** Dan Rea III. **Treasurer:** Jeff White. **Executive Vice President/General Counsel:** Kim Miner. **Senior Vice President/Communications:** Bill Wanless. **Senior Vice President/Corporate Partnerships:** Michael Gwynn. **Senior Vice President/Sales & Marketing:** Rob Crain. **Senior Vice President/Chief Financial & Technology Officer:** Matt Levin. **Vice President/Corporate Partnerships:** Jack Verducci. **Vice President/Marketing:** Brooke Cooper. **Executive Assistant to the Chairman:** Fay Scheer. **Special Assistant to the Chairman & Director of Ballpark Planning:** Bart Harvey. **Special Assistant to the President & Intern Coordinator:** Jackie Wilkes. **Senior Director of Ticket Operations:** Samantha Saccoia-Beggs. **Senior Director of Ticket Sales:** Matt Harper. **Senior Director of Fan Services:** Rick Medeiros. **Director of Baseball Operations & Community Relations:** Joe Bradlee. **Director of Client Services:** Bernadette Provost. **Director of Food & Beverage:** Jenn Boisclair. **Director of Production:** Joe Jacobs. **Director of Special Events:** Hannah Butler. **Office Manager:** Carol Krushnowski. **Corporate & Community Partnerships:** Mike Lyons. **Corporate Event Managers:** Anthony Cahill, Jim Cain. **Group Event Managers:** Ben Proctor, Ryan Meagher. **Staff Accountant:** Dan Fontaine. **Director of Worcester Operations:** Steve Oliveira. **Director of Warehouse Operations:** Jeff Caster. **Facilities Maintenance Manager:** Dave Crowley. **Manager of Merchandising:** Kat Burns. **Community Relations Assistant:** Alex Richardson. **Operations Coordinator, PawSox/WooSox Foundations:** Sabriya Chaudhry. **Manager of Productions:** Tim Quitadamo. **Assistant Box Office Manager:** Matt Vetter. **Field Superintendent:** Matt McKinnon. **Assistant Groundskeeper:** Alex Tedesco. **Clubhouse Manager:** Josh Liebenow. **Radio Broadcasters:** Josh Maurer, Mike Monaco.

FIELD STAFF

Field Manager: Billy McMillon. **Hitting Coach:** Rich Gedman. **Pitching Coach:** Paul Abbott. **Coach:** Bruce Crabbe. **Trainer:** David Herrera. **Strength & Conditioning Coach:** Chris Messina.

GAME INFORMATION

Radio Announcers: Josh Maurer, Mike Monaco. **No. of Games Broadcast:** 140. **Flagship Station:** WHJJ 920-AM. **PA Announcers:** Ben DeCastro. **Official Scorer:** Bruce Guindon.
Stadium Name: McCoy Stadium. **Location:** From north, 95 South to exit 2A in Massachusetts (Newport Ave); follow Newport Ave for 2 miles, right on Columbus Ave, follow one mile, stadium on right; From south, 95 North to exit 28 (School Street); right at bottom of exit ramp, through two sets of lights, left onto Pond Street, right on Columbus Ave, stadium entrance on left; From west (Worcester); 295 North to 95 South and follow directions from north; From east (Fall River); 195 West to 95 North and follow directions from south. **Standard Game Times:** 7 pm, Sat. 6, Sun 1. **Ticket Price Range:** $6-14. **Visiting Club Hotel:** Hampton Inn Pawtucket, 2 George St, Pawtucket, RI 02860. **Telephone:** (401) 723-6700.

ROCHESTER RED WINGS

Address: One Morrie Silver Way, Rochester, NY 14608.
Telephone: (585) 454-1001. **Fax:** (585) 454-1056.
E-Mail: info@redwingsbaseball.com. **Website:** RedWingsBaseball.com.
Affiliation (first year): Minnesota Twins (2003). **Years in League:** 1885-89, 1891-92, 1895-present

OWNERSHIP/MANAGEMENT

Operated by: Rochester Community Baseball, Inc.
President/CEO/COO: Naomi Silver.
Chairman: Gary Larder. **General Manager:** Dan Mason. **Assistant GM:** Will Rumbold. **Controller:** Michelle Schiefer. **Director, Human Resources:** Paula LoVerde. **Ticket Office Mgr. & Business Coordinator:** Dave Welker. **Manager, Operations:** Marcia DeHond. **Director, Communications:** Nate Rowan. **Director, Corporate Development:** Nick Sciarratta. **Manager, Social Media & Promotions:** Tim Doohan. **Director, Group Sales:** Bob Craig. **Group Sales & Tickets Reps:** Kevin Lute & Mike Ewing. **Senior Director, Sales:** Matt Cipro. **Director, Ticket Operations:** Rob Dermody. **Assistant Director, Ticket Operations:** Eric Friedman. **Director, Game Day Operations:** Travis Sick. **Director, Video Production:** John Blotzer. **Director, Merchandising:** Nicole Boyle. **Merchandising Assistant:** Kathy Bills. **Head Groundskeeper:** Gene Buonomo. **Assistant Groundskeeper:** Geno Buonomo. **Office Manager:** Amber Johnson. **GM, Food/Beverage:** Jeff Desantis. **Business Manager, Food/Beverage:** Dave Bills. **Manager, Concessions:** Jeff Savidge. Director, **Catering & Hospitality:** Steve Gonzalez. **Suites Manager & Events Coordinator:** Megan Ridings. **Executive Chef:** Ryan Donalty. **Sous Chef:** Nick Johnson. **Manager, Warehouse:** Tyler Klobusicky.

FIELD STAFF

Manager: Toby Gardenhire. **Hitting Coach:** Matt Borgschulte. **Pitching Coach:** Cibney Bello. **Bullpen Coach:** Mike McCarthy. **Coach:** Robbie Robinson. **Athletic Trainer:** Jason Kirkman. **Strength Coach:** Jacob Dean.

GAME INFORMATION

Radio Announcer: Josh Whetzel. **No. of Games Broadcast:** 140. **Flagship Stations:** WHTK 1280-AM.
PA Announcers: Kevin Spears, Rocky Perrotta. **Official Scorers:** Warren Kozireski, Brendan Harrington, Craig Bodensteiner. **Stadium Name:** Frontier Field. **Location:** I-490 East to exit 12 (Brown/Broad Street) and follow signs; I-490 West to exit 14 (Plymouth Ave) and follow signs. **Standard Game Times:** 7:05 pm, Sun 1:05. **Ticket Price Range:** $9-14. **Visiting Club Hotel:** Holiday Inn Rochester Downtown, 70 State St, Rochester, NY 14608. **Telephone:** (585) 546-3450.

SCRANTON/WILKES-BARRE RAILRIDERS

Address: 235 Montage Mountain Rd., Moosic, PA 18507.
Telephone: (570) 969-2255. **Fax:** (570) 963-6564.
E-Mail Address: info@swbrailriders.com.
Website: www.swbrailriders.com.
Affiliation (first year): New York Yankees (2007). **Years in League:** 1989-

OWNERSHIP/MANAGEMENT

President: John Adams. **General Manager:** Katie Beekman. **Chief Financial Officer/Financial Controller:** Scott A'Hara. **VP, Ticket Sales:** Andrew Yarnall. **Sr. Director, Corporate Services & Design:** Kristina Knight. **Director, Marketing & Media/ Broadcasting:** Adam Marco. **Director, Community Relations:** Jordan Maydole. **Chief Sales Officer:** Sal Lombardo. **Corporate Sales Executive:** Jordan Perrine. **Group Sales Executives:** Kaitlin Hueston, Mike Reviello. **Sr. Director Corporate Services & Design:** Felicia Adamus. **Corporate Service Manager:** Jordan Perrine. **Premium Services Manager:** Michelle Newberry. **Director, Season Ticket Sales & Service:** Kelly Cusick. **Account Executives, Client Retention:** Joe Yudichak, Maggie Merren. **Account Executives, Premium Sales:** Cole Acoveno, Tim Duggan, Joe Tucciarone. **Group Sales Manager:** Mike Harvey. **Director, Youth Baseball & Sports Sales:** Robby Judge. **Business Operations & Pinstripes Foundation Manager:** Amy Miller. **Special Events/ Social Media Manager:** Kat Sokirka. **Administrative Assistant:** Deanna Golden. **Director, Field Operations:** Steve Horne. **Assistant Groundskeeper:** Dustin Spiegel. **Director, Facility Operations:** Joe Villano. **Stadium Operations Manager:** Nick Bolka. **Director of Business Development:** Vince Bulik. **Sales Associate:** Tyler Movessian. **Staff Accountant:** Barbara Verrastro.

FIELD STAFF

Manager: Doug Davis. **Hitting Coach:** Phil Plantier. **Pitching Coach:** Tommy Phelps. **Bullpen Coach:** Doug Davis. **Athletic Trainer:** Darren London. **Strength & Conditioning Coach:** Brad Hyde. **Defensive Coaches:** Aaron Bossi, Raul Dominguez.

GAME INFORMATION

Radio Announcers: Adam Marco. **No. of Games Broadcast:** 140. **Flagship Stations:** 1340 WYCK-AM, 1400 WICK-AM, 1440 WCDL-AM. **Television Announcer:** Adam Marco. **No. of Games Broadcast:** TBA. **Flagship Station:** TBA. **PA Announcers:** Unavailable. **Official Scorers:** Dean Corwin, Dick Devans, Mark Ligi &Armand Rosamilia. **Stadium Name:** PNC Field. **Location:** Exit 182 off Interstate 81; stadium is on Montage Mountain Road. **Standard Game Times:** 6:35 pm

(April/May) 7:05 pm (June-August); Sun. 1:05 pm. **Ticket Price Range:** $10-$16. **Visiting Club Hotel:** Hilton Scranton & Conference Center. **Telephone:** (570) 343-3000.

SYRACUSE METS

Address: One Tex Simone Drive, Syracuse NY, 13208
Telephone: 315-474-7833. **Fax:** 315-474-2658.
E-Mail Address: baseball@syracusemets.com. **website:** syracusemets.com
Affiliation (First year): New York Mets (2019). **Years in league:** 1885-1889, 1891-92, 1894-1901, 1918, 1920-1927, 1934-1955, 1961-present

OWNERSHIP/MANAGEMENT
Operated by: NY Mets. **General Manager:** Jason Smorol. **Assistant GM, Stadium/Baseball Ops:** Clint Cure. **Assistant GM, Business Development:** Katie Berger. **Director, Sales/Marketing:** Kathleen McCormick. **Director, Finance:** Frank Santoro. **Senior Accountant:** Patrick Taylor. **Director, Broadcasting/Media Relations:** Michael Tricarico. **Director, Ticket Operations:** Will Commisso. **Director, Multimedia Production:** Anthony Cianchetta. **Manager, Corporate Sales:** Julie Cardinali. **Manager, Luxury Suites/Hospitality:** Bill Ryan. **Manager, Social Media/Graphics:** Danny Tripodi. **Manager, Equipment/Clubhouse Operations:** Jody Pucello. **Head Groundskeeper/Director, Turf Management:** John Stewart.

FIELD STAFF
Manager: Brian Schneider. **Pitching Coach:** D.J. Carrasco. **Hitting Coach:** Joel Chimelis. **Bench Coach:** Rich Donnelly

GAME INFORMATION
Radio Announcer: Michael Tricarico. **No. of Games Broadcast:** 140. **Flagship Station:** The Score 1260 AM. **PA Announcers:** Nick Aversa. **Official Scorer:** Dom Leo. **Stadium Name:** NBT Bank Stadium. **Location:** New York State Thruway to exit 36 (I-81 South); to 7th North Street exit, left on 7th North, right on Hiawatha Boulevard. **Standard Game Times:** 6:35 pm, Sun. 1:05 pm. **Ticket Price Range:** $10-18. **Visiting Club Hotel:** Embassy Suites @ Destiny USA.

TOLEDO MUD HENS

Address: 406 Washington St., Toledo, OH 43604.
Telephone: (419) 725-4367. **Fax:** (419) 725-4368.
E-Mail Address: mudhens@mudhens.com. **Website:** www.mudhens.com.
Affiliation (first year): Detroit Tigers (1987). **Years in League:** 1889, 1965-

OWNERSHIP/MANAGEMENT
Operated By: Toledo Mud Hens Baseball Club, Inc. **Chairman of the Board:** Michael Miller. **Vice President:** David Huey. **Secretary/Treasurer:** Charles Bracken. **President/CEO:** Joseph Napoli. **GM/Executive Vice President:** Erik Ibsen. **President, Chief Marketing Officer:** Kim McBroom. **CFO:** Brian Leverenz. **Accounting:** Sheri Kelly, Shelly Solis. **Assistant Controller:** Tom Mitchell. **Director, Strategic Planning and Projects:** Michael Keedy. **Director, Communications/ Media:** Andi Roman. **Community Relations Manager:** Rob Wiercinski. **Social Media Coordinator:** Amanda Jerzykowski. **Director, Ticket Sales/Services:** Thomas Townley. **Director of Operations, Food & Beverage:** Chris Shannon. **Manager, Banquets:** Hanna Roberts. **Suites Manager:** Ann Marie Biesiada. **Concessions Manager:** McKenzie Whiteman. **VP of Hospitality:** Benito Suero. **Asst. Director of Operations:** Cory Pleasant. **Gameday Operations Manager:** Greg Setola. **Director Corporate Partnerships:** Ed Sintic. **Game Plan Consultants:** Logan Ankney John Dotson, Becky Fitts, Adam Haman, Clayton Wielinski, Brian Wilson. **Group Sales Manager:** Kyle Moll. **Group Consultant:** Rita Natter, Samanth Roush, Matt Snider. **Manager, Ticket Service Team:** Troy Hammersmith. **Ticket Services Team:** Haley Dennis, Samantha Hoot, Tori Larsick. **Manager, Box Office Sales:** Jennifer Hill. **Assistant Manager Box Office Sales:** Jessica MacFarlane. **Special Events Coordinator:** Emily Croll. **Game Day Coordinator:** Tyler Clark, CJ O'Leary. **Fan Experience Specialist:** Heather Brunsting. **Marketing Coordinator:** Regan Elder. **Director, Broadcast Services:** Greg Tye. **Video Production Coordinator:** Cory Marshall. **Creative Director:** Dan Royer. **Graphic Design Assistants:** Will Melon, Troy Hester. **Director, Merchandise & Licensing:** Craig Katz. **Manager, Swamp Shop:** Aaron Jones. **Office Manager:** Carol Hamilton. **Executive Assistants:** Beth Loy, Brenda Murphy, Pam Miranda. **Turf Manager:** Kyle Leppelmeier. **Asst. Sports Turf Manager:** Cory Myers. **Clubhouse Manager:** Joe Sarkisian. **Team Historian:** John Husman.

FIELD STAFF
Manager: Tom Prince. **Hitting:** Mike Hessman. **Pitching Coach:** Juan Nieves. **Developmental:** CJ Wamsley. **Trainer:** Jason Schwartzman. **Strength and Conditioning:** Dan Morrison. **Baseball Information Assistant:** Correy Ericksen. **Trackman Operator:** Kevin Cleary.

GAME INFORMATION
Radio Announcer: Jim Weber. **No. of Games Broadcast:** 140. **Flagship Station:** WCWA 1230-AM. **TV Announcers:** Jim Weber, Matt Melzak. No. **of Games Broadcast:** 70 (all home games). **TV Flagship:** Buckeye Cable Sports Network (BCSN). **PA Announcer:** Mason. **Official Scorers:** Jeff Businger, Ron Kleinfelter, John Malkoski Jr., John Malkoski Sr., Lee Schuh, Jason Parkins. **Stadium Name:** Fifth Third Field. **Location:** From Ohio Turnpike 80/90, exit 54 (4A) to I-75 North, follow I-75 North to exit 201-B, left onto Erie Street, right onto Washington Street; From Detroit, I-75 South to exit 202-A, right onto Washington Street; From Dayton, I-75 North to exit 201-B, left onto Erie Street, right on Washington Street; From Ann Arbor, Route 23 South to I-475 East, I-475 east to I-75 South, I-75 South to exit 202-A, right onto Washington Street. **Ticket Price Range:** $12. **Visiting Club Hotel:** Park Inn, 101 North Summit, Toledo, OH 43604. **Telephone:** (419) 241-3000.

PACIFIC COAST LEAGUE

Address: One Chisholm Trail, Suite 4200, Round Rock, Texas 78681.
Telephone: (512) 310-2900. **Fax:** (512) 310-8300.
E-Mail Address: office@pclbaseball.com.
Website: www.pclbaseball.com.
President: Branch B. Rickey.

Vice President: Don Logan (Las Vegas).
Directors: John Traub (Albuquerque), Alan Ledford (El Paso), Michael Baker (Fresno), Sam Bernabe (Iowa), Don Logan (Las Vegas), Peter B. Freund (Memphis), Frank Ward (Nashville), Gary Green (Omaha), Michael Byrnes (Oklahoma City), Eric Edelstein (Reno), Chris Almendarez (Round Rock), Jeff Savage (Sacramento), Marc Amicone (Salt Lake), Dave Elmore (San Antonio), Aaron Artman (Tacoma), Lou Schwechheimer (Wichita).
Director, Business: Melanie Fiore. **Vice President, Baseball Operations:** Dwight Hall. Manager, **Communications & Baseball Operations:** Michael Schroeder.
Division Structure: American Conference—Northern: Iowa, Memphis, Nashville, Omaha; **Southern:** Oklahoma City, Round Rock, San Antonio, Wichita. **Pacific Conference—Northern:** Fresno, Reno, Sacramento, Tacoma. **Southern:** Albuquerque, El Paso, Las Vegas, Salt Lake.
Regular Season: 140 games. **2020 Opening Date:** April 9. **Closing Date:** Sept 7.
All-Star Game: July 15 at Scranton/Wilkes-Barre (PCL vs International League).
Playoff Format: Pacific Conference/Northern winner meets Southern winner, and American Conference/Northern winner meets Southern winner in best-of-five semifinal series. Winners meet in best-of-five series for league championship.

Branch Rickey

Triple-A Championship Game: Sept 22 at Las Vegas (PCL vs International League).
Roster Limit: 25. **Player Eligibility Rule:** No restrictions; **Brand of Baseball:** Rawlings ROM.
Umpires: Sean Allen (Fresno, CA), David Arrieta (Maracaibo, Zulia, VZ), Ryan Blakney (Phoenix, AZ), Nestor Ceja (Arleta ,CA), Paul Clemons (Oxford, KS), Ramon De Jesus (Santo Domingo, DR), Derek Eaton (Elk Grove, CA), Reid Gibbs (Glendale, AZ), Clayton Hamm (Spicewood, TX), John Libka (Port Huron, MI), Alex MacKay (Evergreen, CO), Nick Mahrley (Phoenix, AZ), Ben May (Milwaukee, WI), Kyle McCrady (Longview, WA), Jacob Metz (Edmonds, WA), Malachi Moore (Compton, CA), Edwin Moscoso (Santiago, Chile), Cody Oakes (Oelwein, IA), Roberto Ortiz (Kissimmee, FL), Jonathan Parra (Valencia, Carabobo, VZ), Sean Ryan (Waunakee, WI), Chris Segal (Fairfax, VA), Jason Starkovich (San Tan Valley, AZ), Nate Tomlinson (Ogdensburg, WI), Junior Valentine (Maryville, TN), Clint Vondrak (Reno, NV), Lew Williams (Lodi, CA), Matt Winter (Mankato, MN), Tom Woodring (Las Vegas, NV).

STADIUM INFORMATION

Club	Stadium	Opened	LF	CF	RF	Capacity	2019 Att.
Albuquerque	Isotopes Park	2003	340	400	340	13,500	542,832
El Paso	Southwest University Park	2014	322	406	322	8,018	522,894
Fresno	Chukchansi Park	2002	324	400	335	12,500	380,090
Iowa	Principal Park	1992	335	400	335	11,000	489,173
Las Vegas	Cashman Field	1983	328	433	328	11,500	650,934
Memphis	AutoZone Park	2000	319	400	322	10,000	327,753
Nashville	First Tennessee Park	2015	330	405	310	10,000	578,291
Oklahoma City	Chickasaw Bricktown Ballpark	1998	325	400	325	9,000	444,131
Omaha	Werner Park	2011	310	402	315	9,023	328,307
Reno	Aces Ballpark	2009	339	410	340	9,100	336,215
Round Rock	Dell Diamond	2000	330	405	325	8,722	597,928
Sacramento	Raley Field	2000	330	403	325	14,014	549,440
Salt Lake	Smith's Ballpark	1994	345	420	315	14,511	433,596
New Orleans	Shrine on Airline	1997	325	400	325	10,000	337,484
Tacoma	Cheney Stadium	1960	325	425	325	6,500	347,378
Wichita	New Wichita ballpark	2020	N/A	N/A	N/A	10,000	188,092

ALBUQUERQUE ISOTOPES

Address: 1601 Avenida Cesar Chavez SE, Albuquerque, NM 87106
Telephone: (505) 924-2255. **Fax:** (505) 242-8899.
E-Mail Address: info@abqisotopes.com. **Website:** www.abqisotopes.com.
Affiliation (first year): Colorado Rockies (2015). **Years in League:** 1972-2000, 2003-

OWNERSHIP/MANAGEMENT

President: Ken Young. **Vice President/Secretary/Treasurer:** Emmett Hammond. **VP/GM:** John Traub. **VP, Corporate Development:** Nick LoBue. **Assistant GM, Business Operations:** Chrissy Baines. **Assistant GM, Sales/Marketing:** Adam Beggs. **Director, Public Relations:** Kevin Collins. **Director, Retail Operations:** Kara Hayes. **Director, Stadium Operations:** Bobby Atencio. **Director, Accounting/Human Resources:** Cynthia DiFrancesco. **Box Office/Administration Manager:** Mark Otero. **Director, Community Relations:** Michelle Montoya. **Marketing/Promotions**

Manager: Dylan Storm. **Director of Game Production:** Kris Shepard. **Suite Relations Manager:** Lorraine Chavez. **Travel Coordinator/Home Clubhouse Manager:** Ryan Maxwell. **Season Tickets/Group Sales Manager:** Jason Buchta. **Ticket Sales Executives:** Jeremy Lucero, Terry Clark, Aaron Robinson, CJ Scroger, Aly Thomas. **Graphic Designer:** Rebecca Zook. **Communications Coordinator:** Andrew Cockrum. **Front Office Assistant:** Margaret Harris. **Retail Operations Assistant:** Michael Malgieri. **Broadcaster:** Josh Suchon. **Stadium Operations Coordinator:** Phillip Trujillo. **Event Operations Coordinator:** Summer Noelle. **Head Groundskeeper:** Clint Belau. **Assistant Groundskeeper:** Tyler Hutchinson. **GM, Spectra:** Boris Revilla. **Executive Chef, Spectra:** Ryan Kagimoto. **Spectra Office Manager:** Angela Goniea.

FIELD STAFF

Manager: Warren Schaeffer. **Hitting Coach:** Tim Doherty. **Pitching Coach:** Blaine Beatty. **Athletic Trainer:** Heath Townsend. **Physical Performance Coach:** Phil Bailey.

GAME INFORMATION

Radio Announcer: Josh Suchon. **No. of Games Broadcast:** 140. **Flagship Station:** KNML 95.9-FM & 610-AM. **PA Announcer:** Francina Walker. **Official Scorers:** Gary Herron, Brent Carey, John Miller, Frank Mercogliano. **Stadium Name:** Isotopes Park. **Location:** From 1-25, exit east on Avenida Cesar Chavez SE to University Boulevard; From I-40, exit south on UniversityBoulevard SE to Avenida Cesar Chavez. **Standard Game Times:** 6:35 pm / 7:05 pm. **Sun 1:35/6:**05 pm. **Ticket Price Range:** $8-$27. **Visiting Club Hotel:** Sheraton Albuquerque Airport Hotel, 2910 Yale Blvd SE, Albuquerque, NM 87106. **Telephone:** (505) 843-7000.

EL PASO CHIHUAHUAS

Address: 1 Ballpark Plaza, El Paso, TX 79901.
Telephone: (915) 533-2273. **Fax:** (915) 242-2031.
E-Mail Address: info@epchihuahuas.com. **Website:** www.epchihuahuas.com.
Affiliation (first year): San Diego Padres (2014). **Years in League:** 2014-

OWNERSHIP/MANAGEMENT

Owner/Chairman of the Board: Paul Foster. **Owner/CEO/Vice Chairman:** Josh Hunt. **Owners:** Alejandra de la Vega Foster, Woody Hunt. **President:** Alan Ledford. **Senior Vice President/General Manager:** Brad Taylor. **Senior Director, Finance & Administration:** Pamela De La O. **Senior Accounting Manager:** Heather Hagerty. **Accounting Assistant:** Pamela Nieto. **Staff Accountant:** Antonio Mendoza. **Director, Corporate Partnerships & Suite Services:** Judge Scott. **Account Executive, Corporate Partnership & Activation:** Adrian Arvizo. **Manager, Corporate Partnership Activation:** Alex O'Connor. **Account Executive, Corporate Partnerships:** Javier Delgado. **Senior Director, Ticket Sales & Service:** Nick Seckerson. **Manager, Season Seat Sales:** Primo Martinez. **Director, Business Development Analytics & Ticket Operations:** Ross Rotwein. **Manager, Group Sales:** Brittany Morgan. **Supervisor, Group Ticket Services:** Killian Vallieu. **Account Executives, Ticket Sales:** Ethan Andersen, Matt Heiligenberg, Jay Morris. **Account Executives, Group Sales:** Corey Cerrone, Korey Dunn, Austin Weber. **Senior Account Executive, Group Sales:** Janine Quiroz. **Manager, Ticket Operations:** Ruben Armendariz. **Supervisor, Ticket Operations:** Jacob Rock. **Senior Director, Marketing & Communications:** Angela Olivas. **Senior Manager, Video & Digital Production:** Juan Gutierrez. **Senior Manager, Broadcast & Media Relations:** Tim Hagerty. **Director, Promotions & Community Relations:** Andy Imfeld. **Mascot & Entertainment Supervisor:** Grant Gorham. **Production & Social Media Coordinator:** Gage Freeman. **Community Relations & Promotions Coordinator:** Kate Lewis. **Creative Services & Digital Marketing Coordinator:** Ilene Serna.

Senior Director, Guest Services & Baseball Operations: Lizette Espinosa. **Senior Director, Ballpark Operations:** Douglas Galeano. **Manager Grounds, Head Groundskeeper:** Travis Howard. **Assistant Groundskeeper:** Andrew Faust. **Assistant Groundskeeper:** Antonio Tafoya. **Supervisor, Facilities:** Michael Raymundo. **Manager, Guest Services & Operations:** Evan Ruiz. **Baseball Operations & Guest Services Specialist:** Latoya Wright. **Manager, Retail & Merchandise Operations:** Leslie Holt.

FIELD STAFF

Manager: Edwin Rodriguez. **Hitting Coach:** Morgan Burkhart. **Pitching Coach:** Pete Zamora. **Coach:** Lance Burkhart. **Trainers:** Dan Turner, Dan Leja.

GAME INFORMATION

Radio Announcer: Tim Hagerty. **No. of Games Broadcast:** 140. **Flagship Station:** ESPN 600 AM El Paso. **PA Announcer:** Larry Berg. **Official Scorer:** Bernie Ricono. **Stadium Name:** Southwest University Park. **Standard Game Times:** 7:05, Sun 1:05 or 6:05. **Ticket Price Range:** $5-10.50. **Visiting Club Hotel:** Hilton Garden Inn.

FRESNO GRIZZLIES

Address: 1800 Tulare St, Fresno, CA 93721.
Telephone: (559) 320-4487. **Fax:** (559) 264-0795.
E-Mail Address: info@fresnogrizzlies.com. **Website:** www.FresnoGrizzlies.com.
Affiliation (first year): Washington Nationals (2019). **Years in League:** 1998-

OWNERSHIP/MANAGEMENT

Operated By: Fresno Sports & Events
Managing Partner: Michael Baker. **Chief Financial Officer:** Michael Moran.
President: Derek Franks. **Assistant General Manager:** Andrew Milios. **Director, Marketing Creative:** Sam Hansen.
Vice President of Operations: Shaun O'Brien. **Director, Stadium Maintenance:** Harvey Kawasaki. **Director of Gameday Operations:** Steven Andrade. **Stadium Maintenance Manager:** Ira Calvin. **Vice President, Sales:** Jason Hannold. **Manager, Ticket Office:** Eric Moreno. **Director, Ticket Sales:** Brandon Aurecchione. **Group Sales Manager:** Kyle Selna. **Group Account Executive:** Zach Gilman. **Entertainment Manager:** Ray Ortiz. **Media Relations Manager:** Stephen Rice. **Graphic Designer:** Dorian Castro. **Merchandise Manager:** Bayley Coleman. **Ballpark Development Manager:** Jon Stockton. **Controller:** Allison Ferrell. **Entertainment/Mascot Manager:** Troy Simeon. **Community Engagement Coordinator:** Madeline Hamada. **Manager of Corporate Partnerships:** Jazzmine Young. **Head Groundskeeper:** David Jacinto. **Home Clubhouse Manager:** Jeff Little. **Visiting Clubhouse Manager:** Eric Gomez. **Administrative Assistant:** Norma Mata. **Director, Pro Sports Catering:** Kendyl Brown. **Assistant Director, Pro Sports Catering:** Alex Lilley.

FIELD STAFF

Manager: Randy Knorr. **Hitting Coach:** Brian Daubach. **Pitching Coach:** Michael Tejera. **Trainer:** Eric Montague. **Strength & Conditioning:** Mike Warren.

GAME INFORMATION

Radio Announcer: Doug Greenwald. **No. of Games Broadcast:** 140. **Flagship Radio Station:** Unavailable. **Stadium Name:** Chukchansi Park. **Location:** 1800 Tulare St, Fresno, CA 93721. **Directions:** From 99 North, take Fresno Street exit, left on Fresno Street, left on Inyo or Tulare to stadium. From 99 South, take Fresno Street exit, left on Fresno Street, right on Broadway to H Street. From 41 North, take Van Ness exit toward Fresno, left on Van Ness, left on Inyo or Tulare, stadium is straight ahead. From 41 South, take Tulare exit, stadium is located at Tulare and H Streets, or take Van Ness exit, right on Van Ness, left on Inyo or Tulare, stadium is straight ahead. **Ticket Price Range:** $10-19. **Visiting Club Hotel:** Doubletree Downtown Fresno, 2233 Ventura St. Fresno, CA 93721. **Telephone:** (559)-268-1000.

IOWA CUBS

Address: One Line Drive, Des Moines IA 50309.
Telephone: (515) 243-6111. **Fax:** (515) 243-5152.
Website: www.iowacubs.com.
Affiliation (first year): Chicago Cubs (1981). **Years in League:** 1969-

OWNERSHIP/MANAGEMENT

Chairman/Principal Owner: Michael Gartner. **Executive Vice President:** Michael Giudicessi. **President/General Manager:** Sam Bernabe. **Vice Chairman/Shareholder:** Mike C. Gartner. **Shareholder:** Dr. Doug Dorner. **VP/Assistant GM:** Randy Wehofer. **VP/CFO:** Sue Tollefson. **Director, Media Relations:** Shelby Cravens. **Director, Video and Multimedia Arts:** Justin Walters. **Director, Ticket Operations:** Clayton Grandquist. **Director, Broadcasting:** Alex Cohen. **Director, Group Outings:** Jason Gellis. **VP/Director, Luxury Suites:** Brent Conkel. **VP/Stadium Operations:** Jeff Tilley. **Manager, Stadium Operations:** Andrew Quillin, Dustin Halderson. **Account Executive:** John Rodgers, Nick Long. **Group Sales:** Beth Kneeskern. **VP/Head Groundskeeper:** Chris Schlosser. **Assistant Groundskeeper:** Chase Manning. **Director, Merchandise:** Lisa Hufford. **Accounting:** Lori Auten, Amy Bean. **Chief Technology Officer:** Ryan Clutter. **Manager, Social and Digital Media:** Matt Evers. **Director of Miscellaneous Endeavors:** Scott Sailor. **Landscape Coordinator:** Shari Kramer.

FIELD STAFF

Manager: Marty Pevey. **Hitting Coaches:** Desi Wilson, Will Remillard. **Pitching Coach:** Ron Villone. **Athletic Trainers:** Ed Halbur, Toby Williams. **Strength/Conditioning:** Keegan Knoll.

GAME INFORMATION

Radio Announcers: Alex Cohen, Deene Ehlis. No. **of Games Broadcast:** 140. **Flagship Station:** AM 940 KPSZ. **PA Announcers:** Mark Pierce, Corey Coon, Rick Stageman, Joe Hammen. **Official Scorers:** Michael Pecina, James Hilchen, Steve Mohr. **Stadium Name:** Principal Park. **Location:** I-80 or I-35 to I-235, to Third Street exit, south on Third Street, left on Line Drive. **Standard Game Times:** 12:08/7:08 pm, Sun. 1:08. **Ticket Price Range:** $5-35. **Visiting Hotel:** Hampton Inn and Suites Downtown, 120 SW Water Street, Des Moines IA 50309. **Telephone:** (515) 244-1650.

LAS VEGAS AVIATORS

Address: 1650 S. Pavilion Center Drive, Las Vegas, NV 89135.
Telephone: (702) 939-7200. **Fax:** (702) 943-7214.
E-Mail Address: info@aviatorslv.com. **Website:** www.aviatorslv.com.
Affiliation (first year): Oakland Athletics (2019). **Years in League:** 1983 - present (37 years)

OWNERSHIP/MANAGEMEN

Operated By: Summerlin Las Vegas Baseball Club LLC.
President/COO: Don Logan. **General Manager/Vice President, Sales/Marketing:** Chuck Johnson. **Vice President, Ticket Sales:** Erik Eisenberg. **VP of Community Relations & Special Events:** Melissa Harkavy. **Vice President/Accounting:** Scott Montes. **Vice President/Ballpark Support:** Nick Fitzenreider. **Vice President/Stadium Operations:** Jay Cline. **Director, Ticket Operations:** Siobhan Steiermann. **Director, Ticket Sales:** TJ Thedinga. **Director, Sponsorships:** James Jensen. **Director, Broadcasting:** Russ Langer. **Director, Ballpark Operations:** Johnathan Jensen. **Director, Business Development:** Larry Brown. **Media Relations Director:** Jim Gemma. **Director/Game Entertainment:** Gary Arlitz. **Director, Retail Operations:** Jason Weber. **Director/Team Operations:** Steve Dwyer. **Marketing/Social Media Manager:** Heather Henderson. **Senior Account Executive:** Bryan Frey. **Account Executives, Ticket Sales:** Nathan Erbach, Ariel Greenberg, David Moses, Kyle Nakama. **Senior Staff Accountant:** Brian Winslow. **Ballpark Operations Manager:** Deonte Hawkins. **Ballpark Support Manager:** Chip Vespe. **Box Office Manager:** Annette Evans. **Ticket Operations Coordinator:** Michelle Taggart. **Executive Assistant:** Jan Dillard. **Ticket Services & Community Relations Coordinators:** Katie Greener, Hayley Smith. **Administrative Support Specialist:** Kirsten Sheff. **Community Relations & Special Events Assistant:** Jenna Potter. **Team Store Manager:** Edward Dorville. **Retail Coordinator:** Mariz Arellano. **Chief Engineer:** Ronnie Cabrera. **Executive Director Public Safety:** Bill Corder.

FIELD STAFF

Manager: Fran Riordan. **Hitting Coach:** Todd Steverson. **Pitching Coach:** Rick Rodriguez. **Coach:** Hiram Bocachica. **Athletic Trainer:** Justin Whitehouse. **Asst. Athletic Trainer:** Tony Leo. **Strength/Conditioning Coach:** Matt Rutledge.

GAME INFORMATION

Radio Announcer: Russ Langer. **No. of Games Broadcast:** 140. **Flagship Station:** NBC Sports AM 920 'The Game'. **PA Announcer:** Dan Bickmore. **Official Scorer:** Peter Legner. **Stadium Name:** Las Vegas Ballpark. **Location:** I 215 North Beltway to Sahara Avenue (exit east), left on Pavilion Center Drive; 1 215 South Beltway to Charleston Blvd. (exit east), right on Pavilion Center Drive. **Standard Game Time:** 7:05 pm. **Ticket Price Range:** $12-60. **Visiting Club Hotel:** Red Rock Casino Resort & Spa, 11011 W. Charleston Blvd. Las Vegas, NV 89135. **Telephone:** (702) 797-7777.

MEMPHIS REDBIRDS

Office Address: 198 Union, Memphis, TN 38103.
Stadium Address: 198 Union Ave, Memphis, TN 38103.
Telephone: (901) 721-6000. **Fax:** (901) 328-1102. **Website:** www.memphisredbirds.com.
Affiliation (first year): St. Louis Cardinals (1998). **Years in League:** 1998-

OWNERSHIP/MANAGEMENT

Ownership: Peter B. Freund.
President/General Manager: Craig Unger. **Vice President, Marketing and Sales:** Andy Steavens. **Vice President, Stadium and Baseball Operations:** Mike Voutsinas. **Media and Public Relations:** Michael Weisman. **Director, Ticket Sales:** Kyle Krebs. **Director, Field Operations:** Brian Bowe. **Manager, Ticket Operations:** Gian D'Amico. **Manager, Corporate Sales:** Tyler Gilles. **Manager, Marketing:** Nikki Paine. **Manager, Guest Services and Baseball Operations:** Marissa Zvolanek. **Accounting Manager:** Cindy Neal. **Facilities Manager:** Spencer Shields.

FIELD STAFF

Manager: Ben Johnson. **Hitting Coach:** Brandon Allen. **Pitching Coach:** Dernier Orozco. **Trainer:** Dan Martin. **Strength & Conditioning:** Frank Witkowski.

GAME INFORMATION

Radio Announcer: Steve Selby. **No. of Games Broadcast:** 140. **Flagship Station:** online. **PA Announcer:** TBA. **Official Scorers:** J.J. Guinozzo, Eric Opperman. **Stadium Name:** AutoZone Park. **Location:** North on I-240, exit at Union Avenue West, one and half miles to park. **Standard Game Times:** Mon-Wed. 6:35, Thu-Fri. 7:05, Sat. 6:35, Sun 2:05. **Ticket Price Range:** $9-24. **Visiting Club Hotel:** TBA.

NASHVILLE SOUNDS

Address: 19 Junior Gilliam Way, Nashville, TN 37219.
Telephone: (615) 690-HITS. **Fax:** (615) 256-5684.
E-Mail address: info@nashvillesounds.com. **Website:** www.nashvillesounds.com.
Affiliation (first year): Texas Rangers (2019). **Years in League:** 1998-

OWNERSHIP/MANAGEMENT

Operated By: MFP Baseball. **Owners:** Frank Ward, Masahiro Honzawa.
GM/Chief Operating Officer: Adam Nuse. **VP, Operations:** Doug Scopel. **VP, Fan Relations:** Amy Schoch. **VP, Sales:** Bryan Mayhood. **Director, Finance:** Barb Walker. **Director, Sales:** Taylor Fisher. **Director, Corporate Partnerships:** Danielle Gaw. **Director, Media Relations:** Chad Seely. **Director, Marketing:** Alex Wassel. **Director, Entertainment:** Mary Hegley. **Director, Retail:** Katie Ward. **Director, Advertising:** Ryan Madar. **Director, Broadcasting:** Jeff Hem. **Director, Stadium Operations:** Jeremy Wells. **Director, Video and Production:** Neil Rosan. **Manager, Promotions and Activation:** Shannyn Wong. **Manager, Digital Marketing:** Abby Holman. **Manager, Business Development:** Sierra Seigel. **Business Development, Corporate Partnerships:** Jon Brownfield. **Business Development, Corporate Partnerships:** Katie Painter. **Merchandise Manager:** Wade Becker. **Executive Director, Nashville Sounds Foundation:** Destiny Whitmore. **Ticket Operations Manager:** Kyle Hargrove. **Stadium Operations Manager:** Austin Brunk, Caleb Yorks. **Account Executive:** Kelsen Adeni, Wesley Donald, Kevin Kurowski. **Account Executive, Ticket Sales:** Mandy Valentine, Mahalie Shorrock, Anton Calvin. **Ticket Operations Coordinator:** Irving Alvarez. **Ticket Sales Representatives:** Jon Bellis, Randi Bivens, Zach Booth, Nate Card, Hayley Greenwell, Matt Walker. **Ticket Operations Coordinator:** Ben Whalen, Macy Tilton. **Ticket Sales Representative:** Easton Cornelius, Audrey Idol, Andrew Rudolph, Emily Vick. **Partnership Activation Coordinator:** Allie Doheny. **Mascot Coordinator:** Buddy Yelton. **Production Event Coordinator:** Stephen Hart. **Creative Assistant:** RV Oliver. **Graphic Designer:** Joe Masterson. **Fan Services Seasonal Associate:** Travis Williams. **Groundskeeper:** Thomas Trotter. **Assistant Groundskeepers:** Shay Adams, Bryce Huebner. **Clubhouse & Equipment Manager:** Matt Gallant. **Visiting Clubhouse Manager:** Patrick King. **Team Photographer:** Casey Gower.

FIELD STAFF

Manager: Darwin Barney. **Hitting Coach:** Chase Lambin. **Pitching Coach:** Brendan Sagara. **Bullpen Coach:** Eric Gagne. **Coach:** Tyler Graham. **Athletic Trainer:** Carlos Olivas. **Strength/Conditioning Coach:** Al Sandoval.

GAME INFORMATION

Radio Announcer: Jeff Hem. **No. of Games Broadcast:** 140. **Flagship Station:** 97.5 FM. **Official Scorers:** Eric Jones, Cody Bush, Eric Moyer. **Stadium Name:** First Horizon Park. **Location:** I-65 to exit 85 (Rosa L Parks Blvd) and head south; Turn left on Jefferson St, then turn right onto 5th Ave North, then turn left on Jackson St. **Standard Game Times:** 7:05, 6:35, 6:15, 2:05. **Ticket Price Range:** $10-35. **Visiting Club Hotel:** Millennium Maxwell House, 2025 Rosa L Parks Blvd, Nashville, TN, 37228.

OKLAHOMA CITY DODGERS

Address: 2 S Mickey Mantle Dr., Oklahoma City, OK 73104.
Telephone: (405) 218-1000. **Fax:** (405) 218-1001.
E-Mail Address: info@okcdodgers.com. **Website:** www.okcdodgers.com.
Affiliation (first year): Los Angeles Dodgers (2015). **Years in League:** 1963-1968, 1998-

OWNERSHIP/MANAGEMENT

Operated By: MB OKC LLC. **Principal Owner:** Mandalay Baseball
President/General Manager: Michael Byrnes. **Senior Vice President:** Jenna Byrnes. **Vice President, Ticket Sales:** Kyle Daugherty. **Vice President, Corporate Partnerships:** Nick Gates. **Director, Finance/Accounting:** John MacDonald. **Senior Director, Operations:** Mitch Stubenhofer. **Senior Director, Marketing/Communications:** Ben Beecken. **Director, Business Intelligence:** Kyle Logan. **Director, Ticket Operations:** Bethany Staub. **Director, Partner Services:** Katy White. **Director, Facility Operations:** Harlan Budde. **Director, Communications/Broadcasting:** Alex Freedman. **Director, Food Service Operations:** Lindsay Robb. **Executive Director, OKC Dodgers Baseball Foundation:** Carol Herrick. **Communications Coordinator:** Lisa Johnson. **Baseball Operations Coordinator:** Billy Maloney. **Game Presentation Manager:** A.J. Navarro. **Office Manager:** Travis Hunter. **Head Groundskeeper:** Monte McCoy. **Clubhouse Manager:** T.J. Leonard.

FIELD STAFF

Manager: Travis Barbary. **Hitting Coach:** Emmanuel Burriss. **Pitching Coach:** Bill Simas. **Coach:** Mark Kertenian. **Athletic Trainers:** Shawn McDermott and Victor Scarpone. **Performance Coach:** Tyler Norton.

GAME INFORMATION

Radio Announcer: Alex Freedman. **No. of Games Broadcast:** 140. **Station:** KGHM-AM 1340 (www.1340thegame.com). **PA Announcer:** Jared Gallagher. **Official Scorers:** Jim Byers, Mark Heusman, Rich Tortorelli. **Stadium Name:** Chickasaw Bricktown Ballpark. **Location:** Bricktown area in downtown Oklahoma City, near interchange of I-235 and I-40, off I-235 take Sheridan exit to Bricktown; off I-40 take Shields exit, north to Bricktown. **Standard Game Times:** 7:05 pm, Sun 2:05 (April-June), 6:05 (July-Aug). **Ticket Price Range:** $9-28. **Visiting Club Hotel:** Courtyard Oklahoma City Downtown, 2 West Reno Ave., Oklahoma City, OK 73102. **Telephone:** (405) 232-2290.

OMAHA STORM CHASERS

Address: Werner Park, 12356 Ballpark Way, Papillion, NE 68046.
Administrative Office Phone: (402) 734-2550. **Ticket Office Phone:**
(402) 738-5100. **Fax:** (402) 734-7166. **E-mail Address:** info@omahastorm-
chasers.com. **Website:** www.omahastormchasers.com. **Affiliation (first year):** Kansas City Royals (1969). **Years in
League:** 1998-

OWNERSHIP/MANAGEMENT

Operated By: Alliance Baseball Managing Partners. **Owners:** Gary Green, Larry Botel, Brian Callaghan, Eric Foss,
Stephen Alepa, Peter Huff, Evan Friend.
CEO: Gary Green. **President:** Martie Cordaro. **Vice President/General Manager:** Laurie Schlender. **Chief Revenue
Officer:** Ryan Querry. **Assistant GM, Events/Sales:** Andrea Bedore. **Human Resources Manager:** Laura Warnock.
Senior Corporate Sales Executive: Mark Nasser. **Director/Business Development:** Dave Endress. **Director/
Operations:** Steve Farrens. **Head Groundskeeper:** Derek York. **Facilities Manager:** Louie Page. **Broadcaster:** Jake
Eisenberg. **Marketing/Promotions Manager:** Andrew Asbury. **Promotions/Game Operations Manager:** Rachel Rea.
Promotions/Community Events Coordinator: Alvin Garcia. **Client Services Manager:** Mackenzie Parker. **Media/
Public Relations Manager:** Tony Boone. **Creative Services Manager:** Lauren Kirk. **Video/Multimedia Coordinator:**
Scott Popp. **Director/Ticket Operations:** Anna Corbett. **Group Sales Manager:** Zach Ziler. **Corporate Sales Executive:**
Tim Jacob. **Group Sales Executives:** Bradley Divan, Stephen Hough, Sam Olson, Harrison Zornes. **Retail Operations
Manager:** Mitch Cunningham. **Ticket Operations Assistant:** Mason Cole. **Bookkeeper:** Rachel Sefren. **Ballpark
Operations Assistant:** Jordan King. **Grounds Manager:** Tom Walter. **Home Clubhouse Manager:** Mike Brown. **Front
Office Assistant:** Donna Kostal, Michelle VanBemmelen.

FIELD STAFF

Manager: Brian Poldberg. **Hitting Coach:** Brian Buchanan. **Pitching Coach:** Dane Johnson. **Bench coach:** Tony Pena
Jr. **Athletic Trainer:** James Stone. **Strength Coach:** Dwayne Peterson.

GAME INFORMATION

Radio Announcers: Jake Eisenberg. **No. of Games Broadcast:** 140. **Flagship Station:** KZOT-AM 1180.
PA Announcer: Craig Evans & Jake Ryan. **Official Scorers:** Frank Adkisson, Gary Sharp & Ryan White. **Stadium
Name:** Werner Park. **Location:** Highway 370, just east of I-80 (exit 439). **Standard Game Times:** 6:35 pm (April-May),
7:05 (June-Sept), Fri./Sat. 7:05, Sun. 2:05. **Visiting Club Hotel:** Courtyard Omaha La Vista, 12560 Westport Parkway, La
Vista, NE 68128. **Telephone:** (402) 339-4900. **Fax:** (402) 339-4901.

RENO ACES

Address: 250 Evans Ave, Reno, NV 89501.
Telephone: (775) 334-4700. **Fax:** (775) 334-4701.
Website: www.renoaces.com.
Affiliation (first year): Arizona Diamondbacks (2009). **Years in League:** 2009-

OWNERSHIP/MANAGEMENT

President: Eric Edelstein.
General Manager: Emily Jaenson. **Chief Operations Officer:** Chris Holland. **Chief Revenue Officer:** Samantha
Hicks. **Chief Financial Officer:** Stacey Bowman. **VP of Business Development:** Brian Moss. **Director of Ticket
Operations:** Sarah Bliss. **Director of Field Operations:** Joe Hill. **Senior Accountant:** Adam Hyde. **Accounting Clerk:**
Jose Mata. **Communications Manager:** Jake Trybulski. **Senior Marketing Manager:** Vince Ruffino. **Digital Media
Coordinator:** AJ Grimm. **Group Sales Director:** Alex Strathearn. **Entertainment Manager:** Devin Levan-Galang.
Merchandise Manager: Joey Santos. **Ticket Operations Manager:** Kristina Solis. **Fan Experience Manager:** Marisa
Ochoa. **Facilities Manager:** Miguel Paredes. **Creative Manager:** Blake O'Brien. **Corporate Partnerships Director:**
Max Margulies. **Community Relations Manager:** Jared Cooper. **Retail Sales Coordinator:** Nick Pepple. **Corporate
Partnerships Services Account Manager:** Courtney Baker. **Corporate Partnerships Account Manager:** Max Simpson.
Account Executive Corporate Partnerships: Justin Kelleher. **Member Services Coordinator, Aces:** Emily Cryer. **Sales
& Analytics Coordinator:** Emilie Schliksbier. **Stadium Superintendent:** Ben Sanchez. **Account Executive, Group
Sales:** JJ Baldivia. **Account Executive, Group Sales:** Ellie Stockwell. **Sales Academy Rep:** Blake Paris. **Sales Academy
Rep:** Joe Portillo. **Sales Academy Rep:** Kyle Vincent. **Sales Academy Rep:** Scott Whan. **Member Services Director:**
Laura Raymond. **Account Executive, Outside Sales:** Shawnee McFadden. **Account Executive, Outside Sales:** Tyler
Wilson. **Stadium Operations Assistant:** Myles Fresquez. **Senior Account Executive:** Henry Fassinger. **Assistant
Groundskeeper:** Adam Vecitis. **Assistant Groundskeeper:** Leah Withrow. **Human Resources Manager:** Amanda
Littrell. **Visiting Clubhouse Manager:** TBA.

FIELD STAFF

Manager: Chris Cron. **Hitting Coach:** Jason Camilli. **Pitching Coach:** Jeff Bajenaru. **Coach:** Greg Gross. **Athletic
Trainer:** Michael Powell. **Strength & Conditioning Coach:** Steven Candelaria.

GAME INFORMATION

Radio Announcer: Zack Bayrouty. **PA Announcers:** Cory Smith, Chris Payne. **Official Scorers:** Alan Means, Greg Erny, Gregg Zive.

Stadium Name: Greater Nevada Field. **Location: From north, south and east:** I-80 West, Exit 14 (Wells Ave.), left on Wells, right at Kuenzil St., field on right; From West, I-80 East to Exit 13 (Virginia St.), right on Virginia, left on Second, field on left. **Standard Game Times:** 7:05 p.m., 6:35 p.m., 1:05 p.m. **Ticket Price Range:** $8-35.

ROUND ROCK EXPRESS

Address: 3400 East Palm Valley Blvd, Round Rock, TX 78665.
Telephone: (512) 255-2255. **Fax:** (512) 255-1558.
E-Mail Address: info@rrexpress.com. **Website:** www.RRExpress.com.
Affiliation (first year): Houston Astros (2019). **Year in League:** 2005-

OWNERSHIP/MANAGEMENT

Operated By: Ryan Sanders Baseball, LP. **Principal Owners:** Nolan Ryan, Don Sanders. **Owners:** Reese Ryan, Reid Ryan, Brad Sanders, Bret Sanders, Eddie Maloney.

CEO, Ryan Sanders Baseball: Reese Ryan. **Chief Operating Officer, Ryan Sanders Baseball:** JJ Gottsch. **Executive Assistant, Ryan Sanders Baseball:** Debbie Bowman. **Administrative Assistant, Ryan Sanders Baseball:** Jacqueline Bowman. **President:** Chris Almendarez. **General Manager:** Tim Jackson. **Advisor to President/General Manager:** Dave Fendrick. **Senior Vice President, Marketing:** Laura Fragoso. **Vice President, Administration/Accounting:** Debbie Coughlin. **Vice President, Corporate Sales:** Henry Green. **Vice President, Ticket Sales:** Gary Franke. **Assistant General Manager, Sales:** Stuart Scally. **Senior Director, Ticket Operations:** Ross Scott. **Senior Director, United Heritage Center:** Scott Allen. **Director, Ballpark Entertainment:** Steve Richards. **Director, Broadcasting:** Mike Capps. **Director, Community Relations and Special Events:** Elisa Fogle. **Director, Express Select:** Chris Godwin. **Director, IT:** Sam Isham. **Director, Retail Operations:** Joe Belger. **Director, Stadium Maintenance:** Aurelio Martinez. **Director, Stadium Operations:** Gene Kropff. **Manager, Client Services:** Zach Pustka. **Manager, Development & Programs, Nolan Ryan Foundation:** Peyton Chapman. **Manager, Post-Event Cleaning:** Mark Maloney. **Manager, PR/Communications:** Andrew Felts. **Manager, Stadium Operations:** Justin Botkins. **Coordinator, Amateur Baseball:** Chase Almendarez. **Coordinator, Promotional Events:** Casey Wright. **Coordinator, Season Memberships and Suite Services:** Aschley Eschenburg. **Specialist, Brand Marketing:** Julia Price. **Specialist, Digital Content:** Taylor Shipp. **Specialist, Guest Experience:** Jake Foust. **Specialist, IT:** Preston Chapman. **Senior Account Executives:** Alyssa Coggins, Oscar Rodriguez. **Account Executives:** Lucas Allison, Taylor Dillingham, Chaniel Nelson. **Head Groundskeeper:** Nick Rozdilski. **Clubhouse Manager:** Kenny Bufton. **Maintenance Staff:** Ofelia Gonzalez. **Electrician/HVAC Maintenance Staff:** Leslie Hitt. **Technician/Painter:** Roger Calkins. **Office Manager:** Wendy Abrahamsen. **Assistant, Accounting:** Sandy Tucker. **Assistant, Railyard Team Store:** Lisa Martinez.

FIELD STAFF

Manager: Mickey Storey. **Hitting Coach:** Ben Rosenthal. **Pitching Coach:** Drew French. **Development Coach:** Ryan Engels. **Trainer:** John Gregorich. **Strength Coach:** Hazael Wessin.

GAME INFORMATION

Radio Announcers: Mike Capps. **No. of Games Broadcast:** 140. **Flagship Station:** AM 1300 The Zone. **PA Announcer:** Glen Norman. **Official Scorer:** David Boyd.

Stadium Name: Dell Diamond. **Location:** US Highway 79, 3.5 miles east of Interstate 35 (exit 253) or 1.5 miles west of Texas Tollway 130. **Standard Game Times:** 7:05 pm, 6:05, 1:05, 11:35. **Ticket Price Range:** $7-$30.

Visiting Club Hotel: Hilton Garden Inn, 2310 North IH-35, Round Rock, TX 78681. **Telephone:** (512) 341-8200.

SACRAMENTO RIVER CATS

Address: Sutter Health Park - 400 Ballpark Drive, West Sacramento, CA 95691
Telephone: (916) 376-4700. **Fax:** (916) 376-4710.
E-Mail Address: reception@rivercats.com. **Website:** www.rivercats.com
Affiliation (first year): San Francisco Giants (2015). **Years in League:** 1903, 1909-11, 1918-60, 1974-76, 2000-

OWNERSHIP/MANAGEMENT

Majority Owner/CEO: Susan Savage. **President:** Jeff Savage. **General Manager:** Chip Maxson. **Director, Human Resources:** Isabella Guedes. **Coordinator, Human Resources:** Vanessa Villanueva. **Vice President, Finance:** Maddie Strika. **Accounting Coordinator:** Darcy Kooman. **Executive Assistant:** Dawn Lloyd. **Front Desk Administrator:** Liz Phillips. **Vice President, Partner Services:** Greg Coletti. **Director, Corporate Partnerships:** Ryan Maddox. **Manager, Key Accounts:** Ellese Iliff. **Coordinator, Partnership Activation:** Krystal Jones. **Coordinator, Partnership Activation:** Carl Dyer. **Senior Manager, Communications and Baseball Operations:** Danniel Emmons. **Coordinator, Media and Baseball:** Conner Penfold. **Radio Broadcaster:** Johnny Doskow. **Multimedia Designer:** Mike Villarreal. **Graphic Design Coordinator:** Nina Berghausen. **Manager, Marketing:** Melissa Adams. **Marketing Coordinator:** Hannah Burton. **Promotions Manager:** Amber Wyatt. **Director, Ticket Operations:** Joe Carlucci. **Senior Manager, Group Sales:** Jeff Goldsmith. **Manager, Membership Sales:** Troy Loparco. **Manager, Business Development:** Jack Barbour. **Manager, Corporate Sales:** John Watts. **Senior Membership Experience Specialist:** Kyle Strom. **Coordinator, Membership and Suite Services: Kayla Vidal. **Specialist, Membership Experience:** Sarah Romero. **Senior Account Executives, Group Events:** Peyton Burnham, Tyler Kadison. **Account Executives, Group Events:** Justin Wiley, Cassandra Ferree, Evan Grodan, Stephanie Brausch. **Account Executives, Corporate Sales:** Daniel Alonso, Ryan Dehn, Noah Hansler. **Account Executives, Inside Sales:** Ian Pettley, Jared Rebensdorf, Austin Staab, Mohammed Halabi, Kyle Garber, Cheyenne Taylor. **Manager, Merchandise:** Rose Holland. **Manager, Merchandise Marketing & Online Sales:** Erin Kilby. **Coordinator, Website/Research:** Brent Savage. **Vice President, Ballpark Experience:** Corey Brandt. **Director, Events/Entertainment:** Brittney Nizuk. **Senior Coordinator, Events/Entertainment:** Aubrey Schmidt. **Coordinator, Events/Entertainment:** Lauren Baldwin. **Director, Field Operations:** Chris Shastid. **Facility Supervisor:** Anthony Hernandez. **Manager, Security:** Rich Bentley. **Stadium Operations Supervisor:** Mike Correa. **Stadium Operations:** Jack Veasey. **Coordinator, Field Operations:** Marcello Clamar. **Landscaper:** Rafael Quiroz. **Manager, Concessions:** Sean Gerkensmeyer. **Manager, Suites & Premium Hospitality:** Megan Kohl. **Food & Beverage HR Coordinator:** Courtney Cino.

FIELD STAFF
Manager: Dave Brundage. **Hitting Coach:** Damon Minor. **Pitching Coach:** Glen Dishman. **Fundamentals Coach:** Jolbert Cabrera. **Bullpen Coach:** C.J. Picerni. **Athletic Trainers:** David Getsoff, Hiro Sato. **Strength & Conditioning Coach:** Andy King.

GAME INFORMATION
Radio Broadcaster: Johnny Doskow. **No. of Games Broadcast:** 140. **PA Announcer:** Keith Jouganatos. **Official Scorers:** Mark Honbo, Doug Kelly, Robert Barsanti. **Stadium Name:** Sutter Health Park. **Location:** I-5 to Business-80 West, exit at Jefferson Boulevard. **Standard Game Time:** 7:05 p.m. **Ticket Price Range:** $10-$70. **Visiting Club Hotel:** Holiday Inn Sacramento Downtown - Arena.

SALT LAKE BEES

Address: 77 W 1300 South, Salt Lake City, UT 84115.
Telephone: (801) 325-2337. **Fax:** (801) 485-6818.
E-Mail Address: info@slbees.com. **Website:** www.slbees.com.
Affiliation (first year): Los Angeles Angels (2001). **Years in League:** 1915-25, 1958-65, 1970-84, 1994-.

OWNERSHIP/MANAGEMENT
Operated by: Larry H. Miller Baseball Inc.
Principal Owner: Gail Miller. **President, Miller Sports & Entertainment:** Jim Olson. **Chief Revenue Officer:** Don Stirling. **Chief Financial Officer:** John Larson. **President/General Manager:** Marc Amicone. **Assistant GM:** Bryan Kinneberg. **Senior VP, Corporate Partnerships:** Ted Roberts. **Senior VP, Communications:** Frank Zang. **General Counsel:** Sam Harkness. **VP of Corporate Partnerships:** John Kimball. **Director, Broadcasting:** Steve Klauke. **VP Ticket Sales:** Trevor Haws, **Director,Ticket Sales:** Brad Jacoway. **Director, Corporate Partnerships:** Kim Brown. **Director, Marketing:** Brady Brown. **Director, Ticket Operations:** Derrek DeGraaff. **Communications Manager:** Kraig Williams. **Game Operations and Marketing Manager:** Caylor Tarter. **Graphic Designer:** Cody Cunningham. **Youth Programs Coordinator:** Nate Martinez. **Home Clubhouse Manager:** Cole Filosa. **Visiting Clubhouse Manager:** Chris Simonsen. **Head Groundskeeper:** Brian Soukup. **Asst. Head Groundskeeper:** Paul Sheffield.

FIELD STAFF
Manager: Lou Marson. **Hitting Coach:** Brian Betancourth. **Pitching Coach:** Jairo Cuevas. **Trainer:** Brian Reinker.

GAME INFORMATION
Radio Announcer: Steve Klauke. **No. of Games Broadcast:** 140. **Flagship Station:** 1280 AM. **PA Announcer:** Jeff Reeves. **Official Scorers:** Jeff Cluff, Brooke Frederickson. **Stadium Name:** Smith's Ballpark. **Location:** I-15 North/South to 1300 South exit, east to ballpark at West Temple. **Standard Game Times:** 6:35 (Night games), 1:05 Sunday day games, 12:05 (weekday day games). **Ticket Price Range:** $10-24.

SAN ANTONIO MISSIONS

Address: 5757 Highway 90 West, San Antonio, TX 78227.
Telephone: (210) 675-7275. **Fax:** (210) 670-0001.
E-Mail Address: sainfo@samissions.com. **Website:** www.samissions.com.
Affiliation (first year): Milwaukee Brewers (2019). **Years in League:** 2019-

OWNERSHIP/MANAGEMENT
Operated by: Elmore Sports Group. **Principal Owner:** David Elmore.
President: Burl Yarbrough. **General Manager:** Dave Gasaway. **Assistant GMs:** Mickey Holt, Jeff Long, Bill Gerlt. **Director, Baseball Operations:** Rich Weimert. **GM, Diamond Concessions:** Deanna Mierzwa. **Controller:** Eric Olivarez. **Director, Broadcasting:** Mike Saeger. **Office Manager:** Delia Rodriguez. **Director, Operations:** John Hernandez. **Director, Public Relations:** Mark Meyers. **Field Superintendent:** Travis Joslin. **Director, Ticketing:** JJ Jimenez.

FIELD STAFF
Manager: Rick Sweet. **Hitting Coach:** Al LeBoeuf. **Pitching Coach:** Jim Henderson. **Coach:** Ned Yost IV. **Trainer:** Lanning Tucker. **Strength Coach:** Andrew Emmick.

GAME INFORMATION
Radio Announcer: Mike Saeger. **No. of Games Broadcast:** 140. **Flagship Station:** 860-AM.
PA Announcer: Roland Ruiz. **Official Scorer:** David Humphrey.
Stadium Name: Nelson Wolff Stadium. **Location:** From I-10, I-35 or I-37, take US Hwy 90 West to Callaghan Road exit. **Standard Game Times:** 7:05 pm, Sun 2:05pm/6:05pm.
Visiting Club Hotel: Holiday Inn Northwest/Sea World. **Telephone:** (210) 520-2508.

TACOMA RAINIERS

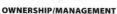

Address: 2502 South Tyler St, Tacoma, WA 98405.
Telephone: (253) 752-7707. **Fax:** (253) 752-7135.
Website: www.tacomarainiers.com
Affiliation (first year): Seattle Mariners (1995). **Years in League:** 1960-Present

OWNERSHIP/MANAGEMENT
Owners: The Baseball Club of Tacoma. **President:** Aaron Artman. **CFO:** Brian Coombe. **Assistant General Manager:** Nick Cherniske. **Vice President, Sales:** Shane Santman. **Director of Administration and Assistant to the President:** Patti Stacy. **Senior Director, Ticket Sales:** Tim O'Hollaren. **Director, Business Development:** Ben Nelson. **Director, Ticket Operations:** Kristin Myers. **Manager, Corporate Sales:** Devon Barker. **Manager, Corporate Sales:** Maggie Baumgarten. **Manager, Corporate Sales:** Kevin Drugge. **Manager, Corporate Sales:** Hank Foster. **Manager, Corporate Sales:** Danny Muno. **Manager, Corporate Sales:** Rocky McNulty. **Manager, Corporate Sales:** Josh Preli. **Inside Sales:** Aaron Oda. **Director, Group Sales and Event Marketing:** Caitlin Calnan. **Manager, Group Sales:** Chris Aubertin. **Premium Experience and Events Manager:** Hannah Hall. **Coordinator, Group Events:** Michael Landrum. **Coordinator, Group Events:** Maddie Miller. **Coordinator, Group Events:** Hayley Hacker. **Vice President, Marketing:** Megan Mead. **Director, Creative:** Casey Catherwood. **Director, Media Relations and Content Development:** AJ Garcia. **Coordinator, Game Entertainment:** Maddie Bukata. **Coordinator, Marketing and Community Outreach:** Fernanda Irish. **Graphic Designer:** Delaney Saul. **Graphic Designer:** Erin Fogerty. **Manager, Marketing:** Reema Patel. **Director, Technical:** Anthony Phinney. **Specialist, Multimedia:** Adam Wygle. **Broadcaster,** Mike Curto. **Director, Partner Services:** Yvette Yzaguirre. **Manager, Partner Services:** Rachel Hansen. **Director, Baseball Ops and Merchandise:** Ashley Schutt. **Manager, Team Store:** Kyle McGilvray. **Manager, Stadium Operations:** Zack Armstrong. **Head Groundskeeper:** Michael Huie. **Manager, Facility Maintenance:** Steffan Drake. **Manager, Box Office:** Michael McCoy. **Director, Finance and Operations:** Jack Kelly. **Coordinator, Front Desk:** Aubrey O'Brien.

FIELD STAFF
Manager: Daren Brown. **Hitting Coach:** Roy Howell. **Pitching Coach:** Rob Marcello. **Trainers:** Tom Newberg and Josh DiLoreto. **Performance Specialist:** Derek Mendoza.

GAME INFORMATION
Radio Broadcaster: Mike Curto. **No. of Games Broadcast:** 140. **Flagship Station:** KHHO 850-AM. **PA Announcer:** Randy McNair. **Official Scorers:** Kevin Kalal, Gary Brooks, Michael Jessee, Jon Gilbert. **Stadium Name:** Cheney Stadium. **Location:** From I-5, take exit 132 (Highway 16 West) for 1.2 miles to 19th Street East exit, merge right onto 19th Street, right onto Clay Huntington Way and follow into parking lot of ballpark. **Standard Game Times:** 7:05, Sun. 1:35. (Monday – Wednesday games start at 6:05pm in April – June). **Ticket Price Range:** $7.50-$25.50. **Visiting Club Hotel:** Hotel Murano, 1320 Broadway Plaza, Tacoma, WA 98402. **Telephone:** (253) 238-8000.

WICHITA WIND SURGE

Address: 300 S. Sycamore Street, Wichita KS 67213
Telephone: (316) 221-8000. **Fax:** TBD
E-Mail Address: info@windsurge.com **Website:** www.windsurge.com
Affiliation (first year): Miami Marlins (2020). **Years in League:** 2020-

OWNERSHIP/MANAGEMENT

Managing General Partner: Lou Schwechheimer. Partner / **Chief Operating Officer:** Matt White. Partner/ **Senior Advisor:** Jordan Kobritz. **Partner / SVP, Community Relations:** Annie Life. **President:** Jay Miller. **SVP-HRJC Hospitality:** Eric Petterson. **SVP-General Manager:** Jared Forma. **SVP- Sports & Entertainment Ventures:** Augusto "Cookie" Rojas. **VP- Game Operations & Entertainment:** Derrick Grubbs. **VP & Assistant General Manager:** Bob Moullette. **Director of Finance:** Lori Engleman, **Director of Broadcasting & Team Travel:** Tim Grubbs. **Director of Stadium Operations:** Alex Knudsen. **Director of Ticket Operations:** Adam Mettler. **Director of Field Operations:** Justin McConnell. **Director of Sales & Marketing:** Brian Turner. **Stadium Operations Manager:** Andrew Crawford. **Clubhouse Manager:** Brett Herbert. **Merchandise Manager:** Maggie Schleismann. **Box Office Manager:** Nick Schriever. **Ticket Sales Account Representative:** Jessi Holman. **Marketing Associate:** Jenn Schwechheimer. **Marketing Associate:** Ryan Pluskis. **Sales & Marketing Associate:** Nick Bernabe. **Assistant Groundskeeper:** Richard Goodyear. **Director of Food & Beverage:** Randy Robinson. **Head Chef:** Kris Anderson. **Hospitality Manager:** Lori Buser.

FIELD STAFF

Manager: Keith Johnson. **Hitting Coach:** Justin Mashore. **Pitching Coach:** Jeremy Powell. **Defensive Coach:** Danny Black. **Athletic Trainer:** Greg Harrel. **Strength & Conditioning:** Robert Reichert.

GAME INFORMATION

Radio Announcers: Tim Grubbs. **No. of Games Broadcast:** 140. **Flagship Station:** KGSO 1410 AM and 93.9 FM. **PA Announcer:** Derrick Grubbs. **Official Scorer:** TBD. **Stadium Name:** TBD. **Location: From Airport:** US-400 E/ US-54 E from Eisenhower Airport Pkwy, Take the Seneca St exit from US-400 E/US-54 E, Continue on S Sycamore St to your destination. **Standard Game Times:** 7:05 pm, Sat. 6:05, Sun. 1:05. **Ticket Price Range:** $8-15. **Visiting Club Hotel:** Hyatt Regency Wichita, 400 W Waterman Street, Wichita, KS 67202. **Telephone:** (316) 293-1234.

EASTERN LEAGUE

Address: 27 Gorham Rd, Suite 221, Scarborough, ME 04074.
Telephone: (207) 289-6206. **Fax:** (207) 219-8958.
E-Mail Address: elpb@easternleague.com.
Website: www.easternleague.com.
Years League Active: 1923-
President/Treasurer: Joe McEacharn.
Vice President/Secretary: Charlie Eshbach. **VP:** Chuck Domino. **Director of Operations:**
Bill Rosario. **Directors:** Fernando Aguirre (Erie), Ken Babby (Akron), Art Solomon (New
Hampshire), Kevin Kulp (Harrisburg), Lou DiBella (Richmond), Geoff Iacuessa (Portland), Joe
Finley (Trenton), John Hughes (Binghamton), Bob Lozinak (Altoona), Brian Shallcross (Bowie),
Josh Solomon (Hartford), Craig Stein (Reading).

Joe McEacharn

Division Structure: Eastern—Binghamton, Hartford, New Hampshire, Portland, Reading,
Trenton. **Western**—Akron, Altoona, Bowie, Erie, Harrisburg, Richmond.
Regular Season: 140 games. **2020 Opening Date:** April 9. **Closing Date:** Sept 7.
All-Star Game: July 15 at Binghamton
Playoff Format: The first half winner and second half winner from each division meet in best-of-five series. Winners
meet in best-of-five series for league championship.
Roster Limit: 25. **Player Eligibility Rule:** No restrictions.
Brand of Baseball: Rawlings.
Umpires: Matt Carlyon (Drums, PA), Trevor Dannegger (Ballwin, MO), Joe Gonzalez (El Monte, CA), Tom Hanahan
(Mentor, OH), Aaron Higgins (Elk Grove, CA), Jude Koury (Youngstown, OH), Lucas Krupa (Sault Ste Marie, MI), Chris
Marco (Waterdown, Ontario), Dave Martinez (Bayonne, NJ), Taka Matsuda (Hamilton, Ontario), Ben Phillips (Cary, NC),
Dane Poncsak (Columbus, OH), Tom Roche (Hamden, CT), Chris Scott (Boston, MA), Sean Shafer-Markle (Grand Rapids,
MI), Mike Snover (Myrtle Beach, SC), Derek Thomas (Cape Coral, FL), Tom West (Scarborough, Australia).

STADIUM INFORMATION

Club	Stadium	Opened	LF	CF	RF	Capacity	2019 Att.
Akron	Canal Park	1997	331	400	337	7,630	340,187
Altoona	Peoples Natural Gas Field	1999	325	405	325	7,210	308,464
Binghamton	NYSEG Stadium	1992	330	400	330	6,012	182,990
Bowie	Prince George's Stadium	1994	309	405	309	10,000	224,686
Erie	UPMC Park	1995	317	400	328	6,000	215,444
Harrisburg	Metro Bank Park	1987	325	400	325	6,300	258,909
Hartford	Dunkin' Donuts Park	2018	325	400	325	6,146	414,946
New Hampshire	Northeast Delta Dental Stadium	2005	326	400	306	6,500	306,511
Portland	Hadlock Field	1994	315	400	330	7,368	357,647
Reading	FirstEnergy Stadium	1951	330	400	330	9,000	398,314
Richmond	The Diamond	1985	330	402	330	9,560	400,321
Trenton	Arm & Hammer Park	1994	330	407	330	6,150	340,705

Dimensions: LF / CF / RF

AKRON RUBBERDUCKS

Address: 300 S Main St, Akron, OH 44308.
Telephone: (330) 253-5151. (855) 97-QUACK. **Fax: (330) 253-3300.**
E-Mail Address: information@akronrubberducks.com.
Website: www.akronrubberducks.com.
Affiliation (first year): Cleveland Indians (1989). **Years in League:** 1989-

OWNERSHIP/MANAGEMENT

Operated By: Fast Forward Sports Group/Akron Baseball, LLC. **Principal Owner/CEO:** Ken Babby.
President: Jim Pfander. **CFO:** Shawn Carlson. **General Manager/COO:** Jim Pfander. **Assistant GM/Vice President,**
Operations: Scott Riley. **Vice President, Sales:** Dave Burke. **Controller:** Leslie Wenzlawsh. **Assistant, Finance:**
Bryson Lenderman. **Manager, Promotions:** Kyle Hixenbaugh. **Coordinator, Media Relations:** Pat McGuire. **Lead**
Broadcaster: Marco LaNave. **Director, Merchandise:** Jeff Campano. **Coordinator, Creative Services:** Gabe Wasylko.
Director, Stadium Operations: Adam Horner. **Head Groundskeeper:** Chris Walsh. **Assistant Groundskeeper:**
James Petrella. **Assistant Director, Ballpark Operations:** James Parsons. **Director, Food/Beverage:** Brian Manning.
Assistant Director, Food/Beverage: Bob Demyan. **Director, Premium Experience:** Sam Dankoff. **Manager, Culinary**
Operations: Louis Willmon-Holland. **Office Manager:** Missy Dies. **Coordinator, Community Relations:** Sonia Gainford.
Manager, Season Ticket Sales & Service: Mitch Cromes. **Senior Manager, Amateur Baseball Development/Group**
Sales & Service: Roy Jacobs. **Assistant Director, Sales/Coordinator Digital Media:** Dominic DeMarco. **Assistant**
Director, Ticket Operations: Sam Cranor. **Ticket Sales Executives:** Ian Wilkinson, Trevor McGuire, TBD. **Manager,**
Corporate Partnerships: Anthony Chadwick. **Coordinator, Corporate Partnerships:** Brian Lobban. **Art Director:**
Scott Watkins. **Director, Player Facilities:** Shad Gross.

FIELD STAFF
Manager: TBD. **Hitting Coach:** TBD. **Pitching Coach:** TBD. **Bench Coach:** TBD. **Trainer:** TBD.

GAME INFORMATION
Radio Announcers: Marco LaNave, Jim Clark. **No. of Games Broadcast:** 140. **Flagship Station:** Fox Sports Radio 1350-AM. **PA Announcer:** DJ Nivens. **Official Scorer:** Chuck Murr. **Stadium Name:** Canal Park. **Location:** From I-76 East or I-77 South, exit onto Route 59 East, exit at Exchange/Cedar, right onto Cedar, left at Main Street; From I-76 West or I-77 North, exit at Main Street/Downtown, follow exit onto Broadway Street, left onto Exchange Street, right at Main Street. **Standard Game Time:** 6:35 (non-fireworks game); 7:05 pm (fireworks games), Sun 2:05. **Ticket Price Range:** $5-11. **Visiting Club Hotel:** Fairfield Inn & Suites by Marriott Akron Fairlawn. **Telephone:** (330) 665-0641.

ALTOONA CURVE

Address: Peoples Natural Gas Field, 1000 Park Avenue, Altoona, PA 16602
Telephone: (814) 943-5400. **Fax:** (814) 942-9132
E-Mail Address: frontoffice@altoonacurve.com. **Website:** www.altoonacurve.com
Affiliation (first year): Pittsburgh Pirates (1999). **Years in League:** 1999-

OWNERSHIP/MANAGEMENT
Operated By: Lozinak Professional Baseball.
Managing Members: Bob and Joan Lozinak. **COO:** David Lozinak. **CFO:** Mike Lozinak. **General Manager:** Derek Martin. **Senior Advisor:** Sal Baglieri. **Assistant General Manager:** Nathan Bowen. **Director of Finance:** Mary Lamb. **Assistant Director of Finance:** Aaron McGuire. **Administrative Assistant:** Michelle Anna. **Director of Communications & Broadcasting:** Garett Mansfield. **Communications & Broadcasting Assistant:** Justin Gallanty. **Director of Ticketing:** Jess Knott. **Box Office Manager:** Bryan Sowers. **Senior Ticket Account Manager:** Ed Moffett. **Ticket Sales Manager:** Kyle Wilson. **Ticket Sales Manager:** Alex Popies. **Ticket Sales Manager:** Corbin Padgett. **Manager of Partnership Services:** Jade Giantini. **Director of Community Relations & Social Media:** Annie Choiniere. **Director of Ballpark Operations:** Doug Mattern. **Head Groundskeeper:** TBD. **Director of Concessions:** Glenn McComas. **Assistant Director of Concessions:** Ashley Daley. **Director of Entertainment and Branding:** Isaiah Arpino. **Director of Creative Services:** Braeden Appleman. **Creative Services Assistant:** Megan Corcoran. Director of Marketing, **Promotions & Special Events:** Mike Kessling. **Director of Merchandise:** Michelle Gravert.

FIELD STAFF
Manager: Dave Turgeon. **Hitting Coach:** David Newhan. **Pitching Coach:** Tom Filer. **Coach:** Gera Alvarez. **Trainer:** Jorge Islas. **Strength/Conditioning:** Joe Schlesinger.

GAME INFORMATION
Radio Announcers: Garett Mansfield and Justin Gallanty. **No. of Games Broadcast:** 140. **Flagship Station:** WRTA 98.5 FM and 1240 AM. **PA Announcer:** Rich DeLeo. **Official Scorers:** Ted Beam, Dick Wagner. **Stadium Name:** Peoples Natural Gas Field. **Location:** Located just off the Frankstown Road Exit off I-99. **Standard Game Times:** 6 p.m. (Weekdays, April-May); 6:30 p.m. (Weekdays, June-August); Fri 7 p.m.; Sat. 4 p.m. and 6 p.m.; Sun 2 p.m. and 6 p.m. **Ticket Price Range:** $8-17. **Visiting Club Hotel:** Microtel Inn & Suites Altoona.

BINGHAMTON RUMBLE PONIES

Office Address: 211 Henry St., Binghamton, NY 13901.
Mailing Address: PO Box 598, Binghamton, NY 13902.
Telephone: (607) 722-3866. **Fax:** (607) 723-7779.
E-Mail Address: info@bingrp.com. **Website:** www.bingrp.com.
Affiliation (first year): New York Mets (1992). **Years in League:** 1923-37, 1940-63, 1966-68, 1992-

OWNERSHIP/MANAGEMENT
President: John Hughes. **Managing Director:** John Bayne. **Director of Business Operations:** Kelly Hust. **Director of Broadcasting & Media Relations:** Jacob Wilkins. **Director of Community Relations and Box Office Manager:** Eddie Saunders. **Director of Video Production:** Chris Ortega. **Director of Marketing & Promotions:** Lorin Williams. **Director of Stadium Operations:** Richard Tylicki. **Director of Sales:** Bill Koehler . **Director of Merchandise & Retail Sales:** Jessica Swartz. **Senior Account Executive:** Tony Rogers. **Scholastic Programs Coordinator:** Lou Ferraro.

FIELD STAFF
Manager: Lorenzo Bundy. **Hitting Coach:** Tony Jaramillo. **Pitching Coach:** Jonathan Hurst. **Bench Coach:** Luis Rivera.

GAME INFORMATION
Radio Announcer: Jacob Wilkins. **No. of Games Broadcast:** 140. **Flagship Station:** WNBF 1290-AM. **PA Announcer:** Frank Perney. **Official Scorer:** Matt Ferraro. **Stadium Name:** NYSEG Stadium. **Location:** I-81 to exit 4S (Binghamton), Route 11 exit to Henry Street. **Standard Game Times:** 6:35, 7:05 (Fri-Sat), 1:05, 2:05 (Day Games). **Ticket Price Range:** $7 - $14. **Visiting Club Hotel:** Holiday Inn Downtown.

BOWIE BAYSOX

Address: Prince George's Stadium, 4101 NE Crain Hwy, Bowie, MD 20716.
Telephone: (301) 805-6000. **Fax:** (301) 464-4911.
E-Mail Address: info@baysox.com. **Website:** www.baysox.com.
Affiliation (first year): Baltimore Orioles (1993). **Years in League:** 1993-

OWNERSHIP/MANAGEMENT
Owned By: Maryland Baseball Holding LLC. **President:** Ken Young. **General Manager:** Brian Shallcross. **Assistant GM:** Phil Wrye. **Business Manager:** Landon Ferrell. **Director, Ticket Operations:** Charlene Fewer. **Director, Sponsorships:** Matt McLaughlin. **Promotions Manager:** Chris Rogers. **Communications Manager:** Robby Veronesi. **Sponsorship Account Manager/Director of Broadcasting:** Adam Pohl. **Assistant Director of Ticket Operations:** Scott Rupp. **Assistant Director of Ticket Operations:** Mauricio Simms. **Box Office Manager:** Aaron Ware.
Director, Video Production: Mitchell Block. **Facility Manager & Head Groundskeeper:** Richard Douglas. **Groundskeeper Assistant:** Darren Blackmon. **Director. Gameday Personnel:** Darlene Mingioli. **Clubhouse Manager:** Dallas Darling.

FIELD STAFF
Manager: Buck Britton. **Hitting Coach:** Tim Gibbons. **Pitching Coach:** Justin Ramsey. **Fundamentals Coach:** Butch Davis. **Athletic Trainer:** Brian Guzman. **Development Coach:** Grant Anders.

GAME INFORMATION
Radio Announcer: Adam Pohl. **No. of Games Broadcast:** 140. **Flagship Station:** www.1430wnav.com. **PA Announcer:** Adrienne Roberson. **Official Scorers:** Dan Gretz, Patrick Stevens. **Stadium Name:** Prince George's Stadium. **Location:** 1/4 mile south of US 50/Route 301 Interchange in Bowie. **Standard Game Times:** Mon-Thu, Sat. 6:35 pm, Fri 7:05 pm, Sun 1:35 pm. **Ticket Price Range:** $8-$18. **Visiting Club Hotel:** Crowne Plaza Annapolis, 173 Jennifer Rd, Annapolis, MD 21401; **Telephone:** (410) 266-3131.

ERIE SEAWOLVES

Address: 110 E 10th St, Erie, PA 16501.
Telephone: (814) 456-1300. **Fax:** (814) 456-7520.
E-Mail Address: seawolves@seawolves.com. **Website:** www.seawolves.com.
Affiliation (first year): Detroit Tigers (2001). **Years in League:** 1999-

OWNERSHIP/MANAGEMENT
Principal Owners: At Bat Group, LLC.
CEO: Fernando Aguirre. **President:** Greg Coleman. **Assistant GM, Communications:** Greg Gania. **Assistant GM, Sales:** Mark Pirrello. **Director, Accounting/Finance:** Amy McArdle. **Director, Operations:** TBA. **Director, Entertainment:** David Micik. **Account Executive:** Joe Peer. **Account Executive:** Jack Gorman. **Community Engagement Manager:** Christopher McDonald. **Director, Merchandise:** Christy Buchar. **Director, Food/Beverage:** Jeff Burgess. **Ticket Operations Manager:** Tom Barnes.

FIELD STAFF
Manager: TBA. **Hitting Coach:** Adam Melhuse. **Pitching Coach:** Mark Johnson. **Developmental Coach:** Tony Smith. **Trainer:** Chris Vick. **Strength/Conditioning Coach:** Phil Hartt.

GAME INFORMATION
Radio Announcer: Greg Gania. **No. of Games Broadcast:** 140. **Flagship Station:** Fox Sports Radio WFNN 1330-AM. **PA Announcer:** Bob Shreve. **Official Scorer:** TBA. **Stadium Name:** UPMC Park. **Location:** US 79 North to East 12th Street exit, left on State Street, right on 10th Street. **Standard Game Times:** 6:05 p.m. (April-May), 7:05 p.m. (June-Aug), Sun 1:35 p.m. **Ticket Price Range:** $10-16. **Visiting Club Hotel:** Baymont Inn & Suites, 8170 Perry Hwy., Erie, PA 16509. **Telephone:** (814) 866-8808.

HARRISBURG SENATORS

Office Address: FNB Field, City Island, Harrisburg, PA 17101.
Mailing Address: PO Box 15757, Harrisburg, PA 17105.
Telephone: (717) 231-4444. **Fax:** (717) 231-4445.
E-Mail address: information@senatorsbaseball.com. **Website:** www.senatorsbaseball.com.
Affiliation (first year): Washington Nationals (2005). **Years in League:** 1924-35, 1987-

OWNERSHIP/MANAGEMENT
President: Kevin Kulp.
General Manager: Randy Whitaker. **Accounting Manager:** Donna Demczak. **Receptionist:** Jill Parrish. **Senior Corporate Sales Executive:** Todd Matthews. **Corporate Sales Executive:** Nathan Rovenolt. **Director, Group Sales:** Jessica Moyer. **Director, Ticket Operations:** Matt McGrady. **Senior Account Executive:** Sage Berry. **Account**

MINOR LEAGUES

Executive: Erin Carr. **Group Sales Account Executives:** Kyle Kondracki. **Account Executive:** Samuel West. **Sales Service Coordinator:** Josh Bleyer. **Director, Marketing:** Ashley Grotte. **Radio Broadcaster:** Terry Byrom. **Director, Merchandise:** Ann Marie Naumes. **Director, Game Entertainment:** Scott Ciaccia. **Game Entertainment Coordinator:** Sami Lesniak. **Director, Community Relations:** JK McKay. **Director of Stadium Operations:** Tim Foreman. **Head Groundskeeper:** Brandon Forsburg. **General Business Interns:** Kaitlin Caringi, Logan Duras, Megan McGloin & Colin Weidman. **Box Office Intern:** Travis Miller. **Graphic Design Intern:** Elyse Jones. **Radio Broadcaster Intern:** Will Greer. **Stadium Operations & Field Interns:** Andrew Berg & Steven Rollins.

FIELD STAFF
Manager: Billy Gardner, Jr. **Coach:** Brian Rupp. **Pitching Coach:** Sam Narron. **Trainer:** T.D. Swinford. **Strength Coach:** R.J. Guyer.

GAME INFORMATION
Radio Announcers: Terry Byrom & Will Greer. **No. of Games Broadcast:** Home-70 Road-70 CBSSports Radio Harrisburg. **PA Announcer:** TBD. **Official Scorers:** Andy Linker and Mick Reinhard. **Stadium Name:** FNB Field. **Location:** I-83, exit 23 (Second Street) to Market Street, bridge to City Island. **Ticket Price Range:** $9-35. **Visiting Club Hotel:** Comfort Inn and Suites Harrisburg Airport, 1589 W. Harrisburg Pike, Middletown, PA 17057. **Telephone:** (717) 857-8776. **Visiting Team Workout Facility:** TBD.

HARTFORD YARD GOATS

Address: Dunkin' Donuts Park, 1214 Main Street, Hartford CT 06103
Telephone: (860) 246-4628. **Fax:** (860) 247-4628
E-Mail Address: info@yardgoatsbaseball.com. **Website:** www.YardGoatsBaseball.com
Affiliation (first year): Colorado Rockies (2015). **Years in League:** 2015-

OWNERSHIP/MANAGEMENT
President: Tim Restall. **General Manager:** Mike Abramson.
Assistant General Manager, Sales: Josh Montinieri. **Assistant General Manager, Operations:** Dean Zappalorti. **Director, Broadcasting & Media Relations:** Jeff Dooley. **Executive Director of Business Development:** Steve Given. **Director of Human Resources:** Thulani LeGrier. **Director of Event Services:** Conor Geary. **Events Marketing Manager:** Jacqueline Crockwell. **Hospitality and External Business Coordinator:** Jessica Gorman. **Director of Stadium Operations:** Ryan Mariotti. **Stadium Operations Manager:** Andrew Girard. **Executive Director, Community Partnerships:** Tiffany Young. **Fundraising and Community Engagement Manager:** Tom Baxter. **Controller:** Jim Bonfiglio. **Director of Client Services & Team Relations:** Amanda Goldsmith. **Promotions & Marketing Manager:** Danielle Chylinski. **Game Production Manager:** Mike Delgado. **Merchandise Manager:** AJ Massaro. **Box Office Manager:** Sage Vigliarolo. **Box Office Coordinator:** Rick Hoffman. **Director of Ticket Sales:** Steve Mekkelsen. **Ticket Sales Account Executive:** Matt DiBona. **Ticket Sales Account Executive:** Shawn Perry. **Ticket Sales Account Executive:** Kyle Abad. **Ticket Sales Account Executive:** Allie Toffolon. **Ticket Sales Account Executive:** Jacob Michney. **Ticket Sales Account Executive:** Jordan Carrion. **Sports Turf Manager:** Kyle Calhoon. **Administrative Assistant:** Shania Myers. **Community and Education Program Manager:** Tetrick Stonar. **Creative Services and Digital Marketing Coordinator:** Riley Hicks. **Stadium Services Technician:** Joe Bombardier. **Assistant Groundskeeper:** Andrew Cebry. **Grounds and Stadium Operations Assistant:** Jaime Torres. **Professional Sports Catering, Regional Vice President:** Scott Gustafson. **Director of Operations:** Jenny Nelson. **Concessions Manager:** Andrew Labov. **Executive Chef:** Joe Bartlett. **Premium Catering Manager:** Angela Kucharski. **Business Manager:** Kevin Molde.

FIELD STAFF
Manager: Chris Denorfia. **Hitting Coach:** Tom Sutaris. **Pitching Coach:** Frank Gonzalez. **Trainer:** Hoshito Mizutani. **Physical Performance Coach:** Mason Rook.

GAME INFORMATION
Radio Announcers: Jeff Dooley, Dan Lovallo. **No. of Games Broadcast:** 140. **Flagship Station:** News Radio 1410*FM 100.9 Spanish Danny Rodriguez, Derik Rodriguez. **PA Announcer:** Jared Doyon. **Official Scorer:** Jim Keener. **Stadium Name:** Dunkin' Donuts Park. **Directions: From the West:** Take 84 East to Exit 50 (Main Street). Take Exit 50 toward Main St. Use the left lane to merge onto Chapel St S. Turn left onto Trumbull St. Use the middle lane to turn left onto Main St. **From the East:** Take 84 West to Exit 50 (US-44 W/Morgan Street). Follow I-91 S/Main St. Take a slight right onto Main St. **From the North:** Take 91 South to Exit 32A - 32B (Trumbull St). Turn left onto Market St. Turn right onto Morgan St. Take a slight right onto Main St. **From the South:** Take 91 North to Exit 32A - 32B (Market St). Use the left lane to take Exit 32A-32B for Trumbull St. Use the middle lane to turn left onto Market St. Turn right onto Morgan St. Take a slight right onto Main St. **Ticket Price Range:** $6-22. **Visiting Club Hotel:** Holiday Inn Express, 2553 Berlin Turnpike, Newington, CT 06111. (860) 372-4000.

NEW HAMPSHIRE
FISHER CATS

Address: 1 Line Dr, Manchester, NH 03101.
Telephone: (603) 641-2005. **Fax:** (603) 641-2055.
E-Mail Address: info@nhfishercats.com. **Website:** www.nhfishercats.com.
Affiliation (first year): Toronto Blue Jays (2004). **Years in League:** 2004-

OWNERSHIP/MANAGEMENT
Operated By: DSF Sports. **Owner:** Art Solomon.
President: Mike Ramshaw. **General Manager:** Jim Flavin. **Senior VP, Sales:** Jeff Tagliaferro. **VP, Stadium Operations:** Tim Hough. **VP, Business Development:** Erik Lesniak. **Executive Director, Ticket Sales:** Jenna Lembo. **Director, Hospitality and Special Events:** Stephanie Fournier. **Director of Promotions & Entertainment:** Tyler Zickel. **Senior Account Executive:** John Evans. **Senior Account Executive:** Nate Newcombe. **Corporate Controller:** Jennifer Egan. **Corporate Sales Manager:** Tom Devarenne. **Box Office Manager:** Tara Leeth. **Marketing and Promotions Manager:** Sarah Lenau. **Broadcasting and Media Relations Manager:** Tyler Murray. **Production Manager:** Evan O'Brien. **Facility Operations Manager:** D.J. Peer. **Merchandise Manager:** Samantha Stawarz. **Turf Manager:** Greg Nigrello. **Corporate Sales and Promotions Coordinator:** Andrew Marais. **Ticket Sales Account Executives:** Andrew Larson. Professional Sports Catering, Director, **Food & Beverage:** Jesse DaSilva.

FIELD STAFF
Manager: Cesar Martin. **Hitting Coach:** Matt Young. **Pitching Coach:** Jim Czajkowski. **Athletic Trainer:** Caleb Daniel. **Strength/Conditioning:** Brian Pike. **Dietitian:** Kat Mangieri. **Position Coach:** Chris Schaeffer.

GAME INFORMATION
Radio Announcers: Tyler Murray, Bob Lipman, Tyler Zickel, Charlie Sherman.
No. of Games Broadcast: 140. **Flagship Station:** WGIR 610-AM. **PA Announcer:** Ben Altsher. **Official Scorers:** Chick Smith, Lenny Parker. **Stadium Name:** Northeast Delta Dental Stadium. **Location:** From I-93 North, take I-293 North to exit 5 (Granite Street), right on Granite Street, right on South Commercial Street, right on Line Drive. **Ticket Price Range:** $12. **Visiting Club Hotel:** Country Inn & Suites, 250 South River Rd., Bedford, N.H. 03110. **Telephone:** (603) 666-4600.

PORTLAND SEA DOGS

Office Address: 271 Park Ave, Portland, ME 04102.
Mailing Address: PO Box 636, Portland, ME 04104.
Telephone: (207) 874-9300. **Fax:** (207) 780-0317.
E-Mail address: seadogs@seadogs.com. **Website:** www.seadogs.com.
Affiliation (first year): Boston Red Sox (2003). **Years in League:** 1994-

OWNERSHIP/MANAGEMENT
Operated By: Portland, Maine Baseball, Inc.
Chairman: Bill Burke. **Treasurer:** Sally McNamara. **President/General Manager:** Geoff Iacuessa. **Senior VP:** John Kameisha. **VP/ Financial Affairs & Game Operations:** Jim Heffley. **VP/ Communications & Fan Experience:** Chris Cameron. **Assistant General Manager/Sales:** Dennis Meehan. **Director, Corporate Sales:** Justin Phillips. **Ticket Office Manager:** Bryan Pahigian. **Assistant Ticket Office Manager:** Allison Casiles. **Director, Creative Services:** Ted Seavey. **Mascot Coordinator:** Tim Jorn. Director, **Media Relations & Broadcasting:** Mike Antonellis. **Director, Food Services:** Mike Scorza. **Assistant Director, Food Services:** Greg Moyes. **Ticket Office Coordinator:** Alan Barker. **Account Executive:** Melissa Mayhew. **Senior Advisor:** Charlie Eshbach. **Clubhouse Manager:** Mike Coziahr. **Head Groundskeeper:** Jason Cooke. **Assistant Groundskeeper:** Andy Cashman.

FIELD STAFF
Manager: Joe Oliver. **Hitting Coach:** Lance Zawadski. **Pitching Coach:** Lance Carter. **Coach:** Frankie Rios. **Athletic Trainer:** Scott Gallon. **Strength & Conditioning Coach:** Ben Chadwick.

GAME INFORMATION
Radio Announcer: Mike Antonellis. **No. of Games Broadcast:** 140. **Flagship Station:** WPEI 95.9 FM. **PA Announcer:** Paul Coughlin. **Official Scorer:** Thom Hinton. **Stadium Name:** Hadlock Field. **Location:** From South, I-295 to exit 5, merge onto Congress Street, left at St John Street, merge right onto Park Ave; From North, I-295 to exit 6A, right onto Park Ave. **Ticket Price Range:** $6-11. **Visiting Club Hotel:** Fireside Inn & Suites, 81 Riverside St., Portland, ME 04103. **Telephone:** (207) 774-5601.

READING FIGHTIN PHILS

Office Address: Route 61 South/1900 Centre Ave, Reading, PA 19605. **Mailing Address:** PO Box 15050, Reading, PA 19612.
Telephone: (610) 370-2255. **Fax:** (610) 373-5868.
E-Mail Address: info@fightins.com. **Website:** www.fightins.com.
Affiliation (first year): Philadelphia Phillies (1967). **Years in League:** 1933-35, 1952-61, 1963-65, 1967-

OWNERSHIP/MANAGEMENT

Operated By: E&J Baseball Club, Inc. **Principal Owner:** Reading Baseball LP. **Managing Partner:** Craig Stein.
General Manager: Scott Hunsicker.
Assistant General Manager: Matt Hoffmaster. **Exec. Director, Sales:** Joe Bialek. **Exec. Director, Baseball Operations:** Kevin Sklenarik. **Exec. Director, Tickets & Groups:** Mike Becker. **Exec. Director, Community & Fan Development:** Mike Robinson. **Exec. Director, Business Development:** Anthony Pignetti. **Controller:** Kris Haver. **Head Groundskeeper:** Dan Douglas. **Chief Director, Promotions:** Todd Hunsicker. **Director, Marketing & Exec. Director, Baseballtown Charities:** Tonya Petrunak. **Video Director:** Andy Kauffman. **Director, Food & Beverage:** Travis Hart. **Office Manager:** Deneen Giesen. **Director, Groups:** Jon Nally. **Director, Public Relations/Media Relations & Radio Broadcaster:** Kirsten Karbach. **Director, Client Fulfillment/Clubhouse Operations:** Andrew Nelson. **Director, Graphic Arts/Merchandise:** Ryan Springborn. **Account Executive:** Nick Helber. **Group Outings Manager:** Nick Mayer. **Extra Events Manager:** Nicole Fetchko. **Stadium Operations Manager:** Heath Skimski. **Diversity Outreach Coordinator:** Roberto Sanchez.

FIELD STAFF

Manager: Kevin Boles. **Hitting Coach:** Tyler Henson. **Pitching Coach:** Jonathan Hurst. **Assistant Coach:** Nelson Prada.

GAME INFORMATION

Radio Announcer: Kirsten Karbach. **No. of Games Broadcast:** 140. **Flagship Station:** 610 ESPN.
Official Scorers: Kyle Matschke, Brian Kopetsky, Josh Leiboff, Dick Shute.
Stadium Name: FirstEnergy Stadium. **Location:** From east, take Pennsylvania Turnpike West to Morgantown exit, to 176 North, to 422 West, to Route 12 East, to Route 61 South exit; From west, take 422 East to Route 12 East, to Route 61 South exit; From north, take 222 South to Route 12 exit, to Route 61 South exit; From south, take 222 North to 422 West, to Route 12 East exit at Route 61 South. **Standard Game Times:** 7:10 pm, 6:45, Sundays 2:15 or 5:15. **Ticket Price Range:** $7-13.
Visiting Club Hotel: Crowne Plaza Reading Hotel 1741 Papermill Road, Wyomissing, PA 19610. **Telephone:** (610) 376-3811.

RICHMOND FLYING SQUIRRELS

Address: 3001 N Boulevard, Richmond, VA 23230.
Telephone: (804) 359-3866. **Fax:** (804) 359-1373.
E-Mail Address: info@squirrelsbaseball.com. **Website:** www.squirrelsbaseball.com.
Affiliation: San Francisco Giants (2010). **Years in League:** 2010-

OWNERSHIP/MANAGEMENT

Operated By: Navigators Baseball LP. **President/Managing Partner:** Lou DiBella.
CEO: Chuck Domino. **Vice President/COO:** Todd "Parney" Parnell.
General Manager: Ben Rothrock. **Controller:** Faith Casey-Harriss. Assistant Controller, Debbie Srock. **Executive Director, Corporate Sales:** Ben Terry. **Executive Director, Business Development:** Marty Steele. **Corporate Sales Executives:** Lydia Novalis, Clint Goulden, Hunter Gray. Executive Director, **Marketing & Promotions:** Anthony Oppermann. **Director of Communications & Broadcasting:** Trey Wilson. **Communications & Broadcasting Assistant:** Blaine McCormick. **Community Relations Manager:** Bailey Johnson. **Community Relations & Promotions Assistant:** Evan Piercy. **Special Events Manager:** Hannah DeFrank. **Social Media & Promo Manager:** Caroline Phipps. **Creative Services & Production Manager:** Nick Elder. **Director, of Group Sales:** Garrett Erwin. **Director of Group Hospitality:** Sam Mireles. **Group Hospitality Sales Executive:** Becca Wenger. **Group Sales Executive:** Donovan Havens. **Group Sales Executive:** Hayden Nachtigal. **Group Sales Associate:** Casey Newton. **Director of Ticketing:** Eric Harrell. **Ticket Sales Manager:** Shelby Moody. **Ticket Sales Assistant:** Deja King. **Director of Food & Beverage:** Josh Barban. **Food & Beverage Operations Manager:** Tom Pritzl. **Food & Beverage Manager:** Nathan Goldenberg. **Director of Stadium Operations:** Evan Smith. **Stadium Operations Assistant:** Ren Miller. **Manager of Field Operations:** Kyle Nichols. **Assistant Manager of Field Operations:** Drew Norris. **Retail & Merchandise Manager:** Jackson Hairfield.

FIELD STAFF

Manager: Jose Alguacil. **Hitting Coach:** Doug Clark. **Pitching Coach:** Steve Kline. **Fundamentals Coach:** Lipso Nava. **Bullpen Catcher:** Victor Cairo. **Athletic Trainer:** Garrett Havig. **Strength Coach:** Mark Spadavecchia.

GAME INFORMATION

Radio Announcers: Trey Wilson, Blaine McCormick. **No. of Games Broadcast:** 140. **Flagship Station:** Sports Radio 910 The Fan WRNL. **PA Announcer:** Anthony Oppermann. **Official Scorer:** Bob Flynn. **Stadium Name:** The Diamond. **Location:** Right off I-64 at the Boulevard exit. **Standard Game Times:** 6:35 pm, Fri., 7:05, Sat. 6:05, Sun. 1:05. **Ticket Price Range:** $8-12. **Visiting Club Hotel:** Fairfield Inn & Suites by Marriott Richmond Short Pump/I-64. **Telephone:** (804) 545-4200.

TRENTON THUNDER

Address: One Thunder Road, Trenton, NJ 08611.
Telephone: (609) 394-3300. **Fax:** (609) 394-9666.
E-Mail address: fun@trentonthunder.com. **Website:** www.trentonthunder.com.
Affiliation (first year): New York Yankees (2003). **Years in League:** 1994-Present

OWNERSHIP/MANAGEMENT

Operated By: Garden State Baseball LLP.
General Manager/ Chief Operating Officer: Jeff Hurley. **Senior Vice President of Corporate Sales & Partnerships:** Eric Lipsman. **Vice President, Marketing and Sponsorships:** Lydia Rios. **Senior Director, Ticket Sales:** Jon Bodnar. **Director, Merchandising:** Joe Pappalardo. **Director, Food & Beverages, Food Service America:** Kelly Kromer. **Director, Entertainment:** Ben Wolverton. **Director, Broadcasting and Media Relations:** Jon Mozes. **Director, Grounds:** Mike Kerns. **Director, Baseball & Stadium Operations:** Bryan Rock. **Director, Finance:** Trevor Hain. **Manager, Box Office:** Jackie Mott. **Manager, Office/Finance:** Morgan Schroll. **Corporate Sales Manager:** Juli Donlen. **Manager, Group Sales:** Brian Davis. **Manager, Ticket Memberships:** Bernadette Marco. **Manager, Corporate Ticket Sales:** Seth English. **Manager, Community Relations:** Casey Borish. **Manager, Stadium Operations:** Shane Eldridge. Manager, **Food & Beverage:** Josh Manion. **Promotions and Social Media Coordinator:** Brady LeDonne. **Production Coordinator:** Marisa Murphy. **Ticket Membership Account Executive:** Tommy Kay. **Ticket Membership Account Executive:** Nick Abela. **Group Sales Account Executive:** Tyler Gleason. **Group Sales Account Executive:** Matt Lutz
Group Sales Account Representative: Haley Hajduk. **Chef:** Corey Anderson. **Home Clubhouse Manager:** Harris Seletsky. **Visiting Clubhouse Manager:** Eric Bjurstrom. **Radio Broadcasters:** Jon Mozes. **PA Announcer:** Kevin Scholla. **Radio Stations:** 920 AM The Jersey (Flagship) / WBCB 1490-AM (Select Games). **Team Photographer:** Mike Dill. **Official Scorers:** Jay Dunn, Greg Zak Jr., Greg Zak Sr. **Bat Dog:** Rookie.

FIELD STAFF

Manager: TBA. **Hitting Coach:** TBA. **Pitching Coach:** TBA. **Defensive Coach:** TBA. **Bullpen Coach:** TBA. **Trainer:** TBA. **Strength/Conditioning Coach:** TBA.

GAME INFORMATION

Radio Announcers: Jon Mozes, TED. **No. of Games Broadcast:** 140. **Flagship Station:** 920 AM The Jersey – Fox Sports Radio. **PA Announcer:** Kevin Scholla. **Official Scorers:** Jay Dunn, Greg Zak, Greg Zak Sr. **Stadium Name:** ARM & HAMMER Park. **Location:** From I-95, take Route 1 North to Route 29 South, stadium entrance just before tunnel; From NJ Turnpike, take Exit 7A and follow I-195 West, Road will become Route 29, Follow through tunnel and ballpark is on left. **Standard Game Times:** Monday-Friday: 10:30, 11:00, 12:00, 7:00. Sat. 5:00, 7:00. Sun 1:00, 5:00. **Ticket Price Range:** $11-13.

SOUTHERN LEAGUE

Telephone: (770) 321-0400. **Fax:** (770) 321-0037.
E-Mail Address: office@southernleague.com.
Website: www.southernleague.com.
Years League Active: 1964-
President: Lori Webb.
   Vice President: Doug Kirchhofer. **Directors:** Hunter Reed (Biloxi), Jonathan Nelson (Birmingham), Jason Freier (Chattanooga), Reese Smith (Jackson), Ken Babby (Jacksonville), Chip Moore (Mississippi), Todd Parnell (Montgomery), Jonathan Griffith (Pensacola), Ralph Nelson (Rocket City), and Doug Kirchhofer (Tennessee).
   Director of Baseball Operations: Donna Musterer.
   Division Structure: North—Birmingham, Chattanooga, Jackson, Rocket City, Tennessee. **South**—Biloxi, Jacksonville, Mississippi, Montgomery, Pensacola.
   Regular Season: 140 games (split schedule). **2019 Opening Date:** April 9. **Closing Date:** Sept. 7. **All-Star Game:** June 23 in Jackson, TN

Lori Webb

   Playoff Format: First-half division winners meet second-half division winners in best-of-five series. Winners meet in best of five series for league championship.
   Roster Limit: 25. **Player Eligibility Rule:** No restrictions.
   Brand of Baseball: Rawlings. **Umpires:** Unavailable at this time.

STADIUM INFORMATION

Club	Stadium	Opened	LF	CF	RF	Capacity	2019 Att.
Biloxi	MGM Park	2015	335	400	335	6,000	146,845
Birmingham	Regions Field	2013	320	400	325	8,500	379,707
Chattanooga	AT&T Field	2000	325	400	330	6,362	228,662
Jackson	The Ballpark at Jackson	1998	310	395	320	6,000	107,131
Jacksonville	Baseball Grounds of Jacksonville	2003	321	420	317	11,000	327,388
Mississippi	Trustmark Park	2005	335	402	332	7,416	163,841
Montgomery	Riverwalk Stadium	2004	314	380	332	7,000	216,839
Pensacola	Blue Wahoos Stadium	2012	325	400	335	6,000	296,095
Rocket City	Madison Ballpark	1997	326	400	326	7,000	95,087
Tennessee	Smokies Stadium	2000	330	400	330	6,000	287,708

Dimensions column spans LF, CF, RF.

BILOXI SHUCKERS

Address: 105 Caillavet Street, Biloxi, MS 39530
Telephone: (228) 233-3465.
E-Mail Address: info@biloxishuckers.com. **Website:** www.biloxishuckers.com.
Affiliation (first year): Milwaukee Brewers (2015). **Years in League:** 2015-present.

OWNERSHIP/MANAGEMENT
   Operated By: Biloxi Baseball LLC.
   President: Ken Young. **General Manager:** Hunter Reed. **Assistant General Manager:** Trevor Matifes. **Media Relations Manager and Broadcaster:** Garrett Greene. **Director of Ticket Operations:** Allan Lusk. **Group Sales Coordinator:** Layton Markwood. **Corporate Partnerships Coordinator:** Stephanie Chapman. **Ticket Sales Executive:** Kory DuMond. **Box Office & Ticket Sales Executive:** Racheal Prosise. **Community Relations & Promotions Manager:** Kelsey Thompson. **Sales & Marketing Coordinator:** Dustin Fishman. **Creative Services Manager:** Stephanie Carr. **Graphic Design & Ticket Sales Executive:** Katy Knauss. **Retail Manager:** Megan Ondrey. **Head Groundkeeper:** TBA. **Human Resources & Accounting Manager:** Lisa Turner. **Stadium Operations Manager:** Kennedy Helms. **Team Ambassador:** Barry Lyons.

FIELD STAFF
   Manager: Mike Guerrero. **Hitting Coach:** Chuckie Caufield. **Pitching Coach:** Fred Dabney. **Coach:** Nestor Corredor. **Athletic Trainer:** Jeff Bodenhamer. **Strength/Conditioning Coach:** Jason Morriss. **Development Coach:** Paul Moeller.

GAME INFORMATION
   PA Announcer: Kyle Curley. **Official Scorer:** Scotty Berkowitz.
   Stadium Name: MGM Park. **Location:** I-10 to I-110 South toward beach, take Ocean Springs exit onto US 90 (Beach Blvd), travel east one block, turn left on Caillavet Street, stadium is on the left. **Ticket Price Range:** $7-$24. **Visiting Club Hotel:** DoubleTree by Hilton Biloxi on Beach Blvd.

BIRMINGHAM BARONS

Office Address: 1401 1st Ave South, Birmingham, AL, 35233. **Mailing Address:** PO Box 877, Birmingham, AL, 35201.
Telephone: (205) 988-3200. **Fax:** (205) 988-9698.
E-Mail Address: barons@barons.com. **Website:** www.barons.com.
Affiliation (first year): Chicago White Sox (1986). **Years in League:** 1964-65, 1967-75, 1981-

OWNERSHIP/MANAGEMENT
Principal Owners: Don Logan, Jeff Logan, Stan Logan.
President/General Manager: Jonathan Nelson. **Vice President of Business Development & Entertainment:** John Cook. **HR & Payroll Manager:** Ty Reed. **Vice President of Finance:** Randy Prince. **Bookkeeping:** Connie Sharp. **Director of Group Sales–Operations:** Tyler Gore. **Director of Group Sales & Sponsorship Coordinator:** Cole Buck. **Group Sales Manager:** Jordan Smith. **Group Sales Manager:** John Hudson. **Group Sales Manager:** Harrison Lindner. **Corporate Sales Manager:** Rich Smyth. **Corporate Sales Manager:** Richard Coats. **Director, Broadcasting:** Curt Bloom. **Marketing & Promotions Manager:** Samantha Beck. **Marketing & Promotions Coordinator:** Hannah Echols. **Director of Season Tickets:** Scout Johnson. **Senior Director of Hospitality & Events:** Jennifer McGee. **Special Events Manager:** Amanda Callahan. **Receptionist:** Ashlee Stegall. **Premium Sales Manager & Group Sales Manager:** Abby Southerland. **Director, Stadium Operations:** Mike Craven. **Director, Customer Service:** George Chavous. **Head Groundskeeper:** Zach Van Voorhees. **General Manager of Food & Beverage:** David Madison. **Concessions Manager:** Andy Jackson. **Director of Catering:** Sarah Spires. **Catering Manager:** Joie Tucker. **Inventory Control Accountant:** Jonathan Judge. **Executive Chef:** Nick Tittle. **Sous Chef:** Vic Arnold.

FIELD STAFF
Manager: Justin Jirschele. **Hitting Coach:** Charlie Romero. **Bench Coach:** Devin DeYoung. **Pitching Coach:** Richard Dotson. **Head Athletic Trainer:** Hyeon Kim. **Performance Coach:** Tim Rodmaker.

GAME INFORMATION
Radio Announcer: Curt Bloom. **No of Games Broadcast:** 140. **Flagship Station:** JOX 94.5-WJOX-FM. **PA Announcers:** Derek Scudder, Andy Parish. **Official Scorers:** Jeff Allison, David Tompkins. **Stadium Name:** Regions Field. **Location:** I-65 (exit 259B) in Birmingham. **Standard Game Times:** 7:05 pm, Sat. 6:30, Sun 4:00. **Ticket Price Range:** $8-15. **Visiting Club Hotel:** Sheraton Birmingham Hotel, 2101 Richard Arrington Junior Boulevard North, Birmingham, AL 35203. **Telephone:** (205) 324-5000.

CHATTANOOGA LOOKOUTS

Office Address: 201 Power Alley, Chattanooga, TN 37402.
Mailing Address: PO Box 11002, Chattanooga, TN 37401.
Telephone: (423) 267-2208. **Fax:** (423) 267-4258.
E-Mail Address: lookouts@lookouts.com. **Website:** www.lookouts.com.
Affiliation (first year): Cincinnati Reds (2019). **Years in League:** 1964-65, 1976-

OWNERSHIP/MANAGEMENT
Operated By: Chattanooga Lookouts, LLC
Principal Owner: Hardball Capital. **Managing Partner:** Jason Freier. **President:** Rich Mozingo. **Public/Media Relations Manager:** Dan Kopf. **Head Groundskeeper:** Mike Showe. **Marketing & Promotions Manager:** Alex Tainsh. **Director of Broadcasting:** Larry Ward. **Operations Manager:** Michael Matheson. **Vice President:** Andrew Zito. **Ticket Partnership Manager:** Jennifer Crum. **Ticket Partnership Manager:** Nolan Turner. **Ticket Partnership Manager:** Jarrah Vella-Wright. **Ticket Operations Manager:** Graham Hartman. **Concessions Manager:** William Marr.

FIELD STAFF
Manager: Ricky Gutierrez. **Hitting Coach:** Daryle Ward. **Pitching Coach:** Seth Etherton. **Coach:** Lenny Harris.

GAME INFORMATION
Radio Announcers: Larry Ward. **No. of Games Broadcast:** 140. **Flagship Station:** 98.1 The LAKE.
PA Announcer: Ron Hall. **Official Scorers:** Howard Runyon, Andy Paul, David Jenkins.
Stadium Name: AT&T Field. **Location:** From I-24, take US 27 North to exit 1C (4th Street), first left onto Chestnut Street, left onto Third Street. **Ticket Price Range:** $5-10. **Visiting Club Hotel:** Holiday Inn, 2232 Center Street, Chattanooga, TN 37421. **Telephone:** (423) 485-1185.

JACKSON GENERALS

Address: 4 Fun Place, Jackson, TN 38305.
Telephone: (731) 988-5299. **Fax:** (731) 988-5246.
E-Mail Address: sarge@jacksongeneralsbaseball.com.
Website: www.jacksongeneralsbaseball.com
Affiliation (fourth year): Arizona Diamondbacks (2017). **Years in League:** 1998-present-

MINOR LEAGUES

OWNERSHIP/MANAGEMENT
Operated by: Jackson Baseball Club LLC.
Chairman: David Freeman. **Owner:** Reese Smith III. **President & General Manager:** Marcus Sabata. **Vice President, Finance:** Charles Ferrell. **Assistant General Manager:** Steve Maloan. **Turf Manager:** None currently. **Manager, Media Relations/Broadcasting:** Andrew Chapman. **Manager, Tickets & Merchandise:** Patrick Adams. **Manager, Stadium Operations & Security:** Matt Malone. **Manager, Catering/Concessions:** Winston Brooks. **Manager of Promotions/Production:** Vincent Zielen. **Sales Exec:** Ryan Whitt.

FIELD STAFF
Manager: Blake Lalli. **Hitting Coach:** Rick Short. **Pitching Coach:** Doug Drabek. **Coach:** Jorge Cortes. **Strength/Conditioning Coach:** Derek Clovis. **Trainer:** Joe Rosauer.

GAME INFORMATION
Radio Announcer: Andrew Chapman. **No. of Games Broadcast:** 140 (Home & Away). **PA Announcer:** Mike Coburn. **Official Scorer:** Mike Henson. **Stadium Name:** The Ballpark at Jackson. **Location:** From I-40, take exit 85 South on FE Wright Drive, left onto Ridgecrest Road. **Standard Game Times:** 6:35, Sun. 2:05 or 6:05. **Ticket Price Range:** $8-12. **Visiting Club Hotel:** Doubletree by Hilton Jackson, 1770 Hwy 45 Bypass, Jackson, TN 38305. **Telephone:** (731) 664-6900.

JACKSONVILLE JUMBO SHRIMP

Office Address: 301 A. Philip Randolph Blvd, Jacksonville, FL 32202.
Telephone: (904) 358-2846. **Fax:** (904) 358-2845.
E-Mail Address: info@jaxshrimp.com. **Website:** www.jaxshrimp.com.
Affiliation (first year): Miami Marlins (2009). **Years In League:** 1970-

OWNERSHIP/MANAGEMENT
Operated by: Jacksonville Baseball LLC
Owner & Chief Executive Officer: Ken Babby. **Executive Assistant to Ken Babby:** Jill Popov. **President, Fast Forward Sports Group:** Jim Pfander. **Chief Financial Officer:** Shawn Carlson. **Executive Vice President/General Manager:** Harold Craw. **Assistant General Manager:** Noel Blaha. **Vice President, Sales and Marketing:** Linda McNabb. **Director, Stadium Operations:** Weill Casey. **Director, Field Operations:** Christian Galen. **Director, Food & Beverage:** Ernest Hopkins. **Director, Corporate Partnerships:** Gary Nevolis. **Director, Community Relations:** Andrea Williams. **Director, Promotions & Special Events:** David Ratz. **Director, Broadcasting:** Roger Hoover. **Assistant Director, Ticket Operations:** Peter Ercey. **Assistant Director, Ticket Sales:** James Abbatinozzi. **Senior Business Development & Military Affairs:** Theresa Viets. **Creative Services Manager:** Brian DeLettre. **Merchandise Manager:** Brennan Earley. **Food/Beverage Manager:** Nevious Love. **Food/Beverage Manager, Suites & Catering:** Chris Harper. **Media/Public Relations Manager:** Scott Kornberg. **Business Manager:** Teresa Lively-Hall. **Assistant Food/Beverage Manager:** Taylor Lee. **Account Executives:** Damon Aultman, Robert Dorfman, Justin Lemminn, Matt Morabito, Tom Snyder, Devin Walker. **Office Manager:** Christine Collins. **Accounting Assistant:** Jacob Yurdakul. **Stadium Operations Assistant:** Matthew Maynard. **Stadium Operations Associate:** Randal "Randy" Civale.

FIELD STAFF
Manager: Kevin Randel. **Pitching Coach:** Bruce Walton. **Hitting Coach:** Scott Seabol. **Defensive Coach:** Jose Ceballos. **Athletic Trainer:** Jason Roberts. **Strength/Conditioning Coach:** Amanda Sartoris. **Video Assistant:** TBA.

GAME INFORMATION
Radio Announcers: Roger Hoover & Scott Kornberg. **No. of Games Broadcast:** 140. **Flagship Station:** 102.3 FM. **PA Announcer:** Thomas Norton. **Official Scorer:** Jason Eliopulos. **Stadium Name:** Bragan Field at The Baseball Grounds of Jacksonville. **Location:** I-95 South to Martin Luther King Parkway exit, follow Gator Bowl Blvd around TIAA Bank Field; I-95 North to Exit 347 (Emerson Street), go right to Hart Bridge Expressway, take Sports Complex exit, left at light to stop sign, take left and follow around TIAA Bank Field; From Mathews Bridge, take A Philip Randolph exit, right on A Philip Randolph, straight to stadium. **Standard Game Times:** 7:05 pm, Sat. 6:35 pm, Sun. 3:05 pm. **Ticket Price Range:** $5-$18. **Visiting Club Hotel:** Doubletree by Hilton Hotel Jacksonville Riverfront, 1201 Riverplace Blvd., Jacksonville, FL 32207. **Telephone:** (904) 398-8800.

MISSISSIPPI BRAVES

Office Address: Trustmark Park, 1 Braves Way, Pearl, MS 39208.
Mailing Address: PO Box 97389, Pearl, MS 39288.
Telephone: (601) 932-8788. **Fax:** (601) 936-3567.
E-Mail Address: mississippibraves@braves.com. **Web site:** www.mississippibraves.com.
Affiliation (first year): Atlanta Braves (2005). **Years in League:** 2005-

OWNERSHIP/MANAGEMENT
Operated By: Atlanta National League Baseball Club Inc.
Vice President & General Manager: Pete Laven. **Assistant General Manager/Director of Sales:** Tim Mueller. **Office Manager:** Christy Shaw. **Ticket Manager:** Jeff Olson. **Account Executive:** Darius Green. **Account Executive:** Daylin Britt. **Account Executive:** Jacob Lord. **Account Executive:** Peyton Cain. **Head Groundskeeper:** Sam Turner.

Director of Group Sales: David Kerr. **Director of Stadium Operations:** Zach Evans. **Director of Communications, Media & Broadcasting:** Chris Harris. **Promotions & Entertainment Manager:** Ali Nerini. **Graphic Design Manager:** Garrett Steiger. **Merchandise Manager:** Rebekah Sones. **Food & Beverage Director:** Felicia Thompson.

FIELD STAFF
Manager: Chris Maloney. **Hitting Coach:** Einar Diaz. **Pitching Coach:** Dave Chavarria. **Coach:** Nestor Perez Jr. **Trainer:** Dave Comeau. **Strength:** Jordan Sidwell.

GAME INFORMATION
Radio Announcer: Chris Harris. **No. of Games Broadcast:** 140. **Flagship Station:** WYAB 103.9 FM. **PA Announcer:** Derrel Palmer. **Official Scorer:** Mark Beason.
Stadium Name: Trustmark Park. **Location:** I-20 to exit 48/Pearl (Pearson Road). **Ticket Price Range:** $6-$25. **Visiting Club Hotel:** Hilton Garden Inn Jackson Flowood, 118 Laurel Park Cove, Flowood, MS 39232. **Telephone:** (601) 487-0800.

MONTGOMERY BISCUITS

Address: 200 Coosa St., Montgomery, AL 36104.
Telephone: (334) 323-2255. **Fax:** (334) 323-2225.
E-Mail address: info@biscuitsbaseball.com. **Website:** www.biscuitsbaseball.com.
Affiliation (first year): Tampa Bay Rays (2004). **Years in League:** 1965-1980, 2004-

OWNERSHIP/MANAGEMENT
Operated By: Biscuits Baseball LLC. **Managing Owner:** Lou DiBella
President: Todd "Parney" Parnell. **Chief Operating Officer:** Brendon Porter. **General Manager:** Michael Murphy. **Executive Consultant:** Greg Rauch. **Corporate & Military Partnerships:** Jay Jones. **Corporate Partnerships Executive:** Haley Toler. **Director of Group Sales:** Chris Walker. **Group Sales Executive:** Daniel Jones. **Community Engagement Coordinator:** Kenny Flores. **Box Office Manager, Season Ticket Coordinator:** Justin Ross. **Marketing & Multimedia:** Jared McCarthy. **Broadcaster, Media Relations:** Chris Adams-Wall. **Retail Manager:** Ashley Williams. **Director, Food & Beverage:** Risa Juliano. **Assistant Director of Food & Beverage:** Michael Parham. **Director, Stadium Operations:** Steve Blackwell. **Stadium Operations Assistant:** Thomas Constant. **Head Groundskeeper:** Alex English. **Business Manager:** Tracy Mims. **Financial Specialist:** Joan Burden. **Executive Administrator:** Jeannie Burke.

FIELD STAFF
Manager: Morgan Ensberg. **Pitching Coach:** RC Lichtenstein. **Coach:** Gary Redus. **Coach:** Jamie Nelson. **Athletic Trainer:** Kris Russell. **Conditioning Coach:** Carlos Gonzalez

GAME INFORMATION
Radio Announcer: Chris Adams-Wall. **No of Games Broadcast:** 140. **Flagship Station:** WMSP 740-AM. **PA Announcer:** Rick Hendrick. **Official Scorer:** Brian Wilson. **Stadium Name:** Montgomery Riverwalk Stadium. **Location:** I-65 to exit 172, east on Herron Street, left on Coosa Street. **Ticket Price Range:** $9-13. **Visiting Club Hotel:** Candlewood Suites, 9151 Boyd-Cooper Pkwy, Montgomery, AL 36117. **Telephone:** (334) 277-0677.

PENSACOLA BLUE WAHOOS

Telephone: (850) 934-8444. **Fax:** (850) 791-6256.
E-Mail Address: info@bluewahoos.com. **Website:** www.bluewahoos.com
Affiliation (first year): Minnesota Twins (2019). **Years in League:** 2012-

OWNERSHIP/MANAGEMENT
Operated by: Northwest Florida Professional Baseball LLC. **Principal Owners:** Quint Studer, Rishy Studer. **Minority Owner:** Bubba Watson, Derrick Brooks. **President:** Jonathan Griffith. **Vice President of Operations:** Donna Kirby. **Vice President of Sales:** Alex Sides. **Receptionist:** Dawn Williams. **Facilities Manager:** Mike Crenshaw. **Head Groundskeeper:** Dustin Hannah. **Director, Human Relations:** Candice Miller. **Media and Public Relations Manager:** Daniel Venn. **Senior Writer:** Bill Vilona. **Broadcaster:** Chris Garagiola. **Creative Services Manager:** Adam Waldron. **Creative Services Assistant Manager:** Derek Diamond. **Merchandise and Community Relations Manager:** Anna Striano. **Ticket Operations Manager:** Kyle Williamson. **Box Office Assistant Manager:** Danny Do. **Group Sales Manager:** Bailie Tate. **Corporate Sales Executive:** Steven Unser. **Season Ticket Concierence:** JP Stanzell. **CFO:** Amber McClure. **Assistant CFO:** Sally Jewell, Pam Handlin.

FIELD STAFF
Manager: Ramon Borrego. **Hitting Coach:** Ryan Smith. **Pitching Coaches:** Luis Ramirez, Nat Ballenberg. **Coach:** Joe Mangiameli. **Athletic Trainer:** Chris McNeely. **Strength & Conditioning Coach:** Travis Koon.

GAME INFORMATION
Radio Announcer: Chris Garagiola. **No. of Games Broadcast:** 140. **Flagship Station:** ESPN Pensacola. **PA Announcer:** Josh Gay, Kevin Peterson, Chris James. **Official Scorer:** Craig Cooper, Don Burns. **Stadium Name:** Blue Wahoos Stadium. **Standard Game Times:** 6:35 pm, Sat. 6:05, Sun. 4:05. **Ticket Price Range:** $5-$19.

ROCKET CITY TRASH PANDAS

Address: 1 Trash Pandas Way. Madison, AL 35758.
Telephone: (256) 325-1403.
E-Mail Address: Info@trashpandasbaseball.com. **Website:** www.trashpandasbaseball.
com.
Affiliation (first year): Los Angeles Angels (2017). **Years in League:** 2020 (first year).

OWNERSHIP/MANAGEMENT

Owned and Operated by: BallCorps, LLC. **President and CEO:** Ralph Nelson. **Executive Vice President and General Manager:** Garrett Fahrmann. **Vice President, Marketing, Promotions and Entertainment:** Lindsey Knupp. **Special Advisor to the President and CEO:** Chuck Domino. **Special Advisor to the President and CEO:** Elizabeth Nelson. **Senior Director, Finance:** Jill Webb. **Director, Stadium and Baseball Operations:** Ken Clary. **Vice President, Food and Beverage Operations:** Mary Nixon. **Senior Account Executive, Partnerships and Groups:** Emo Furfori. **Groundskeeper:** Charlie Weaver.

FIELD STAFF

Manager: Jay Bell. **Hitting Coach:** Matt Spring. **Pitching Coach:** Tim Norton. **Defensive Coach:** Derek Florko. **Team Trainer:** Matt Morrell. **Strength and Conditioning Coach:** Jon Hill.

GAME INFORMATION

Director, Broadcasting and Baseball Information: Josh Caray. **No. of Games Broadcast:** 140. **Radio:** WUMP-FM 103.9. **Website:** www.umpsports.com. **PA Announcer:** Antonio MacBeath. **Official Scorer:** Don Rizzardi. **Stadium Name:** Toyota Field. **Location:** I-565 to exit 1. **Standard Game Times:** 6:35 pm (Weekdays), 7:05 pm (Friday), 6:05 pm (Saturdays), 2:05 pm (Sundays, April-June, Sept.), 5:05 pm (Sundays, July-Aug). **Ticket Price Range:** $8-22. **Visiting Club Hotel:** Best Western Plus Madison/Huntsville, 9035 Madison Blvd., Madison, AL 35758. Phone 256-772-7170, ext. 704.

TENNESSEE SMOKIES

Address: 3540 Line Drive, Kodak, TN 37764.
Telephone: (865) 286-2300. **Fax:** (865) 523-9913.
E-Mail Address: info@smokiesbaseball.com. **Website:** www.smokiesbaseball.com.
Affiliation (first year): Chicago Cubs (2007-). **Years in League:** 1964-67, 1972-

OWNERSHIP/MANAGEMENT

Owners: Randy and Jenny Boyd.
CEO: Doug Kirchhofer. **President/COO:** Chris Allen. **Vice President:** Jeremy Boler. **General Manager:** Tim Volk. **Assistant General Manager, Stadium Operations:** Bryan Webster. **Operations Assistant:** Caleb Miles. **Outside Events & Merchandise Manager:** Alex Eleas. **Director of Broadcasting:** Mick Gillispie. **Head Groundskeeper:** Eric Taylor. **Administrative Assistant:** Tolena Trout. **Director of Corporate Partnerships:** Corey Smart. **Partnership Activation Manager:** Baylor Love. **Partnership Activation Manager:** Kate Farrell. **Business Manager:** Suzanne French. **Admin/Finance Assistant:** Michelle Conway. **Director of Food and Beverage:** Chris Franklin. **Hospitality Manager:** Morgan Messick. **Director of Marketing & Entertainment:** Aris M Theofanopoulos. **Marketing & Community Relations Assistant:** Leslie Soffa. **Creative Services:** Nic Ha. **Director of Ticket & Group Sales:** Andrew O'Gara. **Senior Account Executive:** Matt Graves. **Account Executive/Ticket Operations:** Brett Adams. **Account Executive:** Evan Courtney. **Account Executive:** Joe Snodgrass.

FIELD STAFF

Manager: Mark Johnson. **Hitting Coach:** Chad Allen. **Pitching Coach:** Terry Clark. **Coach:** Ben Carhart. **Strength Coach:** Jason Morriss. **Athletic Trainer:** Toby Williams.

GAME INFORMATION

Radio Announcer: Mick Gillispie. **No. of Games Broadcast:** 140. **Flagship Station:** WNML 99.1-FM/990-AM. **PA Announcer:** George Yardley. **Official Scorer:** Wade Mitchell. **Stadium Name:** Smokies Stadium. **Location:** I-40 to exit 407, Highway 66 North. **Standard Game Times:** 7:00 pm, Sat. 7:00 pm, Sun. 2/5:30. **Ticket Price Range:** $10-$14.
Visiting Club Hotel: Hampton Inn & Suites Sevierville, 105 Stadium Drive, Kodak, TN 37764. **Telephone:** (865) 465-0590.

TEXAS LEAGUE

Mailing Address: 8621 Mid Cities Blvd., Suite 400, North Richland Hills, TX 76182
Telephone: (682) 316-4100
E-Mail Address: office@texasleague.com
Website: www.texasleague.com.
Years League Active: 1888-1890, 1892, 1895-1899, 1902-1942, 1946-

President/Treasurer: Tim Purpura

Vice President: Andy Milovich. **Corporate Secretary:** Wes Weigle. **Assistant to the President:** Sonja Owen. **Directors:** Jon Dandes (Northwest Arkansas), TBD (Corpus Christi), TBD (Springfield), Mike Melega (Tulsa), Chuck Greenberg (Frisco), Miles Prentice (Midland), Russ Meeks (Arkansas), D. G. Elmore (Amarillo).

Division Structure: North—Arkansas, Northwest Arkansas, Springfield, Tulsa. South—Corpus Christi, Frisco, Midland, San Antonio.

Regular Season: 140 games (split-schedule). **2020 Opening Date:** April 9. **Closing Date:** Sept 7.

All-Star Game: June 23 at Amarillo

Playoff Format: First-half division winners play second-half division winners in best-of-five series. Winners meet in best-of-five series for league championship.

Roster Limit: 25. **Player Eligibility Rule:** No restrictions.

Brand of Baseball: Rawlings.

Umpires: Isais Barba, Andrew Barrett, Michael Carroll, Zachary Dobson, Darius Ghani, Luis Hernandez, Steven Jaschinski, Jose Matamoros, Raul Moreno Benitez, Tyler Olson, Michael Rains, Justin Robinson.

Tim Purpura

STADIUM INFORMATION

Club	Stadium	Opened	LF	CF	RF	Capacity	2019 Att.
Amarillo	Hodgetown	2019	—	—	—	7,000	427,791
Arkansas	Dickey-Stephens Park	2007	332	413	330	5,842	311,021
Corpus Christi	Whataburger Field	2005	325	400	315	5,362	323,688
Frisco	Dr Pepper Ballpark	2003	335	409	335	10,216	455,765
Midland	Security Bank Ballpark	2002	330	410	322	4,669	285,368
NW Arkansas	Arvest Ballpark	2008	325	400	325	6,500	284,829
Springfield	John Q. Hammons Field	2003	315	400	330	6,750	328,217
Tulsa	ONEOK Field	2010	330	400	307	7,833	374,501

AMARILLO SOD POODLES

Ballpark Address: 715 S. Buchanan Street, Amarillo, TX 79101
Mailing Address: P.O. Box 9880, Amarillo, TX 79105
Main Phone: (806) 803-7762
Stadium Name: HODGETOWN. **Estimated Capacity:** 7,300
Affiliation (first year): San Diego Padres (2019). **Years in League:** 2019-

OWNERSHIP/MANAGEMENT

Owners: Elmore Sports Group.

President & General Manager: Tony Ensor. **Assistant General Manager, Director of Ticket Sales and Service:** Jeff Turner. **Director of Finance:** Ben Knowles. **Executive Assistant and Merchandise Manager:** Lynn Ensor. **Director of Public Relations and Baseball Operations:** Shane Philipps. **Director of Broadcasting:** Sam Levitt. **Video Production Manager:** Joe Corbisiero. **Director of Marketing:** Tess Bloom. **Director of Partnerships:** Matt Hamilton. **Corporate Activation Specialist:** Kelly Schuberg. **Promotions Manager:** Sierra Todd. **Mascot Entertainment and Community Relations Manager:** Austin Jackson. **Director of Group Sales:** Dustin True. **Ticket Operations Manager:** Nick Yardley. **Partnerships Account Executive:** Jacob Helmus. **Account Executive:** Matt Sutherland. **Group Account Executive:** Zak McGrath **Account Executive:** Michael Little. **Director of Stadium Operations:** Wayne Loeblein. **Operations Manager:** Zack Clark. **Head Groundskeeper:** Zach Severns. **Director of Food and Beverage:** Mike Lindal.

FIELD STAFF

Manager: Phillip Wellman. **Hitting Coach:** Raul Padron. **Pitching Coach:** Jimmy Jones. **Fielding Coach:** Freddy Flores. **Strength & Conditioning Coach:** Sam Hoffman. **Athletic Trainers:** Drew Garner, Allyse Kramer.

GAME INFORMATION

Radio Announcer: Sam Levitt. **No. of Games Broadcast:** 140. **Flagship Station:** KIXZ 940 AM (Townsquare Media Amarillo). **PA Announcer:** N/A. **Official Scorer:** N/A. **Stadium Name:** HODGETOWN. **Standard Game Times:** 11:05 a.m., 1:05 p.m., 6:05 p.m., 7:05 p.m. CT. **Ticket Price Range:** $6-18. **Visiting Club Hotel:** Home2 Suites by Hilton. **Telephone:** 806-803-7762.

ARKANSAS TRAVELERS

Office Address: Dickey-Stephens Park, 400 West Broadway, North Little Rock, AR 72114.
Mailing Address: PO Box 3177, Little Rock, AR 72203.
 Telephone: (501) 664-1555. **Fax:** (501) 664-1834.
 E-Mail address: travs@travs.com. **Website:** www.travs.com.
 Affiliation (first year): Seattle Mariners (2017). **Years in League:** 1966-

OWNERSHIP/MANAGEMENT
 Ownership: Arkansas Travelers Baseball Club, Inc.
 President: Russ Meeks.
 General Manager: Paul Allen. **Assistant GM, Merchandise:** Rusty Meeks. **Broadcaster:** Steven Davis. **Controller:** Brad Eagle. **Director, Finance:** Patti Clark. **Director, In-Game Entertainment:** Tommy Adam. **Park Superintendent:** Greg Johnston. **Assistant Park Superintendent:** Reggie Temple. **Director, Stadium Operations:** Andrew Heideman. **Assistant Grounds Manager: Taylor Woelfel Director, Tickets:** John Sjobeck. **Director, Marketing/Media Relations:** Lance Restum. **Corporate Event Planners:** Cameron Jefferson, Sophie Ozier, Montag Genser. **Director of Luxury Suites:** Mike Johnson. **Receptionist:** Jean Belken. **Director of Food and Beverage:** Ben Hornbrook. **Assistant Director of Food and Beverage:** Hunter Johnston.

FIELD STAFF
 Manager: Dave Berg. **Hitting Coach:** Andy Bissell. **Pitching Coach:** Alon Leichman. **Performance Coach:** Michael Saddler. **Trainer:** Taylor Bennett. **Coach:** Ryan Scott.

GAME INFORMATION
 Radio Announcer: Steven Davis. **No. of Games Broadcast:** 140. **Flagship Station:** KARN 920 AM.
 PA Announcer: Russ McKinney. **Official Scorer:** Tim Cooper. **Stadium Name:** Dickey-Stephens Park. **Location:** I-30 to Broadway exit, proceed west to ballpark, located at Broadway Avenue and the Broadway Bridge. **Standard Game Time:** 7:10 pm. **Ticket Price Range:** $3-13. **Visiting Club Hotel:** Crowne Plaza, 201 S. Shackleford Rd, Little Rock, AR 72211. **Telephone:** (501) 223-3000.

CORPUS CHRISTI HOOKS

Address: 734 East Port Ave, Corpus Christi, TX 78401.
 Telephone: (361) 561-4665. **Fax:** (361) 561-4666.
 E-Mail Address: info@cchooks.com. **Website:** www.cchooks.com.
 Affiliation (first year): Houston Astros (2005). **Years in League:** 1958-59, 2005-

OWNERSHIP/MANAGEMENT
 Owned/Operated By: Houston Astros.
 General Manager: Wes Weigle. **Assistant General Manager:** Brady Ballard.
 Senior Director, Stadium Operations: Jeremy Sturgeon. **Director, Media Relations/Broadcasting:** Michael Coffin. **Director, Marketing:** JD Davis. **Director, Business Development:** Maggie Freeborn. **Account Executive:** Amanda Boman. **Account Executive:** Gabi Cerise. **Ticket Operations Manager:** Ray Cervenka. **Accounting Manager:** Jessica Fearn. **Assistant Groundskeeper:** Anthony Hernandez. **Customer Service Manager:** Brett Howsley. **Ballpark Entertainment Manager:** Amy Johnson. **Special Events/Operations Coordinator:** Jorden Klaevemann. **Head Groundskeeper:** Quince Landry. **Account Executive:** Greg LeMonte. **Community Outreach Coordinator:** Courtney Merritt. **Account Manager:** Chanelle Oberly. **Sales Manager:** Kaley O'Brien. **Receptionist:** Denise Perez. **Ticket Operations Coordinator:** Paul Perez. **Account Executive:** Sean Phelan. **Communications Manager:** Dan Reiner. **Video Editor & Motion Graphics Coordinator:** Alex Sanchez. **Stadium Operations:** Michael Shedd. **Retail Manager:** Rudy Soliz. **Online Retail Manager/Store Supervisor:** Eric Suniga. **Home Clubhouse Manager:** Marcus Tramp. **Receptionist:** Trisha Torres.

FIELD STAFF
 Manager: Gregorio Petit. **Hitting Coach:** TBA. **Pitching Coach:** Graham Johnson. **Trainer:** Christian Bermudez.

GAME INFORMATION
 Radio Announcers: Michael Coffin, Gene Kasprzyk, Dominic Cotroneo. **No. of Games Broadcast:** 140. **Flagship Station:** KKTX-AM 1360. **PA Announcer:** TBA. **Stadium Name:** Whataburger Field. **Location:** I-37 to end of interstate, left at Chaparral, left at Hirsh Ave. **Ticket Price Range:** $6-20. **Visiting Club Hotel:** Holiday Inn Corpus Christi Downtown Marina, 707 North Shoreline Blvd, Corpus Christi, Texas, 78401. **Telephone:** (361) 882-1700.

FRISCO ROUGHRIDERS

Address: 7300 RoughRiders Trail, Frisco, TX 75034.
 Telephone: (972) 731-9200. **Fax:** (972) 731-5355.
 E-Mail Address: info@ridersbaseball.com. **Website:** www.ridersbaseball.com.
 Affiliation (first year): Texas Rangers (2003). **Years in League:** 2003-

OWNERSHIP/MANAGEMENT

Operated by: Frisco RoughRiders LP
Chairman/CEO/General Partner: Chuck Greenberg. **President & General Manager:** Andy Milovich. **Chief Operating Officer:** Scott Burchett. **Chief Business Development Officer:** Erik Haag. **Chief Financial Officer:** Bernie Miller. **Director of Business Intelligence & Strategy:** Ankit Agrawal. **Director, Partner Services:** David Kosydar. **Partner Services Coordinators:** Jenny Katlein, Alexis Summers. **Director, Human Resources:** Kenya Allen. **Customer Service Agents:** Claudia Kipp, Vicki Sohn. **VP, Ticket Sales & Services:** Ross Lanford. **Senior Director, Ticket Sales & Services:** David Dwyer. **Director, Membership Experience:** Tyler Ellis. **Premium Group Sales Manager:** Monica Man. **Sr. Corporate Sales Executive:** Tom Baker. **Corporate Sales Executives:** Ryan Biddlecombe, Brandon Blumstein, Andrew Dance, Kasey Klopfenstein, Sydney Peterson, Gustavo Rodriguez, Skylor Rodriguez, Brett Veater. **Group Sales Executives:** Nate Doederlein, Luke Johnson, Cameron Pipes, Chris Powell, Sydney Ryan, Alex Sandborn. **Membership Experience Specialist:** Rachel Bilke, Ashley Martinez. **Director, Ticket Operations:** Stephen Christ. **Ticket Operations Coordinator:** Katie Castillon. **Director, Marketing:** Jennifer Johnson. **Media/Marketing Coordinator:** Krystin King. **Graphic Design Coordinator:** Duncan Stanley. **Game Entertainment Production Coordinator:** Briana Santiago. **Video Production Coordinator:** Nate Rivard. **VP, Community Development:** Breon Dennis, Jr. **Broadcaster:** Zach Bigley. **VP, Ballpark Operations:** Tim Arseneau. **Operations Coordinator:** Andrew Tittor, Ryan Wojdula. **Operations Assistant:** Eric Smith. Senior Director, **Sports Turf & Grounds Manager:** David Bicknell. **Clubhouse Manager:** Mitch Brasher. **Maintenance Director:** Alfonso Bailon. **Merchandise Manager:** Courtney Ward.

FIELD STAFF

Manager: Bobby Wilson. **Hitting Coach:** Josue Perez. **Pitching Coach:** Jeff Andrews. **Bench Coach:** Jonathan Gelnar. **Athletic Trainer:** Alex Rodriguez. **Strength & Conditioning Coach:** Wade Lamont.

GAME INFORMATION

Broadcaster: Zach Bigley. **No. of Games Broadcast:** 140. **Flagship Station:** www.RidersBaseball.com. **Stadium Name:** Dr Pepper Ballpark. **Location:** Intersection of Dallas North Tollway & State Highway 121. **Standard Game Times:** 7:05 PM, Sunday 4:05 PM (April-May), 6:05 PM (June-September). **Visiting Club Hotel:** Comfort Suites at Frisco Square, 9700 Dallas Parkway, Frisco, TX 75033. **Visiting Club Hotel Phone:** (972) 668-9700. **Visiting Club Hotel Fax:** (972) 668-9701.

MIDLAND ROCKHOUNDS

Address: Security Bank Ballpark, 5514 Champions Drive, Midland, TX 79706.
Telephone: (432) 520-2255. **Fax:** (432) 520-8326.
Website: www.midlandrockhounds.org.
Affiliation (first year): Oakland Athletics (1999). **Years in League:** 1972-

OWNERSHIP/MANAGEMENT

Operated By: Midland Sports, Inc. **Principal Owners:** Miles Prentice, Bob Richmond.
President: Miles Prentice. **Executive Vice President:** Bob Richmond. **General Manager:** Monty Hoppel.
Assistant GM: Jeff VonHolle. **Assistant GM, Marketing/Tickets:** Jamie Richardson. **Assistant GM, Operations:** Ray Fieldhouse. **Director, Broadcasting/Publications:** Bob Hards. **Director, Business Operations:** Eloisa Galvan. **Director, Sales:** Matthew Barnett. **Director, Ticketing/Office Manager:** Ryan Artzer. **Director, Client Services/Sports Complex Marketing:** Shelly Haenggi. **Director, Community Relations:** Rachael DiLeonardo. **Media Relations Coordinator:** Nathan Hymel. **Director, Marketing:** Matt Bari. **Director, Operations:** Cannon Schrank. **Assistant Box Office Manager/Sales Executive:** Joshua Selaya. **Office Manager:** Leslie Martin. **Head Groundskeeper:** Eric Peckham. **Game Entertainment/Video Board Coordinator:** Russ Pinkerton. **Sales Executive:** Will Thomas. **Assistant Concessions Manager:** Al Melville. **Home Clubhouse Manager:** Vernon Koslow. **Visiting Clubhouse Manager:** TBA.

FIELD STAFF

Manager: Scott Steinmann. **Hitting Coach:** Tommy Everidge. **Pitching Coach:** Steve Connelly. **Coach:** Juan Dilone. **Athletic Trainer:** Shane Zdebiak. **Strength/Conditioning Coach:** Matt Mosiman.

GAME INFORMATION

Radio Announcer: Bob Hards. **No. of Games Broadcast:** 140. **Flagship Station:** KCRS 550 AM. **PA Announcer:** Wes Coles. **Official Scorer:** Steve Marcum. **Stadium Name:** Security Bank Ballpark. **Location:** From I-20, exit Loop 250 North to Highway 191 intersection. **Standard Game Times:** Sunday: 2:00 pm, Monday-Wednesday: 6:30 pm, Thursday-Saturday: 7:00 pm. **Ticket Price Range:** $8-16. **Visiting Club Hotel:** Sleep Inn& Suites, 5612 Deauville Blvd, Midland, TX 79706. **Telephone:** (432) 694-4200.

NORTHWEST ARKANSAS NATURALS

Address: 3000 Gene George Blvd, Springdale, AR 72762.
Telephone: (479) 927-4900. **Fax:** (479) 756-8088.
E-Mail Address: tickets@nwanaturals.com. **Website:** www.nwanaturals.com.

Affiliation (first year): Kansas City Royals (1995). **Years in League:** 2008-

OWNERSHIP/MANAGEMENT
Principal Owner: Rich Products Corp. **Owner/President:** Robert Rich Jr. **President, Rich Entertainment Group:** Melinda Rich. **Chief Operating Officer, Rich Entertainment Group:** Joseph Segarra. **President, Rich Baseball Operations:** Mike Buczkowski. **Vice President/General Manager:** Justin Cole. **Director, Sales:** Mark Zaiger. **Director, Business:** Morgan Helmer. **Director, Marketing/PR:** Dustin Dethlefs. **Director, Ballpark Operations:** Jeff Windle. **Ballpark Operations Assistant:** Matthew Holland. **Head Groundskeeper:** Brock White. **Business Department Assistant:** Sarah Giesen. **Ticket Office Manager:** Matt Fanning. **Radio Broadcaster:** Benjamin Kelly. **Promotions Coordinator:** Roxanne Garner. **Creative Services Coordinator:** Adam Annaratone. **Account Executives:** Trey Garner & Josh Hill. **Account Executive/Event Coordinator:** Spencer Lundquist. **Clubhouse Manager:** Danny Helmer.

FIELD STAFF
Manager: Scott Thorman. **Hitting Coach:** Abraham Nunez. **Pitching Coach:** Doug Henry. **Development Coach:** Tony Medina. **Athletic Trainer:** Justin Kemp. **Strength & Conditioning Coach:** Luis Jeronimo.

GAME INFORMATION
Radio Announcer: Benjamin Kelly. **No. of Games Broadcast:** 140. **Flagship:** KQSM 92.1-FM. **PA Announcer:** Bill Rogers. **Official Scorers:** Kyle Stiles, Walter Woodie & Paul Boyd. **Stadium Name:** Arvest Ballpark. **Location:** I-49 to US 412 West (Sunset Ave), Left on Gene George Blvd. **Ticket Price Range:** $8.75-14.75. **Standard Game Times:** 7:05 pm (Monday-Friday), 6:05 pm (Saturday), 2:05 pm (Sunday). **Visiting Club Hotel:** Holiday Inn Springdale, 1500 S 48th St, Springdale, AR 72762. **Telephone:** (479) 751-8300.

SPRINGFIELD CARDINALS

Address: 955 East Trafficway, Springfield, MO 65802.
Telephone: (417) 863-0395. **Fax:** (417) 832-3004.
E-Mail Address: springfield@cardinals.com. **Website:** springfieldcardinals.com.
Affiliation (first year): St. Louis Cardinals (2005). **Years in League:** 2005-

OWNERSHIP/MANAGEMENT
Operated By: St. Louis Cardinals.
Vice President/General Manager: Dan Reiter. **VP, Baseball/Business Operations:** Scott Smulczenski. **Director, Market Development:** Brad Beattie. **Director, Ticket Operations:** Angela Deke. **Manager, Public Relations/Broadcaster:** Andrew Buchbinder. **Public Relations/Digital Media Specialist:** Matt Turer. **Marketing/Event Coordinator:** Regina Norris. **Manager, Production:** Kent Shelton. **Graphic Designer:** T.J. Patton. **Manager, Premium Sales/Marketing:** Zack Pemberton. **Manager, Ticket Sales:** Eric Tomb. **Memberships Coordinator:** Ross Fuller. **Director, Stadium Operations:** Aaron Lowrey. **Head Groundskeeper:** Brock Phipps. **Assistant Head Groundskeeper:** Derek Edwards.

FIELD STAFF
Manager: Joe Kruzel. **Hitting Coach:** Tyger Pederson. **Pitching Coach:** Darwin Marrero. **Trainer:** Chris Whitman.

GAME INFORMATION
Radio Announcer: Andrew Buchbinder. **No. of Games Broadcast:** 140. **Flagship Station:** JOCK 98.7 FM. **PA Announcer:** Eric Tomb. **Official Scorers:** Mark Stillwell, Tim Tourville, Phillip Dowden. **Stadium Name:** Hammons Field. **Location:** Highway 65 to Chestnut Expressway exit, west to National, south on National, west on Trafficway. **Standard Game Time:** 7:10 pm. **Ticket Price Range:** $7-28. **Visiting Club Hotel:** University Plaza Hotel, 333 John Q Hammons Parkway, Springfield, MO 65806. **Telephone:** (417) 864-7333.

TULSA DRILLERS

Address: 201 N. Elgin Ave, Tulsa, OK 74120.
Telephone: (918) 744-5998. **Fax:** (918) 747-3267.
E-Mail Address: mail@tulsadrillers.com. **Website:** www.tulsadrillers.com.
Affiliation (first year): Los Angeles Dodgers (2015). **Years in League:** 1933-42, 1946-65, 1977-

OWNERSHIP/MANAGEMENT
Operated By: Tulsa Baseball Inc.
Co-Chairman: Dale Hubbard. **Co-Chairman:** Jeff Hubbard. **President/GM:** Mike Melega. **Executive VP/Assistant GM:** Jason George. **Vice President, Operations:** Mark Hilliard. **Vice President, Media & Public Relations:** Brian Carroll. **Vice President, Ticket Sales:** Eric Newendorp. **Vice President, Marketing:** Justin Gorski. **Vice President, Food Service:** Robert Founds. **Director of Merchandise:** Tom Jones. **Director, Operations:** Marshall Schellhardt. **Manager, Ticket Sales:** Joanna Hubbard. **Manager, Senior Accounts:** Phil Sidoti. **Manager, Corporate Partnerships:** Cameron Gordon. **Account Executives:** Katy Pace, Nick Hill, Justin Perkins. **Manager, Graphic Design:** Danielle Hepburn. **Manager, Community Relations:** Taylor Levacy. **Accountant:** Jenna Savill. **Ticket Operations Assistants:** Terry Jenner, Lana Mark. **Ticket Sales Assistants:** Levi Cook, Drew Kilgore, Aki Miwa, Corey Wilson. **Promotions Assistant:** Alex Kossakoski. **Media & Public Relations Assistant:** Brandon Hawkins. **Graphic Design & Social Media Assistant:** Montel Vidot. **Video Production Assistants:** Sam Cohen, Will Leggett. **Assistant Accountant:** Katie Martin. **Executive**

Assistant: Lynda Davis. **Receptionist & Events Coordinator:** Kelsi Tulk. **Head Groundskeeper:** Gary Shepherd. **Facilities Manager:** Micah Wade. **Mascot Coordinator:** Chris Carozza. **Director, Culinary Operations:** Chris Bullis. **Director, Hospitality:** Amanda Coe. **Team Photographers:** Rich Crimi, Tim Campbell.

FIELD STAFF

Manager: Scott Hennessey. **Hitting Coach:** Brett Pill. **Pitching Coach:** Dave Borkowski. **Coach:** Jeremy Rodriguez. **Performance Coach:** Garrett Lloyd. **Strength Coach:** Noah Huff. **Athletic Trainer:** Yuya Mukaihara.

GAME INFORMATION

Radio Announcer: Dennis Higgins. **No. of Games Broadcast:** 140. **Flagship Station:** KTBZ 1430-AM.

PA Announcer: Kirk McAnany. **Official Scorers:** Bruce Howard, Duane DaPron, Larry Lewis, Barry Lewis.

Stadium Name: ONEOK Field. **Location:** I-244 to Cincinnati/Detroit Exit (6A), north on Detroit Ave, right onto John Hope Franklin Blvd, right on Elgin Ave. **Standard Game Times:** 7:00 pm, Sun. 1:00 (April-June), 7:00 (July-Aug). **Visiting Club Hotel:** Marriott Tulsa Hotel Southern Hills, 1902 E 71st Street, Tulsa, OK 74136. **Telephone:** (918) 493-7000.

CALIFORNIA LEAGUE

Address: 3600 South Harbor Blvd, Suite 122, Oxnard, CA 93035.
Telephone: (805) 985-8585. **Fax:** (805) 985-8580.
Website: www.californialeague.com.
E-Mail: info@californialeague.com.
Years League Active: 1941-1942, 1946-
President: Charlie Blaney.
Vice President: Tom Volpe. **Directors:** Bobby Brett (Rancho Cucamonga), Jake Kerr (Lancaster), Dave Elmore (Inland Empire), Gary Jacobs (Lake Elsinore), Mike Savit (Modesto), Elliott Sigal (Visalia), Tom Volpe (Stockton), Dan Orum (San Jose).
Director, Operations: Matt Blaney. **Historian:** Chris Lampe.
Legal Counsel: Jonathan Light. **CPA:** Mike Owen.
Division Structure: North—Modesto, San Jose, Stockton, Visalia. **South**—Inland Empire, Lake Elsinore, Lancaster, Rancho Cucamonga.
Regular Season: 140 games (split schedule).
2018 Opening Date: April 9. **Closing Date:** Sept 7.
Playoff Format: Four teams make the playoffs. First-half winners in each division play second-half winners (or wild card if the same team wins both halves) in best-of-five semifinals. Winners meet in best-of-five series for league championship.
All-Star Game: June 23 at Stockton.
Roster Limit: 25 active (35 under control). **Player Eligibility:** No more than two players and one player/coach on active list may have more than six years experience.
Brand of Baseball: Rawlings. **Umpires:** TBD.

Charlie Blaney

STADIUM INFORMATION

Club	Stadium	Opened	Dimensions			Capacity	2019 Att.
			LF	CF	RF		
Inland Empire	San Manuel Stadium	1996	330	410	330	5,000	181,253
Lake Elsinore	The Diamond	1994	330	400	310	7,866	172,280
Lancaster	The Hangar	1996	350	410	350	4,500	161,595
Modesto	John Thurman Field	1952	312	400	319	4,000	139,762
Rancho Cucamo.	LoanMart Field	1993	335	400	335	6,615	162,085
San Jose	Municipal Stadium	1942	320	390	320	5,208	155,253
Stockton	Banner Island Ballpark	2005	300	399	326	5,200	179,465
Visalia	Recreation Ballpark	1946	320	405	320	2,468	129,118

INLAND EMPIRE 66ERS

Address: 280 South E St., San Bernardino, CA 92401.
Telephone: (909) 888-9922. **Fax:** (909) 888-5251. **Website:** www.66ers.com.
Affiliation (first year): Los Angeles Angels (2011). **Years in League:** 1941, 1987-

OWNERSHIP/MANAGEMENT

Operated by: Inland Empire 66ers Baseball Club of San Bernardino. **Principal Owners:** David Elmore, Donna Tuttle. **President:** David Elmore. **Chairman:** Donna Tuttle. **General Manager:** Joe Hudson. **Assistant GM:** Steve Pellé. **Assistant GM:** Daniel Vazquez. **Director, Broadcasting:** Steve Wendt. **Director, Community Relations:** Stephanie O'Quinn. **Director, Group Sales:** Hollee Haines. **Director, Ticket Operations/Sales:** Sean Peterson. **Manager, Creative Services:** Dusty Ferguson. **Manager, Promotions:** Anna Forslin. **Account Executives:** Jarrett Stark, Yanney Ponce, Mary Grinnan. **Administrative Assistant:** Marlena Garcia. **Manager, Facility:** Richard Morales. **Head Groundskeeper:** Dominick Guerrero. **Accountant:** Karly Strahl. **Director, Food & Beverage (Diamond Creations):** Ryan Liptrot. **Operations Manager, Food & Beverage (Diamond Creations):** Mike Liotta.

FIELD STAFF

Manager: Jack Santora. **Hitting Coach:** Kenny Hook. **Pitching Coach:** Michael Wuertz. **Defensive Coach:** Franklin Navarro. **Athletic Trainer:** Yusuke Takahashi. **Strength and Conditioning Coach:** Ryan Orr.

GAME INFORMATION

Radio Announcer: Steve Wendt. **Flagship Station:** 66ers Radio on TuneIn. **PA Announcer:** Renaldo Gonzales. **Official Scorer:** Bill Maury-Holmes. **Stadium Name:** San Manuel Stadium. **Location:** From south, I-215 to 2nd Street exit, east on 2nd, right on G Street; from north, I-215 to 3rd Street exit, left on Rialto, right on G Street. **Standard Game Times:** Mon.-Sat. 7:05 pm; Sun. 2:05 pm (1st Half) 5:35 pm (2nd Half). **Ticket Price Range:** $12-$18. **Visiting Club Hotel:** Holiday Inn Express & Suites. **Telephone:** (909) 796-1000.

LAKE ELSINORE STORM

Address: 500 Diamond Drive, Lake Elsinore, CA 92530
Telephone: (951) 245-4487. **Fax:** (951) 245-0305.
E-Mail Address: info@stormbaseball.com. **Website:** www.stormbaseball.com.
Affiliation (first year): San Diego Padres (2001). **Years in League:** 1994-

OWNERSHIP/MANAGEMENT

Owners: Gary Jacobs, Len Simon. **CEO/Co-General Manager:** Shaun Brock. **CFO/Co-General Manager:** Christine Kavic. Asst. **GM Baseball & Events/Marketing Director:** Mark Beskid. **Assistant CFO:** Andres Pagan. **Director of Community Relations/Promo Manager:** Karen Lovett. **Director of Broadcasting:** Sean McCall. **Director of Merchandising:** Arlene Spahn. **Director of Ticketing:** Eric Colunga. **Senior Group Sales Executive:** Eric Theiss. Social Media/ Jr. **Group Sales Executive:** Alexandra Ortiz. **Senior Corporate Sales/Brand Ambassador/Clubhouse Manager:** Terrance Tucker. **Junior Group Sales Executive:** Krista Williams. **Fulfillment and Processing:** Natalie Gates. **Junior Corporate Sales Associate:** Kaz Egan. **Diversity and Corporate Sales Associate:** Arthur Romero. **Production Manager:** Jon Gripe. **Director of Mascot Relations:** Stephen Webster. **Front Office Manager:** Peggy Mitchell. **Director of Stadium Operations/Head Groundskeeper:** Tyler Beckas. **Stadium Operations Manager:** Daniel Limon. **Grounds Crew:** Brandon Castaneda. **Grounds Crew:** Anthony Anaya. **Food & Beverage Operations:** Steve Bearse. **Catering Manager:** Candice Nicholas. **Concessions Manager:** Jason Natale. **Tap Room Manager:** Jason Wozniak.

FIELD STAFF

Manager: Mike McCoy. **Hitting Coach:** Patrick O'Sullivan. **Pitching Coach:** TBA. **Fielding Coach:** Felipe Blanco. **Strength Coach:** Corey Measner. **Trainer:** Maritza Castro.

GAME INFORMATION

Radio Announcer: Sean McCall. **No. of Games Broadcast:** 140. **Flagship Station:** Radio 94.5. **PA Announcer:** Dave McCrory. **Official Scorer:** Lloyd Nixon. **Stadium Name:** The Diamond. **Location:** From I-15, exit at Diamond Drive, west one mile to stadium. **Standard Game Times:** Mon.-Thurs. 6 p.m. Fri. 7pm Sat. 6 p.m. Sunday 1pm. **Ticket Price Range:** $5-$20. **Visiting Club Hotel:** Econo Lodge Lake Elsinore Casino, 20930 Malaga St, Lake Elsinore, CA 92530. **Telephone:** (951) 674-3101.

LANCASTER JETHAWKS

Address: 45116 Valley Central Way, Lancaster, CA 93536.
Telephone: (661) 726-5400. **Fax:** (661) 726-5406.
Email Address: info@jethawks.com. **Website:** www.jethawks.com.
Affiliation (first year): Colorado Rockies (2017). **Years in League:** 1996-

OWNERSHIP/MANAGEMENT

Operated By: JetHawks Baseball, LP. **Principal Owner/Managing General Partner:** Jake Kerr. **Partner:** Jeff Mooney. **President:** Andy Dunn. **Executive Vice President/General Manager:** Tom Backemeyer. **Assistant General Manager:** Katie Woods Director, **Facility/Baseball Operations:** John Laferney. **Director, Broadcasting & Media Relations:** Jason Schwartz. **Box Office/Merchandise Manager:** Taylor Dunn. **Sr Director, Corporate Partnerships:** Chuck Lang. **Ticket Sales Account Executive:** Nicklaus DiPaola. **Ticket Sales Account Executive:** Adan Rodriguez. **Special Advisor:** Mark Bozigian.

FIELD STAFF

Developmental Supervisor: TBD. **Manager:** Scott Little. **Hitting Coach:** TBD. **Pitching Coach:** TBD. **Athletic Trainer:** Josh Guterman. **Clubhouse Manager:** Joey Scott.

GAME INFORMATION

Radio Announcer: Jason Schwartz. **No. of Games Broadcast:** 140. **Flagship Station:** www.jethawks.com. **PA Announcer:** TBD. **Official Scorer:** David Guenther. **Stadium Name:** The Hangar. **Location:** Highway 14 in Lancaster to Avenue I exit, west one block to stadium. **Standard Game Times:** 6:35 pm, Sun. 2:05pm (April-June), 5:05pm (July-Sept). **Ticket Price Range:** $10-17. **Visiting Club Hotel:** Comfort Inn, 1825 W Avenue J-12, Lancaster CA 93534. **Telephone:** (661) 723-2001.

MODESTO NUTS

Office Address: 601 Neece Dr, Modesto, CA 95351. **Mailing Address:** PO Box 883, Modesto, CA 95353.
Telephone: (209) 572-4487. **Fax:** (209) 572-4490
E-Mail Address: fun@modestonuts.com. **Website:** www.modestonuts.com.
Affiliation (first year): Seattle Mariners (2017). **Years in League:** 1946-64, 1966-

OWNERSHIP/MANAGEMENT

Operated by: HWS Group IV. **Majority Owners:** Seattle Mariners.

MINOR LEAGUES

General Manager: Zach Brockman. **Director of Marketing & Promotions:** Veronica Hernandez. **Head Groundskeeper:** Alan Jones. **Account Executive:** Dylan Queary. **Community Relations Manager:** Amber Lingley. **Director of Ticket Sales:** Chris Fleischmann. **Ticket Sales Manager:** Steven Webster. **In-Game Entertainment Manager:** TBD. **Director of Broadcasting:** Keaton Gillogly. **Office Manager:** Kate Mendoza. **Food and Beverage Manager:** Robert Provencio. **Stadium Operations Managers:** TBD.

FIELD STAFF

Manager: Denny Hocking. **Pitching Coach:** TBD. **Hitting Coach:** TBD. **Trainer:** TBD.

GAME INFORMATION

Radio Announcer: Keaton Gillogly. **PA Announcer:** Unavailable. **Official Scorer:** Unavailable. **Stadium Name:** John Thurman Field. **Location:** Highway 99 in southwest Modesto to Tuolumne Boulevard exit, west on Tuolumne for one block to Neece Drive, left for 1/4 mile to stadium. **Standard Game Times:** 7:05 pm, Sun. 2:05pm/6:05 pm. **Ticket Price Range:** $8-14. **Visiting Club Hotel:** Unavailable.

RANCHO CUCAMONGA
QUAKES

Office Address: 8408 Rochester Ave., Rancho Cucamonga, CA 91730.
Mailing Address: P.O. Box 4139, Rancho Cucamonga, CA 91729.
Telephone: (909) 481-5000. **Fax:** (909) 481-5005.
E-Mail Address: info@rcquakes.com. **Website:** www.rcquakes.com.
Affiliation (first year): Los Angeles Dodgers (2011). **Years in League:** 1993-

OWNERSHIP/MANAGEMENT

Operated By: Bobby Brett. **Principal Owner:** Bobby Brett.
President: Brent Miles. **Vice President/General Manager:** Grant Riddle. **Vice President/Tickets:** Monica Ortega. **Vice President/Groups:** Linda Rathfon. **Vice President/Sponsorships:** Chris Pope. **Director of Sponsorships:** David Fields. **Sponsorship Service Coordinator:** Karen DeYoung. **Promotions Coordinator:** Chloe Melanson. **Director, Fan Engagement:** Bobbi Salcido. **Director, Group Sales:** Kyle Burleson. **Director, Season Tickets/Operations:** Eric Jensen. **Group Sales Coordinator:** Emily Lokovic, Sarah Mansour. **Director, Accounting:** Amara McCellan. **Director, Public Relations/Voice of the Quakes:** Mike Lindskog. **Office Manager:** Shelley Scebbi. **Director, Food/Beverage:** Michael Garcia.

FIELD STAFF

Manager: TBD. **Hitting Coach:** Dustin Kelly. **Pitching Coach:** TBD. **Assistant Coach:** TBD.

GAME INFORMATION

Radio Announcer: Mike Lindskog. **No. of Games Broadcast:** 140. **Flagship Station:** NewsTalk AM 1290 PA. **Announcer:** Chris Albaugh. **Official Scorer:** Steve Wishek/Curt Christiansen. **Stadium Name:** LoanMart Field. **Location:** I-10 to I-15 North, exit at Foothill Boulevard, left on Foothill, left on Rochester to Stadium. **Standard Game Times:** 7:05 pm; **First Half Sundays** at 2:05 pm (April through June 21); **Second Half Sundays** 5:05 pm (June 28 through Sept. 6). **Visiting Club Hotel:** Best Western Heritage Inn, 8179 Spruce Ave, Rancho Cucamonga, CA 91730. **Telephone:** (909) 466-1111.

SAN JOSE GIANTS

Office Address: 588 E Alma Ave, San Jose, CA 95112.
Mailing Address: PO Box 21727, San Jose, CA 95151.
Telephone: (408) 297-1435. **Fax:** (408) 297-1453.
E-Mail Address: info@sjgiants.com. **Website:** www.sjgiants.com.
Affiliation (first year): San Francisco Giants (1988). **Years in League:** 1942, 1947-58, 1962-76, 1979-

OWNERSHIP/MANAGEMENT

Operated by: Progress Sports Management. **Principal Owners:** San Francisco Giants, Heidi Stamas, Richard Beahrs. **President/CEO:** Daniel Orum. **General Manager:** Mark Wilson. **Chief Operating Officer:** Ben Taylor. **VP, Sales:** Jeff Di Giorgio. **VP, Marketing:** Matt Alongi. **VP, Game Day Operations and Human Resources:** Tara Tallman. **Director, Player Personnel:** Linda Pereira. **Director, Broadcasting:** Joe Ritzo. **Director, Media Relations:** Justin Allegri. **Manager, Ticketing:** Ryan Anthony. **Manager, Retail/Merchandise:** Sierra Hanley. **Manager, Food and Beverage:** Ramiro Mijares. **Coordinator, Marketing and Community Relations:** David Baez. **Account Executive:** Benji Meshek. **Coordinator, Finance:** Riley Jacobs.

FIELD STAFF

Manager: Dennis Pelfrey. **Hitting Coach:** Pat Burrell. **Pitching Coach:** Matt Yourkin. **Fundamentals Coach:** Gary Davenport. **Athletic Trainer:** Ryo Watanabe. **Strength & Conditioning Coach:** Jesse White. **Bullpen Coach:** Ray Ortega.

GAME INFORMATION

Radio Announcers: Joe Ritzo, Justin Allegri. **No. of Games Broadcast:** 140. **Flagship:** sjgiants.com. **Television Announcers:** Joe Ritzo, 70 home games on MiLB.TV. **PA Announcer:** Russ Call. **Official Scorer:** Mike Hohler. **Stadium Name:** Excite Ballpark. **Location:** South on **I-280:** Take 10th/11th Street Exit, turn right on 10th Street, turn left on Alma Ave. North on **I-280:** Take the 10th/11th Street Exit, Turn left on 10th Street, turn left on Alma Ave. **Standard Game Times:** 7 p.m., 6:30 p.m, Sat. 6 p.m., Sun 1 p.m. (5 p.m. after May 24). **Ticket Price Range:** $8-24.

STOCKTON PORTS

Address: 404 W Fremont St, Stockton, CA 95203.
Telephone: (209) 644-1900. **Fax:** (209) 644-1931.
E-Mail Address: info@stocktonports.com. **Website:** www.stocktonports.com.
Affiliation (first year): Oakland Athletics (2005). **Years in League:** 1941, 1946-72, 1978-

OWNERSHIP/MANAGEMENT

Operated By: 7th Inning Stretch LLC. **Chairman/CEO:** Tom Volpe.
President: Pat Filippone. **Assistant General Manager:** Justice Hoyt. **Director of Corporate Partnerships:** Gary Olson. **Director of Operations/Special Events:** Luke Johnson. **Community Relations Manager:** Paige Kiesewetter. **Group Sales Manager:** Doren Weil. **Box Office Manager:** Christine Bowling. **Marketing Manager:** Katie Schulz. **Ticket Sales and Merchandise Executive:** Owen Hopkins. **Account Executive:** Malcolm Boehm. **Front Office Manager:** Christa Leri. **Finance Manager:** Lyla Jacobson.

FIELD STAFF

Manager: Bobby Crosby. **Hitting Coach:** Brian McArn. **Pitching Coach:** Chris Smith. **Coach:** Javier Herrera. **Athletic Trainer:** Nick Voelker. **Strength & Conditioning Coach:** Henry Torres. **Club House Manager:** Vic Zapien.

GAME INFORMATION

Radio Announcer: Zack Bayrouty. **No of Games Broadcast:** 140. **Flagship Station:** TuneIn App. **PA Announcer:** Gary Ellenbolt. **Official Scorer:** Paul Muyskens. **Stadium Name:** Banner Island Ballpark. **Location:** From I-5/99, take Crosstown Freeway (Highway 4) exit El Dorado Street, north on El Dorado to Fremont Street, left on Fremont. **Standard Game Times:** 7:10 pm. **Ticket Price Range:** $10-$20. **Visiting Club Hotel:** Best Western, 111 E March Lane, Stockton, CA 95207. **Telephone:** 209-474-3301.

VISALIA RAWHIDE

Address: 300 N Giddings St, Visalia, CA 93291.
Telephone: (559) 732-4433. **Fax:** (559) 739-7732.
E-Mail Address: info@rawhidebaseball.com.
Website: www.rawhidebaseball.com.
Affiliation (first year): Arizona Diamondbacks (2007). **Years in League:** 1946-62, 1968-75, 1977-

OWNERSHIP/MANAGEMENT

Owner: First Pitch Entertainment, LLC. **Vice President and General Manager:** Jennifer Reynolds. **Assistant General Manager:** Mike Candella and Julian Rifkind. **Director of Ticketing:** Markus Hagglund. **Director of Broadcasting & Media Relations:** Jill Gearin. **Head Groundskeeper:** James Templeton. **Director of Ballpark Operations:** Brady Hochhalter. **Community Partnership Manager:** Joe Ross. **Merchandise Manager:** Shawna Steinway. **Director of Ballpark Events:** Cassie Sandrini. **Ballpark Operations Assistant:** Dakota Gentry. **Ticketing and Community Partnerships Assistant:** TBA.

FIELD STAFF

Manager: Shawn Roof. **Hitting Coach:** Travis Denker. **Pitching Coach:** Shane Loux. **Coach:** Carlos Mesa. **Trainer:** Damon Reel.

GAME INFORMATION

Radio Announcers: Jill Gearin. **No. of Games Broadcast:** 100. **Flagship Station:** Unavailable.
PA Announcer: Brian Anthony. **Official Scorer:** Harry Kargenian and Mark "Scooter" Cossentine. **Stadium Name:** Rawhide Ballpark. **Location:** From Highway 99, take 198 East to Mooney Boulevard exit, left at second signal on Giddings; four blocks to ballpark. **Standard Game Times:** 7 pm, Sun. 1pm (first half), 6 pm (second half). **Ticket Price Range:** $9-30. **Visiting Club Hotel:** Quality Inn, 1010 E Prosperity Ave, Tulare, CA 93274.

CAROLINA LEAGUE

Address: 3206 Buena Vista Road, Winston-Salem, NC 27106
Telephone: (336) 691-9030. **Fax:** (336) 464-2737.
E-Mail Address: office@carolinaleague.com.
Website: www.carolinaleague.com.
Years League Active: 1945-
President/Treasurer: Geoff Lassiter.
Vice President: Billy Prim (Winston-Salem). **Executive VP:** Tim Zue (Salem). **Corporate Secretary:** Ken Young (Frederick). **Directors:** DG Elmore (Lynchburg), Chuck Greenberg (Myrtle Beach), Dave Ziedelis (Frederick), Tyler Barnes (Carolina), Dave Heller (Wilmington), Billy Prum (Winston-Salem), Art Silber (Potomac), David Lane (Fayetteville), Joe Januszeswki (Down East).
Media Director: Brian Boesch. **Division Structure: North**—Frederick, Fredericksburg, Lynchburg, Salem, Wilmington. **South**—Carolina, Down East, Fayetteville, Myrtle Beach, Winston-Salem.
Regular Season: 140 games (split schedule).

Geoff Lassiter

2020 Opening Date: April 9. **Closing Date:** Sept 7.
All-Star Game: South Division vs. North Division at Lynchburg, June 23.
Playoff Format: First-half division winners play second-half division winners in best-of- three series. If a team wins both halves it plays division opponent with next-best second- half record. Division series winners meet in best-of-five series for Mills Cup. **Roster Limit:** 25 active. **Player Eligibility Rule:** No age limit. No more than two players and one player/coach on active list may have six or more years of prior minor league service. **Brand of Baseball:** Rawlings. **Umpires:** Unavailable.

STADIUM INFORMATION

Club	Stadium	Opened	Dimensions LF	CF	RF	Capacity	2019 Att.
Carolina	Five County Stadium	1991	330	400	309	6,500	193,568
Down East	Grainger Stadium	1949	335	390	335	4,100	110,619
Fayetteville	SEGRA Stadium	2019	319	400	330	4,786	246,961
Frederick	Harry Grove Stadium	1990	325	400	325	5,400	263,528
Fredericksburg	Northwest Federal Field	1984	315	400	315	6,000	192,474
Lynchburg	City Stadium	1939	325	390	325	4,000	117,029
Myrtle Beach	TicketReturn.com Field	1999	308	400	328	5,200	226,247
Salem	Salem Memorial Stadium	1995	325	401	325	6,415	171,866
Wilmington	Frawley Stadium	1993	325	400	325	6,532	231,325
Winston-Salem	BB&T Ballpark	2010	315	399	323	5,500	264,879

CAROLINA MUDCATS

Office Address: 1501 NC Hwy 39, Zebulon, NC 27597.
Mailing Address: PO Drawer 1218, Zebulon, NC 27597.
Telephone: (919) 269-2287. **Fax:** (919) 269-4910.
E-Mail Address: muddy@carolinamudcats.com.
Website: www.carolinamudcats.com.
Affiliation (first year): Milwaukee Brewers (2017-). **Years in League:** 2012-

OWNERSHIP/MANAGEMENT

Ownership: Milwaukee Brewers Baseball Club
Operated by: Milwaukee Brewers Baseball Club
Vice President/General Manager: Joe Kremer. **Assistant General Manager, Operations:** Eric Gardner. **Assistant GM, Sales:** David Lawrence. **Business Manager:** Joshua Perry. **Manager, Ticket Package Sales:** Taylor Gustafson. Jason Leone, Coordinator - Box Office. Manager, **Group Sales & Business Development:** Mitchell Lister. **Associate, Business Development:** Ryder Barrett. **Associate, Business Development:** Brandon Diorio. **Associate, Business Development:** Thomas Eatman. **Director, Promotions and Fan Experience:** Patrick Ennis. **Director of Marketing & Community Relations:** Samantha Barry. **Manager, Multimedia:** Evan Moesta. **Coordinator, Social Media/Marketing/Graphics:** Aaron Bayles. **Manager, Merchandise:** Amy Peterson. **Coordinator, Stadium Operations:** Michael Lincoln. **Director, Food and Beverage:** Dwayne Lucas. **Coordinator, Food and Beverage:** Josh Clark. **Director, Broadcasting and Media Relations:** Greg Young. **Manager, Grounds:** John Packer.

FIELD STAFF

Manager: Joe Ayrault. **Pitching Coach:** Nick Childs. **Hitting Coach:** Bobby Spain. **Coach:** David Tufo. **Development Coach:** Michael O'Neal. **Athletic Trainer:** Matt Deal. **Strength & Conditioning Specialist:** Jonah Mergen.

GAME INFORMATION

Radio Announcer: Greg Young. **No. of Games Broadcast:** 140. **Flagship Station:** TuneIn Radio. **PA Announcer:** Hayes Permar. **Official Scorer:** Bill Woodward. **Stadium Name:** Five County Stadium.
Location: From Raleigh, US 64 East to 264 East, exit at Highway 39 in Zebulon. **Standard Game Times:** 7:00, Sat. 5:00, Sun. 2:00. **Ticket Price Range:** $11-13. **Visiting Club Hotel:** Holiday Inn Raleigh.

DOWN EAST WOOD DUCKS

Address: 400 East Grainger Avenue, Kinston, NC 28502
Telephone: (252) 686-5165
E-Mail Address: jbullock@woodducksbaseball.com. **Website:** woodducksbaseball.com
Affiliation (first year): Texas Rangers (2017). **Years in League:** 2017-

OWNERSHIP/MANAGEMENT
Operated By: Texas Rangers, LLC.
Chief Operating Officer & Chairman, Ownership Committee: Neil Leibman. **Executive Vice President, Sports & Entertainment:** Sean Decker. **Vice President:** Wade Howell. **Assistant GM of Operations:** Janell Bullock. **Assistant GM Of Sales:** Jon Clemmons. **Creative Services Director:** Matthew Edwards. **Director of Marketing:** Alexa Kay. **Director of Broadcasting:** Matt Present. **Group Sales Executive:** Jackson Cook. **Group Sales Executive:** John McCormick. **Head Groundskeeper:** Stephen Watson.

FIELD STAFF
Manager: Joshua Johnson. **Hitting Coach:** Jared Goedert. **Pitching Coach:** Steve Mintz. **Trainer:** Luke Teeters. **Strength & Conditioning Coach:** Jon Nazarko.

GAME INFORMATION
Radio Announcer: Matt Present. **PA Announcer:** Bryan Hanks. **Stadium Name:** Grainger Stadium.
Standard Game Times: 7:00 (weekdays), 6:00 (Saturdays), 2:00 (Sundays). **Ticket Price Range:** $7-11.
Visiting Club Hotel: Mother Earth Motor Lodge, 501 N Herritage St., Kinston, NC 28501.

FAYETTEVILLE WOODPECKERS

Address: 460 Hay St., Fayetteville, NC 28301
Telephone: 910-339-1989.
E-Mail Address: Woodpeckers@astros.com. **Website:** fayettevillewoodpeckers.com.
Affiliation (first year): Houston Astros (2019). **Years in League:** 2019-

OWNERSHIP/MANAGEMENT
Principal Owner: Houston Astros.
President: Mark Zarthar. **General Manager:** David Lane. **Vice President, Sales and Marketing:** Austin Schwartz. **Director, Finance:** Jennifer Carpenter. **Director, Sales:** Chaz Dawson. **Director, Marketing:** Pete Subsara. **Director, Stadium Operations:** Chris Cominse. **Director, Field Operations:** Alpha Jones. **Manager, Marketing and Communications:** Ben Hughes. **Manager, Retail:** Brittany Tschida. **Manager, Corporate Partnerships:** Sarah Suggs. **Manager, Baseball Operations:** Mike Montesino. **Manager, Ticket Operations:** Gabriel Evans. **Manager, Events:** Rachel Smith. **Manager, Creative Services:** Ryan LeFevre. **Manager, Community Relations & Media Relations:** **Manager, Facility Operations:** Victoria Huggins. **Account Executive, Ticketing:** Elizabeth Adams. **Account Executive, Sponsorships:** Kevin Hughes. **Account Executive, Ticketing:** Travis Gortman.

FIELD STAFF
Manager: Nate Shaver. **Hitting Coach:** Rafael Peña. **Pitching Coach:** Thomas Whitsett.

GAME INFORMATION
Radio Announcer: Matt Dean. **No. of Games Broadcast:** 140. **Flagship Station:** N/A.
PA Announcer: Ray Thomas. **Official Scorer:** Eddy Southard. **Stadium Name:** Segra Stadium. **Standard Game Times:** M-F 7pm, Sat. 5pm, Sun. 2pm. **Visiting Club Hotel:** Fairfield Inn. **Telephone:** 910-223-7867.

FREDERICK KEYS

Address: 21 Stadium Dr., Frederick, MD 21703.
Telephone: (301) 662-0013. **Fax:** (301) 662-0018.
E-Mail Address: info@frederickkeys.com. **Website:** www.frederickkeys.com.
Affiliation: Baltimore Orioles (1989). **Years in League:** 1989-

OWNERSHIP/MANAGEMENT
Ownership: Maryland Baseball Holding LLC.
President: Ken Young. **General Manager:** Dave Ziedelis. **Assistant General Manager:** Andrew Klein. **Director of Marketing:** Maci Hill. **Broadcasting & Public Relations Manager:** TBA. **Digital Content Coordinator:** Katey Ladika. **Director of Stadium Operations:** Kari Collins. **Ticket Operations Manager:** Jackson Bushong-Taylor. **Sponsorship Sales Account Managers:** Casey O'Brien, Patrick Koogle. **Group Sales Manager:** Meghan Walling. **Group Sales Account Managers:** Layla Adinolfi, Rob Brown. **Broadcasting/PR/CR Assistant:** TBA. **Marketing Assistant:** Morgan Crow. **Head Groundskeeper:** Mike Dunn. **Clubhouse Manager:** Jared Weiss. **Director of Finance & Human Resources:** Tami Hetrick. **General Manager, Spectra:** Ben Stechschulte.

FIELD STAFF
   Manager: Kyle Moore. **Hitting Coach:** Tom Eller. **Pitching Coach:** Josh Conway. **Development Coach:** David Barry.
Fundamentals Coach: Collin Woody. **Athletic Trainer:** Marty Brinker.

GAME INFORMATION
   Radio Announcers: TBA. **PA Announcer:** Andy Redmond. **Official Scorers:** Luke Stillson, Dave Musil, Geoff Goyne,
Ben Trittipoe, Dennis Hetrick. **Stadium Name:** Harry Grove Stadium. **Location:** From I-70, take exit 54 (Market Street),
left at light; From I-270, take exit 32 (I-70Baltimore/Hagerstown toward Baltimore (I-70), to exit 54 at Market Street.
Ticket Price Range: $9-15. **Visiting Club Hotel:** Comfort Inn Frederick, 7300 Executive Way, Frederick, MD 21704.
Telephone: (301) 668-7272.

FREDERICKSBURG NATIONALS

   Office Address: 42 Jackie Robinson Way, Fredericksburg, VA 22401
   Mailing Address: 42 Jackie Robinson Way, Fredericksburg, VA 22401
   Telephone: (540) 858-4242.
   E-Mail Address: info@frednats.com.
   Website :www.frednats.com.
   Affiliation (first year): Washington Nationals (2005). **Years in League:** 1978-

OWNERSHIP/MANAGEMENT
   Operated By: SAJ Baseball LLC. **Principal Owner:** Art Silber.
President: Lani Silber Weiss. **Executive VP/General Manager: Nick Hall, Director of Partnerships:** Tory Goodman.
Partnership Account Executive: Callie Sullivan. **Manager of Partnership Fulfillment:** Gibson Stoffer. **Director of
Ticket Operations:** Alec Manriquez. **Director of Ticket & Hospitality Sales:** Arnold Malloy. **Ticket Sales Manager:**
Matt LeBlanc. **Hospitality Fulfillment Manager:** Devin Monahan. **Ticket Sales Account Executive:** Rich Crosslin.
Ticket Sales Account Executive: Jimmy Burns. **Ticket Sales Account Executive:** Ally Chism. **VP of Operations:** Aaron
Johnson. **Director of Stadium Operations:** Will Darmstead. **Director of Merchandise:** McKenzie Goodman. **Head
Groundskeeper:** LJ Black/ **Business Operations Manager:** Theresa Coffey. **Office Manager & Accounting Assistant:**
Kathy Roman. **VP of Creative Services:** Robert Perry. **Director of Design:** Alexis Deegan. **Marketing Coordinator:**
Paige Honaker. **Community & Mascot Relations Director:** Nathan Gunnels.

FIELD STAFF
   Manager: Tripp Keister. **Hitting Coach:** Luis Ordaz. **Pitching Coach:** Justin Lord. **Athletic Trainer:** Don Neidig.
Strength & Conditioning Coach: Shane Hill.

GAME INFORMATION
   Radio Announcer: Erik Bremer. **No. of Games Broadcast:** 140. **Flagship:** www.frednats.com. **PA Announcer:** TBD.
Official Scorer: TBD. **Stadium Name:** TBD. **Location:** From I-95, take exit 130B onto VA-3W/Plank Road for 0.7 miles.
Turn right onto Carl D. Silver Pkwy. Stay straight for 1.8 miles until you reach stadium parking lot. **Standard Game
Times:** TBD. **Ticket Price Range:** TBD. **Visiting Club Hotel:** TBD.

LYNCHBURG HILLCATS

   Address: Lynchburg City Stadium, 3180 Fort Ave, Lynchburg, VA 24501.
   Telephone: (434) 528-1144. **Fax:** (434) 846-0768.
   E-Mail Address: info@lynchburg-hillcats.com. **Website:** www.Lynchburg-hillcats.com.
   Affiliation (first year): Cleveland Indians (2015). **Years in League:** 1966-

OWNERSHIP/MANAGEMENT
   Operated By: Elmore Sports Group.
   President and General Manager: Chris Jones. **Assistant General Manager:** Matt Klein. **Assistant General
Manager:** Peter Billups. **Account Executive and Box Office Manager:** Hanna Tyree. **Director of Field Operations:**
Joseph Knight. **Director of Food and Beverage:** Matt Ramstead. **Director of Broadcasting and Media Relations:**
Maura Sheridan. **Director of Entertainment and Promotions: Jeff Raymond, Social Media Coordinator:** Megan
Davis. **Operations/Clubhouse Manager:** Ryan Henson. **Director of Accounting:** Austin Amos. **Account Executive:**
Kyle Taylor. **Promotions Assistant:** Vivian Colangelo. **Video Production Assistant:** Ian Kocis. **Video Production
Assistant:** Drew Melton. **Operations Assistant:** Casey Pendry.

FIELD STAFF
   Manager: Dennis Malavé. **Hitting Coach:** Grant Fink. **Pitching Coach:** Owen Dew. **Bench Coach:** Juan De Le Cruz.
Strength & Conditioning Coach: Eric Ortego. **Athletic Trainer:** Jake Legan.

GAME INFORMATION
   Radio Announcer: Maura Sheridan. **No. of Games Broadcast:** 140. **PA Announcer:** Jeff Raymond. **Official Scorers:**
Dan Fallen. **Stadium Name:** Calvin Falwell Field at Lynchburg City Stadium. **Location:** US 29 Business South to
Lynchburg City Stadium (exit 6); US 29 Business North to Lynchburg City Stadium (exit 4). **Ticket Price Range:** $5-15.
Visiting Club Hotel: La Quinta Inn & Suites, 3320 Candlers Mountain Rd., Lynchburg, VA 24502. **Telephone:** (434) 847-
8655.

MYRTLE BEACH PELICANS

Mailing Address: 1251 21st Avenue N. Myrtle Beach, SC 29577.
Telephone: (843) 918-6000. **Fax:** (843) 918-6001.
E-Mail Address: info@myrtlebeachpelicans.com.
Website: www.myrtlebeachpelicans.com.
Affiliation: (first year): Chicago Cubs (2015). **Years in League:** 1999-

OWNERSHIP/MANAGEMENT

Owners, Greenberg Sports Group: Chuck Greenberg. **President, Greenberg Sports Group:** Andy Milovich. **General Manager:** Ryan Moore. **Assistant General Manager:** Kristin Call. **Sr. Director, Finance:** Anne Frost. **Administrative Assistant:** Beth Freitas. **Director of Sales:** Ryan Cannella. **Director, Business Development:** Ryan Waters. **Sports & Tourism Sales Manager:** Todd Chapman. **Corporate Sales Representative:** Robert Buchanan. **Box Office Manager:** Shannon Barbee. **Fan Engagement:** Hunter Horenstein. **AGM of Operations:** Mike Snow. **Merchandise Manager/Pro Shop:** Dan Bailey. **Director, Food & Beverage:** Brad Leininger **Sports Turf Manager:** JC Blackhurst. **Director of Video Productions:** Kyle Guertin. **Media Relations:** Noah Cloonan.

FIELD STAFF

Manager: Steve Lerud. **Pitching Coach:** Anderson Tavarez. **Hitting Coach:** Paul McAnulty. **Assistant Hitting Coach:** Will Skett. **Athletic Trainer:** Logan Severson.

GAME INFORMATION

PA Announcer: TBA. **Official Scorer:** TBA. **Stadium Name:** Ticketreturn.com Field at Pelicans Ballpark. **Location:** US Highway 17 Bypass to 21st Ave. North, half mile to stadium. **Standard Game Times:** 7:05 p.m. **Ticket Pirce Range:** $9-$15. **Visiting Club Hotel:** Doubletree Resorts, 3200 South Ocean Blvd., Myrtle Beach, S.C., 29577. **Telephone:** (843) 315-7100.

SALEM RED SOX

Office Address: 1004 Texas St., Salem, VA 24153.
Mailing Address: PO Box 842, Salem, VA 24153.
Telephone: (540) 389-3333. **Fax:** (540) 389-9710.
E-Mail Address: info@salemsox.com. **Website:** www.salemsox.com.
Affiliation (first year): Boston Red Sox (2009). **Years in League:** 1968-

OWNERSHIP/MANAGEMENT

Operated By: Carolina Baseball LLC/Fenway Sports Group.
Managing Director: Jeff White. **General Manager:** Allen Lawrence. **VP of Tickets:** Blair Hoke. **VP of Corporate Partnerships:** Steven Elovich. **Marketing/Promotions Manager:** Emily Wydo. **Facilities Manager/Head Groundskeeper:** Joey Elmore. **Director of Ticket Sales:** Charlie Umland. **Ticket Operations Manager:** Lior Bittan. **Food/Beverage Manager:** Gregory Shoukas. **Group Sales Manager:** Alex Michel. **Bookkeeper:** Barry Stephens. **Video Production Manager:** Cameron Moist. **Business Development Manager:** Kris North. **Merchandise & Special Events Manager:** Kayla Keegan. **Clubhouse Manager:** Tom Wagner.

FIELD STAFF

Manager: Corey Wimberly. **Hitting Coach:** Nelson Paulino. **Pitching Coach:** TBA. **Trainer:** Nick Kuchwara.

GAME INFORMATION

Radio Announcer: Melanie Newman. **No. of Games Broadcast:** 140. **Flagship Station:** 1240 AM. **PA Announcer:** Emile Brown. **Official Scorer:** Billy Wells. **Stadium Name:** Haley Toyota Field at Salem Memorial Ballpark. **Location:** I-81 to exit 141 (Route 419), follow signs to Salem Civic Center Complex. **Standard Game Times:** 7:05 pm, Sat./Sun. 6:05/4:05. **Ticket Price Range:** $7-15. **Visiting Club Hotel:** Comfort Suites Ridgewood Farms, 2898 Keagy Rd., Salem, VA 24153. **Telephone:** (540) 375-4800.

WILMINGTON BLUE ROCKS

Address: 801 Shipyard Drive, Wilmington, DE 19801.
Telephone: (302) 888-2015. **Fax:** (302) 888-2032.
E-Mail Address: info@bluerocks.com. **Website:** www.bluerocks.com.
Affiliation (first year): Kansas City Royals (2007). **Years in League:** 1993-present

OWNERSHIP/MANAGEMENT

Operated by: Wilmington Blue Rocks LP. **Honorary President:** Matt Minker. **Club President:** Clark Minker. **Owners:** Main Street Baseball. **Managing Partner/League Director & CEO, Main Street Baseball:** Dave Heller. **General Manager:** Andrew Layman. **Director of Broadcasting & Video:** Cory Nidoh. **Director of Media Relations:** Matt Janus. **Director, Merchandise:** Jim Beck. **Director, Community Affairs:** Kevin Linton. **Director of Web and Creative Services:** Mike Diodati. **Director of Business Development:** Robert Ford. **Director of Ticket Operations:**

Joe McCarthy. **Director of Marketing:** Liz Welch. **Ticket Sales Manager:** Brett Leichtman. **Group Sales Executives:** Stephanie Garafolo, Mike Rice and Antoine Ray.

FIELD STAFF

Manager: Chris Widger. **Hitting Coach:** Andy LaRoche. **Pitching Coach:** Steve Luebber. **Athletic Trainer:** Daniel Accola.

GAME INFORMATION

Radio Announcer: Cory Nidoh. **No. of Games Broadcast:** 140. **Flagship Station:** 89.7 WGLS-FM. **PA Announcer:** Kevin Linton. **Official Scorer:** Dick Shute. **Stadium Name:** Judy Johnson Field at Daniel S. Frawley Stadium. **Location:** I-95 North to Maryland Ave (exit 6), right on Maryland Ave, and through traffic light onto Martin Luther King Blvd, right at traffic light on Justison St, follow to Shipyard Dr; I-95 South to Maryland Ave (exit 6), left at fourth light on Martin Luther King Blvd, right at fourth light on Justison St, follow to Shipyard Dr. **Standard Game Times:** 6:35 pm, (Mon-Thur) 7:05 (Fri) 6:05 (Sat) Sun. 1:35 p.m. **Ticket Price Range:** $6-$15. **Visiting Club Hotel:** Quality Inn & Suites Skyways 147 North Dupont Highway New Castle, DE 19720 (302) 328-6666.

WINSTON-SALEM DASH

Office Address: 926 Brookstown Ave, Winston-Salem, NC 27101.
Stadium Address: 951 Ballpark Way, Winston-Salem, NC 27101.
Telephone: (336) 714-2287. **Fax:** (336) 714-2288.
E-Mail Address: info@wsdash.com. **Website:** www.wsdash.com.
Affiliation (first year): Chicago White Sox (1997). **Years in League:** 1945-

OWNERSHIP/MANAGEMENT

Operated by: W-S Dash. **Principal Owner:** Billy Prim.
President: CJ Johnson. **VP, Chief Financial Officer:** Kurt Gehsmann. **VP, Baseball Operations:** Ryan Manuel. **VP, Corporate Partnerships:** Dean Kessel. **Chief Financial Officer:** Kurt Gehsmann. **Director of Ballpark Experience and Branding:** Jessica Aveyard. **General Manager-Legends:** Kit Edwards. **Catering manager:** Beverly Becker. **Concessions Manager:** Zachary Mounce. **Director of Ticket Sales:** Paul Stephens. **Director of Corporate Partnership Services:** Ayla Acosta. **Broadcast and Media Relations Manager:** Joe Weil. **Head Groundskeeper:** Corey Church. **Accounting Manager:** Amanda Elbert. **Corporate Partnerships Assistant:** Andrew Key. **Group Sales Representatives:** Ben Underwood, Tyler Hess. **Business Development Representatives:** Tomas Miller, Corey Cook. **Sales Coordinator:** Rosanna Stewart. **Ticket Sales & Service Representative:** Taylor Hodges. **Box Office Manager:** Drew Fisch. **Box Office Assistant:** Mario Fischer

FIELD STAFF

Manager: Ryan Newman. **Hitting Coach:** Charlie Poe. **Pitching Coach:** Danny Faquhar. **Trainer:** Carson Wooten. **Strength Coach:** George Timke.

GAME INFORMATION

Radio Announcer: Joe Weil. **No. of Games Broadcast:** 140. **Flagship Station:** The Triad Sports Hub - 101.5 FM & 600 AM (Thursdays) or wsdash.com (all games). **PA Announcer:** Jeffrey Griffin. **Official Scorer:** TBD. **Stadium Name:** BB&T Ballpark. **Location:** I-40 Business to Peters Creek Parkway exit (exit 5A). **Standard Game Times:** M-F 7 p.m., Sat. 6 p.m., Sun. 2 p.m. **Visiting Club Hotel:** Best Western Plus- University Inn.

FLORIDA STATE LEAGUE

Office Address: 3901 26th St., Vero Beach, FL 32960.
Mailing Address: 3901 26th St., Vero Beach, FL 32960.
Telephone: (772) 257-8423.
E-Mail Address: office@floridastateleague.com.
Website: www.floridastateleague.com.
Years League Active: 1919-1927, 1936-1941, 1946- .
Chairman/President/Treasurer: Terry Reynolds.
Executive Vice President: John Timberlake. **VPs: North**—Ron Myers. **South**—Mike Bauer.
Corporate Secretary: Steve Smith.
Mike Bauer (Jupiter/Palm Beach), Shelby Nelson (Dunedin), Jordan Kobritz (Charlotte), Jeff Podobnik (Bradenton), Andrew Kaufmann (Fort Myers), Reese Smith, III (Daytona), Ron Myers (Lakeland), David Freeman (North Port), Vance Smith (Tampa), Traer Van Allen (St. Lucie), John Timberlake (Clearwater). **League Executive Assistant:** Laura LeCras.
Division Structure: North— Clearwater, Daytona, Dunedin, Lakeland, North Port, Tampa.
South—Bradenton, Charlotte, Fort Myers, Jupiter, Palm Beach, St. Lucie.
Regular Season: 140 games (split schedule). **2020 Opening Date:** April 9. **Closing Date:** September 6. **All-Star Game:** June 23 at Daytona.
Playoff Format: First-half division winners meet second-half winners in best of three series. Winners meet in best of five series for league championship. **Roster Limit:** 25. **Player Eligibility Rule:** No age limit. No more than two players and one player-coach on active list may have six or more years of prior minor league service.
Brand of Baseball: Rawlings.
Umpires: Harley Acosta Mercedes, Jonathon Benken, Brandon Blome, Edwin Jimenez Pernalete, Ben Fernandez, James Jean, Dexter Kelley, Marcelo Alfonzo Lozano, Tanner Moore, Taylor Payne, Kelvis Velez Caminero, Justin Whiddon.

Terry Reynolds

STADIUM INFORMATION

Club	Stadium	Opened	Dimensions LF	CF	RF	Capacity	2019 Att.
Bradenton	McKechnie Field	1923	335	400	335	8,654	71,284
Charlotte	Charlotte Sports Park	2009	343	413	343	5,028	91,349
Clearwater	Spectrum Field	2004	330	400	330	8,500	180,069
Daytona	Jackie Robinson Ballpark	1930	317	400	325	4,200	143,189
Dunedin	Florida Auto Exchange Stadium	1977	335	400	327	5,509	11,757
Florida	Cool Today Park	2019	335	400	335	8,000	19,615
Fort Myers	Hammond Stadium	1991	330	405	330	7,900	108,800
Jupiter	Roger Dean Chevrolet Stadium	1998	330	400	325	6,871	62,684
Lakeland	Publix Field at Joker Marchant Stadium	1966	340	420	340	7,961	50,770
Palm Beach	Roger Dean Chevrolet Stadium	1998	330	400	325	6,871	57,418
St. Lucie	First Data Field	1988	338	410	338	7,000	82,581
Tampa	Steinbrenner Field	1996	318	408	314	10,270	61,290

BRADENTON MARAUDERS

Address: 1701 27th Street East, Bradenton, FL 34208.
Telephone: (941) 747-3031. **Fax:** (941) 747-9442.
E-Mail Address: MaraudersInfo@pirates.com
Website: bradentonmarauders.com
Affiliation (first year): Pittsburgh Pirates (2010). **Years in League:** 1919-20, 1923-24, 1926, 2010-.

OWNERSHIP/MANAGEMENT
Operated By: Pittsburgh Associates of Florida
VP, Florida & Dominican Operations: Jeff Podobnik. **General Manager/Director of Sales & Marketing:** Craig Warzecha. **Director, Florida Operations:** Ray Morris. **Director, Concessions & Retail:** Chuck Knapp. **Assistant General Manager/Manager, Ticket Sales:** Jackie Riggleman. **Coordinator, Corporate Partnerships & Ticketing:** Zach Henkel. **Account Manager, Ticket Sales:** Nick Nelson. **Account Manager, Ticket Sales:** Taylor Fraise; **Coordinator, Marketing/Community Relations:** Mary Lanzino. **Coordinator, Stadium Operations:** Drew Pirritano. **Manager, Game Presentation:** Rebekah Rivette. **Head Groundskeeper:** Marc Sundeen.

FIELD STAFF
Manager: Wyatt Toregas. **Hitting Coach:** Butch Wynegar. **Pitching Coach:** Drew Benes. **Athletic Trainer:** Matt DenBleyker.

GAME INFORMATION
PA Announcer: Jeff Phillips. **Official Scorer:** Dave Taylor. **Stadium Name:** LECOM Park. **Location:** I-75 to exit 220 (220B from I-75N) to SR 64 West/Manatee Ave, Left onto 9th St West, LECOM PARK on the left. **Standard Game Times:** 6:30 pm, Sun. 1:00 pm. **Ticket Price Range:** $6-10. **Visiting Club Hotel:** Holiday Inn Express West, 4450 47th St W,

Bradenton, FL 34210. **Telephone:** (941) 747-3031.

CHARLOTTE STONE CRABS

Address: 2300 El Jobean Road, Building A, Port Charlotte, FL 33948.
Telephone: (941) 206-4487. **Fax:** (941) 421-7413.
E-Mail Address: info@stonecrabsbaseball.com. **Website:** www.stonecrabsbaseball.com.
Affiliation (first year): Tampa Bay Rays (2009). **Years in League:** 2009-

OWNERSHIP/MANAGEMENT
Operated By: CBI-Rays.
General Manager: Jeffrey Cook. **Assistant GM:** Jeff Cook. **Finance Director:** Lori Engleman. **Director of Ticket Operations:** Hallie Rubins. **Director of Fan Engagement:** Ashley Stephenson. **Director of Food & Beverage:** Brittany Jones. **Stadium Operations Manager:** Andrew Crawford. **Broadcasting & Media Relations Manager:** John Vittas. **Video Production Manager:** Chance Fernandez. **Box Office Manager:** Jennifer Lundrigan.

FIELD STAFF
Manager: Jeff Smith. **Pitching Coach:** Steve "Doc" Watson. **Coach:** Brady North. **Coach:** Jeremy Owens.

GAME INFORMATION
PA Announcer: Josh Grant. **Official Scorer:** Steve Posilovich. **Scoreboard Stats:** R.J. Fraser. **Gameday Stringer:** Jack Melton. **Stadium Name:** Charlotte Sports Park. **Location:** I-75 to Exit 179, turn left onto Toledo Blade Blvd then right on El Jobean Rd. **Ticket Price Range:** $8-12. **Visiting Club Hotel:** Sleep Inn, 806 Kings Hwy., Port Charlotte, FL 33980. **Phone:** 941-613-6300.

CLEARWATER THRESHERS

Address: 601 N Old Coachman Road, Clearwater, FL 33765.
Telephone: (727) 712-4300. **Fax:** (727) 712-4498.
Website: www.threshersbaseball.com.
Affiliation (first year): Philadelphia Phillies (1985). **Years in League:** 1985-

OWNERSHIP/MANAGEMENT
Operated by: Philadelphia Phillies.
Director of Florida Operations: John Timberlake. **General Manager of Clearwater Threshers:** Jason Adams. **Senior Manager of Corporate Partnerships:** Dan McDonough. **Business Manager:** Dianne Gonzalez. **General Manager, Spectrum Field:** Doug Kemp. **Assistant GM, Clearwater Threshers:** Dan Madden. **Ballpark Operations Manager:** Jay Warren. **Community Engagement/Media Manager:** Robert Stretch. **Food and Beverage Manager:** Justin Gunsaulus. **Assistant Food and Beverage Manager:** Justin Stone. **Office Manager:** DeDe Angelillis. **Senior Sales Associate:** Bobby Mitchell. **Corporate Sales Associate:** Cory Sipe. **Merchandise Manager:** Robin Warner. **Clubhouse Manager:** Mark Meschede. **Bar Manager:** Damian Heinz. **Manager, Ticket Operations:** Pat Prevelige. **Assistant Manager, Ticket Operations:** Kyle Webb. **Facility and Operations Coordinator:** Sean McCarthy. **Manager, Promotions and Game Entertainment:** Dominic Repper. **Field Supervisor:** Opie Cheek. **Suites Coordinator:** Wendy Smith. **Merchandise Assistant:** Shan Isett. **Group Sales Assistant:** Victoria Phipps. **Fun Team Coordinator:** Lindsey Settlemire. **Operations Assistant:** Will Priest. **Threshers Broadcaster:** Thaddeus Krzus.

FIELD STAFF
Manager: TBA. **Hitting Coach:** TBA. **Pitching Coach:** TBA.

GAME INFORMATION
PA Announcer: Don Guckian. **Official Scorer:** Larry Wiederecht. **Stadium Name:** Spectrum Field. **Location:** US 19 North and Drew Street in Clearwater. **Standard Game Times:** Mon.-Thu. 7 pm, Fri.-Sat. 6:30 pm, Sun. 1 p.m., most Wednesdays are day games. **Ticket Price Range:** $6-10. **Visiting Club Hotel:** La Quinta Inn, 21338 US Highway 19 N, Clearwater, FL 33765. **Telephone:** (727) 799-1565.

DAYTONA TORTUGAS

Address: 110 E Orange Ave, Daytona Beach, FL 32114.
Telephone: (386) 257-3172. **Fax:** (386) 523-9490.
E-Mail Address: info@daytonatortugas.com. **Website:** www.daytonatortugas.com.
Affiliation (first year): Cincinnati Reds (2015). **Years in League:** 1920-24, 1928, 193_ 41, 1946-73, 1977-87, 1993-

OWNERSHIP/MANAGEMENT
Operated By: Tortugas Baseball Club LLC. **Principal Owner/President:** Reese Smith III. **Co-Owners:** Bob Fregolle, Rick French. **President:** Ryan Keur. **General Manager:** Jim Jaworski. **Assistant General Manager:** Austin Scher. **Director of Corporate Partnerships:** Anderson Rathbun. **Partnership Fulfillment and Promotions Manager:** Amy

Cecil. **Director of Ticket Operations:** Paul Krenzer. **Director of Ticket Sales:** Melissa Balbach. **Ticket Sales Executive:** Max Furbee. **Community Relations Manager:** Josh McCann. **Creative Services Manager:** Bella Crispino. **Broadcaster and Media Relations Manager:** Justin Rocke. **Director of Stadium Operations and Events:** Thomas Vickers. **Head Groundskeeper:** Collin Tyzinski.

FIELD STAFF
Manager: Dick Schofield. **Bench Coach:** Darren Bragg. **Hitting Coach:** Alex Peláez. **Pitching Coach:** Tom Brown. **Athletic Trainer:** Ryan Ross. **Strength & Conditioning Coach:** TBA.

GAME INFORMATION
Radio Announcer: Justin Rocke. **No. of Games Broadcast:** 140. **Flagship Station:** TuneIn only. **PA Announcer:** Tim Lecras. **Official Scorer:** Don Roberts. **Stadium Name:** Jackie Robinson Ballpark. **Location:** I-95 to International Speedway Blvd Exit, east to Beach Street, south to Magnolia Ave east to ballpark; A1A North/South to Orange Ave west to ballpark. **Standard Game Time:** 7:05 p.m. (Mon-Sat); 5:35 p.m. (Sun). **Ticket Price Range:** $7-13.00. **Visiting Club Hotel:** Holiday Inn Resort Daytona Beach Oceanfront, 1615 S. Atlantic Ave Daytona Beach, FL 32118. **Telephone:** (386) 255-0921.

DUNEDIN BLUE JAYS

Address: 373 Douglas Ave Dunedin, FL 34698.
Telephone: (727) 733-9302. **Fax:** (727) 734-7661.
E-Mail Address: dunedin@bluejays.com. **Website:** dunedinbluejays.com.
Affiliation (first year): Toronto Blue Jays (1987). **Years in League:** 1978-79, 1987-

OWNERSHIP/MANAGEMENT
Director Florida Operations: Shelby Nelson. **General Manager:** Mike Liberatore. **Accounting Manager:** Gayle Gentry. **Manager, Retail Sales and Community Relations:** Kathi Beckman. **Supervisor, Ticket and Box Office Operations:** Craig Ball. **Administrative Assistant/Receptionist:** Dea Jones. **Manager, Security and Stadium Operations:** Zac Phelps. **Head Superintendent:** Patrick Skunda.

FIELD STAFF
Manager: Donnie Murphy. **Hitting Coach:** Matt Hague. **Pitching Coach:** Antonio Caceres. **Position Coach:** George Carroll. **Strength & Conditioning Coach:** Justin Batcher. **Athletic Trainer:** Luke Greene.

GAME INFORMATION
PA Announcer: Bill Christie. **Official Scorer:** Steven Boychuk. **Stadium Name:** TD Ballpark. **Location:** From I-275, north on Highway 19, exit on Drew Street, right on North Keene Road, left onto Union Street. Right onto Douglas Avenue and stadium is on the right. **Standard Game Times:** 6:30 pm, Sun. 1:00 pm. **Ticket Price Range:** $8-$12. **Visiting Club Hotel:** La Quinta, 21338 US Highway 19 North, Clearwater, FL. **Telephone:** (727) 799-1565.

FLORIDA FIRE FROGS

Address: 18800 South, W Villages Pkwy, Venice, FL 34293
Telephone: (941) 413-5000. **E-Mail Address:** info@floridafirefrogs.com.
Website: www.floridafirefrogs.com.
Affiliation (first year): Atlanta Braves (2017). **Years in League:** 2017-

OWNERSHIP/MANAGEMENT
Operated By: Atlanta National League Baseball Club Inc. **Chairman: CEO:** TBA. **GM:** Christina Shaw. **Assistant General Manager:** TBA. **Clubhouse Manager:** Jeff Pink. **Head Groundskeeper:** Matt Taylor.

FIELD STAFF
Manager: Barrett Kleinknecht. **Pitching Coach:** Dan Meyer. **Hitting Coach:** Danny Santiesteban.

GAME INFORMATION
PA Announcer: TBA. **Official Scorer:** TBA. **Radio Broadcaster:** NA. **Radio Station:** NA. **Stadium Name:** Cool Today Park. **Location:** From **I-75S:** Take Exit 191 (River Rd Englewood/North Port). Keep Right onto River Road for 3.9 miles. Turn Right onto US 41/Tamiami Trail. In 1.5 miles take a left onto W. Villages Pkwy. Continue on W. Villages Pkwy for .75 miles. From **I-75N:** Take Exit 191 (River Rd Englewood/North Port). Turn left onto River Road. Continue for 3.9 miles. Turn Right onto US 41/Tamiami Trail. In 1.5 miles take a left onto W. Villages Pkwy. Continue on W. Villages Pkwy for .75 miles.

FORT MYERS MIGHTY MUSSELS

Address: 14400 Six Mile Cypress Pkwy, Fort Myers, FL 33912.
Telephone: (239) 768-4210. **Fax:** (239) 768-4211.
E-Mail Address: frontdesk@mightymussels.com.
Website: www.mightymussels.com.
Affiliation (first year): Minnesota Twins (1992). **Years in League:** 1926, 1978-87, 1992-

OWNERSHIP/MANAGEMENT

Operated By: Kaufy Baseball, LLC. **Owner:** Andrew Kaufmann. **Partner:** Jason Hochberg
President: Bob Ohrablo. **Executive Vice President:** Scott Einhorn. **VP of Sponsorship & Baseball Ventures:**
Chris Peters. **General Manager, Director of Operations:** Judd Loveland. **Director of Marketing:** Lauren Muni. **Chief
Financial Officer:** Kim Baldini. **Manager of Corporate Partnerships:** Andy Wood. **Sales Manager:** Marinda Kitchen.
Senior Account Executive: Jeremy Ramey. **Account Executive:** Brittany Bowen. **Account Executive:** Julius van
Rooyen. **Broadcast & Media Relations Manager:** Marshall Kelner. **Graphic Designer:** Shannon Rankin. **Director of
Food & Beverage:** Loren Merrigan. **Assistant Director of Food & Beverage:** Micah Beutell. **Operations Assistant:**
Frankie Martello. **Merchandise Manager:** Lynn Izzo.

FIELD STAFF

Manager: Aaron Sutton. **Hitting Coach:** Nate Rasmussen. **Hitting Coach:** Brian Meyer. **Pitching Coach:** Virgil
Vazquez. **Pitching Coach:** Carlos Hernandez. **Athletic Trainer:** Ben Myers. **Strength & Conditioning Coach:** Chuck
Bradway.

GAME INFORMATION

Radio Announcer: Marshall Kelner. **No. of Games Broadcast:** 140. **Internet Broadcast:** www.mightymussels.com.
PA Announcer: Allen Woodard. **Official Scorer:** Scott Pedersen. **Stadium Name:** William H. Hammond Stadium at the
CenturyLink Sports Complex. **Location:** Exit 131 off I-75, west on Daniels Parkway, left on Six Mile Cypress Parkway.
Standard Game Times: Mon-Fri 6:30 or 7:00 pm, Sat. 7:00; Sun. 2:00. **Ticket Price Range:** $10-$15. **Visiting Club Hotel:**
Fairfield Inn & Suites Fort Myers Cape Coral, 7090 Cypress Terrace, Fort Myers, FL 33907.

JUPITER HAMMERHEADS

Address: 4751 Main Street, Jupiter, FL 33458.
Telephone: (561) 775-1818. **Fax:** (561) 691-6886.
E-Mail Address: PalmBeachCardinals@rogerdeanchevroletstadium.com.
Affiliation (first year): Miami Marlins (1998). **Years in League:** 1998-

OWNERSHIP/MANAGEMENT

Owned By: St. Louis Cardinals, Jupiter Stadium, LTD.
General Manager, Jupiter Stadium, LTD: Mike Bauer. **General Manager:** Jamie Toole. **Executive Assistant:** Lynn
Besaw. **Media Relations Coordinator:** Andrew Miller. **Media Relations Assistant:** Ryer Gardenswartz. **Director of
Accounting:** Pam Satory. **Accounting Specialist:** Alexa Harshbarger. **Director of Corporate Partnerships:** Jamie Toole.
Director of Events: Andrew Seymour. **Marketing & Promotions Manager:** Sarah Campbell. **Building Manager:** Walter
Herrera. **Director, Grounds & Facilities:** Jordan Treadway. **Assistant Director, Grounds & Facilities:** Mitchell Moenster.
Merchandise Manager: Susan Crawford. **Ticket Office Manager:** Louis Reyes. **Ticket Office Assistant Manager:**
Kaitlyn Kilcoyne.

FIELD STAFF

Manager: TBA. **Pitching Coach:** TBA. **Hitting Coach:** TBA. **Strength & Conditioning Coach:** TBA. **Athletic Trainer:**
TBA. **Defensive Coach:** TBA.

GAME INFORMATION

PA Announcers: John Frost, Jay Zeager. **Official Scorer:** Brennan McDonald. **Stadium Name:** Roger Dean Chevrolet
Stadium. **Location:** I-95 to exit 83, east on Donald Ross Road for 1/4 mile, left on Parkside Dr. **Standard Game Times:**
6:30 pm, Sat. 5:30pm, Sun. 1:00pm. **Ticket Price Range:** $7- $10. **Visiting Club Hotel:** Fairfield Inn by Marriott, 6748
Indiantown Road, Jupiter, FL 33458. **Telephone:** (561) 748-5252.

LAKELAND FLYING TIGERS

Address: 2301 Lakeland Hills Blvd., Lakeland, FL 33805.
Telephone: (863) 686-8075. **Fax:** (863) 687-4127.
Website: www.lakelandflyingtigers.com.
Affiliation (first year): Detroit Tigers (1967). **Years in League:** 1919-26, 1953-55, 1960, 1962-64, 1967-

OWNERSHIP/MANAGEMENT

Owned By: Detroit Tigers, Inc.
President and CEO, Ilitch Holdings, Inc. and Chairman and CEO, Detroit Tigers: Christopher Ilitch. **Director,
Florida Operations:** Ron Myers. **General Manager:** Zach Burek. **Manager, Administration/Operations Manager:**
Shannon Follett. **Ticket Manager:** Ryan Eason. **Assistant General Manager:** Dan Lauer. **Administration/ Operations
Assistant:** Alison Streicher. **Sales Representatives:** Chimere Butler, Clarissa Skillman.

FIELD STAFF

Manager: Andrew Graham. **Hitting Coach:** Bill Springman. **Pitching Coach:** Jorge Cordova. **Developmental Coach:**
Ollie Kadey. **Athletic Trainer:** Sean McFarland. **Strength & Conditioning Coach:** Dax Fiore. **Clubhouse Manager:** Pete
Mancuso.

GAME INFORMATION

PA Announcer: Unavailable. **Official Scorer:** Joe Falatek. **Stadium Name:** Publix Field at Joker Marchant Stadium.

Location: Exit 33 on I-4 to 33 South (Lakeland Hills Blvd.), 1.5 miles on left. **Standard Game Times:** Mon.-Fri. 6:30, Sat. 6:00, Sun. 1:00. **Ticket Price Range:** $5-10. **Visiting Club Hotel:** Extended Stay America Lakeland, 4360 Lakeland Park Drive, Lakeland, FL 33809. **Telephone:** (863) 904-2050.

PALM BEACH CARDINALS

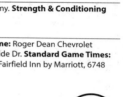

Address: 4751 Main Street, Jupiter, FL 33458.
Telephone: (561) 775-1818. **Fax:** (561) 691-6886.
E-Mail Address: PalmBeachCardinals@rogerdeanchevroletstadium.com.
Affiliation (first year): St. Louis Cardinals (2003). **Years in League:** 2003-

OWNERSHIP/MANAGEMENT

Owned By: St. Louis Cardinals, Jupiter Stadium, LTD.
General Manager, Jupiter Stadium, LTD: Mike Bauer. **General Manager:** Andrew Seymour. **Executive Assistant:** Lynn Besaw. **Media Relations Coordinator:** Andrew Miller. **Media Relations Assistant:** Ryer Gardenswartz. **Director of Accounting:** Pam Satory. **Accounting Specialist:** Alexa Harshbarger. **Director of Corporate Partnerships:** Jamie Toole. **Director of Events:** Andrew Seymour. **Marketing & Promotions Manager:** Sarah Campbell. **Building Manager:** Walter Herrera. **Director, Grounds & Facilities:** Jordan Treadway. **Assistant Director, Grounds & Facilities:** Mitchell Moenster. **Merchandise Manager: Susan Crawford Ticket Office Manager:** Louis Reyes.

FIELD STAFF

Manager: Dann Bilardello. **Pitching Coach:** Rick Harig. **Hitting Coach:** Brian Burgamy. **Strength & Conditioning Coach:** Ross Hasegawa. **Certified Athletic Trainer:** Alex Wolfinger.

GAME INFORMATION

PA Announcers: John Frost, **Jay Zeager, Official Scorer: Lou Villano Stadium Name:** Roger Dean Chevrolet Stadium. **Location:** I-95 to exit 83, east on Donald Ross Road for 1/4 mile, left on Parkside Dr. **Standard Game Times:** 6:30 pm, Sat. 5:30pm, Sun. 1:00pm. **Ticket Price Range:** $7- $10. **Visiting Club Hotel:** Fairfield Inn by Marriott, 6748 Indiantown Road, Jupiter, FL 33458. **Telephone:** (561) 748-5252.

ST. LUCIE METS

Address: 525 NW Peacock Blvd., Port St Lucie, FL 34986.
Telephone: (772) 871-2100. **Fax:** (772) 878-9802.
Website: www.stluciemets.com.
Affiliation (first year): New York Mets (1988). **Years in League:** 1988-

OWNERSHIP/MANAGEMENT

Operated by: Sterling Mets LP.
Chairman/CEO: Fred Wilpon. **President:** Saul Katz. **COO:** Jeff Wilpon. **Executive Director, Minor League Facilities:** Paul Taglieri. **General Manager:** Traer Van Allen. **Executive Assistant:** Mary O'Brien. **Coordinator, Group Sales:** Josh Sexton. **Staff Accountant:** Shannon Murray. **Accounting Clerk:** Christina Rivera. **Director, Sales/Corporate Partnerships:** Lauren DeAcetis. **Director, Ticketing/Merchandise:** Kyle Gleockler. **Manager, Media/Broadcast Relations:** Adam MacDonald. **Director, Group Sales/Community Relations:** Kasey Blair. **Coordinator, Social Media and Graphic Design:** Marissa Kappus. **Maintenance:** Jeff Montpetit.

FIELD STAFF

Manager: Chad Kreuter. **Hitting Coach:** Bruce Fields. **Pitching Coach:** Royce Ring. **Bench Coach:** Endy Chavez. **Trainer:** Hiroto Kawamura. **Performance Coach:** Kory Wan.

GAME INFORMATION

PA Announcer: Evan Nine. **Official Scorer:** Bill Whitehead. **Stadium Name:** First Data Field. **Location:** Exit 121 (St Lucie West Blvd) off I-95, east 1/2 mile, left on NW Peacock Blvd. **Standard Game Times:** 6:30 pm, Sun 12:00 pm. **Ticket Price Range:** $6 - $10. **Visiting Club Hotel:** SpringHill Suites by Marriott, 2000 NW Courtyard Circle, Port St Lucie, FL 34986. **Telephone:** (772) 871-2929.

TAMPA TARPONS

Address: One Steinbrenner Drive, Tampa, FL 33614.
Telephone: (813) 875-7753. **Fax:** (813) 673-3186
E-Mail Address: vsmith@yankees.com. **Website:** tarponsbaseball.com
Affiliation (first year): New York Yankees (1994). **Years in League:** 1919-27, 1957-1988, 1994-

OWNERSHIP/MANAGEMENT

Operated by: Florida Bomber Baseball LLC. **VP Business Operations:** Vance Smith. **General Manager:** Matt Gess. **Assistant GM:** Jeremy Ventura. **Premium Ticket Services:** Jennifer Magliocchetti. **Digital/Social Media Coordinator:** Maddie Erhardt. **Operations Coordinator:** Kate Harvey. **Director, Grounds:** Ritchie Anderson. **Stadium Supervisor:** Ron Kaufman. **Head Groundskeeper:** Jeff Eckert.

FIELD STAFF

Manager: David Adams. **Pitching Coach:** Jose Rosado. **Hitting Coach:** Joe Migliaccio. **Defensive Coach:** Kevin Mahoney. **Defensive Coach:** Jason Phillips. **Athletic Trainer:** Michael Becker. **Strength & Conditioning Coach:** Jacob Dunning. **Clubhouse Manager:** J.R. Bassett. **Video Manager:** Mike Triller. **Advance Scouting Analyst:** Matt Reiland.

GAME INFORMATION

Radio: Unavailable. **PA Announcer:** Unavailable. **Official Scorer:** Unavailable. **Stadium Name:** George M Steinbrenner Field. **Location:** I-275 to Dale Mabry Hwy, North on Dale Mabry Hwy (Facility is at corner of West Martin Luther King Blvd/Dale Mabry Hwy). **Standard Game Times:** Mon - Sat. 6:30pm, Sun 1pm. **Ticket Price Range:** $5-8. **Visiting Club Hotel:** Double Tree by Hilton Tampa Airport - Westshore.

MIDWEST LEAGUE

Address: 210 S. Michigan St., South Bend, Ind. 46601.
Telephone: (574) 234-3000. **Fax:** (574) 234-4220.
E-Mail Address: mwl@midwestleague.com, dickn@sni-law.com.
Website: www.midwestleague.com.
Years League Active: 1947-
President/Legal Counsel/Secretary: Richard A. Nussbaum, II.
Vice President: Lew Chamberlin. **Directors:** Andrew Berlin (South Bend). Jack Blackstock (Bowling Green). Kim Parker (Burlington). Lew Chamberlin (West Michigan). Dennis Conerton (Beloit). Paul Davis (Clinton). Tom Dickson (Lansing). Jason Freier (Fort Wayne). David Heller (Quad Cities). Doug Nelson (Cedar Rapids). Greg Rosenbaum (Dayton). Peter Carfagna (Lake County). Brad Tammen (Great Lakes). Jason Mott (Peoria). Dr. Bob Froehlich (Kane County). Rob Zerjav (Wisconsin). **Director Emeritus:** Dave Walker. **League Administrator:** Holly Voss.
Division Structure: East—Bowling Green, Dayton, Fort Wayne, Lake County, Lansing, South Bend, Great Lakes, West Michigan. **West**—Beloit, Burlington, Cedar Rapids, Clinton, Kane County, Peoria, Quad Cities, Wisconsin.

Richard Nussbaum

Regular Season: 140 games (split schedule). **Opening Date:** April 9. **Closing Date:** Sept 7. **All-Star Game:** June 23 at Bowling Green, Kentucky. **Playoff Format:** Eight teams qualify. First-half and second-half division winners and wild-card teams meet in best of three quarterfinal series. Winners meet in best of three series for division championships. Division champions meet in best-of-five series for league championship. **Roster Limit:** 25 active. **Player Eligibility Rule:** No age limit. No more than two players and one player-coach on active list may have more than five years experience. **Brand of Baseball:** Rawlings ROM-MID. **Umpires:** Unavailable.

STADIUM INFORMATION

Club	Stadium	Opened	Dimensions LF	CF	RF	Capacity	2019 Att.
Beloit	Pohlman Field	1982	325	380	325	3,500	73,200
Bowling Green	Bowling Green Ballpark	2009	318	400	326	4,559	190,877
Burlington	Community Field	1947	338	403	318	3,200	67369
Cedar Rapids	Veterans Memorial Stadium	2002	315	400	325	5,300	150,278
Clinton	Ashford University Field	1937	335	401	325	5,000	121,325
Dayton	Fifth Third Field	2000	338	402	338	6,830	545,108
Fort Wayne	Parkview Field	2009	336	400	318	8,100	371,259
Great Lakes	Dow Diamond	2007	332	400	325	5,200	195,904
Kane County	Northwestern Medicine Field	1991	335	400	335	10,973	350,305
Lake County	Classic Park	2003	320	400	320	6,157	200,756
Lansing	Cooley Law School Stadium	1996	305	412	305	11,000	311,028
Peoria	Dozer Park	2002	310	400	310	7,000	198,545
Quad Cities	Modern Woodmen Park	1931	343	400	318	7,140	150,905
South Bend	Four Winds Fields	1987	336	405	336	5,000	319,616
West Michigan	Fifth Third Ballpark	1994	317	402	327	9,281	360,295
Wisconsin	Neuroscience Group Field	1995	325	400	325	5,170	218,037

BELOIT SNAPPERS

Office Address: 2301 Skyline Drive, Beloit, WI 53511.
Mailing Address: P.O. Box 855, Beloit, WI 53512.
Telephone: (608) 362-2272. **Fax:** (608) 362-0418.
E-Mail: snappy@snappersbaseball.com. **Website:** www.snappersbaseball.com.
Affiliation (first year): Oakland Athletics (2013). **Years in League:** 1982-

OWNERSHIP/MANAGEMENT
General Manager: Jeff Gray. **Marketing and Media Manager:** TBD. **Tickets and Group Sales Manager:** Tommy Himebaugh. **Corporate Partnerships Manager:** TBD. **Head Groundskeeper:** TBD.

FIELD STAFF
Manager: Lloyd Turner. **Hitting Coach:** Javier Godard. **Pitching Coach:** Don Schulze. **Assistant Coach:** Craig Conklin. **Athletic Trainer:** Brian Thorson. **Strength & Conditioning Coach:** Kevin Guild.

GAME INFORMATION
Radio Announcer: TBD. **No. of Games Broadcast:** TBD. **Flagship Station:** TBD. **PA Announcer:** TBD. **Official Scorer:** TBD. **Stadium Name:** Pohlman Field. **Location:** I-90 to exit 185-A, right at Cranston Road for 1 1/2 miles; I-43 to Wisconsin 81 to Cranston Road, right at Cranston for 1 1/2 miles. **Standard Game Times:** 6:30 pm, Sat. 4 pm (April), Sun 2 pm. **Ticket Price Range:** $8-$12.00. **Visiting Club Hotel:** Rodeway Inn, 2956 Milwaukee Rd, Beloit, WI 53511. **Telephone:** (608) 364-4000.

BOWLING GREEN HOT RODS

Address: Bowling Green Ballpark, 300 8th Avenue, Bowling Green, KY 42101.
Telephone: (270) 901-2121. **Fax:** (270) 901-2165.
E-Mail Address: fun@bghotrods.com. **Website:** www.bghotrods.com.
Affiliation (first year): Tampa Bay Rays (2009). **Years in League:** 2010-

OWNERSHIP/MANAGEMENT

Operated By: BG SKY, LLC.
President/Managing Partner: Jack Blackstock. **General Manager/COO:** Eric C. Leach. **Assistant General Manager:** Matt Ingram. **Director, Sales:** Kyle Wolz. **Director, Stadium Operations:** Brock Wilson. **Assistant Director, Stadium Operations:** David Heimerdinger. **Director, Creative Services:** Nick Jourdan. **Head Groundskeeper:** Tradd Jones. Manager, **Broadcasting & Media Relations:** Shawn Murnin. Manager, **Social Media & Marketing:** Holli Hawkins. **Manager of Fun:** Jamie Vanaman. **Manager, Corporate Marketing:** Shelby Cohen. **Manager, Corporate Marketing:** Alex Ortiz. **Account Executive & Retail Store Manager:** Aidan Hickey. **Account Executive:** Luke Easley. **Promotions & Community Engagement Assistant:** Blake Mayfield. **Creative Services Assistant:** Haley Schoengart. **Video Production Assistant:** Blake Forshee. **Bookkeeper:** Kim Myers.

FIELD STAFF

Manager: Blake Butera. **Pitching Coach:** Jim Paduch. **Assistant Coaches:** Wuarnner Rincones, Skeeter Barnes. **Athletic Trainer:** Brian Newman. **Strength & Conditioning Coach:** Jordan Brown.

GAME INFORMATION

Radio Announcer: Shawn Murnin. **No. of Games Broadcast:** 140. **Flagship Station:** WBGN 94.1 FM.
PA Announcer: Unavailable. **Official Scorer:** Unavailable. **Stadium Name:** Bowling Green Ballpark. **Location:** From I-65, take Exit 26 (KY-234/Cemetery Road) into Bowling Green for 3 miles, left onto College Street for .2 miles, right onto 8th Avenue. **Standard Game Times:** Mon.-Sat., 6:35 pm, Sun., 4:05 pm. **Ticket Price Range:** $8-24. **Visiting Club Hotel:** Tru by Hilton. **Telephone:** (270) 904-2260.

BURLINGTON BEES

Office Address: 2712 Mount Pleasant St., Burlington, IA 52601.
Mailing Address: PO Box 824, Burlington, IA 52601.
Telephone: (319) 754-5705. **Fax:** (319) 754-5882.
E-Mail Address: staff@gobees.com. **Website:** www.gobees.com.
Affiliation (first year): Los Angeles Angels (2013). **Years in League:**1962-

OWNERSHIP/MANAGEMENT

Operated By: Burlington Baseball Association Inc.
President: Scott Zaiser. **General Manager:** Kim Parker. **Director of Ticketing & Front Office Administrator:** Jill Mason. **Sales/Stadium Operations Executive:** Tad Lowary. **Sales/Stadium Operations Executive:** Nick Carey. **Director Media Relations:** Ted Gutman. **Groundskeeper:** Jordan Barr. **Clubhouse Manager:** Michael Wilkes.

FIELD STAFF

Manager: Jack Howell. **Hitting Coach:** Will Bradley. **Pitching Coach:** Tyler Anderson. **Defensive Coach:** Trevor Nyp. **Trainer:** Nick Faciana. **S & C Coach:** Andrea Nunez.

GAME INFORMATION

Radio Announcer: RJ Larson. **No. of Games Broadcast:** 71 home games. **PA Announcer:** Marty Mogk. **Official Scorer:** Ted Gutman/Terry Abrisz. **Stadium Name:** Community Field. **Location:** From US 34, take US 61 North to Mt. Pleasant St, east 1/8 mile. **Standard Game Times:** Mon.-Sat., 6:30 pm, Sat., 5:00 pm (April-May) Sun., 2 pm. **Ticket Price Range:** $5-10. **Visiting Club Hotel:** Pzazz Best Western FunCity, 3001 Winegard Dr., Burlington, IA 52601. **Telephone:** (319) 753-2223.

CEDAR RAPIDS KERNELS

Office Address: 950 Rockford Road SW, Cedar Rapids, IA 52404.
Mailing Address: PO Box 2001, Cedar Rapids, IA 52406.
Telephone: (319) 363-3887. **Fax:** (319) 363-5631.
E-Mail: kernels@kernels.com. **Website:** www.kernels.com.
Affiliation (first year): Minnesota Twins (2013). **Years in League:** 1962-

OWNERSHIP/MANAGEMENT

President: Greg Seyfer. **Chief Executive Officer:** Doug Nelson. **General Manager:** Scott Wilson. **Senior Director of Ticket/Group Sales:** Andrea Brommelkamp. **Senior Director of Corporate Sales & Marketing:** Jessica Fergesen. **Senior Director of Food and Beverage:** Nathan Varner. **Controller/Human Relations:** Cindy Oldfather. **Community Relations Manager:** Aron Brecht. **Director of Food & Beverage:** Brett Heikkila. **Sales & Marketing Coordinator:** Lakin

Goodman. **Group Sales Coordinator:** Morgan Johnson. **Food & Beverage Staffing Manager:** Daniel Eggers. **Stadium Operations Manager:** Brad Mochal. **Office Manager/Donations Coordinator:** Sherry Downey. **Sports Turf Manager:** Jesse Roeder. **Radio Broadcaster:** Chris Kleinhans-Schulz. **Clubhouse Manager:** Mason Steinberg.

FIELD STAFF

Field Manager: Brian Dinkelman. **Hitting Coach:** Bryce Berg. **Pitching Coach:** Peter Larson. **Pitching Coach:** Calvin Maduro. **Coach:** Luis Rodriguez. **Trainer:** Tyler Blair. **Strength Coach:** Colin Feikles.

GAME INFORMATION

Radio Announcer: Chris Kleinhans-Schulz. **No. of Games Broadcast:** 140. Streaming Internet Only. **PA Announcer:** David Schulte. **Official Scorers:** TBD. **Stadium Name:** Perfect Game Field at Veterans Memorial Stadium. **Directions to Stadium:** From I-380 North, take the Wilson Ave exit, turn left on Wilson Ave, after the railroad tracks, turn right on Rockford Road, proceed .8 miles, stadium is on left; from I-380 South, exit at First Avenue West (exit 19b), Go west to 15th street and turn left. Turn left onto 8th Ave, then right onto Kurt Warner Way (tennis courts). **Standard Game Times:** Mon.-Sat., 6:35 pm, Sun. 2:05 pm. **Ticket Price Range:** $9-13 in advance, $10-14 day of game. **Visiting Club Hotel:** Comfort Inn & Suites, 2025 Werner Ave NE, Cedar Rapids, IA 52402. **Telephone:** (319) 378-8888.

CLINTON LUMBERKINGS

Office Address: 537 Ball Park Drive, Clinton, IA 52732.
Mailing Address: PO Box 1295, Clinton, IA 52733.
Telephone: (563) 242-0727. **Fax:** (563) 242-1433.
E-Mail Address: lumberkings@lumberkings.com. **Website:** www.lumberkings.com.

OWNERSHIP/MANAGEMENT

Operated By: Clinton Baseball Club Inc.
President: Paul Davis. **General Manager:** Ted Tornow. **Director, Broadcasting/Media Relations:** Michael Broskowski. **Director, Operations:** Tyler Oehmen. **Head Groundskeeper:** Jack Bondy. **Accountant:** Ryan Marcum. **Assistant Directors, Operations:** Morty Kriner and Nick Irwin. **Director, Facility Compliance:** Tom Whaley. **Office Procurement Manager:** Les Moore. **Community Service Representative:** Tammy Johnson. **Assistant Groundskeeper:** Matt Dunbar. **Special Events Coordinator:** Tom Krogman.

FIELD STAFF

Manager: Tom Lawless. **Hitting Coach:** Matt Snyder. **Pitching Coach:** Mark DiFelice. **Athletic Trainer:** Melissa Hampton. **Strength & Conditioning Coach:** Sam Saver. **Coach:** Frank Moore.

GAME INFORMATION

Radio Announcer: Michael Broskowski. **No. of Games Broadcast:** 140. **Flagship Station:** WCCI 100.3 FM. **PA Announcer:** Brad Seward. **Official Scorer:** Alex Miller. **Stadium Name:** NelsonCorp Field. **Location:** Highway 67 North to Sixth Ave. North, right on Sixth, cross railroad tracks, stadium on right. **Standard Game Times:** 6:30 pm. **Saturday:** 5 p.m. **Sunday:** 2:00. **Ticket Price Range:** $5-8. **Visiting Club Hotel:** Econo Lodge, 2300 Lincoln Way, Clinton Iowa 52732. **Telephone:** (563) 321-4886.

DAYTON DRAGONS

Office Address: Fifth Third Field, 220 N. Patterson Blvd., Dayton,OH 45402.
Mailing Address: PO Box 2107, Dayton, OH 45401.
Telephone: (937) 228-2287. **Fax:** (937) 228-2284.
E-Mail Address: dragons@daytondragons.com. **Website:** www.daytondragons.com.
Affiliation (first year): Cincinnati Reds (2000). **Years in League:** 2000-

OWNERSHIP/MANAGEMENT

Operated By: Palisades Arcadia Baseball LLC.
President & General Manager: Robert Murphy. **Executive Vice President:** Eric Deutsch. **Office Manager/Executive Assistant to the President:** Leslie Stuck. **VP, Assistant General Manager:** Brandy Guinaugh. **VP, Accounting/Finance:** Mark Schlein. **VP, Corporate Partnerships:** Brad Eaton, Trafton Eutsler. Director, **Media Relations & Broadcasting:** Tom Nichols. **Senior Director, Operations:** John Wallace. **Director, Facility Operations:** Jason Fleenor. **Senior Director, Entertainment:** Kaitlin Rohrer. **Director, Entertainment:** Katrina Gibbs. **Director, Ticket Operations:** Stefanie Mitchell. **Director, Ticket Sales:** Andrew Hayes. **Director, Group Sales:** Carl Hertzberg. **Senior Inside Sales Manager:** Mandy Roselli. **Group Sales Managers:** Nicholas Fryman, Grant Hall, Andrew Majzan, Ben Shockley, Nicholas Zaleski. **Business Development Managers:** Dosh Hyde, Keenan Young, Andrew Zellers. **Corporate Partnerships Managers:** Christine Burns, Megan Norkunas, Brandon Rexin, Brittany Snyder, Alex Wilker. **Ticket Operations Manager:** Jordyn Lewis. **Ticket Operations Coordinator:** Cody Messal. **Graphic Designer:** Ashley Donahue. **Sports Turf Manager:** Tanner Turner. **Manager of Retail Operations:** Kyle Dunlap. **Media Relations Assistant:** Jack Kizer. **Entertainment Assistant:** Jamie Penwell. **Staff Accountant:** Dawn Reed. **Administrative Assistant:** Erica Szente. **Clubhouse Manager:** Austin Coleman.

FIELD STAFF

Manager: Gookie Dawkins. **Hitting Coach:** Darryl Brinkley. **Pitching Coach:** Brian Garman. **Bench Coach:** Hernan

Iribarren. **Trainer:** Andrew Cleves. **Strength/Conditioning:** Dan Donahue.

GAME INFORMATION

Radio Announcers: Tom Nichols and Jack Kizer. **No. of Games Broadcast:** 140. **Flagship Station:** WONE 980 AM. **Television Announcer:** Tom Nichols and Jack Pohl. **No. of Games Broadcast:** Home-25. **Flagship Station:** WBDT Channel 26. **PA Announcer:** Ben Oburn. **Official Scorers:** Matt Lindsay, Mike Lucas, Matt Zircher. **Stadium Name:** Fifth Third Field. **Location:** I-75 South to downtown Dayton, left at First Street; I-75 North, right at First Street exit. **Ticket Price Range:** $9-$19. **Visiting Club Hotel:** Courtyard by Marriott, 100 Prestige Place, Miamisburg, OH 45342. **Telephone:** 937-433-3131. **Fax:** 937-433-0285.

FORT WAYNE TINCAPS

Address: 1301 Ewing St., Fort Wayne, IN 46802.
Telephone: (260) 482-6400. **Fax:** (260) 471-4678.
E-Mail Address: info@tincaps.com. **Website:** www.tincaps.com.
Affiliation (first year): San Diego Padres (1999). **Years in League:** 1993-

OWNERSHIP/MANAGEMENT

Operated By: Hardball Capital. **Owner:** Jason Freier.
President: Mike Nutter. **Vice President, Corporate Partnerships:** David Lorenz. **VP, Finance:** Brian Schackow. **VP, Marketing & Promotions:** Michael Limmer. **Creative Director:** Tony DesPlaines. **Director of Video Production:** Melissa Darby. **Assistant Video Production Manager:** Tim Bajema. **Broadcasting/Media Relations Manager:** John Nolan. **Assistant Director of Marketing & Promotions:** Morgan Olson. **Digital Content Manager:** Cory Stace. **Community & Fan Engagement Manager:** Brenda Feasby. **Group Sales Director:** Jared Parcell. **Group Sales Assistant Director:** Brent Harring. **Senior Ticket Account Manager:** Austin Allen. **Ticket Account Manager:** Dalton McGill. **Ticket Account Manager:** Jenn Sylvester. **Ticket Account Manager:** Tyler Lantz. **Ticketing Director:** Paige Watson. **Reading Program Director/Assistant Director of Ticketing:** Kade Zvokel. **Corporate Partnerships Manager:** Devon Merder. **Special Events Coordinator:** Holly Raney. **Banquet Event Manager:** Alexis Strabala. **Food/ Beverage Director:** Bill Lehn. **Executive Chef/Culinary Director:** Pisarn Amornarthakij. **Food/Beverage Operations Manager:** Dominick Catanzarite. **VIP Services Manager:** Rebekah Carr. **Commissary Manager:** Michael Shidler. **Head Groundskeeper:** Keith Winter. **Facilities Director:** Tim Burkhart. **Accounting Manager/Facilities Manager:** Erik Lose. **Groundskeeping/Ballpark Operations Assistant:** Jake Sperry. **Groundskeeping Assistant:** Jackson Boyce. **Merchandise Manager:** Emma Reese. **Human Resources/Office Manager:** Cathy Tinney.

FIELD STAFF

Manager: Anthony Contreras. **Hitting Coach:** Jonathan Matthews. **Pitching Coach:** Leo Rosales. **Fielding Coach:** Jonathan Meyer. **Athletic Trainer:** Nick Coberly. **Strength & Conditioning Coach:** Ben Loftis.

GAME INFORMATION

Radio Announcers: John Nolan, Mike Maahs. **No. of Radio Games Broadcast:** 140. **Flagship Station:** WKJG 1380-AM/100.9-FM. **TV Announcers:** John Nolan, Brett Rump, Tracy Coffman. **No. of TV Games Broadcast:** Home–70. **Flagship Station:** Comcast Network 81. **PA Announcer:** Jared Parcell. **Official Scorers:** Rich Tavierne, Bill Scott, Dan Watson. **Stadium Name:** Parkview Field. **Location:** 1301 Ewing St., Fort Wayne, IN, 46802. **Ticket Price Range:** $6-$15. **Visiting Club Hotel:** Quality Inn, 1734 West Washington Center Rd., Fort Wayne, IN, 46818. **Telephone:** (260-489-5554).

GREAT LAKES LOONS

Address: 825 East Main St., Midland, MI 48640.
Telephone: (989) 837-2255. **Fax:** (989) 837-8780.
E-Mail Address: info@loons.com. **Website:** www.loons.com.
Affiliation (first year): Los Angeles Dodgers (2007). **Years in League:** 2007-

OWNERSHIP/MANAGEMENT

Stadium Ownership: Michigan Baseball Foundation. **Founder, CEO:** William Stavropoulos. **President, GM:** Brad Tammen. **Vice President, CFO:** Jana Chotivkova. **Vice President, CRO:** Chris Mundhenk. **Director, ESPN 100.9-FM Sales:** Jay Arons. **Manager, Promotions:** Cameron Bloch. **Coordinator, ESPN 100.9-FM Radio Traffic:** Andrew Booms. **Assistant GM, Marketing & Communication:** Matt DeVries. **Manager, Retail Operations:** Kimberley Emerick. **Coordinator, ESPN 100.9-FM Content & Play-by-Play Broadcaster:** Blake Froling. **Director, Group Sales:** Tony Garant. **General Manager, Dow Diamond Events:** Dave Gomola. **Associate, Ticket Sales:** Glyn Hunt. **Administrative Support Assistant:** Melissa Kehoe. **Director, Partnership Activation:** Tyler Kring. **Executive Chef:** Andrea Noonan. **Director, ESPN 100.9-FM Production & Operations:** Jerry O'Donnell. **Manager, Group Ticket Sales:** Riley Paulus. **Director, Ticket Operations:** Sam PeLong. **Sr. Director, Community Impact & Engagement:** Thom Pepe. **Director, Business Applications & Analytics:** Eric Ramseyer. **Head Groundskeeper:** Kelly Rensel. **Coordinator, Group Ticket Sales:** Rickey Rissman. **Director, Creative Services:** Alex Seder. **Manager, Accounting:** Holly Snow. **Manager, Human Resources:** Stacy Sprunger. **Director, Accounting:** Jamie Start. **Assistant GM, Facility Operations:** Dan Straley. **Manager, Catering:** Ryan Teeple. **Manager, ESPN 100.9-FM Programming & Play-by-Play Broadcaster:** Brad Tunney. **Corporate Account Executive:** Joe Volk. **Vice President, Baseball Operations & Gameday Experience:** Tiffany Wardynski.

FIELD STAFF

Manager: John Shoemaker. **Hitting Coach:** TBA. **Pitching Coach:** TBA. **Bench Coach:** TBA.

GAME INFORMATION

Play-by-Play Broadcaster: Brad Tunney & Blake Froling. **No. of Games Broadcast:** 140. **Flagship Station:** WLUN, ESPN 100.9-FM (ESPN1009.com). **PA Announcer:** Jerry O'Donnell. **Official Scorers:** Steve Robb, Jason Wirtz. **Stadium Name:** Dow Diamond. **Location:** I-75 to US-10 W, Take the M-20/US-10 Business exit on the left toward downtown Midland, Merge onto US-10 W/MI-20 W (also known as Indian Street), Turn left onto State Street, the entrance to the stadium is at the intersection of Ellsworth and State Streets. **Standard Game Times:** Mon.-Sat., 6:05 pm (April), 7:05 pm (May-Sept), Sun. 2:05 pm. **Ticket Price Range:** $7-13. **Visiting Club Hotel:** Holiday Inn, 810 Cinema Drive, Midland, MI 48642. **Telephone:** (989) 794-8500.

KANE COUNTY COUGARS

Address: 34W002 Cherry Lane, Geneva, IL 60134.
Telephone: (630) 232-8811. **Fax:** (630) 232-8815.
Website: www.kccougars.com.
Affiliation (first year): Arizona Diamondbacks (2015). **Years in League:** 1991-

OWNERSHIP/MANAGEMENT

Operated By: Cougars Baseball Partnership/American Sports Enterprises, Inc. **Chairman/Chief Executive Officer/ President:** Dr. Bob Froehlich. **Owners:** Dr. Bob Froehlich, Cheryl Froehlich. **Board of Directors:** Dr. Bob Froehlich, Cheryl Froehlich, Stephanie Froehlich, Chris Neidhart, Marianne Neidhart. **Vice President/General Manager:** Curtis Haug. **Senior Director, Finance/Administration:** Douglas Czurylo. **Finance/Accounting Manager:** Lance Buhmann. **Accounting:** Sally Sullivan. **Senior Director, Ticketing:** R. Michael Patterson. **Senior Ticket Sales Representative:** Alex Miller. **Sales Representatives:** Dave Grochowski, Kelton Zimmerman, Jeff Weaver. **Director, Ticket Services/Community Relations:** Amy Mason. **Assistant Director of Ticket Operations:** Paul Quillia. **Ticket Operations Representative:** Ashley Kouba. **Director, Security:** Dan Klinkhamer. **Promotions Director:** Caela McBride. **Communications Coordinator:** Jacquie Boatman. **Design/Graphics:** Emmet Broderick. **Media Placement Coordinator:** Bill Baker. **Office Manager:** Sherri Johnson. **Video Director:** Andy Cozzi. **Director, Food/Beverage:** Jon Nekolny. **Assistant Director of Food & Beverage:** Jim Szymanski. **Senior Director, Stadium Operations:** Mike Klafehn. **Director, Maintenance:** Jeff Snyder. **Head Groundskeeper:** Sean Ehlert.

FIELD STAFF

Manager: Vince Harrison. **Hitting Coach:** K.C. Judge. **Pitching Coach:** Barry Enright . **Bench Coach:** Juan Francia. **Athletic Trainer:** Daniel Fifer. **Strength & Conditioning Coach:** Logan Jones. **Clubhouse Manager:** TBD.

GAME INFORMATION

Radio Announcer: Joe Brand. **No. of Games Broadcast:** 140. **Flagship Station:** WBIG 1280-AM. **Official Scorer:** Bill Baker. **Stadium Name:** Northwestern Medicine Field. **Location:** From east or west, I-88 Ronald Reagan Memorial Tollway) to Farnsworth Ave. North exit, north five miles to Cherry Lane, left into stadium; from northwest, I-90 (Jane Addams Memorial Tollway) to Randall Rd. South exit, south to Fabayan Parkway, east to Kirk Rd., north to Cherry Lane, left into stadium complex. **Standard Game Times:** Mon.-Sat., 6:30 pm, Sun., 1 pm. **Ticket Price Range:** $9-15. **Visiting Club Hotel:** My Place Hotel, 1000 Kilbery Lane - North Aurora, IL 60542. **Telephone:** (630) 256-8485.

LAKE COUNTY CAPTAINS

Address: 35300 Vine St., Eastlake, OH 44095-3142.
Telephone: (440) 975-8085. **Fax:** (440) 975-8958.
E-Mail Address: jyorko@captainsbaseball.com
Website: www.captainsbaseball.com
Affiliation (first year): Cleveland Indians (2003). **Years in League:** 2010-

OWNERSHIP/MANAGEMENT

Operated By: Cascia LLC. **Owners:** Peter and Rita Carfagna, Ray and Katie Murphy. **Chairman/Secretary/Treasurer:** Peter Carfagna. **Vice Chairman:** Rita Carfagna. **Vice President:** Ray **Murphy.** **General Manager:** Jen Yorko. **Assistant General Manager, Sales, Media Relations & Production:** Tim O'Brien. **Assistant General Manager, Food, Beverage & Operations:** John Klein. **Director, Ticket Sales:** Kate Roth. **Director, Turf Operations:** Charlie Erlenbach. **Director, Finance:** Nicole Owens. **Director, Game Entertainment & Partnerships:** Casey Rusnak. **Manager, Stadium Operations:** Kasey Konte. **Manager, Box Office & Special Events:** Zach Smith. **Asst. Manager, Food and Beverage:** Tim Machin. **Ticket Sales Account Executive:** Olivia Vocke. **Ticket Sales Account Executive:** Kevin **Clements.Ticket Sales Account Executive:** Patrick Schommer. **Ticket Sales Account Executive:** Brendan Whitney. **Manager of Broadcasting & Media Relations:** Andrew Luftglass. **Office Assistant:** Jim Carfagna.

FIELD STAFF

Field Manager: Greg DiCenzo. **Hitting Coach:** Mike Mergenthaler. **Pitching Coach:** Jason Blanton. **Bench Coach:** Vance Law. **Athletic Trainer:** Patrick Reynolds. **Strength & Conditioning Coach:** Paul Synenkyj.

GAME INFORMATION

Radio Announcer: Andrew Luftglass. **No. of Games Broadcast:** 140. **Flagship Station:** allsportscleveland.net. **PA Announcer:** Jasen Sokol. **Official Scorers:** Mike Mohner, Chuck Murr. **Stadium Name:** Classic Park. **Location:** From Ohio State Route 2 East, exit at Ohio 91, go left and the stadium is 1/4 mile north on your right; From Ohio State Route 90 East, exit at Ohio 91, go right and the stadium in approximately five miles north on your right. **Standard Game Times:** Mon.-Sat., 6:30 pm (April-May), Mon.-Sat., 7:00 pm (June-Sept), Sun. 1:30 pm. **Visiting Club Hotel:** Red Roof Inn 4166 State Route 306, Willoughby, Ohio 44094. **Telephone:**(440)-946-9872.

LANSING LUGNUTS

Address: 505 E. Michigan Ave., Lansing, MI 48912.
Telephone: (517) 485-4500. **Fax:** (517) 485-4518.
E-Mail Address: info@lansinglugnuts.com. **Website:** www.lansinglugnuts.com.
Affiliation (first year): Toronto Blue Jays (2005). **Years in League:** 1996-

OWNERSHIP/MANAGEMENT

Operated By: Take Me Out to the Ballgame LLC. **Principal Owners:** Tom Dickson, Sherrie Myers.
General Manager: Tyler Parsons. **Vice President of Business Development:** Steve Malliet. **Director of Human Resource and Business Operations:** Angela Sees. **Director of Finance:** Brianna Pfeil. **Director of Sales:** Ross Combs. **Group Sales Manager, Senior Manager of Sales and Ticket Services:** Eric Pionk. **Box Office Supervisor:** Keith Schwartz. **Director of Retail:** Matt Hicks. **Director of Stadium Operations:** Dennis Busse. **Senior VP of Operations Food & Beverage:** Patrick Day. **Food/Beverage Director:** Anthony Hilla. **Concessions Manager:** April Griffus. **Director of Special Events & Meetings Manager:** Malinda Barr. **Special Events Coordinator:** Erika Witte. **Production Manager:** Terry Alapert. **Marketing Manager:** Bill Getschman. **Corporate Partnerships Manager:** Ashley Loudan. **Head Grounds Manager:** Paul Kuhna.

FIELD STAFF

Manager: Luis Hurtado. **Hitting Coach:** Ryan Wright. **Pitching Coach:** Phil Cundari. **Position Player Coach:** Dave Pano. **Athletic Trainer:** Hiroki Yoshimoto. **Strength & Conditioning Coach:.** Casey Callison.

GAME INFORMATION

Radio Announcer: Jesse Goldberg-Strassler. **No. of Games Broadcast:** 140. **Flagship Station:** WQTX 92.1-FM. **PA Announcer:** Unavailable. **Official Scorer:** Timothy Zeko. **Stadium Name:** Cooley Law School Stadium. **Location:** I-96 East/West to US 496, exit at Larch Street, north of Larch, stadium on left. **Ticket Price Range:** $8-$36. **Visiting Club Hotel:** Radisson Hotel.

PEORIA CHIEFS

Address: 730 SW Jefferson, Peoria, IL 61605.
Telephone: (309) 680-4000. **Fax:** (309) 680-4080.
E-Mail Address: feedback@chiefsnet.com. **Website:** www.peoriachiefs.com.
Affiliation (first year): St. Louis Cardinals (2013). **Years in League:** 1983-

OWNERSHIP/MANAGEMENT

Operated By: Peoria Chiefs Community Baseball Club LLC.
General Manager: Jason Mott. **Manager, Box Office:** Ryan Sivori. **Director, Media/Baseball Ops/Community Engagement:** Nathan Baliva. **Director, Creative Services:** Allison Rhoades. **Director, Stadium Operations:** Patrick Walker. **Director, Corporate Partnerships:** Ben Garrod. **Manager, Merchandise & Game Presentation:** Austin Shone. **Account Executive:** Matt Champeau, Nolan Ard. **Inside Sales Representative:** Kenton Smith, Dylan Schild, Cody Schindler. **Head Groundskeeper:** Mike Reno.

FIELD STAFF

Manager: Erick Almonte. **Hitting Coach:** Cody Gabella. **Pitching Coach:** Adrian Martin
Athletic Trainer: Chris Walsh. **Strength & Conditioning Coach:** Kyle Richter.

GAME INFORMATION

Radio Announcer: Nathan Baliva. **No. of Games Broadcast:** 140. **Flagship Station:** www.peoriachiefs.com, Tune-In Radio. **4PA Announcer:** Dustin Fitzpatrick, Rodney Knuppel. **Official Scorers:** Nathan Baliva & TBA. **Stadium Name:** Dozer Park. **Location:** From South/East, I-74 to exit 93 (Jefferson St), continue one mile, stadium is one block on left; From North/West, I-74 to Glen Oak Exit, turn right on Glendale, which turns into Kumpf Blvd, turn right on Jefferson, stadium on left. **Standard Game Times:** Mon.-Sat., 6:35 p.m. Sun., 1:35 p.m. **Ticket Price Range:** $9-15. **Visiting Club Hotel:** Quality Inn & Suites, 4112 Brandywine Dr, Peoria, IL, 61614. **Telephone:** (309) 685-2556.

QUAD CITIES RIVER BANDITS

Address: 209 S. Gaines St., Davenport, IA 52802.
Telephone: (563) 324-3000. **Fax:** (563) 324-3109.
E-Mail Address: bandit@riverbandits.com. **Website:** www.riverbandits.com.
Affiliation (first year): Houston Astros (2013-). **Years in League:** 1960-

OWNERSHIP/MANAGEMENT

Operated by: Main Street Iowa LLC, Dave Heller, Roby Smith. **General Manager:** Joe Kubly. **VP, Sales:** Shawn Brown. **Assistant GM, Baseball Operations:** Paul Kleinhans-Schulz. **Assistant GM, Ballpark Operations:** Seth Reeve. **Executive Director, Special Events:** Taylor Satterly. **Director, Amusements:** TBD. **Director, Finance and HR:** Julie James. **Director, Marketing and Community Relations:** Kaylee Golden. **Manager, Promotions:** Allie Bettenhausen. **Director, Media Relations:** TBD. **Manager, Creative Services and Production:** Evan Wiseman. **Director, Merchandise:** Darren Pitra. **Manager, First Impressions:** Rae Mittan. **Director, Ticketing:** Julia McNeil. **Head Groundskeeper:** TBD. **Director, Food/Beverage:** Kyle Lindquist. **Account Executive, Group Sales:** Micheal Plummer. **Account Executive, Group Sales; Coordinator, Fulfillment:** Aaron Wilson .

FIELD STAFF

Manager: TBD **Hitting Coach:** TBD **Pitching Coach:** TBD.

GAME INFORMATION

Radio Announcer: TBD. **No. of Games Broadcast:** 140. **Flagship Station:** 1170-AM KBOB. **PA Announcer:** Unavailable. **Official Scorer:** Unavailable. **Stadium Name:** Modern Woodmen Park. **Location:** From I-74, take Grant Street exit left, west onto River Drive, left on South Gaines Street; from I-80, take Brady Street exit south, right on River Drive, left on S. Gaines Street. **Standard Game Times:** Mon.-Sat., 6:35 pm; Sun. 1:05 pm (April and Sept.), Sun. 5:05 pm (May-August). **Ticket Price Range:** $5-$20. **Visiting Club Hotel:** Radisson Quad City Plaza Hotel,111 E. 2nd St, Davenport, IA 52801. **Telephone:** (563) 322-2200.

SOUTH BEND CUBS

Office Address: 501 W. South St., South Bend, IN 46601.
Mailing Address: PO Box 4218, South Bend, IN 46634.
Telephone: (574) 235-9988. **Fax:** (574) 235-9950.
E-Mail Address: cubs@southbendcubs.com. **Website:** www.southbendcubs.com
Affiliation (first year): Chicago Cubs (2015). **Years in League:** 1988-

OWNERSHIP/MANAGEMENT

Owner: Andrew Berlin. **President:** Joe Hart. **Vice President/General Manager, Business Development:** Nick Brown. **Assistant GM, Tickets:** Andy Beuster. **Director, Ticket Operations and Customer Service:** Devon Hastings. **Senior Account Executive:** Logan Lee. **Account Executives:** Dan Harazin, Zack Bucher, Kyle Cavanaugh, Ryan Coleman. **Director, Finance/Human Resources:** TBD. **Director, Food/Beverage:** Nick Barkley. **Catering/Business Manager:** Kelly Kalsch. **Executive Chief:** Josh Farmer. **Concession Manager:** Kyle Hoffmann. **Director, Media/Promotions:** Chris Hagstrom-Jones. **Promotions Assistant & Office Manager:** Sydney Ezell. **Merchandise Manager:** Mary-Lou Pallo. **Assistant GM, Operations:** Peter Argueta. **Stadium Operations Assistant:** Josh Stephens. **Head Groundskeeper:** T.J. Wohlever. **Groundskeeper:** Jeremy Harper.

FIELD STAFF

Manager: Buddy Bailey. **Hitting Coach:** Dan Puente. **Pitching Coach:** Jamie Vermilyea. **Bench Coach:** Ricardo Medina. **Athletic Trainer:** Matt Hussey. **Strength & Conditioning Coach:** TBD..

GAME INFORMATION

Radio Announcer: Darin Pritchett. **Flagship Station:** 96.1 FM WSBT. **PA Announcer:** Gregg Sims, Jon Thompson. **Official Scorer:** Peter Yarbro. **Stadium Name:** Four Winds Field. **Location:** I-80/90 toll road to exit 77, take US 31/33 south to South Bend to downtown (Main Street), to Western Ave., right on Western, left on Taylor. **Standard Game Times:** Mon.-Sat., 7:05 pm, Sun. 2:05 pm. **Ticket Price Range:** Advance $11-13, Day of Game $12-14. **Visiting Club Hotel:** Aloft South Bend. **Hotel Telephone:** (574) 288-8000.

WEST MICHIGAN WHITECAPS

Office Address: 4500 West River Dr., Comstock Park, MI 49321.
Mailing Address: PO Box 428, Comstock Park, MI 49321.
Telephone: (616) 784-4131. **Fax:** (616) 784-4911.
E-Mail Address: playball@whitecapsbaseball.com.
Website: www.whitecapsbaseball.com.
Affiliation (first year): Detroit Tigers (1997). **Years in League:** 1994-

OWNERSHIP/MANAGEMENT

President: Steve McCarthy. **Vice President:** Jim Jarecki. **Vice President, Sales Dan Morrison Facility Events Manager:** Mike Klint. **Operations Manager:** Bret Frieze . **Director, Food/Beverage:** Matt Timon. **Community Relations Manager:** Jenny Garone. **Director, Marketing/Media:** Steve VanWagoner. **Promotions Manager:** Ben Love. **Creative and Digitial Design Manager:** Elaine Boonenberg. **Box Office Manager:** Shaun Pynnonen. **Groundskeeper:** Mitch Hooten. **Facility Maintenance Manager: Kip Jelinski Director, Ticket Sales:** Chad Sayen.

FIELD STAFF

Manager: Brayan Pena. **Hitting Coach:** John Murrian. **Pitching Coach:** Willie Blair. **Bench Coach:** TBD .**Athletic Trainer:** Cody Derby

GAME INFORMATION

Radio Announcers: Dan Hasty. **No. of Games Broadcast:** 140. **Flagship Station:** The TICKET Grand Rapids. **PA Announcers:** Mike Newell, Bob Wells. **Official Scorers:** Mike Dean, Don Thomas. **Stadium Name:** Fifth Third Ballpark. **Location:** US 131 North from Grand Rapids to exit 91 (West River Drive). **Ticket Price Range:** $9-18. **Visiting Club Hotel:** Hampton Inn 500 Center Dr NW . **Telephone:** (616) 647-1000.

WISCONSIN TIMBER RATTLERS

Office Address: 2400 N. Casaloma Dr., Appleton, WI 54913.
Mailing Address: PO Box 7464, Appleton, WI 54912.
Telephone: (920) 733-4152. **Fax:** (920) 733-8032.
E-Mail Address: info@timberrattlers.com. **Website:** www.timberrattlers.com.
Affiliation (first year): Milwaukee Brewers (2009). **Years in League:** 1962-

OWNERSHIP/MANAGEMENT

Operated By: Appleton Baseball Club, Inc.
Chairman: Tom Lehr. **President/General Manager:** Rob Zerjav. **Vice President/Assistant GM:** Aaron Hahn. **Vice President, Tickets:** Ryan Moede. **Director, Marketing/ Assistant GM:** Hilary Bauer. **Director, Food/Beverage:** Ryan Grossman. **Director, Security:** Scott Hoelzel. **Director, Community Relations:** Dayna Baitinger. **Director, Corporate Partnerships:** Ryan Cunniff. **Director of Grounds:** Kyle Slaton. **Director, Merchandise:** Jay Gruszncki. **Director, Media Relations:** Chris Mehring. **Senior Manager, Ticket Sales & Service:** Kyle Fargen. **Ticket Account Executives:** Kat Cera, Brett Kirmse. **Corporate Marketing Manager:** Seth Merrill. **Box Office Manager:** Trevor Wetzel. **Controller:** Eric Dresang. **Director of Catering & Events:** Kim Chonos. **Wedding Sales & Events Manager:** Kim McGownd. **Executive Chef:** Charles Behrmann. **Executive Sous Chef:** Chris Gosz. **Assistant, Food/Beverage Director:** Megan Andrews. **Stadium Operations Manager:** Justin Peterson. **Creative Director:** Ann Lindeman. **Entertainment Coordinator:** Jacob Jirschele. **Graphic Designer:** Nick Guenther. **Accounting/Human Resources Manager:** Brooke Brefczynski. **Production Manager:** Jerred Drake. **Clubhouse Manager:** Mason Kubly. **Office Manager:** Mary Robinson.

FIELD STAFF

Manager: Matt Erickson. **Hitting Coach:** Dave Joppie. **Pitching Coach:** Carson Cross. **Athletic Trainer:** Jeff Paxson.

GAME INFORMATION

Radio Announcer: Chris Mehring. **No. of Games Broadcast:** 140. **Flagship Station:** WNAM 1280-AM. **Television Announcer:** Chris Mehring (Radio Simulcast). **Television Affiliates:** WACY-TV. No. **of Games Broadcast:** 14. **PA Announcer:** Joey D. **Official Scorer:** Jay Grusznski. **Stadium Name:** Neuroscience Group Field at Fox Cities Stadium. **Location:** Highway 41 to Highway 15 (00) exit, west to Casaloma Drive, left to stadium. **Standard Game Times:** Mon.-Fri., 6:35 pm (April-May), 7:05 pm (June-Sept.), Sat., 6:35 pm, Sun., 1:05 pm. **Ticket Price Range:** $9-31. **Visiting Club Hotel:** TBA.

SOUTH ATLANTIC LEAGUE

Address: 2451 N. McMullen Booth Rd., Ste. 245, Clearwater, FL, 33759.
Telephone: (727) 538-4270. **Fax:** (727) 499-6853.
E-Mail Address: office@saloffice.com.
Website: www.southatlanticleague.com.
Years League Active: 1904-1964, 1979-
President/Secretary/Treasurer: Eric Krupa.
First Vice President: Chip Moore (Rome). **Second Vice President:** Craig Brown (Greenville).
Directors: Brian DeWine (Asheville), Jeff Eiseman (Augusta), Marvin Goldklang (Charleston), Jason Freier (Columbia), Tom Volpe (Delmarva), Wes Elingburg (Greensboro), Craig Brown (Greenville), Bruce Quinn (Hagerstown), Neil Leibman (Hickory), Andrew Sandler (Kannapolis), Art Matin (Lakewood), Andy Shea (Lexington), Chip Moore (Rome), Tim Wilcox (West Virginia).
Division Structure: North—Delmarva, Greensboro, Hagerstown, Hickory, Kannapolis, Lakewood, West Virginia. **South**—Asheville, Augusta, Charleston, Columbia, Greenville, Lexington, Rome.

Eric Krupa

Regular Season: 140 games (split schedule).
2020 Opening Date: April 9. **Closing Date:** September 7. **All-Star Game:** June 23 at Rome. **Playoff Format:** First-half and second-half division winners meet in best-of-three series. Winners meet in best of five series for league championship.
Roster Limit: 25 active. **Player Eligibility Rule:** No age limit. No more than two players and one player-coach on active list may have more than five years of experience.
Brand of Baseball: Rawlings. **Umpires:** Sean Cassidy (Arlington, VA), Adam Clark (Toney, AL), Nolan Earley (Kennewick, WA), Rene Gallegos (San Antonio, TX), Mitchell Leikam (Fort Belvoir, VA), Jose Lozada Bermudez (Las Piedras, PR), Thomas O'Neil (Lexington, KY), Jen Pawol (Decatur, IL), Adam Pierce (Ayden, NC), Cliburn Rondon Romero (Guatire/ Miranda, Venezuela), Caleb Stone (Graham, NC), Kyle Stutz (Leander, TX), Bryan Van Vranken (Sarasota, FL), Tyler Witte (Pearl River, NY).

STADIUM INFORMATION

| | | | Dimensions | | | | |
Club	Stadium	Opened	LF	CF	RF	Capacity	2019 Att.
Asheville	McCormick Field	1992	326	373	297	4,000	187,718
Augusta	SRP Park	2018	330	395	318	4,782	266,569
Charleston	Joseph P. Riley, Jr. Ballpark	1997	306	386	336	5,800	301,320
Columbia	Segra Park	2016	319	400	330	7,501	245,522
Delmarva	Arthur W. Perdue Stadium	1996	309	402	309	5,200	218,794
Greensboro	First National Bank Field	2005	322	400	320	7,599	306,136
Greenville	Fluor Field at the West End	2006	310	400	302	5,000	329,733
Hagerstown	Municipal Stadium	1931	335	400	330	4,600	59,682
Hickory	L.P. Frans Stadium	1993	330	401	330	5,062	137,546
Kannapolis	Intimidators Stadium	1995	330	400	310	4,700	75,931
Lakewood	FirstEnergy Park	2001	325	400	325	6,588	308.318
Lexington	Whitaker Bank Ballpark	2001	320	401	318	6,033	270,221
Rome	State Mutual Stadium	2003	335	400	330	5,100	152,874
West Virginia	Appalachian Power Park	2005	330	400	320	4,300	118,444

ASHEVILLE TOURISTS

Address: McCormick Field, 30 Buchanan Place, Asheville, NC 28801.
Telephone: (828) 258-0428. **E-Mail Address:** info@theashevilletourists.com.
Website: www.theashevilletourists.com.
Affiliation (first year): Colorado Rockies (1994). **Years in League:** 1976-

OWNERSHIP/MANAGEMENT

Operated By: DeWine Seeds Silver Dollar Baseball, LLC. **President:** Brian DeWine. **General Manager:** Larry Hawkins. **Assistant General Manager:** Sam Fischer. **Senior Sales Executive:** Chris Smith. **Director of Broadcasting/ Media Relations:** Doug Maurer. **Stadium Operations Director:** Eliot Williams. **Director of Food & Beverage:** Tyler Holt. **Director of Ticket Operations:** Hannah Martin. **Group Sales Associates:** Michael Grimes, Robert Mantey, Avery Page. **Head Groundskeeper:** Matt Dierdorff. **Outside Sales Associate:** Bob Jones. **Executive Assistant:** Samantha Cook. **Merchandise Manager:** Kali DeWine. **Publications:** Bill Ballew.

FIELD STAFF

Manager: Robinson Cancel. **Development Supervisor:** Randy Ingle. **Hitting Coach:** Zach Osborne. **Pitching Coach:** Mark Brewer. **Athletic Trainer:** Kelsey Branstetter.

GAME INFORMATION

Radio Announcer: Doug Maurer. **No. of Games Broadcast:** 140. **Flagship Station:** Asheville Tourists Online Radio Network. **PA Announcer:** Tim Lolley. **Official Scorer:** Steven Grady, Bob Rose. **Stadium Name:** McCormick Field.

Location: I-240 to Charlotte Street South exit, south one mile on Charlotte, left on McCormick Place. **Ticket Price Range:** $6.50-13.50. **Visiting Club Hotel:** Holiday Inn. **Telephone:** (818) 298-5611.

AUGUSTA GREENJACKETS

Office Address: 187 Railroad Ave. North Augusta, SC 29841.
Mailing Address: 187 Railroad Ave. North Augusta, SC 29841.
Telephone: (803) 349-9467. **Fax:** (803) 349-9434.
E-Mail Address: info@greenjacketsbaseball.com. **Website:** www.greenjacketsbaseball.com.
Affiliation (first year): San Francisco Giants (2005). **Years in League:** 1988-

OWNERSHIP/MANAGEMENT

Ownership Group: AGON Sports & Entertainment. **Owner:** Chris Schoen.
President: Jeff Eiseman. **HR & Business Operations:** Missy Martin. **Vice President:** Tom Denlinger. **General Manager:** Brandon Greene. **Director of Ticket Sales:** Matt Szczupakowski. **Accounting:** Debbie Brown. **Director of Stadium Operations:** Billy Nowak. **Director of Marketing, Promotions & Community Relations Manager:** Catie Graf. **Director of Corporate Partnerships:** Greg Dietz. **Member & Ticket Sales Manager:** Troy Pakusch. **Director of Group Sales:** Yari Natal. **Senior Group Sales Executive:** James Mullins. **Event Sales Manager:** Erin Bunts. **Ticket & Group Sales Executive:** D'Shaun Booker. **Sales & Event Services Coordinator:** Marquisha Grovner. **Ticket & Group Sales Executive:** Austin Lowndes. **Multimedia Video & Creative Services Specialist:** Alexis Ludovici. **Stadium Operations Coordinator:** Zach Balden. **Ticket Operations Manager:** Tyler Henderson. **Director of Retail & Merchandise Sales:** Chelsea Galbraith. **Director of Food & Beverage Director:** John Schow. **Food & Beverage Manager:** David Hutto. **Groundskeeper:** Darrell Lemmer.

FIELD STAFF

Manager: Carlos Valderrama. **Hitting Coach:** Jake Fox. **Pitching Coach:** Alain Quijano. **Fundamentals Coach:** Willie Romero.

GAME INFORMATION

PA Announcer: Unavailable. **Stadium Name:** SRP Park. **Standard Game Times:** Mon.-Fri., 7:05 pm, Sat., 6:05 pm, Sun., 2:05 pm through All Star Break, Sun., 5:05 pm after All Star Break. **Ticket Price Range:** $9-$28. **Visiting Club Hotel:** Comfort Suites, 2911 Riverwest Dr, Augusta, GA. **Telephone:** (706) 434-2540.

CHARLESTON RIVERDOGS

Office Address: 360 Fishburne St, Charleston, SC 29403.
Mailing Address: PO Box 20849, Charleston, SC 29403.
Telephone: (843) 723-7241. **Fax:** (843) 723-2641.
E-Mail Address: admin@riverdogs.com. **Website:** www.riverdogs.com.
Affiliation (first year): New York Yankees (2005). **Years in League:** 1973-78, 1980-

OWNERSHIP/MANAGEMENT

Operated by: The Goldklang Group/South Carolina Baseball Club LP.
Chairman: Marv Goldklang. **President:** Jeff Goldklang. **Club President/General Manager:** Dave Echols. **President Emeritus:** Mike Veeck. **Director, Fun:** Bill Murray. **Co-Owners:** Peter Freund, Gene Budig, Al Phillips. **VP, Corporate Sales:** Andy Lange. **Assistant GM:** Ben Abzug. **Director of Client Services:** Melissa Azevedo. **Director, Promotions:** Nate Kurant. **Director, Broadcasting/Media Relations:** Matt Dean. **Director, Food/Beverage:** Jesse White. **Director, Community Relations:** Walter Nolan-Cohn. **Director, Ticket Sales:** Garret Randle. **Director, Operations:** Josh Otterline. **Director, Special Events:** Lisa Dingman. **Director, Video Production:** Jeremy Schrank. **Business Manager:** Dale Stickney. **Box Office Manager:** Morgan Powell. **Marketing & Creative Services Manager:** Courtney Lewis. **Special Events Manager:** Kayli Varner. **Riley Park Club Events Manager:** Bailey Linderman. **Food/Beverage Manager:** Kristina Wilkins. **Hospitality Manager:** Sara Carpenter. **Operations Manager:** Jordan Wiley. **Sales Representative:** Daniel Armas, Claudia Davis, Mike Ryan, Serg Saradjian, Jake Terrell. **Office Manager:** Cynthia Linhart. **Head Groundskeeper:** Kevin Coyne. **Clubhouse Manager:** Matt Seletsky.

FIELD STAFF

Manager: Julio Mosquera. **Hitting Coach:** Greg Colbrunn. **Pitching Coach:** Gabe Luckert. **Defensive Coaches:** Travis Chapman, Francisco Leandro. **Athletic Trainer:** Michael Sole. **Strength & Conditioning Coach:** Danny Russo.

GAME INFORMATION

Radio Announcer: Matt Dean. **No. of Games Broadcast:** 140. **Flagship Station:** WTMA 1250-AM. **PA Announcer:** Ken Carrington. **Official Scorer:** Mike Hoffman. **Stadium Name:** Joseph P. Riley, Jr. **Location:** 360 Fishburne St, Charleston, SC 29403, From US 17, take Lockwood Dr. North, right on Fishburne St. **Standard Game Times:** Mon.-Fri., 7:05pm, Sat. 6:05 pm, Sun. 5:05 pm. **Ticket Price Range:** $8-20. **Visiting Club Hotel:** Aloft Charleston Airport.

COLUMBIA FIREFLIES

Office Address: 1640 Freed Street, Columbia, SC 29201.
Mailing Address: 1640 Freed Street, Columbia, SC 29201.
Telephone: (803) 726-4487.
E-Mail Address: info@columbiafireflies.com. **Website:** www.columbiafireflies.com.
Affiliation (first year): New York Mets (2016). **Years in League:** 2016-

OWNERSHIP/MANAGEMENT

Operated By: Columbia Fireflies Baseball, LLC.
President: John Katz. **Executive Vice President:** Brad Shank. **Senior Vice President/Food & Beverage:** Scott Burton. **Vice President of Corporate Partnerships:** Blake Buchanan. Director, **Accounting & Baseball Operations:** Jonathan Mercier. **Director, Marketing:** Ashlie DeCarlo. **Office Manager:** Katie Maroney. **Director, Ticketing:** Joe Shepard. **Director, Group Sales:** Juan Encarnacion. **Senior Corporate Account Manager:** Jeff Berger, Scott Rhodes. **Ticket Account Manager:** Nick Spano, Derrick Bradford, Ty Jamieson. **Graphics Manager:** Casey Vecchio. **Promotions Manager:** Brooke Buckley. **Digital Content Manager:** Brendan McDowell. **Community Engagement Manager:** McKenzie Brown. **Merchandise Manager:** Mallory Turnbull. **Executive Chef:** Bobby Hunter. **Food & Beverage Manager:** Michael Bolt. **Director of Stadium Operations:** Anthony Altamura. **Assistant Director of Stadium Operations:** Matt Lundquist. **Stadium Operations Manager:** Tyler Restrepo. **Head Groundskeeper:** Drew Tice. **Assistant Groundskeeper:** Joe Golding. **Corporate Partnerships Account Executive:** Jason Haller. **Director of Special Events:** Allison Abercrombie.

FIELD STAFF

Manager: Reid Brignac. **Hitting Coach:** Mariano Duncan. **Pitching Coach:** Jerome Williams. **Bench Coach:** Jay Pecci. **Athletic Trainer:** Vanessa Weisbach. **Performance Coach:** Jeff Teitz.

GAME INFORMATION

Radio Announcer: Unavailable. **No. of Games Broadcast:** 140. **Flagship Station:** Unavailable. **PA Announcer:** Bryan Vacchio. **Official Scorer:** Unavailable. **Stadium Name:** Segra Park. **Location:** 1640 Freed Street, Columbia, SC 29201. **Standard Game Times:** Mon.-Fri., 7:05pm, Sat. 6:05pm, Sun. 2:05 pm first half, 5:05pm second half. **Ticket Price Range:** $5-$10. **Visiting Club Hotel:** Hyatt Place Columbia/Harbison, 1130 Kinley Road, Irmo, SC 29063.

DELMARVA SHOREBIRDS

Office Address: 6400 Hobbs Rd, Salisbury, MD 21804.
Mailing Address: PO Box 1557, Salisbury, MD 21802.
Telephone: (410) 219-3112. **Fax:** (410) 219-9164.
E-Mail Address: info@theshorebirds.com. **Website:** www.theshorebirds.com.
Affiliation: Baltimore Orioles (1997). **Years in League:** 1996-

OWNERSHIP/MANAGEMENT

Operated By: 7th Inning Stretch, LP. **Owner:** Tom Volpe. **President:** Pat Filippone. **General Manager:** Chris Bitters. **Assistant GM:** Jimmy Sweet. **Director of Business Development:** Andrew Bryda. **Director of Marketing:** Ben Vigliarolo. **Director of Broadcasting & Communications:** Will DeBoer. **Community Relations Manager:** Chip Woytowitz. **Director of Tickets:** Brandon Harms. **Director of Ticket & Merchandise Operations:** Benjamin Posner. **Ticket Sales Account Executive:** Joe DeLucia. **Ticket Sales Account Executive:** Nikki Meredith. **Ticket Sales Account Executive:** Chris Borysewicz. **Director of Stadium Operations:** Billy Blackwell. **Head Groundskeeper:** Caroline Beauchamp. **Accounting Manager:** Matt Figard.

FIELD STAFF

Manager: Dave Anderson. **Pitching Coach:** Robbie Alvies. **Hitting Coach:** Ryan Fuller. **Fundamentals Coach:** Jeff Kunkel. **Development Coach:** Matt Packer. **Athletic Trainer:** Adam Sparks.

GAME INFORMATION

Radio Announcer: Will DeBoer. **No. of Games Broadcast:** 140. **Flagship Station:** Fox Sports 960 WTGM. **PA Announcer:** Tyler Horton. **Stadium Name:** Arthur W. Perdue Stadium. **Location:** From US 50 East, right on Hobbs Rd; From US 50 West, left on Hobbs Road. **Standard Game Time:** 7:05 pm. **Ticket Price Range:** $8-13. **Visiting Club Hotel:** Sleep Inn, 406 Punkin Court, Salisbury, MD 21804. **Telephone:** (410) 572-5516..

GREENSBORO GRASSHOPPERS

Address: 408 Bellemeade St, Greensboro, NC 27401.
Telephone: (336) 268-2255. **Fax:** (336) 273-7350.
E-Mail Address: info@gsohoppers.com. **Website:** www.gsohoppers.com.
Affiliation (first year): Pittsburgh Pirates (2019) **Years in League:** 1979-

OWNERSHIP/MANAGEMENT

Operated By: Greensboro Baseball LLC. **Principal Owners:** Wes Elingburg, Cooper Brantley, Len White. **President/General Manager:** Donald Moore. **Vice President, Baseball Operations:** Katie Dannemiller. **Assistant General Manager:** Tim Vangel. **Chief Financial Officer:** Brad Falkiewicz. **Director of Sales:** Todd Olson. **Director, Ticket Sales/Services:** Erich Dietz. **Director, Creative Services:** Amanda Williams. **Coordinator, Promotions/Community Relations:** Stephen Johnson. **Manager, Video Production:** Jak Kerley. **Director, Merchandise:** Tyler Metcalf. **Sales Associates:** Dylan James, Chase Shuford. **Director, Stadium Operations:** TBD. **Groundskeeper:** Anthony Alejo, Kyle Boesel.

FIELD STAFF

Manager: Kieran Mattison **Hitting Coach:** Johnny Tucker. **Pitching Coach:** Stan Kyles. **Coach:** Sal Panigua. **Athletic Trainer:** Matt McNamee. **Strength & Conditioning Coach:** Adam Marso.

GAME INFORMATION

Radio Announcer: Andy Durham. **No. of Games Broadcast:** 140. **Flagship Station:** WPET 950-AM. **PA Announcer:** Stuart Barefoot . **Official Scorer:** Wesley Gullet. **Stadium Name:** First National Bank Field. **Location:** From I-85, take Highway 220 South (exit 36) to Coliseum Blvd, continue on Edgeworth Street, ballpark at corner of Edgeworth and Bellemeade Streets. **Standard Game Times:** Mon.-Sat., 7 pm, Sun., 2 pm (April, May, June and July 5th), Sun., 4 pm (July 12 and 26, Aug.)**Ticket Price Range:** $7-11. **Visiting Club Hotel:** LaQuinta Inn @ **Greensboro Airport**— 7905 Triad Center Drive, Greensboro, NC 27409. **Telephone:** (336) 840.1550.

GREENVILLE DRIVE

Address: 935 South Main St, Suite 202, Greenville, SC 29601
Telephone: (864) 240-4500.
E-Mail Address: info@greenvilledrive.com. **Website:** www.greenvilledrive.com.
Affiliation (first year): Boston Red Sox (2005). **Years in League:** 2005-

OWNERSHIP/MANAGEMENT

Owner: Andrew Berlin. **President:** Joe Hart. **Vice President/General Manager, Business Development:** Nick Brown. **Assistant GM, Tickets:** Andy Beuster. **Director, Ticket Operations and Customer Service:** Devon Hastings. **Senior Account Executive:** Logan Lee. **Account Executives:** Dan Harazin, Zack Bucher, Kyle Cavanaugh, Ryan Coleman. **Director, Finance/Human Resources:** TBD. **Director, Food/Beverage:** Nick Barkley. **Catering/Business Manager:** Kelly Kalsch. **Executive Chief:** Josh Farmer. **Concession Manager:** Kyle Hoffmann. **Director, Media/Promotions:** Chris Hagstrom-Jones. **Promotions Assistant & Office Manager:** Sydney Ezell. **Merchandise Manager:** Mary-Lou Pallo. **Assistant GM, Operations:** Peter Argueta. **Stadium Operations Assistant:** Josh Stephens. **Head Groundskeeper:** T.J. Wohlever. **Groundskeeper:** Jeremy Harper.

FIELD STAFF

Manager: Buddy Bailey. **Hitting Coach:** Dan Puente. **Pitching Coach:** Jamie Vermilyea. **Bench Coach:** Ricardo Medina. **Athletic Trainer:** Matt Hussey. **Strength & Conditioning Coach:** TBD..

GAME INFORMATION

Radio Announcer: Darin Pritchett. **Flagship Station:** 96.1 FM WSBT. **PA Announcer:** Gregg Sims, Jon Thompson. **Official Scorer:** Peter Yarbro. **Stadium Name:** Four Winds Field. **Location:** I-80/90 toll road to exit 77, take US 31/33 south to South Bend to downtown (Main Street), to Western Ave., right on Western, left on Taylor. **Standard Game Times:** Mon.-Sat., 7:05 pm, Sun. 2:05 pm. **Ticket Price Range:** Advance $11-13, Day of Game $12-14. **Visiting Club Hotel:** Aloft South Bend. **Hotel Telephone:** (574) 288-8000.

HAGERSTOWN SUNS

HAGERSTOWN SUNS

Address: 274 E Memorial Blvd, Hagerstown, MD 21740.
Telephone: (301) 791-6266. **Fax:** (301) 791-6066.
E-Mail Address: info@hagerstownsuns.com. **Website:** www.hagerstownsuns.com.
Affiliation (first year): Washington Nationals (2007). **Years in League:** 1993-

OWNERSHIP/MANAGEMENT

Principal Owner/Operated by: Hagerstown Baseball LLC.
President: Tim McDulin. **General Manager:** Travis Painter. **Assistant GM/Head Groundskeeper:** Brian Saddler.
Director, Media Relations: John Kocsis Jr. **F&B Operations:** Center Plate. **Manager, Promotions/Game Day Production:** Tom Burtman. **Manager, Box Office/Ticket Operations:** Unavailable. **Sales Executive:** Ross Jones.

FIELD STAFF

Manager: Mario Lisson. **Hitting Coach:** Jorge Mejia. **Pitching Coach:** Pat Rice. **Trainer:** Darren Yoos. **Strength & Conditioning Coach:** Will Lindholm.

GAME INFORMATION

Radio Announcer: John Kocsis Jr. **No. of Games Broadcast:** Home-70. **Flagship Station:** Unavailable. **PA Announcer:** Johnny Castle. **Official Scorer:** Will Kauffman. **Stadium Name:** Municipal Stadium. **Location:** Exit 32B (US 40 West) on I-70 West, left at Eastern Boulevard; Exit 6A (US 40 East) on I-81, right at Eastern Boulevard. **Standard Game Times:** Mon.-Fri., 6:35 pm (April 6:05 pm), Sat., 6:05 pm (April 4:05 pm), Sun. 2:05 pm. **Ticket Price Range:** $10-13.

HICKORY CRAWDADS

Office Address: 2500 Clement Blvd. NW, Hickory, NC 28601.
Mailing Address: 2500 Clement Blvd. NW, Hickory, NC 28601.
Telephone: (828) 322-3000.
E-Mail Address: crawdad@hickorycrawdads.com.
Website: www.hickorycrawdads.com.
Affiliation (first year): Texas Rangers (2009). **Years in League:** 1952, 1960, 1993-

OWNERSHIP/MANAGEMENT

Operated by: Hickory Baseball Inc. **Principal Owners:** Texas Rangers.
President: Neil Leibman. **General Manager:** Douglas Locascio. **Assistant GM:** Skip Moser. **Business Manager:** Donna White. **Director of Promotions and Community Relations:** Chris Dillon. **Director of Creative Services and Media Relations:** Ashley Salinas. **Director of Sales:** Robby Willis. **Director of Group Sales:** Daniel Barkley. **Head Groundskeeper:** Cody Bryant. **Group Sales Executives:** Kristen Buynar, Samantha Baldini. **General Manager of Food and Beverage:** Ryan Spangler.

FIELD STAFF

Manager: Carlos Cardoza. **Hitting Coach:** Jason Hart. **Pitching Coach:** Jose Jaimes. **Bench Coach:** Jay Sullenger.
Athletic Trainer: Tyler Voas. **Strength and Conditioning Coach:** Andy Earp.

GAME INFORMATION

PA Announcers: Jason Savage, Rob Eastwood. **Official Scorers:** Mark Parker. **Stadium Name:** LP Frans Stadium.
Location: I-40 to exit 123 (Lenoir North), 321 North to Clement Blvd, left for 1/2 mile. **Standard Game Times: First half**—Mon.-Wed. & Sat., 6:30 pm, Thur. & Fri., 7 pm, Sun., 3 pm; **Second half**—Mon.-Sat., 7 pm, Sun., 5 pm. **Visiting Club Hotel:** Crowne Plaza, 1385 Lenior-Rhyne Boulevard SE, Hickory, NC 28602. **Telephone:** (828) 323-1000.

KANNAPOLIS CANNON BALLERS

Office Address: 216 West Ave. Kannapolis, NC 28081
Mailing Address: 216 West Ave. Kannapolis, NC 28081
Telephone: (704) 932-3267
Email Address: info@kcballers.com. **Website:** kcballers.com
Affiliation (first year): Chicago White Sox (2001). **Years in the League:** 1995-present-

OWNERSHIP/MANAGEMENT

Operated by: Temerity Baseball Club, LLC. **Operating Partner:** Scotty Brown. **Premier Partnerships:** Chris Semmens. **General Manager:** Matt Millward. **Assistant GM:** Vince Marcucci. **Account Executive:** Walker Brooke. **Broadcasting & Baseball Operations Manager:** Trevor Wilt. **Director of Retail Operations:** Tayler Gainer. **Sales & Retail Coordinator:** Emily Goddard. **Director of Tickets & Development:** Jake "The Ticket Leprechaun" Brewer. **Director of Finance & Administration:** Paige Tamaro. **Special Events Manager:** Rachel Kilinski. **Director of Stadium Operations:** Michael Wolf. **Director of Entertainment:** Blair Jewell. **Digital Media & Creative Designer:** Caitlyn Gardner. **Head Groundskeeper:** Billy Ball. **Assistant Groundskeeper:** Erik Salmon. **Director of Video Production:** Melissa Clark. **Director of Food & Beverage Operations:** Chris Beasley.

MINOR LEAGUES

FIELD STAFF
Manager: Guillermo Quiroz. **Pitching Coach:** José Bautista. **Hitting Coach:** Cole Armstrong. **Coach:** Patrick Leyland. **Trainer:** Joe Geck. **Performance Coach:** Kevin Childs.

GAME INFORMATION
Radio Announcer: Trevor Wilt. **No. of Games Broadcast:** 70. **Flagship Station:** kcballers.com / Tuneln Radio App. **PA Announcer:** Jordan Connell. **Official Scorer:** Jimmy Lewis. **Stadium Name:** TBA. **Location:** Exit 58 on I-85, turn west on to South Cannon Blvd., continue straight until left turn on Dale Earnhardt Blvd., take right on Vance, then left on West Ave. **Standard Game Times:** Mon-Sat: 7:00p.m. / Sun: 1:30p.m. **Ticket Price Range:** $9-$15. **Visiting Club Hotel:** TBA.

LAKEWOOD BLUECLAWS

Address: 2 Stadium Way, Lakewood, NJ 08701.
Telephone: (732) 901-7000. **Fax:** (732) 901-3967.
E-Mail Address: info@blueclaws.com. **Website:** www.blueclaws.com
Affiliation (first year): Philadelphia Phillies (2001). **Years in League:** 2001-

OWNERSHIP/MANAGEMENT
Managing Partner/Shore Town Baseball: Art Matin. **President/General Manager:** Joe Ricciutti. **Assistant General Manager:** Kevin Fenstermacher. **Sr. VP, Ticket Sales:** Bob McLane. **VP, Ticket Sales:** Jim McNamara. **VP, Commnity Relations:** Jim DeAngelis. **VP, Finance:** Don Rodgers. **Sr. Director, Sponsorship:** Rob Vota. **Director of Communications:** Greg Giombarrese. **Director of Production:** Kirsten Boye. **Director, Marketing & Promotions:** Jamie Stone. **Director, Food & Beverage:** Brian Genis. **Director, Partnership Services:** Zack Nicol. **Director, Merchandise:** Ben Cecil. **Director, Season Tickets:** Rob McGillick. **Corporate Sales Manager:** Anthony Arena, Mike Kasel. **Senior Sales Executive:** Craig Ebinger. **Ticket Sales Manager:** Juwan Jackson, Michael Troy. **Ticket Memberships Manager:** Joel Podos, Elias Riginos. **Group Sales Executive:** Brian O'Shaughnessy, Dave McKurth. **Ticket Operations Manager:** Garrett Herr. **Food & Beverage Manager:** Kathryn Raso. **Events & Operations Manager:** Steve Woloshin, Kevin McNellis. **Accounting Manager:** Annette Clark. **Ticket Operations Coordinator:** Tyler Odle. **Partnership Services Coordinator:** Arielle Roth. **Heads Groundskeeper:** Mike Morvay. **Front Office Manager:** JoAnne Bell.

FIELD STAFF
Manager: TBA. **Hitting Coach:** TBA. **Pitching Coach:** TBA. **Coach:** TBA. **Trainer:** TBA. **Strength & Conditioning Coach:** TBA.

GAME INFORMATION
Radio Announcers: Greg Giombarrese. **No. of Games Broadcast:** 140. **Flagship Station:** WOBM 1160-AM. **PA Announcers:** Jeff Fromm. **Official Scorers:** Joe Bellina. **Stadium Name:** FirstEnergy Park. **Location:** Route 70 to New Hampshire Avenue, North on New Hampshire for 2.5 miles to ballpark. **Standard Game Times:** 7:05 pm, 6:35 pm (April-May); Sun 1:05. **Ticket Price Range:** $7-15. **Visiting Team Hotel:** Days Hotel, Toms River...290 NJ-37, Toms River, NJ 08753...732-244-4000.

LEXINGTON LEGENDS

Address: 207 Legends Lane, Lexington, KY 40505.
Telephone: (859) 252-4487. **Fax:** (859) 252-0747.
E-Mail Address: community@lexingtonlegends.com.
Website: www.lexingtonlegends.com.
Affiliation (first year): Kansas City Royals (2013). **Years in League:** 2001-

OWNERSHIP/MANAGEMENT
Operated By: STANDS LLC. **Principal:** Susan Martinelli.
President/CEO: Andy Shea. **Executive Vice President:** Gary Durbin. **Vice President, Operations:** Shannon Kidd. **Accounting and Business Operations Manager:** Leslie Taylor. **Director of Marketing:** Anne Mapson. **Director, Corporate Sales:** Jesse Scaglion. **Director of Ticket Sales:** Mike Allison. **Premium Ticket Sales Manager:** Colin Dodd. **Ticket Operations Manager:** Ian Ueltschi. **Director, Broadcasting/Media Relations:** Emma Tiedemann. **Retail Manager:** Sidney Laughlin. **Director, Special Events:** Kara Shepherd. **Ticket Sales Account Executive:** Adam Vrzal. **Ticket Sales Account Executive:** Zach Booth. **Ticket Sales Account Executive:** Luke Lancaster. **Senior Account Executive:** Ron Borkowski. **Head Groundskeeper:** Johnny Youngblood. **Facility Specialist:** Steve Moore.

FIELD STAFF
Manager: Brooks Conrad. **Hitting Coach:** Jesus Azuaje. **Pitching Coach:** Carlos Martinez. **Bench Coach:** Glenn Hubbard. **Athletic Trainer:** Gavin Grosh.

GAME INFORMATION
Radio Announcer: Emma Tiedemann. **PA Announcer:** Unavailable. **Official Scorer:** Joseph Hardiman. **Stadium Name:** Whitaker Bank Ballpark. **Location:** From I-64/75, take exit 113, right onto North Broadway toward downtown Lexington for 1.2 miles, past New Circle Road (Highway 4), right into stadium, located adjacent to Northland Shopping Center. **Standard Game Times:** Mon., Tues., Thurs., Fri., 7:05 pm, Wed., 12:35 pm, Sat., 6:35 pm. Sun., 2:05 pm. **Ticket Price Range:** $5-$25.

ROME BRAVES

Office Address: State Mutual Stadium, 755 Braves Blvd, Rome, GA 30161.
Mailing Address: PO Box 1915, Rome, GA 30162-1915.
Telephone: (706) 378-5100. **Fax:** (706) 368-6525.
E-Mail Address: romebraves@braves.com. **Website:** www.romebraves.com.
Affiliation (first year): Atlanta Braves (2003). **Years in League:** 2003-

OWNERSHIP MANAGEMENT

Operated By: Atlanta National League Baseball Club Inc. **VP and General Manager:** David Cross. **Assistant General Manager:** Miranda Black. **Director, Stadium Operations:** Morgan McPherson. **Ticket Manager:** Jalaam Robinson. **Community Relations and Special Events:** Lori George. Manager, **Suites & Catering:** Anna Winstead. **Graphic Design Manager:** Drew Gibby. **Account Representative:** Katie Aspin. **Account Representative:** Matt Pinson. **Field Turf Manager:** Joseph Brooks. **Retail Manager:** Starla Roden. **Warehouse Operations Manager:** Tyler Stinson. **Food and Beverage Director:** Jonathan Jackson. **Culinary Director:** Owen Reppert.

FIELD STAFF

Manager: Matt Tuiasosopo. **Hitting Coach:** Mike Bard. **Pitching Coach:** Kanekoa Texeira. **Coach:** Wiggy Nevarez. **Athletic Trainer:** Koji Kanemura. **Strength Coach:** Ryan Meehan.

GAME INFORMATION

Radio Announcer: Kevin Karel. **No. of Games Broadcast:** 140. **Flagship Station:** 99.5 FM The Jock, RomeBraves.com (home games). **PA Announcer:** Anthony McIntosh, Sr. **Official Scorers:** Jim O'Hara, Lyndon Huckaby. **Stadium Name:** State Mutual Stadium. **Location:** I-75 North to exit 190 (Rome/Canton), left off exit and follow Highway 411/Highway 20 to Rome, right at intersection on Highway 411 and Highway 1 (Veterans Memorial Highway), stadium is at intersection of Veterans Memorial Highway and Riverside Parkway. **Ticket Price Range:** $5-12. (purchased in advance). **Visiting Club Hotel:** Days Inn, 840 Turner McCall Blvd, Rome, GA 30161. **Telephone:** (706) 295-0400.

WEST VIRGINIA POWER

Address: 601 Morris St, Suite 201, Charleston, WV 25301.
Telephone: (304) 344-2287. **Fax:** (304) 344-0083.
E-Mail Address: info@wvpower.com. **Website:** www.wvpower.com.
Affiliation (first year): Seattle Mariners (2019). **Years in League:** 1987-

OWNERSHIP MANAGEMENT

Operated By: West Virginia Baseball, LLC.
Managing Partner: Tim Wilcox. **General Manager:** Jeremy Taylor. **Assistant General Manager/Director of Food & Beverage:** Aaron Simmons. **Accountant:** Darren Holstein. **Broadcast & Media Relations Manager:** David Kahn. **Head Groundskeeper:** TBD. **Box Office Manager:** Zach Kurdin. **Director of Sales:** George Levandoski. **Stadium Operations Manager:** Jesus Paez. **Food & Beverage Assistant:** Nathan Richard. **Game Entertainment/Production Manager:** TBD. **Community Outreach Manager:** Lindsey Webb.

FIELD STAFF

Manager: Eric Farris. **Hitting Coach:** Rob Benjamin. **Pitching Coach:** Nathan Bannister.

GAME INFORMATION

Radio Announcer: David Kahn. **No. of Games Broadcast:** 140. **Flagship Stations:** The Jock-WJYP-1300 AM & WMON-1340 AM. **PA Announcer:** Unavailable. **Official Scorer:** Unavailable. **Stadium Name:** Appalachian Power Park. **Location:** I-77 South to Capitol Street exit, left on Lee Street, left on Brooks Street. **Standard Game Times:** Mon.-Sat., 7:05 pm, Sun., 2:05 pm. **Ticket Price Range:** $8-11. **Visiting Club Hotel:** Holiday Inn Civic Center, 100 Civic Center Drive, Charleston, WV 25301. **Telephone:** (304) 345-0600.

NEW YORK-PENN LEAGUE

Address: 204 37th Ave. N., #366, St. Petersburg, Florida 33704.
Telephone: NA. **Fax:** NA.
Website: www.newyork-pennleague.com.
Years League Active: 1939-
President: Ben J. Hayes, J.D.
President Emeritus: Robert Julian. **Treasurer:** Jon Dandes (West Virginia). **Corporate Secretary:** Doug Estes (Williamsport).
League Administrator: Laurie Hayes. **League Media Associate:** Tricia Burrows.
Directors: Matt Slatus (Aberdeen), Jeff Dygert (Auburn), None (Batavia), Steve Cohen (Brooklyn), E. Miles Prentice (Connecticut), Marvin Goldklang (Hudson Valley), Dave Heller (Lowell), Michael Savit (Mahoning Valley), Chuck Greenberg (State College), Glenn Reicin (Staten Island), Bill Gladstone (Tri-City), Kyle Bostwick (Vermont), Jon Dandes (West Virginia), Peter Freund (Williamsport).

Ben Hayes

Division Structure: McNamara—Aberdeen, Brooklyn, Hudson Valley, Staten Island. **Pinckney**—Auburn, Batavia, Mahoning Valley, State College, West Virginia, Williamsport. **Stedler**—Lowell, Connecticut, Tri-City, Vermont. **Regular Season:** 76 games. **2019 Opening Date:** June 18. **Closing Date:** Sept 7.
All-Star Game: Aug. 18, Lowell.
Playoff Format: Division winners and wild-card team meet in best of three series. Winners meet in best of three series for league championship. **Roster Limit:** 35 active and eligible to play in any given game. **Player Eligibility Rule:** No more than four players 23 or older; no more than three players on active list may have four or more years of prior service. **Brand of Baseball:** Rawlings. **Umpires:** Unavailable.

STADIUM INFORMATION

Club	Stadium	Opened	Dimensions			Capacity	2019 Att.
			LF	CF	RF		
Aberdeen	Ripken Stadium	2002	310	400	310	6,000	118,357
Auburn	Falcon Park	1995	330	400	330	2,800	39,381
Batavia	Dwyer Stadium	1996	325	400	325	2,600	43,118
Brooklyn	KeySpan Park	2001	315	412	325	7,500	174,522
Connecticut	Dodd Stadium	1995	309	401	309	6,270	66,532
Hudson Valley	Dutchess Stadium	1994	325	400	325	4,494	148,158
Lowell	Edward LeLacheur Park	1998	337	400	301	4,842	100,687
Mahoning Valley	Eastwood Field	1999	335	405	335	6,000	98,833
State College	Medlar Field at Lubrano Park	2006	325	399	320	5,412	119,120
Staten Island	Richmond County Bank Ballpark	2001	325	400	325	6,500	66,520
Tri-City	Joseph L. Bruno Stadium	2002	325	400	325	5,000	131,529
Vermont	Centennial Field	1922	323	405	330	4,000	83,122
West Virginia	WVU Baseball Park	2015	325	400	325	3,500	62,846
Williamsport	Bowman Field	1923	345	405	350	4,200	64,148

ABERDEEN IRONBIRDS

Address: 873 Long Drive, Aberdeen, MD 21001
Telephone: (410) 297-9292. **Fax:** (210) 297-6653
E-Mail Address: Info@ironbirdsbaseball.com. **Website:** ironbirdsbaseball.com
Affiliation (first year): Baltimore Orioles (2002). **Years in league:** 2002-

OWNERSHIP/MANAGEMENT
Operated By: Ripken Professional Baseball LLC. **Principal Owner:** Cal Ripken Jr. **Co-Owner/Executive Vice President:** Bill Ripken. **General Manager:** Jack Graham. **Director, Ticketing:** Adam Barbato. **Director, Creative Services:** Kevin Jimenez. **Manager, Event Operations:** Jessie Rushing. **Director, Corporate Partnerships:** Ryan Christy. **Manager, Corporate Partnerships:** George Cluster. **Director, Finance & Administration:** Wayne Leonard. **Manager, Community Relations and Retail:** Amelia Adams. **Sports Turf Superintendent:** Todd Bradley. **Manager, Facilities:** Larry Gluch. **Facilities Assistant:** David Dawson. **Sr. Box Office Coordinator:** Nat Giblin. **Sr. Marketing Manager:** Tyler Weigandt. **Manager, Membership Services & Retention:** Justin Gentilcore. **Coordinator, Memberships Services & Retention:** Micki Quartucci. **Account Executive:** Brian O'Shaughnessy.

FIELD STAFF
Manager: Kevin Bradshaw. **Hitting Coach:** Anthony Villa. **Pitching Coach:** Joe Haumacher. **Fundamentals Coach:** Branden Becker. **Development Coach:** Joseph Botelho. **Athletic Trainer:** Gary Smith. **Strength & Conditioning:** TBA

GAME INFORMATION
Radio Announcer: Michael Lehr. **No. of Games Broadcast:** 76. **Flagship Station:** WAMD 970 AM. **PA Announcer:**

Ray Atkinson. **Official Scorer:** Joe Stetka. **Stadium Name:** Leidos Field at Ripken Stadium. **Location:** I-95 to exit 85 (route 22), west on 22, right onto long drive. **Ticket Price Range:** $5-$39. **Visiting Club Hotel:** Comfort Inn-Aberdeen.

AUBURN DOUBLEDAYS

Address: 130 N Division St, Auburn, NY 13021. **Telephone:** (315) 255-2489.
E-Mail Address: info@auburndoubledays.com. **Website:** www.auburndoubledays.com.
Affiliation (first year): Washington Nationals (2011). **Years in League:** 1958-80, 1982-

OWNERSHIP/MANAGEMENT
Owned by: City of Auburn. **Operated by:** Auburn Community Baseball, LLC. **President:** Jeff Dygert.
General Manager: Robert Scarbrough. **Assistant General Managers:** David Lindberg.

FIELD STAFF
Manager: Patrick Anderson. **Hitting Coach:** Mark Harris. **Pitching Coach:** Franklin Bravo.

GAME INFORMATION
Radio Announcer: Frankie Vernouski , Cooper Boardman. **No. of Games Broadcast:** 44. **Flagship Station:** Fingerlakes1.com. **PA Announcer:** Dan Wallace. **Official Scorer:** Terry Clifford. **Stadium Name:** Leo Pinckney Field at Falcon Park. **Location:** I-90 to exit 40, right on Route 34 South for 8 miles to York Street, right on York, left on North Division Street. **Standard Game Times:** Unavailable. **Ticket Price Range:** $6-11. **Visiting Club Hotel:** Unavailable.

BATAVIA MUCKDOGS

Address: Dwyer Stadium, 299 Bank St, Batavia, NY 14020.
Telephone: 585-483-3647. **E-Mail Address:** bkelly@muckdogs.com.
Website: www.muckdogs.com.
Affiliation (first year): Miami Marlins (2013). **Years in League:** 1939-53, 1957-59, 1961-

OWNERSHIP/MANAGEMENT
Operated By: Batavia Muckdogs, Inc. **General Manager:** Brendan Kelly. **Sales and Marketing Coordinator:** Kerri Schmidt. **Director of Grounds:** Cooper Thomson.

FIELD STAFF
Manager: Jorge Hernandez. **Hitting Coach:** Nathan Mikolas. **Pitching Coach:** Gabe Luckert. **Athletic Trainer:** TBA. **Strength & Conditioning Coach:** TBA.

GAME INFORMATION
Radio Announcer: Unavailable. **No. of Games Broadcast:** Home-38. **Flagship Station:** WBTA 1490- AM/100.1 FM. **PA Announcer:** Paul Spiotta. **Official Scorer:** Paul Spiotta. **Stadium Name:** Dwyer Stadium. **Location:** I-90 to exit 48, left on Route 98 South, left on Richmond Avenue, left on Bank Street. **Standard Game Times:** Mon.-Sat., 7:05 pm, Sun., 5:05 pm. **Ticket Price Range:** $7-9 (in advance), $8-$10 (day of). **Visiting Club Hotel:** Red Roof Inn.

BROOKLYN CYCLONES

Address: 1904 Surf Ave, Brooklyn, NY 11224.
Telephone: (718) 372-5596. **Fax:** (718) 449-6368.
E-Mail Address: info@brooklyncyclones.com. **Website:** www.brooklyncyclones.com.
Affiliation (first year): New York Mets (2001) **Years in League:** 2001-

OWNERSHIP/MANAGEMENT
Chairman, CEO: Fred Wilpon. **President:** Saul Katz. **COO:** Jeff Wilpon. **Vice President:** Steve Cohen. **General Manager:** Kevin Mahoney. **Assistant GM:** Gary Perone. **Director, Communications:** Billy Harner. **Operations Manager:** Vladimir Lipsman. **Box Office Manager:** Nick Monteleone. **Marketing Manager:** Alyssa Morel. **Director, Community Relations:** Christina Moore. **Community Outreach/Promotions:** King Henry. **Account Executives:** Tommy Cardona, Mordechai Twersky, Bryan Wynne, Keith Raad, Jeremy Allen, Anthony Genna, Ricky Viola. **Staff Accountant:** Tatiana Isdith. **Administrative Assistant, Community Relations:** Sharon Lundy.

FIELD STAFF
Manager: Ed Blankmeyer. **Hitting Coach:** Rafael Fernandez. **Pitching Coach:** Josh Towers. **Bench Coach:** Benny DiStefano. **Athletic Trainer:** Anthony Olivieri. **Performance Coach:** Wyatt Briggs

GAME INFORMATION
Radio Announcer: Keith Raad. **No. of Games Broadcast:** 76. **Flagship Station:** Web Streaming Only. **PA Announcer:** Mark Frotto. **Official Scorer:** Howard Kaplan, Patrick McCormack. **Stadium Name:** MCU Park. **Location:** Belt Parkway to Cropsey Ave South, continue on Cropsey until it becomes West 17th St, continue to Surf Ave, stadium on south side of Surf Ave; By subway, west/south to Stillwell Ave./Coney Island station. **Ticket Price Range:** $10-17. **Visiting Club Hotel:** Unavailable.

NORWICH SEA UNICORNS

Address: 14 Stott Avenue, Norwich, CT 06360.
Telephone: (860) 887-7962. **Fax:** (860) 886-5996.
E-Mail Address: info@goseaunicorns.com. **Website:** www.goseaunicorns.com.
Affiliation (first year): Detroit Tigers (1999). **Years in League:** 2010-

OWNERSHIP/MANAGEMENT
Operated By: Oneonta Athletic Corp. **President:** Miles Prentice. **Senior Vice President:** CJ Knudsen. **General Manager:** Dave Schermerhorn. **Director, Concessions/Merchandise:** Heather Bartlett. **Box Office Manager:** Marissa Dagliere. **Business Development Manager:** Lee Walter, Jr. **Head Groundskeeper:** Ryan Lefler.

FIELD STAFF
Manager: Gary Cathcart. **Hitting Coach:** Chase Rowe. **Pitching Coach:** Carlos Bohorquez. **Athletic Trainer:** Erick Flores. **Strength & Conditioning Coach:** Francisco Rivas.

GAME INFORMATION
PA Announcer: Ed Weyant. **Official Scorer:** Chris Cote. **Stadium Name:** Dodd Stadium. **Location:** Exit 14 (old exit 82) off I-395. **Standard Game Times:** Mon.-Fri., 7:05 pm, Sat., 6:05 pm, Sun., 4:05 pm. **Ticket Price Range:** $10-20.
Visiting Club Hotel: Holiday Inn Norwich.

HUDSON VALLEY RENEGADES

Office Address: Dutchess Stadium, 1500 Route 9D, Wappingers Falls, NY 12590.
Mailing Address: PO Box 661, Fishkill, NY 12524.
Telephone: (845) 838-0094. **Fax:** (845) 838-0014.
E-Mail Address: info@hvrenegades.com. **Website:** www.hvrenegades.com.
Affiliation (first year): Tampa Bay Rays (1996). **Years in League:** 1994-

OWNERSHIP/MANAGEMENT
Operated by: Keystone Professional Baseball Club Inc. **Principal Owner:** Marv Goldklang.
President/General Manager: Steve Gliner. **Vice President:** Rick Zolzer. **Vice President of Community Partnerships:** Kristen Huss. **Director, Baseball Operations:** Joe Ausanio. **Director, Business Operations:** Vicky DeFreese. **Director, Food & Beverage/Merchandise:** Teri Bettencourt. **Manager, Marketing:** Morgan Rumpf. **Manager, New Business Development:** Dave Neff. **Head Groundskeeper:** Tom Hubmaster. **Manager, Box Office and Account Executive:** Kyler DeMale. **Senior Account Executive:** Bill Levy. **Manager, Community Engagement and Account Exectuvie:** Luis Flores. **Promotions Manager:** Patsy Marotto.

FIELD STAFF
Manager: Rafael Valenzuela. **Pitching Coach:** R.C. Lichenstein. **Coach:** Joe Szekely. **Coach:** German Melendez. **Athletic Trainer:** Tsutomu Kamiya. **Strength & Conditioning Coach:** Dan Rousseau. **Clubhouse Manager:** John Horaz.

GAME INFORMATION
Radio Announcer: Rob Adams **No. of Games Broadcast: Home**—38 at hvrenegades.com. **PA Announcer:** Rick Zolzer. **Official Scorer:** Mike Ferraro. **Stadium Name:** Dutchess Stadium. **Location:** I-84 to exit 11 (Route 9D North), north one mile to stadium. **Standard Game Times:** Mon.-Fri., 7:05 pm, Sat, 6:05 pm, Sun., 4:35 pm. **Visiting Club Hotel:** Courtyard By Marriott Fishkill, 17 Westage Drive, Fishkill, NY, 12524. **Telephone:** (845) 897-2400.

LOWELL SPINNERS

Address: 450 Aiken St, Lowell, MA 01854.
Telephone: (978) 459-2255. **Fax:** (978) 459-1674.
E-Mail Address: info@lowellspinners.com. **Website:** www.lowellspinners.com.
Affiliation (first year): Boston Red Sox (1996). **Years in League:** 1996-

OWNERSHIP/MANAGEMENT
Operated by: Main Street Baseball. **Owner:** Dave Heller.
President/General Manager: Shawn Smith. **Vice President:** Brian Lindsay. **VP, Finance:** Priscilla Harbour. **Group Sales Manager:** Riley Robar. **Creative Services Representative:** Erin Reynolds. **Grounds Manager:** Kyle Wood. **Director of Grounds Management:** Jack Schmidgall. **Director of Merchandise:** Shawn Bergeron. **Manager of Marketing Partnerships:** Frank Pimentel. **Manager of Operations:** Kristin Kinchla.

FIELD STAFF
Manager: Luke Montz. **Hitting Coach:** Nate Spears. **Pitching Coach:** Nick Green. **Athletic Trainer:** Taylor Boucher.

GAME INFORMATION
Radio Announcer: John Leahy. **No. of Games Broadcast:** 76. **Flagship Station:** WCAP 980-AM. **PA Announcer:** Kyle

Wescott. **Official Scorer:** David Rourke. **Stadium Name:** Edward A LeLacheur Park. **Location:** From Route 495 and 3, take exit 35C (Lowell Connector), follow connector to exit 5B (Thorndike Street) onto Dutton Street, left onto Father Morrissette Boulevard, right on Aiken Street. **Standard Game Times:** 7:05 pm. **Ticket Price Range:** $7-10 (advance); $9-12 (day of game). **Visiting Club Hotel:** Radisson of Chelmsford, 10 Independence Dr, Chelmsford, MA 01879. **Telephone:** (978) 356-080.

MAHONING VALLEY
SCRAPPERS

Address: 111 Eastwood Mall Blvd, Niles, OH 44446.
Telephone: (330) 505-0000. **Fax:** (303) 505-9696.
E-Mail Address: info@mvscrappers.com. **Website:** www.mvscrappers.com.
Affiliation (first year): Cleveland Indians (1999). **Years in League:** 1999-

OWNERSHIP/MANAGEMENT
Operated By: HWS Baseball Group. **Managing General Partner:** Michael Savit. **Vice President, HWS Baseball/ General Manager:** Jordan Taylor. **Assistant GM, Marketing:** Heather Sahli. **Assistant GM, Sales:** Matt Thompson. **Director of Tickets & Game Operations:** Kate Walsh. **Director of Ticket Sales:** Kaylin Rose. **Manager, Group Sales:** Clayton Sibilla. **Manager, Box Office:** George Kirby. **Assistant GM, Operations:** Brad Hooser. **Head Groundskeeper:** Kyle Nagy. **Manager, Accounting & Human Resources:** Roxanne Polichetti. **Manager, Production:** Drew Masirovits.

FIELD STAFF
Manager: Luke Carlin. **Hitting Coach:** Craig Massoni. **Pitching Coach:** Kevin Erminio. **Bench Coach:** J.T. Maquire. **Athletic Trainer:** Franklin Sammons. **Strength & Conditioning Coach:** Juan Acevedo.

GAME INFORMATION
Radio Announcer: Tim Pozsgai. **No. of Games Broadcast:** 76. **Flagship Station:** TBD. **PA Announcer:** Robb Schmidt. **Official Scorer:** Craig Antush. **Stadium Name:** Eastwood Field. **Location:** I-80 to 11 North to 82 West to 46 South; stadium located behind Eastwood Mall. **Ticket Price Range:** $8-12. **Visiting Club Hotel:** Fairfield by Marriott, 1860 Niles Cortland Road SE, Warren, OH 44484. **Telephone:** 330-544-5774.

STATE COLLEGE SPIKES

Address: 112 Medlar Field at Lubrano Park, University Park, PA 16802.
Telephone: (814) 272-1711. **Fax:** (814) 272-1718.
Website: www.statecollegespikes.com.
Affiliation (first year): St. Louis Cardinals (2013). **Years in League:** 2006-

OWNERSHIP/MANAGEMENT
Operated By: Spikes Baseball LP. **Chairman/Managing Partner:** Chuck Greenberg.
General Manager: Scott Walker. **Assistant GM, Operations:** Dan Petrazzolo. **Director of Ticket Sales:** David Woodard. **Business Development Manager:** Taylor Young. **Ticket Account Executive:** Bo Dinger. **Ticket Sales Associates:** Matt Deutch, Kenny McKernan, Christa Wagner. **Accounting & Box Office Specialist:** Robert DeLusa. **Senior Sports Turf Manager:** Matt Neri. **Director of Food & Beverage:** Gary Straight. **Director of In-Game Entertainment:** John Foreman. **Director of Communications:** Joe Putnam. **Director of Merchandise:** Julie Henry.

FIELD STAFF
Manager: Jose Leon. **Hitting Coach:** Jason Broussard. **Pitching Coach:** Dean Kiekhefer. **Athletic Trainer:** Joey Olsiewicz. **Strength & Conditioning Coach:** Don Trapp.

GAME INFORMATION
PA Announcer: Jeff Brown. **Official Scorers:** Dave Baker, John Dixon. **Stadium Name:** Medlar Field at Lubrano Park. **Location:** From west, US 322 to Mount Nittany Expressway, I-80 to exit 158 (old exit 23/Milesburg), follow Route 150 South to Route 26 South; From east, I-80 to exit 161 (old exit 24/Bellefonte) to Route 26 South or US 220/I-99 South. **Standard Game Times:** Mon.-Sat., 7:05 pm, Sun., 6:05 pm. **Ticket Price Range:** $8-18. **Visiting Club Hotel:** Ramada Conference & Golf Hotel, 1450 Atherton St, State College, PA 16801. **Telephone:** (814) 238-3001.

STATEN ISLAND YANKEES

Stadium Address: 75 Richmond Terrace, Staten Island, NY 10301.
Telephone: (718) 720-9265. **Fax:** (718) 273-5763. **Website:** www.siyanks.com.
Affiliation (first year): New York Yankees (1999). **Years in League:** 1999-Present.

OWNERSHIP/MANAGEMENT
Principal Owners: Nostalgic Partners. **President/Operating Partner:** Will Smith. **General Manager:** T.J. Jahn. **Vice President of Baseball Operations:** Jane Rogers. **COO:** Jason Nazzaro. **Director of Corporate Partnerships:** Mary

Almonte. **Director of Concessions:** Duane Hand. **Ticket Operations Manager:** Jesse Lopresti. **Ticket Sales & Service Manager:** Megan Bloyd. **Community Relations & Group Tickets Manager:** David Budash. **Group Sales Executives:** Jackie D'Elia, Michael Santeramo. **Production & Marketing Manager:** Michael Galayda. **Head Groundskeeper:** Brett Franklin. **Stadium Operations Director:** Anthony Polito.

FIELD STAFF
Manager: Dan Fiorito. **Hitting Coach:** Ryan Chipka. **Pitching Coach:** Dustin Glant.

GAME INFORMATION
Radio Announcer: Unavailable. **No. of Games Broadcast:** Unavailable. **Flagship Station:** Unavailable. **PA Announcer:** Unavailable. **Official Scorer:** Unavailable. **Stadium Name:** Richmond County Bank Ballpark at St. George. **Location:** 75 Richmond Terrace, Staten Island, NY 10301 (located next to Staten Island Ferry and Staten Island Railway-St. George). **Standard Game Times:** Mon-Sat., 7 p.m., Sun., 1 p.m. **Visiting Club Hotel:** Unavailable.

TRI-CITY VALLEYCATS

Office Address: Joseph L Bruno Stadium, 80 Vandenburg Ave, Troy, NY 12180.
Mailing Address: PO Box 694, Troy, NY 12181.
Telephone: (518) 629-2287. **Fax:** (518) 629-2299.
E-Mail Address: info@tcvalleycats.com. **Website:** www.tcvalleycats.com.
Affiliation (first year): Houston Astros (2002). **Years in League:** 1999-

OWNERSHIP/MANAGEMENT
Operated By: Tri-City ValleyCats Inc. **Principal Owners:** Martin Barr, John Burton, William Gladstone, Rick Murphy, Alfred Roberts, Stephen Siegel. **President:** William Gladstone. **Executive Vice President/Chief Operating Officer:** Rick Murphy. **General Manager:** Matt Callahan. **Assistant GM:** Michelle Skinner. **Media Relations Manager:** Chris Chenes. **Ticket Office and Operations Manager:** Jessica Guido. **Food & Beverage Manager:** Missy Henry. **Community & Promotions Coordinator:** Elyse Zima. **Account Executive:** Matt Sammarco. **Sales & Operations Associate:** Jordan Mitchell. **Cilent Services Associate:** Lizzy Tripoli.

FIELD STAFF
Manager: Wladimir Sutil. **Hitting Coach:** Ernesto Irizarry. **Pitching Coach:** John Kovalik.

GAME INFORMATION
Radio Announcer: Unavailable. **No. of Games Broadcast:** 38. **Flagship Station:** MiLB.com. **PA Announcer:** Anthony Pettograsso. **Official Scorer:** Jim Pertierra. **Stadium Name:** Joseph Bruno Stadium. **Location:** From north, I-87 to exit 7 (Route 7), go east 1 1⁄2 miles to I-787 South, to Route 378 East, go over bridge to Route 4, right to Route 4 South, one mile to Hudson Valley Community College campus on left; From south, I-87 to exit 23 (I-787), I-787 north six miles to exit for Route 378 east, over bridge to Route 4, right to Route 4 South, one mile to campus on left; From east, Massachusetts Turnpike to exit B-1 (I-90), nine miles to Exit 8 (Defreestville), left off ramp to Route 4 North, five miles to campus on right; From west, I-90 to exit 24 (I-90 East), I-90 East for six miles to I-787 North (Troy), 2.2 miles to exit for Route 378 East, over bridge to Route 4, right to Route 4 south for one mile to campus on left. **Standard Game Times:** 7pm, Sun. 5 pm. **Ticket Price Range:** $5.50-$12.50. **Visiting Club Hotel:** The Desmond Hotel Albany, 660 Albany-Shaker Road, Albany, NY 12211. **Telephone:** (518) 869-8100.

VERMONT LAKE MONSTERS

Address: 1 King Street Ferry Dock, Burlington, VT 05401.
Telephone: (802) 655-4200. **Fax:** (802) 655-5660.
E-Mail Address: info@vermontlakemonsters.com.
Website: www.vermontlakemonsters.com.
Affiliation (first year): Oakland Athletics (2011). **Years in League:** 1994-

OWNERSHIP/MANAGEMENT
Operated by: Vermont Expos Inc.
Principal Owner/President: Ray Pecor Jr. **Vice President:** Kyle Bostwick. **General Manager:** Joe Doud. **Assistant General Manager:** Adam Matth. **Executive Director of Business Development:** Nate Cloutier. **Marketing and In-Game Promotions Manager:** Jeff Kent. **Box Office and Team Operations Manager:** Hannah Carlin. **Director of Hospitality:** Naomi Desranleau. **Staff Accountant:** Heather Regnaud. **Director, Media Relations:** Paul Stanfield. **Clubhouse Operations:** Jack Zagursky, Alex Lefebvre. **Head Groundskeeper:** John Thibeault.

FIELD STAFF
Manager: Rick Magnante. **Hitting Coach:** Francisco Santana. **Pitching Coach:** Carlos Chavez. **Bench Coach:** Anthony Phillips.

GAME INFORMATION
Radio Announcers: George Commo. **No. of Games Broadcast:** Home-38 (Internet Only). **PA Announcer:** Rich Haskell, Jamey McGowan. **Official Scorer:** Bruce Bosley. **Stadium Name:** Centennial Field. **Location:** I-89 to exit 14W, right on East Avenue for one mile, right at Colchester Avenue. **Standard Game Times:** Mon.-Fri., 7:05 pm, Sat., 6:05 pm, Sun., 5:05 pm. **Ticket Price Range:** $5-15. **Visiting Club Hotel:** Doubletree By Hilton (formerly Sheraton). **Telephone:** (802) 865-6600.

WEST VIRGINIA BLACK BEARS

Office Address: 2040 Jedd Gyorko Drive, Granville, WV 26534
Mailing Address: PO Box 4680 Morgantown, WV 26504.
Telephone: (304) 293-7910. **Website:** www.westvirginiablackbears.com
Affiliation (first year): Pittsburgh Pirates (2015). **Years in League:** 2015-

OWNERSHIP/MANAGEMENT

Operated By: Rich Baseball Operations. **President:** Robert Rich Jr. **Chief Operating Officer:** Jonathan Dandes.
General Manager: Matthew Drayer. **Assistant GM:** Jackie Riggleman. **Sponsorship & Promotions Manager:** Travis O'Neal. **Stadium Manager:** Craig McIntosh. **Groundskeeper:** Logan Elliott.

FIELD STAFF

Manager: TBA. **Hitting Coach:** TBA. **Pitching Coach:** TBA.

GAME INFORMATION

PA Announcer: Bill Nevlin. **Official Scorer:** Unavailable. **Stadium Name:** Monongalia County Ballpark. **Standard Game Times:** Mon.-Fri., 6:35 pm, Sat., 7:05 pm, Sun., TBA. **Visiting Club Hotel:** Fairfield Inn & Suites by Marroitt.

WILLIAMSPORT CROSSCUTTERS

Office Address: BB&T Ballpark at Historic Bowman Field, 1700 W Fourth St, Williamsport, PA 17701. **Mailing Address:** PO Box 3173, Williamsport, PA 17701.
Telephone: (570) 326-3389. **Fax:** (570) 326-3494.
E-Mail Address: mail@crosscutters.com. **Website:** www.crosscutters.com.
Affiliation (first year): Philadelphia Phillies (2007). **Years in League:** 1968-72, 1994-

OWNERSHIP/MANAGEMENT

Operated By: Cutting Edge Baseball, LLC. **Principal Owner:** Peter Freund.
Vice President/General Manager: Doug Estes. **Vice President, Marketing/Public Relations:** Gabe Sinicropi.
Director, Food/Beverage: Bill Gehron. **Director, Ticket Operations/Community Relations:** Sarah Budd. **Director, Client Services: Nate Schneider, Production Director:** Justin Hawkins, **Director of Smiles:** Rhashan West-Bey. **Head Groundskeeper:** Cam Richardson.

FIELD STAFF

Manager: Milver Reyes. **Hitting Coach:** TBA. **Pitching Coach:** Hector Berrios. **Coach:** TBA.

GAME INFORMATION

Radio Announcers: TBA. **No. of Games Broadcast:** 76. **Flagship Station:** WLYC 1050-AM & 104.1 FM (FoxSports Williamsport). **Stadium Name:** BB&T Ballpark at Historic Bowman Field. **Location:** 1700 W. Fourth St., Williamsport, Pa. **From the North:** Follow Route 15 South. Take the Fourth Street exit. Turn left onto Fourth Street. Ballpark will be on your left. **From the South:** Follow Route 15 North. Cross the Susquehanna River via the Market Street Bridge and follow into Downtown Williamsport. At the second traffic light, turn left onto Fourth Street. Follow approx. 3 miles. Ballpark will be on your right. Ballpark will be your right. **Ticket Price Range:** $8-$15. **Visiting Club Hotel:** Best Western, 1840 E Third St, Williamsport, Pa., 17701. **Telephone:** (570) 326-1981.

NORTHWEST LEAGUE

Address: PO Box 18847, Panama City Beach, FL 32417
Telephone: (805) 588-6205
E-Mail Address: njohnsonnwl@gmail.com
Website: www.northwestleague.com.
Years League Active: 1954-
President/Treasurer: North Johnson
Vice President: Jeff Eiseman (Boise) **Corporate Secretary:** Jerry Walker (Salem-Keizer).
Directors: Dave Elmore (Eugene), Bobby Brett (Spokane), Charlton Volpe (Everett), Jake Kerr (Vancouver), Mike McMurray (Hillsboro), Brent Miles (Tri-City), Jerry Walker (Salem-Keizer), Jeff Eiseman (Boise).
Division Structure: South—Boise, Hillsboro, Eugene, Salem-Keizer. **North**—Everett, Spokane, Tri-City, Vancouver. **Regular Season:** 76 games (split schedule).

North Johnson

2020 Opening Date: June 17. **Closing Date:** Sept. 7. **All-Star Game:** Aug. 4 at Rocky Mountain (Northwest League vs. Pioneer Baseball League). **Playoff Format:** First-half division winners meet second-half division winners in best-of-three series. Winners meet in best-of-five series for league championship. **Roster Limit:** 35 active, 35 under control. **Player Eligibility Rule:** No more than three players on active list may have four or more years of prior service. **Brand of Baseball:** Rawlings. **Umpires:** Unavailable.

STADIUM INFORMATION

Club	Stadium	Opened	LF	CF	RF	Capacity	2019 Att.
Boise	Memorial Stadium	1989	335	400	335	3,426	129,805
Eugene	PK Park	2010	335	400	325	4,000	131,467
Everett	Everett Memorial Stadium	1984	324	380	330	3,682	116,630
Hillsboro	Hillsboro Ballpark	2013	325	400	325	4,500	133,605
Salem-Keizer	Volcanoes Stadium	1997	325	400	325	4,100	80,833
Spokane	Avista Stadium	1958	335	398	335	7,162	200,273
Tri-City	Dust Devils Stadium	1995	335	400	335	3,700	87,021
Vancouver	Nat Bailey Stadium	1951	335	395	335	6,500	235,980

Dimensions

BOISE HAWKS

Address: 5600 N. Glenwood St. Boise, ID 83714.
Telephone: (208) 322-5000. **Fax:** (208) 322-6846.
Website: www.boisehawks.com.
Affiliation (first year): Colorado Rockies (2015).
Years in League: 1975-76, 1978, 1987-

OWNERSHIP/MANAGEMENT

Operated by: Boise Professional Baseball LLC. **President:** Jeff Eiseman. **HR & Operations:** Missy Martin. **Vice President:** Bob Flannery. **General Manager:** Mike Van Hise. **Director, Stadium Ops/Food & Beverage:** Jake Lusk. **Manager, Accounting/Office:** Judy Peterson. **Corporate Sales Manager:** Matt Osbon. **Ticket Sales Manager:** Jon Jensen. **Group Event Executive:** Colton Hampson. **Account Executive:** Kristi Croteau, Justin Lako. **Box Office Manager:** Reilly Raube. **Assistant Director, Stadium Operations:** Christian Lomeli. **Food and Beverage Coordinator:** Adam Pinckard. **Media Relations/Marketing Manager:** Carly McCullough. **Marketing and Community Relations Specialist:** Paige Plotzke. **Graphics/Video Production Coordinator:** TBD. **Media Relations & Play-by-Play Broadcaster:** Leonard Barry. **Head Groundskeeper:** John Gides.

FIELD STAFF

Manager: TBD. **Hitting Coach:** TBD. **Pitching Coach:** TBD. **Athletic Trainer:** Mickey Clarizio. **Development Supervisor:** Fred Ocasio.

GAME INFORMATION

Radio Announcer: Leonard Barry . **No. of Games Broadcast:** 76. **Flagship Station:** KTIK 1350 AM. **PA Announcer:** Jeremy Peterson. **Official Scorer:** Curtis Haines. **Stadium Name:** Memorial Stadium. **Location:** I-84 to Cole Rd., north to Western Idaho Fairgrounds at 5600 North Glenwood St. **Standard Game Time:** 7:15 pm. **Ticket Price Range:** $8-35. **Visiting Club Hotel:** Simple Suites

EUGENE EMERALDS

Office Address: 2760 Martin Luther King Jr. Blvd, Eugene, OR 97401.
Mailing Address: PO Box 10911, Eugene, OR 97440.
Telephone: (541) 342-5367. **Fax:** (541) 342-6089.
E-Mail Address: info@emeraldsbaseball.com. **Website:** www.emeraldsbaseball.com.
Affiliation (first year): Chicago Cubs (2015). **Years in League:** 1955-68, 1974-

OWNERSHIP/MANAGEMENT

Operated By: Elmore Sports Group Ltd. **Principal Owner:** David Elmore.
General Manager: Allan Benavides. **Assistant GM:** Matt Dompe. **Director, Food/Beverage:** Turner Elmore.
Director, Tickets: David Roth. **Event Manager:** Chris Bowers. **Graphic Designer:** Danny Cowley. **Director, Community Affairs:** Anne Culhane. **Ticket Sales:** Andrew Brown, Cam LaFerle, Kindra Bates. **Merchandise and Social Media:** Shelby Holteen. **Sponsorship Sales:** Patrick Zajac. **Home Radio:** Matt Dompe. **Away Radio:** Alex Stimson.

FIELD STAFF

Manager: Lance Rymel. **Hitting Coach:** Osmin Melendez. **Pitching Coach:** Armando Gabino. **Assistant Coach:** Travis Fitta. **Athletic Trainer:** Sean Folan.

GAME INFORMATION

Radio Announcer: Matt Dompe. **No. of Games Broadcast:** 76. **Flagship Station:** 95.3-FM The Score. **PA Announcer:** Ted Welker. **Official Scorer:** George McPherson. **Stadium Name:** PK Park. **Standard Game Time:** Mon.-Sat., 7:05 p.m., Sun., 5:05pm. **Ticket Price Range:** $8-$15. **Visiting Club Hotel:** Holiday Inn, Eugene Springfield.

EVERETT AQUASOX

Mailing Address: 3802 Broadway, Everett, WA 98201.
Telephone: (425) 258-3673. **Fax:** (425) 258-3675.
E-Mail Address: info@aquasox.com. **Website:** www.aquasox.com.
Affiliation (first year): Seattle Mariners (1995). **Years in League:** 1984-

OWNERSHIP/MANAGEMENT

Operated by: 7th Inning Stretch, LLC.
Directors: Tom Volpe, Pat Filippone. **General Manager:** Danny Tetzlaff. **Assistant GM:** Rick Maddox. **Director, Corporate Partnerships/Broadcasting:** Pat Dillon. **Director, Tickets:** Bryan Martin. **Corporate Partnership and Team Operations Manager:** Alex Clausius. **Director of Community Relations & Merchandise:** Ashlea LaPlant. **Marketing & Social Media Manager:** Sarah Newgarde. **Account Executives:** Scott Brownlee, Conner Grant, Kieran McMahon.

FIELD STAFF

Manager: Louis Boyd. **Hitting Coach:** Joe Thurston. **Pitching Coach:** Ari Ronick.

GAME INFORMATION

Radio Announcer: Pat Dillon. **No. of Games Broadcast:** 76. **Flagship Station:** KRKO 1380-AM, 95.3-FM. **PA Announcer:** Tom Lafferty. **Official Scorer:** Patrick Lafferty. **Stadium Name:** Everett Memorial Stadium. **Location:** I-5, exit 192. **Standard Game Times:** Mon.-Sat., 7:05 pm, Sun., 4:05 pm. **Ticket Price Range:** $8-18. **Visiting Club Hotel:** Best Western Cascadia Inn, 2800 Pacific Ave, Everett, WA 98201. **Telephone:** (425) 258-4141.

HILLSBORO HOPS

Address: 4460 NE Century Blvd., Hillsboro, OR, 97124. **Telephone:** (503) 640-0887.
E-Mail Address: info@hillsborohops.com. **Website:** www.hillsborohops.com.
Affiliation (first year): Arizona Diamondbacks (2001). **Years in League:** 2013-

OWNERSHIP/MANAGEMENT

Operated by: Short Season LLC. **Managing Partners:** Mike McMurray, Josh Weinman, Myron Levin.
Chairman and CEO: Mike McMurray. **President and General Manager:** K.L. Wombacher. **Chief Financial Officer:** Laura McMurray. **Director, Ballpark Operations:** Adam Good. **Vice President, Tickets:** Jason Gavigan. **Senior Director, Merchandise:** Shantel Gritsch. **Manager, Marketing and Communications:** Casey Sawyer. **Director, Broadcasting:** Rich Burk.

FIELD STAFF

Manager: Javier Colina. **Hitting Coach:** Franklin Stubbs. **Pitching Coach:** Mike Parrott. **Coach:** Mark Reed. **Coach:** Ben Petrick.

GAME INFORMATION

PA Announcer: Jason Swygard. **Official Scorer:** Blair Cash. **Stadium Name:** Ron Tonkin Field. **Location:** 4460 NE Century Blvd., Hillsboro, OR. 97124. **Standard Game Times:** Mon.-Sat., 7:05 pm, Sun., 4:05 pm. **Ticket Price Range:** $7-$20. **Visiting Club Hotel:** Extended Stay America—Portland/Hillsboro, Hillsboro, OR. **Telephone:** (503) 221-0140.

SALEM-KEIZER VOLCANOES

Office Address: 6700 Field of Dreams Way, Keizer, OR 97303.
Mailing Address: PO Box 20936, Keizer, OR 97307.
Telephone: (503) 390-2225. **Fax:** (503) 390-2227.
E-Mail Address: Volcanoes@volcanoesbaseball.com. **Website:** www.volcanoesbaseball.com.
Affiliation (first year): San Francisco Giants (1997). **Years in League:** 1997-

OWNERSHIP/MANAGEMENT

Operated By: Sports Enterprises Inc. **Principal Owners:** Jerry Walker, Lisa Walker. **President/General Manager:** Jerry Walker. **Vice President:** Lisa Walker. **CEO:** Mickey Walker. **President, Business Operations:** Mitche Graf. **President, Stadium Operations Emeritus:** Rick Nelson. **Senior Account Executive, Game Day Operations:** Jerry Howard. **Director of Tickets:** Stephen Lilly. **Director, Business Development:** Justin Lacche.

FIELD STAFF

Manager: Lenn Sakata. **Hitting Coach:** Michael Brdar. **Pitching Coach:** Paul Oseguera. **Fundamentals Coach:** Eliezer Zambrano. **Trainer:** Tim Vigue.

GAME INFORMATION

Radio Announcer: Unavailable. **No. of Games Broadcast:** 76. **Flagship Station:** Unavailable. **PA Announcer:** Unavailable. **Official Scorer:** Scott Sepich. **Stadium Name:** Volcanoes Stadium. **Location:** I-5 to exit 260 (Chemawa Road), west one block to Stadium Way NE, north six blocks to stadium. **Standard Game Times:** Mon.-Sat., 6:35 pm, Sun., 5:05 p.m. **Ticket Price Range:** $7-22. **Visiting Club Hotel:** Comfort Suites, 630 Hawthorne Ave SE, Salem, OR 97301. **Telephone:** (503) 585-9705.

SPOKANE INDIANS

Office Address: Avista Stadium, 602 N Havana, Spokane, WA 99202.
Mailing Address: PO Box 4758, Spokane, WA 99220.
Telephone: (509) 535-2922. **Fax:** (509) 534-5368.
E-Mail Address: mail@spokaneindians.com. **Website:** www.spokaneindians.com.
Affiliation (first year): Texas Rangers (2003). **Years in League:** 1972, 1983-Present-

OWNERSHIP/MANAGEMENT

Operated By: Longball Inc. **Principal Owner:** Bobby Brett. **Co-Owner/Senior Advisor:** Andrew Billig. **President:** Chris Duff. **Senior Vice President:** Otto Klein. **VP, Concessions & Hospitality:** Josh Roys. **VP, Business Operations:** Lesley DeHart. **General Manager:** Kyle Day. **Assistant General Manager:** Sean Bozigian. **Assistant GM, Tickets:** Nick Gaebe. **Director, Concessions & Hospitality:** Darby Moore. **Business Operations Manager:** MacKenzie White. **Business Operations Coordinator:** Kayla Rott. **Partner Services Coordinator:** Gina Giesseman. **Promotions and Sustainability Coordinator:** Annie Wissmiller. **Director of Public Relations:** John Collett. **Communications Consultant:** Bud Bareither. **Assistant Director of Tickets:** Jake Browne. **Account Executives:** Devyn Kelly, James Lange. **Director of Group Sales:** Sean Dorsey. **Group Sales Coordinators:** Becca Collins, Jamie Isaacson. **Personal Account Managers:** Trey Endris, Ryan Songey. **Chief Financial Officer:** Greg Sloan. **Controller:** Tim Gittel. **Director of Facilities & Grounds:** Tony Lee. **Assistant Director, Stadium Operations:** Larry Blumer.

FIELD STAFF

Manager: Sean Cashman. **Pitching Coach:** Brian Conger. **Hitting Coach:** Sharnol Adriana. **Coach:** Pat Brady. **Strength & Conditioning Coach:** Ed Yong. **Athletic Trainer:** Yuichi Takizawa.

GAME INFORMATION

Radio Announcer: Mike Boyle. **No. of Games Broadcast:** 76. **Flagship Station:** 1510 AM/103.5 FM. **PA Announcer:** Unavailable. **Official Scorer:** Todd Gilkey. **Stadium Name:** Avista Stadium. **Location:** From west, I-90 to exit 283B (Thor/Freya), east on Third Avenue, left onto Havana; From east, I-90 to Broadway exit, right onto Broadway, left onto Havana. **Standard Game Time:** Mon.-Sat., 6:30 pm, Sun., 3:30 pm. **Ticket Price Range:** $5-13. **Visiting Club Hotel:** Mirabeau Park Hotel & Convention Center, 1100 N. Sullivan Rd, Spokane, WA 99037. **Telephone:** (509) 924-9000.

TRI-CITY DUST DEVILS

Address: 6200 Burden Blvd, Pasco, WA 99301.
Telephone: (509) 544-8789. **Fax:** (509) 547-9570.
E-Mail Address: info@dustdevilsbaseball.com.
Website: www.dustdevilsbaseball.com.
Affiliation (first year): San Diego Padres (2015).
Years in League: 1955-1974, 1983-1986, 2001-

OWNERSHIP/MANAGEMENT

Operated by: Northwest Baseball Ventures. **Principal Owners:** George Brett, Yoshi Okamoto, Brent Miles.

President: Brent Miles. **Vice President/General Manager:** Derrel Ebert. **Assistant General Manager, Business Operations:** Trevor Shively. **Assistant General Manager, Sponsorships:** Ann Shively. **Assistant General Manager, Tickets:** Riley Shintaffer. **Sponsorships Account Executive:** Michael Allen. **Sponsorships Account Executive/ Beverage Service Manager:** Brennan McIntire. **Ticket Sales/Stadium Operations Manager:** Marcus Manderbach. **Group Sales Coordinator:** Alex Cornwell. **Account Executive:** Selina Koon. **Head Groundskeeper:** Michael Angel.

FIELD STAFF

Manager: Vinny Lopez. **Hitting Coach:** Raul Gonzalez. **Pitching Coach:** Gorman Heimueller. **Fielding Coach:** Luis Mendez.

GAME INFORMATION

Radio Announcer: Chris King. **No. of Games Broadcast:** 76. **Flagship Station:** 870-AM KFLD. **PA Announcer:** Patrick Harvey. **Official Scorers:** Tony Wise, Scott Tylinski. **Stadium Name:** Gesa Stadium. **Location:** I-182 to exit 9 (Road 68), north to Burden Blvd, right to stadium. **Standard Game Time:** 7:15 pm. **Ticket Price Range:** $8-12. **Visiting Club Hotel:** Hampton Inn & Suites Pasco/Tri-Cities, 6826 Burden Blvd., Pasco, WA 99301. **Telephone:** (509) 792-1660.

VANCOUVER CANADIANS

Address: Scotiabank Field at Nat Bailey Stadium, 4601 Ontario St, Vancouver, B.C. V5V 3H4.
Telephone: (604) 872-5232. **Fax:** (604) 872-1714.
E-Mail Address: staff@canadiansbaseball.com.
Website: www.canadiansbaseball.com.
Affiliation (first year): Toronto Blue Jays (2011). **Years in League:** 2000-

OWNERSHIP/MANAGEMENT

Operated by: Vancouver Canadians Professional Baseball LLP. **Managing General Partner:** Jake Kerr. **Co-Owner:** Jeff Mooney. **President:** Andy Dunn. **General Manager:** Allan Bailey. **Assistant General Manager:** Stephani Ellis. **Financial Controller:** Brenda Chmiliar. **VP, Sales/Marketing:** Graham Wall. **Director, Communications:** Rob Fai. **Senior Advisor:** Walter Cosman. **Director, Sales/Game Day Operations:** Michael Richardson. **Manager, Sales & Marketing:** Chelsea Jenner. **Manager, Ticket Operations:** Stephen Maisey. **Coordinator, Sales & Game Day Operations:** Jordan Skavinsky. **Coordinator, Sales & Marketing:** Jonah Morris. **Coordinator, Sales & Marketing:** Rachel Jawandha. **Assistant Financial Controller:** Charlene Shamku. **Head Groundskeeper:** Ross Baron. **Manager, Ballpark Operations/Home Clubhouse Attendant:** John Stewart. **Manager, Concessions:** Iain Graham (Aramark).

FIELD STAFF

Manager: Brent Lavallee. **Hitting Coach:** Andy Fermin. **Pitching Coach:** Demetre Kokoris.

GAME INFORMATION

Radio/TV Announcer: Rob Fai (14th season). **No. of Games Broadcast:** 76. **Flagship Station:** Sportsnet650 AM. **PA Announcer:** Niall O'Donohoe. **Official Scorer:** Mike Hanafin. **Stadium Name:** Nat Bailey **Stadium.Location:** From downtown, take Cambie Street Bridge, left on East 29th Ave., left on Ontario St. to stadium; From south, take Highway 99 to Oak Street, right on 41st Ave, left on Cambie St. right on East 29th Ave., left on Ontario St to stadium. **Standard Game Times:** Mon.-Sat., 7:05 pm, Sun., 1:05 pm. **Ticket Price Range:** $16-27. **Visiting Club Hotel:** Sandman Hotel Vancouver Airport, 3233 St. Edwards Dr., Richmond, B.C., V6X 1N4. **Telephone:** (604) 303-8888.

APPALACHIAN LEAGUE

Mailing Address: 1340 Environ Way, Chapel Hill, NC 27517
Telephone: 919-913-4590. **E-Mail Address:** dan@appyleague.com
Website: www.appyleague.com.
Years League Active: 1921-25, 1937-55, 1957-
President/Treasurer: Dan Moushon.
Corporate Secretary: Jeremy Boler (Elizabethton). **League Publicist:** Betsy Haugh (Pulaski).
President Emeritus: Lee Landers.
Directors: Charlie Wilson (Toronto), Larry Broadway (Pittsburgh), Alec Zumwalt (Kansas City), Ron Knight (Atlanta), Alex Hassan (Minnesota), Eric Lee (Cincinnati), Gary LaRocque (St. Louis), Jared Banner (New York Mets), Jeff McLerran (Tampa Bay), Eric Schmitt (New York Yankees).
Executive Committee: Mike Mains (Elizabethton), Brian Paupeck (Kingsport), Betsy Haugh (Pulaski), Gary La Rocque (St. Louis), Charlie Wilson (Toronto), Larry Broadway (Pittsburgh).
Board of Trustees Representative: Mitch Lukevics (Tampa Bay).
Baseball Chapel Representative: Brandon Bennett (Danville).
Division Structure: East—Bluefield, Burlington, Danville, Princeton, Pulaski. **West**—Bristol, Elizabethton, Greeneville, Johnson City, Kingsport.
Regular Season: 68 games. **2020 Opening Date:** June 22. **Closing Date:** Sept. 1.
All-Star Game: None. **Playoff Format:** First-and second-place teams in each division play each other in best-of-three series. Winners meet in best-of-three series for league championship. **Roster Limit:** 35 active, 35 under control.
Player Eligibility Rule: No more than three players on the active roster may have three or more years of prior minor league service. **Brand of Baseball:** Rawlings. **Umpires:** Unavailable.

Dan Moushon

STADIUM INFORMATION

Club	Stadium	Opened	Dimensions LF	Dimensions CF	Dimensions RF	Capacity	2019 Att.
Bluefield	Bowen Field	1939	335	400	335	2,046	20,909
Bristol	DeVault Memorial Stadium	1969	325	400	310	2,000	18,750
Burlington	Burlington Athletic Stadium	1960	335	410	335	3,216	40,142
Danville	Dan Daniel Memorial Park	1993	330	400	330	2,755	30,007
Elizabethton	Joe O'Brien Field	1974	335	414	326	1,500	27,569
Greeneville	Pioneer Park	2004	331	400	331	2,672	43,617
Johnson City	TVA Credit Union Ballpark	1956	320	410	320	2,897	80,612
Kingsport	Hunter Wright Stadium	1995	330	410	330	2,418	29,553
Princeton	Hunnicutt Field	1988	330	396	330	2,000	24,133
Pulaski	Calfee Park	1935	335	405	310	2,912	95,897

BLUEFIELD BLUE JAYS

Office Address: Stadium Drive, Bluefield, WV 24701. **Mailing Address:** PO Box 356, Bluefield, WV 24701. **Telephone:** (304) 324-1326. **Fax:** (304) 324-1318.
E-Mail Address: babybirds1@comcast.net. **Website:** www.bluefieldjays.com.
Affiliation (first year): Toronto Blue Jays (2011). **Years in League:** 1946-55, 1957-

OWNERSHIP/MANAGEMENT
Director: Charlie Wilson (Toronto Blue Jays). **President:** George McGonagle. **Vice President:** David Kersey. **Counsel:** Brian Cochran. **General Manager:** Patrick (Rocky) Malamisura.

FIELD STAFF
Manager: Jose Mayorga. **Hitting Coach:** Paul Elliott. **Pitching Coach:** Rafael Lazo. **Position Player Coach:** Aaron Mathews. **Athletic Trainer:** Roelvis Vargas. **Strength & Conditioning Coach:** Tommy LaBriola.

GAME INFORMATION
PA Announcer: Unavailable. **Official Scorer:** Unavailable. **Stadium Name:** Bowen Field. **Location:** I-77 to Bluefield exit 1, Route 290 to Route 460 West, fourth light right onto Leatherwood Lane, left at first light, past Hometown Shell station and turn right, stadium quarter-mile on left. **Ticket Price Range:** $6. **Visiting Club Hotel:** Quality Inn Bluefield, 3350 Big Laurel Highway/460 West, Bluefield, WV 24701. **Telephone:** (304) 325-6170.

BRISTOL PIRATES

Office Address: 1501 Euclid Ave, Bristol, VA 24201.
Mailing Address: PO Box 1434, Bristol, VA 24203.
Telephone: (276) 206-9946. **Fax:** (423)-968-2636.
E-Mail Address: gm@bristolbaseball.com. **Website:** www.bristolpiratesbaseball.com.
Twitter: @BriBucs. **Facebook:** www.facebook.com/bristolpiratesbaseball.
Affiliation (first year): Pittsburgh Pirates (2014). **Years in League:** 1921-25, 1940-55, 1969-

OWNERSHIP/MANAGEMENT
Owned by: Pittsburgh Pirates. **Director:** Larry Broadway (Pittsburgh Pirates). **Operated by:** Bristol Baseball Inc.
President/General Manager: Mahlon Luttrell. **Vice President:** Craig Adams, Mark Young. **Treasurer:** Delma Luttrell.
Secretary: Connie Kinkead.

FIELD STAFF
Manager: TBA. **Hitting Coach:** TBA. **Pitching Coach:** TBA. **Athletic Trainer:** TBA. **Strength & Conditioning Coach:**
TBA.

GAME INFORMATION
Radio: milb.com. **PA Announcer:** Unavailable. **Official Scorer:** Connie Kinkead. **Stadium Name:** DeVault Memorial
Stadium. **Location:** I-81 to exit 3 onto Commonwealth Ave, right on Euclid Ave for half-mile. **Standard Game Times:**
Mon.-Sat., 7 pm, Sun., 6 pm. **Ticket Price Range:** $4-$8. **Visiting Club Hotel:** Holiday Inn, 3005 Linden Drive Bristol, VA
24202. **Telephone:** (276) 466-4100.

BURLINGTON ROYALS

Office Address: 1450 Graham St, Burlington, NC 27217.
Mailing Address: PO Box 1143, Burlington, NC 27216. **Telephone:** (336) 222-0223.
E-Mail Address: info@burlingtonroyals.com. **Website:** www.burlingtonroyals.com
Affiliation (first year): Kansas City Royals (2007). **Years in League:** 1986-

OWNERSHIP/MANAGEMENT
Operated by: Burlington Baseball Club Inc. **Director:** Mitch Maier (Kansas City)
President: Miles Wolff. **General Manager:** Mikie Morrison. **Assistant GM:** Lauren Wagaman.
Director of Operations: Brett Burke.

FIELD STAFF
Manager: Tony Pena Jr. **Hitting Coach:** Ramon Castro. **Pitching Coach:** John Habyan.

GAME INFORMATION
Radio Announcer: Alex Feuz. **No. of Games Broadcast:** Home-34, Away-4. **Flagship:** www.burlingtonroyals.com.
PA Announcer: Unavailable. **Official Scorer:** Unavailable. **Stadium Name:** Burlington Athletic Stadium. **Location:**
I-40/85 to exit 145, north on Route 100 (Maple Avenue) for 1.5 miles, right on Mebane Street for 1.5 miles, right on
Beaumont, left on Graham. **Standard Game Time:** 6:30 pm. **Ticket Price Range:** $6-10. **Visiting Club Hotel:** Best
Western Plus Burlington.

DANVILLE BRAVES

Office Address: Dan Daniel Memorial Park, 302 River Park Dr, Danville, VA 24540.
Mailing Address: PO Box 378, Danville, VA 24543.
Telephone: (434) 797-3792. **Fax:** (434) 797-3799.
E-Mail Address: danvillebraves@braves.com. **Website:** www.dbraves.com.
Affiliation (first year): Atlanta Braves (1993). **Years in League:** 1993-

OWNERSHIP/MANAGEMENT
Operated by: Atlanta National League Baseball Club LLC.
Director: Ben Sestanovich (Atlanta Braves). **VP/General Manager:** Brandon Bennett. **Assistant GM:** Stephen
Brunson. **Head Groundskeeper:** Ryan Brown.

FIELD STAFF
Manager: Michael Saunders. **Hitting Coach:** Connor Narron. **Pitching Coach:** TBA. **Bench Coach:** TBA. **Athletic
Trainer:** TBA. **Strength & Conditioning Coach:** TBA.

GAME INFORMATION
Radio Announcer: Nick Pierce. **No. of Games Broadcast:** Home-34. **Flagship Station:** www.dbraves.com.
PA Announcer: Jay Stephens. **Official Scorer:** TBD. **Stadium Name:** American Legion Field Post 325 Field at Dan
Daniel Memorial Park. **Location:** US 29 Bypass to River Park Drive/Dan Daniel Memorial Park exit; follow signs to park.
Standard Game Times: Mon.-Sat., 6:30 pm, Sun. June & July 6:30 pm; August 2:00 pm. **Ticket Price Range:** $5-10.
Visiting Club Hotel: Comfort Inn & Suites, 100 Tower Drive, Danville, VA 24540.

ELIZABETHTON TWINS

Office Address: 804 Holly Lane., Elizabethton, TN 37643.
Stadium Address: 804. Holly Lane, Elizabethton, TN 37643.
Mailing Address: 804 Holly Lane, Elizabethton, TN 37643.
Telephone: (423) 547-6443.
Affiliation (first year): Minnesota Twins (1974). **Years in League:** 1937-42, 1945-51, 1974-

OWNERSHIP/MANAGEMENT
Operated by: Boyd Sports LLC. **Director:** Alex Hassan. **President:** Chris Allen. **Vice President:** Jeremy Boler. **General Manager:** Brice Ballentine.

FIELD STAFF
Manager: Ray Smith. **Hitting Coach:** Jeff Reed. **Pitching Coach:** Richard Salazar. **Athletic Trainer:** Matt Smith. **Strength & Conditioning Coach:** Cesar Castillo. **Coach:** Jimmy Alvarez.

GAME INFORMATION
Radio Announcer: TBD. **No. of Games Broadcast:** 34–Home, 34–Away. **Flagship Station:** Elizabethtontwins.com. **PA Announcer:** Tom Banks. **Official Scorer:** Gene Renfro. **Stadium Name:** Northeast Community Credit Union Ballpark. **Location:** I-81 to Highway I-26, exit at Highway 321/67, left on Holly Lane. **Standard Game Times:** 6:30 pm. **Ticket Price Range:** $5-7. **Visiting Club Hotel:** Holiday Inn, 101 W Springbrook Dr, Johnson City, TN 37601. **Telephone:** (423) 282-4611.

GREENEVILLE REDS

Office Address: 135 Shiloh Road, Greeneville, TN 37745
Mailing Address: 135 Shiloh Road, Greeneville, TN 37745
Telephone: (423) 609-7400. **E-Mail Address:** contact@greenevillereds.com.
Website: www.greenevillereds.com.

OWNERSHIP/MANAGEMENT
Owned by: Boyd Sports, LLC. **Director:** Shawn Pender (Cincinnati Reds). **General Manager:** Kristen Atwell.

FIELD STAFF
Manager: Derrin Ebert. **Hitting Coach:** Luis Terrero. **Pitching Coach/Assistant to the Pitching Coordinator:** Chris Booker. **Bench Coach:** Reggie Williams. **Athletic Trainer:** Wade Hebrink. **Strength & Conditioning Coach:** Joel Canacoo.

GAME INFORMATION
Radio Announcer: Unavailable. **Flagship Station:** greenevillereds.com. **PA Announcer:** TBD. **Official Scorer:** TBD. **Stadium Name:** Pioneer Park. **Location:** On the campus of Tusculum University, 135 Shiloh Rd Greeneville, TN 37745. **Standard Game Time:** Mon-Fri., 6:30 pm, Sat., 6:30 pm, Sun., 5 pm. **Ticket Price Range:** $5 group discount, $7 reserved, $8 premium.

JOHNSON CITY CARDINALS

Office Address: 510 Bert St., Johnson City, TN 37601.
Mailing Address: PO Box 179, Johnson City, TN 37605.
Telephone: (423) 461-4866. **E-Mail Address:** contact@jccardinals.com.
Website: www.jccardinals.com. **Affiliation (first year):** St. Louis Cardinals (1975).
Years in League: 1911-13, 1921-24, 1937-55, 1957-61, 1964-

OWNERSHIP/MANAGEMENT
Owned by: St. Louis Cardinals. **Operated by:** Boyd Sports, LLC. **President:** Chris Allen. **Director:** Gary Larocque. **General Manager:** Zac Clark. **Assistant General Manager:** Kat Deal.

FIELD STAFF
Manager: Roberto Espinoza. **Hitting Coach:** Daniel Nicolaisen. **Pitching Coach:** Renee Cortez. **Athletic Trainer:** Justin Wilson. **Strength and Conditioning Coordinator:** Jaqueline Gover.

GAME INFORMATION
PA Announcer: Unavailable. **Official Scorer:** Unavailable. **Stadium Name:** TVA Credit Union Ballpark. **Location:** I-26 to exit 23, left on East Main, through light onto Legion Street. **Standard Game Time:** 7 pm. **Ticket Price Range:** $6-$9. **Visiting Club Hotel:** Holiday Inn, 101 W Springbrook Dr, Johnson City, TN 37601. **Telephone:** (423) 282-4611.

KINGSPORT METS

Address: 800 Granby Rd, Kingsport, TN 37660.
Telephone: (423) 224-2626. **Fax:** (423) 224-2625.
E-Mail Address: info@kmets.com. **Website:** www.kmets.com
Affiliation (first year): New York Mets (1980).
Years in League: 1921-25, 1938-52,1957, 1960-63, 1969-82, 1984-

OWNERSHIP/MANAGEMENT
Owner/Operated By: New York Mets. **Director:** Jared Banner. **General Manager:** Brian Paupeck. **Staff:** Josh Lawson, Taylor Koesters. **Clubhouse Manager:** Carlos Martell.

FIELD STAFF
Manager: Chris Newell. **Hitting Coach:** Trey Hannam. **Pitching Coach:** Glenn Abbott. **Bench Coach:** Gilbert Gomez. **Athletic Trainer:** Austin Dayton. **Performance Coach:** Ayram Texidor.

GAME INFORMATION
PA Announcer: Marty Murr. **Official Scorer:** Zeke Newton. **Stadium Name:** Hunter Wright Stadium. **Location:** I-26, Exit 1 (Stone Drive), left on West Stone Drive (US 11W), right on Granby Road. **Standard Game Times:** Mon-Sat., 6:30pm, Sun., 2pm. **Doubleheaders**—Mon-Sat. 4 pm, Sun. 2pm. **Ticket Price Range:** $5.50-$8. **Visiting Club Hotel:** Quality Inn, 3004 Bays Mountain Plaza, Kingsport, TN 37664. **Telephone:** (423) 230-0534.

PRINCETON RAYS

Office Address: 345 Old Bluefield Rd, Princeton, WV 24739.
Mailing Address: PO Box 5646, Princeton, WV 24740. **Telephone:** (304) 487-2000.
Fax: (304) 487-8762. **E-Mail Address:** princetonrays@frontier.com. **Website:** www.princetonrays.net.
Affiliation (first year): Tampa Bay Rays (1997). **Years in League:** 1988-

OWNERSHIP/MANAGEMENT
Operated By: Princeton Baseball Association Inc. **Director:** Jeff McLerran. **President:** Dewey Russell. **General Manager:** Danny Shingleton. **Director, Stadium Operations:** Adam Sarver, Rusty Sarver. **Chaplain:** Craig Stout.

FIELD STAFF
Manager: Sean Smedley. **Hitting Coach:** Manny Castillo. **Pitching Coach:** Alberto Bastardo. **Coach:** Frank Jagoda. **Athletic Trainer:** Ruben Santiago.

GAME INFORMATION
Radio Announcer: Wes McKinney (Home), Kyle Cooper (Away). **No. of Games Broadcast:** 34–Away. **Flagship Station:** WAEY-103.3FM. **PA Announcer:** Tommy Lester. **Official Scorer:** TBD. **Stadium Name:** Hunnicutt Field. **Location:** Exit 9 off I-77, US 460 West to downtown exit, left on Stafford Drive; stadium located behind Mercer County Technical Education Center. **Standard Game Times:** Mon.-Sat., 6:30 pm, Sun., 5 pm. **Ticket Price Range:** $5-8. **Visiting Club Hotel:** Sleep Inn, 1015 Oakvale Rd, Princeton, WV 24740. **Telephone:** (304) 431-2800.

PULASKI YANKEES

Office Address: 529 Pierce Avenue, Pulaski, VA 24301.
Mailing Address: PO Box 852, Pulaski, VA 24301. **Telephone:** (540) 980-1070.
Email Address: info@pulaskiyankees.net. **Affiliation (first season):** New York Yankees (2015).
Years in League: 1942-1951, 1952-55, 1957-58, 1969-77, 1982-92, 1997-2002, 2003-2006, 2008-2014, 2015-

OWNERSHIP/MANAGEMENT
Operated By: Calfee Park Baseball Inc. **Park Owners:** David Hagan, Larry Shelor. **General Manager:** Betsy Haugh.

FIELD STAFF
Manager: TBA. **Hitting Coach:** Kevin Martir. **Pitching Coach:** Gerardo Casadiego. **Athletic Trainer:** TBA. **Strength & Conditioning Coach:** TBA.

GAME INFORMATION
PA Announcer: Unavailable. **Official Scorer:** Unavailable. **Stadium Name:** Historic Calfee Park. **Location:** Interstate 81 to Exit 89-B (Route 11), north to Pulaski, right on Pierce Avenue. **Ticket Price Range:** $5-11. **Visiting Club Hotel:** Quality Inn, Dublin, Va.

PIONEER BASEBALL LEAGUE

Office Address: 812 W. 30th Avenue, Spokane, WA 99203.
Mailing Address: PO Box 2564, Spokane, WA 99220.
Telephone: (509) 456-7615. **Fax:** (509) 456-0136.
E-Mail Address: fanmail@pioneerleague.com.
Website: www.pioneerleague.com.
Years League Active: 1939-42, 1946-
President: Jim McCurdy.

Jim McCurdy

Directors: Dave Baggott (Ogden), Peter C. Davis (Missoula), Gant Elmore (Colorado Springs), Kevin Greene (Idaho Falls), Michael Baker (Grand Junction), Jeff Katofsky (Orem), Vinny Purpura (Great Falls), Dave Heller (Billings). **League Administrator:** Teryl MacDonald.
Executive Director: Mary Ann McCurdy.
Division Structure: North—Billings, Great Falls, Idaho Falls, Missoula. **South**— Grand Junction, Ogden, Orem, Rocky Mountain.
Regular Season: 76 games (split schedule). **2020 Opening Date:** June 19. **Closing Date:** Sept. 12. **All-Star Game:** Aug. 4 at Rocky Mountain (Pioneer Baseball League vs. Northwest League).
Playoff Format: First-half division winners meet second-half division winners in best of three series. Winners meet in best-of-three series for league championship. **Roster Limit:** 35 active, 35 dressed for each game. **Player Eligibility Rule:** No player on active list may have three or more years of prior minor league service. **Brand of Baseball:** Rawlings.
Umpires: Unavailable.

STADIUM INFORMATION

Club	Stadium	Opened	Dimensions			Capacity	2019 Att.
			LF	CF	RF		
Billings	Dehler Park	2008	329	410	350	3,071	96,594
Grand Junction	Sam Suplizio Field	1949	302	400	333	7,014	102,015
Great Falls	Centene Stadium at Legion Park	1956	335	414	335	3,800	83,826
Idaho Falls	Melaleuca Field	1976	340	400	350	3,400	81,870
Missoula	Ogren Park at Allegiance Field	2004	309	398	287	3,500	87,981
Ogden	Lindquist Field	1997	335	396	334	5,000	88,751
Orem	Home of the Owlz	2005	305	408	312	4,500	109,635
Rocky Mountain	Security Service Field	1988	350	410	350	8,500	88,112

BILLINGS MUSTANGS

Office Address: Dehler Park, 2611 9th Avenue North, Billings, MT 59101.
Mailing Address: PO Box 1553, Billings, MT 59103-1553.
Telephone: (406) 252-1241. **Fax:** (406) 252-2968.
E-Mail Address: mustangs@billingsmustangs.com. **Website:** billingsmustangs.com.
Affiliation (first year): Cincinnati Reds (1974). **Years in League:** 1948-63, 1969-

OWNERSHIP/MANAGEMENT

Operated By: Mustangs Baseball LLC.
President/CEO: Dave Heller. **General Manager:** Gary Roller. **Director, Corporate Sales/Partnerships:** Chris Marshall. **Director, Stadium Operations:** Matt Schoonover. **Director, Broadcasting/Media Relations:** Dustin Daniel. **Director, Food and Beverage Services:** Curt Prchal. **Director, Field Operations:** Jeff Limburg.

FIELD STAFF

Manager: Bryan LaHair. **Hitting Coach:** Jordan Stouffer. **Pitching Coach:** Forrest Herrmann. **Bench Coach:** Julio Morillo. **Athletic Trainer:** Josh Hobson. **Strength & Conditioning Coach:** Kyle Laughlin.

GAME INFORMATION

Radio Broadcaster: Dustin Daniel. **No. of Games Broadcast:** 76. **Flagship Station:** ESPN 910-AM KBLG. **PA Announcer:** Sarah Spangle. **Official Scorer:** George Kimmet. **Stadium Name:** Dehler Park. **Location:** I-90 to Exit 450, north on 27th Street North to 9th Avenue North. **Standard Game Times:** Mon.–Sat., 6:35 pm, Sun., 1:05 pm. **Ticket Price Range:** $5-$11.

GRAND JUNCTION ROCKIES

Address: 1315 North Ave., Grand Junction, CO, 81501
Telephone: (970) 255-7625. **Fax:** (970) 241-2374
Email: mritter@gjrockies.com. **Website:** www.gjrockies.com
Affiliation (first year): Colorado Rockies (2001). **Years in League:** 2001–

OWNERSHIP/MANAGEMENT
Principal Owners/Operated by: GJR, LLC. **President:** Mick Ritter. **Assistant GM:** Matt Allen. **Director of Broadcasting and Sales:** Kyle Kercheval.

FIELD STAFF
Manager: Jake Opitz. **Hitting Coach:** Trevor Burmeister. **Pitching Coach:** Helmis Rodriguez. **Supervisor:** TBA.

GAME INFORMATION
Radio Announcer: Kyle Kercheval . **No. of Games Broadcast:** 76. **Flagship Station:** MiLB.TV, gjrockies.com. **Television Announcer:** Kyle Kercheval. **No. of Games Televised:** Unavailable. **Flagship:** KGJT—My Network, Dish Network. **Produced by:** Colorado Mesa University. **PA Announcer:** Tim Ray. **Official Scorers:** Unknown. **Stadium Name:** Suplizio Field. **Location:** 1315 North Ave. Grand Junction, CO 81501. **Standard Game Times:** 6:40 pm. **Ticket Price Range:** $7-$11.

GREAT FALLS VOYAGERS

Address: 1015 25th St N, Great Falls, MT 59401.
Telephone: (406) 452-5311. **Fax:** (406) 454-0811.
E-Mail Address: voyagers@gfvoyagers.com. **Website:** www.gfvoyagers.com.
Affiliation (first year): Chicago White Sox (2003).
Years in League: 1948-1963, 1969-

OWNERSHIP/MANAGEMENT
Operated By: Great Falls Baseball Club.
CEO: Vinny Purpura. **President:** Scott Reasoner. **General Manager:** Scott Lettre.

FIELD STAFF
Manager: Mike Gellinger. **Hitting Coach:** Cameron Seitzer. **Pitching Coach:** John Ely.

GAME INFORMATION
Radio Announcer: Shawn Tiemann. **No. of Games Broadcast:** 76. **Flagship Station:** KXGF-1400 AM. **PA Announcer:** Chris Evans. **Official Scorer:** Mike Lewis. **Stadium Name:** Centene Stadium. **Location:** From I-15 to exit 281 (10th Ave S), left on 26th, left on Eighth Ave North, right on 25th, ballpark on right, past railroad tracks. **Ticket Price Range:** $5-12. **Visiting Club Hotel:** Days Inn, 101 14th Ave NW, Great Falls, MT 59404. **Telephone:** (406) 727-6565

IDAHO FALLS CHUKARS

Office Address: 900 Jim Garchow Way, Idaho Falls, ID 83402.
Mailing Address: PO 2183, Idaho, ID 83403.
Telephone: (208) 522-8363. **Fax:** (208) 522-9858.
E-Mail Address: chukarsbaseball@gmail.com. **Website:** www.ifchukars.com.
Affiliation (first year): Kansas City Royals (2004). **Years in League:** 1940-42, 1946-

OWNERSHIP/MANAGEMENT
Operated By: The Elmore Sports Group. **Principal Owner:** David Elmore.
President/General Manager: Kevin Greene. **Vice President:** Paul Henderson. **Assistant GM:** Josh Michalsen. **Director, Operations:** Aaron Madero. **Clubhouse Manager:** Patrick Greene. **Head Groundskeeper:** TBA.

FIELD STAFF
Manager: Omar Ramirez. **Hitting Coach:** Chris Nelson. **Pitching Coach:** Clayton Mortensen.

GAME INFORMATION
Radio Announcer: John Balginy. **No. of Games Broadcast:** 76. **Flagship Station:** ESPN 980-AM & 94.5 and 105.1FM. **PA Announcer:** Javier Hernandez. **Official Scorer:** John Balginy. **Stadium Name:** Melaleuca Field. **Location:** I-15 to West Broadway exit, left onto Memorial Drive, right on Mound Avenue, 1/4 mile to the stadium. **Standard Game Times:** Mon.-Sat., 7:15 pm, Sun., 4:00 pm. **Ticket Price Range:** $8-12. **Visiting Club Hotel:** Le Ritz Hotel, 720 Lindsay Blvd, Idaho Falls, ID 83402. **Telephone:** (208) 528-0880.

MISSOULA PADDLEHEADS

Address: 140 N Higgins, Suite 201, Missoula, MT 59802. **Telephone:** (406) 543-3300. **E-Mail Address:** trush@gopaddleheads.com. **Website:** www. gopaddleheads.com.
Affiliation (first year): Arizona Diamondbacks (1999). **Years in League:** 1956-60, 1999-

OWNERSHIP/MANAGEMENT
Operated By: Big Sky Professional Baseball LLC. **Co-Chairs:** Peter & Susan Crampton Davis.
Vice President: Matt Ellis. **Director of Marketing & PR:** Taylor Rush. **Director/Sales:** Tyler Hill. **Office Manager/Bookkeeper:** Nola Hunter. **Director/ Retail:** Kim Klages Johns.
Ticket Sales & Box Office Specialist: Robert Rink. **Entertainment and Promotions Manager:** Sam Boyd. **Stadium Operations Specialist:** Brett Shure.

FIELD STAFF
Manager: Darrin Garner. **Hitting Coach:** Jose Amado. **Pitching Coach:** Manny Garcia. **Bench Coach:** Mike Benjamin. **Athletic Trainer:** Chris Schepel. **Strength & Conditioning Coach:** TBD.

GAME INFORMATION
Radio Announcer: Unavailable. **No. of Games Broadcast:** 76. **Flagship Station:** ESPN 102.9 FM. **PA Announcer:** RJ Hentz. **Official Scorer:** Unavailable. **Stadium Name:** Ogren Park Allegiance Field. **Location:** Take Orange Street to Cregg Lane, west on Cregg Lane, stadium west of McCormick Park past railroad trestle. **Standard Game Times:** Mon.-Sat., 7:05 pm, Sun., 5:05 pm. **Ticket Price Range:** $8-14. **Visiting Club Hotel:** TBD.

OGDEN RAPTORS

Address: 2330 Lincoln Ave, Ogden, UT 84401. **Telephone:** (801) 393-2400. **Fax:** (801) 393-2473.
E-Mail Address: homerun@ogden-raptors.com. **Website:** www.ogden-raptors.com.
Affiliation (first year): Los Angeles Dodgers (2003). **Years in League:** 1939-42, 1946-55, 1966-74, 1994-

OWNERSHIP/MANAGEMENT
Operated By: Ogden Professional Baseball, Inc. **Principal Owners:** Dave Baggott, John Lindquist.
President/General Manager: Dave Baggott. **Director, Media Relations/Broadcaster:** Andrew Haynes. **Director, Food Services:** Trever Wilson. **Director, Security:** Scott McGregor. **Director, Social Media:** Kevin Johnson. **Director, Information Technology:** Chris Greene. **Public Relations:** Pete Diamond. **Groundskeeper:** Kenny Kopinski. **Assistant Groundskeeper:** Bob Richardson.

FIELD STAFF
Manager: Tony Cappuccilli. **Hitting Coach:** Dylan Nasiatka. **Pitching Coach:** Dean Stiles. **Clubhouse Manager:** Dave "MacGyver" Ackerman.

GAME INFORMATION
Radio Announcer: Andrew Haynes. **No. of Games Broadcast:** 76. **Flagship Station:** ogden-raptors.com. **PA Announcer:** Pete Diamond. **Official Scorer:** Dennis Kunimura. **Stadium Name:** Lindquist Field. **Location:** I-15 North to 21th Street exit, east to Lincoln Avenue, south three blocks to park. **Standard Game Times:** Mon.-Sat., 7 pm, Sun., 4pm. **Ticket Price Range:** $4-10. **Visiting Club Hotel:** Unavailable.

OREM OWLZ

Address: 970 W. University Parkway, Orem, UT 84058. **Telephone:** (801) 377-2255.
E-Mail Address: matt@oremowlz.com. **Website:** www.oremowlz.com.
Affiliation (first year): Los Angeles Angels (2001). **Years in League:** 2001-

OWNERSHIP/MANAGEMENT
Operated By: Bery Bery Gud To Me LLC. **Principal Owner:** Jeff Katofsky.
General Manager: Rick Berry. **Assistant GM:** Julie Hatch. **Director, Sales & Social Media:** Tim Morrissey.

FIELD STAFF
Manager: Andy Schatzley. **Hitting Coach:** Ryan Sebra/Daniel Ortega. **Pitching Coach:** James Fort/Bo Martino.

GAME INFORMATION
Radio Announcer: David Korzeniowski. **No. of Games Broadcast:** 76. **Flagship Station:** Unavailable. **PA Announcer:** TBD. **Official Scorer:** TBD. **Stadium Name:** Home of the Owlz. **Location:** Exit 269 (University Parkway) off I-15 at Utah Valley University campus. **Ticket Price Range:** $6-11. **Visiting Club Hotel:** La Quinta Inn & Suites Orem University Parkway, 521 W Universtiy Prky, Orem, UT 84058. **Telephone:** (801) 226-0440.

ROCKY MOUNTAIN VIBES

Address: 4385 Tutt Blvd., Colorado Springs, CO 80922.
Telephone: (719) 597-1449. **Fax:** (719) 597-2491.
E-Mail address: info@vibesbaseball.com. **Website:** www.vibesbaseball.com.
Affiliation (first year): Milwaukee Brewers (2015). **Years in League:** 2019-

OWNERSHIP/MANAGEMENT

Operated By: Rocky Mountain Vibes. **Principal Owner:** Dave Elmore. **President/General Manager:** Chris Phillips. **Assistant GM:** Keith Hodges. **Director, Baseball Operations & Communications:** Travis Arnold. **Manager, Ticketing/Merchandise:** Aaron Griffith. **Director, Accounting:** Ed Duffett. **Director, Ballpark Entertainment:** Abby Kappel. **Director, Marketing:** Kyle Fritzke. **VP, Field Operations:** Steve DeLeon. **Manager, Community Relations:** Crystal Mazey. **Manager, Group Sales/Military Liaison:** Jonathan Basil. **Manager, Group Sales:** Jake Hathaway. **Event Manager:** Brien Smith. **Executive Chef:** Chris Evans. **Clubhouse Manager:** TBD.

FIELD STAFF

Manager: Nestor Corredor. **Hitting Coach:** Liu Rodriguez. **Pitching Coach:** Rolando Valles.

GAME INFORMATION

No. of Games Broadcast: 76. **Flagship Station:** TuneIn. **PA Announcer:** TBD. **Official Scorer:** Marty Grantz. **Stadium Name:** UCHealth Park. **Location:** I-25 South to Woodmen Road exit, east on Woodmen to Powers Blvd., right on Powers to Barnes Road. **Standard Game Times:** Mon.-Fri., 6:40 pm, Sat., 6:00 pm, Sun., 1:30 pm. **Ticket Price Range:** $5-15.

ARIZONA LEAGUE

Office Address: 620 W Franklin St., Boise, ID 83702. **Mailing Address:** PO Box 1645, Boise, ID 83701.
Telephone: (208) 429-1511. **Fax:** (208) 429-1525. **E-Mail Address:** bobrichmond357@gmail.com.
Years League Active: 1988- **President/Treasurer:** Bob Richmond. **Vice President:** Mike Bell (D-backs).
Corporate Secretary: Zak Basch. **Administrative Assistant:** Rob Richmond.
Divisional Alignment: East—Athletics Green, Athletics Gold, Cubs Red, Cubs Blue, Giants Orange, Giants Black, Angels and Diamondbacks. **Central**—Brewers Gold, Dodgers 2, Indians Blue, Padres 2, White Sox, and Reds. **West**—Brewers Blue, Dodgers 1, Indians Red, Padres 1, Mariners, Royals, and Rangers. **Regular Season:** 56 games (split schedule).
2018 Opening Date: June 24. **Closing Date:** Sept. 2. **Playoff Format:** Six teams qualify. The three division champions from each half qualify for the single-elimination playoffs. If the same team wins a division in both halves, the team with the second-best overall record from the other division teams would qualify as the second team from that division. The two clubs with the best overall records receive first-round byes. Quarterfinal winners advance to a one-game playoff against one of the clubs that received a bye. Semifinal winners meet in a best-of-three series for the league championship. **All-Star Game:** None. **Roster Limit:** 35 active. **Player Eligibility Rule:** No player may have three or more years of prior minor league service.

Clubs	Playing Site	Manager	Hitting Coach	Pitching Coach
Angels	Angels Complex, Tempe	David Stapleton	T. Jeske/C.Shaw	Reklaitis/Baumann
Athletics Green	Fitch Park, Mesa	Eddie Menchaca	Ruben Escalera	Gabriel Ozuna
Athletics Gold	Fitch Park, Mesa	Webster Garrison	Kevin Kouzmanoff	Bryan Corey
Brewers Blue	Maryvale Baseball Complex, Phoenix	Rafael Neda	Brenton Del Chiaro	Hiram Burgos
Brewers Gold	Maryvale Baseball Complex, Phoenix	Nick Stanley	Brandon Macias	Michael Schlact
Cubs Red	Cubs Park, Mesa	Carmelo Martinez	J. Rogers/R. Folden	Doug Willey
Cubs Blue	Cubs Park, Mesa	Jimmy Gonzalez	E. Patterson/C. Rojas	Tony Cougoule
D-backs	Salt River Fields at Talking Stick	Nick Evans	Micah Franklin	Hatuey Mendoza
Dodgers	Camelback Ranch, Phoenix	Jair Fernandez	Jarek Cunningham	Rob Ellis
Giants Orange	Giants Complex, Scottsdale	Tony Diggs	TBD	Mike Couchee
Giants Black	Giants Complex, Scottsdale	Jose Montilla	Juan Parra	O. Matos
Indians 1	Goodyear Ballpark	Ken Knutson	Chris Smith	TBD
Indians 2	Goodyear Ballpark	Jerry Owens	Jordan Becker	Mike Steele
Mariners	Peoria Sports Complex	Zac Livingston	Jose Umbria	Yoel Monzon
Padres 1	Peoria Sports Complex	Aaron Levin	Doug Banks	Christian Wonders
Padres 2	Peoria Sports Complex	Oscar Salazar	Jed Morris	John Halama
Rangers	Surprise Recreation Campus	Sean Cashman	Sharnol Adriana	Bryan Conger
Reds	Goodyear Ballpark	Jose Moreno	Todd Takayoshi	Elmer Dessens
Royals	Surprise Recreation Campus	M. Bernard	A. David	Davis/Pimentel
White Sox	Camelback Ranch, Phoenix	Ever Magallanes	Drew Hasler	Felipe Lira

GULF COAST LEAGUE

Operated By: Minor League Baseball.
Office Address: 9550 16th Street North, St Petersburg, FL 33716.
Telephone: 727-456-1734. **Fax:** 727-456-1745. **Website:** www.milb.com. **Email Address:** gcl@milb.com.
Senior Vice President, Baseball & Business Operations: Tim Brunswick. **Assistant Director, Baseball & Business Operations:** Andy Shultz. **2019 Opening Date:** June 24. **Closing Date:** August 31. **Regular Season:** 56 Games (East, South)/52 Games (North). **Divisional Alignment: East**—Astros, Cardinals, Marlins, Mets, Nationals. **North**—Blue Jays, Phillies East, Phillies West, Tigers East, Tigers West, Yankees East, Yankees West. **South**—Braves, Orioles, Pirates, Rays, Red Sox, Twins. **Playoff Format:** The division winner with the best winning percentage plays the wild card (the non-division winner with best winning percentage) and the other two division winners meet in a one game semifinal. The winners meet in a best-of-three series for the Gulf Coast League championship. **All-Star Game:** None. **Roster Limit:** 35 active and in uniform and eligible to play in any given game. At least 10 must be pitchers as of July 1. **Player Eligibility Rule:** No player may have three or more years of prior minor league service. **Brand of Baseball:** Rawlings. **Statistician:** Major League Baseball Advanced Media.

Clubs	Playing Site	Manager	Hitting Coach	Pitching Coach
Astros	The Ballpark of the Palm Beaches	Ricardo Rivera	Rene Rojas	Jose Rada
Blue Jays	Bobby Mattick Training Center,	Dennis Holmberg	Michel Abreu	Cory Popham
Braves	Braves Complex,	Anthony Nunez	B. Moore/O. Rosario	Elvin Nina
Cardinals	Cardinals Complex	Joe Hawkins	T. Wolfe/B. Gilkey	Giovanni Carrara
Marlins	Roger Dean Stadium Complex	John Pachot	Jesus Merchan	Jason Erickson
Mets	Mets Complex	David Davalillo	Joel Fuentes	Josue Matos
Nationals	The Ballpark of the Palm Beaches	Rocket Wheeler	Amaury Garcia	Larry Pardo
Orioles	Ed Smith Stadium Complex	Alan Mills	Patrick Jones	Adam Bleday
Phillies E.	Carpenter Complex, Clearwater	Roly deArmas	Rafael DeLima	Pat Robles
Phillies W.	Carpenter Complex, Clearwater	Bobby Wernes	Zack Jones	Bruce Billings
Pirates	Pirate City, Bradenton	TBA	TBA	TBA
Rays	Charlotte Sports Park	Reinaldo Ruiz	F. Maldonado	M. DeMerritt/ J.Gonzalez
Red Sox	Jet Blue Park, Fort Myers	Tom Kotchman	Junior Zamora	Miguel Bonilla
Tigers East	Tigertown, Lakeland	Luis Lopez	Rafael Gil	Carlos Bohorqueza
Tigers West	Tigertown, Lakeland	Gary Cathcart	Bill Springman	Mike Alvarez
Twins	Lee County Sports Complex,	T. Miyoshi	Schlecter/Rodriguez	Moriarity /Urbina
Yankees E.	Himes Complex, Tampa	Travis Chapman	Aaron Leanhardt	Ben Buck
Yankees W.	Himes Complex, Tampa	TBD	Jake Hirst	Preston Claiborne

TEAM
SCHEDULES

TRIPLE-A

INTERNATIONAL LEAGUE

BUFFALO BISONS

APRIL	
9-12	at Scranton/WB
13-16	at Pawtucket
17-19	Rochester
20-22	Scranton/WB
24-26	at Rochester
27-30	Durham

MAY	
1-3	Louisville
5-7	at Indianapolis
8-10	at Louisville
11-14	Pawtucket
15-17	Lehigh Valley
19-21	at Scranton/WB
22-25	at Lehigh Valley
26-28	Scranton/WB
29-31	at Rochester

JUNE	
2-4	Norfolk
5-7	Indianapolis
9-11	at Norfolk
12-14	at Durham
15-17	Scranton/WB
18-21	Pawtucket
23-25	at Lehigh Valley
26-28	at Pawtucket
29-30	Lehigh Valley

JULY	
1	Lehigh Valley
2-3	Syracuse
4-6	at Syracuse
7-9	at Scranton/WB
10-12	Rochester
16-19	Syracuse
20-23	at Columbus
24-26	at Toledo
28-30	Gwinnett
31	Toledo

AUGUST	
1-2	Toledo
3-5	Rochester
6	at Rochester
7-9	at Syracuse
10-13	Charlotte
14-16	Columbus
18-20	at Charlotte
21-23	at Gwinnett
25-27	Lehigh Valley
28-30	Rochester
31	at Pawtucket

SEPTEMBER	
1-2	at Pawtucket
3-4	at Syracuse
5-7	at Rochester

CHARLOTTE KNIGHTS

APRIL	
9-12	at Durham
13-15	at Norfolk
16-19	Durham
20-22	Norfolk
24-26	at Louisville
27-30	Indianapolis

MAY	
1-3	Pawtucket
5-7	at Scranton/WB
8-10	at Pawtucket
11-14	Durham
15-17	Gwinnett
19-21	at Louisville
22-25	at Toledo
26-28	Durham
29-31	at Norfolk

JUNE	
2-4	Rochester
5-7	Scranton/WB
9-11	at Columbus
12-14	at Indianapolis
15-17	Norfolk
18-21	at Gwinnett
23-25	Louisville
26-28	Toledo
29-30	at Durham

JULY	
1	at Durham
2-3	Gwinnett
4-6	at Gwinnett
7-9	at Durham
10-12	Indianapolis
16-19	Gwinnett
20-23	at Syracuse
24-26	at Rochester
28-30	Syracuse
31	Columbus

AUGUST	
1-2	Columbus
3-5	at Gwinnett
6-9	Norfolk
10-13	at Buffalo
14-16	at Lehigh Valley
18-20	Buffalo
21-23	Lehigh Valley
25-27	at Norfolk
28-30	at Durham
31	Norfolk

SEPTEMBER	
1-2	Norfolk
3-4	at Gwinnett
5-7	Gwinnett

COLUMBUS CLIPPERS

APRIL	
9-10	Louisville
11-12	at Louisville
13-15	at Indianapolis

27-30	Rochester

MAY	
1-3	Scranton/WB
5-7	at Rochester
8-10	at Scranton/WB
11-14	Indianapolis
15-17	Toledo
19-21	at Durham
22-25	at Gwinnett
26-28	Louisville
29-31	Toledo

JUNE	
2-4	at Lehigh Valley
5-7	at Syracuse
9-11	Charlotte
12-14	Syracuse
15-17	at Indianapolis
18-21	at Toledo
23-25	Durham
26-28	Gwinnett
29-30	at Louisville

JULY	
1	at Louisville
2-3	at Toledo

DURHAM BULLS

APRIL	
9-12	Charlotte
13-15	Gwinnett
16-19	at Charlotte
20-22	at Gwinnett
24-26	Columbus
27-30	at Buffalo

MAY	
1-3	at Syracuse
5-7	Toledo
8-10	Syracuse
11-14	at Charlotte
15-17	at Norfolk
19-21	Columbus
22-25	Indianapolis
26-28	at Charlotte
29-31	Gwinnett

JUNE	
2-4	at Toledo
5-7	at Louisville
9-11	Lehigh Valley
12-14	Buffalo
15-17	at Gwinnett
18-21	Norfolk
23-25	at Columbus
26-28	at Indianapolis
29-30	Charlotte

JULY	
1	Charlotte
2-3	at Norfolk
4-6	Norfolk
7-9	Charlotte
10-12	at Toledo
16-19	at Indianapolis
20-23	Pawtucket
24-26	Louisville
28-30	at Pawtucket
31	at Lehigh Valley

AUGUST	
1-2	at Lehigh Valley
3-5	Norfolk
6-9	at Gwinnett
10-13	Rochester
14-16	Scranton/WB
18-20	at Rochester
21-23	at Scranton/WB
25-27	Gwinnett
28-30	Charlotte
31	at Gwinnett

SEPTEMBER	
1-2	at Gwinnett
3-4	Norfolk
5-7	at Norfolk

GWINNETT STRIPERS

APRIL	
9-12	at Norfolk
13-15	at Durham
16-19	Norfolk
20-22	Durham
24-26	Toledo
27-30	at Syracuse

MAY	
1-3	at Lehigh Valley
5-7	Syracuse
8-10	Toledo
11-14	at Norfolk
15-17	at Charlotte

4-6	Toledo
7-9	Gwinnett
10-12	at Louisville
16-19	at Indianapolis
20-23	Buffalo
24-26	Lehigh Valley
28-30	at Norfolk
31	at Charlotte

AUGUST	
1-2	at Charlotte
3-5	Louisville
6-9	Indianapolis
10-13	at Pawtucket
14-16	at Buffalo
18-20	Pawtucket
21-23	Norfolk
25-27	at Toledo
28-30	Louisville
31	at Indianapolis

SEPTEMBER	
1-2	at Indianapolis
3-4	Toledo
5-7	at Toledo

JULY	
1	Charlotte
2-3	at Norfolk
4-6	Norfolk
7-9	Charlotte
10-12	at Toledo
16-19	at Indianapolis
20-23	Pawtucket
24-26	Louisville
28-30	at Pawtucket
31	at Lehigh Valley

16-17	Louisville
18-19	at Louisville
20-22	Indianapolis
24-26	at Durham

19-21	Indianapolis
22-25	Columbus
26-28	at Norfolk
29-31	at Durham

JUNE	
2-4	Scranton/WB
5-7	Rochester
9-11	at Scranton/WB
12-14	at Rochester
15-17	Durham
18-21	Charlotte
23-25	at Indianapolis
26-28	at Columbus

29-30 . . . . Norfolk	3-5 . . . . Charlotte
	6-9 . . . . Durham
JULY	10-13 . . . . .at Toledo
1 . . . . Norfolk	14-16 . . . . . . .at Louisville
2-3 . . . . at Charlotte	18-20 . . . . . Lehigh Valley
4-6 . . . . Charlotte	21-23 . . . . Buffalo
7-9 . . . . at Columbus	25-27 . . . . . . .at Durham
10-12 . . . . Norfolk	28-30 . . . . . . at Norfolk
16-19 . . . . . . at Charlotte	31 . . . . Durham
20-23 . . . . . . Louisville	
24-26 . . . . . . Pawtucket	**SEPTEMBER**
28-30 . . . . . . at Buffalo	1-2 . . . . Durham
31 . . . . . . at Pawtucket	3-4 . . . . Charlotte
	5-7 . . . . . . .at Charlotte
AUGUST	
1-2 . . . . . . at Pawtucket	

INDIANAPOLIS INDIANS

APRIL	**JULY**
9-12 . . . . Toledo	1 . . . . .at Toledo
13-15 . . . . Columbus	2-3 . . . . at Louisville
16-19 . . . . .at Toledo	4-6 . . . . Louisville
20-22 . . . . at Columbus	7-9 . . . . Toledo
24-26 . . . . Norfolk	10-12 . . . . . at Charlotte
27-30 . . . . . .at Charlotte	16-19 . . . . . . Columbus
	20-23 . . . . . at Rochester
MAY	24-26 . . . . at Scranton/WB
1-3 . . . . at Norfolk	28-30 . . . . . Rochester
5-7 . . . . Buffalo	31 . . . . Scranton/WB
8-10 . . . . . . Lehigh Valley	
11-14 . . . . . at Columbus	**AUGUST**
15-17 . . . . Louisville	1-2 . . . . Scranton/WB
19-21 . . . . . .at Gwinnett	3-5 . . . . Toledo
22-25 . . . . . . .at Durham	6-9 . . . . . at Columbus
26-28 . . . . Toledo	10-13 . . . . at Lehigh Valley
29-31 . . . . Louisville	14-16 . . . . . at Pawtucket
	18-20 . . . . Norfolk
JUNE	21-23 . . . . . . .Pawtucket
2-4 . . . . at Syracuse	25-27 . . . . at Louisville
5-7 . . . . at Buffalo	28-30 . . . . . . .at Toledo
9-11 . . . . Syracuse	31 . . . . Columbus
12-14 . . . . . . Charlotte	
15-17 . . . . Columbus	**SEPTEMBER**
18-21 . . . . at Louisville	1-2 . . . . Columbus
23-25 . . . . . . Gwinnett	3-4 . . . . Louisville
26-28 . . . . . . Durham	5-7 . . . . . . .at Louisville
29-30 . . . . .at Toledo	

LEHIGH VALLEY IRONPIGS

APRIL	**JULY**
9-12 . . . . . . at Rochester	1 . . . . at Buffalo
13-16 at Scranton/Wilkes-Barre	2-3 . . . . Rochester
17-19 . . . . . . .Pawtucket	4-6 . . . . . . at Rochester
20-22 . . . . . . Rochester	7-9 . . . . . . at Pawtucket
24-26 . . . . . at Pawtucket	10-12 Scranton/Wilkes-Barre
27-30 . . . . . . Louisville	16-19 . . . . . Rochester
	20-23 . . . . . . .at Toledo
MAY	24-26 . . . . . at Columbus
1-3 . . . . Gwinnett	28-30 . . . . Toledo
5-7 . . . . . at Louisville	31 . . . . Durham
8-10 . . . . . at Indianapolis	
11-14 Scranton/Wilkes-Barre	**AUGUST**
15-17 . . . . . . at Buffalo	1-2 . . . . Durham
19-21 . . . . Syracuse	3-6 . . . . at Syracuse
22-25 . . . . Buffalo	7-9 at Scranton/Wilkes-Barre
26-28 . . . . at Syracuse	10-13 . . . . . .Indianapolis
29-31 . . . . . at Pawtucket	14-16 . . . . . Charlotte
	18-20 . . . . . at Gwinnett
JUNE	21-22 . . . . .at Charlotte
2-4 . . . . Columbus	25-27 . . . . . . at Buffalo
5-7 . . . . Norfolk	28-30 . . . . . . .Pawtucket
9-11 . . . . t Durham	31 . . . . Syracuse
12-14 . . . . . at Norfolk	
15-17 . . . . . .Pawtucket	**SEPTEMBER**
18-21 . . . . . at Syracuse	1-2 . . . . Syracuse
23-25 . . . . Buffalo	3-4 at Scranton/Wilkes-Barre
26-28 . . . . . Syracuse	5-7 . . Scranton/Wilkes-Barre
29-30 . . . . . . at Buffalo	

LOUISVILLE BATS

APRIL	29-30 . . . . Columbus
9-10 . . . . . . at Columbus	**JULY**
11-12 . . . . . . Columbus	1 . . . . Columbus
13-15 . . . . Toledo	2-3 . . . . .Indianapolis
16-17 . . . . at Columbus	4-6 . . . . . at Indianapolis
18-19 . . . . . . Columbus	7-9 . . . . . . at Norfolk
20-22 . . . . . . .at Toledo	10-12 . . . . . . Columbus
24-26 . . . . . . Charlotte	16-19 . . . . Toledo
27-30 . . . . at Lehigh Valley	20-23 . . . . . at Gwinnett
MAY	24-26 . . . . . .at Durham
1-3 . . . . at Buffalo	28-30 . . . . . Scranton/WB
5-7 . . . . . Lehigh Valley	31 . . . . Rochester
8-10 . . . . Buffalo	**AUGUST**
11-14 . . . . . . .at Toledo	1-2 . . . . Rochester
15-17 . . . . at Indianapolis	3-5 . . . . . . at Columbus
19-21 . . . . . . Charlotte	6-9 . . . . .at Toledo
22-25 . . . . Norfolk	10-13 . . . . . . Syracuse
26-28 . . . . at Columbus	14-16 . . . . . Gwinnett
29-31 . . . . at Indianapolis	18-20 . . . . . at Syracuse
JUNE	21-23 . . . . at Rochester
2-4 . . . . .Pawtucket	25-27 . . . . .Indianapolis
5-7 . . . . Durham	28-30 . . . . at Columbus
9-11 . . . . . at Pawtucket	31 . . . . Toledo
12-14 . . . . at Scranton/WB	**SEPTEMBER**
15-17 . . . . Toledo	1-2 . . . . Toledo
18-21 . . . . . .Indianapolis	3-4 . . . . . at Indianapolis
23-25 . . . . at Charlotte	5-7 . . . . . . .Indianapolis
26-28 . . . . . at Norfolk	

NORFOLK TIDES

APRIL	**JULY**
9-12 . . . . Gwinnett	1 . . . . at Gwinnett
13-15 . . . . . . Charlotte	2-3 . . . . Durham
16-19 . . . . . at Gwinnett	4-6 . . . . .at Durham
20-22 . . . . . .at Charlotte	7-9 . . . . Louisville
24-26 . . . . at Indianapolis	10-12 . . . . . at Gwinnett
27-30 . . . . . . .Pawtucket	16-19 . . . . Durham
MAY	20-23 . . . . at Scranton/WB
1-3 . . . . . . .Indianapolis	24-26 . . . . . at Syracuse
5-7 . . . . . . at Pawtucket	28-30 . . . . . Columbus
8-10 . . . . . . at Rochester	31 . . . . Syracuse
11-14 . . . . . . Gwinnett	**AUGUST**
15-17 . . . . Durham	1-2 . . . . Syracuse
19-21 . . . . . . .at Toledo	3-5 . . . . .at Durham
22-25 . . . . at Louisville	6-9 . . . . at Charlotte
26-28 . . . . . . Gwinnett	10-13 . . . . . Scranton/WB
29-31 . . . . . . Charlotte	14-16 . . . . Rochester
JUNE	18-20 . . . . at Indianapolis
2-4 . . . . at Buffalo	21-23 . . . . at Columbus
5-7 . . . . at Lehigh Valley	25-27 . . . . . Charlotte
9-11 . . . . Buffalo	28-30 . . . . . Gwinnett
12-14 . . . . . Lehigh Valley	31 . . . . .at Charlotte
15-17 . . . . at Charlotte	**SEPTEMBER**
18-21 . . . . . at Durham	1-2 . . . . . . .at Charlotte
23-25 . . . . Toledo	3-4 . . . . .at Durham
26-28 . . . . . . Louisville	5-7 . . . . Durham
29-30 . . . . at Gwinnett	

PAWTUCKET RED SOX

APRIL	8-10 . . . . Charlotte
9-12 . . . . Syracuse	11-14 . . . . at Buffalo
13-16 . . . . Buffalo	15-17 . . . . at Syracuse
17-19 . . . . at Lehigh Valley	19-21 . . . . . Rochester
20-22 . . . . at Syracuse	22-25 . . . . Syracuse
24-26 . . . . . Lehigh Valley	26-28 . . . . . at Rochester
27-30 . . . . at Norfolk	29-31 . . . . Lehigh Valley
MAY	**JUNE**
1-3 . . . . .at Charlotte	2-4 . . . . at Louisville
5-7 . . . . .Norfolk	5-7 . . . . .at Toledo

9-11 . . . . Louisville
12-14 . . . . Toledo
15-17 . . . at Lehigh Valley
18-21 . . . . at Buffalo
23-25 . . . . Rochester
26-28 . . . . Buffalo
29-30 . . . . . at Rochester

JULY
1 . . . . at Rochester
2-3 . . . . . . Scranton/WB
4-6 . . . . at Scranton/WB
7-9 . . . . . Lehigh Valley
10-12 . . . . . at Syracuse
16-19 . . . . Scranton/WB
20-23 . . . . . . .at Durham
24-26 . . . at Gwinnett
28-30 . . . . . . Durham

ROCHESTER RED WINGS

APRIL
9-12 . . . . . Lehigh Valley
13-15 . . . . Syracuse
17-19 . . . . . . at Buffalo
20-22 . . at Lehigh Valley
24-26 . . . . Buffalo
27-30 . . . . . at Columbus

MAY
1-3 . . . . .at Toledo
5-7 . . . . Columbus
8-10 . . . . Norfolk
11-14 . . . . . at Syracuse
15-17 . . . Scranton/WB
19-21 . . . . at Pawtucket
22-25 . . at Scranton/WB
26-28 . . . . . .Pawtucket
29-31 . . . . Buffalo

JUNE
2-4 . . . . . . at Charlotte
5-7 . . . . . . at Gwinnett
9-11 . . . . Toledo
12-14 . . . . . . Gwinnett
15-17 . . . . at Syracuse
18-21 . . . . Scranton/WB
23-25 . . . at Pawtucket
26-28 . . at Scranton/WB
29-30 . . . . . Pawtucket

SCRANTON/WILKES-BARRE RAILRIDERS

APRIL
9-12 . . . . Buffalo
13-16 . . . . Lehigh Valley
17-19 . . . . . at Syracuse
20-22 . . . . . at Buffalo
24-26 . . . . . . Syracuse
27-30 . . . . . . .at Toledo

MAY
1-3 . . . . . . at Columbus
5-7 . . . . Charlotte
8-10 . . . . Columbus
11-14 . . at Lehigh Valley
15-17 . . . at Rochester
19-21 . . . . Buffalo
22-25 . . . . . Rochester
26-28 . . . . at Buffalo
29-31 . . . . . . Syracuse

JUNE
2-4 . . . . . .at Gwinnett
5-7 . . . . . . .at Charlotte
9-11 . . . . . . Gwinnett
12-14 . . . . . . Louisville

31 . . . . Gwinnett

AUGUST
1-2 . . . . Gwinnett
3-6 . . . . at Scranton/WB
7-9 . . . . . . at Rochester
10-13 . . . . . Columbus
14-16 . . . . . .Indianapolis
18-20 . . . . at Columbus
21-23 . . . at Indianapolis
25-27 . . . . Scranton/WB
28-30 . . at Lehigh Valley
31 . . . . Buffalo

SEPTEMBER
1-2 . . . . Buffalo
3-4 . . . . . at Rochester
5-7 . . . . Syracuse

JULY
1 . . . . .Pawtucket
2-3 . . . at Lehigh Valley
4-6 . . . . Lehigh Valley
7-9 . . . . Syracuse
10-12 . . . . at Buffalo
16-19 . . at Lehigh Valley
20-23 . . . . .Indianapolis
24-26 . . . . . Charlotte
28-30 . . at Indianapolis
31 . . . . .at Louisville

AUGUST
1-2 . . . . . at Louisville
3-5 . . . . . . at Buffalo
6 . . . . Buffalo
7-9 . . . . . . .Pawtucket
10-13 . . .at Durham
14-16 . . . . at Norfolk
18-20 . . . . Durham
21-23 . . . . . Louisville
24-27 . . . . . Syracuse
28-30 . . . . at Buffalo
31 . . . . at Scranton/WB

SEPTEMBER
1-2 . . . . at Scranton/WB
3-4 . . . . . .Pawtucket
5-7 . . . . Buffalo

15-17 . . . . . at Buffalo
18-21 . . . . at Rochester
23-25 . . . . . Syracuse
26-28 . . . . . . Rochester
29-30 . . . . . at Syracuse

JULY
1 . . . . at Syracuse
2-3 . . . . . at Pawtucket
4-6 . . . . . . .Pawtucket
7-9 . . . . Buffalo
10-12 . . at Lehigh Valley
16-19 . . . . at Pawtucket
20-23 . . . . . . .Norfolk
24-26 . . . . .Indianapolis
28-30 . . . .at Louisville
31 . . . . at Indianapolis

AUGUST
1-2 . . . at Indianapolis
3-6 . . . . . . .Pawtucket
7-9 . . . . . Lehigh Valley
10-13 . . . . at Norfolk
14-16 . . . .at Durham
18-20 . . . . Toledo

21-23 . . . . Durham
25-27 . . . . at Pawtucket
28-30 . . . . . at Syracuse
31 . . . . Rochester

SYRACUSE METS

APRIL
9-12 . . . . at Pawtucket
13-15 . . . . . at Rochester
17-19 . . . . Scranton/WB
20-22 . . . . . .Pawtucket
24-26 . . at Scranton/WB
27-30 . . . . . Gwinnett

MAY
1-3 . . . . Durham
5-7 . . . . . . .at Gwinnett
8-10 . . . . .at Durham
11-14 . . . . . . Rochester
15-17 . . . . . .Pawtucket
19-21 . . at Lehigh Valley
22-25 . . . . at Pawtucket
26-28 . . . . Lehigh Valley
29-31 . . . at Scranton/WB

JUNE
2-4 . . . . . . .Indianapolis
5-7 . . . . Columbus
9-11 . . . . at Indianapolis
12-14 . . . . at Columbus
15-17 . . . . . . Rochester
18-21 . . . . Lehigh Valley
23-25 . . . at Scranton/WB
26-28 . . at Lehigh Valley
29-30 . . . . Scranton/WB

TOLEDO MUD HENS

APRIL
9-12 . . . . . at Indianapolis
13-15 . . . . .at Louisville
16-19 . . . . .Indianapolis
20-22 . . . . . . Louisville
24-26 . . . . . .at Gwinnett
27-30 . . . . Scranton/WB

MAY
1-3 . . . . Rochester
5-7 . . . . .at Durham
8-10 . . . . . . .at Gwinnett
11-14 . . . . . . Louisville
15-17 . . . at Columbus
19-21 . . . . .Norfolk
22-25 . . . . . . Charlotte
26-28 . . . . at Indianapolis
29-31 . . . . . at Columbus

JUNE
2-4 . . . . Durham
5-7 . . . . .Pawtucket
9-11 . . . . . . at Rochester
12-14 . . . . at Pawtucket
15-17 . . . .at Louisville
18-21 . . . . . Columbus
23-25 . . . . . at Norfolk
26-28 . . . at Charlotte
29-30 . . . .Indianapolis

SEPTEMBER
1-2 . . . . Rochester
3-4 . . . . . Lehigh Valley
5-7 . . . . at Lehigh Valley

JULY
1 . . . . Scranton/WB
2-3 . . . . at Buffalo
4-6 . . . . Buffalo
7-9 . . . . . . at Rochester
10-12 . . . . .Pawtucket
16-19 . . . . . at Buffalo
20-23 . . . . . . Charlotte
24-26 . . . . . . Norfolk
28-30 . . . at Charlotte
31 . . . . at Norfolk

AUGUST
1-2 . . . . . . at Norfolk
3-6 . . . . Lehigh Valley
7-9 . . . . Buffalo
10-13 . . . . at Louisville
14-16 . . . . . .at Toledo
18-20 . . . . . Louisville
21-23 . . . . Toledo
24-27 . . . . at Rochester
28-30 . . . Scranton/WB
31 . . . . at Lehigh Valley

SEPTEMBER
1-2 . . . . at Lehigh Valley
3-4 . . . . Buffalo
5-7 . . . . . . at Pawtucket

JULY
1 . . . . .Indianapolis
2-3 . . . . Columbus
4-6 . . . . . at Columbus
7-9 . . . . at Indianapolis
10-12 . . . . . . Durham
16-19 . . . . .at Louisville
20-23 . . . . Lehigh Valley
24-26 . . . . Buffalo
28-30 . . . at Lehigh Valley
31 . . . . at Buffalo

AUGUST
1-2 . . . . . . at Buffalo
3-5 . . . . .at Indianapolis
6-9 . . . . Louisville
10-13 . . . . . . Gwinnett
14-16 . . . . . Syracuse
18-20 . . at Scranton/WB
21-23 . . . . . Syracuse
25-27 . . . . . Columbus
28-30 . . . .Indianapolis
31 . . . . . .at Louisville

SEPTEMBER
1-2 . . . . . .at Louisville
3-4 . . . . . . at Columbus
5-7 . . . . Columbus

PACIFIC COAST LEAGUE

ALBUQUERQUE ISOTOPES

APRIL
10-14 . . . . . . .at Las Vegas
15-17 . . . . Salt Lake
18-20 . . . . Las Vegas
22-24 . . . . .at Reno
25-27 . . . . . at Tacoma
30 . . . . Reno

MAY
2-3 . . . . Reno
5-7 . . . . .at Fresno
9-11 . . . . . . Las Vegas
13-16 . . . . El Paso
17-19 . . . . .at Fresno
22-25 . . . . at Sacramento
27-30 . . . . .Tacoma
31 . . . . at El Paso

JUNE
1-3 . . . . at El Paso
4-7 . . . . .Salt Lake
10-12 . . . . . .at Okla. City
13-15 . . . . . . .at Wichita
18-20 . . . . Memphis

21-23 . . . . .Nashville
26-29 . . . . .at Reno

JULY
1-4 . . . . at Tacoma
5-8 . . . . El Paso
9-12 . . . . . . .Sacramento
17-19 . . . . at Salt Lake
21-24 . . . . Fresno
25-27 . . . .at Las Vegas
29-31 . . . . .Omaha

AUGUST
1-4 . . . . Iowa
6-8 . . . . at San Antonio
9-12 . . . . at Round Rock
14-17 . . . . .Tacoma
18-21 . . . . . at El Paso
22-24 . . . . . Sacramento
26-28 . . . . Reno
29-30 . . . . at Sacramento

SEPTEMBER
1-4 . . . . . at Salt Lake
5-7 . . . . Fresno

EL PASO CHIHUAHUAS

APRIL
10-14 . . . . . . at Salt Lake
15-17 . . . . Las Vegas
18-20 . . . . Salt Lake
22-24 . . . . .at Tacoma
25-27 . . . . . .at Reno
30 . . . . .Tacoma

MAY
1-3 . . . . .Tacoma
5-8 . . . . .at Las Vegas
9-12 . . . . . . .Sacramento
13-16 . . . at Albuquerque
17-19 . . . . .Salt Lake
22-25 . . . . .at Fresno
27-30 . . . at Sacramento
31 . . . . Albuquerque

JUNE
1-3 . . . . . . Albuquerque
4-8 . . . . Las Vegas
10-12 . . . . at Wichita
13-16 . . . . . .at Okla. City
18-20 . . . . .Nashville
21-24 . . . . Memphis

26-30 . . . . at Tacoma

JULY
1-4 . . . . Reno
5-8 . . at Albuquerque
9-13 . . . . Fresno
17-20 . . . . .at Las Vegas
21-24 . . . . . . .Sacramento
25-26 . . . . at Salt Lake
29-31 . . . . Iowa

AUGUST
1-4 . . . . Omaha
6-8 . . . . at Round Rock
9-12 . . . . . at San Antonio
14-17 . . . . Reno
18-21 . . . . . Albuquerque
22-24 . . . . . . .at Fresno
26-28 . . . . .Tacoma
29-31 . . . . Fresno

SEPTEMBER
1-4 . . . . .at Reno
5-7 . . . . at Sacramento

FRESNO GRIZZLIES

APRIL
10-14 . . . . . . .at Tacoma
15-17 . . . . Reno
18-20 . . . . .Tacoma
22-23 . . . . . at Salt Lake
25-28 . . . . .at Las Vegas
30 . . . . .Salt Lake

MAY
1-3 . . . . Salt Lake
5-7 . . . . . . Albuquerque
9-11 . . . . .at Reno
13-16 . . . . at Sacramento
17-19 . . . . . Albuquerque
22-25 . . . . El Paso
27-30 . . . . .at Reno
31 . . . . .Sacramento

JUNE
2-3 . . . . .Sacramento

4-7 . . . . Reno
10-12 . . . . . at Nashville
13-15 . . . . . .at Memphis
18-20 . . . . .Wichita
21-24 . . . . Okla. City
26-30 . . . . at Salt Lake

JULY
1-4 . . . . . . .at Las Vegas
5-6 . . . . . . .Sacramento
9-13 . . . . at El Paso
17-20 . . . . .Tacoma
21-24 . . . at Albuquerque
25-26 . . . . . . at Tacoma
29-31 . . . . . .Round Rock

AUGUST
1-4 . . . . . . San Antonio
6-8 . . . . .at Iowa
9-11 . . . . at Omaha

IOWA CUBS

APRIL
9-13 . . . . at Nashville
14-16 . . . . . San Antonio
18-20 . . . . . . Round Rock
22-24 . . . . at San Antonio
25-27 . . . . at Round Rock
29-30 . . . . .Nashville

MAY
2-3 . . . . .Nashville
4-7 . . . . Okla. City
9-11 . . . . at Omaha
13-16 . . . . .at Okla. City
17-19 . . . . .Omaha
22-25 . . . . at San Antonio
27-30 . . . . . at Wichita
31 . . . . .Round Rock

JUNE
2 . . . . .Round Rock
4-7 . . . . .Wichita
10-12 . . . .at Las Vegas
13-16 . . . . at Salt Lake
18-20 . . . . Reno
21-23 . . . . .Tacoma

26-29 . . . . . .at Memphis

JULY
1-4 . . . . at Omaha
5-7 . . . . Memphis
9-12 . . . . . San Antonio
17-19 . . . . . at Round Rock
21-24 . . . . .at Okla. City
25-26 . . . . .Wichita
29-31 . . . . . . at El Paso

AUGUST
1-4 . . . . at Albuquerque
6-8 . . . . Fresno
9-11 . . . . . . .Sacramento
14-16 . . . . . at Wichita
18-19 . . . . . .Nashville
21-23 . . . . . . Memphis
26-28 . . . . at Nashville
29-30 . . . . .at Memphis

SEPTEMBER
1-3 . . . . Okla. City
5-7 . . . . .Omaha

LAS VEGAS AVIATORS

APRIL
10-14 . . . . . Albuquerque
15-17 . . . . at El Paso
18-20 . . . . at Albuquerque
22-24 . . . . . Sacramento
25-28 . . . . Fresno
30 . . . . . . at Sacramento

MAY
1-3 . . . . . at Sacramento
5-8 . . . . El Paso
9-11 . . . . at Albuquerque
13-16 . . . . . . Salt Lake
16-19 . . . . . . .at Reno
22-25 . . . . .Tacoma
27-30 . . . . at Salt Lake
31 . . . . Reno

JUNE
2-3 . . . . Reno
4-8 . . . . at El Paso
10-12 . . . . Iowa
13-16 . . . . .Omaha
18-20 . . . . . at Round Rock
21-24 . . . .at San Antonio

26-30 . . . . . .Sacramento

JULY
1-4 . . . . Fresno
5-7 . . . . at Salt Lake
9-12 . . . . . . .at Tacoma
17-20 . . . . . . El Paso
21-24 . . . . .at Reno
25-27 . . . . Albuquerque
29-31 . . . . . . at Wichita

AUGUST
1-4 . . . .at Okla. City
6-8 . . . . .Nashville
9-12 . . . . . . Memphis
14-17 . . . . . . .at Fresno
18-21 . . . . Reno
22-23 . . . . . . at Tacoma
26-28 . . . . at Sacramento
29-31 . . . . .Tacoma

SEPTEMBER
1-4 . . . . .at Fresno
5-7 . . . . Salt Lake

MEMPHIS REDBIRDS

APRIL
10-13 . . . . .Omaha
15-17 . . . . . . at Wichita
18-20 . . . .at Okla. City
21-24 . . . . .Wichita
25-27 . . . . . Okla. City
29-30 . . . . . at Omaha

MAY
2-3 . . . . . . at Omaha
5-8 . . . . at Round Rock
9-11 . . . . . San Antonio
12-16 . . . . .Round Rock
16-19 . . . . . . at Nashville

22-25 . . . . .Wichita
26-29 . . . . .Nashville
31 . . . . .at Okla. City

JUNE
2-3 . . . . . at Okla. City
4-7 . . . .at San Antonio
9-12 . . . . . . .Sacramento
13-15 . . . . Fresno
18-20 . . . . at Albuquerque
21-24 . . . . . at El Paso
26-29 . . . . Iowa
30 . . . . San Antonio

JULY
1-3	San Antonio
5-7	at Iowa
9-12	at Wichita
17-19	Okla. City
21-24	at Nashville
25-26	at San Antonio
28-31	Tacoma

AUGUST
1-3	Reno

6-8	at Salt Lake
9-12	at Las Vegas
14-16	Round Rock
18-20	at Omaha
21-23	at Iowa
25-28	Omaha
29-30	Iowa

SEPTEMBER
1-4	at Round Rock
5-7	Nashville

NASHVILLE SOUNDS

APRIL
9-13	Iowa
15-17	at Okla. City
18-20	at Wichita
21-23	Okla. City
24-27	Wichita
29-30	at Iowa

MAY
2-3	at Iowa
4-7	San Antonio
8-11	Round Rock
12-16	at Omaha
16-19	Memphis
21-25	Okla. City
26-29	at Memphis
30-31	at Wichita

JUNE
2	at Wichita
4-7	at Round Rock
10-12	Fresno
13-16	Sacramento
18-20	at El Paso
21-23	at Albuquerque

26-30	Omaha

JULY
1-4	Round Rock
4-8	at San Antonio
9-12	at Okla. City
17-19	Wichita
21-24	Memphis
25-26	at Round Rock
29-31	Reno

AUGUST
1-4	Tacoma
6-8	at Las Vegas
9-12	at Salt Lake
14-16	San Antonio
18-19	at Iowa
21-23	at Omaha
26-28	Iowa
29-30	Omaha

SEPTEMBER
1-4	at San Antonio
5-7	at Memphis

OKLAHOMA CITY DODGERS

APRIL
10-13	at San Antonio
15-17	Nashville
18-20	Memphis
21-23	at Nashville
25-27	at Memphis
30	San Antonio

MAY
1-3	San Antonio
4-7	at Iowa
9-11	Wichita
13-16	Iowa
16-19	at Wichita
21-25	at Nashville
27-30	Omaha
31	Memphis

JUNE
2-3	Memphis
4-7	at Omaha
10-12	Albuquerque
13-16	El Paso
18-20	at Sacramento
21-24	at Fresno

26-30	Round Rock

JULY
1-4	Wichita
5-8	at Round Rock
9-12	Nashville
17-19	at Memphis
21-24	Iowa
25-26	at Omaha
29-31	Salt Lake

AUGUST
1-4	Las Vegas
6-8	at Tacoma
9-12	at Reno
14-16	at Omaha
18-20	at San Antonio
21-23	at Round Rock
26-28	San Antonio
29-30	Round Rock

SEPTEMBER
1-3	at Iowa
5-7	at Wichita

OMAHA STORM CHASERS

APRIL
10-13	at Memphis
14-16	Round Rock
18-20	San Antonio
22-24	at Round Rock
25-27	at San Antonio
29-30	Memphis

MAY
2-3	Memphis
5-8	at Wichita
9-11	Iowa
12-16	Nashville
17-19	at Iowa
22-25	at Round Rock
27-30	at Okla. City
31	San Antonio

JUNE
2	San Antonio
4-7	Okla. City
10-11	at Salt Lake
13-16	at Las Vegas
18-20	Tacoma
21-23	Reno

26-30	at Nashville

JULY
1-4	Iowa
4-8	at Wichita
9-12	Round Rock
17-19	at San Antonio
21-24	Wichita
25-26	Okla. City
29-31	at Albuquerque

AUGUST
1-4	at El Paso
6-8	Sacramento
9-11	Fresno
14-16	at Okla. City
18-20	Memphis
21-23	Nashville
25-28	at Memphis
29-30	at Nashville

SEPTEMBER
1-4	Wichita
5-7	at Iowa

RENO ACES

APRIL
9-13	Sacramento
15-17	at Fresno
18-20	at Sacramento
22-24	Albuquerque
25-27	El Paso
30	at Albuquerque

MAY
2-3	at Albuquerque
5-8	Tacoma
9-11	Fresno
13-16	at Tacoma
16-19	Las Vegas
22-25	at Salt Lake
27-30	Fresno
31	at Las Vegas

JUNE
2-3	at Las Vegas
4-7	at Fresno
10-12	Round Rock
13-16	San Antonio
18-20	at Iowa

21-23	at Omaha
26-29	Albuquerque

JULY
1-4	at El Paso
5-8	Tacoma
9-12	Salt Lake
17-19	at Sacramento
21-24	Las Vegas
25-26	Sacramento
29-31	at Nashville

AUGUST
1-3	at Memphis
6-8	Wichita
9-12	Okla. City
14-17	at El Paso
18-21	at Las Vegas
22-23	Salt Lake
26-28	at Albuquerque
29-30	at Salt Lake

SEPTEMBER
1-4	at El Paso
5-7	at Tacoma

ROUND ROCK EXPRESS

APRIL
10-13	Wichita
14-16	at Omaha
18-20	at Iowa
22-24	Omaha
25-27	Iowa
30	at Wichita

MAY
1-3	at Wichita
5-8	Memphis
8-11	at Nashville
12-16	at Memphis
16-20	San Antonio
22-25	Omaha
27-30	at San Antonio
31	at Iowa

JUNE
2	at Iowa

4-7	Nashville
10-12	at Reno
13-16	at Tacoma
18-20	Las Vegas
21-24	Salt Lake
26-30	at Okla. City

JULY
1-4	at Nashville
5-8	Okla. City
9-12	at Omaha
17-19	Iowa
21-24	at San Antonio
25-26	Nashville
29-31	at Fresno

AUGUST
1-3	at Sacramento
6-8	El Paso
9-12	Albuquerque

14-16 . . . . . . .at Memphis
18-20 . . . . .Wichita
21-23 . . . . Okla. City
26-28 . . . . . . at Wichita

29-30 . . . . . . .at Okla. City

SEPTEMBER
1-4 . . . . Memphis
5-7 . . . . . . San Antonio

SACRAMENTO RIVER CATS

APRIL
9-13 . . . . .at Reno
15-17 . . . . . . .Tacoma
18-20 . . . . Reno
22-24 . . . .at Las Vegas
25-28 . . . . . at Salt Lake
30 . . . . Las Vegas

MAY
1-3 . . . . Las Vegas
5-7 . . . . . . at Salt Lake
9-12 . . . . . . at El Paso
13-16 . . . . Fresno
17-19 . . . . . at Tacoma
22-25 . . . .Albuquerque
27-30 . . . . El Paso
31 . . . . .at Fresno

JUNE
2-3 . . . . .at Fresno
4-7 . . . . .Tacoma
9-12 . . . . . at Memphis
13-16 . . . . at Nashville
18-20 . . . . . Okla. City

21-23 . . . . .Wichita
26-30 . . . . . .at Las Vegas

JULY
1-4 . . . . .Salt Lake
5-6 . . . . .at Fresno
9-12 . . . . at Albuquerque
17-19 . . . . Reno
21-24 . . . . . . at El Paso
25-26 . . . . .at Reno
29-31 . . . . . San Antonio

AUGUST
1-3 . . . . .Round Rock
6-8 . . . . . . at Omaha
9-11 . . . . .at Iowa
14-16 . . . . . . .Salt Lake
18-21 . . . . Fresno
22-24 . . . .at Albuquerque
26-28 . . . . . Las Vegas
29-30 . . . . Albuquerque

SEPTEMBER
1-4 . . . . .at Tacoma
5-7 . . . . .El Paso

SALT LAKE BEES

APRIL
10-14 . . . . El Paso
15-17 . . . . at Albuquerque
18-20 . . . . . . at El Paso
22-23 . . . . Fresno
25-28 . . . . . .Sacramento
30 . . . . .at Fresno

MAY
1-3 . . . . .at Fresno
5-7 . . . . .Sacramento
9-12 . . . . .Tacoma
13-16 . . . . . .at Las Vegas
17-19 . . . . . at El Paso
22-25 . . . . Reno
27-30 . . . . . . Las Vegas
31 . . . . at Tacoma

JUNE
2 . . . . .at Tacoma
4-7 . . . . at Albuquerque
10-11 . . . . .Omaha
13-16 . . . . Iowa
18-20 . . . . at San Antonio
21-24 . . . . at Round Rock

26-30 . . . . Fresno

JULY
1-4 . . . . . at Sacramento
5-7 . . . . Las Vegas
9-12 . . . . .at Reno
17-19 . . . . . Albuquerque
21-24 . . . . at Tacoma
25-26 . . . . El Paso
29-31 . . . . . .at Okla. City

AUGUST
1-3 . . . . at Wichita
6-8 . . . . Memphis
9-12 . . . . .Nashville
14-16 . . . . at Sacramento
18-21 . . . . .Tacoma
22-23 . . . . . .at Reno
26-28 . . . .at Fresno
29-30 . . . . Reno

SEPTEMBER
1-4 . . . . Albuquerque
5-7 . . . . . . .at Las Vegas

SAN ANTONIO MISSIONS

APRIL
10-13 . . . . . . Okla. City
14-16 . . . . at Iowa
18-20 . . . . . at Omaha
22-24 . . . . Iowa
25-27 . . . . .Omaha
30 . . . . . . .at Okla. City

MAY
1-3 . . . . . . .at Okla. City
4-7 . . . . at Nashville
9-11 . . . . . . .at Memphis

13-16 . . . . .Wichita
16-20 . . . . . at Round Rock
22-25 . . . . Iowa
27-30 . . . . . .Round Rock
31 . . . . at Omaha

JUNE
2 . . . . .at Omaha
4-7 . . . . Memphis
10-12 . . . . at Tacoma
13-16 . . . . . . .at Reno
18-20 . . . . . .Salt Lake
21-24 . . . . Las Vegas

26-29 . . . . at Wichita
30 . . . . .at Memphis

JULY
1-3 . . . . . . .at Memphis
4-8 . . . . .Nashville
9-12 . . . . at Iowa
17-19 . . . . .Omaha
21-24 . . . . . .Round Rock
25-26 . . . . Memphis
29-31 . . . . . at Sacramento

TACOMA RAINIERS

APRIL
10-14 . . . . Fresno
15-17 . . . . at Sacramento
18-20 . . . . . . .at Fresno
22-24 . . . . . . El Paso
25-27 . . . Albuquerque
30 . . . . at El Paso

MAY
1-3 . . . . at El Paso
5-8 . . . . .at Reno
9-12 . . . . . at Salt Lake
13-16 . . . . Reno
17-19 . . . . . .Sacramento
22-25 . . . .at Las Vegas
27-30 . . . . at Albuquerque
31 . . . . .Salt Lake

JUNE
2 . . . . .Salt Lake
4-7 . . . . at Sacramento
10-12 . . . . . San Antonio
13-16 . . . . . .Round Rock
18-20 . . . . at Omaha

21-23 . . . . .at Iowa
26-30 . . . . El Paso

JULY
1-4 . . . . . . Albuquerque
5-8 . . . . .at Reno
9-12 . . . . . . Las Vegas
17-20 . . . . . .at Fresno
21-24 . . . . . .Salt Lake
25-26 . . . . . . Fresno
28-31 . . . . . .at Memphis

AUGUST
1-4 . . . . . . at Nashville
6-8 . . . . Okla. City
9-11 . . . . .Wichita
14-17 . . . at Albuquerque
18-21 . . . . at Salt Lake
22-23 . . . . . . Las Vegas
26-28 . . . . . at El Paso
29-31 . . . . . .at Las Vegas

SEPTEMBER
1-4 . . . . .Sacramento
5-7 . . . . Reno

WICHITA WIND SURGE

APRIL
9-13 . . . . . at Round Rock
14-16 . . . . Memphis
17-20 . . . . . . .Nashville
21-23 . . . . . .at Memphis
24-27 . . . . . at Nashville
29-30 . . . . . .Round Rock

MAY
1-3 . . . . .Round Rock
4-7 . . . . .Omaha
8-11 . . . . .at Okla. City
12-15 . . . . at San Antonio
16-19 . . . . . Okla. City
21-25 . . . . .at Memphis
26-29 . . . . Iowa
30-31 . . . . .Nashville

JUNE
1-2 . . . . .Nashville
3-7 . . . . .at Iowa
9-11 . . . . El Paso
12-15 . . . . . Albuquerque
17-19 . . . . . .at Fresno
20-23 . . . . at Sacramento
25-29 . . . . . . San Antonio

30 . . . . .at Okla. City

JULY
1-3 . . . . .at Okla. City
4-7 . . . . .Omaha
8-12 . . . . Memphis
16-19 . . . . . . at Nashville
20-23 . . . . . . at Omaha
24-26 . . . . .at Iowa
28-30 . . . . . Las Vegas
31 . . . . .Salt Lake

AUGUST
1-3 . . . . .Salt Lake
5-7 . . . . .at Reno
8-11 . . . . . at Tacoma
13-16 . . . . Iowa
17-19 . . . . at Round Rock
20-23 . . . . at San Antonio
25-27 . . . . .Round Rock
28-30 . . . . . San Antonio
31 . . . . at Omaha

SEPTEMBER
1-3 . . . . at Omaha
4-7 . . . . Okla. City

DOUBLE-A

EASTERN LEAGUE

AKRON RUBBERDUCKS

APRIL
9-11 . . . . . at Binghamton
13-15 . . . . . . at Reading
17-19 . . . . . . Binghamton
20-22 . . . . Altoona
23-26 . . . . at Bowie
27-29 . . . . . at Altoona

MAY
1-3 . . . . Bowie
4-6 . . . . Trenton
7-10 . . . . at Bowie
11-13 . . . . at Erie
14-17 . . . . Bowie
19-21 . . . . . at Altoona
22-25 . . . . . . Richmond
26-28 . . . . Erie
29-31 . . . . . at Reading

JUNE
1-4 . . . . . . Binghamton
5-7 . . . . Harrisburg
9-11 . . . . . . at Hartford
12-14 . . . . . . at Trenton
15-17 . . . New Hampshire
19-22 . . . . at Erie
23-26 . . . . at Binghamton
27-29 . . . . Altoona

30 . . . . Binghamton

JULY
1-3 . . . . . . Binghamton
4-6 . . . . at Bowie
7-9 . . . . Altoona
10-12 . . . . at Erie
16-19 . . . . Erie
20-22 . . . . . at Richmond
23-26 . . . . . at Altoona
27-29 . . . . . Richmond
30-31 . . . . Trenton

AUGUST
1-2 . . . . Trenton
4-6 . . . . . . at Portland
7-9 . . at New Hampshire
11-13 . . . . Portland
14-16 . . . . Hartford
18-20 . . at Harrisburg
21-23 . . . . Reading
24-26 . . . . Erie
27-30 . . . . . at Reading
31 . . . . at Richmond

SEPTEMBER
1-3 . . . . . . at Richmond
4-7 . . . . Erie

ALTOONA CURVE

APRIL
9-11 . . . . Erie
13-15 . . . . . . Richmond
16-19 . . . . at Erie
20-22 . . . . . . at Akron
23-26 . . . . . Harrisburg
27-29 . . . . Akron

MAY
1-3 . . . . . . at Harrisburg
4-6 . . . . . . at Richmond
7-10 . . . . Erie
11-13 . . . . Hartford
14-17 . . at Harrisburg
19-21 . . . . Akron
22-25 . . . . at Erie
26-28 . . . . at Richmond
29-31 . . . . . . Portland

JUNE
2-4 . . . . . . at Reading
5-7 . . . . at Trenton
9-11 . . . . Reading
12-14 . . . New Hampshire
16-18 . . . . at Hartford
19-22 . . . . Reading
23-26 . . . . Erie
27-29 . . . . at Akron
30 . . . . . . at Harrisburg

JULY
1-3 . . . . . at Harrisburg
4-6 . . . . Erie
7-9 . . . . at Akron
10-12 . . . . Bowie
16-19 . . . . . at Bowie
20-22 . . . . . at Trenton
23-26 . . . . . . Akron
27-29 . . . . . . Trenton
30-31 . . . . . at Bowie

AUGUST
1-2 . . . . . . at Bowie
4-6 . . . . Hartford
7-9 . . . . at Binghamton
11-13 . . . . . Harrisburg
14-16 . . . . . Richmond
18-20 . . . . at Portland
21-23 . . at New Hampshire
24-26 . . . . . at Bowie
27-30 . . . . Binghamton
31 . . . . Harrisburg

SEPTEMBER
1-3 . . . . Harrisburg
4-7 . . . . . . at Richmond

BINGHAMTON RUMBLE PONIES

APRIL
9-11 . . . . Akron
13-15 . . . . Portland
17-19 . . . . at Akron
20-21 . . . . at Erie
23-26 . . . New Hampshire

27-29 . . . . Erie

MAY
1-3 . . . at New Hampshire
4-6 . . . . . . at Portland
7-10 . . . . New Hampshire

11-13 . . . . . . Richmond
14-17 . . at New Hampshire
19-21 . . . . . . Harrisburg
22-25 . . . . Reading
26-28 . . . . . . at Trenton
29-31 . . . . . . at Bowie

JUNE
1-4 . . . . at Akron
5-7 . . . . Bowie
9-11 . . . . Trenton
12-14 . . . . at Richmond
16-18 . . . . at Harrisburg
19-22 . . . . Portland
23-26 . . . . Akron
27-29 . . . . . at Erie
30 . . . . at Akron

JULY
1-3 . . . . at Akron
4-6 . . . . Hartford
7-9 . . . . Erie
10-12 . . . at Portland

BOWIE BAYSOX

APRIL
9-11 . . . . Richmond
13-15 . . . . Erie
16-19 . . . . at Richmond
20-22 . . . . at Harrisburg
23-26 . . . . Akron
27-29 . . . . . Harrisburg

MAY
1-3 . . . . at Akron
4-6 . . . . at Erie
7-10 . . . . Akron
11-13 . . . . . Harrisburg
14-17 . . . . . . at Akron
19-21 . . . . . . Richmond
22-25 . . . . at Harrisburg
26-28 . . . . . at Hartford
29-31 . . . . . Binghamton

JUNE
2-4 . . . . at Trenton
5-7 . . . . at Binghamton
9-11 . . . . Harrisburg
12-14 . . . . Portland
15-17 . . . . at Erie
19-22 . . . . . . Hartford
23-26 . . . . . Harrisburg
27-29 . . . . . at Reading

30 . . . . at Erie

JULY
1-3 . . . . at Erie
4-6 . . . . Akron
7-9 . . . . Richmond
10-12 . . . . . at Altoona
16-19 . . . . Altoona
20-22 . . . . at Hartford
23-26 . . . . at Trenton
27-29 . . . . Erie
30-31 . . . . Altoona

AUGUST
1-2 . . . . Altoona
4-6 . . . at New Hampshire
7-9 . . . . . . at Portland
11-13 . . . . . . Reading
14-16 . . . . New Hampshire
18-20 . . . . at Hartford
21-23 . . . . at Richmond
24-26 . . . . . Altoona
27-30 . . . . . Trenton
31 . . . . at Erie

SEPTEMBER
1-3 . . . . at Erie
4-7 . . . . . at Binghamton

ERIE SEAWOLVES

APRIL
9-11 . . . . at Altoona
13-15 . . . . at Bowie
16-19 . . . . Altoona
20-21 . . . . . Binghamton
23-26 . . . . . . at Trenton
27-29 . . . . at Binghamton

MAY
1-3 . . . . Trenton
4-6 . . . . Bowie
7-10 . . . . . . at Altoona
11-13 . . . . Akron
14-17 . . . . . at Trenton
18-20 . . . . . at Hartford
22-25 . . . . Altoona
26-28 . . . . . . at Akron

29-31 . . . . . . Harrisburg

JUNE
2-4 . . . at New Hampshire
5-7 . . . . . . at Portland
9-11 . . . . New Hampshire
12-14 . . . . at Harrisburg
15-17 . . . . Bowie
19-22 . . . . Akron
23-26 . . . . . at Altoona
27-29 . . . . Binghamton
30 . . . . Bowie

JULY
1-3 . . . . Bowie
4-6 . . . . . . at Altoona
7-9 . . . . at Binghamton
10-12 . . . . Akron

RICHMOND
11-13 . . . . . . Richmond
14-17 . . at New Hampshire
19-21 . . . . . . Harrisburg
22-25 . . . . Reading
26-28 . . . . . . at Trenton
29-31 . . . . . at Bowie

JUNE
1-4 . . . . at Akron
5-7 . . . . Bowie
9-11 . . . . Trenton
12-14 . . . . at Richmond
16-18 . . . . at Harrisburg
19-22 . . . . Portland
23-26 . . . . Akron
27-29 . . . . . at Erie
30 . . . . at Akron

JULY
1-3 . . . . at Akron
4-6 . . . . Hartford
7-9 . . . . Erie
10-12 . . . at Portland

HARTFORD
16-19 . . . . Hartford
20-22 . . . . . . at Portland
23-26 . . . . . at Hartford
27-29 . . . . Portland
30-31 . . . . . at Reading

AUGUST
1-2 . . . . at Reading
3-6 . . . . at Erie
7-9 . . . . Altoona
11-13 . . . . Trenton
14-16 . . . . at Harrisburg
18-20 . . at New Hampshire
21-23 . . . . . . Harrisburg
24-26 . . . New Hampshire
27-30 . . . . . at Altoona
31 . . . . at Hartford

SEPTEMBER
1-3 . . . . at Hartford
4-7 . . . . Bowie

16-19 . . . . at Akron
20-22 . . . . Reading
23-26 . . . . . . Richmond
27-29 . . . . . . at Bowie
30-31 . . . . at Richmond

AUGUST
1-2 . . . . . . at Richmond
3-6 . . . . . . Binghamton
7-9 . . . . . . at Reading
11-13 . . . . Hartford

HARRISBURG SENATORS

APRIL
9-11 . . . . at Trenton
13-15 . . . . . . at Hartford
16-19 . . . . Reading
20-22 . . . . Bowie
23-26 . . . . . at Altoona
27-29 . . . . at Bowie

MAY
1-3 . . . . Altoona
4-6 . . . . Hartford
7-10 . . . . . at Reading
11-13 . . . . at Bowie
14-17 . . . . Altoona
19-21 . . at Binghamton
22-25 . . . . Bowie
26-28 . . . . . . Portland
29-31 . . . . . . at Erie

JUNE
2-4 . . . . Hartford
5-7 . . . . at Akron
9-11 . . . . . . at Bowie
12-14 . . . . Erie
16-18 . . . . . Binghamton
19-22 . . . . at Richmond
23-26 . . . . at Bowie
27-29 . . . . . . Richmond

HARTFORD YARD GOATS

APRIL
9-11 . . . . Portland
13-15 . . . . . . Harrisburg
16-19 . . at New Hampshire
20-22 . . . . . . at Portland
23-26 . . . . . Richmond
27-29 . . . New Hampshire

MAY
1-3 . . . . . . at Richmond
4-6 . . . . at Harrisburg
7-10 . . . . . . Portland
11-13 . . . . . at Altoona
14-17 . . . . at Richmond
18-20 . . . . Erie
22-25 . . . . . at Portland
26-28 . . . . Bowie
29-31 . . . New Hampshire

JUNE
2-4 . . . . . . at Harrisburg
5-7 . . . . Reading
9-11 . . . . Akron
12-14 . . . . at Reading
16-18 . . . . Altoona
19-22 . . . . at Bowie
23-26 . . . . at Trenton
27-29 . . . New Hampshire

14-16 . . . . Portland
18-20 . . . . . at Reading
21-23 . . . . . . Trenton
24-26 . . . . . at Akron
27-30 . . . . Harrisburg
31 . . . . Bowie

SEPTEMBER
1-3 . . . . Bowie
4-7 . . . . at Akron

30 . . . . Altoona
JULY
1-3 . . . . Altoona
4-6 . . . . at Richmond
7-9 . . . . Trenton
10-12 . . . . . at Hartford
16-19 . . . . . Richmond
20-22 . . at New Hampshire
23-26 . . . . . at Portland
27-29 . . . . . . Reading
30-31 . . . New Hampshire

AUGUST
1-2 . . . . New Hampshire
4-6 . . . . . at Trenton
7-9 . . . . . . Richmond
11-13 . . . . . at Altoona
14-16 . . . . . Binghamton
18-20 . . . . Akron
21-23 . . at Binghamton
24-26 . . . . . Richmond
27-30 . . . . . at Erie
31 . . . . at Altoona

SEPTEMBER
1-3 . . . . . at Altoona
4-7 . . . . Hartford

30 . . . . Trenton
JULY
1-3 . . . . Trenton
4-6 . . . . at Binghamton
7-9 . . . at New Hampshire
10-12 . . . . . Harrisburg
16-19 . . . at Binghamton
20-22 . . . . Bowie
23-26 . . . . . Binghamton
27-29 . . at New Hampshire
30-31 . . . . . . Portland

AUGUST
1-2 . . . . Portland
4-6 . . . . at Altoona
7-9 . . . . Trenton
11-13 . . . . at Erie
14-16 . . . . . at Akron
18-20 . . . . Bowie
21-23 . . . . at Portland
24-26 . . . . at Trenton
27-30 . . . . . Richmond
31 . . . . . . Binghamton

SEPTEMBER
1-3 . . . . . Binghamton
4-7 . . . . . at Harrisburg

NEW HAMPSHIRE FISHER CATS

APRIL
9-11 . . . . . . at Reading
13-15 . . . . . . at Trenton
16-19 . . . . Hartford
20-22 . . . . Trenton
23-26 . . at Binghamton
27-29 . . . . . at Hartford

MAY
1-3 . . . . . . Binghamton
4-6 . . . . Reading
7-10 . . . . at Binghamton
11-13 . . . . at Portland
14-17 . . . . . Binghamton
19-21 . . . . . at Reading
22-25 . . . . . . Trenton
26-28 . . . . . . Reading
29-31 . . . . at Hartford

JUNE
2-4 . . . . Erie
5-7 . . . . Richmond
9-11 . . . . at Erie
12-14 . . . . at Altoona
15-17 . . . . . at Akron
19-22 . . . . . . Trenton
23-26 . . . . . . Portland
27-29 . . . . at Hartford

30 . . . . at Portland
JULY
1-3 . . . . . . at Portland
4-6 . . . . Reading
7-9 . . . . Hartford
10-12 . . . . . at Trenton
16-19 . . . . . . Portland
20-22 . . . . . Harrisburg
23-26 . . . . . at Reading
27-29 . . . . . . Hartford
30-31 . . . at Harrisburg

AUGUST
1-2 . . . . . . at Harrisburg
4-6 . . . . Bowie
7-9 . . . . Akron
11-13 . . . . . at Richmond
14-16 . . . . . . at Bowie
18-20 . . . . . Binghamton
21-23 . . . . Altoona
24-26 . . . at Binghamton
27-30 . . . . Portland
31 . . . . at Trenton

SEPTEMBER
1-3 . . . . at Trenton
4-7 . . . . . . at Portland

PORTLAND SEA DOGS

APRIL
9-11 . . . . . . at Hartford
13-15 . . . . at Binghamton
16-19 . . . . Trenton
20-22 . . . . Hartford
23-26 . . . . . at Reading
27-29 . . . . . at Trenton

MAY
1-3 . . . . Reading
4-6 . . . . . . Binghamton
7-10 . . . . at Hartford
11-13 . . . New Hampshire
14-17 . . . . . . Reading
19-21 . . . . . at Trenton
22-25 . . . . . . Hartford
26-28 . . at Harrisburg
29-31 . . . . at Altoona

JUNE
2-4 . . . . Richmond
5-7 . . . . Erie
9-11 . . . . . at Richmond
12-14 . . . . . at Bowie
16-18 . . . . . . Trenton
19-22 . . . at Binghamton
23-26 . . at New Hampshire
27-29 . . . . Trenton

30 . . . . . New Hampshire
JULY
1-3 . . . . New Hampshire
4-6 . . . . . at Trenton
7-9 . . . . . at Reading
10-12 . . . . Binghamton
16-19 . . at New Hampshire
20-22 . . . . . Binghamton
23-26 . . . . . Harrisburg
27-29 . . at Binghamton
30-31 . . . . at Hartford

AUGUST
1-2 . . . . . . at Hartford
4-6 . . . . Akron
7-9 . . . . Bowie
11-13 . . . . . at Akron
14-16 . . . . . . at Erie
18-20 . . . . Altoona
21-23 . . . . Hartford
24-26 . . . . . at Reading
27-30 . . at New Hampshire
31 . . . . Reading

SEPTEMBER
1-3 . . . . Reading
4-7 . . . . New Hampshire

READING FIGHTIN PHILS

APRIL
9-11 . . . . New Hampshire
13-15 . . . . Akron
16-19 . . . . at Harrisburg
20-22 . . . . at Richmond
23-26 . . . . . Portland
27-29 . . . . . . Richmond

MAY
1-3 . . . . . . at Portland
4-6 . . . at New Hampshire
7-10 . . . . . . Harrisburg
11-13 . . . . . . Trenton

14-17 . . . . . . at Portland
19-21 . . . New Hampshire
22-25 . . . at Binghamton
26-28 . . at New Hampshire
29-31 . . . . . . Akron

JUNE
2-4 . . . . Altoona
5-7 . . . . . at Hartford
9-11 . . . . at Altoona
12-14 . . . . . . Hartford
16-18 . . . . . Richmond
19-22 . . . . at Altoona

23-26 . . . . . at Richmond
27-29 . . . . Bowie
30 . . . . Richmond

JULY
1-3 . . . . Richmond
4-6 . . . at New Hampshire
7-9 . . . . Portland
10-12 . . . at Richmond
16-19 . . . . . . Trenton
20-22 . . . . . . at Erie
23-26 . . . New Hampshire
27-29 . . . . . at Harrisburg
30-31 . . . . . Binghamton

AUGUST
1-2 . . . . Binghamton
4-6 . . . . . . at Richmond
7-9 . . . . Erie
11-13 . . . . at Bowie
14-16 . . . . . . at Trenton
18-20 . . . . Erie
21-23 . . . . . . at Akron
24-26 . . . . . . Portland
27-30 . . . . Akron
31 . . . . at Portland

SEPTEMBER
1-3 . . . . at Portland
4-7 . . . . at Trenton

RICHMOND FLYING SQUIRRELS

APRIL
9-11 . . . . at Bowie
13-15 . . . . . . at Altoona
16-19 . . . . Bowie
20-22 . . . . . . Reading
23-26 . . . . . at Hartford
27-29 . . . . . at Reading

MAY
1-3 . . . . Hartford
4-6 . . . . Altoona
7-10 . . . . . . at Trenton
11-13 . . . . at Binghamton
14-17 . . . . . . Hartford
19-21 . . . . . at Bowie
22-25 . . . . . at Akron
26-28 . . . . . Altoona
29-31 . . . . . . Trenton

JUNE
2-4 . . . . at Portland
5-7 . . at New Hampshire
9-11 . . . . Portland
12-14 . . . . . Binghamton
16-18 . . . . . at Reading
19-22 . . . . . Harrisburg
23-26 . . . . . . Reading
27-29 . . . . at Harrisburg

30 . . . . at Reading

JULY
1-3 . . . . at Reading
4-6 . . . . . . Harrisburg
7-9 . . . . at Bowie
10-12 . . . . . . Reading
16-19 . . . at Harrisburg
20-22 . . . . Akron
23-26 . . . . . at Erie
27-29 . . . . . at Akron
30-31 . . . . Erie

AUGUST
1-2 . . . . Erie
4-6 . . . . Reading
7-9 . . . . at Harrisburg
11-13 . . . New Hampshire
14-16 . . . . . at Altoona
18-20 . . . . . . Trenton
21-23 . . . . Bowie
24-26 . . . . at Harrisburg
27-30 . . . . at Hartford
31 . . . . Akron

SEPTEMBER
1-3 . . . . Akron
4-7 . . . . Altoona

TRENTON THUNDER

APRIL
9-11 . . . . Harrisburg
13-15 . . . New Hampshire
16-19 . . . . . at Portland
20-22 . . at New Hampshire
23-26 . . . . Erie
27-29 . . . . Portland

MAY
1-3 . . . . at Erie
4-6 . . . . at Akron
7-10 . . . . . . Richmond
11-13 . . . . . at Reading
14-17 . . . . Erie
19-21 . . . . . . Portland
22-25 . . at New Hampshire
26-28 . . . . . Binghamton
29-31 . . . . at Richmond

JUNE
2-4 . . . . Bowie
5-7 . . . . Altoona
9-11 . . . . at Binghamton
12-14 . . . . Akron
16-18 . . . . . at Portland
19-22 . . at New Hampshire
23-26 . . . . Hartford
27-29 . . . . at Portland
30 . . . . at Hartford

JULY
1-3 . . . . . . at Hartford
4-6 . . . . Portland
7-9 . . . . . at Harrisburg
10-12 . . . New Hampshire
16-19 . . . . at Reading
20-22 . . . . . . Altoona
23-26 . . . . Bowie
27-29 . . . . . at Altoona
30-31 . . . . . . at Akron

AUGUST
1-2 . . . . at Akron
4-6 . . . . . . Harrisburg
7-9 . . . . . . at Hartford
11-13 . . . at Binghamton
14-16 . . . . . . Reading
18-20 . . . . at Richmond
21-23 . . . . . . at Erie
24-26 . . . . . Hartford
27-30 . . . . . at Bowie
31 . . . . New Hampshire

SEPTEMBER
1-3 . . . . New Hampshire
4-7 . . . . Reading

SOUTHERN LEAGUE

BILOXI SHUCKERS

APRIL
9-13 . . . . . Montgomery
15-19 . . . . at Jacksonville
20-24 . . . . . at Pensacola
25-29 . . . . . Jacksonville
30 . . . . . at Montgomery

MAY
1-4 . . . . at Montgomery
6-10 . . . . . . Chattanooga
11-15 . . . . at Jacksonville
16-20 . . . . . Montgomery
21-25 . . . . at Rocket City
27-31 . . . . . Mississippi

JUNE
1-5 . . . . at Jackson
6-10 . . . . Rocket City
11-15 . . at Chattanooga
17-21 . . . . . . Pensacola
26-30 . . . . at Birmingham

30 . . . . Mississippi

JULY
1-3 . . . . Mississippi
4-9 . . . . . at Pensacola
10-14 . . . . . Birmingham
16-19 . . . . at Tennessee
21-26 . . . . Jackson
28-31 . . . at Birmingham

AUGUST
1 . . . . . . at Birmingham
1-5 . . . . . . at Mississippi
6-10 . . . . . Jacksonville
12-16 . . . . . . Tennessee
18-22 . . . at Montgomery
23-27 . . . . Jackson
28-31 . . . at Mississippi

SEPTEMBER
1 . . . . at Mississippi
3-7 . . . . Pensacola

BIRMINGHAM BARONS

APRIL
10-13 . . . . . Rocket City
15-19 . . . . . . at Jackson
21-25 . . . . . Tennessee
25-29 . . . at Chattanooga

MAY
1-4 . . . . . Mississippi
6-10 . . . . . . at Jackson
12-16 . . . . Rocket City
16-20 . . . . at Tennessee
21-25 . . at Chattanooga
28-31 . . . . Jackson

JUNE
1-5 . . . . . at Mississippi
6-10 . . . . . Chattanooga
12-16 . . . . . Montgomery
17-21 . . . . at Tennessee
26-30 . . . . Biloxi
30 . . . . . . at Rocket City

JULY
1-4 . . . . . at Rocket City
4-10 . . . . . . Jacksonville
10-14 . . . . . at Biloxi
17-19 . . . . Chattanooga
21-26 . . . . at Jacksonville
28-31 . . . . Biloxi

AUGUST
1 . . . . Biloxi
1-6 . . . . Pensacola
6-10 . . . . . at Rocket City
12-16 . . . . at Pensacola
19-22 . . . . Jackson
23-27 . . . at Jacksonville
29-30 . . . . . Tennessee

SEPTEMBER
1-2 . . . . Tennessee
3-7 . . . . at Montgomery

CHATTANOOGA LOOKOUTS

APRIL
9-13 . . . . Jackson
15-19 . . . . at Tennessee
20-24 . . . . . Rocket City
25-29 . . . . . Birmingham
30 . . . at Jacksonville

MAY
1-4 . . at Jacksonville
6-10 . . . . at Biloxi
11-15 . . . . Jackson
16-20 . . . . at Rocket City
21-25 . . . . . Birmingham
27-31 . . . . . at Pensacola

JUNE
1-5 . . . . . Montgomery
6-10 . . . . at Birmingham
11-15 . . . . Biloxi
17-21 . . . . at Montgomery
25-29 . . . . . Jacksonville

30 . . . . Tennessee

JULY
1-3 . . . . Tennessee
4-9 . . . . . . at Jackson
10-14 . . . . . Mississippi
17-19 . . . at Birmingham
21-26 . . . . . Pensacola
27-31 . . . . . at Jackson

AUGUST
1-5 . . . . . . Tennessee
6-10 . . . . at Montgomery
12-16 . . . . at Mississippi
18-22 . . . . . Rocket City
23-27 . . . at Tennessee
28-31 . . . . . Jacksonville

SEPTEMBER
1 . . . . Jacksonville
3-7 . . . . . at Rocket City

JACKSON GENERALS

APRIL
9-13 . . . . . at Chattanooga
15-19 . . . . . . Birmingham
20-24 . . . . . at Mississippi
25-29 . . . . . . Tennessee
30 . . . . at Pensacola

MAY
1-4 . . . . . at Pensacola
6-10 . . . . . . Birmingham
11-15 . . at Chattanooga
16-20 . . . . . . Mississippi
21-25 . . . . . . Tennessee
28-31 . . . . at Birmingham

JUNE
1-5 . . . . Biloxi
6-10 . . . . . at Tennessee
11-15 . . . . . . Pensacola
17-21 . . . at Rocket City
25-29 . . . . . . Tennessee

30 . . . . . at Montgomery

JULY
1-3 . . . . . at Montgomery
4-9 . . . . . . Chattanooga
11-14 . . . at Rocket City
16-19 . . . Montgomery
21-26 . . . . at Biloxi
27-31 . . . Chattanooga

AUGUST
1-5 . . . . Rocket City
6-10 . . . . at Tennessee
12-16 . . . . . Montgomery
19-22 . . . at Birmingham
23-27 . . . . . . at Biloxi
28-31 . . . . . Rocket City

SEPTEMBER
1 . . . . Rocket City
3-7 . . . . . at Jacksonville

JACKSONVILLE JUMBO SHRIMP

APRIL
9-13 . . . . . at Mississippi
15-19 . . . . Biloxi
20-24 . . . . at Montgomery
25-29 . . . . . . at Biloxi
30 . . . . Chattanooga

MAY
1-4 . . . . . Chattanooga
6-10 . . . . at Tennessee
11-15 . . . . Biloxi
16-20 . . . . at Pensacola
21-25 . . . . Montgomery
27-31 . . . at Tennessee

JUNE
1-5 . . . . Pensacola
6-10 . . . . at Montgomery
11-15 . . . . Rocket City
17-21 . . . . . Mississippi
25-29 . . . at Chattanooga

30 . . . . Pensacola

JULY
1-3 . . . . Pensacola
4-10 . . . at Birmingham
10-14 . . . . . Tennessee
16-19 . . . at Mississippi
21-26 . . . Birmingham
27-31 . . . at Pensacola

AUGUST
1-5 . . . . . Montgomery
6-10 . . . . . . at Biloxi
12-16 . . . at Rocket City
18-22 . . . . Mississippi
23-27 . . . . Birmingham
28-31 . . . at Chattanooga

SEPTEMBER
1 . . . . . at Chattanooga
3-7 . . . . Jackson

MISSISSIPPI BRAVES

APRIL
9-13 . . . . . . Jacksonville
15-19 . . . at Rocket City
20-24 . . . . . . Jackson
25-29 . . . . . . Pensacola

MAY
1-4 . . . . at Birmingham
6-10 . . . Montgomery
11-15 . . at Pensacola
16-20 . . . . . at Jackson
21-25 . . . . Pensacola
27-31 . . . . . at Biloxi

JUNE
1-5 . . . . . . Birmingham
6-10 . . . . at Pensacola
11-15 . . . . . Tennessee
17-21 . . . at Jacksonville
25-29 . . . Rocket City
30 . . . . at Biloxi

JULY
1-3 . . . . at Biloxi
4-9 . . . . . Montgomery
10-14 . . . at Chattanooga
16-19 . . . Jacksonville
21-26 . . . at Montgomery
27-31 . . . . . Rocket City

AUGUST
1-5 . . . . Biloxi
6-10 . . . at Pensacola
12-16 . . . Chattanooga
18-22 . . . at Jacksonville
23-27 . . . at Montgomery
28-31 . . . . Biloxi

SEPTEMBER
1 . . . . Biloxi
3-7 . . . . . at Tennessee

MONTGOMERY BISCUITS

APRIL
9-13 . . . . at Biloxi

15-19 . . . . . . Pensacola
20-24 . . . . . Jacksonville

25-29 . . . . at Rocket City
30 . . . . Biloxi

MAY
1-4 . . . . Biloxi
6-10 . . . . at Mississippi
11-15 . . . . Tennessee
16-20 . . . . . at Biloxi
21-25 . . at Jacksonville
27-31 . . . . Rocket City

JUNE
1-5 . . . . at Chattanooga
6-10 . . . . . Jacksonville
12-16 . . at Birmingham
17-21 . . . . Chattanooga
25-29 . . . at Pensacola
30 . . . . Jackson

25-29 . . . . at Rocket City
30 . . . . Biloxi

MAY
1-4 . . . . Biloxi
6-10 . . . . at Mississippi
11-15 . . . . . Tennessee
16-20 . . . . . at Biloxi
21-25 . . . at Jacksonville
27-31 . . . . Rocket City

JUNE
1-5 . . . . at Chattanooga
6-10 . . . . . Jacksonville
12-16 . . at Birmingham
17-21 . . . . Chattanooga
25-29 . . . at Pensacola
30 . . . . Jackson

JULY
1-3 . . . . Jackson
4-9 . . . . . at Mississippi
10-14 . . . . . Pensacola
16-19 . . . . . at Jackson
21-26 . . . . . Mississippi
27-31 . . . . at Tennessee

AUGUST
1-5 . . . . at Jacksonville
6-10 . . . . . Chattanooga
12-16 . . . . . at Jackson
18-22 . . . . Biloxi
23-27 . . . . Mississippi
28-31 . . . . at Pensacola

SEPTEMBER
1 . . . . at Pensacola
3-7 . . . . . . Birmingham

PENSACOLA BLUE WAHOOS

APRIL
9-13 . . . . Tennessee
15-19 . . . at Montgomery
20-24 . . . . Biloxi
25-29 . . at Mississippi
30 . . . . Jackson

MAY
1-4 . . . . Jackson
6-10 . . . at Rocket City
11-15 . . . . Mississippi
16-20 . . . . Jacksonville
21-25 . . . at Mississippi
27-31 . . . . Chattanooga

JUNE
1-5 . . . . at Jacksonville
6-10 . . . . Mississippi
11-15 . . . . at Jackson
17-21 . . . . . at Biloxi
25-29 . . . Montgomery

30 . . . . . at Jacksonville

JULY
1-3 . . . . at Jacksonville
4-9 . . . . Biloxi
10-14 . . . at Montgomery
16-19 . . . . Rocket City
21-26 . . at Chattanooga
27-31 . . . . Jacksonville

AUGUST
1-6 . . . . at Birmingham
6-10 . . . . . Mississippi
12-16 . . . . Birmingham
18-22 . . . at Tennessee
23-27 . . at Rocket City
28-31 . . . Montgomery

SEPTEMBER
1 . . . . . . Montgomery
3-7 . . . . at Biloxi

ROCKET CITY TRASH PANDAS

APRIL
10-13 . . . . at Birmingham
15-19 . . . . Mississippi
20-24 . . . at Chattanooga
25-29 . . . . Montgomery
30 . . . . at Tennessee

MAY
1-4 . . . . . . at Tennessee
6-10 . . . . . Pensacola
12-16 . . . at Birmingham
16-20 . . . Chattanooga
21-25 . . . . Biloxi
27-31 . . at Montgomery

JUNE
1-6 . . . . Tennessee
6-10 . . . . . . at Biloxi
11-15 . . at Jacksonville
17-21 . . . . . Jackson
25-29 . . at Mississippi

30 . . . . Birmingham

JULY
1-4 . . . . . . Birmingham
4-9 . . . . . at Tennessee
11-14 . . . . . . Jackson
16-19 . . . at Pensacola
21-26 . . . . . Tennessee
27-31 . . at Mississippi

AUGUST
1-5 . . . . . at Jackson
6-10 . . . . Birmingham
12-16 . . . . Jacksonville
18-22 . . at Chattanooga
23-27 . . . . Pensacola
28-31 . . . . at Jackson

SEPTEMBER
1 . . . . at Jackson
3-7 . . . . . . Chattanooga

TENNESSEE SMOKIES

APRIL
9-13 . . . . . at Pensacola
15-19 . . . . Chattanooga
21-25 . . . at Birmingham
25-29 . . . . at Jackson
30 . . . . Rocket City

MAY
1-4 . . . . Rocket City
6-10 . . . . Jacksonville
11-15 . . . at Montgomery
16-20 . . . . Birmingham
21-25 . . . . at Jackson

27-31 . . . . . . Jacksonville

JUNE
1-6 . . . . . at Rocket City
6-10 . . . . Jackson
11-15 . . . . . at Mississippi
17-21 . . . . . Birmingham
25-29 . . . . . . at Jackson
30 . . . . . at Chattanooga

JULY
1-3 . . . . . at Chattanooga
4-9 . . . . . . Rocket City
10-14 . . . . . at Jacksonville
16-19 . . . . Biloxi

21-26 . . . . . at Rocket City
27-31 . . . . . . Montgomery

AUGUST
1-5 . . . . . at Chattanooga
6-10 . . . . Jackson
12-16 . . . . at Biloxi
18-22 . . . . . . Pensacola
23-27 . . . . Chattanooga
29-30 . . . at Birmingham

SEPTEMBER
1-2 . . . . . at Birmingham
3-7 . . . . Mississippi

TEXAS LEAGUE

AMARILLO SOD POODLES

APRIL
10-11 . . . . at Arkansas
12-15 . . . . at Tulsa
17-19 . . . . Arkansas
19-22 . . . . Tulsa
24-26 . . . . Midland
28-30 . . at Corpus Christi

MAY
2-4 . . . . at Midland
6-8 . . . . . Corpus Christi
9-10 . . . . Frisco
11-14 . . . . at Corpus Christi
16-17 . . . . at Frisco
19-22 . . . . . NW Arkansas
23-24 . . . . Arkansas
27-29 . . . at NW Arkansas
30-31 . . . . . at Arkansas

JUNE
3-5 . . . . Frisco
6-7 . . . . Midland
9-12 . . . . at Frisco
13-14 . . . . . . at Midland
16-19 . . . . Corpus Christi
20-21 . . . . Frisco
26-28 . . . . . . at Frisco

28-30 . . . at Corpus Christi

JULY
1-4 . . . . at Midland
5-7 . . . . Frisco
9-11 . . . . Springfield
12-14 . . . . Tulsa
15-18 . . . . . at Springfield
19-21 . . . . at Tulsa
23-25 . . . . Corpus Christi
26-28 . . . . at Frisco
29-31 . . . . Midland

AUGUST
1-2 . . . . at Frisco
3-6 . . . . at Corpus Christi
8-9 . . . . at Midland
11-14 . . . . Corpus Christi
15-16 . . . . Frisco
19-21 . . . at NW Arkansas
22-23 . . . . at Springfield
26-29 . . . . Corpus Christi
30-31 . . . . Midland

SEPTEMBER
2-4 . . . . . NW Arkansas
5-7 . . . . Springfield

ARKANSAS TRAVELERS

APRIL
10-11 . . . . Amarillo
14-15 . . . . Frisco
17-19 . . . . . . at Amarillo
19-22 . . . . at Frisco
24-26 . . . . at Tulsa
29 . . . . . . NW Arkansas

MAY
1 . . . . NW Arkansas
2-5 . . . . Springfield
6-8 . . . . at Tulsa
8-10 . . . . . at Springfield
12-15 . . . . Tulsa
16-17 . . . . Springfield
18-22 . . . . . at Midland
23-24 . . . . . at Amarillo
27-29 . . . . Midland
30-31 . . . . Amarillo

JUNE
2-5 . . . . . at Springfield
6-7 . . . . at Tulsa
9-12 . . . . Springfield
13-14 . . . . Tulsa
16-19 . . . . at NW Arkansas
20-21 . . . . at Tulsa
26-27 . . . . . at Springfield

29-30 . . . . . NW Arkansas

JULY
1 . . . . NW Arkansas
2-4 . . . . Springfield
4-7 . . . . at NW Arkansas
9-11 . . . . Frisco
11-14 . . . . Corpus Christi
16-18 . . . . at Frisco
18-20 . . . at Corpus Christi
23-25 . . . . Tulsa
25-28 . . . at NW Arkansas
28-31 . . . . . at Springfield

AUGUST
1-2 . . . . . NW Arkansas
4-7 . . . . Tulsa
8-9 . . . . at NW Arkansas
10-12 . . . . at Springfield
14-16 . . . . . NW Arkansas
18-20 . . . at Corpus Christi
22-23 . . . . . . at Midland
26-28 . . . . . . at Tulsa
29-30 . . . . . . Springfield

SEPTEMBER
1 . . . . Springfield
2-4 . . . . . Corpus Christi
5-7 . . . . Midland

CORPUS CHRISTI HOOKS

APRIL
9-11 . . . . . NW Arkansas
12-14 . . . . . . Springfield
16-18 . . . at NW Arkansas
19-22 . . . . at Springfield
24-26 . . . . at Frisco
28-30 . . . . Amarillo

MAY
1-4 . . . . Frisco
6-8 . . . . at Amarillo
9-10 . . . . . . at Midland
11-14 . . . . Amarillo
15-17 . . . . Midland
18-22 . . . . . at Springfield
23-25 . . . . at Tulsa
26-28 . . . . . Springfield
29-31 . . . . Tulsa

JUNE
2-5 . . . . at Midland
5-7 . . . . Frisco
8-11 . . . . Midland
13-14 . . . . . . at Frisco
16-19 . . . . . at Amarillo
20-21 . . . . . at Midland
25-27 . . . . Midland

28-30 . . . . Amarillo

JULY
2-4 . . . . at Frisco
4-6 . . . . Midland
9-11 . . . . at NW Arkansas
11-14 . . . . . at Arkansas
15-17 . . . . NW Arkansas
18-20 . . . . Arkansas
23-25 . . . . . at Arkansas
26-27 . . . . . . at Midland
28-30 . . . . Frisco
31 . . . . Midland

AUGUST
1-2 . . . . Midland
3-6 . . . . Amarillo
8-9 . . . . at Frisco
11-14 . . . . . at Amarillo
14-16 . . . . Midland
18-20 . . . . Arkansas
21-23 . . . . Tulsa
26-29 . . . . . at Midland
29-31 . . . . Frisco

SEPTEMBER
2-4 . . . . . at Arkansas
5-7 . . . . at Tulsa

FRISCO ROUGHRIDERS

APRIL
10-12 . . . . at Tulsa
14-15 . . . . . at Arkansas
17-19 . . . . Tulsa
19-22 . . . . . . Arkansas
24-26 . . . . Corpus Christi
28-29 . . . . . . at Midland

MAY
1 . . . . at Midland
1-4 . . . at Corpus Christi
6-8 . . . . Midland
9-10 . . . . . . at Amarillo
12-15 . . . . Midland
16-17 . . . . Amarillo
19-22 . . . . . . at Tulsa
23-24 . . . . at Springfield
27-29 . . . . Tulsa
30-31 . . . . . . Springfield

JUNE
3-5 . . . . . . at Amarillo
5-7 . . . at Corpus Christi
9-12 . . . . Amarillo
13-14 . . . . Corpus Christi
15-19 . . . . . at Midland
20-21 . . . . . at Amarillo

26-28 . . . . Amarillo
28-30 . . . . . . at Midland

JULY
2-4 . . . . . Corpus Christi
5-7 . . . . . . at Amarillo
9-11 . . . . . at Arkansas
11-14 . . . at NW Arkansas
16-18 . . . . . . Arkansas
19-21 . . . . NW Arkansas
22-25 . . . . . at Midland
26-28 . . . . . . Amarillo
28-30 . . at Corpus Christi

AUGUST
1-2 . . . . Amarillo
3-7 . . . . at Midland
8-9 . . . . Corpus Christi
11-14 . . . . Midland
15-16 . . . . . at Amarillo
18-21 . . . . at Springfield
22-23 . . . at NW Arkansas
26-29 . . . . Midland
29-31 . . . at Corpus Christi

SEPTEMBER
2-4 . . . . Springfield
5-7 . . . . . NW Arkansas

MIDLAND ROCKHOUNDS

APRIL
10-12 . . . . . . Springfield
12-14 . . . . NW Arkansas
16-18 . . . . at Springfield
19-22 . . . at NW Arkansas
24-26 . . . . . at Amarillo
28-29 . . . . Frisco

MAY
1 . . . . Frisco
2-4 . . . . Amarillo
6-8 . . . . at Frisco
9-10 . . . . Corpus Christi
12-15 . . . . . . at Frisco

15-17 . . . at Corpus Christi
18-22 . . . . Arkansas
23-24 . . . NW Arkansas
27-29 . . . . . at Arkansas
30-31 . . . at NW Arkansas

JUNE
2-5 . . . . . Corpus Christi
6-7 . . . . . . at Amarillo
8-11 . . . at Corpus Christi
13-14 . . . . Amarillo
15-19 . . . . Frisco
20-21 . . . . Corpus Christi
25-27 . . . at Corpus Christi

28-30 .... Frisco

JULY
1-4 .... Amarillo
4-6 .... at Corpus Christi
8-11 .... Tulsa
12-13 ...... Springfield
16-18 ...... at Tulsa
18-20 .... at Springfield
22-25 .... Frisco
26-27 .... Corpus Christi
29-31 ...... at Amarillo
31 .... at Corpus Christi

NORTHWEST ARKANSAS NATURALS

APRIL
9-11 .... at Corpus Christi
12-14 ...... at Midland
16-18 .... Corpus Christi
19-22 ...... Midland
23-26 .... at Springfield
29 ...... at Arkansas

MAY
1 ...... at Arkansas
2-4 .... Tulsa
5-7 ..... at Springfield
9-10 ...... at Tulsa
12-15 ...... Springfield
16-17 .... Tulsa
19-22 .... at Amarillo
23-24 .... at Midland
27-29 .... Amarillo
30-31 .... Midland

JUNE
3 .... at Tulsa
4 .... Tulsa
6-7 ..... at Springfield
9-12 .... Tulsa
13-14 ...... Springfield
16-19 ...... Arkansas
20-21 .... at Springfield
26-27 .... Tulsa

SPRINGFIELD CARDINALS

APRIL
10-12 ...... at Midland
12-14 ... at Corpus Christi
16-18 ...... Midland
19-22 ..... Corpus Christi

AUGUST
1-2 .... at Corpus Christi
3-7 .... Frisco
8-9 .... Amarillo
11-14 ...... at Frisco
14-16 ... at Corpus Christi
18-21 .... Tulsa
22-23 ...... Arkansas
26-29 ..... at Frisco
30-31 ...... Amarillo

SEPTEMBER
2-4 .... at Tulsa
5-7 ..... at Arkansas

28 .... at Tulsa
29-30 .... at Arkansas

JULY
1 .... at Arkansas
2-4 .... at Tulsa
4-7 .... Arkansas
9-11 ...... Corpus Christi
11-14 .... Frisco
15-17 ... at Corpus Christi
19-21 ...... at Frisco
23-25 ...... Springfield
25-28 ...... Arkansas
29-31 ...... at Tulsa

AUGUST
1-2 .... at Arkansas
4-7 .... Springfield
8-9 .... Arkansas
11-13 ...... at Tulsa
14-16 .... at Arkansas
19-21 ...... Amarillo
22-23 .... Frisco
25-28 .... at Springfield
29-30 .... Tulsa

SEPTEMBER
1 .... Tulsa
2-4 ...... at Amarillo
5-7 .... at Frisco

23-26 ..... NW Arkansas
29 .... at Tulsa

MAY
1 .... at Tulsa
2-5 .... at Arkansas

5-7 ...... NW Arkansas
8-10 .... Arkansas
12-15 .... at NW Arkansas
16-17 ...... at Arkansas
18-22 ...... Corpus Christi
23-24 .... Frisco
26-28 ... at Corpus Christi
30-31 .... at Frisco

JUNE
2-5 .... Arkansas
6-7 ...... NW Arkansas
9-12 .... at NW Arkansas
13-14 .... at NW Arkansas
15-19 .... Tulsa
20-21 ..... NW Arkansas
26-27 ...... Arkansas
28-30 .... at Tulsa

JULY
1 .... at Tulsa
2-4 .... at Arkansas
4-6 .... Tulsa

TULSA DRILLERS

APRIL
10-12 .... Frisco
12-15 .... Amarillo
17-19 .... at Frisco
19-22 ...... at Amarillo
24-26 .... Arkansas
29 .... Springfield

MAY
1 .... Springfield
2-4 ..... at NW Arkansas
6-8 .... Arkansas
9-10 ..... NW Arkansas
12-15 ..... at Arkansas
16-17 .... at NW Arkansas
19-22 .... Frisco
23-25 ..... Corpus Christi
27-29 ...... at Frisco
29-31 ... at Corpus Christi

JUNE
3 .... NW Arkansas
4 .... at NW Arkansas
6-7 .... Arkansas
9-12 ..... at NW Arkansas
13-14 ..... at Arkansas
15-19 .... at Springfield
20-21 .... Arkansas
26-27 .... at NW Arkansas
28 ...... NW Arkansas
28-30 .... Springfield

9-11 .... at Amarillo
12-13 ...... at Midland
15-18 .... Amarillo
18-20 .... Midland
23-25 .... at NW Arkansas
25-27 .... Tulsa
28-31 ...... Arkansas

AUGUST
1-3 .... at Tulsa
4-7 .... at NW Arkansas
8-9 .... Tulsa
10-12 ...... Arkansas
14-17 ...... at Tulsa
18-21 .... Frisco
22-23 ...... Amarillo
25-28 .... NW Arkansas
29-30 .... at Arkansas

SEPTEMBER
1 .... at Arkansas
2-4 .... at Frisco
5-7 ...... at Amarillo

JULY
1 .... Springfield
2-4 ...... NW Arkansas
4-6 ..... at Springfield
8-11 .... at Midland
12-14 ...... at Amarillo
16-18 .... Midland
19-21 .... Amarillo
23-25 ..... at Arkansas
25-27 .... at Springfield
29-31 ..... NW Arkansas

AUGUST
1-3 .... Springfield
4-7 ...... at Arkansas
8-9 ..... at Springfield
11-13 .... NW Arkansas
14-17 ...... Springfield
18-21 ...... at Midland
21-23 ... at Corpus Christi
26-28 ...... Arkansas
29-30 .... at NW Arkansas

SEPTEMBER
1 .... at NW Arkansas
2-4 .... Midland
5-7 ...... Corpus Christi

HIGH CLASS A

CALIFORNIA LEAGUE

INLAND EMPIRE 66ERS

APRIL
9-11 ..... at Rancho Cuca.
14-17 ..... at Lancaster
17-19 .... Visalia
20-23 ...... Rancho Cuca.
24-26 .... at Lake Elsinore
28-30 ..... Rancho Cuca.

MAY
2-3 .... at San Jose
4-7 .... at Modesto

8-10 .... San Jose
11-13 ...... Lancaster
14-17 ...... at Visalia
19-21 .... Stockton
22-25 ..... Lake Elsinore
26-28 .... at Rancho Cuca.
30-31 ...... at Lancaster

JUNE
1-4 .... Modesto
5-7 .... Visalia

10-12 ...... at Lancaster
12-16 ...... at Stockton
17-21 .... Lancaster
25-27 .... Lake Elsinore
28-30 .... at Rancho Cuca.

JULY
1-3 .... at Lake Elsinore
4-6 ...... Rancho Cuca.
7-9 .... Modesto
10-13 .... at Visalia
15-17 ..... Rancho Cuca.
18-20 .... at Lake Elsinore
21-23 .... at Rancho Cuca.
24-26 .... Lake Elsinore
29-30 ...... at San Jose

31 .... at Visalia

AUGUST
1-2 .... at Visalia
4-6 ...... Rancho Cuca.
7-9 .... Visalia
11-13 ...... at Stockton
15-16 ...... at Lancaster
17-20 .... Stockton
21-23 ..... Lake Elsinore
25-27 .... at Lake Elsinore
28-31 .... Lancaster

SEPTEMBER
1-3 ...... Lake Elsinore
5-7 ...... at Lancaster

LAKE ELSINORE STORM

APRIL
9-11 . . . . Modesto
13-16 . . . . Stockton
18-19 . . . . . . at San Jose
20-23 . . . . . at Modesto
24-26 . . . . . Inland Empire
29-30 . . . . . at Lancaster

MAY
1 . . . . at Lancaster
1-3 . . . . at Rancho Cuca.
4-7 . . . . Lancaster
8-10 . . . . Visalia
11-13 . . at Rancho Cuca.
14-17 . . . . San Jose
20-22 . . . . at Lancaster
22-25 . . at Inland Empire
26-28 . . . . . Lancaster
29-31 . . . . Rancho Cuca.

JUNE
1-4 . . . . at Stockton
6-8 . . . . at San Jose
9-11 . . . . . Rancho Cuca.
12-16 . . . . Visalia
17-21 . . . at Rancho Cuca.
25-27 . . at Inland Empire

28-30 . . . . Lancaster

JULY
1-3 . . . . . . Inland Empire
4-6 . . . . at Modesto
7-9 . . . . at Visalia
10-13 . . . . San Jose
16-18 . . . . at Lancaster
18-20 . . . . Inland Empire
21-23 . . . . . . Lancaster
24-26 . . at Inland Empire
28-30 . . . . Stockton
31 . . . . Modesto

AUGUST
1-2 . . . . Modesto
4-6 . . . . . . at Stockton
7-9 . . . . . . at Modesto
11-13 . . . . . . Lancaster
14-16 . . . . Rancho Cuca.
18-21 . . . . at Lancaster
21-23 . . at Inland Empire
25-27 . . . . Inland Empire
28-31 . . . . Rancho Cuca.

SEPTEMBER
1-3 . . . . at Inland Empire
4-7 . . . . at Rancho Cuca.

LANCASTER JETHAWKS

APRIL
10-12 . . . . San Jose
14-17 . . . . . Inland Empire
17-19 . . . . . . at Modesto
21-24 . . . . Visalia
24-26 . . . at Rancho Cuca.
29-30 . . . . . Lake Elsinore

MAY
1 . . . . . . Lake Elsinore
1-3 . . . . at Stockton
4-7 . . . . at Lake Elsinore
9-10 . . . . . Rancho Cuca.
11-13 . . . at Inland Empire
14-17 . . . at Rancho Cuca.
20-22 . . . . Lake Elsinore
23-25 . . . . Stockton
26-28 . . at Lake Elsinore
30-31 . . . . Inland Empire

JUNE
2-4 . . . . at San Jose
5-7 . . . . at Stockton
10-12 . . . Inland Empire
13-17 . . . . San Jose
17-21 . . . at Inland Empire
26-28 . . . . Rancho Cuca.

28-30 . . . at Lake Elsinore

JULY
1-3 . . . at Rancho Cuca.
5-7 . . . . Visalia
8-10 . . . . San Jose
10-13 . . . . . at Stockton
16-18 . . . . Lake Elsinore
18-20 . . . at Rancho Cuca.
21-23 . . at Lake Elsinore
25-26 . . . . Rancho Cuca.
28-30 . . . . . . at Visalia

AUGUST
1-3 . . . . at San Jose
5-7 . . . . Visalia
8-9 . . . . . Rancho Cuca.
11-13 . . at Lake Elsinore
15-16 . . . . Inland Empire
18-21 . . . . . Lake Elsinore
21-23 . . . . . at Modesto
26-28 . . . . . Modesto
28-31 . . at Inland Empire

SEPTEMBER
1-3 . . at Rancho Cuca.
5-7 . . . . . Inland Empire

MODESTO NUTS

APRIL
9-11 . . . . at Lake Elsinore
13-16 . . . . at Visalia
17-19 . . . . . . Lancaster
20-23 . . . . . Lake Elsinore
24-26 . . . . . . at Stockton
28-30 . . . . Stockton

MAY
1-3 . . . . at Visalia
4-7 . . . . . Inland Empire
8-10 . . . . Stockton
12-13 . . . . . . at San Jose
14-17 . . . . . . at Stockton
19-21 . . . . Visalia

22-25 . . . . Rancho Cuca.
26-28 . . . . at Visalia
29-31 . . . . San Jose

JUNE
1-4 . . . . at Inland Empire
5-7 . . . . at Rancho Cuca.
9-11 . . . . Stockton
12-16 . . . . Rancho Cuca.
18-22 . . . . at San Jose
25-27 . . . . Stockton
28-30 . . . . San Jose

JULY
1-3 . . . . at Stockton

RANCHO CUCAMONGA QUAKES

APRIL
9-11 . . . . . Inland Empire
13-16 . . . . San Jose
17-19 . . . . . at Stockton
20-23 . . at Inland Empire
24-26 . . . . . . Lancaster
28-30 . . at Inland Empire

MAY
1-3 . . . . . Lake Elsinore
4-7 . . . . . . at Visalia
9-10 . . . . at Lancaster
11-13 . . . . Lake Elsinore
14-17 . . . . . . Lancaster
20-22 . . . . at San Jose
22-25 . . . . at Modesto
26-28 . . . . Inland Empire
29-31 . . at Lake Elsinore

JUNE
1-4 . . . . Visalia
5-7 . . . . Modesto
9-11 . . at Lake Elsinore
12-16 . . . . at Modesto
17-21 . . . . Lake Elsinore
26-28 . . . . at Lancaster
28-30 . . . . Inland Empire

JULY
1-3 . . . . Lancaster
4-6 . . . at Inland Empire
7-9 . . . . . at Stockton
10-13 . . . . . . Modesto
15-17 . . at Inland Empire
18-20 . . . . . Lancaster
21-23 . . . . Inland Empire
25-26 . . . . at Lancaster
28-30 . . . . . Modesto
31 . . . . Stockton

AUGUST
1-2 . . . . Stockton
4-6 . . . at Inland Empire
8-9 . . . . . at Lancaster
11-13 . . . . . . San Jose
14-16 . . . . at Lake Elsinore
18-20 . . . . at San Jose
21-23 . . . . . . Stockton
25-27 . . . . at Visalia
28-31 . . . at Lake Elsinore

SEPTEMBER
1-3 . . . . Lancaster
4-7 . . . . . Lake Elsinore

SAN JOSE GIANTS

APRIL
10-12 . . . . . at Lancaster
13-16 . . . at Rancho Cuca.
18-19 . . . . . Lake Elsinore
21-23 . . . . . . Stockton
24-26 . . . . at Visalia
29-30 . . . . Visalia

MAY
1 . . . . Visalia
2-3 . . . . . Inland Empire
4-7 . . . . . . at Stockton
8-10 . . . at Inland Empire
12-13 . . . . Modesto
14-17 . . at Lake Elsinore
20-22 . . . . Rancho Cuca.
23-26 . . . . Visalia
26-28 . . . . at Stockton
29-31 . . . . . . at Modesto

JUNE
2-4 . . . . Lancaster
6-8 . . . . . . Lake Elsinore
9-11 . . . . at Visalia
13-17 . . . . . at Lancaster
18-22 . . . . . Modesto
26-28 . . . . Visalia

28-30 . . . . . at Modesto

JULY
1-3 . . . . at Visalia
5-5 . . . . Stockton
8-10 . . . . at Lancaster
10-13 . . . at Lake Elsinore
16-18 . . . . Visalia
18-20 . . . . . at Stockton
22-23 . . . . . Modesto
24-26 . . . at Stockton
29-30 . . . . Inland Empire

AUGUST
1-3 . . . . Lancaster
4-6 . . . . at Modesto
8-10 . . . . . . Stockton
11-13 . . . at Rancho Cuca.
14-16 . . . . . . at Visalia
18-20 . . . . Rancho Cuca.
22-24 . . . . Visalia
25-27 . . . . at Stockton
29-31 . . . . . Modesto

SEPTEMBER
2-4 . . . . Stockton
4-7 . . . . . . at Modesto

STOCKTON PORTS

APRIL
9-11 . . . . at Visalia
13-16 . . . . at Lake Elsinore
17-19 . . . . . Rancho Cuca.
21-23 . . . . . . at San Jose
24-26 . . . . Modesto
28-30 . . . . . . at Modesto

MAY
1-3 . . . . Lancaster
4-7 . . . . San Jose
8-10 . . . . at Modesto
11-13 . . . . Visalia
14-17 . . . . Modesto
19-21 . . . at Inland Empire
23-25 . . . . at Lancaster
26-28 . . . . . . San Jose
29-31 . . . . . . at Visalia

JUNE
1-4 . . . . . . Lake Elsinore
5-7 . . . . Lancaster
9-11 . . . . . . at Modesto
12-16 . . . . Inland Empire
17-21 . . . . . . at Visalia
25-27 . . . . . at Modesto
28-30 . . . . Visalia

JULY
1-3 . . . . Modesto
5-5 . . . . at San Jose
7-9 . . . . . Rancho Cuca.
10-13 . . . . Lancaster
15-17 . . . . . at Modesto
18-20 . . . . . . San Jose
21-23 . . . . . . at Visalia
24-26 . . . . . . San Jose
28-30 . . . at Lake Elsinore
31 . . . . . at Rancho Cuca.

AUGUST
1-2 . . . . at Rancho Cuca.
4-6 . . . . . Lake Elsinore
8-10 . . . . at San Jose
11-13 . . . . Inland Empire
14-16 . . . . Modesto
17-20 . . . at Inland Empire
21-23 . . . at Rancho Cuca.
25-27 . . . . . . San Jose
28-31 . . . . Visalia

SEPTEMBER
2-4 . . . . at San Jose
4-7 . . . . at Visalia

VISALIA RAWHIDE

APRIL
9-11 . . . . Stockton
13-16 . . . . Modesto
17-19 . . . at Inland Empire
21-24 . . . . . at Lancaster
24-26 . . . . . . San Jose
29-30 . . . . . . at San Jose

MAY
1 . . . . at San Jose
1-3 . . . . Modesto
4-7 . . . . . Rancho Cuca.
8-10 . . . . at Lake Elsinore
11-13 . . . . . . at Stockton
14-17 . . . . Inland Empire
19-21 . . . . . . at Modesto
23-26 . . . . . at San Jose
26-28 . . . . . . Modesto
29-31 . . . . Stockton

JUNE
1-4 . . . . . at Rancho Cuca.
5-7 . . . . at Inland Empire
9-11 . . . . San Jose
12-16 . . . . at Lake Elsinore
17-21 . . . . Stockton
26-28 . . . . at San Jose
28-30 . . . . . . at Stockton

JULY
1-3 . . . . San Jose
5-7 . . . . . . at Lancaster
7-9 . . . . . . Lake Elsinore
10-13 . . . . Inland Empire
16-18 . . . . . at San Jose
18-20 . . . . Modesto
21-23 . . . . . . Stockton
24-26 . . . . . at Modesto
28-30 . . . . . . Lancaster
31 . . . . . . Inland Empire

AUGUST
1-2 . . . . . Inland Empire
5-7 . . . . . . at Lancaster
7-9 . . . at Inland Empire
11-13 . . . . Modesto
14-16 . . . . San Jose
17-20 . . . . . at San Jose
22-24 . . . . . . at San Jose
25-27 . . . . Rancho Cuca.
28-31 . . . . . . at Stockton

SEPTEMBER
1-3 . . . . at Modesto
4-7 . . . . Stockton

CAROLINA LEAGUE

CAROLINA MUDCATS

APRIL
9-12 . . . . . Winston-Salem
13-15 . . . . . . Wilmington
16-19 . . . . . at Lynchburg
20-22 . . . . at Fayetteville
23-26 . . . . Down East
28-30 . . . . . Myrtle Beach

MAY
1-3 . . . . at Salem
4-7 . . . . at Fredericksburg
8-10 . . . . Down East
12-14 . . . . . . Wilmington
15-17 . . . . . at Fayetteville
18-20 . . . . . at Down East
21-24 . . . . Winston-Salem
25-28 . . . . Fredericksburg
29-31 . . . . at Salem

JUNE
2-4 . . . . Myrtle Beach
5-7 . . . . Fayetteville
9-11 . . . . at Myrtle Beach
12-14 . . . . . at Down East
15-17 . . . . Salem
18-21 . . . . at Fayetteville
25-28 . . . . . . Lynchburg
30 . . . . . . at Down East

JULY
1-3 . . . . . . at Down East
4-6 . . . . . . Fayetteville
7-9 . . . . . . Wilmington
10-13 . . . . at Lynchburg
15-17 . . . . . . Frederick
18-20 . . . . at Wilmington
21-23 . . . . . at Frederick

DOWN EAST WOOD DUCKS

APRIL
9-12 . . . . Fredericksburg
13-15 . . . . . Fayetteville
16-19 . . . at Winston-Salem
20-22 . . . . . Lynchburg
23-26 . . . . . at Carolina
28-30 . . . . Salem

MAY
1-3 . . . . . . at Lynchburg
4-7 . . . . Fayetteville
8-10 . . . . . . at Carolina
12-14 . . . at Myrtle Beach
15-17 . . . . . Wilmington
18-20 . . . . . . Carolina
21-24 . . . . at Salem
25-28 . . . . . . Frederick
29-31 . . . at Fayetteville

JUNE
2-4 . . . . Winston-Salem
5-7 . . . . at Salem
9-11 . . . . at Fayetteville
12-14 . . . . . . Carolina
15-17 . . at Fredericksburg
18-21 . . . . . Wilmington
25-28 . . . at Winston-Salem

FAYETTEVILLE WOODPECKERS

APRIL
9-12 . . . . Frederick
13-15 . . . . . at Down East
16-19 . . . . Fredericksburg
20-22 . . . . . . Carolina
23-26 . . . . at Wilmington
28-30 . . . . at Frederick

MAY
1-3 . . . . Wilmington
4-7 . . . . . . at Down East
8-10 . . . Myrtle Beach
12-14 . . . at Fredericksburg
15-17 . . . . . . Carolina
18-20 . . . . . . at Salem
21-24 . . . . . at Frederick
25-28 . . . . Salem
29-31 . . . . . Down East

JUNE
2-4 . . . . . . at Lynchburg
5-7 . . . . . at Carolina
9-11 . . . . . . Down East
12-14 . . . . Fredericksburg
15-17 . . at Winston-Salem
18-21 . . . . . . Carolina

(continued columns)
24-26 . . . . . Myrtle Beach
28-30 . . . . . Lynchburg
31 . . . . . at Winston-Salem

AUGUST
1-2 . . . at Winston-Salem
3-5 . . . . . at Myrtle Beach
6-9 . . . . . Winston-Salem
11-13 . . . . at Salem
14-16 . . . . . Myrtle Beach
17-19 . . . . . . Lynchburg
20-23 . . . . . at Down East
25-27 . . . . at Fayetteville
28-31 . . . . Frederick

SEPTEMBER
1-3 . . . at Winston-Salem
4-7 . . . . . . at Frederick

30 . . . . Carolina

JULY
1-3 . . . . Carolina
4-6 . . . . Salem
7-9 . . . at Fredericksburg
10-13 . . . at Frederick
15-17 . . . Winston-Salem
18-20 . . . Myrtle Beach
21-23 . . at Fredericksburg
24-26 . . . . . Fayetteville
28-30 . . . . at Myrtle Beach
31 . . . . Wilmington

AUGUST
1-2 . . . . Wilmington
3-5 . . . . . . at Frederick
6-9 . . . . at Wilmington
11-13 . . . at Winston-Salem
14-16 . . . . . Lynchburg
17-19 . . . . at Fayetteville
20-23 . . . . Carolina
25-27 . . at Winston-Salem
28-31 . . . Myrtle Beach

SEPTEMBER
1-3 . . . . . Fredericksburg
4-7 . . . . at Myrtle Beach

25-28 . . . . at Myrtle Beach
30 . . . . . Winston-Salem

JULY
1-3 . . . . . Winston-Salem
4-6 . . . . at Carolina
7-9 . . . . Salem
10-13 . . . Winston-Salem
15-17 . . . at Myrtle Beach
18-20 . . . . . . at Salem
21-23 . . . . . Lynchburg
24-26 . . . . . at Down East
28-30 . . at Winston-Salem
31 . . . . . at Myrtle Beach

AUGUST
1-2 . . . . at Myrtle Beach
3-5 . . . . . . Wilmington
6-9 . . . . . Myrtle Beach
11-13 . . . at Lynchburg
14-16 . . . . Wilmington
17-19 . . . . . Down East
20-23 . . at Winston-Salem
25-27 . . . . . . Carolina
28-31 . . at Fredericksburg

FREDERICK KEYS

SEPTEMBER	
1-3	Myrtle Beach
4-7	at Lynchburg

APRIL	
9-12	at Fayetteville
13-15	at Lynchburg
16-19	Myrtle Beach
20-22	Wilmington
23-26	at Fredericksburg
28-30	Fayetteville

MAY	
1-3	at Fredericksburg
4-7	Lynchburg
8-10	Winston-Salem
12-14	at Salem
15-17	Fredericksburg
18-20	at Wilmington
21-24	Fayetteville
25-28	at Down East
29-31	at Myrtle Beach

JUNE	
2-4	Salem
5-7	Fredericksburg
9-11	at Lynchburg
12-14	Wilmington
15-17	Myrtle Beach
18-21	at Lynchburg
25-28	at Wilmington

30	Lynchburg

JULY	
1-3	Lynchburg
4-6	at Fredericksburg
7-9	at Winston-Salem
10-13	Down East
15-17	at Carolina
18-20	at Winston-Salem
21-23	Carolina
24-26	Salem
28-30	at Wilmington
31	at Salem

AUGUST	
1-2	at Salem
3-5	Down East
6-9	at Salem
11-13	Fredericksburg
14-16	Winston-Salem
17-19	at Wilmington
20-23	Fredericksburg
25-27	at Myrtle Beach
28-31	at Carolina

SEPTEMBER	
1-3	Salem
4-7	Carolina

FREDERICKSBURG NATIONALS

APRIL	
9-12	at Down East
13-15	at Myrtle Beach
16-19	at Fayetteville
20-22	at Winston-Salem
23-26	Frederick
28-30	at Winston-Salem

MAY	
1-3	Frederick
4-7	Carolina
8-10	at Wilmington
12-14	Fayetteville
15-17	at Frederick
18-20	Myrtle Beach
21-24	Lynchburg
25-28	at Carolina
29-31	Lynchburg

JUNE	
2-4	at Wilmington
5-7	at Frederick
9-11	Winston-Salem
12-14	at Fayetteville
15-17	Down East
18-21	Wilmington
25-28	at Salem
30	at Wilmington

JULY	
1-3	at Wilmington
4-6	Frederick
7-9	Down East
10-13	at Wilmington
15-17	Salem
18-20	at Lynchburg
21-23	Down East
24-26	Wilmington
28-30	at Salem
31	at Lynchburg

AUGUST	
1-2	at Lynchburg
3-5	Winston-Salem
6-9	Lynchburg
11-13	at Frederick
14-16	Salem
17-19	at Myrtle Beach
20-23	at Frederick
25-27	Wilmington
28-31	Fayetteville

SEPTEMBER	
1-3	at Down East
4-7	Salem

LYNCHBURG HILLCATS

APRIL	
9-12	at Salem
13-15	Frederick
16-19	Carolina
20-22	at Down East
23-26	at Salem
28-30	Wilmington

MAY	
1-3	Down East
4-7	at Frederick
8-10	Salem
12-14	at Winston-Salem
15-17	at Myrtle Beach
18-20	Winston-Salem
21-24	at Fredericksburg

25-28	Wilmington
29-31	at Fredericksburg

JUNE	
2-4	Fayetteville
5-7	at Wilmington
9-11	Frederick
12-14	Myrtle Beach
15-17	at Wilmington
18 (21)	Frederick
25-28	at Carolina
30	at Frederick

JULY	
1-3	at Frederick
4-6	Wilmington
7-9	at Myrtle Beach
10-13	Carolina
15-17	Wilmington
18-20	Fredericksburg

MYRTLE BEACH PELICANS

APRIL	
9-12	Wilmington
13-15	Fredericksburg
16-19	at Frederick
20-22	at Salem
23-26	Winston-Salem
28-30	at Carolina

MAY	
1-3	at Winston-Salem
4-7	Salem
8-10	at Fayetteville
12-14	Down East
15-17	Lynchburg
18-20	at Fredericksburg
21-24	at Wilmington
25-28	at Winston-Salem
29-31	Frederick

JUNE	
2-4	at Carolina
5-7	at Winston-Salem
9-11	Carolina
12-14	at Lynchburg
15-17	at Frederick
18-21	Salem
25-28	Fayetteville

30	Salem

JULY	
1-3	Salem
4-6	at Winston-Salem
7-9	Lynchburg
10-13	at Salem
15-17	Fayetteville
18-20	at Down East
21-23	Winston-Salem
24-26	at Carolina
28-30	Down East
31	Fayetteville

AUGUST	
1-2	Fayetteville
3-5	Carolina
6-9	at Fayetteville
11-13	Wilmington
14-16	at Carolina
17-19	Fredericksburg
20-23	at Lynchburg
25-27	Frederick
28-31	at Down East

SEPTEMBER	
1-3	at Fayetteville
4-7	Down East

SALEM RED SOX

APRIL	
9-12	Lynchburg
13-15	Winston-Salem
16-19	at Wilmington
20-22	Myrtle Beach
23-26	Lynchburg
28-30	at Down East

MAY	
1-3	Carolina
4-7	at Myrtle Beach
8-10	at Lynchburg
12-14	Frederick
15-17	at Winston-Salem
18-20	Fayetteville
21-24	Down East
25-28	at Fayetteville
29-31	Carolina

JUNE	
2-4	at Frederick
5-7	Down East
9-11	Wilmington
12-14	at Winston-Salem
15-17	at Carolina

18-21	at Myrtle Beach
25-28	Fredericksburg
30	at Myrtle Beach

JULY	
1-3	at Myrtle Beach
4-6	at Down East
7-9	at Fayetteville
10-13	Myrtle Beach
15-17	at Fredericksburg
18-20	Fayetteville
21-23	at Wilmington
24-26	at Frederick
28-30	Fredericksburg
31	Frederick

AUGUST	
1-2	Frederick
3-5	at Lynchburg
6-9	Frederick
11-13	Carolina
14-16	at Fredericksburg
17-19	Winston-Salem
20-23	at Wilmington
25-27	Lynchburg

28-31 . . . . . . Wilmington

1-3 . . . . at Frederick

WILMINGTON BLUE ROCKS

APRIL
9-12 . . . . at Myrtle Beach
13-15 . . . . . at Carolina
16-19 . . . . Salem
20-22 . . . . at Frederick
23-26 . . . . . Fayetteville
28-30 . . . . . at Lynchburg

MAY
1-3 . . . . . at Fayetteville
4-7 . . . . . Winston-Salem
8-10 . . . . . Fredericksburg
12-14 . . . . at Carolina
15-17 . . . at Down East
18-20 . . . . . . Frederick
21-24 . . . . Myrtle Beach
25-28 . . . . at Lynchburg
29-31 . . at Winston-Salem

JUNE
2-4 . . . . . Fredericksburg
5-7 . . . . Lynchburg
9-11 . . . . . . at Salem
12-14 . . . . at Frederick
15-17 . . . . . Lynchburg
18-21 . . . at Fredericksburg
25-28 . . . . . . Frederick

30 . . . . . Fredericksburg

JULY
1-3 . . . . Fredericksburg
4-6 . . . . . . at Lynchburg
7-9 . . . . . at Carolina
10-13 . . . . Fredericksburg
15-17 . . . . . at Lynchburg
18-20 . . . . . . Carolina
21-23 . . . . Salem
24-26 . . at Fredericksburg
28-30 . . . . . . Frederick
31 . . . . at Down East

AUGUST
1-2 . . . . . . at Down East
3-5 . . . . . at Fayetteville
6-9 . . . . . . Down East
11-13 . . . . at Myrtle Beach
14-16 . . . . at Fayetteville
17-19 . . . . . . Frederick
20-23 . . . . Salem
25-27 . . at Fredericksburg
28-31 . . . . . . at Salem

SEPTEMBER
1-3 . . . . . . Lynchburg
4-7 . . . . . Winston-Salem

WINSTON-SALEM DASH

APRIL
9-12 . . . . . . at Carolina
13-15 . . . . . . at Salem
16-19 . . . Down East
20-22 . . . Fredericksburg
23-26 . . . at Myrtle Beach
28-30 . . . Fredericksburg

MAY
1-3 . . . . Myrtle Beach
4-7 . . . . . at Wilmington
8-10 . . . at Frederick
12-14 . . . . . Lynchburg
15-17 . . . . Salem
18-20 . . . at Lynchburg
21-24 . . . . at Carolina
25-28 . . . . Myrtle Beach
29-31 . . . . . Wilmington

JUNE
2-4 . . . . . at Down East
5-7 . . . . . Myrtle Beach
9-11 . . at Fredericksburg
12-14 . . . . Salem
15-17 . . . . . Fayetteville
18-21 . . . at Down East
25-28 . . . . . Down East

30 . . . . . at Fayetteville

JULY
1-3 . . . . . at Fayetteville
4-6 . . . . . Myrtle Beach
7-9 . . . . Frederick
10-13 . . . . at Fayetteville
15-17 . . . . . at Down East
18-20 . . . . . . Frederick
21-23 . . . at Myrtle Beach
24-26 . . . . . . Lynchburg
28-30 . . . . . Fayetteville
31 . . . . Carolina

AUGUST
1-2 . . . . Carolina
3-5 . . at Fredericksburg
6-9 . . . . . . at Carolina
11-13 . . . . . Down East
14-16 . . . . . at Frederick
17-19 . . . . . . at Salem
20-23 . . . . Fayetteville
25-27 . . . . . Down East
28-31 . . . . . at Lynchburg

SEPTEMBER
1-3 . . . . Carolina
4-7 . . . . . at Wilmington

FLORIDA STATE LEAGUE
BRADENTON MARAUDERS

APRIL
9-10 . . . . Charlotte
11 . . . . at Charlotte
13-15 . . . . . . at St. Lucie
16-19 . . . . . Tampa
20-23 . . . . . . Florida

24-26 . . . . at Palm Beach
28-30 . . . . at Jupiter

MAY
1-3 . . . . St. Lucie
4-6 . . . . at Dunedin
7-9 . . . . Fort Myers

11-14 . . . . . . Dunedin
15-17 . . . at Clearwater
18-21 . . . . at Daytona
22-24 . . . . . . Jupiter
26-28 . . . . Palm Beach
29-31 . . . . at Tampa

JUNE
1-4 . . . . Lakeland
5-7 . . . . . . Daytona
8-10 . . . at Fort Myers
11-14 . . . . at Charlotte
15-17 . . . . Palm Beach
18-21 . . . . . at Florida
25-28 . . . . . . Charlotte
29-30 . . . at Palm Beach

JULY
1-3 . . . . at Palm Beach
4-6 . . . . . Clearwater
8-10 . . . . . at Jupiter
11-13 . . . . Tampa
14-16 . . . . at Fort Myers

CHARLOTTE STONE CRABS

APRIL
9-10 . . . . . at Bradenton
11 . . . . Bradenton
13-15 . . . . . Clearwater
16-19 . . . . at Daytona
20-23 . . . at Lakeland
24-26 . . . . Fort Myers
28-30 . . . Palm Beach

MAY
1-3 . . . . at Fort Myers
4-6 . . . . . at Palm Beach
7-9 . . . . Tampa
11-14 . . . . Jupiter
15-17 . . . . at St. Lucie
18-21 . . . . . at Jupiter
22-24 . . . . . Clearwater
26-28 . . . . . . Tampa
29-31 . . . . at Palm Beach

JUNE
1-4 . . . . St. Lucie
5-7 . . . . at Clearwater
8-10 . . . . . . at Tampa
11-14 . . . . . Bradenton
15-17 . . . . . at Jupiter
18-21 . . . . . Daytona
25-28 . . . . at Bradenton
29-30 . . . . . . Florida

JULY
1-3 . . . . Florida
4-6 . . . . . . at Fort Myers
8-10 . . . . at Tampa
11-13 . . . . St. Lucie
14-16 . . . . at Palm Beach
17-19 . . . . at Dunedin
21-23 . . . . Jupiter
24-26 . . . . . . Dunedin
27-29 . . . . at St. Lucie
30-31 . . . . . . at Florida

AUGUST
1-2 . . . . at Florida
4-6 . . . . . . Fort Myers
7-9 . . . . . Palm Beach
10-12 . . . . at St. Lucie
13-16 . . . . at Dunedin
17-19 . . . . . Bradenton
20-23 . . . . . . Lakeland
25-27 . . . at Clearwater
28-30 . . . . Jupiter
31 . . . . Dunedin

SEPTEMBER
1-2 . . . . Dunedin
3-4 . . . . . . at Fort Myers
5-6 . . . . . . Fort Myers

CLEARWATER THRESHERS

APRIL
9-10 . . . . . . Dunedin
11 . . . . . . at Dunedin
13-15 . . . . at Charlotte
16-19 . . . . Palm Beach
20-23 . . . . . St. Lucie
24 . . . . at Tampa
25 . . . . Tampa
26 . . . . at Tampa
28-30 . . . . at St. Lucie

MAY
1-3 . . . . Dunedin
4-6 . . . . . . at Lakeland
7-9 . . . . . . at Dunedin
11-13 . . . . . . Tampa
14 . . . . . . at Tampa
15-17 . . . . . Bradenton
18-21 . . . . at St. Lucie
22-24 . . . at Charlotte
26-28 . . . . . Lakeland
29-31 . . . at Fort Myers

JUNE
1-4 . . . . . . Daytona
5-7 . . . . . . Charlotte
8-10 . . . . at Daytona
11-14 . . . . . . Florida
15-17 . . . . at Fort Myers

17-19 . . . . . . at St. Lucie
21-23 . . . . Fort Myers
24-26 . . . . . . Jupiter
27-29 . . . . at Dunedin
30-31 . . . . . at Lakeland

AUGUST
1-2 . . . . at Lakeland
4-6 . . . . St. Lucie
7-9 . . . . . . at Tampa
10-12 . . . . . Daytona
13-16 . . . . . at Jupiter
17-19 . . . . at Charlotte
20-23 . . . . . . Dunedin
25-27 . . . . at Daytona
28-30 . . . . Fort Myers
31 . . . . Jupiter

SEPTEMBER
1-2 . . . . Jupiter
3-4 . . . . . at Clearwater
5-6 . . . . . . Clearwater

18-21 . . . . . at Dunedin
25-28 . . . . . . Tampa
29-30 . . . . . Jupiter

JULY
1-3 . . . . Jupiter
4-6 . . . . at Bradenton
8-10 . . . . at Daytona
11-13 . . . . . Lakeland
14-16 . . . . . at Tampa
17-19 . . . . at Fort Myers
21-23 . . . . . . Florida
24-26 . . . . Fort Myers
27-29 . . . . at Lakeland
30-31 . . . . . . Jupiter

AUGUST
1-2 . . . . . . at Jupiter
4-6 . . . . Dunedin
7-9 . . . . . . Daytona
10-12 . . . . at Florida
13-16 . . . . . St. Lucie
17-19 . . . . Fort Myers
20-23 . . . at Palm Beach
25-27 . . . . . Charlotte
28-30 . . . . at Florida
31 . . . . at Tampa

SEPTEMBER
1-2 . . . . Fort Myers

4-7 . . . . at Fredericksburg

3-4 . . . . Bradenton   5-6 . . . . . . at Bradenton

DAYTONA TORTUGAS

APRIL	
9-11 . . . . Florida	
13-15 . . . . at Tampa	
16-19 . . . . Charlotte	
20-23 . . . . . . Palm Beach	
24-26 . . . . . . at Dunedin	
28-30 . . . . . . at Florida	

MAY	
1-3 . . . . Tampa	
4-6 . . . . St. Lucie	
7-9 . . . . at Jupiter	
11-14 . . . . at Palm Beach	
15-17 . . . . . at Lakeland	
18-21 . . . . . . Bradenton	
22-24 . . . . Lakeland	
26-28 . . . . . at St. Lucie	
29-31 . . . . Dunedin	

JUNE	
1-4 . . . . . at Clearwater	
5-7 . . . . . at Bradenton	
8-10 . . . . . . Clearwater	
11-14 . . . . . Fort Myers	
15-17 . . . . . at Dunedin	
18-21 . . . . . at Charlotte	
25-28 . . . . Dunedin	
29-30 . . . . Tampa	

JULY	
1-3 . . . . Tampa	
4-6 . . . . at Jupiter	
8-10 . . . . Clearwater	
11-13 . . . . Jupiter	
14-16 . . . . . . at Lakeland	
17-19 . . . . at Florida	
21-23 . . . . St. Lucie	
24-26 . . . . Lakeland	
27-29 . . . . at Jupiter	
30-31 . . . . . at Fort Myers	

AUGUST	
1-2 . . . . . . at Fort Myers	
4-6 . . . . Jupiter	
7-9 . . . . at Clearwater	
10-12 . . . . . at Bradenton	
13-16 . . . . Florida	
17-19 . . . . . Palm Beach	
20-23 . . . . . . at St. Lucie	
25-27 . . . . . . Bradenton	
28-30 . . . . at Tampa	
31 . . . . at Florida	

SEPTEMBER	
1-2 . . . . at Florida	
3-4 . . . . Palm Beach	
5-6 . . . . . at Palm Beach	

DUNEDIN BLUE JAYS

APRIL	
9-10 . . . . . . at Clearwater	
11 . . . . Clearwater	
13-15 . . . . Lakeland	
16-19 . . . . . . at Jupiter	
20-23 . . . . . at Fort Myers	
24-26 . . . . Daytona	
28-30 . . . . Lakeland	

MAY	
1-3 . . . . . at Clearwater	
4-6 . . . . Bradenton	
7-9 . . . . Clearwater	
11-14 . . . . at Bradenton	
15-17 . . . . at Tampa	
18-21 . . . . Florida	
22-24 . . . . . . Fort Myers	
26-28 . . . . . . at Florida	
29-31 . . . . . . at Daytona	

JUNE	
1-4 . . . . Jupiter	
5-7 . . . . Tampa	
8-10 . . . . . . at Lakeland	
11-14 . . . . at Palm Beach	
15-17 . . . . Daytona	
18-21 . . . . . . Clearwater	
25-28 . . . . . at Daytona	
29-30 . . . . St. Lucie	

JULY	
1-3 . . . . St. Lucie	
4-6 . . . . at Florida	
8-10 . . . . . . at Lakeland	
11-13 . . . . . . Fort Myers	
14-16 . . . . . at St. Lucie	
17-19 . . . . Charlotte	
21-23 . . . . at Tampa	
24-26 . . . . . at Charlotte	
27-29 . . . . . . Bradenton	
30-31 . . . . . . Palm Beach	

AUGUST	
1-2 . . . . Palm Beach	
4-6 . . . . . . at Clearwater	
7-9 . . . . Lakeland	
10-12 . . . . at Fort Myers	
13-16 . . . . Charlotte	
17-19 . . . . St. Lucie	
20-23 . . . . . at Bradenton	
25-27 . . . . Florida	
28-30 . . . . . at St. Lucie	
31 . . . . at Charlotte	

SEPTEMBER	
1-2 . . . . at Charlotte	
3-4 . . . . Tampa	
5-6 . . . . at Tampa	

FLORIDA FIRE FROGS

APRIL	
9-11 . . . . at Daytona	
13-15 . . . . Jupiter	
16-19 . . . . . at Fort Myers	
20-23 . . . . . at Bradenton	
24-26 . . . . Lakeland	
28-30 . . . . Daytona	

MAY	
1-3 . . . . at Lakeland	
4-6 . . . . at Tampa	
7-9 . . . . Palm Beach	
11-14 . . . . St. Lucie	
15-17 . . . . . . at Jupiter	
18-21 . . . . . . at Dunedin	

22-24 . . . . Tampa
26-28 . . . . Dunedin
29-31 . . . . . . at St. Lucie

JUNE	
1-4 . . . . Fort Myers	
5-7 . . . . Lakeland	
8-10 . . . . at Jupiter	
11-14 . . . . at Clearwater	
15-17 . . . . Tampa	
18-21 . . . . Bradenton	
25-28 . . . . at Palm Beach	
29-30 . . . . . at Charlotte	

JULY	
1-3 . . . . at Charlotte	
4-6 . . . . Dunedin	
8-10 . . . . at St. Lucie	
11-13 . . . . at Palm Beach	
14-16 . . . . Jupiter	
17-19 . . . . Daytona	
21-23 . . . . at Clearwater	
24-26 . . . . at Tampa	
27-29 . . . . . Palm Beach	
30-31 . . . . Charlotte	

AUGUST	
1-2 . . . . Charlotte	

FORT MYERS MIGHTY MUSSELS

APRIL	
9-10 . . . . St. Lucie	
11 . . . . at St. Lucie	
13-15 . . . . at Palm Beach	
16-19 . . . . Florida	
20-23 . . . . Dunedin	
24-26 . . . . . at Charlotte	
28-30 . . . . . . at Tampa	

MAY	
1-3 . . . . Charlotte	
4-6 . . . . Jupiter	
7-9 . . . . . at Bradenton	
11-14 . . . . Lakeland	
15-17 . . . . . Palm Beach	
18-21 . . . . at Tampa	
22-24 . . . . . . at Dunedin	
26-28 . . . . at Jupiter	
29-31 . . . . . . Clearwater	

JUNE	
1-4 . . . . at Florida	
5-7 . . . . Palm Beach	
8-10 . . . . Bradenton	
11-14 . . . . . . at Daytona	
15-17 . . . . . . Clearwater	
18-21 . . . . . . at St. Lucie	
25-28 . . . . Jupiter	
29-30 . . . . . . at Lakeland	

JULY	
1-3 . . . . at Lakeland	
4-6 . . . . Charlotte	
8-10 . . . . Palm Beach	
11-13 . . . . . . at Dunedin	
14-16 . . . . Bradenton	
17-19 . . . . Clearwater	
21-23 . . . . . at Bradenton	
24-26 . . . . . at Clearwater	
27-29 . . . . Tampa	
30-31 . . . . Daytona	

AUGUST	
1-2 . . . . Daytona	
4-6 . . . . at Charlotte	
7-9 . . . . at Jupiter	
10-12 . . . . Dunedin	
13-16 . . . . Tampa	
17-19 . . . . . at Clearwater	
20-23 . . . . at Florida	
25-27 . . . . St. Lucie	
28-30 . . . . . at Bradenton	
31 . . . . at Palm Beach	

SEPTEMBER	
1-2 . . . . . . at Palm Beach	
3-4 . . . . Charlotte	
5-6 . . . . at Charlotte	

JUPITER HAMMERHEADS

APRIL	
9-10 . . . . Palm Beach	
11 . . . . . . at Palm Beach	
13-15 . . . . at Florida	
16-19 . . . . Dunedin	
20-23 . . . . Tampa	
24-26 . . . . . . at St. Lucie	
28-30 . . . . . . Bradenton	

MAY	
1-3 . . . . . at Palm Beach	
4-6 . . . . . at Fort Myers	
7-9 . . . . Daytona	
11-14 . . . . . at Charlotte	
15-17 . . . . Florida	
18-21 . . . . Charlotte	
22-24 . . . . at Bradenton	
26-28 . . . . . . Fort Myers	
29-31 . . . . . at Lakeland	

JUNE	
1-4 . . . . at Dunedin	
5-7 . . . . St. Lucie	
8-10 . . . . Florida	
11-14 . . . . . . at Lakeland	
15-17 . . . . Charlotte	
18-21 . . . . Lakeland	
25-28 . . . . . at Fort Myers	
29-30 . . . . . at Clearwater	

JULY	
1-3 . . . . at Clearwater	
4-6 . . . . Daytona	
8-10 . . . . Bradenton	
11-13 . . . . . at Daytona	
14-16 . . . . . . at Florida	
17-19 . . . . . Palm Beach	
21-23 . . . . . at Charlotte	
24-26 . . . . . at Bradenton	
27-29 . . . . Daytona	
30-31 . . . . . . Clearwater	

AUGUST	
1-2 . . . . Clearwater	
4-6 . . . . at Daytona	
7-9 . . . . Fort Myers	
10-12 . . . . at Palm Beach	
13-16 . . . . Bradenton	
17-19 . . . . Lakeland	
20-23 . . . . at Tampa	
25-27 . . . . . . Palm Beach	
28-30 . . . . . at Charlotte	
31 . . . . at Bradenton	

SEPTEMBER	
1-2 . . . . at Bradenton	
3-4 . . . . St. Lucie	
5-6 . . . . at St. Lucie	

LAKELAND FLYING TIGERS

APRIL
9-10 . . . . Tampa
11 . . . . at Tampa
13-15 . . . . . . at Dunedin
16-19 . . . . . . St. Lucie
20-23 . . . . . . Charlotte
24-26 . . . . . . at Florida
28-30 . . . . . . at Dunedin

MAY
1-3 . . . . Florida
4-6 . . . . Clearwater
7-9 . . . . at St. Lucie
11-14 . . . . at Fort Myers
15-17 . . . . Daytona
18-21 . . . . Palm Beach
22-24 . . . . . at Daytona
26-28 . . . . at Clearwater
29-31 . . . . Jupiter

JUNE
1-4 . . . . at Bradenton
5-7 . . . . at Florida
8-10 . . . . Dunedin
11-14 . . . . Jupiter
15-17 . . . . . at St. Lucie
18-21 . . . . . . at Jupiter
25-28 . . . . . . St. Lucie
29-30 . . . . . Fort Myers

JULY
1-3 . . . . Fort Myers
4 . . . . Tampa
5-6 . . . . at Tampa
8-10 . . . . Dunedin
11-13 . . . . at Clearwater
14-16 . . . . Daytona
17 . . . . Tampa
18 . . . . Tampa
19 . . . . Tampa
21-23 . . . . at Palm Beach
24-26 . . . . . . at Daytona
27-29 . . . . . Clearwater
30-31 . . . . . . Bradenton

AUGUST
1-2 . . . . Bradenton
4-6 . . . . at Tampa
7-9 . . . . at Dunedin
10-12 . . . . Tampa
13-16 . . . . . Palm Beach
17-19 . . . . . . at Jupiter
20-23 . . . . . at Charlotte
25-27 . . . . Tampa
28-30 . . . . at Palm Beach
31 . . . . at St. Lucie

SEPTEMBER
1-2 . . . . at St. Lucie
3-4 . . . . Florida
5-6 . . . . at Florida

PALM BEACH CARDINALS

APRIL
9-10 . . . . at Jupiter
11 . . . . Jupiter
13-15 . . . . . Fort Myers
16-19 . . . . . at Clearwater
20-23 . . . . . at Daytona
24-26 . . . . . Bradenton
28-30 . . . . at Charlotte

MAY
1-3 . . . . Jupiter
4-6 . . . . Charlotte
7-9 . . . . at Florida
11-14 . . . . Daytona
15-17 . . . . at Fort Myers
18-21 . . . . . . at Lakeland
22-24 . . . . . . St. Lucie
26-28 . . . . at Bradenton
29-31 . . . . . . Charlotte

JUNE
1-4 . . . . Tampa
5-7 . . . . . . at Fort Myers
8-10 . . . . . at St. Lucie
11-14 . . . . Dunedin
15-17 . . . . at Bradenton
18-21 . . . . . . at Tampa
25-28 . . . . Florida
29-30 . . . . . Bradenton

JULY
1-3 . . . . Bradenton
4-6 . . . . at St. Lucie
8-10 . . . . . at Fort Myers
11-13 . . . . Florida
14-16 . . . . Charlotte
17-19 . . . . . . at Jupiter
21-23 . . . . . . Lakeland
24-26 . . . . . . St. Lucie
27-29 . . . . . at Florida
30-31 . . . . . . at Dunedin

AUGUST
1-2 . . . . at Dunedin
4-6 . . . . Florida
7-9 . . . . at Charlotte
10-12 . . . . Jupiter
13-16 . . . . . at Lakeland
17-19 . . . . . . Daytona
20-23 . . . . . Clearwater
25-27 . . . . . . at Jupiter
28-30 . . . . . . Lakeland
31 . . . . Fort Myers

SEPTEMBER
1-2 . . . . Fort Myers
3-4 . . . . at Daytona
5-6 . . . . Daytona

ST. LUCIE METS

APRIL
April
9-10 . . . . . at Fort Myers
11 . . . . Fort Myers
13-15 . . . . . . Bradenton
16-19 . . . . . at Lakeland
20-23 . . . . at Clearwater
24-26 . . . . Jupiter
28-30 . . . . . Clearwater

MAY
1-3 . . . . . . at Bradenton
4-6 . . . . at Daytona
7-9 . . . . Lakeland
11-14 . . . . . at Florida
15-17 . . . . . Charlotte
18-21 . . . . . Clearwater

22-24 . . . . at Palm Beach
26-28 . . . . Daytona
29-31 . . . . Florida

JUNE
1-4 . . . . at Charlotte
5-7 . . . . at Jupiter
8-10 . . . . . Palm Beach
11-14 . . . . . at Tampa
15-17 . . . . . Lakeland
18-21 . . . . Fort Myers
25-28 . . . . at Lakeland
29-30 . . . . at Dunedin

JULY
1-3 . . . . . . at Dunedin
4-6 . . . . . Palm Beach
8-10 . . . . Florida

APRIL
11-13 . . . . . at Charlotte
14-16 . . . . . . Dunedin
17-19 . . . . . . Bradenton
21-23 . . . . . at Daytona
24-26 . . . . at Palm Beach
27-29 . . . . . Charlotte
30-31 . . . . . . Tampa

AUGUST
1-2 . . . . Tampa
4-6 . . . . . at Bradenton
7-9 . . . . at Florida

JULY
10-12 . . . . . . Charlotte
13-16 . . . . at Clearwater
17-19 . . . . . at Dunedin
20-23 . . . . . . Daytona
25-27 . . . . at Fort Myers
28-30 . . . . . . Dunedin
31 . . . . Lakeland

SEPTEMBER
1-2 . . . . Lakeland
3-4 . . . . at Jupiter
5-6 . . . . Jupiter

TAMPA TARPONS

APRIL
9-10 . . . . . . at Lakeland
11 . . . . Lakeland
13-15 . . . . . . Daytona
16-19 . . . . at Bradenton
20-23 . . . . . at Jupiter
24 . . . . Clearwater
25 . . . . . at Clearwater
26 . . . . . . Clearwater
28-30 . . . . . Fort Myers

MAY
1-3 . . . . at Daytona
4-6 . . . . Florida
7-9 . . . . at Charlotte
11-13 . . . . at Clearwater
14 . . . . Clearwater
15-17 . . . . . . Dunedin
18-21 . . . . Fort Myers
22-24 . . . . . at Florida
26-28 . . . . at Charlotte
29-31 . . . . . Bradenton
June
1-4 . . . . at Palm Beach
5-7 . . . . at Dunedin
8-10 . . . . . . Charlotte
11-14 . . . . . . St. Lucie
15-17 . . . . . at Florida
18-21 . . . . Palm Beach
25-28 . . . . at Clearwater
29-30 . . . . . at Daytona

JULY
1-3 . . . . at Daytona
4 . . . . at Lakeland
5-6 . . . . Lakeland
8-10 . . . . . . Charlotte
11-13 . . . . at Bradenton
14-16 . . . . . Clearwater
17 . . . . . . at Lakeland
18 . . . . Lakeland
19 . . . . . at Lakeland
21-23 . . . . . . Dunedin
24-26 . . . . Florida
27-29 . . . . at Fort Myers
30-31 . . . . . at St. Lucie

AUGUST
1-2 . . . . at St. Lucie
4-6 . . . . Lakeland
7-9 . . . . Bradenton
10-12 . . . . . at Lakeland
13-16 . . . . at Fort Myers
17-19 . . . . Florida
20-23 . . . . Jupiter
25-27 . . . . . at Lakeland
28-30 . . . . . . Daytona
31 . . . . Clearwater

SEPTEMBER
1-2 . . . . Clearwater
3-4 . . . . at Dunedin
5-6 . . . . Dunedin

LOW CLASS A

MIDWEST LEAGUE

BELOIT SNAPPERS

APRIL
9-11	Clinton
13-15	at Peoria
16-19	at Burlington
20-22	Cedar Rapids
23-26	Peoria
28-30	at Fort Wayne

MAY
1-3	at Lake County
4-6	Great Lakes
7-9	Lansing
11-13	at Peoria
14-16	at Clinton
17-19	Burlington
20-22	at Wisconsin
23-25	Clinton
26-28	Wisconsin
29-31	at Burlington

JUNE
2-4	Quad Cities
5-7	Cedar Rapids
8-10	at Quad Cities
11-14	Kane County
15-17	at Cedar Rapids
18-21	at Kane County
25-28	Wisconsin

29-30	at Clinton

JULY
1	at Clinton
2-3	Cedar Rapids
4-5	at Cedar Rapids
7-9	Peoria
10-13	at Burlington
15-17	Dayton
18-20	Bowling Green
21-23	at South Bend
24-26	at West Michigan
28-30	Cedar Rapids

AUGUST
1-2	at Wisconsin
4-6	at Peoria
7-9	Quad Cities
10-12	Clinton
13-16	at Peoria
18-20	Wisconsin
21-24	Burlington
25-27	at Quad Cities
28-31	Kane County

SEPTEMBER
1-3	at Clinton
4-7	at Kane County

BOWLING GREEN HOT RODS

APRIL
9-11	Fort Wayne
13-15	Great Lakes
16-19	at Fort Wayne
20-22	at Dayton
23-26	Lansing
28-30	at Clinton

MAY
1-3	at Burlington
4-6	Peoria
7-9	Cedar Rapids
11-13	at Great Lakes
14-16	at Lake County
17-19	Fort Wayne
20-22	Lake County
23-25	at South Bend
26-28	at West Michigan
29-31	Great Lakes

JUNE
2-4	West Michigan
5-7	at Lake County
8-10	Dayton
11-14	South Bend
15-17	at West Michigan
18-21	at Lansing
25-28	Dayton

29-30	at South Bend

JULY
1	at South Bend
2-3	at Dayton
4-5	Dayton
7-9	Lake County
10-13	Fort Wayne
16-18	at Wisconsin
18-20	at Beloit
21-23	Kane County
24-26	Quad Cities
28-30	at Great Lakes
31	at West Michigan

AUGUST
1-2	at West Michigan
4-6	Lansing
7-9	Lake County
10-12	South Bend
13-16	at Dayton
18-20	at Lake County
21-24	at Fort Wayne
25-27	Great Lakes
28-31	West Michigan

SEPTEMBER
1-3	at Dayton
4-7	at South Bend

BURLINGTON BEES

APRIL
9-11	at Wisconsin
13-15	Clinton
16-19	Beloit
20-22	at Clinton
23-26	at Kane County
28-30	Dayton

MAY
1-3	Bowling Green

4-6	at South Bend
7-9	at West Michigan
11-13	Kane County
14-16	Quad Cities
17-19	at Beloit
20-22	at Cedar Rapids
23-25	at Quad Cities
26-28	Peoria
29-31	Beloit

JUNE
2-4	at Clinton
5-7	Wisconsin
8-10	at Peoria
11-14	at Cedar Rapids
15-17	Peoria
18-21	Cedar Rapids
25-28	at Quad Cities
29-30	Wisconsin

JULY
1	Wisconsin
2-3	Clinton
4-5	at Clinton

CEDAR RAPIDS KERNELS

APRIL
9-11	at Kane County
13-15	Wisconsin
16-19	Quad Cities
20-22	at Beloit
23-26	at Wisconsin
28-30	South Bend

MAY
1-3	West Michigan
4-6	at Dayton
7-9	at Bowling Green
11-13	Wisconsin
14-16	Kane County
17-19	at Quad Cities
20-22	Burlington
23-25	Peoria
26-28	at Kane County
29-31	at Clinton

JUNE
2-4	at Peoria
5-7	at Beloit
8-10	Clinton
11-14	Burlington
15-17	Beloit
18-21	at Burlington
25-28	Peoria

29-30	Quad Cities

JULY
1	Quad Cities
2-3	at Beloit
4-5	Beloit
7-10	at Wisconsin
10-13	Kane County
15-17	at Great Lakes
18-20	at Lansing
21-23	Fort Wayne
24-26	Lake County
28-30	at Beloit
31	at Kane County

AUGUST
1-2	at Kane County
4-6	Wisconsin
7-9	Clinton
10-13	at Wisconsin
13-16	at Burlington
18-20	Kane County
21-24	at Quad Cities
25-27	Burlington
28-31	Quad Cities

SEPTEMBER
1-3	at Peoria
4-7	at Clinton

CLINTON LUMBERKINGS

APRIL
9-11	at Beloit
13-15	at Burlington
16-19	Wisconsin
20-22	Burlington
23-26	at Quad Cities
28-30	Bowling Green

MAY
1-3	Dayton
4-6	at West Michigan
7-9	at South Bend
11-13	Quad Cities
14-16	Beloit
17-19	at Wisconsin

20-22	Kane County
23-25	at Beloit
26-28	at Quad Cities
29-31	Cedar Rapids

JUNE
2-4	Burlington
5-7	at Kane County
8-10	at Cedar Rapids
11-14	Peoria
15-17	Wisconsin
18-21	at Peoria
25-28	at Kane County
29-30	Beloit

4-6	at South Bend
7-9	at West Michigan
11-13	Kane County
14-16	Quad Cities
17-19	at Beloit
20-22	at Cedar Rapids
23-25	at Quad Cities
26-28	Peoria
29-31	Beloit

JUNE
2-4	at Clinton
5-7	Wisconsin
8-10	at Peoria
11-14	at Cedar Rapids
15-17	Peoria
18-21	Cedar Rapids
25-28	at Quad Cities

29-30	Wisconsin

JULY
1	Wisconsin
2-3	Clinton
4-5	at Clinton

JULY
1	Beloit
2-3	at Burlington
4-5	Burlington
7-9	at Quad Cities
10-13	Wisconsin
15-17	at Fort Wayne
18-19	at Lake County
21-23	Great Lakes
24-26	Lansing
28-30	at Quad Cities
31	Peoria

AUGUST
1-2	Peoria
4-6	Quad Cities
7-9	at Cedar Rapids
10-12	at Beloit
13-16	Kane County
18-20	Peoria
21-24	at Kane County
25-27	at Peoria
29-31	at Wisconsin

SEPTEMBER
1-3	Beloit
4-7	Cedar Rapids

DAYTON DRAGONS

APRIL
9-11	Great Lakes
13-15	at Fort Wayne
16-19	at Lansing
20-22	Bowling Green
23-26	Lake County
28-30	at Burlington

MAY
1-3	at Clinton
4-6	Cedar Rapids
7-9	Peoria
11-13	at Lake County
14-16	at Great Lakes
17-19	Lake County
20-22	at Lansing
23-25	West Michigan
26-28	South Bend
29-31	at West Michigan

JUNE
2-4	at Fort Wayne
5-7	West Michigan
8-10	at Bowling Green
11-14	Lansing
15-17	Fort Wayne
18-21	at South Bend
25-28	at Bowling Green

29-30	Fort Wayne

JULY
1	Fort Wayne
2-3	Bowling Green
4-5	at Bowling Green
7-9	at Fort Wayne
10-13	Lake County
15-17	at Beloit
18-20	at Wisconsin
21-23	Quad Cities
24-26	Kane County
28-30	at Fort Wayne
31	South Bend

AUGUST
1-2	South Bend
4-6	Great Lakes
7-9	at South Bend
10-12	at Great Lakes
13-16	Bowling Green
18-20	West Michigan
21-24	at Lansing
25-27	at West Michigan
28-31	Great Lakes

SEPTEMBER
1-3	Bowling Green
4-7	at Lake County

FORT WAYNE TINCAPS

APRIL
9-11	at Bowling Green
13-15	Dayton
16-19	Bowling Green
20-22	at Great Lakes
23-26	at South Bend
28-30	Beloit

MAY
1-3	Wisconsin
4-6	at Quad Cities
7-9	at Kane County
11-13	South Bend
14-16	West Michigan
17-19	at Bowling Green
20-22	Great Lakes
23-25	at Lake County
26-28	at Great Lakes
29-31	Lansing

JUNE
2-4	Dayton
5-7	at Lansing
8-10	Lake County
11-14	at West Michigan
15-17	at Dayton
18-21	Great Lakes
25-28	South Bend
29-30	at Dayton

JULY
1	at Dayton
2-3	at Lake County
4-5	Lake County
7-9	Dayton
10-13	at Bowling Green
15-17	Clinton
18-20	Burlington
21-23	at Cedar Rapids
24-26	at Peoria
28-30	Dayton
31	at Lake County

AUGUST
1-2	at Lake County
4-6	at West Michigan
7-9	Great Lakes
10-12	West Michigan
13-16	at South Bend
18-20	Lansing
21-24	Bowling Green
25-27	at South Bend
28-31	at Lansing

SEPTEMBER
1-3	at Great Lakes
4-7	West Michigan

GREAT LAKES LOONS

APRIL
9-11	at Dayton
13-15	at Bowling Green
16-19	West Michigan
20-22	Fort Wayne
23-26	at West Michigan
28-30	Quad Cities

MAY
1-3	Kane County
4-6	at Beloit
7-9	at Wisconsin
11-13	Bowling Green
14-16	Dayton
17-19	at South Bend
20-22	at Fort Wayne
23-25	Lansing
26-28	Fort Wayne
29-31	at Bowling Green

JUNE
2-4	at Lake County
5-7	South Bend
8-10	at Lansing
11-14	Lake County
15-17	South Bend
18-21	at Fort Wayne
25-28	West Michigan

29-30	at Lake County

JULY
1	at Lake County
2-3	Lansing
4-5	at Lansing
7-9	South Bend
10-13	at West Michigan
15-17	Cedar Rapids
18-20	Peoria
21-23	at Clinton
24-26	at Burlington
28-30	Bowling Green
31	Lansing

AUGUST
1-2	Lansing
4-6	at Dayton
7-9	at Fort Wayne
10-12	Dayton
13-16	at Lake County
18-20	at South Bend
21-24	Lake County
25-27	at Bowling Green
28-31	at Dayton

SEPTEMBER
1-3	Fort Wayne
4-7	Lansing

KANE COUNTY COUGARS

APRIL
9-11	Cedar Rapids
13-15	Quad Cities
16-19	at Peoria
20-22	at Quad Cities
23-26	Burlington
28-30	at Lansing

MAY
1-3	at Great Lakes
4-6	Lake County
7-9	Fort Wayne
11-13	at Burlington
14-16	at Cedar Rapids
17-19	Peoria
20-22	at Clinton
23-25	Wisconsin
26-28	Cedar Rapids
29-31	at Peoria

JUNE
2-5	at Wisconsin
5-7	Clinton
8-11	at Wisconsin
11-14	at Beloit
15-17	Quad Cities
18-21	Beloit
25-28	Clinton

29-30	at Peoria

JULY
1	at Peoria
2-3	Quad Cities
4-5	at Quad Cities
7-9	at Cedar Rapids
10-13	at Cedar Rapids
15-17	South Bend
18-20	West Michigan
21-23	at Bowling Green
24-26	at Dayton
28-30	Peoria
31	Cedar Rapids

AUGUST
1-2	Cedar Rapids
4-6	at Burlington
7-9	at Peoria
10-12	Burlington
13-16	at Clinton
18-20	at Cedar Rapids
21-24	Clinton
25-27	Wisconsin
28-31	at Beloit

SEPTEMBER
1-3	at Wisconsin
4-7	Beloit

LAKE COUNTY CAPTAINS

APRIL
9-11	at South Bend
13-15	West Michigan
16-19	South Bend
20-22	at West Michigan
23-26	at Dayton
28-30	Wisconsin

MAY
1-3	Beloit
4-6	at Kane County
7-9	at Quad Cities

11-13	Dayton
14-16	Bowling Green
17-19	at Dayton
20-22	at Bowling Green
23-25	Fort Wayne
26-28	at Lansing
29-31	at South Bend

JUNE
2-4	Great Lakes
5-7	Bowling Green
8-10	at Fort Wayne

LANSING LUGNUTS

APRIL
- 9-11 at West Michigan
- 13-15 at South Bend
- 16-19 Dayton
- 20-22 South Bend
- 23-26 at Bowling Green
- 28-30 Kane County

MAY
- 1-3 Quad Cities
- 4-6 at Wisconsin
- 7-9 at Beloit
- 11-13 West Michigan
- 14-16 South Bend
- 17-19 at West Michigan
- 20-22 Dayton
- 23-25 at Great Lakes
- 26-28 Lake County
- 29-31 at Fort Wayne

JUNE
- 2-4 at South Bend
- 5-7 Fort Wayne
- 8-10 Great Lakes
- 11-14 at Dayton
- 15-17 at Lake County
- 18-21 Bowling Green
- 25-28 Lake County
- 29-30 at West Michigan

JULY
- 1 at West Michigan
- 2-3 at Great Lakes
- 4-5 Great Lakes
- 7-9 West Michigan
- 10-13 at South Bend
- 15-17 Peoria
- 18-20 Cedar Rapids
- 21-23 at Burlington
- 24-26 at Clinton
- 28-30 South Bend
- 31 at Great Lakes

AUGUST
- 1-2 at Great Lakes
- 4-6 at Bowling Green
- 7-9 West Michigan
- 10-12 Lake County
- 13-16 at West Michigan
- 18-20 at Fort Wayne
- 21-24 Dayton
- 25-27 at Lake County
- 28-31 Fort Wayne

SEPTEMBER
- 1-3 South Bend
- 4-7 at Great Lakes

PEORIA CHIEFS

APRIL
- 9-11 at Quad Cities
- 13-15 Beloit
- 16-19 Kane County
- 20-22 at Wisconsin
- 23-26 at Beloit
- 28-30 West Michigan

MAY
- 1-3 South Bend
- 4-6 at Bowling Green
- 7-9 at Dayton
- 11-13 Beloit
- 14-16 Wisconsin
- 17-19 at Kane County
- 20-22 Quad Cities
- 23-25 at Cedar Rapids
- 26-28 at Burlington
- 29-31 Kane County

JUNE
- 2-4 Cedar Rapids
- 5-7 at Quad Cities
- 8-10 Burlington
- 11-14 at Clinton
- 15-17 at Burlington
- 18-21 Clinton
- 25-28 at Cedar Rapids
- 29-30 Kane County

JULY
- 1 Kane County
- 2-3 at Wisconsin
- 4-5 Wisconsin
- 7-9 at Beloit
- 10-13 Quad Cities
- 15-17 at Lansing
- 18-20 at Great Lakes
- 21-23 Lake County
- 24-26 Fort Wayne
- 28-30 at Kane County
- 31 at Clinton

AUGUST
- 1-2 at Clinton
- 4-6 Beloit
- 7-9 Kane County
- 10-12 at Quad Cities
- 13-16 Beloit
- 18-20 at Clinton
- 22-24 at Wisconsin
- 25-27 Clinton
- 28-31 at Burlington

SEPTEMBER
- 1-3 Cedar Rapids
- 4-7 Burlington

QUAD CITIES RIVER BANDITS

APRIL
- 9-11 Peoria
- 13-15 at Kane County
- 16-19 at Cedar Rapids
- 20-22 Kane County
- 23-26 Clinton
- 28-30 at Great Lakes

MAY
- 1-3 at Lansing
- 4-6 Fort Wayne
- 7-9 Lake County
- 11-13 at Clinton
- 14-16 at Burlington
- 17-19 Cedar Rapids
- 20-22 at Peoria
- 23-25 Burlington
- 26-28 Clinton
- 29-31 at Wisconsin

JUNE
- 2-4 at Beloit
- 5-7 Peoria
- 8-10 Beloit

- 12-14 at Wisconsin
- 15-17 at Kane County
- 18-21 Wisconsin
- 25-28 Burlington
- 29-30 at Cedar Rapids

JULY
- 1 at Cedar Rapids
- 2-3 at Kane County
- 4-5 Kane County
- 7-9 Clinton
- 10-13 at Peoria
- 15-17 West Michigan
- 18-20 South Bend
- 21-23 at Dayton
- 24-26 at Bowling Green
- 28-30 Clinton
- 31 Burlington

AUGUST
- 1-2 Burlington
- 4-6 at Clinton
- 7-9 at Beloit
- 10-12 Peoria
- 14-16 at Wisconsin
- 18-20 at Burlington
- 21-24 Cedar Rapids
- 25-27 Beloit
- 28-31 at Cedar Rapids

SEPTEMBER
- 1-3 at Burlington
- 4-7 Wisconsin

SOUTH BEND CUBS

APRIL
- 9-11 Lake County
- 13-15 Lansing
- 16-19 at Lake County
- 20-22 at Lansing
- 23-26 Fort Wayne
- 28-30 at Cedar Rapids

MAY
- 1-3 at Peoria
- 4-6 Burlington
- 7-9 Clinton
- 11-13 at Fort Wayne
- 14-16 at Lansing
- 17-19 Great Lakes
- 20-22 at West Michigan
- 23-25 Bowling Green
- 26-28 at Dayton
- 29-31 Lake County

JUNE
- 2-4 Lansing
- 5-7 at Great Lakes
- 8-10 West Michigan
- 11-14 at Bowling Green
- 15-17 at Great Lakes
- 18-21 Dayton
- 25-28 at Fort Wayne
- 29-30 Bowling Green

JULY
- 1 Bowling Green
- 2-3 West Michigan
- 4-5 at West Michigan
- 7-9 at Great Lakes
- 10-13 Lansing
- 15-17 at Kane County
- 18-20 at Quad Cities
- 21-23 Beloit
- 24-26 Wisconsin
- 28-30 at Lansing
- 31 at Dayton

AUGUST
- 1-2 at Dayton
- 4-6 Lake County
- 7-9 Dayton
- 10-12 at Bowling Green
- 13-16 Fort Wayne
- 18-20 Great Lakes
- 21-24 at West Michigan
- 25-27 Fort Wayne
- 28-31 at Lake County

SEPTEMBER
- 1-3 at Lansing
- 4-7 Bowling Green

WEST MICHIGAN WHITECAPS

APRIL
- 9-11 Lansing
- 13-15 at Lake County
- 16-19 at Great Lakes
- 20-22 Lake County
- 23-26 Great Lakes
- 28-30 at Peoria

MAY
- 1-3 at Cedar Rapids
- 4-6 Clinton
- 7-9 Burlington
- 11-13 at Lansing
- 14-16 at Fort Wayne
- 17-19 Lansing
- 20-22 South Bend
- 23-25 at Dayton
- 26-28 Bowling Green
- 29-31 Dayton

JUNE
- 2-4 at Bowling Green
- 5-7 at Dayton
- 8-10 at South Bend
- 11-14 Fort Wayne
- 15-17 Bowling Green
- 18-21 at Lake County
- 25-28 at Great Lakes
- 29-30 Lansing

JULY
- 1 Lansing
- 2-3 at South Bend
- 4-5 South Bend
- 7-9 at Lansing
- 10-13 Great Lakes
- 15-17 at Quad Cities
- 18-20 at Kane County
- 21-23 Wisconsin
- 24-26 Beloit
- 28-30 at Lake County
- 31 Bowling Green

AUGUST
- 1-2 Bowling Green
- 4-6 Fort Wayne
- 7-9 at Lansing
- 10-12 at Fort Wayne
- 13-16 Lansing
- 18-20 at Dayton
- 21-24 South Bend
- 25-27 Dayton

SCHEDULES

28-31 . . . at Bowling Green

SEPTEMBER
1-3 . . . . . . Lake County
4-7 . . . . . at Fort Wayne

WISCONSIN TIMBER RATTLERS

APRIL
9-11 . . . . Burlington
13-15 . . . . at Cedar Rapids
16-19 . . . . at Clinton
20-22 . . . . Peoria
23-26 . . . . . Cedar Rapids
28-30 . . . . at Lake County

MAY
1-3 . . . . . . at Fort Wayne
4-6 . . . . Lansing
7-9 . . . . . . Great Lakes
11-13 . . . . at Cedar Rapids
14-16 . . . . . . at Peoria
17-19 . . . . . . Clinton
20-22 . . . . Beloit
23-25 . . . . at Kane County
26-28 . . . . at Beloit
29-31 . . . . . Quad Cities

JUNE
2-5 . . . . . . Kane County
5-7 . . . . . . at Burlington
8-11 . . . . . . Kane County
12-14 . . . . . . at Clinton
15-17 . . . . . Quad Cities
18-21 . . . . at Quad Cities
25-28 . . . . . . at Beloit

29-30 . . . . . at Burlington

JULY
1 . . . . at Burlington
2-3 . . . . Peoria
4-5 . . . . at Peoria
7-10 . . . . . Cedar Rapids
10-13 . . . . . . at Clinton
16-18 . . . . Bowling Green
18-20 . . . . Dayton
21-23 . . . at West Michigan
24-26 . . . . at South Bend
28-31 . . . . . . Burlington

AUGUST
1-2 . . . . Beloit
4-6 . . . . at Cedar Rapids
7-9 . . . . . at Burlington
10-13 . . . . . Cedar Rapids
14-16 . . . . . Quad Cities
18-20 . . . . . . at Beloit
22-24 . . . . Peoria
25-27 . . . at Kane County
29-31 . . . . Clinton

SEPTEMBER
1-3 . . . . . Kane County
4-7 . . . . . at Quad Cities

SOUTH ATLANTIC LEAGUE

ASHEVILLE TOURISTS

APRIL
9-11 . . . . . . at Delmarva
13-15 . . . at West Virginia
16-19 . . . . Columbia
20-22 . . . . Rome
23-26 . . . . . at Lexington
27-29 . . . . . at Augusta
30 . . . . Delmarva

MAY
1-3 . . . . Delmarva
5-7 . . . . . at Columbia
8-10 . . . . at Greensboro
12-14 . . . . . West Virginia
15-17 . . . . . . Lexington
19-21 . . . . . . at Rome
22-24 . . . . . at Columbia
25-28 . . . . . . Lexington
29-31 . . . . . . Greenville

JUNE
1 . . . . Greenville
2-4 . . . . . at Kannapolis
5-7 . . . . . at Delmarva
9-11 . . . . . . Greenville
12-14 . . . . at Columbia
15-17 . . . . at Charleston
18-21 . . . . Rome

25-27 . . . . . . Lexington
28-30 . . . . at Charleston

JULY
1-3 . . . . at West Virginia
4-7 . . . . Lexington
8-10 . . . . . at Greenville
11-14 . . . . Rome
16-19 . . . . at Columbia
21-23 . . . . Hagerstown
24-26 . . . . . . Hickory
28-30 . . . at Kannapolis
31 . . . . . at Charleston

AUGUST
1-2 . . . . . at Charleston
4-6 . . . . . Hagerstown
7-9 . . . . . . at Augusta
10-13 . . . . . at Lexington
14-16 . . . . . . Columbia
17-19 . . . . at Augusta
20-23 . . . . . Charleston
24-27 . . . . . . Columbia
28-30 . . . . at Greenville

SEPTEMBER
1-4 . . . . Augusta
5-7 . . . . . . Charleston

AUGUSTA GREENJACKETS

APRIL
9-12 . . . . . at Columbia
13-15 . . . . at Greensboro
16-19 . . . . Rome
20-22 . . . . . . Lexington
23-26 . . . . at Charleston
27-29 . . . . . . Asheville
30 . . . . at Hickory

MAY
1-3 . . . . at Hickory
5-7 . . . . Lakewood
8-10 . . . . . Kannapolis
12-14 . . . at Hagerstown
15-17 . . . . at Lakewood
19-21 . . . . . Greenville
22-24 . . . . . Charleston
25-28 . . . . at Hickory
29-31 . . . . Kannapolis

JUNE
1 . . . . Kannapolis
2-4 . . . . West Virginia
5-7 . . . . at Charleston
9-11 . . . . . . Delmarva
12-14 . . . at Greenville
15-17 . . . . . at Rome
18-21 . . . . Charleston

25-27 . . . . . at Greenville
28-30 . . . . at Lexington

JULY
1-3 . . . . Charleston
4-7 . . . . at Rome
8-10 . . . . . . Greensboro
11-14 . . . . . Charleston
16-19 . . . at Kannapolis
21-23 . . . . . Columbia
24-26 . . . . Hagerstown
28-30 . . . at Delmarva
31 . . . . . at Kannapolis

AUGUST
1-2 . . . . . at Kannapolis
4-6 . . . . Columbia
7-9 . . . . Asheville
10-13 . . . . at Charleston
14-16 . . . . . Greenville
17-19 . . . . . Asheville
20-23 . . . . at Columbia
24-27 . . . . . at Rome
28-30 . . . . Delmarva

SEPTEMBER
1-4 . . . . . at Asheville
5-7 . . . . . West Virginia

CHARLESTON RIVERDOGS

APRIL
9-12 . . . . Kannapolis
13-15 . . . . . . Hickory
16-19 . . . at Greenville
20-22 . . . at Kannapolis
23-26 . . . . . . Augusta
27-29 . . . . at Hickory
30 . . . . . . Greensboro

MAY
1-3 . . . . . Greensboro
5-7 . . . . . . at Rome
8-10 . . . . at Columbia
13-14 . . . . Lexington
15-17 . . . . Delmarva
19-21 . . . at West Virginia
22-24 . . . at Augusta
25-28 . . . . Columbia
29-31 . . . . . . Rome

JUNE
1 . . . . Rome
2-4 . . . . at Greenville
5-7 . . . . . . Augusta
9-11 . . . . at Columbia
12-14 . . . . at Rome
15-17 . . . . Asheville
18-21 . . . at Augusta

25-27 . . . . . . Hickory
28-30 . . . . . Asheville

JULY
1-3 . . . . . at Augusta
4-7 . . . . . . Greenville
8-10 . . . . at Hickory
11-14 . . . . at Augusta
16-19 . . . . . Greenville
21-23 . . . at Lakewood
24-26 . . . at Greensboro
28-30 . . . . West Virginia
31 . . . . Asheville

AUGUST
1-2 . . . . Asheville
4-6 . . . . . at Lexington
7-9 . . . . . at Greenville
10-13 . . . . . Augusta
14-16 . . . . . . Rome
17-19 . . . . at Columbia
20-23 . . . at Asheville
24-27 . . . . Greenville
28-30 . . . . at Rome

SEPTEMBER
1-4 . . . . . Kannapolis
5-7 . . . . . at Asheville

COLUMBIA FIREFLIES

APRIL
9-12 . . . . . . Augusta
13-15 . . . . Kannapolis
16-19 . . . at Asheville
20-22 . . . at Hickory
23-26 . . . Hagerstown
27-29 . . . at Greensboro
30 . . . . . at Lakewood

MAY
1-3 . . . . . at Lakewood
5-7 . . . . . . Asheville
8-10 . . . . Charleston
12-14 . . . at Kannapolis

15-17 . . . . at Greenville
19-21 . . . . Hagerstown
22-24 . . . . Asheville
25-28 . . . at Charleston
29-31 . . . at West Virginia

JUNE
1 . . . . . at West Virginia
2-4 . . . . . . Lexington
5-7 . . . . . . at Rome
9-11 . . . . Charleston
12-14 . . . . Asheville
15-17 . . . at Hagerstown
18-21 . . . at Lakewood

196 · Baseball America 2020 Directory   BaseballAmerica.com

25-27 . . . . Rome	
28-30 . . . . . . Kannapolis	

JULY

1-3 . . . . . . at Greenville	
4-7 . . . . Hickory	
8-10 . . . . at Rome	
11-14 . . . . . at Greenville	
16-19 . . . . Asheville	
21-23 . . . . . . at Augusta	
24-26 . . . . at West Virginia	
28-30 . . . . Greenville	
31 . . . . Lexington	

AUGUST

1-2 . . . . Lexington	
4-6 . . . . at Augusta	
7-9 . . . . Rome	
10-13 . . . . Greenville	
14-16 . . . . . . at Asheville	
17-19 . . . . . . Charleston	
20-23 . . . . Augusta	
24-27 . . . . . . at Asheville	
28-30 . . . . . at Lexington	

SEPTEMBER

1-4 . . . . Greenville	
5-7 . . . . . at Hagerstown	

DELMARVA SHOREBIRDS

APRIL

9-11 . . . . Asheville	
13-15 . . . . Lakewood	
16-19 . . . . at Hagerstown	
20-22 . . . . . at Lakewood	
23-26 . . . . Hickory	
27-29 . . . . at Kannapolis	
30 . . . . at Asheville	

MAY

1-3 . . . . at Asheville	
5-7 . . . . Greenville	
8-10 . . . . . . Hagerstown	
12-14 . . . . . . at Hickory	
15-17 . . . . at Charleston	
19-21 . . . . . . Kannapolis	
22-24 . . . . . . Greensboro	
25-28 . . . . . at Lakewood	
29-31 . . . . at Greensboro	

JUNE

1 . . . . at Greensboro	
2-4 . . . . Lakewood	
5-7 . . . . Asheville	
9-11 . . . . at Augusta	
12-14 . . . at West Virginia	
15-17 . . . . . . Lakewood	
18-21 . . . . . . at Hickory	

25-27 . . . . . Hagerstown	
28-30 . . . . . Greensboro	

JULY

1-3 . . . . . . at Lakewood	
4-7 . . . . Hagerstown	
8-10 . . . . . at Lakewood	
11-14 . . . . at Greensboro	
16-19 . . . . . West Virginia	
21-23 . . . . at Lexington	
24-26 . . . . at Greenville	
28-30 . . . . Augusta	
31 . . . . Greensboro	

AUGUST

1-2 . . . . . . Greensboro	
4-6 . . . . at West Virginia	
7-9 . . . . . . Kannapolis	
10-13 . . . . . Greensboro	
14-16 . . . . at Hagerstown	
17-19 . . . . . . Lakewood	
20-23 . . . . . Hagerstown	
24-27 . . . . at Kannapolis	
28-30 . . . . . at Augusta	

SEPTEMBER

1-4 . . . . Lexington	
5-7 . . . . at Hickory	

GREENSBORO GRASSHOPPERS

APRIL

9-12 . . . . Lakewood	
13-15 . . . . Augusta	
16-19 . . . . . at Lakewood	
20-22 . . . . at Hagerstown	
23-26 . . . . Greenville	
27-29 . . . . Columbia	
30 . . . . . . at Charleston	

MAY

1-3 . . . . . at Charleston	
5-7 . . . . . . Hagerstown	
8-10 . . . . Asheville	
12-14 . . . . at Greenville	
15-17 . . . . at Kannapolis	
19-21 . . . . Hickory	
22-24 . . . . at Delmarva	
25-28 . . . . . Hagerstown	
29-31 . . . . . . Delmarva	

JUNE

1 . . . . Delmarva	
2-4 . . . . at Rome	
5-7 . . . . . at Greenville	
9-11 . . . . . . Hagerstown	
12-14 . . . . Hickory	
15-17 . . . . . Kannapolis	
18-21 . . . at West Virginia	

25-27 . . . . . . Lakewood	
28-30 . . . . . at Delmarva	

JULY

1-3 . . . . . at Hagerstown	
4-7 . . . . Lakewood	
8-10 . . . . . . at Augusta	
11-14 . . . . . . Delmarva	
16-19 . . . . at Hagerstown	
21-23 . . . . . . Kannapolis	
24-26 . . . . . . Charleston	
28-30 . . . . . at Hickory	
31 . . . . at Delmarva	

AUGUST

1-2 . . . . . . at Delmarva	
4-6 . . . . Rome	
7-9 . . . . Lakewood	
10-13 . . . . . at Delmarva	
14-16 . . . . . at Lakewood	
17-19 . . . . . . Kannapolis	
20-23 . . . . . . Lexington	
24-27 . . . . . at Lakewood	
28-30 . . . . . West Virginia	

SEPTEMBER

1-4 . . . . at Hickory	
5-7 . . . . . at Kannapolis	

GREENVILLE DRIVE

APRIL

9-12 . . . . . at Lexington	
13-15 . . . . at Rome	
16-19 . . . . . Charleston	
20-22 . . . . . West Virginia	
23-26 . . . . at Greensboro	
27-29 . . . . . . Lexington	
30 . . . . Rome	

MAY

1-3 . . . . Rome	
5-7 . . . . . . at Delmarva	
8-10 . . . . at West Virginia	
12-14 . . . . . Greensboro	
15-17 . . . . Columbia	
19-21 . . . . . at Augusta	
22-24 . . . . . at Rome	
25-28 . . . . . West Virginia	
29-31 . . . . at Asheville	

JUNE

1 . . . . at Asheville	
2-4 . . . . Charleston	
5-7 . . . . Greensboro	
9-11 . . . . . . at Asheville	
12-14 . . . . Augusta	
15-17 . . . . West Virginia	
18-21 . . . . at Lexington	

25-27 . . . . Augusta	
28-30 . . . . at Rome	

JULY

1-3 . . . . Columbia	
4-7 . . . . . at Charleston	
8-10 . . . . Asheville	
11-14 . . . . . . Columbia	
16-19 . . . . at Charleston	
21-23 . . . . Hickory	
24-26 . . . . . . Delmarva	
28-30 . . . . . Columbia	
31 . . . . . at Hagerstown	

AUGUST

1-2 . . . . at Hagerstown	
4-6 . . . . Hickory	
7-9 . . . . . . Charleston	
10-13 . . . . . at Columbia	
14-16 . . . . . at Augusta	
17-19 . . . . . . Lexington	
20-23 . . . . . at Rome	
24-27 . . . . at Charleston	
28-30 . . . . . . Asheville	

SEPTEMBER

1-4 . . . . . at Columbia	
5-7 . . . . Rome	

HAGERSTOWN SUNS

APRIL

9-12 . . . . at Rome	
13-15 . . . . . at Lexington	
16-19 . . . . . . Delmarva	
20-22 . . . . . Greensboro	
23-26 . . . . at Columbia	
27-29 . . . . . . Lakewood	
30 . . . . West Virginia	

MAY

1-3 . . . . . West Virginia	
5-7 . . . . at Greensboro	
8-10 . . . . . . at Delmarva	
12-14 . . . . . . Augusta	
15-17 . . . . Rome	
19-21 . . . . at Columbia	
22-24 . . . . . Lakewood	
25-28 . . . at Greensboro	
29-31 . . . . at Lakewood	

JUNE

1 . . . . at Lakewood	
2-4 . . . . Hickory	
5-7 . . . . . . Lexington	
9-11 . . . . at Greensboro	
12-14 . . . . at Lakewood	
15-17 . . . . . . Columbia	
18-21 . . . . Kannapolis	
25-27 . . . . . at Delmarva	

28-30 . . . . . at Lakewood	

JULY

1-3 . . . . . . Greensboro	
4-7 . . . . . at Delmarva	
8-10 . . . . . . Kannapolis	
11-14 . . . at West Virginia	
16-19 . . . . . Greensboro	
21-23 . . . . . at Asheville	
24-26 . . . . at Augusta	
28-30 . . . . . Lexington	
31 . . . . . . Greenville	

AUGUST

1-2 . . . . . Greenville	
4-6 . . . . . at Asheville	
7-9 . . . . . . at Hickory	
10-13 . . . . . Lakewood	
14-16 . . . . . Delmarva	
17-19 . . . at West Virginia	
20-23 . . . . at Delmarva	
24-27 . . . . . Hickory	
28-30 . . . at Kannapolis	

SEPTEMBER

1-4 . . . . . . Lakewood	
5-7 . . . . Columbia	

HICKORY CRAWDADS

APRIL
9-12 . . . . . at West Virginia
13-15 . . . . . . at Charleston
16-19 . . . . Lexington
20-22 . . . . Columbia
23-26 . . . . at Delmarva
27-29 . . . . Charleston
30 . . . . Augusta

MAY
1-3 . . . . Augusta
5-7 . . . . at Lexington
8-10 . . . . at Rome
12-14 . . . . Delmarva
15-17 . . . . . West Virginia
19-21 . . . . at Greensboro
22-24 . . . . at Kannapolis
25-28 . . . . Augusta
29-31 . . . . at Lexington

JUNE
1 . . . . at Lexington
2-4 . . . . . at Hagerstown
5-7 . . . . . West Virginia
9-11 . . . . . . at Lakewood
12-14 . . . . at Greensboro
15-17 . . . . Lexington
18-21 . . . . Delmarva

25-27 . . . . . at Charleston
28-30 . . . . . West Virginia

JULY
1-3 . . . . Kannapolis
4-7 . . . . at Columbia
8-10 . . . . Charleston
11-14 . . . . . at Lexington
16-19 . . . . . . Lakewood
21-23 . . . . at Greenville
24-26 . . . . . at Asheville
28-30 . . . . Greensboro
31 . . . . Lakewood

AUGUST
1-2 . . . . Lakewood
4-6 . . . . . at Greenville
7-9 . . . . . . Hagerstown
10-13 . . . at Kannapolis
14-16 . . . . at Lexington
17-19 . . . . Rome
20-23 . . . . . Kannapolis
24-27 . . . . at Hagerstown
28-30 . . . . at Lakewood

SEPTEMBER
1-4 . . . . . . Greensboro
5-7 . . . . Delmarva

KANNAPOLIS CANNON BALLERS

APRIL
9-12 . . . . . at Charleston
13-15 . . . . . at Columbia
16-19 . . . . West Virginia
20-22 . . . . Charleston
23-26 . . . . at Rome
27-29 . . . . . Delmarva
30 . . . . Lexington

MAY
1-3 . . . . Lexington
5-7 . . . . at West Virginia
8-10 . . . . . . at Augusta
12-14 . . . . . . Columbia
15-17 . . . . . Greensboro
19-21 . . . . at Delmarva
22-24 . . . . Hickory
25-28 . . . . Rome
29-31 . . . . at Augusta

JUNE
1 . . . . at Augusta
2-4 . . . . . . Asheville
5-7 . . . . . . Lakewood
9-11 . . . at West Virginia
12-14 . . . . at Lexington
15-17 . . . . Greensboro
18-21 . . . . at Hagerstown

25-27 . . . . . West Virginia
28-30 . . . . . at Columbia

JULY
1-3 . . . . at Hickory
4-7 . . . . . . West Virginia
8-10 . . . . at Hagerstown
11-14 . . . . at Lakewood
16-19 . . . . . Augusta
21-23 . . . at Greensboro
24-26 . . . at Lakewood
28-30 . . . . . Asheville
31 . . . . Augusta

AUGUST
1-2 . . . . Augusta
4-6 . . . . . at Lakewood
7-9 . . . . . at Delmarva
10-13 . . . . . Hickory
14-16 . . . West Virginia
17-19 . . . at Greensboro
20-23 . . . . . at Hickory
24-27 . . . . . Delmarva
28-30 . . . . Hagerstown

SEPTEMBER
1-4 . . . . . at Charleston
5-7 . . . . . Greensboro

LAKEWOOD BLUECLAWS

APRIL
9-12 . . . . . at Greensboro
13-15 . . . . at Delmarva
16-19 . . . . Greensboro
20-22 . . . . Delmarva
23-26 . . . at West Virginia
27-29 . . . at Hagerstown
30 . . . . Columbia

MAY
1-3 . . . . Columbia
5-7 . . . . at Augusta
8-10 . . . . . at Lexington
12-14 . . . . Rome

15-17 . . . . Augusta
19-21 . . . . at Lexington
22-24 . . . . at Hagerstown
25-28 . . . . . Delmarva
29-31 . . . . Hagerstown

JUNE
1 . . . . Hagerstown
2-4 . . . . . at Delmarva
5-7 . . . . at Kannapolis
9-11 . . . . . . Hickory
12-14 . . . . Hagerstown
15-17 . . . at Delmarva
18-21 . . . . . Columbia

25-27 . . . . . at Greensboro
28-30 . . . . Hagerstown

JULY
1-3 . . . . Delmarva
4-7 . . . . at Greensboro
8-10 . . . . . . Delmarva
11-14 . . . . Kannapolis
16-19 . . . . at Hickory
21-23 . . . . . Charleston
24-26 . . . . Kannapolis
28-30 . . . . . at Rome
31 . . . . at Hickory

AUGUST
1-2 . . . . at Hickory
4-6 . . . . . . Kannapolis
7-9 . . . . at Greensboro
10-13 . . . at Hagerstown
14-16 . . . . Greensboro
17-19 . . . at Delmarva
20-23 . . . at West Virginia
24-27 . . . Greensboro
28-30 . . . . . . Hickory

SEPTEMBER
1-4 . . . at Hagerstown
5-7 . . . . Lexington

LEXINGTON LEGENDS

APRIL
9-12 . . . . Greenville
13-15 . . . . Hagerstown
16-19 . . . . . at Hickory
20-22 . . . . at Augusta
23-26 . . . . . Asheville
27-29 . . . at Greenville
30 . . . . . at Kannapolis

MAY
1-3 . . . . . at Kannapolis
5-7 . . . . Hickory
8-10 . . . . . Lakewood
13-14 . . . at Charleston
15-17 . . . . at Asheville
19-21 . . . . . Lakewood
22-24 . . . . West Virginia
25-28 . . . . at Asheville
29-31 . . . . . . Hickory

JUNE
1 . . . . Hickory
2-4 . . . . . at Columbia
5-7 . . . at Hagerstown
9-11 . . . . Rome
12-14 . . . . Kannapolis
15-17 . . . . at Hickory
18-21 . . . . . Greenville

25-27 . . . . . at Asheville
28-30 . . . . . Augusta

JULY
1-3 . . . . Rome
4-7 . . . . . . at Asheville
8-10 . . . . at West Virginia
11-14 . . . . . . Hickory
16-19 . . . . . at Rome
21-23 . . . . . Delmarva
24-26 . . . . Rome
28-30 . . . . Hagerstown
31 . . . . . at Columbia

AUGUST
1-2 . . . . . at Columbia
4-6 . . . . . . Charleston
7-9 . . . at West Virginia
10-13 . . . . . Asheville
14-16 . . . . . . Hickory
17-19 . . . at Greenville
20-23 . . . at Greensboro
24-27 . . . . West Virginia
28-30 . . . . . Columbia

SEPTEMBER
1-4 . . . . . at Delmarva
5-7 . . . . . at Lakewood

ROME BRAVES

APRIL
9-12 . . . . . Hagerstown
13-15 . . . . . . Greenville
16-19 . . . . . at Augusta
20-22 . . . . at Asheville
23-26 . . . . . Kannapolis
27-29 . . . at West Virginia
30 . . . . . at Greenville

MAY
1-3 . . . . . at Greenville
5-7 . . . . . . Charleston
8-10 . . . . Hickory
12-14 . . . . at Lakewood
15-17 . . . at Hagerstown
19-21 . . . . . . Asheville
22-24 . . . . . . Greenville
25-28 . . . at Kannapolis
29-31 . . . . at Charleston

JUNE
1 . . . . . . at Charleston
2-4 . . . . . . Greensboro
5-7 . . . . . . Columbia
9-11 . . . . at Lexington
12-14 . . . . Charleston
15-17 . . . . . . Augusta
18-21 . . . . at Asheville

25-27 . . . . . at Columbia
28-30 . . . . Greenville

JULY
1-3 . . . . . at Lexington
4-7 . . . . Augusta
8-10 . . . . . . Columbia
11-14 . . . . at Asheville
16-19 . . . . . Lexington
21-23 . . . at West Virginia
24-26 . . . at Lexington
28-30 . . . . Lakewood
31 . . . . . . West Virginia

AUGUST
1-2 . . . . . West Virginia
4-6 . . . . at Greensboro
7-9 . . . . at Columbia
10-13 . . . West Virginia
14-16 . . . at Charleston
17-19 . . . . at Hickory
20-23 . . . . . Greenville
24-27 . . . . . Augusta
28-30 . . . . Charleston

SEPTEMBER
1-4 . . . at West Virginia
5-7 . . . . at Greenville

WEST VIRGINIA POWER

APRIL		
9-12	. . . .	Hickory
13-15	. . . .	Asheville
16-19	. . . .	at Kannapolis
20-22	. . . .	at Greenville
23-26	. . . . . .	Lakewood
27-29	. . . .	Rome
30	. . . . . .	at Hagerstown

MAY		
1-3	. . . . .	at Hagerstown
5-7	. . . .	Kannapolis
8-10	. . . .	Greenville

12-14	. . . . . .	at Asheville
15-17	. . . . . .	at Hickory
19-21	. . . . . .	Charleston
22-24	. . . . .	at Lexington
25-28	. . . . .	at Greenville
29-31	. . . . . .	Columbia

JUNE		
1	. . . .	Columbia
2-4	. . . .	at Augusta
5-7	. . . .	at Hickory
9-11	. . . .	Kannapolis
12-14	. . . . . .	Delmarva

15-17	. . . . .	at Greenville
18-21	. . . . . .	Greensboro
25-27	. . . .	at Kannapolis
28-30	. . . . .	at Hickory

JULY		
1-3	. . . .	Asheville
4-7	. . . .	at Kannapolis
8-10	. . . .	Lexington
11-14	. . . . . .	Hagerstown
16-19	. . . . .	at Delmarva
21-23	. . . .	Rome
24-26	. . . . .	Columbia
28-30	. . . .	at Charleston
31	. . . .	at Rome

AUGUST		
1-2	. . . .	at Rome
4-6	. . . .	Delmarva
7-9	. . . .	Lexington
10-13	. . . . . .	at Rome
14-16	. . . .	at Kannapolis
17-19	. . . .	Hagerstown
20-23	. . . . .	Lakewood
24-27	. . . .	at Lexington
28-30	. . .	at Greensboro

SEPTEMBER		
1-4	. . . .	Rome
5-7	. . . . . .	at Augusta

SHORT SEASON

NEW YORK-PENN LEAGUE

ABERDEEN IRONBIRDS

JUNE		
18-20	. . . .	Hudson Valley
21-23	. . . .	Brooklyn
24-26	. . .	at State College
27-29	. . .	Mahoning Valley

JULY		
1-3	. . . .	at Brooklyn
4-6	. . . . .	West Virginia
7-9	. . . .	at State College
10-12	. . . .	at Staten Island
13-16	. . .	at West Virginia
17-19	. . . .	at Williamsport
21-24	. . . .	Vermont
25-27	. . .	at Staten Island
28-30	. . . . .	West Virginia

31	. . . .	Brooklyn

AUGUST		
1-2	. . . .	Brooklyn
4-7	. .	at Mahoning Valley
8-10	. . . .	Norwich
11-13	. . .	at Hudson Valley
14-16	. . . .	at Vermont
19-21	. . . .	Auburn
22-24	. . . . .	at Norwich
25-27	. . . .	State College
28-30	. . . . .	at Tri-City

SEPTEMBER		
1-4	. . . .	Norwich
5-7	. . .	at Hudson Valley

AUBURN DOUBLEDAYS

JUNE		
18-20	. . . . . .	at Batavia
21-23	. . .	State College
24-26	. .	at Mahoning Valley
27-29	. . .	at West Virginia

JULY		
1-3	. . . .	Tri-City
4-6	. . .	Mahoning Valley
7-9	. . . . . .	at Lowell
10-12	. . . . .	Vermont
13-16	. .	at Mahoning Valley
17-19	. . .	at West Virginia
21-24	. . . .	Lowell
25-27	. . . .	at Vermont
28-30	. . . . .	Staten Island

31	. . . .	at Batavia

AUGUST		
1-2	. . . .	at Batavia
4-7	. . . .	Vermont
8-10	. . . .	at Staten Island
11-13	. . . . . .	Batavia
14-16	. . . .	West Virginia
19-21	. . . .	at Aberdeen
22-24	. . . .	Staten Island
25-27	. . .	at Williamsport
28-30	. . . .	West Virginia

SEPTEMBER		
1-4	. . . .	at Lowell
5-7	. . . .	Batavia

BATAVIA MUCKDOGS

JUNE		
18-20	. . . . . .	Auburn
21-23	. . .	Mahoning Valley
24-26	. . .	at West Virginia
27-29	. . . .	State College

JULY		
1-3	. . .	at Hudson Valley
4-6	. . . . . .	Vermont
7-9	. .	at Mahoning Valley
10-12	. . . .	West Virginia
13-16	. . . .	at Vermont
17-19	. . . . . .	at Lowell
21-24	. . . .	Hudson Valley
25-27	. . .	at West Virginia
28-30	. . . .	Williamsport

31	. . . .	Auburn

AUGUST		
1-2	. . . .	Auburn
4-7	. . . .	at State College
8-10	. . . .	Tri-City
11-13	. . . .	at Auburn
14-16	. . . . .	at Norwich
19-21	. .	Mahoning Valley
22-24	. . . .	at Tri-City
25-27	. . . .	Hudson Valley
28-30	.	at Mahoning Valley

SEPTEMBER		
1-4	. . . . . .	State College
5-7	. . . . . .	at Auburn

BROOKLYN CYCLONES

JUNE		
18	. . . . . .	Staten Island
19	. . . . .	at Staten Island
20	. . . . . .	Staten Island
21 - 23	. . . .	at Aberdeen
24 - 26	. . . . .	Norwich
27 - 29	. . . .	at Tri-City

JULY		
1 - 3	. . . . . .	Aberdeen
4 - 6	. . . . .	Hudson Valley
7 - 9	. . .	at Williamsport
10 - 12	. . . . . .	Lowell
13 - 16	. .	at Hudson Valley
17 - 19	. . . .	at Vermont
21 - 24	. . . .	Williamsport
25 - 27	. . . . .	at Lowell
28 - 30	. .	Mahoning Valley
31	. . . . .	at Aberdeen

AUGUST		
1 - 2	. . . . .	at Aberdeen
4 - 7	. . . . .	West Virginia
8 - 10	. . . . . .	at Lowell
11	. . . . .	Staten Island
12	. . .	at Staten Island
13	. . . . .	Staten Island
14 -16	. .	at Hudson Valley
19 - 21	. . .	State College
22 - 24	. . . .	Vermont
25	. . .	at Staten Island
26	. . . .	Staten Island
27	. . .	at Staten Island
28 - 30	. . . . .	Lowell

SEPTEMBER		
1 - 4	. . . .	at West Virginia
5	. . . .	at Staten Island
6	. . . . .	Staten Island
7	. . . .	at Staten Island

HUDSON VALLEY RENEGADES

JUNE		
18-20	. . . . .	at Aberdeen
21-23	. . .	at Staten Island
24-26	. . . . .	Vermont
27-29	. . . . .	at Lowell

JULY		
1-3	. . . .	Batavia
4-6	. . . . . .	at Brooklyn
7-9	. . . .	Tri-City
10-12	. . . .	at Norwich
13-16	. . . . .	Brooklyn
17-19	. . . .	State College
21-24	. . . . .	at Batavia
25-27	. . . . .	Norwich
28-30	. . .	at State College

31	. . . .	at West Virginia

AUGUST		
1-2	. . . .	at West Virginia
4-7	. . . .	Lowell
8-10	. . . . .	at Vermont
11-13	. . . . .	Aberdeen
14-16	. . . . .	Brooklyn
19-21	. . . . .	at Tri-City
22-24	. . . . . .	Lowell
25-27	. . . .	at Batavia
28-30	. . . .	Williamsport

SEPTEMBER		
1-4	. . . . . .	at Vermont
5-7	. . . . . .	Aberdeen

LOWELL SPINNERS

JUNE		
18-20	. . . . .	Norwich
21-23	. . . . .	at Vermont
24-26	. . .	Staten Island
27-29	. . .	Hudson Valley

JULY		
1-3	. . .	at State College
4-6	. . .	at Staten Island
7-9	. . . . . .	Auburn
10-12	. . . .	at Brooklyn
13-16	. . . . .	Tri-City
17-19	. . . . .	Batavia
21-24	. . . .	at Auburn
25-27	. . . . .	Brooklyn
28-30	. . . .	at Norwich

31	. . . .	Tri-City

AUGUST		
1-2	. . . .	Tri-City
4-7	. . .	at Hudson Valley
8-10	. . . . . .	Brooklyn
11-13	. . . .	at Tri-City
14-16	. . .	at Williamsport
19-21	. . . . .	Vermont
22-24	. .	at Hudson Valley
25-27	. . . . .	Norwich
28-30	. . . .	at Brooklyn

SEPTEMBER		
1-4	. . . . . .	Auburn
5-7	. . . . .	at Norwich

MAHONING VALLEY SCRAPPERS

JUNE
18-20 . . . . at West Virginia
21-23 . . . . at Batavia
24-26 . . . . Auburn
27-29 . . . . . at Aberdeen

JULY
1-3 . . . . Vermont
4-6 . . . . at Auburn
7-9 . . . . Batavia
10-12 . . . at State College
13-16 . . . . Auburn
17-19 . . . . Norwich
21-24 . . . . . . at Tri-City
25-27 . . . . State College
28-30 . . . . . at Brooklyn

31 . . . . . . at Staten Island

AUGUST
1-2 . . . . at Staten Island
4-7 . . . . Aberdeen
8-10 . . . . at Williamsport
11-13 . . . . West Virginia
14-16 . . . . Staten Island
19-21 . . . . . . at Batavia
22-24 . . . . . Williamsport
25-27 . . . . at West Virginia
28-30 . . . . Batavia

SEPTEMBER
1-4 . . . . . at Williamsport
5-7 . . . . West Virginia

NORWICH SEA UNICORNS

JUNE
18-20 . . . . at Lowell
21-23 . . . . Tri-City
24-26 . . . . . at Brooklyn
27-29 . . . . at Staten Island

JULY
1-3 . . . . . . West Virginia
4-6 . . . . . . Williamsport
7-9 . . . . . . at Vermont
10-12 . . . . Hudson Valley
13-16 . . . . at Williamsport
17-19 . . at Mahoning Valley
21-24 . . . . . Staten Island
25-27 . . . at Hudson Valley
28-30 . . . . Lowell

31 . . . . at Vermont

AUGUST
1-2 . . . . at Vermont
4-7 . . . . Williamsport
8-10 . . . . . at Aberdeen
11-13 . . . . Vermont
14-16 . . . . Batavia
19-21 . . . . at Staten Island
22-24 . . . . Aberdeen
25-27 . . . . . at Lowell
28-30 . . . . Vermont

SEPTEMBER
1-4 . . . . . . at Aberdeen
5-7 . . . . Lowell

STATE COLLEGE SPIKES

JUNE
18 . . . . Williamsport
19-20 . . . . at Williamsport
21-23 . . . . . at Auburn
24-26 . . . . . . Aberdeen
27-29 . . . . . . at Batavia

JULY
1-3 . . . . Lowell
4-6 . . . . at Tri-City
7-9 . . . . Aberdeen
10-12 . . . Mahoning Valley
13-16 . . . . at Staten Island
17-19 . . at Hudson Valley
21-24 . . . . West Virginia
25-27 . at Mahoning Valley
28-30 . . . . Hudson Valley

31 . . . . . at Williamsport

AUGUST
1-2 . . . . . at Williamsport
4-7 . . . . Batavia
8-10 . . . . at West Virginia
11-13 . . . . . Williamsport
14-16 . . . . Tri-City
19-21 . . . . . at Brooklyn
22-24 . . . . West Virginia
25-27 . . . . at Aberdeen
28-30 . . . . Staten Island

SEPTEMBER
1-4 . . . . at Batavia
5 . . . . . . at Williamsport
6-7 . . . . . Williamsport

STATEN ISLAND YANKEES

JUNE
18 . . . . at Brooklyn
19 . . . . Brooklyn
20 . . . . at Brooklyn
21-23 . . . . Hudson Valley
24-26 . . . . . . at Lowell
27-29 . . . . Norwich

JULY
1-3 . . . . at Williamsport
4-6 . . . . Lowell
7-9 . . . . at West Virginia
10-12 . . . . . at Aberdeen

13-16 . . . . . State College
17-19 . . . . Tri-City
21-24 . . . . . . at Norwich
25-27 . . . . Aberdeen
28-30 . . . . . at Auburn
31 . . . . . Mahoning Valley

AUGUST
1-2 . . . Mahoning Valley
4-7 . . . . . at Tri-City
8-10 . . . . Auburn
11 . . . . at Brooklyn
12 . . . . Brooklyn

13 . . . . at Brooklyn
14-16 . . at Mahoning Valley
19-21 . . . . Norwich
22-24 . . . . . . at Auburn
25 . . . . Brooklyn
26 . . . . at Brooklyn
27 . . . . Brooklyn

TRI-CITY VALLEYCATS

JUNE
18-20 . . . . . at Vermont
21-23 . . . . . at Norwich
24-26 . . . . . Williamsport
27-29 . . . . . . Brooklyn

JULY
1-3 . . . . at Auburn
4-6 . . . . . . State College
7-9 . . at Hudson Valley
10-12 . . . . . Williamsport
13-16 . . . . . at Lowell
17-19 . . . at Staten Island
21-24 . . . Mahoning Valley
25-27 . . . at Williamsport
28-30 . . . . Vermont

31 . . . . at Lowell

AUGUST
1-2 . . . . at Lowell
4-7 . . . . . Staten Island
8-10 . . . . . . at Batavia
11-13 . . . . Lowell
14-16 . . . . at State College
19-21 . . . . Hudson Valley
22-24 . . . . Batavia
25-27 . . . . . at Vermont
28-30 . . . . . . Aberdeen

SEPTEMBER
1-4 . . . . at Staten Island
5-7 . . . . Vermont

VERMONT LAKE MONSTERS

JUNE
18-20 . . . . Tri-City
21-23 . . . . Lowell
24-26 . . . at Hudson Valley
27-29 . . . . . Williamsport

JULY
1-3 . . at Mahoning Valley
4-6 . . . . at Batavia
7-9 . . . . Norwich
10-12 . . . . . . at Auburn
13-16 . . . . Batavia
17-19 . . . . . . Brooklyn
21-24 . . . . . at Aberdeen
25-27 . . . . . . Auburn
28-30 . . . . . at Tri-City

31 . . . . Norwich

AUGUST
1-2 . . . . Norwich
4-7 . . . . at Auburn
8-10 . . . . Hudson Valley
11-13 . . . . at Norwich
14-16 . . . . . . Aberdeen
19-21 . . . . . at Lowell
22-24 . . . . at Brooklyn
25-27 . . . . . . Tri-City
28-30 . . . . at Norwich

SEPTEMBER
1-4 . . . . . Hudson Valley
5-7 . . . . at Tri-City

WEST VIRGINIA BLACK BEARS

JUNE
18-20 . . . Mahoning Valley
21-23 . . . . at Williamsport
24-26 . . . . . . Batavia
27-29 . . . . . . Auburn

JULY
1-3 . . . . . . at Norwich
4-6 . . . . . . at Aberdeen
7-9 . . . . . Staten Island
10-12 . . . . . at Batavia
13-16 . . . . . Aberdeen
17-19 . . . . . . Auburn
21-24 . . . at State College
25-27 . . . . . . Batavia
28-30 . . . . at Aberdeen

31 . . . . . Hudson Valley

AUGUST
1-2 . . . . . Hudson Valley
4-7 . . . . . . at Brooklyn
8-10 . . . . . State College
11-13 . . at Mahoning Valley
14-16 . . . . . at Auburn
19-21 . . . . Williamsport
22-24 . . . at State College
25-27 . . . Mahoning Valley
28-30 . . . . . at Auburn

SEPTEMBER
1-4 . . . . Brooklyn
5-7 . . . at Mahoning Valley

WILLIAMSPORT CROSSCUTTERS

JUNE	
18	at State College
19-20	State College
21-23	West Virginia
24-26	at Tri-City
27-29	at Vermont

JULY	
1-3	Staten Island
4-6	at Norwich
7-9	Brooklyn
10-12	at Tri-City
13-16	Norwich
17-19	Aberdeen
21-24	at Brooklyn
25-27	Tri-City
28-30	at Batavia

31	State College

AUGUST	
1-2	State College
4-7	at Norwich
8-10	Mahoning Valley
11-13	at State College
14-16	Lowell
19-21	at West Virginia
22-24	at Mahoning Valley
25-27	Auburn
28-30	at Hudson Valley

SEPTEMBER	
1-4	Mahoning Valley
5	State College
6-7	at State College

NORTHWEST LEAGUE

BOISE HAWKS

JUNE	
17-21	at Tri-City
22-24	Salem-Keizer
25-29	at Everett

JULY	
1-3	Hillsboro
4-8	at Spokane
9-13	Everett
15-17	at Hillsboro
18-22	Spokane
23-25	Eugene
26-28	at Salem-Keizer
29-31	Vancouver

AUGUST	
1-2	Vancouver
6-8	at Eugene
9-11	Salem-Keizer
12-16	Tri-City
18-20	at Hillsboro
21-25	at Vancouver
26-28	at Salem-Keizer
29-31	at Eugene

SEPTEMBER	
1-3	Hillsboro
4-6	Eugene

EUGENE EMERALDS

JUNE	
17-21	at Vancouver
22-24	at Hillsboro
25-29	Tri-City

JULY	
1-3	Salem-Keizer
4-8	at Everett
9-13	Spokane
15-17	at Salem-Keizer
18-22	Everett
23-25	at Boise
26-28	Hillsboro
29-31	at Spokane

AUGUST	
1-2	at Spokane
6-8	Boise
9-11	at Hillsboro
12-16	Vancouver
18-20	Salem-Keizer
21-25	at Tri-City
26-28	Hillsboro
29-31	Boise

SEPTEMBER	
1-3	at Salem-Keizer
4-6	at Boise

EVERETT AQUASOX

JUNE	
17-21	at Salem-Keizer
22-24	Vancouver
25-29	Boise

JULY	
1-3	at Tri-City
4-8	Eugene
9-13	at Boise
15-17	Tri-City
18-22	at Eugene
23-25	at Spokane
26-28	Spokane
29-31	Salem-Keizer

AUGUST	
1-2	Salem-Keizer
6-8	at Tri-City
9-11	at Vancouver
12-16	Hillsboro
18-20	at Vancouver
21-25	at Hillsboro
26-28	Tri-City
29-31	Spokane

SEPTEMBER	
1-3	at Spokane
5-7	Vancouver

HILLSBORO HOPS

JUNE	
17-21	at Spokane
22-24	Eugene
25-29	Spokane

JULY	
1-3	at Boise
4-8	Vancouver
9-13	at Tri-City
15-17	Boise
18-22	at Vancouver
23-25	Salem-Keizer
26-28	at Eugene
29-31	Tri-City

AUGUST	
1-2	Tri-City
6-8	at Salem-Keizer
9-11	Eugene
12-16	at Everett
18-20	Boise
21-25	Everett
26-28	at Eugene
29-31	Salem-Keizer

SEPTEMBER	
1-3	at Boise
4-6	at Salem-Keizer

SALEM-KEIZER VOLCANOES

JUNE	
17-21	Everett
22-24	at Boise
25-29	Vancouver

JULY	
1-3	at Eugene
4-8	Tri-City
9-13	at Vancouver
15-17	Eugene
18-22	at Tri-City
23-25	at Hillsboro
26-28	Boise
29-31	at Everett

AUGUST	
1-2	at Everett
6-8	Hillsboro
9-11	at Boise
12-16	Spokane
18-20	at Eugene
21-25	at Spokane
26-28	Boise
29-31	at Hillsboro

SEPTEMBER	
1-3	Eugene
4-6	Hillsboro

SPOKANE INDIANS

JUNE	
17-21	Hillsboro
22-24	Tri-City
25-29	at Hillsboro

JULY	
1-3	at Vancouver
4-8	Boise
9-13	at Eugene
15-17	Vancouver
18-22	at Boise
23-25	Everett
26-28	at Everett
29-31	Eugene

AUGUST	
1-2	Eugene
6-8	at Vancouver
9-11	Tri-City
12-16	at Salem-Keizer
18-20	at Tri-City
21-25	Salem-Keizer
26-28	Vancouver
29-31	at Everett

SEPTEMBER	
1-3	Everett
4-6	at Tri-City

TRI-CITY DUST DEVILS

JUNE	
17-21	Boise
22-24	at Spokane
25-29	at Eugene

JULY	
1-3	Everett
4-8	at Salem-Keizer
9-13	Hillsboro
15-17	at Everett
18-22	Salem-Keizer
23-25	at Vancouver
26-28	Vancouver
29-31	at Hillsboro

AUGUST	
1-2	at Hillsboro
6-8	Everett
9-11	at Spokane
12-16	at Boise
18-20	Spokane
21-25	Eugene
26-28	at Everett
29-31	at Vancouver

SEPTEMBER	
1-3	Vancouver
4-6	Spokane

VANCOUVER CANADIANS

JUNE		JULY	
17-21 . . . . .Eugene		1-3 . . . . Spokane	
22-24 . . . . . . at Everett		4-8 . . . . at Hillsboro	
25-29 . . . . at Salem-Keizer		9-13 . . . . . . Salem-Keizer	
		15-17 . . . . . . at Spokane	

18-22 . . . . .Hillsboro
23-25 . . . . Tri-City
26-28 . . . . at Tri-City
29-31 . . . . at Boise

AUGUST
1-2 . . . . at Boise
6-8 . . . . Spokane
9-11 . . . . Everett

12-16 . . . . at Eugene
18-20 . . . . Everett
21-25 . . . . Boise
26-28 . . . . . . at Spokane
29-31 . . . . Tri-City

SEPTEMBER
1-3 . . . . at Tri-City
5-7 . . . . at Everett

ROOKIE

APPALACHIAN LEAGUE

BLUEFIELD BLUE JAYS

JUNE
22-23 . . . . . .at Princeton
24-26 . . . . . . .at Danville
27-29 . . . . Pulaski

JULY
1-3 . . . . Princeton
4-6 . . . . . . at Burlington
7-8 . . . . . . .at Princeton
9-10 . . . . . . Princeton
11-13 . . . . . . Danville
15-17 . . . . . . Bristol
18-20 . . . .at Greeneville
21-23 . . . . . .at Danville
24-26 . . . . Elizabethton
27-29 . . . . . .Burlington

30-31 . . . . at Pulaski
AUGUST
1 . . . . at Pulaski
3-4 . . . . Princeton
5-7 . . . . at Bristol
8-10 . . . . .at Elizabethton
11-13 . . . . Johnson City
14-16 . . . . . . Greeneville
18-20 . . . . . at Kingsport
21-23 . . . . at Johnson City
24-26 . . . . Danville
27-29 . . . . at Burlington
30-31 . . . . Kingsport

SEPTEMBER
1 . . . . Kingsport

BRISTOL PIRATES

JUNE
22-23 . . . . . . at Pulaski
24-26 . . . . . .at Princeton
27-29 . . . . . Greeneville

JULY
1-2 . . . . . . at Kingsport
3 . . . . . . at Johnson City
4-6 . . . . . . Johnson City
7-8 . . . . Pulaski
9-10 . . . . . . at Pulaski
11-13 . . . . . Elizabethton
15-17 . . . . at Bluefield
18-20 . . . . . . Kingsport
21-23 . . . . at Johnson City
24-26 . . . . at Burlington
27-29 . . . . . . Princeton
30 . . . . . . .at Greeneville

31 . . . . Greeneville
AUGUST
1 . . . . .at Greeneville
3-4 . . . . Pulaski
5-7 . . . . Bluefield
8-10 . . . . .at Danville
11-13 . . . . . .Burlington
14-16 . . . . . . Danville
18-20 . . . .at Greeneville
21-23 . . . . at Kingsport
24-26 . . . . . Elizabethton
27 . . . . Greeneville
28 . . . . . . .at Greeneville
29 . . . . Greeneville
30-31 . . . .at Elizabethton

SEPTEMBER
1 . . . . .at Elizabethton

BURLINGTON ROYALS

JUNE
22 . . . . .at Danville
23 . . . . Danville
24-26 . . . . . at Kingsport
27-29 . . . . Princeton

JULY
1-3 . . . . at Pulaski
4-6 . . . . Bluefield
7-8 . . . . Danville
9-10 . . . . . .at Danville
11-13 . . . . . . Pulaski
15-17 . . . . .at Greeneville
18-20 . . . .at Elizabethton
21-23 . . . . Greeneville
24-26 . . . . . . Bristol

27-29 . . . . . . at Bluefield
30-31 . . . . . .at Princeton
AUGUST
1 . . . . .at Princeton
3-4 . . . . Danville
5-7 . . . . Elizabethton
8-10 . . . . at Pulaski
11-13 . . . . . .at Bristol
14-16 . . . . . . Kingsport
18-20 . . . . Johnson City
21-23 . . . . . .at Princeton
24-26 . . . . at Johnson City
27-29 . . . . .Bluefield
30 . . . . .at Danville
31 . . . . Danville

SEPTEMBER
1 . . . . Danville

DANVILLE BRAVES

JUNE
22 . . . . .Burlington
23 . . . . at Burlington
24-26 . . . . . . .Bluefield
27-29 . . . . at Johnson City

JULY
1-3 . . . . Greeneville
4-6 . . . . . .at Elizabethton
7-8 . . . . . . at Burlington
9-10 . . . . . . .Burlington
11-13 . . . . . at Bluefield
15-17 . . . . . . Princeton
18-20 . . . . . at Pulaski
21-23 . . . . . . Bluefield
24-26 . . . . Pulaski
27-29 . . . . .at Greeneville

30-31 . . . . . Johnson City
AUGUST
1 . . . . Johnson City
3-4 . . . . . . at Burlington
5-7 . . . . . . at Kingsport
8-10 . . . . Bristol
11-13 . . . . . . Kingsport
14-16 . . . . . at Bristol
17-19 . . . . . .at Princeton
21-23 . . . . Elizabethton
24-26 . . . . at Bluefield
27-29 . . . . . . Pulaski
30 . . . . .Burlington
31 . . . . . . at Burlington

SEPTEMBER
1 . . . . at Burlington

ELIZABETHTON TWINS

JUNE
22-23 . . . . . Greeneville
24-26 . . . . . . at Pulaski
27 . . . . at Kingsport
28 . . . . Kingsport
29 . . . . at Kingsport

JULY
1-2 . . . . . at Johnson City
3 . . . . Kingsport
4-6 . . . . Danville
7-10 . . . .at Greeneville
11-13 . . . . . .at Bristol
15 . . . . at Kingsport
16-17 . . . . . . Kingsport
18-20 . . . . . .Burlington
21-23 . . . . .at Princeton
24-26 . . . . . . at Bluefield

27-29 . . . . . Johnson City
30-31 . . . . . Kingsport
AUGUST
1 . . . . at Kingsport
3-4 . . . . . . Greeneville
5-7 . . . . . at Burlington
8-10 . . . . . . .Bluefield
11-13 . . . . at Johnson City
14-16 . . . . at Johnson City
18-20 . . . . . . Pulaski
21-23 . . . . .at Danville
24-26 . . . . . at Bristol
27-29 . . . . Johnson City
30-31 . . . . Bristol

SEPTEMBER
1 . . . . Bristol

GREENEVILLE REDS

JUNE
22-23 . . . .at Elizabethton
24 . . . . . at Johnson City
25-26 . . . . Johnson City
27-29 . . . . at Bristol

JULY
1-3 . . . . . . .at Danville
4-6 . . . . Kingsport
7-10 . . . . Elizabethton
11-13 . . . at Johnson City
15-17 . . . . . .Burlington
18-20 . . . . . Elizabethton
21-23 . . . .at Burlington
24-26 . . . . at Kingsport

27-29 . . . . Danville
30 . . . . Bristol
31 . . . . .at Bristol
AUGUST
1 . . . . Bristol
3-4 . . . . .at Elizabethton
5 . . . . Johnson City
6-7 . . . . at Johnson City
8-10 . . . . . . Princeton
11-13 . . . . . . Pulaski
14-16 . . . . at Bluefield
18-20 . . . . Bristol
21-23 . . . . at Pulaski
24-26 . . . . . . Kingsport

27 . . . . at Bristol	30-31 . . . . . .at Princeton
28 . . . . Bristol	**SEPTEMBER**
29 . . . . at Bristol	1 . . . . .at Princeton

JOHNSON CITY CARDINALS

JUNE	
22-23 . . . . Kingsport	30-31 . . . . . .at Danville
24 . . . . Greeneville	**AUGUST**
25-26 . . . . .at Greeneville	1 . . . . .at Danville
27-29 . . . . . . Danville	3 . . . . . . at Kingsport
JULY	4 . . . . Kingsport
1-2 . . . . . . Elizabethton	5 . . . . . .at Greeneville
3 . . . . Bristol	6-7 . . . . . . Greeneville
4-6 . . . . at Bristol	8-10 . . . . . at Kingsport
7-8 . . . . . at Kingsport	11-13 . . . . at Bluefield
9 . . . . . . Kingsport	14-16 . . . . . Elizabethton
10 . . . . . at Kingsport	18-20 . . . . at Burlington
11-13 . . . . . . Greeneville	21-23 . . . . . .Bluefield
15-17 . . . . . at Pulaski	24-26 . . . . . .Burlington
18-20 . . . . . .at Princeton	27-29 . . . .at Elizabethton
21-23 . . . . Bristol	30-31 . . . . Pulaski
24-26 . . . . . . Princeton	**SEPTEMBER**
27-29 . . . .at Elizabethton	1 . . . . Pulaski

KINGSPORT METS

JUNE	
22-23 . . . . at Johnson City	24-26 . . . . . . Greeneville
24-26 . . . . . .Burlington	27-29 . . . . . at Pulaski
27 . . . . Elizabethton	30-31 . . . .at Elizabethton
28 . . . . . .at Elizabethton	**AUGUST**
29 . . . . . . Elizabethton	1 . . . . Elizabethton
JULY	3 . . . . Johnson City
1-2 . . . . Bristol	4 . . . . . . at Johnson City
3 . . . . . .at Elizabethton	5-7 . . . . Danville
4-6 . . . . .at Greeneville	8-10 . . . . . . Johnson City
7-8 . . . . . Johnson City	11-13 . . . . . .at Danville
9 . . . . . at Johnson City	14-16 . . . . at Burlington
10 . . . . . Johnson City	18-20 . . . . . . .Bluefield
11-13 . . . . . .at Princeton	21-23 . . . . Bristol
15 . . . . . Elizabethton	24-26 . . . .at Greeneville
16-17 . . . .at Elizabethton	27-29 . . . . . . Princeton
18-20 . . . . at Bristol	30-31 . . . . . at Bluefield
21-23 . . . . Pulaski	**SEPTEMBER**
	1 . . . . at Bluefield

PRINCETON RAYS

JUNE	
22-23 . . . . Bluefield	30-31 . . . . . .Burlington
24-26 . . . . Bristol	**AUGUST**
27-29 . . . . . at Burlington	1 . . . . .Burlington
JULY	3-4 . . . . at Bluefield
1-3 . . . . at Bluefield	5-7 . . . . Pulaski
4-6 . . . . Pulaski	8-10 . . . . .at Greeneville
7-8 . . . . Bluefield	11-13 . . . .at Elizabethton
9-10 . . . . . . at Bluefield	14-16 . . . . . at Pulaski
11-13 . . . . . Kingsport	17-19 . . . . . . Danville
15-17 . . . .at Danville	21-23 . . . . . . .Burlington
18-20 . . . . . Johnson City	24-26 . . . . . . at Pulaski
21-23 . . . . . Elizabethton	27-29 . . . . at Kingsport
24-26 . . . . at Johnson City	30-31 . . . . . Greeneville
27-29 . . . . .at Bristol	**SEPTEMBER**
	1 . . . . Greeneville

PULASKI YANKEES

JUNE	**AUGUST**
22-23 . . . . Bristol	1 . . . . .Bluefield
24-26 . . . . . Elizabethton	3-4 . . . . .at Bristol
27-29 . . . . . . at Bluefield	5-7 . . . . . . .at Princeton
JULY	8-10 . . . . . . .Burlington
1-3 . . . . .Burlington	11-13 . . . . .at Greeneville
4-6 . . . . . . .at Princeton	14-16 . . . . . Princeton
7-8 . . . . at Bristol	18-20 . . . .at Elizabethton
9-10 . . . . Bristol	21-23 . . . . . Greeneville
11-13 . . . . at Burlington	24-26 . . . . . . Princeton
15-17 . . . . . Johnson City	27-29 . . . . . .at Danville
18-20 . . . . . . Danville	30-31 . . . . at Johnson City
21-23 . . . . at Kingsport	**SEPTEMBER**
24-26 . . . .at Danville	1 . . . . at Johnson City
27-29 . . . . . . Kingsport	
30-31 . . . . Bluefield	

PIONEER LEAGUE

BILLINGS MUSTANGS

JUNE	**AUGUST**
19-21 . . . . . . Great Falls	1-2 . . . . Idaho Falls
22-23 . . . . . . Missoula	7-10 . . . . Missoula
25-28 . . . . . at Great Falls	12-15 . . . . at Orem
29-30 . . . . . at Missoula	16-19 . . . . . . at Ogden
JULY	21-24 . . . . . Idaho Falls
1-3 . . . . . . at Idaho Falls	25-26 . . . . . Great Falls
4-7 . . . . Missoula	27-30 . . . . at Idaho Falls
8-9 . . . . . . Great Falls	31 . . . . at Great Falls
10-13 . . . . at Missoula	**SEPTEMBER**
15-18 . . . . . . Ogden	1-2 . . . . . at Idaho Falls
19-22 . . . . . .Orem	3-5 . . . . . . Great Falls
24-27 . . . . at Missoula	7-9 . . . . . . Idaho Falls
28-30 . . . at Idaho Falls	10-12 . . . at Great Falls
31 . . . . . . Idaho Falls	

GRAND JUNCTION ROCKIES

JUNE	**AUGUST**
19-21 . . . . .Orem	1-2 . . . . at Orem
22-24 . . . . at Ogden	6-7 . . . . Orem
26-28 . . . . .Orem	8-10 . . . . Ogden
29-30 . . . . Ogden	12-15 . . . . at Idaho Falls
JULY	16-19 . . . . at Missoula
1 . . . . Ogden	21-24 . . . . Ogden
2-3 . . . at Rocky Mountain	25-26 . . . . .Orem
4-6 . . . . Rocky Mountain	27-29 . . . . at Orem
7-9 . . . . at Ogden	31 . . . . . Rocky Mountain
10-13 . . . . . . at Orem	**SEPTEMBER**
15-18 . . . . . Missoula	1 . . . . . . Rocky Mountain
19-22 . . . . . Idaho Falls	2-5 . . . . at Ogden
24-27 . at Rocky Mountain	6-7 . . . . Rocky Mountain
28-30 . . . Rocky Mountain	9-12 . . . at Rocky Mountain
31 . . . . at Orem	

GREAT FALLS VOYAGERS

JUNE	15-18 . . . . .Orem
19-21 . . . . . . at Billings	19-22 . . . . Ogden
22-23 . . . . . at Idaho Falls	24-27 . . . . . at Idaho Falls
25-28 . . . . Billings	28-30 . . . . . . at Missoula
29-30 . . . . . . Idaho Falls	31 . . . . Missoula
JULY	**AUGUST**
1-3 . . . . at Missoula	1-2 . . . . Missoula
4-7 . . . . . . Idaho Falls	7-10 . . . . . . Idaho Falls
8-9 . . . . at Billings	12-15 . . . . . . at Ogden
10-13 . . . . . at Idaho Falls	16-19 . . . . at Orem

21-24 . . . . Missoula	
25-26 . . . . . . at Billings	
27-30 . . . . . at Missoula	
31 . . . . Billings	

SEPTEMBER

1-2 . . . . Billings	
3-5 . . . . at Billings	
7-9 . . . . Missoula	
10-12 . . . . Billings	

IDAHO FALLS CHUKARS

JUNE		AUGUST	
19-21 . . . . . . at Missoula		1-2 . . . . at Billings	
22-23 . . . . . . Great Falls		7-10 . . . . . at Great Falls	
24-27 . . . . . . Missoula		12-15 . . . Grand Junction	
29-30 . . . . . at Great Falls		16-19 . . Rocky Mountain	
JULY		21-24 . . . . . at Billings	
1-3 . . . . Billings		25-26 . . . . . at Missoula	
4-7 . . . . . at Great Falls		27-30 . . . . Billings	
8-9 . . . . . . at Missoula		31 . . . . Missoula	
10-13 . . . . . . Great Falls		**SEPTEMBER**	
15-18 . . at Rocky Mountain		1-2 . . . . Missoula	
19-22 . . at Grand Junction		4-6 . . . . . at Missoula	
24-27 . . . . . Great Falls		7-9 . . . . . . at Billings	
28-30 . . . . . . Billings		10-12 . . . . . Missoula	
31 . . . . at Billings			

MISSOULA PADDLEHEADS

JUNE		AUGUST	
19-21 . . . . . . Idaho Falls		1-2 . . . . . at Great Falls	
22-23 . . . . . at Billings		7-10 . . . . . . at Billings	
24-27 . . at Idaho Falls		12-15 . . Rocky Mountain	
29-30 . . . . . . Billings		16-19 . . . . Grand Junction	
JULY		21-24 . . . . at Great Falls	
1-3 . . . . Great Falls		25-26 . . . . . Idaho Falls	
4-7 . . . . . . at Billings		27-30 . . . . . Great Falls	
8-9 . . . . . . Idaho Falls		31 . . . . . . at Idaho Falls	
10-13 . . . . Billings		**SEPTEMBER**	
15-18 . . at Grand Junction		1-2 . . . . . at Idaho Falls	
19-22 . at Rocky Mountain		4-6 . . . . . . Idaho Falls	
24-27 . . Billings		7-9 . . . . . at Great Falls	
28-30 . . . . . Great Falls		10-12 . . . . at Idaho Falls	
31 . . . . at Great Falls			

OGDEN RAPTORS

JUNE		
19-21 . . . Rocky Mountain		31 . . . . . Rocky Mountain
22-24 . . . Grand Junction		**AUGUST**
26-28 . . at Rocky Mountain		1-2 . . . . . Rocky Mountain
29-30 . . at Grand Junction		6-7 . . . at Rocky Mountain
JULY		8-10 . . . at Grand Junction
1 . . . . at Grand Junction		12-15 . . . . . Great Falls
3 . . . . at Orem		16-19 . . . . Billings
4-5 . . . . at Orem		21-24 . . at Grand Junction
6 . . . . at Orem		25-29 . . at Rocky Mountain
7-9 . . . . . . Grand Junction		31 . . . . Orem
10-13 . . . Rocky Mountain		**SEPTEMBER**
15-18 . . . . . . at Billings		1 . . . . Orem
19-22 . . at Great Falls		2-5 . . . . . Grand Junction
24 . . . . at Orem		6-8 . . . . . . at Orem
25 . . . . Orem		9-11 . . . . at Orem
26-28 . . . . at Orem		12 . . . . at Orem
29-30 . . . . Orem		

OREM OWLZ

JUNE		JULY	
19-21 . . at Grand Junction		1 . . . . at Rocky Mountain	
22-24 . . . Rocky Mountain		3 . . . . Ogden	
26-28 . . at Grand Junction		4-5 . . . . . . at Ogden	
29-30 . . at Rocky Mountain		6 . . . . Ogden	
		7-9 . . . . Rocky Mountain	

10-13 . . . Grand Junction	
15-18 . . . at Great Falls	
19-22 . . . . . . at Billings	
24 . . . . Ogden	
25 . . . . at Ogden	
26-28 . . . . Ogden	
29-30 . . . . . at Ogden	
31 . . . . . Grand Junction	

AUGUST

1-2 . . . . Grand Junction	
6-7 . . . at Grand Junction	
8-10 . . . at Rocky Mountain	

ROCKY MOUNTAIN VIBES

JUNE		AUGUST	
19-21 . . . . at Ogden		1-2 . . . . at Ogden	
22-24 . . . . . . at Orem		6-7 . . . . Ogden	
26-28 . . . . Ogden		8-10 . . . . Orem	
29-30 . . . . Orem		12-15 . . . . at Missoula	
JULY		16-19 . . . at Idaho Falls	
1 . . . . Orem		21-24 . . . . . . Orem	
2-3 . . . . Grand Junction		25-29 . . . . . . Ogden	
4-6 . . . at Grand Junction		31 . . . . at Grand Junction	
7-9 . . . . at Orem		**SEPTEMBER**	
10-13 . . . . . at Ogden		1 . . . . . at Grand Junction	
15-18 . . . . Idaho Falls		2-5 . . . . at Orem	
19-22 . . . . . Missoula		6-7 . . . at Grand Junction	
24-27 . . at Grand Junction		9-12 . . . . Grand Junction	
28-30 . . at Grand Junction			
31 . . . . at Ogden			

ARIZONA LEAGUE

AZL ANGELS
Home Games Only

JUNE			
22 . . . . Giants Black		28 . . . . Giants Black	
25 . . . . Cubs Red		31 . . . . Cubs Red	
27 . . . . Padres 1		**AUGUST**	
28 . . . . Indians Blue		2 . . . . Giants Black	
JULY		3 . . . . Indians Blue	
2 . . . . White Sox		7 . . . . Royals	
5 . . . . . . Athletics Gold		10 . . . . . Athletics Gold	
8 . . . . Mariners		13 . . . . Reds	
9 . . . . . . Brewers Gold		14 . . . . Dodgers 1	
12 . . . . Padres 2		17 . . . . Dodgers 2	
16 . . . . Cubs Blue		20 . . . . Cubs Blue	
19 . . . . . Giants Orange		23 . . . . . Giants Orange	
20 . . . . Athletics Green		24 . . . . Athletics Green	
24 . . . . . Indians Red		28 . . . . Rangers	
25 . . . . D-backs		29 . . . . D-backs	

AZL ATHLETICS GREEN

JUNE			
22 . . . . Cubs Blue		28 . . . . Cubs Blue	
25 . . . . . . Brewers Gold		31 . . . . Padres 2	
27 . . . . Dodgers 1		**AUGUST**	
29 . . . . . Giants Orange		2 . . . . Royals	
30 . . . . . Indians Blue		4 . . . . . Giants Orange	
JULY		5 . . . . Cubs Blue	
5 . . . . . . Brewers Blue		10 . . . . White Sox	
7 . . . . Dodgers 2		12 . . . . D-backs	
9 . . . . Giants Black		14 . . . . Giants Black	
11 . . . . Rangers		16 . . . . Padres 1	
15 . . . . Cubs Red		19 . . . . Cubs Red	
16 . . . . D-backs		20 . . . . D-backs	
21 . . . . Angels		25 . . . . Angels	
22 . . . . . Athletics Gold		26 . . . . Athletics Gold	
27 . . . . Reds		31 . . . . Mariners	

LEGENDARY QUALITY
SINCE 1960

JONATHON LUCROY
Pro Catcher

WWW.ALL-STARSPORTS.COM

MOVE FORWARD > RISE ABOVE

AZL BREWERS GOLD

JUNE	
24	Royals
26	Cubs Blue
28	Dodgers 1
29	Dodgers 2

JULY	
3	Padres 2
5	Indians Red
10	Angels
11	Giants Orange
13	White Sox
16	Reds
20	Brewers Blue
21	Indians Blue
24	Rangers
26	White Sox
30	Athletics Green

AUGUST	
1	Dodgers 2
3	Padres 2
4	Dodgers 2
8	Padres 2
10	Padres 1
15	Cubs Red
16	Mariners
18	Indians Blue
20	Reds
24	Brewers Blue
25	Indians Blue
28	Giants Orange
30	White Sox

AZL CUBS BLUE

JUNE	
24	Angels
25	Athletics Gold
29	D-backs

JULY	
2	Indians Blue
5	Rangers
7	Royals
10	Brewers Blue
12	Dodgers 2
15	Giants Orange
17	Cubs Red
22	Giants Orange
23	Athletics Green
25	Giants Black

26	Padres 1
30	Angels
31	Athletics Gold

AUGUST	
4	Brewers Blue
7	Padres 2
10	Indians Red
12	Dodgers 2
15	White Sox
17	Reds
19	Giants Orange
21	D-backs
26	Brewers Gold
27	Athletics Green
29	Giants Black
30	Cubs Red

AZL GIANTS BLACK

JUNE	
23	Angels
24	Brewers Blue
26	D-backs
29	Athletics Gold

JULY	
2	Padres 2
4	Dodgers 2
6	Indians Red
7	Cubs Red
11	Cubs Blue
15	Rangers
18	Athletics Green
19	White Sox
22	Reds
24	Giants Orange

29	Angels
30	Giants Orange

AUGUST	
1	D-backs
4	Athletics Gold
7	Cubs Red
9	Mariners
11	Giants Orange
12	Cubs Red
16	Dodgers 1
19	Brewers Gold
22	Athletics Green
23	Reds
26	Padres 2
28	Padres 1

AZL MARINERS

JUNE	
22	White Sox
24	Dodgers 1
26	Padres 1
29	Royals

JULY	
2	Reds
3	Indians Red
7	D-backs
9	Cubs Blue
13	Padres 2

15	Brewers Gold
17	Rangers
19	Dodgers 2
22	Cubs Red
24	Brewers Blue
28	Indians Blue
30	Dodgers 1

AUGUST	
1	Padres 1
4	Royals
7	Athletics Green

8	Indians Red
12	Angels
14	Athletics Gold
18	Reds

AZL PADRES 1

JUNE	
22	Dodgers 1
25	White Sox
28	Rangers

JULY	
2	Royals
3	Brewers Blue
6	Padres 2
7	Athletics Gold
12	Giants Black
13	Angels
16	Royals
19	Indians Red
21	Reds
22	Brewers Gold

27	Mariners
28	Dodgers 1
31	D-backs

AUGUST	
3	Rangers
7	Dodgers 2
8	Brewers Blue
11	Cubs Blue
12	Giants Orange
17	Cubs Red
18	Padres 2
20	Royals
23	Indians Red
25	Athletics Gold
26	Indians Blue
30	Athletics Green

AZL RANGERS

JUNE	
23	Padres 1
26	Brewers Blue
29	Cubs Red

JULY	
1	Mariners
3	Dodgers 1
6	Athletics Green
8	Brewers Gold
10	White Sox
13	Reds
16	Indians Red
21	Athletics Gold
22	Indians Blue
26	Royals
27	Cubs Blue

29	Padres 1

AUGUST	
1	Brewers Blue
4	Angels
6	Mariners
8	Dodgers 1
11	Padres 2
13	Giants Black
15	D-backs
18	Dodgers 2
20	Indians Red
25	Brewers Blue
26	Reds
30	Royals
31	Padres 1

AZL ROYALS

JUNE	
22	Reds
25	D-backs
28	Mariners
30	Cubs Blue

JULY	
4	Angels
5	White Sox
8	Padres 1
10	Indians Red
13	Brewers Blue
15	Dodgers 1
18	Giants Orange
19	Padres 2
23	Indians Red
25	Rangers

28	Athletics Gold
31	Brewers Gold

AUGUST	
3	Mariners
5	Brewers Gold
9	Rangers
10	Cubs Red
13	Padres 1
15	Athletics Green
18	Brewers Blue
19	Dodgers 1
22	Padres 1
23	Dodgers 2
27	Giants Black
29	Rangers

AZL DODGERS 2

JUNE	
22	Indians Blue
24	Athletics Green
27	Mariners
28	Reds

JULY	
1	Brewers Gold
3	Giants Black
8	Reds
9	Rangers
11	Indians Red

15 . . . . White Sox
18 . . . . Indians Blue
20 . . . . Dodgers 1
22 . . . . Padres 2
23 . . . . Angels
28 . . . . Padres 2
30 . . . . Royals

AUGUST
2 . . . . Padres 1
3 . . . . Reds

AZL INDIANS RED

JUNE
22 . . . . Padres 2
25 . . . . Rangers
28 . . . . . Brewers Blue
30 . . . . Padres 1

JULY
2 . . . . . . Athletics Green
7 . . . . . . Giants Orange
8 . . . . Dodgers 1
10 . . . . Cubs Red
13 . . . . Dodgers 2
17 . . . . . . Indians Blue
18 . . . . Mariners
21 . . . . Royals
22 . . . . D-backs

27 . . . . . . Brewers Gold
28 . . . . White Sox
31 . . . . Rangers

AUGUST
3 . . . . Brewers Blue
5 . . . . Padres 1
7 . . . . Reds
12 . . . . Royals
13 . . . . Dodgers 1
15 . . . . Angels
18 . . . . . . Giants Black
21 . . . . . Athletics Green
22 . . . . Mariners
25 . . . . Royals
26 . . . . D-backs
31 . . . . Cubs Blue

AZL PADRES 2

JUNE
23 . . . . Mariners
26 . . . . Dodgers 2
27 . . . . . Athletics Gold
30 . . . . White Sox

JULY
1 . . . . D-backs
5 . . . . Reds
8 . . . . . . Indians Blue
10 . . . . . Athletics Green
11 . . . . . Brewers Blue
17 . . . . . . Brewers Gold
18 . . . . Padres 1
23 . . . . Dodgers 1
24 . . . . Royals
26 . . . . Cubs Red

29 . . . . . Giants Orange

AUGUST
1 . . . . Cubs Blue
2 . . . . Indians Red
5 . . . . White Sox
6 . . . . Giants Black
10 . . . . Reds
13 . . . . . . Indians Blue
15 . . . . Padres 1
16 . . . . . . Indians Red
21 . . . . . . Brewers Gold
22 . . . . Dodgers 1
27 . . . . Angels
28 . . . . Dodgers 2
31 . . . . Dodgers 2

AZL GIANTS ORANGE

JUNE
22 . . . . D-backs
27 . . . . . . Indians Red
28 . . . . . . Giants Black

JULY
1 . . . . . Athletics Green
3 . . . . Angels
8 . . . . White Sox
9 . . . . Dodgers 1
12 . . . . . . Cubs Red
13 . . . . . . Indians Blue
17 . . . . Padres 1
20 . . . . . . Cubs Blue
23 . . . . Mariners
25 . . . . . . Dodgers 2
27 . . . . . Athletics Gold

28 . . . . D-backs

AUGUST
2 . . . . . . Athletics Gold
3 . . . . . . Giants Black
6 . . . . . Athletics Green
8 . . . . Royals
13 . . . . . Brewers Gold
14 . . . . Rangers
17 . . . . . Giants Black
18 . . . . Angels
21 . . . . . . Cubs Red
24 . . . . . . Cubs Blue
27 . . . . . . Cubs Red
29 . . . . . Athletics Green
31 . . . . . Athletics Gold

AZL INDIANS BLUE

JUNE
23 . . . . . Giants Orange
26 . . . . Reds
27 . . . . . . White Sox

JULY
1 . . . . . . Giants Black
3 . . . . Royals
5 . . . . Cubs Red
6 . . . . D-backs
11 . . . . . Athletics Gold
12 . . . . . Indians Red
16 . . . . . . Padres 2
19 . . . . . Brewers Gold
23 . . . . . . Padres 1
24 . . . . . . Dodgers 2

26 . . . . . Brewers Blue
29 . . . . . . Mariners

AUGUST
1 . . . . Reds
2 . . . . White Sox
6 . . . . . . Dodgers 1
8 . . . . Angels
10 . . . . Rangers
11 . . . . D-backs
16 . . . . . Cubs Blue
17 . . . . Royals
20 . . . . . . Padres 2
23 . . . . . Brewers Gold
27 . . . . . . Dodgers 1
28 . . . . . Indians Red
30 . . . . . Brewers Blue

AZL ATHLETICS GOLD

JUNE
24 . . . . Giants Orange
26 . . . . . Athletics Green

JULY
1 . . . . . . Dodgers 1
2 . . . . Cubs Red
4 . . . . Rangers
6 . . . . . . Dodgers 2
10 . . . . . . Padres 1
12 . . . . . . Mariners
17 . . . . . Giants Black
18 . . . . . Cubs Blue
20 . . . . Royals
23 . . . . . . D-backs
25 . . . . . Cubs Red
26 . . . . . . Angels

30 . . . . . Brewers Blue

AUGUST
1 . . . . . Athletics Green
6 . . . . . Cubs Blue
7 . . . . . White Sox
9 . . . . . . Angels
11 . . . . . Indians Red
15 . . . . . Indians Blue
17 . . . . . Padres 2
21 . . . . . Giants Black
22 . . . . . Cubs Blue
24 . . . . . Mariners
27 . . . . . D-backs
29 . . . . Brewers Gold
30 . . . . Indians Red

AZL DODGERS 1

JUNE
23 . . . . Royals
26 . . . . Indians Red
29 . . . . Brewers Blue

JULY
2 . . . . . . Dodgers 2
4 . . . . . Giants Orange
6 . . . . . Cubs Blue
7 . . . . . . Angels
12 . . . . . . Reds
13 . . . . Giants Black
17 . . . . D-backs
19 . . . . Rangers
24 . . . . Padres 1
25 . . . . Mariners

27 . . . . . Padres 2
29 . . . . . Royals

AUGUST
1 . . . . . Indians Red
4 . . . . . Cubs Red
7 . . . . . Indians Blue
9 . . . . Athletics Green
11 . . . . Brewers Gold
12 . . . . Athletics Gold
17 . . . . Mariners
18 . . . . White Sox
21 . . . . Padres 1
23 . . . . Rangers
28 . . . . . Royals
29 . . . . Mariners
31 . . . . Indians Blue

AZL BREWERS BLUE

JUNE
23 . . . . . . Indians Red
25 . . . . . . Padres 2
30 . . . . . . Rangers

JULY
1 . . . . Padres 1
4 . . . . . . Cubs Blue
6 . . . . . . Mariners
8 . . . . . . Giants Black
9 . . . . Royals
15 . . . . . Angels
17 . . . . Athletics Green

19 . . . . . . Reds
22 . . . . . Dodgers 1
25 . . . . Brewers Gold
27 . . . . Dodgers 2
29 . . . . Indians Red
31 . . . . White Sox

AUGUST
5 . . . . . Rangers
6 . . . . . Padres 1
9 . . . . Giants Orange
11 - 13 . . . Mariners
14 . . . . . Royals

19 . . . . Angels	26 . . . . Dodgers 1
21 . . . . Indians Blue	29 . . . . Cubs Red
23 . . . . Padres 2	31 . . . . Reds

AZL REDS

JUNE	
23 . . . . Brewers Gold	26 . . . . . . Athletics Green
25 . . . . Indians Blue	29 . . . . Brewers Gold
27 . . . . Giants Black	31 . . . . Indians Blue
30 . . . . . . Athletics Gold	**AUGUST**
JULY	2 . . . . Mariners
1 . . . . Cubs Blue	5 . . . . Indians Blue
6 . . . . . . Giants Orange	6 . . . . Indians Red
7 . . . . Padres 2	11 . . . . Dodgers 2
10 . . . . D-backs	12 . . . . Padres 2
11 . . . . Padres 1	15 . . . . Brewers Blue
17 . . . . Dodgers 2	16 . . . . Rangers
18 . . . . Dodgers 1	21 . . . . Dodgers 2
23 . . . . Cubs Red	22 . . . . White Sox
24 . . . . White Sox	27 . . . . Mariners
	28 . . . . White Sox
	30 . . . . Angels

AZL D-BACKS

JUNE	
24 . . . . Cubs Red	27 . . . . Indians Blue
27 . . . . Cubs Blue	30 . . . . Rangers
30 . . . . . . Brewers Gold	**AUGUST**
JULY	2 . . . . Cubs Blue
2 . . . . . . Giants Orange	5 . . . . . . Athletics Gold
4 . . . . Mariners	7 . . . . . . Giants Orange
5 . . . . Padres 1	9 . . . . Dodgers 2
11 . . . . Dodgers 1	10 . . . . Brewers Blue
12 . . . . . . Athletics Green	16 . . . . . . Giants Orange
15 . . . . . . Athletics Gold	17 . . . . . . Athletics Green
18 . . . . Angels	19 . . . . . . Athletics Gold
20 . . . . . . Giants Black	22 . . . . Angels
21 . . . . Brewers Blue	24 . . . . Giants Black
26 . . . . Indians Red	25 . . . . Reds
	30 . . . . Padres 2
	31 . . . . . . Brewers Gold

AZL CUBS RED

JUNE	
22 . . . . . . Athletics Gold	28 . . . . Reds
26 . . . . . . Giants Orange	**AUGUST**
27 . . . . Royals	1 . . . . Giants Orange
30 . . . . Angels	2 . . . . Dodgers 1
JULY	5 . . . . Angels
1 . . . . Indians Red	6 . . . . D-backs
4 . . . . . . Athletics Green	9 . . . . Cubs Blue
6 . . . . . . Brewers Gold	11 . . . . . . Athletics Green
9 . . . . D-backs	14 . . . . D-backs
11 . . . . Mariners	16 . . . . . . Brewers Blue
16 . . . . . . Athletics Gold	20 . . . . . . Athletics Gold
18 . . . . White Sox	22 . . . . . . Giants Orange
20 . . . . Rangers	24 . . . . Royals
21 . . . . Cubs Blue	25 . . . . Cubs Blue
27 . . . . . . Giants Black	31 . . . . . . Giants Black

AZL WHITE SOX

JUNE	
23 . . . . Dodgers 2	4 . . . . Brewers Gold
24 . . . . Rangers	7 . . . . Indians Blue
28 . . . . Padres 2	9 . . . . . . Athletics Gold
29 . . . . Angels	12 . . . . Royals
JULY	16 . . . . . . Brewers Blue
3 . . . . Reds	20 . . . . Mariners
	21 . . . . Padres 2
	23 . . . . . . Giants Black

25 . . . . . Athletics Green	12 . . . . . . Indians Blue
29 . . . . Dodgers 2	14 . . . . . . Brewers Gold
30 . . . . Cubs Red	17 . . . . Indians Red
AUGUST	20 . . . . . . Brewers Blue
3 . . . . Dodgers 1	24 . . . . Rangers
4 . . . . D-backs	25 . . . . Padres 2
8 . . . . Reds	27 . . . . Padres 1
9 . . . . Brewers Gold	29 . . . . Dodgers 2

GULF COAST LEAGUE

GCL ASTROS   *Home Games Only

JUNE	AUGUST
29 . . . . Cardinals	2 . . . . Mets
30 . . . . Nationals	5 . . . . Marlins
JULY	8 . . . . Cardinals
3 . . . . Mets	9 . . . . Nationals
6 . . . . Marlins	12 . . . . Mets
9 . . . . Cardinals	15 . . . . Marlins
10 . . . . Nationals	18 . . . . . . Cardinals
13 . . . . Mets	19 . . . . Nationals
16 . . . . Marlins	22 . . . . Mets
19 . . . . . . Cardinals	25 . . . . Marlins
20 . . . . Nationals	28 . . . . . . Cardinals
23 . . . . Mets	29 . . . . . . Nationals
26 . . . . Marlins	**SEPTEMBER**
29 . . . . . . Cardinals	1 . . . . Mets
30 . . . . Nationals	4 . . . . Marlins

GCL BLUE JAYS

JUNE	AUGUST
29 . . . . Tigers West	4 . . . . Phillies West
JULY	6 . . . . Yankees East
2 . . . . Phillies West	10 . . . . . . Phillies East
4 . . . . Yankees East	11 . . . . . . Yankees East
8 . . . . Phillies East	13 . . . . Tigers East
9 . . . . . . Yankees West	17 . . . . . . Tigers West
15 . . . . Tigers West	20 . . . . . . Phillies West
18 . . . . . . Phillies West	22 . . . . . . Yankees East
20 . . . . Tigers East	26 . . . . . . Phillies East
21 . . . . . . Yankees East	27 . . . . . . Yankees East
24 . . . . . . Phillies East	29 . . . . . . Tigers East
25 . . . . . . Yankees West	**SEPTEMBER**
28 . . . . Tigers East	2 . . . . Tigers West
31 . . . . . . Tigers West	5 . . . . . . Phillies West

GCL BRAVES

JUNE	AUGUST
30 . . . . Orioles	1 . . . . Rays
JULY	4 . . . . Pirates
4 . . . . Rays	6 . . . . Twins
7 . . . . Pirates	7 . . . . Rays
9 . . . . Twins	10 . . . . Orioles
10 . . . . Rays	12 . . . . Red Sox
13 . . . . Orioles	15 . . . . Rays
15 . . . . Red Sox	17 . . . . Pirates
18 . . . . Rays	19 . . . . Twins
20 . . . . Pirates	21 . . . . Rays
22 . . . . Twins	25 . . . . Orioles
24 . . . . Rays	27 . . . . Red Sox
28 . . . . Orioles	29 . . . . Rays
30 . . . . Red Sox	**SEPTEMBER**
	1 . . . . Pirates
	4 . . . . Rays

GCL CARDINALS

JULY	
2 . . . . Nationals	
4 . . . . Astros	
5 . . . . Mets	
8 . . . . Marlins	
12 . . . . Nationals	
14 . . . . Astros	
15 . . . . Mets	
18 . . . . Marlins	
22 . . . . Nationals	
24 . . . . Astros	
25 . . . . Mets	
28 . . . . Marlins	

AUGUST	
1 . . . . Nationals	

| 3 . . . . Astros |
| 4 . . . . Mets |
| 7 . . . . Marlins |
| 11 . . . . Nationals |
| 13 . . . . Astros |
| 14 . . . . Mets |
| 17 . . . . Marlins |
| 21 . . . . Nationals |
| 23 . . . . Astros |
| 24 . . . . Mets |
| 27 . . . . Marlins |
| 31 . . . . Nationals |

SEPTEMBER	
2 . . . . Astros	
3 . . . . Mets	

GCL MARLINS

JUNE	
29 . . . . Nationals	

JULY	
1 . . . . Astros	
3 . . . . Cardinals	
7 . . . . Mets	
9 . . . . Nationals	
11 . . . . Astros	
13 . . . . Cardinals	
17 . . . . Mets	
19 . . . . Nationals	
21 . . . . Astros	
23 . . . . Cardinals	
27 . . . . Mets	
29 . . . . Nationals	
31 . . . . Astros	

AUGUST	
2 . . . . Cardinals	
6 . . . . Mets	
8 . . . . Nationals	
10 . . . . Astros	
12 . . . . Cardinals	
16 . . . . Mets	
18 . . . . Nationals	
20 . . . . Astros	
22 . . . . Cardinals	
26 . . . . Mets	
28 . . . . Nationals	
30 . . . . Astros	

SEPTEMBER	
1 . . . . Cardinals	
5 . . . . Mets	

GCL METS

JUNE	
30 . . . . Cardinals	

JULY	
2 . . . . Marlins	
6 . . . . Nationals	
8 . . . . Astros	
10 . . . . Cardinals	
12 . . . . Marlins	
16 . . . . Nationals	
18 . . . . Astros	
20 . . . . Cardinals	
22 . . . . Marlins	
26 . . . . Nationals	
28 . . . . Astros	
30 . . . . Cardinals	

AUGUST	
1 . . . . Marlins	
5 . . . . Nationals	
7 . . . . Astros	
9 . . . . Cardinals	
11 . . . . Marlins	
15 . . . . Nationals	
17 . . . . Astros	
19 . . . . Cardinals	
21 . . . . Marlins	
25 . . . . Nationals	
27 . . . . Astros	
29 . . . . Cardinals	
31 . . . . Marlins	

SEPTEMBER	
4 . . . . Nationals	

GCL NATIONALS

JULY	
1 . . . . Mets	
4 . . . . Marlins	
5 . . . . Astros	
7 . . . . Cardinals	
11 . . . . Mets	
14 . . . . Marlins	
15 . . . . Astros	
17 . . . . Cardinals	
21 . . . . Mets	
24 . . . . Marlins	
25 . . . . Astros	
27 . . . . Cardinals	

| 31 . . . . Mets |

AUGUST	
3 . . . . Marlins	
4 . . . . Astros	
6 . . . . Cardinals	
10 . . . . Mets	
13 . . . . Marlins	
14 . . . . Astros	
16 . . . . Cardinals	
20 . . . . Mets	
23 . . . . Marlins	
24 . . . . Astros	

GCL ORIOLES

JUNE	
29 . . . . Braves	

JULY	
1 . . . . Twins	
3 . . . . Pirates	
7 . . . . Red Sox	
9 . . . . Rays	
10 . . . . Pirates	
14 . . . . Braves	
16 . . . . Twins	
17 . . . . Pirates	
20 . . . . Red Sox	
22 . . . . Rays	
24 . . . . Pirates	
27 . . . . Braves	
29 . . . . Twins	

| 31 . . . . Pirates |

AUGUST	
4 . . . . Red Sox	
6 . . . . Rays	
8 . . . . Pirates	
11 . . . . Braves	
14 . . . . Pirates	
17 . . . . Red Sox	
19 . . . . Rays	
22 . . . . Pirates	
24 . . . . Braves	
26 . . . . Twins	
28 . . . . Pirates	

SEPTEMBER	
1 . . . . Red Sox	
5 . . . . Pirates	

GCL PHILLIES EAST

JUNE	
30 . . . . Blue Jays	

JULY	
2 . . . . Tigers West	
3 . . . . Yankees East	
6 . . . . Yankees West	
7 . . . . Tigers East	
9 . . . . Phillies West	
11 . . . . Yankees East	
16 . . . . Blue Jays	
18 . . . . Tigers West	
22 . . . . Yankees West	
23 . . . . Tigers East	
25 . . . . Phillies West	

AUGUST	
1 . . . . Blue Jays	
4 . . . . Tigers West	
5 . . . . Yankees East	
7 . . . . Yankees West	
8 . . . . Tigers East	
11 . . . . Phillies West	
18 . . . . Blue Jays	
20 . . . . Tigers West	
21 . . . . Yankees East	
24 . . . . Yankees West	
25 . . . . Tigers East	
27 . . . . Phillies West	

SEPTEMBER	
3 . . . . Blue Jays	
5 . . . . Tigers West	

GCL PHILLIES WEST

JUNE	
29 . . . . Yankees East	

JULY	
1 . . . . Phillies East	
8 . . . . Tigers West	
10 . . . . Blue Jays	
13 . . . . Yankees West	
14 . . . . Tigers East	
15 . . . . Yankees East	
17 . . . . Phillies East	
24 . . . . Tigers West	
27 . . . . Blue Jays	
29 . . . . Yankees West	
30 . . . . Tigers East	
31 . . . . Yankees East	

AUGUST	
3 . . . . Phillies East	
10 . . . . Tigers West	
12 . . . . Blue Jays	
14 . . . . Yankees West	
15 . . . . Tigers East	
17 . . . . Yankees East	
19 . . . . Phillies East	
26 . . . . Tigers West	
28 . . . . Blue Jays	
31 . . . . Yankees West	

SEPTEMBER	
1 . . . . Tigers East	
2 . . . . Yankees East	
4 . . . . Phillies East	

GCL PIRATES

JUNE	
30 . . . . Twins	

JULY	
4 . . . . Orioles	
6 . . . . Braves	
8 . . . . Red Sox	
11 . . . . Orioles	

| 13 . . . . Twins |
| 15 . . . . Rays |
| 18 . . . . Orioles |
| 21 . . . . Braves |
| 25 . . . . Orioles |
| 28 . . . . Twins |
| 30 . . . . Rays |

(GCL Cardinals continued)
| 26 . . . . Cardinals |
| 30 . . . . Mets |

SEPTEMBER	
2 . . . . Marlins	
3 . . . . Astros	
5 . . . . Cardinals	

AUGUST
1 . . . . Orioles
3 . . . . Braves
5 . . . . Red Sox
7 . . . . Orioles
10 . . . . Twins
12 . . . . Rays
15 . . . . Orioles
18 . . . . Braves
20 . . . . Red Sox
21 . . . . Orioles
25 . . . . Twins
27 . . . . Rays
29 . . . . Orioles
31 . . . . Braves
SEPTEMBER
2 . . . . Red Sox
4 . . . . Orioles

GCL RAYS

JUNE
29 . . . . Red Sox
JULY
1 . . . . Pirates
3 . . . . Braves
6 . . . . Twins
8 . . . . Orioles
11 . . . . Braves
14 . . . . Red Sox
16 . . . . Pirates
17 . . . . Braves
21 . . . . Twins
25 . . . . Braves
27 . . . . Red Sox
29 . . . . Pirates
31 . . . . Braves
AUGUST
3 . . . . Twins
5 . . . . Orioles
8 . . . . Braves
11 . . . . Red Sox
14 . . . . Braves
18 . . . . Twins
20 . . . . Orioles
22 . . . . Braves
24 . . . . Red Sox
26 . . . . Pirates
28 . . . . Twins
31 . . . . Twins
SEPTEMBER
2 . . . . Orioles
5 . . . . Braves

GCL RED SOX

JUNE
30 . . . . Rays
JULY
1 . . . . Braves
4 . . . . Twins
6 . . . . Orioles
9 . . . . Pirates
10 . . . . Twins
13 . . . . Rays
16 . . . . Braves
18 . . . . Twins
21 . . . . Orioles
22 . . . . Pirates
24 . . . . Twins
28 . . . . Rays
29 . . . . Braves
AUGUST
1 . . . . Twins
3 . . . . Orioles
6 . . . . Pirates
7 . . . . Twins
10 . . . . Rays
15 . . . . Twins
18 . . . . Orioles
19 . . . . Pirates
21 . . . . Twins
25 . . . . Rays
26 . . . . Braves
29 . . . . Twins
31 . . . . Orioles
SEPTEMBER
4 . . . . Twins

GCL TIGERS EAST

JUNE
29 . . . . Phillies East
JULY
1 . . . . Yankees East
3 . . . . Blue Jays
6 . . . . Phillies West
8 . . . . Yankees West
11 . . . . Blue Jays
13 . . . . Tigers West
15 . . . . Phillies East
17 . . . . Yankees East
22 . . . . Phillies West
24 . . . . Yankees West
29 . . . . Tigers West
31 . . . . Phillies East
AUGUST
3 . . . . Yankees East
5 . . . . Blue Jays
7 . . . . Phillies West
10 . . . . Yankees West
14 . . . . Tigers West
17 . . . . Phillies East
19 . . . . Yankees East
21 . . . . Blue Jays
24 . . . . Phillies West
26 . . . . Yankees West
31 . . . . Tigers West
SEPTEMBER
2 . . . . Phillies East
4 . . . . Yankees East

GCL TIGERS WEST

JUNE
30 . . . . Phillies West
JULY
4 . . . . Tigers East

7 . . . . Blue Jays
10 . . . Phillies East
14 . . . . . . Yankees East
16 . . . . . . Phillies West
20 . . . . . . Yankees West
21 . . . . Tigers East
23 . . . . Blue Jays
27 . . . . . . Phillies East
28 . . . . . . Yankees West
30 . . . . . . Yankees East
AUGUST
1 . . . . Phillies West
6 . . . . Tigers East

GCL TWINS

JUNE
29 . . . . Pirates
JULY
3 . . . . Red Sox
7 . . . . Rays
8 . . . .\. . . Braves
11 . . . . Red Sox
14 . . . . Pirates
15 . . . . Orioles
17 . . . . Red Sox
20 . . . . Rays
25 . . . . Red Sox
27 . . . . Pirates
30 . . . . Orioles
31 . . . . Red Sox
AUGUST
4 . . . . Rays
5 . . . . Braves
8 . . . . Red Sox
11 . . . . Pirates
12 . . . . Orioles
14 . . . . Red Sox
17 . . . . Rays
20 . . . . Braves
22 . . . . Red Sox
24 . . . . Pirates
27 . . . . Orioles
28 . . . . Red Sox
SEPTEMBER
1 . . . . Rays
2 . . . . Braves
5 . . . . Red Sox

GCL YANKEES EAST

JULY
2 . . . . Yankees West
6 . . . . Tigers West
7 . . . . Phillies West
9 . . . . Tigers East
13 . . . . Blue Jays
18 . . . . Yankees West
20 . . . . Phillies East
22 . . . . Tigers West
23 . . . . Phillies West
25 . . . . Tigers East
28 . . . . Phillies East
29 . . . . Blue Jays
AUGUST
4 . . . . . . Yankees West
7 . . . . Tigers West
8 . . . . Phillies West
11 . . . . Tigers East
13 . . . . Phillies East
14 . . . . Blue Jays
20 . . . . . . Yankees West
24 . . . . Tigers West
25 . . . . . . Phillies West
27 . . . . Tigers East
29 . . . . . . Phillies East
31 . . . . Blue Jays
SEPTEMBER
5 . . . . Yankees West

GCL YANKEES WEST

JUNE
30 . . . . Tigers East
JULY
1 . . . . Blue Jays
3 . . . . Tigers West
4 . . . . Phillies West
10 . . . . . . Yankees East
11 . . . . Tigers West
14 . . . . Phillies East
16 . . . . Tigers East
17 . . . . Blue Jays
21 . . . . . . Phillies West
27 . . . . . . Yankees East
30 . . . . . . Phillies East
AUGUST
1 . . . . Tigers East
3 . . . . Blue Jays
5 . . . . Tigers West
6 . . . . Phillies West
12 . . . . . . Yankees East
15 . . . . . . Phillies East
18 . . . . Tigers East
19 . . . . Blue Jays
21 . . . . Tigers West
22 . . . . . . Phillies West
28 . . . . . . Yankees East
SEPTEMBER
1 . . . . Phillies East
3 . . . . Tigers West
4 . . . . Blue Jays

INDEPENDENT

AMERICAN ASSOCIATION

CLEBURNE

MAY	
16-19	Sioux Falls
20-22	Winnipeg
28-30	Fargo-Moorhead
31	St. Paul

JUNE	
1-2	St. Paul
11-13	Kansas City
14-17	Sioux City
18-20	Texas
25-27	Cleburne

JULY	
2-4	Chicago
5-7	Gary SouthShore
16-18	Lincoln
19-21	Milwaukee

AUGUST	
3-5	Sioux Falls
6-8	Kansas City
15-17	Sioux City
24-26	Texas

FARGO-MOORHEAD

MAY	
20-23	Fargo-Moorhead
24-26	Texas

JUNE	
3-5	Lincoln
18-20	Gary SouthShore
21-23	Chicago
28-30	St. Paul

JULY	
4	Lincoln
5-7	Milwaukee

9-11	Sioux City
12-13	Lincoln
19-21	St. Paul
30-31	Chicago

AUGUST	
15-17	Sioux Falls
18-20	Gary SouthShore
24-26	Winnipeg
31	Cleburne

SEPTEMBER	
1-2	Cleburne

GARY SOUTHSHORE

MAY	
21-23	Sioux City
24-26	Sioux Falls

JUNE	
3-6	Chicago
11-13	Winnipeg
14-16	St. Paul
28-30	Kansas City

JULY	
12-14	Cleburne
15-18	Fargo-Moorhead

19-21	Chicago
30-31	Winnipeg

AUGUST	
1	Winnipeg
2-4	Milwaukee
6-8	Fargo-Moorhead
12-14	Texas
15-17	Milwaukee
21-23	St. Paul
31	Lincoln

SEPTEMBER	
1-2	Lincoln

LINCOLN

MAY	
23-26	Cleburne
27-29	St. Paul

JUNE	
6-9	Texas
18-20	Milwaukee
21-23	Texas
28-30	Sioux City

JULY	
5-7	Kansas City

9-11	Winnipeg
24-26	Fargo-Moorhead
30-31	Sioux City

AUGUST	
1	Sioux City
2-4	Kansas City
9-11	Sioux Falls
12-14	Chicago
15-17	St. Paul
25-26	Gary SouthShore
28-30	Cleburne

MILWAUKEE

MAY	
24-26	Chicago
31	Lincoln

JUNE	
1-2	Lincoln

3-6	Kansas City
11-13	Sioux Falls
14-16	Winnipeg
24-27	Gary SouthShore

JULY	
9-11	Cleburne
12-14	Sioux City
27-29	Gary SouthShore
30-31	St. Paul

AUGUST	
1	St. Paul
9-11	Winnipeg

12-14	Fargo-Moorhead
18-20	Chicago
21-23	Fargo-Moorhead
24-26	Sioux Falls
31	Texas

SEPTEMBER	
1-2	Texas

ST. PAUL

MAY	
16-19	Milwaukee
21-23	Chicago
24-26	Sioux City

JUNE	
7-9	Milwaukee
11-13	Fargo-Moorhead
21-23	Gary SouthShore
24-26	Texas

JULY	
1-3	Lincoln

12-14	Winnipeg
16-18	Kansas City
24-26	Cleburne
28-29	Kansas City

AUGUST	
9-11	Gary SouthShore
12-14	Winnipeg
24-27	Chicago
28-30	Fargo-Moorhead

SEPTEMBER	
1-2	Cleburne

SIOUX CITY

MAY	
16-19	Lincoln
28-30	Texas

JUNE	
7-9	Fargo-Moorhead
10-13	Lincoln
21-23	Sioux Falls
25-27	Winnipeg

JULY	
2-4	Milwaukee

15-17	Chicago
19-21	Sioux Falls
24-26	Gary SouthShore
27-29	Texas

AUGUST	
6-8	St. Paul
9-11	Cleburne
19-20	Kansas City
21-23	Cleburne
24-26	Kansas City

SIOUX FALLS

MAY	
31	Winnipeg

JUNE	
1-2	Winnipeg
3-6	Cleburne
7-9	Fargo-Moorhead
14-16	Lincoln
17-20	St. Paul
24-27	Fargo-Moorhead
28-30	Milwaukee

JULY	
5-7	Sioux City
8-11	Texas
12-14	Chicago
24-26	Kansas City
27-29	Lincoln

AUGUST	
12-13	Sioux City
18-20	Cleburne
21-23	Texas
27-29	Sioux City

TEXAS

MAY	
16-19	Winnipeg
20-22	Sioux Falls
31	Fargo-Moorhead

JUNE	
1-2	Fargo-Moorhead
3-5	St. Paul
14-16	Kansas City
28-30	Cleburne

JULY	
1	Cleburne

2-4	Gary SouthShore
5-7	Chicago
16-18	Milwaukee
19-21	Lincoln
31	Cleburne

AUGUST	
1-2	Cleburne
3-5	Sioux City
6-8	Sioux Falls
16-17	Kansas City
18-20	Lincoln
27-29	Kansas City

JULY

9-11	Cleburne
12-14	Sioux City
27-29	Gary SouthShore
30-31	St. Paul

AUGUST

1	St. Paul
9-11	Winnipeg

SEPTEMBER

1-2	Texas

WINNIPEG

MAY	
24-26	Kansas City
28-30	Gary SouthShore

JUNE	
3-6	Sioux City
7-9	Cleburne
18-20	Chicago
21-23	Milwaukee

JULY	
1-3	Fargo-Moorhead
4-8	St Paul

16-18	Sioux Falls
24-26	Texas
27-28	Fargo-Moorhead

AUGUST	
6-8	Lincoln
15-17	Chicago
18-19	St. Paul
27-29	Gary SouthShore
30-31	Sioux Falls

SEPTEMBER	
1-2	Sioux Falls

ATLANTIC LEAGUE

HIGH POINT ROCKERS

MAY	
2-5	Sugar Land
6-8	New Britain
17-19	Southern Maryland
21-23	Long Island
31	New Britain

JUNE	
1-2	New Britain
3-6	York
14-16	Long Island
18-20	Lancaster

JULY	
1-4	Lancaster
5-7	Somerset

19-21	Somerset
25-28	Sugar Land
29-31	Southern Maryland

AUGUST	
1	Southern Maryland
6-8	Sugar Land
9-11	York
16-18	Long Island
23-25	York
27-29	New Britain

SEPTEMBER	
1-5	Southern Maryland
11-12	Lancaster
13-16	Somerset

LANCASTER BARNSTORMERS

APRIL	
26-28	High Point
29-30	Long Island

MAY	
1-2	Long Island
7-8	Sugar Land
17-19	Somerset
21-23	New Britain
31	Southern Maryland

JUNE	
1-2	Southern Maryland
4-6	Sugar Land
14-16	York
25-27	Somerset
28-30	Southern Maryland

JULY	
5-7	York
16-18	High Point
23-25	Somerset
26-28	Southern Maryland

AUGUST	
6-8	New Britain
9-11	Long Island
19-22	High Point
23-25	Sugar Land
30-31	New Britain

SEPTEMBER	
1	New Britain
2-5	Long Island
13-15	York

LONG ISLAND DUCKS

MAY	
3-5	York
7-9	Southern Maryland
17-19	New Britain
24-26	Sugar Land
27-30	Lancaster

JUNE	
7-9	High Point
11-13	Somerset
21-23	Lancaster
25-27	New Britain

JULY	
1-4	Sugar Land

5-7	Southern Maryland
19-21	Lancaster
22-25	New Britain

AUGUST	
2-4	High Point
13-15	York
19-22	Somerset
26-29	Southern Maryland
30-31	Somerset

SEPTEMBER	
1	Somerset
6-8	Sugar Land
9-12	York
20-22	High Point

NEW BRITAIN BEES

MAY	
3-5,	Somerset
14-16	Lancaster
24-26	High Point
28-30	York

JUNE	
3-6	Long Island
7-9	Lancaster
18-20	Southern Maryland
21-23	Sugar Land

JULY	
1-4	Somerset
5-7	Sugar Land

16-18	Southern Maryland
19-21	York
30-31	Long Island

AUGUST	
1	Long Island
2-4	York
9-11	Southern Maryland
12-15	High Point
23-25	Long Island

SEPTEMBER	
2-5	Somerset
6-8	Lancaster
13-16	Sugar Land
17-19	High Point

SOMERSET PATRIOTS

APRIL	
26-28	New Britain
29-30	High Point

MAY	
1	High Point
9-12	Lancaster
14-16	High Point
21-23	Sugar Land

JUNE	
4-6	Southern Maryland
7-9	York
14-16	Southern Maryland
18-20	Long Island
28-30	Long Island

JULY	
12-14	New Britain
15-18	York
26-28	Long Island
30-31	York

AUGUST	
1	York
9-11	Sugar Land
13-15	Lancaster
23-25	Southern Maryland
26-29	Lancaster

SEPTEMBER	
6-8	High Point
10-12	Sugar Land
20-22	New Britain

SOUTHERN MARYLAND

MAY	
3-5	Lancaster
10-12	New Britain
13-16	Long Island
24-26	Somerset
27-30	High Point

JUNE	
7-9	Sugar Land
10-13	New Britain
21-23	High Point
24-26	York

JULY	
2-4	York
12-14	Lancaster

19-21	Sugar Land
22-24	High Point

AUGUST	
2-4	Somerset
5-8	Long Island
12-15	Sugar Land
16-18	Somerset
30-31	York

SEPTEMBER	
1	York
10-12	New Britain
13-15	Long Island
16-19	Lancaster

SUGAR LAND

APRIL	
25-30	Southern Maryland

MAY	
1	Southern Maryland
10-12	Long Island
13-19	York
27-31	Somerset

JUNE	
1-2	Somerset
10-13	Lancaster
14-17	New Britain
25-30	High Point

JULY	
12-17	Long Island
29-31	Lancaster

AUGUST	
1-4	Lancaster
16-22	New Britain
30-31	High Point

SEPTEMBER	
1	High Point
3-5	York
17-19	Somerset
20-22	Southern Maryland

YORK

APRIL	
26-28	Long Island

30	New Britain

MAY
1-2 . . . . New Britain
6-8 . . . . Somerset
9-12 . . . . .High Point
20-23 . . Southern Maryland
24-26 . . . . Lancaster
31 . . . . Long Island

JUNE
1-2 . . . . Long Island
10-13 . . . . . . .High Point
18-20 . . . . Sugar Land
21-23 . . . . Somerset
28-30 . . . . . . New Britain

JULY
12-14 . . . . . . .High Point
22-24 . . . . . Sugar Land
26-28 . . . . . New Britain

AUGUST
5-8 . . . . Somerset
16-18 . . . . Lancaster
19-22 . . Southern Maryland
26-29 . . . . . . Sugar Land

SEPTEMBER
6-8 . . . . . Southern Maryland
16-19 . . . . Long Island
20-22 . . . . Lancaster

AMERICAN ASSOCIATION

CHICAGO

MAY
17-19 . . . . .Gary
27-29 . . . . Sioux Falls
31 . . . . Sioux City

JUNE
1-2 . . . . Sioux City
10-12 . . . . Texas
14-16 . . . .Fargo-Moorhead
24-27 . . . . . . Kansas City
28-30 . . . . Winnipeg

JULY
9-11 . . . . .Gary

24-26 . . . . . . Milwaukee
27-29 . . . . . . .Cleburne

AUGUST
2-4 . . . . St. Paul
6-8 . . . . Milwaukee
9-11 . . . .Fargo-Moorhead
21-23 . . . . . . Winnipeg
28-30 . . . . . . Milwaukee
31 . . . . St. Paul

SEPTEMBER
1-2 . . . . St. Paul

CLEBURNE

MAY
16-19 . . . . . . Sioux Falls
20-22 . . . . Winnipeg
28-30 . . .Fargo-Moorhead
31 . . . . St. Paul

JUNE
1-2 . . . . St Paul
11-13 . . . . . . Kansas City
14-17 . . . . . . Sioux City
18-20 . . . . Texas
25-27 . . . . Lincoln

JULY
2-4 . . . . Chicago
5-7 . . . . .Gary
16-18 . . . . .Lincoln
19-21 . . . . . . Milwaukee

AUGUST
3-5 . . . . Sioux Falls
6-8 . . . . Kansas City
15-17 . . . . . . Sioux City
24-26 . . . . Texas

FRONTIER LEAGUE

EVANSVILLE

MAY
10-12 . . . .Southern Illinois
17-19 . . . . Florence
28-30 . . . . . .Washington

JUNE
11-13 . . . . . . Windy City
14-16 . . . . . Schaumburg
25-27 . . . . . Schaumburg
28-30 . . . . . . River City

JULY
12-14 . . . . .Lake Erie
16-18 . . . . .Joliet
26-28 . . . . . Windy City

AUGUST
2-4 . . . . .Southern Illinois
6-8 . . . . .Lake Erie
13-15 . . . . River City
16-18 . . . . Gateway
23-25 . . . . Florence
27-29 . . . . Gateway

FLORENCE

MAY
9 . . . . .Lake Erie
10-12 . . . . Joliet
15-16 . . . . River City
24-26 . . .Southern Illinois
31 . . . . Evansville

JUNE
1-2 . . . . Evansville
5-6 . . . . Windy City

11-13 . . . . . Schaumburg
14-16 . . . . . Lake Erie
21-24 . . . . . . Gateway

JULY
2-4 . . . . . .Southern Illinois
5-6 . . . . .Lake Erie
19-21 . . . . . . Evansville
31 . . . . Gateway

AUGUST
1 . . . . Gateway
2-4 . . . . .Washington

GATEWAY

MAY
10-12 . . . . . Schaumburg
21-23 . . . . . . Evansville
28-30 . . . . Florence
31 . . . . .Washington

JUNE
1-2. . . . . .Washington
11-13 . . . . . . River City
14-16 . . . . . . Windy City
28-30 . . .Southern Illinois

JULY
2-4 . . . . Evansville

16-18 . . . . River City
21-22 . . . . . .Washington
27-29 . . . . Joliet

12-14 . . . . Florence
23-25 . . . . . . .Lake Erie
26-28 . . . . Joliet

AUGUST
6-8 . . . . . Southern Illinois
9-11 . . . . . . Windy City
20-22 . . . . . Schaumburg
23-25 . . . . . River City
30-31 . . . . .Washington

SEPTEMBER
1 . . . . .Washington

JOLIET

MAY
9 . . . . Windy City
14-16 . . . . . Gateway
17-19 . . . . . Schaumburg
28-29 . . . . . Windy City

JUNE
4-6 . . . . Evansville
11-13 . . . . . .Lake Erie
14-16 . . . . . .Washington
21-23 . . . . . . River City
25-27 . . . . Florence

JULY
2-4 . . . . River City
5-7 . . . . Windy City
19-21 . . . . . . Gateway
23-25 . . . . . . Evansville

AUGUST
2-4 . . . . Schaumburg
13-15 . . . . . .Washington
16-18 . . . . Southern Illinois
30-31 . . . . . .Lake Erie

SEPTEMBER
1 . . . . .Lake Erie

LAKE ERIE

MAY
10-12 . . . . Windy City
14-16 . . . Southern Illinois
28-30 . . . . . Schaumburg

JUNE
1-2 . . . . Joliet
7-9 . . . . Southern Illinois
18-20 . . . . Gateway
21-23 . . . . . . Evansville

JULY
2-4 . . . . .Washington

16-18 . . . . Florence
19-21 . . . . . . .Washington
30-31 . . . . Evansville

AUGUST
1 . . . . Evansville
2-4 . . . . River City
9-11 . . . . Joliet
13-15 . . . . Gateway
20-22 . . . . Windy City
23-25 . . . . . Schaumburg

NEW JERSEY

MAY
22-24 . . . . . . Quebec
26-28 . . . . . .Washington
29-31 . . . . . . Windy City

JUNE
3 . . . . New York
9 . . . . New York
11 . . . . New York
12-14 . . . . . Trois-Rivieres
26-28 . . . . Florence
30 . . . . New York

JULY
1-2 . . . . New York
7-9 . . . . Joliet
21-23 . . . . . .Lake Erie
24-26 . . . . . . Gateway
31 . . . . Quebec

AUGUST
1-2 . . . . Quebec
3-5 . . . . Schaumburg
7-9 . . . . . Trois-Rivieres
21-23 . . . . . Sussex County
25-27 . . . . . .Washington
28-30 . . . . Sussex County

NEW YORK

MAY	
15-17 . . . . . .Washington	
19-21 . . . Southern Illinois	
22-24 . . . . Lake Erie	

JUNE	
2 . . . . New Jersey	
4 . . . . New Jersey	
5-7 . . . . . . Trois-Rivieres	
10 . . . . New Jersey	
16-18 . . . . . . Washington	
19-21 . . . . Evansville	
26-28 . . . . Joliet	

JULY	
3-5. . . . . Quebec	
21-23 . . . . Gateway	
24-26 . . . . Florence	

AUGUST	
4-6. . . . . Quebec	
7-9. . . . . . Sussex County	
18-20 . . . . Sussex County	
28-30 . . . . . Trois-Riveries	

SEPTEMBER	
1-3. . . . . New Jersey	

QUEBEC

MAY	
26-28 . . . . Evansville	
29-31 . . . . Florence	

JUNE	
16-18 . . . . . New Jersey	
19-21 . . . Southern Illinois	
23-25 . . . . New York	
26-28 . . . . Gateway	

JULY	
17-19 . . . . Trois-Rivieres	

21-23 . . . Sussex County	
24-26 . . . . . .Washington	

AUGUST	
7-9. . . . . .Washington	
11-13 . . . . . . New York	
18-20 . . . . Windy City	
21-23 . . . . . Schaumburg	
25-27 . . . . Trois-Rivieres	

SEPTEMBER	
1-3. . . . . Sussex County	
4-6. . . . . . . New Jersey	

RIVER CITY

MAY	
9-12 . . . . . . .Washington	
17-19 . . . . Gateway	
21-23 . . . Southern Illinois	
24-26 . . . . Evansville	

JUNE	
5-6. . . . . Lake Erie	
7-9. . . . . Joliet	
18-20 . . . . Florence	
26-27 . . . . Gateway	

JULY	
5-7. . . . . Evansville	
17-18 . . . . Schaumburg	
19-21 . . . Southern Illinois	
26-28 . . . . . . .Lake Erie	

AUGUST	
7-8. . . . . . . Windy City	
9-11 . . . . Florence	
21-22 . . . . Joliet	
28-29 . . . . . .Washington	

SCHAUMBURG

MAY	
14-16 . . . . . . .Washington	
21-23 . . . . .Lake Erie	
24-27 . . . . Joliet	

JUNE	
4-6. . . . . Gateway	
7-9. . . . . Evansville	
19-20 . . . . Joliet	
21-23 . . . Southern Illinois	
28-30 . . . . Florence	

JULY	
2-4. . . . . . . Windy City	
12-14 . . . . . .Washington	
19-21 . . . . . Windy City	
23-25 . . . Southern Illinois	
29-31 . . . . . . River City	

AUGUST	
1 . . . . River City	
6-8. . . . . Florence	
16-18 . . . . . .Lake Erie	
30-31 . . . . . . River City	

SOUTHERN ILLINOIS

MAY	
17-19 . . . . . . Windy City	
28-30 . . . . . . River City	
31 . . . . Schaumburg	

JUNE	
1-2. . . . . . . Schaumburg	
11-13 . . . . . .Washington	
14-16 . . . . . . River City	
25-27 . . . . . . Windy City	

JULY	
5-7. . . . . Gateway	
12-14 . . . . Joliet	
16-17 . . . . Gateway	
26-27 . . . . Florence	
30-31 . . . . Joliet	

AUGUST	
1 . . . . Joliet	
9-11 . . . . . . Schaumburg	
13-15 . . . . Florence	

20-22 . . . . Evansville	
27-29 . . . . . . .Lake Erie	
30-31 . . . . Evansville	

SEPTEMBER	
1 . . . . Evansville	

SUSSEX COUNTY

MAY	
14 . . . . New York	
19-21 . . . . . . .Lake Erie	
22-24 . . . . Gateway	

JUNE	
5-7. . . . . . . New Jersey	
15-18 . . . . . . Evansville	
19-21 . . . . . .Washington	
23-25 . . . . Florence	
30 . . . . Qubec	

JULY	
1-2. . . . . Quebec	

3-5. . . . . New Jersey	
10-12 . . . . Joliet	
17-19 . . . . New York	
28-30 . . . . Quebec	

AUGUST	
31 . . . . . . Trois-Riveres	
1-2. . . . . . Trois-Riveres	
4-6. . . . . . . Windy City	
11-13 . . . . Trois-Riveres	
26-28 . . . . . . New York	

SEPTEMBER	
4-6. . . . . . . .Washington	

TROIS-RIVIERES

MAY	
26-28 . . . . Evansville	
29-31 . . . . Florence	

JUNE	
16-18 . . . . Southern Illinois	
19-21 . . . . . .Washington	
23-25 . . . . Gateway	
26-28 . . . . Sussex County	

JULY	
7-9. . . . . Quebec	
10-12 . . . . . . New Jersey	

21-23 . . . . . . .Washington	
24-26 . . . . Sussex County	
28-30 . . . . New York	

AUGUST	
4-6. . . . . . . .Washington	
14-16 . . . . Quebec	
18-20 . . . . Schaumburg	
21-23 . . . . Windy City	

SEPTEMBER	
4-6. . . . . New York	

WASHINGTON

MAY	
17-19 . . . . .Lake Erie	
22-23 . . . . Florence	
24-26 . . . . Gateway	

JUNE	
4-6. . . . Southern Illinois	
7-9. . . . . Florence	
18-20 . . . . Evansville	
25-27 . . . . . . .Lake Erie	
28-30 . . . . Joliet	

JULY	
5-7. . . . . . . Schaumburg	
16-18 . . . . . Windy City	
23-25 . . . . . River City	
26-28 . . . . . Schaumburg	

AUGUST	
6-8. . . . . Joliet	
9-11 . . . . . . Evansville	
16-18 . . . . . Windy City	
23-25 . . . Southern Illinois	

WINDY CITY

MAY	
14-16 . . . . Evansville	
21-23 . . . . Joliet	
24-26 . . . . . . .Lake Erie	
31 . . . . River City	

JUNE	
1-2. . . . . River City	
7-9. . . . . Gateway	
18-20 . . . Southern Illinois	
21-23 . . . . .Washington	
28-30 . . . . . . .Lake Erie	

JULY	
12-14 . . . . . . River City	
23-25 . . . . . . Florence	
30-31 . . . . .Washington	

AUGUST	
1 . . . . .Washington	
2-4. . . . . Gateway	
13-15 . . . . . Schaumburg	
23-25 . . . . Joliet	
27-29 . . . . . Schaumburg	
30-31 . . . . Florence	

INDEPENDENT LEAGUES

AMERICAN ASSOCIATION

Mailing and Street Address: PO Box 995, Moorhead, MN 56561-0995.
Telephone: (218) 512-0380.
Email: info@aaipb.com
Website: americanassociationbaseball.com.
Year Founded: 2005.
Commissioner: Joshua E. Schaub. **Executive Director:** Josh Buchholz. **Director of Umpires:** Ronnie Teague.
Directors: Jim Abel, Mark Brandmeyer, Daryn Eudaly, Marv Goldklang, Shawn Hunter, Sam Katz, Mark Ogren, John Roost, Patrick Salvi, Scott Sonju, Bruce Thom and Mike Zimmerman.
Opening Date: May 19. **Closing Date:** September 7.
Regular Season: 100 games.
Division Structure: North—Chicago Dogs, Gary SouthShore RailCats, Fargo-Moorhead RedHawks, Milwaukee Milkmen, St. Paul Saints, Winnipeg Goldeyes. **South**—Cleburne Railroaders, Kansas City T-Bones, Lincoln Saltdogs, Sioux City Explorers, Sioux Falls Canaries, Texas AirHogs.
Playoff Format: Top two teams in each division play in best-of-five series. Winners play in best-of-five American Association Finals. **Roster Limit:** 23.
Player Eligibility Rule: Minimum of five first-year players; maximum of five veterans (at least six or more years of professional service).
Brand of Baseball: Rawlings.
Statistician: Pointstreak.com, Stack Sports, 5360 Legacy Dr #150, Plano, TX 75024.

STADIUM INFORMATION

Club	Stadium	Opened	LF	CF	RF	Capacity	2018 Att.
Chicago	Impact Field	2018	313	389	294	6,300	166,672
Cleburne	The Depot at Cleburne Station	2017	335	400	320	3,750	78,624
Fargo-Moorhead	Newman Outdoor Field	1996	314	408	318	4,172	161,857
Gary SouthShore	U.S. Steel Yard	2002	320	400	335	6,139	167,887
Kansas City	T-Bones Stadium	2003	300	396	328	6,270	156,058
Lincoln	Haymarket Park	2001	335	403	325	4,500	168,394
Milwaukee	Routine Field	2019	330	407	330	4,000	59,459
St. Paul	CHS Field	2015	330	396	320	7,140	394,970
Sioux City	Mercy Field at Lewis and Clark Park	1993	330	400	330	3,800	51,618
Sioux Falls	Sioux Falls Stadium	1964	313	410	312	4,462	114,452
Texas	AirHogs Stadium	2008	330	400	330	4,500	59,471
Winnipeg	Shaw Park	1999	325	400	325	7,481	195,787

Dimensions: LF, CF, RF

CHICAGO DOGS

Office Address: 9800 Balmoral Avenue, Rosemont, IL, 60018
Telephone: 847.636.5450.
E-mail: info@thechicagodogs.com. **Website:** thechicagodogs.com.
Owners: Shawn Hunter, Steven Gluckstern.
Chief Operating Officer: Trish Zuro. **Baseball Operations:** Ron Stern.
Corporate Sponsorships: Julia Brady. **Corporate Sales Manager:** Scott Foley. **Sales and Event Manager:** Evan Gersonde. **Senior Account Executive:** Kyle McKenna, Jon Ryan, Mackenzie Thomas. **Account Executive:** Jason Mandell.
Director of Game Entertainment and PA Announcer: Kevin Sullivan. **Media Relations:** Alexandra Jakubiak.
Community Relations: Daniela Barrios. **Broadcast and Media Relations Manager:** Sam Brief. **Website Design/ Photographer:** Matt Zuro.
Retail Director: Jeff Chapman. **Director of Operations:** Mark Viniard. **Assistant Director of Operations:** Kyle Lindquist. **Executive Chef:** Mike Blase.
Manager: Butch Hobson. **Clubhouse Manager:** Daniel Langston.

GAME INFORMATION

Stadium Name: Impact Field, 9800 Balmoral Avenue, Rosemont, IL 60018.
Standard Game Times: Mon.-Sat., 7:05 pm, Sun., 3:05 pm (July-Sept.)

CLEBURNE RAILROADERS

Office Address: 1906 Brazzle Boulevard, Cleburne, TX 76033.
Telephone: (817) 945-8705.
Email address: info@railroaderbaseball.com. **Website:** railroaderbaseball.com.
President/Co-Owner: John Junker. **Co-Owner:** Daryn Eudaly.
General Manager: Josh Robertson. **Director of Business Operations:** Bill Adams.
Director of Sales: David Kirk. **Ticket Office Manager:** Hollie Bunn. **Facility and Maintenance Manager:** Jon Stark.
Director of Broadcasting and Media Relations: Brad Allred. **Broadcasting and Media Relations Manager:** Denning Gerig.
Field Manager: Brent Clevlen. **Pitching Coach:** Mike Jeffcoat. **Hitting Coach:** John Rodriguez.

GAME INFORMATION
Broadcasters: Brad Allred and Denning Gerig. **Games Broadcast:** 100. **Webcast Address:** www.953khits.com.
Stadium Name: The Depot at Cleburne Station. **Directions:** From Chisholm Trail Parkway (toll road) continue south across US HWY 67, turn left onto Cleburne Station Boulevard. From US HWY 67 South, exit Nolan River Road, turn left onto Nolan River Road, turn left onto Cleburne Station Boulevard. From US HWY 67 North, exit Nolan River Road, turn right onto Nolan River Road, turn left onto Cleburne Station Boulevard. **Standard Game Times:** Mon.-Sat., 7:06 PM, Sun., 2/5 PM

FARGO-MOORHEAD REDHAWKS

Office Address: 1515 15th Ave N Fargo, ND 58102
Telephone: (701) 235-6161. **Fax:** (701) 297-9247.
Email Addresses: redhawks@fmredhawks.com media@fmredhawks.com.
Website: fmredhawks.com
Operated by: Fargo Baseball LLC. **Chairman of the Board:** N. Bruce Thom. **President & CEO:** Brad Thom.
General Manager: Matt Rau. **Vice President, Finance:** Rick Larson. **Assistant General Manager:** Karl Hoium.
Director of Communications: Chad Ekren. **Director of Ticket Operations:** Isaac Olson.
Group Sales Manager: Cole Milberger. **Director of Food and Beverage:** Derek Wang. **Community Relations and Merchandise Manager:** Ashley McCoy. **Stadium Superintendent/Head Groundskeeper:** Tom Drietz.
Field Manager: Jim Bennett. **Bench Coach:** Chris Coste. **Hitting Coach:** Anthony Renz. **Bullpen Coach:** Robbie Lopez.
Clubhouse Manager: Brennan Cozier. **Player Personnel Consultant:** Jeff Bittiger

GAME INFORMATION
Radio Announcers: Jack Michaels & Chase Miller. **Games Broadcasted:** 100. **Flagship Station:** 740 THE FAN (KNFL-740AM, K297BW 107.3FM). **Stadium Name:** Newman Outdoor Field (1996). **Location:** I-29 North to exit 67, east on 19th Ave North, right on Albrecht Boulevard. **Standard Game Times:** M-F. 7:02 pm Sat.: 6 pm, Sun.: 1:00 pm.

GARY SOUTHSHORE RAILCATS

Office Address: One Stadium Plaza, Gary, IN 46402.
Telephone: (219) 882-2255. **Fax:** (219) 882-2259.
Email Address: info@railcatsbaseball.com. **Website:** railcatsbaseball.com.
Operated by: Salvi Sports Enterprises.
Owner/CEO: Pat Salvi. **Owner:** Lindy Salvi.
President, Salvi Sports Enterprises: Brian Lyter. **General Manager:** Brian Flenner. **Director of Sales:** Daniel Faulkner. **Director of Ticket Operations:** Hisham Abad. **Marketing Consultant:** Renee Connelly.
Senior Director of Operations/Head Groundskeeper: Noah Simmons. **Manager of Marketing and Promotions:** Ashley Nylen. **Director of Food and Beverage:** Michael Dortch. **Account Executive:** Matt Santiago.
Field Manager: Greg Tagert.

GAME INFORMATION
Games Broadcast: 100. **Flagship Station:** WEFM 95.9-FM. **Stadium Name:** US Steel Yard. **Location:** Take I-65 North to end of highway at U.S. 12/20 (Dunes Highway). Turn left on U.S. 12/20 heading west for 1.5 miles (three stop lights). Stadium is on left side. **Standard Game Times:** Mon.-Tues., Thurs.-Fri., 7:10 pm, Wed., 6:45 pm, Sat., 6:10 pm, Sun., 2:10 pm.

KANSAS CITY T-BONES

Office Address: 1800 Village West Parkway, Kansas City, KS 66111.
Telephone: 913-328-5618.
Email: tickets@tbonesbaseball.com. **Web:** tbonesbaseball.com.
Operated by: Max Fun Entertainment, LLC.
Principal Owner: Mark Brandmeyer. **President:** Matt Perry.
General Manager/Vice President: Chris Browne. **Chief Monetary Officer:** Mark McKee.
Director, Group Sales: Nick Restivo. **Director, Marketing and Promotions:** Morgan Kolenda.
Dir. Ticket Sales/Merch: Kacy Muller. **Box Office Manager:** Cameron Eiseman. **Director, Stadium Operations and Grounds:** Nathan Miller.
Field Manager: Joe Calfapietra. **Coaches:** Frank White, Bill Sobbe. **Equipment Manager:** John West.

GAME INFORMATION
Radio Announcer: Dan Vaughan. **Games broadcast:** 100. **Site:** www.tbonesbaseball.com. **Stadium Name:** T-Bones Stadium. **Location:** State Avenue West off I-435 and State Ave. **Standard Game Times:** Mon-Sat., 7:05 pm, Sun., 1:05 pm.

LINCOLN SALTDOGS

Office Address: 403 Line Drive Circle, Suite A, Lincoln, NE 68508.
Telephone: (402) 474-2255. **Fax:** (402) 474-2254.
Email Address: info@saltdogs.com. **Website:** saltdogs.com.
Chairman: Jim Abel. **President/GM:** Charlie Meyer.
Director, Marketing: Bret Beer. **Director, Broadcasting/Communications:** Michael Dixon. **Director, Stadium Operations:** Dave Aschwege. **Director, Sales:** Steve Zoucha. **Director, Video Production:** Cade McFadden. **Assistant Director, Stadium Operations:** Dan Busch. **Manager, Ticket Sales:** Colter Clarke. **Group Sales Executive:** Daniel Thomas. **Athletic Turf Manager:** Jeremy Johnson. **Assistant Turf Manager:** Jen Roeber.
Office Manager: Kaydra Brodine. **Director of Operations for Concessions:** Steve Deriese. **Director of Kitchen Operations:** Katie Wilkinson.
Manager: James Frisbie. **Coach:** Tommy Gregg. **Coach:** Brad Weitzel.

GAME INFORMATION
Public Address Announcer: Heath Kramer. **Broadcast Team:** Jeff Briden, Jack Bockoven, Ryan Swanigan, Danny Burke. **No. of Games Broadcast:** 100. **Flagship Station:** KLMS 1480AM & ESPN101.5 FM. **Webcast Address:** www.americanassociationbaseball.com. **Stadium Name:** Haymarket Park. **Location:** I-80 to Cornhusker Highway West, left on First Street, right on Sun Valley Boulevard, left on Line Drive. **Standard Game Times:** Mon.-Sat., 7:05 pm, Sun., 1:35 pm.

MILWAUKEE MILKMEN

Website: milwaukeemilkmen.com.
Owner: Michael Zimmerman.
Corporate Partnership/Ticket Sales: Joe Zimmerman. **Entertainment & Events:** Scot Johnson. **Finance:** Tom Johns. **Administration:** Dan Kuenzi. **Medical Staff:** Midwest Orthopedic Speciality Hospital.
Manager: Anthony Barone.

GAME INFORMATION
Ballpark Location: 7035 S. Ballpark Drive, Franklin, WI 53132. **Main Office:** 7044 S. Ballpark Drive, Ste 300, Franklin WI 53132. **Standard Game Times:** Mon.-Fri., 7:05 pm. Sat., 6:05 pm. Sun., 1:05 pm.

ST. PAUL SAINTS

Office Address: 360 Broadway Street, St. Paul, MN 55101.
Telephone: (651) 644-3517. **Fax:** (651) 644-1627.
Email Address: funisgood@saintsbaseball.com.
Website: saintsbaseball.com.
Principal Owners: Marv Goldklang, Jeff Goldklang, Gerald Goldklang, Mike Goldklang, Bill Murray, Mike Veeck, Larry Eagel, Tom Whaley, Alton Phillips. **Chairman:** Marv Goldklang. **President:** Jeff Goldklang.
Executive VP/General Manager: Derek Sharrer. **Executive VP:** Tom Whaley. **Senior VP/Assistant GM:** Chris Schwab.
Vice President/Director, Broadcast/Media Relations: Sean Aronson. **Director, Promotions/Marketing:** Sierra Bailey.
Director, Corporate Partnerships: Tyson Jeffers. **Director of Sales:** Zane Heinselman. **Ticket Sales Executive:** Abbie Farrell. **Ticket Sales Executive:** Michael Villafana. **Ticket Office Manager:** Aaron Boettger. **Director, Operations:**

Curtis Nachtsheim. **Marketing and Creative Services Manager:** Rob Thompson. **Director, Digital Media and Video Production:** Jordan Lynn. **Multi-Media Content Producer:** Zach Neubauer. **Director, Community Partnerships/Fan Services:** Eddie Coblentz. **Business Manager:** Krista Schnelle. **Office Manager:** Gina Kray. **Events Manager:** Anna Gutknecht. **Director, Food/Beverage:** Justin Grandstaff, Gregg Kraly. **Head Groundskeeper:** Marcus Campbell.
Field Manager: George Tsamis. **Coaches:** Kerry Ligtenberg, Ole Sheldon. **Athletic Trainer:** Jason Ellenbecker.

GAME INFORMATION
Radio Announcer: Sean Aronson. **Games Broadcast:** 100. **Flagship Station:** KFAN+ 96.7 FM. **Webcast Address:** www.saintsbaseball.com. **Stadium Name:** CHS Field. **Location:** From the west take I-94 to the 7th St. Exit and head south to 5th & Broadway. From the east take I-94 to the Mounds Blvd/US-61N exit. Turn left on Kellogg and a right on Broadway until you reach 5th St. **Standard Game Times:** Mon.-Sat., 7:05 pm, Sun., 5:05 pm.

SIOUX CITY EXPLORERS

Office Address: 3400 Line Drive, Sioux City, IA 51106.
Telephone: (712) 277-9467. **Fax:** (712) 277-9406.
Email Address: promotions@xsbaseball.com. **Website:** www.xsbaseball.com.
President: Matt Adamski.
Director, Stadium Operations and Baseball Operations: Boyd Pitkin.
Field Manager: Steve Montgomery. **Coaches:** Bobby Post, Derek Wolfe. **Athletic Trainer:** Bruce Fischbach.
Clubhouse Manager: Robby Loraditch.

GAME INFORMATION
Radio Announcer: Connor Ryan. **No. of Games Broadcast:** 100. **Flagship Station:** KSCJ 1360-AM. **Webcast Address:** www.xsbaseball.com. **Stadium Name:** Mercy Field at Lewis and Clark Park. **Location:** I-29 to Singing Hills Blvd, North, right on Line Drive. **Standard Game Times:** Mon.-Fri., 7:12 pm, Sat., 6:05 pm, Sun., 4:02 pm.

SIOUX FALLS CANARIES

Office Address: 1001 N West Ave, Sioux Falls, SD 57104.
Telephone: (605) 336-6060.
Email Address: info@sfcanaries.com. **Website:** www.sfcanaries.com.
Operated by: Canaries Baseball, LLC. **CEO/Managing Partner:** Tom Garrity.
General Manager: Duell Higbe. **Sales:** Christopher Plucker, Andrew Candela.
Field Manager: Mike Meyer.

GAME INFORMATION
Radio Announcer: Carter Woodiel. **No. of Games Broadcast:** 100. **Flagship Station:** KWSN 1230-AM. **Webcast Address:** www.kwsn.com. **Stadium Name:** Sioux Falls Stadium. **Location:** I-29 to Russell Street, east one mile, south on West Avenue. **Standard Game Times:** Mon.-Fri., 7:05 pm, Sat., 6:05 pm, Sun., 1:05 pm.

TEXAS AIRHOGS

Office Address: 1600 Lone Star Parkway, Grand Prairie, TX 75050.
Telephone: (972) 521-6730. **Fax:** (972) 504-2288.
Website: www.airhogsbaseball.com. **Email:** info@airhogsbaseball.com.
General Manager: Nate Gutierrez. **Asst. General Manager:** Justin Terry. **Senior Director of Sales and Broadcasting:** Tim Costello. **Director of Baseball Operations:** Billy Martin, Jr. **Community Relations & PR Specialist:** Kelsey Armand. **Group Sales Executives:** Zachary Lee, Alexis Elizondo. **Director of Stadium Operations:** Buddy Craig. **Marketing Specialist:** Danielle Bassetti. **Field Manager:** Chris Bando.

GAME INFORMATION
Broadcaster: Tim Costello. **Games Broadcast:** 100. **Webcast:** www.airhogsbaseball.com. **Stadium Name:** AirHogs Stadium. **Location:** From I-30, take Beltline Road exit going north, take Lone Star Park entrance towards the stadium. **Standard Game Times:** Mon.-Sat. 7:05 p.m. Sun. 5:05 p.m..

WINNIPEG GOLDEYES

Office Address: One Portage Ave E, Winnipeg, Manitoba R3B 3N3.
Telephone: (204) 982-2273. **Fax:** (204) 982-2274.
Email Address: goldeyes@goldeyes.com. **Website:** www.goldeyes.com.
Operated by: Winnipeg Goldeyes Baseball Club, Inc.
Principal Owner/President: Sam Katz. **General Manager:** Andrew Collier. **Vice President & COO:** Regan Katz.
CFO: Jason McRae-King. **Director, Sales/Marketing:** Dan Chase. **Manager, Box Office:** Paul Duque. **Coordinator,**

Food/Beverage: Melissa Schlichting. **Account Executive:** Steve Schuster. **Suite Manager/Sales & Marketing:** Angela Sanche. **Media Coordinator:** Nigel Batchelor. **Manager, Retail:** Kendra Gibson. **Controller:** Kim Saito. **Facility Manager:** Don Ferguson. **Executive Assistant:** Sherri Rheubottom. **Administrative Assistant:** Lindsay Jestin.
   Manager/Director, Player Procurement: Rick Forney. **Coach:** Kash Beauchamp. **Clubhouse Manager:** Jamie Samson.

GAME INFORMATION

   Radio Announcer: Steve Schuster. No. **of Games Broadcast:** 100. **Flagship Station:** CJNU 93.7 FM. **Stadium Name:** Shaw Park. **Location:** North on Pembina Highway to Broadway, East on Broadway to Main Street, North on Main Street to Water Avenue, East on Water Avenue to Westbrook Street, North on Westbrook Street to Lombard Avenue, East on Lombard Avenue to Mill Street, South on Mill Street to ballpark. **Standard Game Times:** Mon.-Fri., 7:00 pm, Sat., 6:00 pm, Sun., 1:00 pm.

ATLANTIC LEAGUE

Mailing Address: PO Box 5190, Lancaster, Pa., 17606.
Telephone: (303) 915-8414 or (978) 790-5421.
Email Address: suggestions@atlanticleague.com . **Website:** atlanticleague.com.
Year Founded: 1998.
Founder/Chairman: Frank Boulton.
Executive Committee: Frank Boulton, Bill Shipley, Bob Zlotnik.
President: Rick White. **League Administrator:** Emily Merrill.
Division Structure: Freedom—Lancaster, Southern Maryland, Sugar Land, York.
Liberty—High Point, Long Island, Road Warriors, Somerset.
Regular Season: 126 games (split-schedule).
2020 Opening Date: April 30. **Closing Date:** Sept. 20. **All-Star Game:** July 14, at Southern Maryland.
Playoff Format: First-half division winners meet second-half winners in best-of-five series; Winners meet in best-of-five final for league championship.
Roster Limit: 25. Teams may keep 27 players from start of season until May 31. **Eligibility Rule:** No restrictions; MLB and MiLB suspensions honored.
Brand of Baseball: Rawlings. **Statistical Service:** Major League Baseball.

STADIUM INFORMATION

Club	Stadium	Opened	Dimensions LF	CF	RF	Capacity	2019 Att.
High Point Rockers	BB&T Point	2019	336	400	339	4,024	144,486
Lancaster	Clipper Magazine Stadium	2005	372	400	300	6,000	285,441
Long Island	Bethpage Ballpark	2000	325	400	325	6,002	328,194
Somerset	TD Bank Ballpark	1999	317	402	315	6,100	344,641
So. Maryland	Regency Furniture Stadium	2008	305	400	320	6,000	200,889
Sugar Land	Constellation Field	2012	348	405	325	7,500	304,753
York	PeoplesBank Park	2007	300	400	325	5,000	199,045

HIGH POINT ROCKERS

Office Address: 301 N. Elm Street, High Point, NC 27262.
Telephone: (336) 888-1000.
E-Mail Address: info@highpointrockers.com. **Website:** highpointrockers.com
Owner: High Point Baseball, Inc.
Assistant General Manager: Christian Heimall. **Director of Ticket Sales:** Susan Ormond. **Ticket Operations Manager:** Leighton Foster. **Facilities Operations Manager:** Shane Poling. **Account Executive:** Matthew Scott. **Account Executive:** Caroline Cooling.
Promotions Manager: Mackenzie Barnes. **Corporate Sales Manager:** David Martin. **Director of Corporate Growth & Fulfillment:** Caroline Keating. **Accountant:** Matthew McCree.
Field Manager: Jamie Keefe. **Pitching Coach:** Frank Viola. **Bench Coach & Player Procurement:** Billy Horn. **Athletic Trainer:** Zac Schner. **Clubhouse Manager:** Kevin Pearman.

GAME INFORMATION
Games Broadcast: 126. **Flagship Station:** highpointrockers.com. **Stadium Name:** BB&T Point. **Location:** 301 N. Elm Street, High Point, NC 27262. **Standard Game Times:** Mon.-Sat., 7:05 pm, Sun., 5:05 pm. **Visiting Club Hotel:** Red Lion Hotel. 135 S. Main Street, High Point, NC 27262..

LANCASTER BARNSTORMERS

Office Address: 650 North Prince Street, Lancaster, PA 17603..
Telephone: (717) 509-4487.
Website: lancasterbarnstormers.com
General Manager: Michael Reynolds. **VP, Marketing:** Kristen Simon. **Vice President of Finance:** Pamela Raffensberger. **Corporate Sales Manager:** Melissa Tucker. **Director of Community Relationships:** Maureen Wheeler.
Director, Media Relations/Broadcasting: Dave Collins. **Vice President of Stadium Operations:** Mike Logan. **Vice President Ticket Sales:** Charlie Hildbold. **Human Resource Generalist:** Tania Atkinson. **Box Office Manager:** Adam Smith. **Business Development Specialist, Groups:** Brendan Dudek. **Promotions & Sponsorship Fulfillment Manager:** Alexandra Bunn. **Business Development Specialist, Groups:** Jack Elliott.
Operations Manager: Tim Snyder. **Business Development Specialist, Groups:** Kyle Witman. **Senior Staffing and Mascot Coordinator:** Lori Krchnar. **Cleaning Services Supervisor:** Miggy Rosado. **Creative Services Coordinator:** Ryan Cortazzo.

Group Sales Manager: Samantha Biastre. **Director of Marketing:** Michael Whisler, **Business Development Specialist, Season Tickets:** Christopher Heal. **Business Development Specialist, Season Tickets:** Taylor Gunden. **Business Development Specialist, Season Tickets:** Erica Giuliani.

Business Development Specialist, Season Tickets: Conner Wylie. **Business Development Specialist, Season Tickets:** Alyssa Worthington. **Assistant to the General Manager:** Yvette Ramos.

Manager: Ross Peeples. **Baseball Operations Manager:** Troy Steffy.

GAME INFORMATION

Stadium: Clipper Magazine Stadium. **Location:** 650 North Prince Street, Lancaster, PA 17603. **Standard Game Times:** Mon-Sat., 6:30 pm, Sun., 1 pm..

LONG ISLAND DUCKS

Mailing Address: 3 Court House Dr, Central Islip, NY 11722.
Telephone: (631) 940-3825. **Fax:** (631) 940-3800.
Email Address: info@liducks.com. **Website:** liducks.com.
Operated by: Long Island Ducks Professional Baseball Club, LLC.
Founder/CEO: Frank Boulton. **Owner/Chairman:** Seth Waugh. **Owner:** Bud Harrelson. **President/General Manager:** Michael Pfaff. **Assistant GM/Senior VP, Sales:** Doug Cohen. **Senior Director, Administration:** Gerry Anderson. **VP, Sales/Operations:** John Wolff. **Director, Season Sales:** Brad Kallman.

Director, Media Relations/Broadcasting: Michael Polak. **Director, Marketing/Promotions:** Jordan Schiff. **Staff Accountant:** Annmarie DeMasi. **Manager, Group Sales:** Sean Smith. **Manager, Stadium Operations:** DJ Bornschein. **Manager, Merchandise/Client Services:** Katelyn Paquette.

Head Groundskeeper: Andrew Wright. **Coordinator, Administration:** Michelle Jensen. **Account Executives:** Anthony Fiorelli, Jack Fagan, Don Kennedy. **GM, Food & Beverage, Great South Bay Hospitality, LLC:** Alan Goodman.

Field Manager: Wally Backman. **Coaches:** Mauro "Goose" Gozzo, Lew Ford. **Coordinator, Medical Services:** Tony Amin. **Head Trainer:** Dotty Pitchford. **Assistant Trainer:** Deanna Reynolds.

GAME INFORMATION

Radio Announcers: Michael Polak, Chris King, David Weiss. **No. of Games Broadcast:** 126 on LIDucks.com, Facebook Live and YouTube. **Official Scorer:** Michael Polak.

SOMERSET PATRIOTS

Office Address: One Patriots Park, Bridgewater, NJ 08807.
Telephone: (908) 252-0700. **Fax:** (908) 252-0776.
Website: somersetpatriots.com.
Operated by: Somerset Baseball Partners, LLC. **Principal Owners:** Steve Kalafer, Josh Kalafer, Jonathan Kalafer. **Chairman Emeritus:** Steve Kalafer. **Chairmen:** Josh Kalafer and Jonathan Kalafer. **President/GM:** Patrick McVerry. **Senior VP, Marketing:** Dave Marek. **VP, Public Relations:** Marc Russinoff. **VP, Operations:** Bryan Iwicki. **VP, Ticket Operations:** Matt Kopas.

Senior Director, Merchandise: Rob Crossman. **Director, Tickets:** Nick Cherrillo. **Director, Broadcasting & Media Relations:** Marc Schwartz. **Director, Marketing:** Hal Hansen.

Director, Operations: Zach Keller. **Director, Administration:** Michele DaCosta. **Corporate Sales Manager:** Ken Smith. **Group Sales Managers:** Matt Hayden, Nate Roe, Mike Seppi. **Ticket Office, Manager:** Tim O'Leary. **Controller:** Suzanne Colon. **Accountant:** Stephanie DePass.

GM, HomePlate Catering/Hospitality: Mike McDermott. **Assistant GM, HomePlate Catering/Hospitality:** Jimmy Search. **Head Groundskeeper:** Dan Purner.

Field Manager: Brett Jodie. **Pitching Coach/Director, Baseball Operations:** Jon Hunton. **Hitting/Third Base Coach:** Ty Wright. **Athletic Trainer:** TBD. **Manager Emeritus:** Sparky Lyle.

GAME INFORMATION

Radio Announcer: Marc Schwartz. **No. of Games Broadcast:** Home-72, Away-54. **Flagship Station:** WCTC 1450-AM. **Video Streams:** SPN.tv. **Ballpark Name:** TD Bank Ballpark. **Standard Game Times:** Mon.- Thurs. 6:35 pm/ 7:05 pm, Fri & Sat., 7:05 pm, Sun., 1:05 pm/ 5:05 pm.

SOUTHERN MARYLAND
BLUE CRABS

Office Address: 11765 St. Linus Drive, Waldorf, Maryland 20602.
Telephone: (301) 638-9788.
Principal Owners: Crabs On Deck LLC.
General Manager: Courtney Knichel. **Marketing Manager:** Sam Rubin. **Director, Sales:** Tom Fink. **Box Office Manager:** Stephen Thomson. **Sales Executive:** Mario Pietroluongo. **Sales Executive:** Seth Distler. **Director of Operations:** Tim Lillis. **Groundskeeper:** Ben Baker.
Field Manager: Stan Cliburn. **Bench Coach:** Joe Walsh. **Pitching Coach:** Daryl Thompson

GAME INFORMATION
Radio Announcer: Andrew Bandstra. **Stadium Name:** Regency Furniture Stadium.
Standard Game Times: Mon.-Sat., 6:35 pm; Sun. 2:05 pm..

SUGAR LAND SKEETERS

Office Address: 1 Stadium Drive, Sugar Land, Texas, 77498.
Telephone: (281) 240-4487.
Owners: Bob, Kevin and Marcie Zlotnik. **President:** Christopher Hill. **Special Advisor:** Deacon Jones. **General Manager:** Tyler Stamm. **Senior Vice President, Sales and Marketing:** Bob Merril. **Vice President, Community:** Kyle Dawson.
Office Administrator: Ashley Richter. **Director of Finance:** Greg Hodges. **Executive Advisor:** Larry Lobue. **Director, Ticket Sales:** Jennifer Schwarz. **Box Office Manager:** Kaitlin Nieberding. **Head Groundskeeper:** Brad Detmore. **Assistant Groundskeeper:** Austin Baudler.
Vice President, Events: Matt Thompson. **Special Events Manager:** Eddy Juarez. **Event Operations Manager:** Russell Wohldmann. **Stadium and Event Operations:** Douglas Failing, Andrew Wagar. **Senior Business Development Manager:** Sunny Okpon. **Business Development Managers:** Dolores Townley, Cassie Turzillo, Kimberly Munroy. **Vice President, Sponsorship Sales:** Chris Parsons.
Director of Special Projects: Teneisha Richardson. **Marketing/Digital Media Coordinator:** Megan Murnane. **Marketing Coordinator:** Erin Keir. **Media Relations Director/Broadcaster:** Ryan Posner. **Community Relations Manager:** Sallie Weir.
Video Production Coordinator: Troy Young. **Graphics Coordinator:** Shay Villarreal. **Mascot Coordinator:** Megan Brown. **Legends General Manager:** Greg Hernandez. **Legends Events Manager:** Jay Lero. **Legends Accountant:** Andrea Jennings. **Legends Operations Manager:** Ginavieve Strickland. **Executive Chef:** Eric Robison.
Field Manager: Pete Incaviglia. **Team Doctor:** V. Joseph Mandola, M.D. **Athletic Trainer:** Max Mahaffey.

GAME INFORMATION
Radio Announcer: Ryan Posner. **No. of Games Broadcast:** 70. **Flagship Streaming Station:** YouTube. **Standard Game Times:** Mon.-Fri., 7:05 pm, Sat., 6:05 pm, Sun., 2:05 pm. **Visiting Club Hotel:** Sugar Land Marriott Town Square. **Telephone:** (281) 275-8400.

YORK REVOLUTION

Office Address: 5 Brooks Robinson Way, York, PA 17401.
Telephone: (717) 801-4487. **Fax:** (717) 801-4499.
Email Address: info@yorkrevolution.com. **Website:** yorkrevolution.com.
Operated by: York Professional Baseball Club, LLC. **Principal Owners:** York Professional Baseball Club, LLC.
President: Eric Menzer. **General Manager/Vice President, Operations:** John Gibson. **VP, Business Development:** Nate Tile. **Finance Coordinator:** Jen Martin. **Finance Assistant:** Mike Allen. **Director, Ticketing:** Cindy Brown. **Director, Marketing/Communications:** Doug Eppler. **Creative Director:** Cody Bannon. **Marketing Manager:** Sarah Dailey. **Senior Account Executive:** Brandon Tesluk. **Account Executives:** Allyson Stough, Morgan Day, Devin Kolodziej, Rachel Mohre, Heather Ramp. **Director, Client Services:** Tylor Toll. **Director, Operations:** David Dicce. **Director, Special Events:** Adam Nugent. **Revolution Hospitality GM:** Rob Wilson. **Revolution Hospitality Catering Manager:** Kate Hammond. **Revolution Hospitality Chef:** Tiffany Livering. **Revolution Hospitality Concessions Manager:** Amanda Shusko. **Revolution Retail Manager:** Kelsey Dorner.
Field Manager: Mark Mason. **Bench/Third Base Coach:** Enohel Polanco.

GAME INFORMATION
WOYK GM/Broadcaster: Darrell Henry. **No. of Games Broadcast:** 140. **Flagship Station:** WOYK 1350 AM. **Official Scorer:** Brian Wisler. **Stadium Name:** PeoplesBank Park. **Standard Game Times:** Mon.-Sat., 6:30 pm, Sun., 2:00 pm. **Visiting Club Hotel:** Wyndham Garden York, 2000 Loucks Road, York, PA 17408. **Telephone:** (717) 846-9500..

FRONTIER LEAGUE

Office Address: 2041 Goose Lake Rd Suite 2A, Sauget, IL 62206.
Telephone: (618) 215-4134. **Fax:** (618) 332-2115.
Email Address: office@frontierleague.com. **Website:** www.frontierleague.com.
Year Founded: 1993.
Commissioner: Bill Lee.
Deputy Commissioners: Kevin Winn, Steve Tahsler.
President: Rich Sauget (Gateway). **Vice President, Operations:** Brian Lyter (Schaumburg). **Vice President, Marketing:** John Stanley (Evansville)
Board of Directors: David DelBello (Florence), Nick Semaca (Joliet), Tom Kramig (Lake Erie), Greg Lockhard (New Jersey), Shawn Reilly (Rockland), Michel Laplante (Quebec), Mike Pinto (Southern Illinois), Al Dorso (Sussex County), Rene Martin (Trois-Rivieres), Stu Williams (Washington), Al Oremus (Windy City).
Division Structure: Can-Am —Lake Erie, New Jersey, New York, Quebec, Sussex County, Trois-Rivieres, Washington. Windy City. **Midwestern** —Evansville, Florence, Gateway, Joliet, Schaumburg, Southern Illinois, Windy City.
Regular Season: 96 games. **2019 Opening Date:** May 14. **Closing Date:** Sept 6.
All-Star Game: Wednesday, July 15 at Washington.
Playoff Format: 2nd and 3rd place teams in play-in game. Winner vs. Division Winner in best-of-3. Best 3-of-5 Championship Series.
Roster Limit: 24. **Eligibility Rule:** Minimum of ten Rookie 1/Rookie 2 players. Maximum of four players born before October 1, 1991. **Brand of Baseball:** Rawlings.
Statistician: Pointstreak/Stack Sports, 5360 Legacy Drive, Suite #150, Plano, TX 75024.

STADIUM INFORMATION

Club	Stadium	Opened	Dimensions LF	CF	RF	Capacity	2018 Att.
Evansville	Bosse Field	1915	315	415	315	5,110	100,051
Florence	UC Health Stadium	2004	325	395	325	4,200	99,308
Gateway	GCS Ballpark	2002	318	395	325	5,500	112,252
Joliet	DuPage Medical Group Field	2002	330	400	327	6,229	121,730
Lake Erie	Sprenger Stadium	2009	325	400	325	5,000	100,915
New Jersey	Yogi Berra Stadium	1998	308	398	308	3,784	76,658
New York	Provident Bank Park	2011	323	403	313	4,750	123,999
Quebec	Stade Canac de Québec	1938	315	385	315	4,500	119,060
Schaumburg	Schaumburg Stadium	1999	355	400	353	8,107	156,383
So. Illinois	Rent One Park	2007	325	400	330	4,500	101,441
Sussex County	Skylands Stadium	1994	330	392	330	4,200	72,594
Trois-Rivieres	Stade Quillorama	1938	342	372	342	4,500	85,506
Washington	Wild Things Park	2002	325	400	325	3,200	90,638
Windy City	Ozinga Field	1999	335	390	335	2,598	79,171

EVANSVILLE OTTERS

Mailing Address: 23 Don Mattingly Way, Evansville, IN 47711.
Telephone: (812) 435-8686. **Website:** www.evansvilleotters.com.
Facebook—Evansville Otters, **Twitter**—@EvilleOtters, **Instagram**—@evansvilleotters
Operated by: Evansville Baseball, LLC. **Owner:** Bussing family. **President:** John Stanley.
Vice President, Sales: Joel Padfield. **Assistant General Manager:** Elspeth Urbina. **Director of Communications:** Preston Leinenbach. **PA Announcer:** Zane Clodfelter. **Gift Shop Manager:** Rhonda Trail. **Account Executive:** Keith Millikan. **Account Executive/Social Media Coordinator:** Maci Hill. **Groundskeeper:** Lance Adler.
Field Manager: Andy McCauley.

GAME INFORMATION

No. of Games Broadcast: Home-48, Away-48. **Radio/Video Stream:** evansvilleotters.com (Otters Digital Network).
Stadium Name: Bosse Field (Opened in 1915). **Directions:** US 41 to Lloyd Expressway West (IN-62), Main St Exit, Right on Main St, ahead 1 mile to Bosse Field. **Standard Game Times:** Mon.-Sat., 6:35 pm, Sun., **12:35, 5**:05. **Doubleheaders:** 5:35 p.m. **Visiting Club Hotel:** The Comfort Inn & Suites, 3901 Highway 41 North, Evansville, IN 47711. Phone 812-423-5818.

FLORENCE Y'ALLS

Office Address: 7950 Freedom Way, Florence, KY, 41042.
Telephone: (859) 594-4487. **Fax:** (859) 594-3194.
Email Address: info@florenceyalls.com.
Operated by: Freedom Baseball Club, LLC.
President/CEO: David DelBello
VP/General Manager: Josh Anderson. **Director of Merchandising & Premium Fan Experience:** Amanda Sipple.
Director of Business Development: Knicko Hartung. **Director of Fan Communications:** Hannah Siefert. **Ticket Sales & Operations Executive:** Aaron Luken. **Director of Business Operations:** Max Johnson. **Group Sales Executive:** Eric Quallen.
Field Manager: Brian White

GAME INFORMATION
Stadium: UC Health Stadium. **Location:** I-71/75 South to exit 180, left onto US 42, right on Freedom Way; I-71/75 North to exit 180. **Standard Game Times:** Mon.-Thurs., 6:35 pm, Fri., 7:05 pm, Sat., 6:35, Sun., 3:05 pm. **Visiting Club Hotel:** Microtel Inn & Suites, Florence, KY

GATEWAY GRIZZLIES

Telephone: (618) 337-3000. **Fax:** (618) 332-3625.
Email Address: info@gatewaygrizzlies.com. **Website:** www.gatewaygrizzlies.com.
Owner: Rich Sauget.
General Manager: Steve Gomric. **Assistant General Manager:** Kurt Ringkamp. **Assistant General Manager:** James Caldwell. **Marketing Director:** Collin Vieth.
Director of Group Sales and Business Development: Brady Huber. **Operations & Events Assistant:** Brenndon Tindall. **Box Office and Business Manager:** Justin Dettmann.
Director of Promotions and Fan Engagement: Jennifer Wunder. **Assistant Box Office Manager:** Houston Kruse.
Manager: Phil Warren. **Pitching Coach:** Steve Brook. **Hitting Coach:** Darin Kinsolving. **Director of Player Personnel:** Bobby Brown. **Bench Coach:** Scott Brown.

GAME INFORMATION
No. of Games Broadcast: Home-50, Away-48. **PA Announcer:** Tom Calhoun. **Stadium Name:** GCS Ballpark.
Location: I-255 at exit 15 (Mousette Lane). **Standard Game Times:** Mon.-Sat., 7:05 pm, Sun., 6:05 pm.

JOLIET SLAMMERS

Office Address: 1 Mayor Art Schultz Dr, Joliet, IL 60432
Telephone: (815) 722-2287
E-Mail Address: info@jolietslammers.com. **Website:** www.jolietslammers.com.
Owner: Joliet Community Baseball & Entertainment, LLC.
General Manager: Heather Mills. **Vice President, Sales & Marketing:** John Wilson. **Director of Food & Beverage:** Tom Fremarek.
Director of Tournaments and Special Events: Cori Herbert. **Director of Community Relations:** Ken Miller.
Marketing Manager: Rachel Buonafede. **Group Sales Manager:** Lauren Rhodes.
Corporate Sales and Service Manager: Christine Bialobok.
Box Office Manager: Chris Habecker. **Operations Manager:** Chase Steininger. **Team Photographer:** Adam Jomant.
Field Manager/Director, Baseball Operations: Jeff Isom. **Coach:** Jerry McDowell.

GAME INFORMATION
No. of Games Broadcast: 96. **Flagship Station:** www.jolietslammers.com. **Stadium Name:** Joliet Route 66 Stadium.
Location: 1 Mayor Art Schultz Drive, Joliet, IL 60432. **Standard Game Times:** Mon.-Fri., 7:05 pm, Sat., 6:05 pm., Sun., 1:05 pm.

LAKE ERIE CRUSHERS

Address: 2009 Baseball Boulevard. Avon, Ohio 44011.
Telephone: 440-934-3636. **Website:** www.lakeeriecrushers.com.
Operated by: Blue Dog Baseball, LLC. **Managing Officer:** Tom Kramig.
VP Operations: Paul Siegwarth. **Accountant:** DJ Saylor. **Director, Concessions/**
Catering: Greg Kobunski. **Digital Marketing Manager:** Eric Davies.
Director of Promotions: Allison Albers. **Director of Ticketing:** Taylor Adrian.
Account Executives: Ryan Acus, Chris Smith, Kyle Wagoner, Jack Goold. **Director, Broadcasting:** Andy Barch.
Field Manager: Dan Rohn.

GAME INFORMATION:
Stadium Name: Sprenger Health Care Stadium. **Location:** Intersection of I-90 and Colorado Ave in Avon, OH.
Standard Game Times: Mon.-**Friday, 7:05 pm, Saturday 6:**05 pm, Sun., 2:05 pm.

NEW JERSEY JACKALS

Office Address: 8 Yogi Berra Drive, Little Falls, NJ 07424. **Telephone:** (973) 746-7434.
Email Address: contact@jackals.com. **Website:** www.jackals.com.
Owner/President: Al Dorso. **President, Baseball Operations:** Gregory Lockard.
Sr. Vice President, Operations: Al Dorso Jr. **Vice President, Marketing:** Mike Dorso. **General Manager:** Gil Addeo.
Coordinator, Group Sales: Nicole Cartaino. **Director, Creative Services:** William Romano. **Public Relations:** Steven Solomon.
Field Manager: Brooks Carey.

GAME INFORMATION
No. of Games Broadcast: 100. **Webcast Address:** www.jackals.com. **Stadium Name:** Yogi Berra Stadium. **Location:** On the campus of Montclair State University; Route 80 or Garden State Parkway to Route 46, take Valley Road exit to Montclair State University. **Standard Game Times:** Mon.-Fri., 7:05 pm, Sat., 6:05 pm., Sun., 2:05 pm.

QUEBEC CAPITALES

Owners: Jean Tremblay, Pierre Tremblay, Marie-Pierre Simard
President: Michel Laplante. **General Manager:** Charles Demers. **Vice-President:** Bobby Baril.
Director of baseball operations and media relations: Jean Grignon-Francke. **Accounting:**
Koralie Tanguay. **Ticketing coordinator:** Philippe Turmel.
Promotions and community coordinator: Janel Laplante. **Administrative assistant:** Francine Gendron. **Victoria Baseball Complex:** Alexandre Harvey. **Graphic consultant:** Frédéric Gariépy. **Social media and marketing coordinator:** Andréanne Gagnon. **Gift shop manager:** Jean-Philippe Otis.
Party Deck coordinator: Frédérick Plamondon. **Marketing assistant:** Marie-Pier Gosselin. **Marketing consultant:** Annie-Pier Couture.
Field manager: Patrick Scalabrini.

GAME INFORMATION
Stadium Name: Stade Canac de Québec. **Location:** Highway 40 to Highway 173 (Centre-Ville) exit 2 to Parc Victoria.
Standard Game Times: Mon.-Fri., 7:05 pm, Sat., 6:05 pm, Sun., 1:05 pm.

NEW YORK BOULDERS

Office Address: 1 Palisades Credit Union Park Drive, Pomona, NY 10970.
Telephone: (845) 364-0009. **Fax:** (845) 364-0001.
E-Mail Address: info@nyboulders.com. **Website:** nyboulders.com.
Team President/Managing Partner: Shawn Reilly. **Assistant GM/Box Office Digital Media Manager:** Megan Ciampo. **Director of Business Development:** Seth Cantor. **Director of Finance:** Michele Almash.
Media Coordinator/PA Announcer: Steve Balsan. **Ticket Sales Manager:** Karen McCombs. **Assistant Ticket Sales Manager:** Courtney Vardi. **Account Executive:** Michael O'Brien.
Promotions and Entertainment Coordinator: Julie Trainor. **Media Liaison/Play-By-Play:** Marc Ernay. **Facilities and Operations Coordinator:** Bobby Nodelman. **Educational Director:** Gail Gultz.
Community Relations Manager: Vanessa Mauriello. **Audio/Visual Specialist:** Jim Houston. **Director of Security and Parking:** Jeff Rinaldi. **Retail Store Manager:** Deidra Verona. **Ambassador:** John Thompson.
Manager: Kevin Baez. **Pitching Coach:** Zach Jemiola. **Athletic Trainer:** Louise Inch. **Player Development:** Kevin Tuve.

GAME INFORMATION

Broadcaster: Marc Ernay. **Stadium Name:** Palisades Credit Union Park. **Location:** Take Palisades Parkway Exit 12 towards Route 45, make left at stop sign on Conklin Road, make left on Route 45, turn right on Pomona Road, take 1st right on Fireman's Memorial Drive. **Standard Game Times:** Mon-Fri., **Varies between 10:**30 am, 11 am and 7 pm. **Sat:** 6:30 p.m. **Sun:** 1:30 p.m..

SCHAUMBURG BOOMERS

Office Address: 1999 Springinsguth Road, Schaumburg, IL 60193
Email Address: info@boomersbaseball.com. **Website:** www.boomersbaseball.com.
Owned by: Pat and Lindy Salvi.
General Manager: Michael Larson. **Assistant GM:** Anthony Giammanco. **Director of Facilities:** Mike Tlusty. **Director Food/Beverage:** Devin Maney. **Broadcaster:** Tim Calderwood.
Box Office Manager: Alec Marovitz. **Director of Promotions:** Lexi Fiolka. **Director of Community Relations:** Peter Long.
Director of Stadium Operations: Collin Cunningham. **Account Executive:** Hanna Olson. **Corporate Sales Executive:** Pete Thompson.
Field Manager: Jamie Bennett.

GAME INFORMATION

Broadcaster: Tim Calderwood. **No. of Games Broadcast:** Home-48, Away-48. **Flagship Station:** WRMN 1410 AM Elgin. **Stadium:** Schaumburg Boomers Stadium. **Location:** I-290 to Thorndale Ave Exit, head West on Elgin-O'Hare Expressway until Springinsguth Road Exit, second left at Springinsguth Road (shared parking lot with Schaumburg Metra Station). **Visiting Club Hotel:** Indian Lakes Resort, 250 W Schick Rd, Bloomingdale, IL 60108.

SOUTHERN ILLINOIS MINERS

Office Address: Rent One Park, 1000 Miners Drive, Marion, IL 62959.
Telephone: (618) 998-8499. **Fax:** (618) 969-8550.
Email Address: info@southernillinoisminers.com. **Website:** southernillinoisminers.com.
Operated by: Southern Illinois Baseball Group. **Owner:** Jayne Simmons.
Chief Operating Officer: Mike Pinto. **General Manager:** Cathy Perry. **Assistant General Manager:** Will Niermann. **Stadium Operations:** Joe Klinger.
Director, Ticket Operations: Pat McCarthy. **Director, Video Production/Creative Services:** Jon Weaver. **Director, Promotions:** Jake Varney.
Director, Radio Broadcasting/Media Relations: Jason Guerette. **Account Executives:** James Felton, Cole Landon, Nate Vicini.
Field Manager: Mike Pinto. **Hitting Coach:** Steve Marino. **Instructor:** Ralph Santana. **Strength & Conditioning Coordinator:** Chris Stone.

GAME INFORMATION

Games Broadcast: www.103.5espn.com. **Stadium Name:** Rent One Park. **Location:** US 57 to Route 13 East, right at Halfway Road to Fairmont Drive. **Standard Game Times:** Mon-Fri., 7:05 pm, Sat., 6:05 pm, Sun., 5:05 pm. **Visiting Club Hotel:** Best Western, 400 Comfort Drive, Marion, IL 62959 618-998-1220.

SUSSEX COUNTY MINERS

Owner, President: Al Dorso Sr.
President, Baseball Operations: Greg Lockard. **Vice President, Operations:** Al Dorso Jr. **Vice President, Marketing:** Mike Dorso. **General Manager:** Justin Ferrarella. **Director, Broadcasting and Media Relations:** Bret Leuthner.
Manager, Corporate Sales: Joann Ciancitto. **Youth Programs Coordinator:** Adrienne Lina. **Senior Graphic Design:** Will Romano. **Media Relations Manager:** Steven Solomon. **Broadcasting & Media Relations:** Sean Bretherick.
Social Media Coordinator: Carolyn Clites. **Manager, Facilities:** Shane White. **Group Sales Coordinator:** Alex Kashman.
Field Manager/Director of Baseball Operations: Bobby Jones.

GAME INFORMATION

Broadcaster: Bret Leuthner. **No. of Games Broadcast:** 100. **Webcast Address:** www.scminers.com. **Stadium Name:** Skylands Stadium. **Location:** In New Jersey, I-80 to exit 34B (Route 15 North) to Route 565 North; From Pennsylvania, I-84 to Route 6 (Matamoras) to Route 206 North to Route 565 North. **Standard Game Times:** Mon.-Fri., 7:05 pm, Sat., 6:05 pm, Sun., 2:05 pm (May-June, Sept.), 4:05 pm (July-August).

TROIS-RIVIÈRES AIGLES

Office Address: 1760 Avenue Gilles-Villeneuve, Trois-Rivières, QC G9A 5K8.
Telephone: (819) 379-0404. **Email Address:** info@lesaiglestr.com.
Website: www.lesaiglestr.com
Owners: Côté-Reco Group and Vertdure Group
President: Paul Poisson. **General Manager:** René Martin.
Director, Marketing: Zoé Newbury. **Administrative Director:** Frédérik Bélanger.
Advisor, Partnerships And Events: Marie-Hélène Lavoie. **Ticketing Coordinator:** Sylvie Dubé.
Field Manager: T.J. Stanton. **Coaches:** Kole Zimmeman.

GAME INFORMATION
No. of Games Broadcast: 65. **Webcast Address:** www.cfou.ca/direct.php.
Stadium Name: Stade de Trois-Rivières. **Location:** Take Hwy 40 West, exit Boul. des Forges/Centre-ville, keep right, turn right at light, turn right at stop sign.

WASHINGTON WILD THINGS

Office Address: One Washington Federal Way, Washington, PA 15301.
Telephone: (724) 250-9555. **Fax:** (724) 250-2333.
Email Address: info@washingtonwildthings.com. **Website:** washingtonwildthings.com.
Owned by: Sports Facility, LLC. **Operated by:** Washington Frontier League Baseball, LLC.
Managing Partner: Francine W. Williams. **Executive Director:** Steve Zavacky.
President/General Manager: Tony Buccilli. **Director of Marketing/Communications/Corporate Relations:** Christine Blaine. **Director of Ticket Sales:** Edwin Valentin. **Corporate Account Executive:** Debra Lavelle. **Community Sales Manager:** Hanna Luckenbach. **Ticket Manager:** Austin Snodgrass. **Ticket Account Executive:** Austin Weekly and Wally Luckachesky. **Vice President, Finance:** JJ Heider. **Creative Services:** Craig Lion.
Field Manager: Gregg Langbehn.

GAME INFORMATION
Stadium Name: Wild Things Park. **Location:** I-70 to exit 15 (Chestnut Street), right on Chestnut Street to Washington Crown Center Mall, right at mall entrance, right on to Mall Drive to stadium. **Standard Game Times:** Mon.-Sat., 7:05 pm, Sun., 5:35 pm. **Visiting Club Hotel:** Red Roof Inn.

WINDY CITY THUNDERBOLTS

Office Address: 14011 South Kenton Avenue, Crestwood, IL 60418
Telephone: (708) 489-2255. **Fax:** (708) 489-2999.
Email Address: info@wcthunderbolts.com. **Website:** www.wcthunderbolts.com.
Owned by: Crestwood Professional Baseball, LLC.
General Manager: Mike VerSchave. **Assistant GM:** Bill Waliewski. **Director, Community Relations:** Johnny Sole. **Director, Group Sales:** Kenny Thorne. Director, **Not-For-Profit Events:** Karen Engel.
Field Manager: Brian Smith.

GAME INFORMATION
Radio Announcer: Terry Bonadonna. **No. of Games Broadcast:** 96. **Flagship Station:** WXAV, 88.3 FM. **Official Scorer:** Chris Gbur. **Stadium Name:** Ozinga Field. **Location:** I-294 to South Cicero Ave, exit (Route 50), south for 1 1/2 miles, left at Midlothian Turnpike, right on Kenton Ave; I-57 to 147th Street, west on 147th to Cicero, north on Cicero, right on Midlothian Turnpike, right on Kenton. **Standard Game Times:** Mon.-Fri., 7:05 pm, Sat., 6:05 pm, Sun., 2:05 pm. **Visiting Club Hotel:** Georgio's Quality Inn & Suites, 8800 W 159th St, Orland Park, IL 60462. **Telephone:** (708) 403-1100.

ADDITIONAL LEAGUES

EMPIRE LEAGUE BASEBALL

Address: PO Box 89173, Tampa, FL 33689.

Email: baseball@empireproleague.com.

Owner/President/CEO: Eddie Gonzalez. **Owner/VP/Director of Player Personnel:** Jerry Gonzalez. **Owner:** Matt Joyce. **Owner:** Livio Forte.

Legal Consultant: Jason Sampson. **Scouting Executive:** Angel Flores. **International Scouting Executive:** Ken Matsuzaka. **Scouting and Pitching Rover:** Joe Gannon.

Year Founded: 2015.

Teams: Georgia Rhinos, New Hampshire Wild, Plattsburgh Thunderbirds, Puerto Rico Islanders, Sarnack Lake Surge, Tupper Lake Riverpigs.

Regular Season: 50 games. **Playoffs:** Top four advance. Single-game semifinal. Three-game championship series.

PECOS LEAGUE

Website: www.PecosLeague.com.

Address: PO Box 271489, Houston, TX 77277.

Telephone: (575) 680-2212.

E-mail: info@pecosleague.com.

Commissioner: Andrew Dunn.

Pacific All Star Game Monterey July 5

Mountain All Star Game (site TBA) July 12

Mountain Division—Alpine Cowboys, Alpine, Texas; Garden City Wind, Garden City, Kan.; Santa Fe Fuego, Santa Fe, N.M.; Trinidad Triggers, Trinidad, Colo.; Roswell Invaders, Roswell, N.M.; Tucson Saguaros, Tucson, Ariz.

Pacific Division—Bakersfield Train Robbers, Bakersfield, Calif.; Monterey Amberjacks, Monterey, Calif.; Wasco Reserves, Wasco Calif.; Martinez Sturgeon, Martinez, Calif.; Pittsburg Anchors, Pittsburg, Calif.; Santa Cruz Seaweed, Santa Cruz, Calif.

Year Founded: 2010.

Regular Season: 64 games. **Start Date:** May 30.

Playoff Format: First round—Best-of-three. **Second round**—Best-of-three. **Finals**—Best-of-three.

Roster Limit: 22 (no designated hitter).

Eligibility Rules: 25 and under.

Brand of Baseball: Rawlings-National League.

UNITED SHORE PROFESSIONAL BASEBALL LEAGUE

Location: Jimmy Johns Field. 7171 Auburn Rd, Utica, MI. 48317

Telephone: (248) 601-2400

Email: baseballoperations@uspbl.com. **Website:**www.uspbl.com

Ownership Group: General Sports & Entertainment. **CEO:** Andrew D. Appelby. **COO:** Dana L. Schmitt.

Director of Premium Sales and Services: Jonathon Hebel. **VP of Groups Sales & Events:** Theresa Doan. **VP of Client Services:** Jeremiah Hergott. **Director of Ballpark Operations:** Dillon Dubois. **Senior Director of Marketing & PR:** Katie Page. **Director of Food & Beverage:** Nathan Liska.

Director of Baseball Operations: Justin Orenduff. **Director of Baseball Administration:** Mike Zielinski. **Fielding Coordinator:** Paul Niggebrugge.

Pitching Coordinator: Shane McCatty. **Assistant Pitching Coordinator:** Alan Oaks.

Teams: Birmingham-Bloomfield Beavers, Eastside Diamond Hoppers, Utica Unicorns, Westside Woolly Mammoths.

Roster Limit: 20. **Eligibility Rules:** Players must be between 18 and 26-years-old.

2020 Start Date: May 8th. **Season length:** 50 games per team. **Playoff Format:** Single-game elimination.

AMERICAS

MEXICO
MEXICAN LEAGUE

MEMBER, NATIONAL ASSOCIATION
NOTE: The Mexican League is a member of the National Association of Professional Baseball Leagues and has a Triple-A classification. However, its member clubs operate largely independent of the 30 major league teams, and for that reason the league is listed in the international section.

Address: Adolfo López Mateos #172 Piso 3. Col. Merced Gómez. C.P. 03930, Benito Juárez, Ciudad de México. **Telephone:** 52-55-8310-5200. **Fax:** 52-55-5395-2454. **E-Mail Address:** oficina@lmb.com.mx. **Website:** lmb.com.mx.

Years League Active: 1955-.

President: Horacio De la Vega Flores. **Director, Administration:** Oscar Neri Rojas Salazar.

Division Structure: North—Durango, Laguna, Monclova, Monterrey, Saltillo, Tijuana. **South**—Campeche, Leon, Mexico City, Oaxaca, Puebla, Quintana Roo, Tabasco, Yucatan.

Regular Season: 114 games (split-schedule). **2020 Opening Date:** April 6. **Closing Date:** Aug. 6.

All-Star Game: June 12-14. **Playoff Format:** Five teams from each division qualify for a four-round playoff. Championship round is best-of-seven series.

Roster Limit: 28. **Roster Limit, Imports:** 7.

CAMPECHE PIRATAS
Office Address: Calle Filiberto Qui Farfan No. 2, Col. Camino Real, CP 24020, Campeche, Campeche. **Telephone:** (52) 981-827-4759. **Fax:** (52) 981-827-4767. **E-Mail Address:** piratas@prodigy.net.mx. **Website:** piratasdecampeche.mx.

President: Gabriel Escalante Castillo. **General Manager:** Gabriel Lozano Berron.

Manager: Jesus Sommers.

DURANGO GENERALES
Office Address: De Los Deportes, Unidad Deportiva, 98065_00 Zacatecas, ZAC. **Telephone:**(52) 667-788-9900. **E-Mail Address:** info@generales.mx. **Website:** generales.mx.

President: Virgilio Ruiz Isassi.

Manager: Juan Pacho.

LAGUNDA ALGODONEROS
Office Address: Algodoneros Unión Laguna Juan Gutemberg s/n C.P. 27000 Torreón, Coah. Estadio Revolución. **Telephone:** (52) 871-718-5515. **E-Mail Address:** info@unionlaguna.mx. **Website:** unionlaguna.mx.

President: Francisco Orozco Marín. **General Manager:** Jorge Luis Lechuga Torres.

Manager: Jonathan Martinez.

LEON BRAVES
Office Address: Estadio Domingo Santana Boulevard Congreso de Chilpancingo 803, Unidad Deportiva. León Guanajuato, México. CP 37237. **Telephone:** (52) 477-272-8675. **E-Mail Address:** contacto@bravosdeleon.mx. **Website:** bravosdeleon.com.

President: Arturo Blanco Díaz. **General Manager:** Daniel Espino.

Manager: Tim Johnson.

MEXICO CITY DIABLOS ROJOS
Office Address: Av río Churubusco #1001, Colonia ex-ejidos de la Magdalena Mixhuca, Alcaldía Iztacalco, C.P. 08010 CDMX. **Telephone:** (56) 91-28-72-92. **E-Mail Address:** contacto@diablos-rojos.com. **Website:** diablos.com.mx.

President: Alfredo Harp Helu. **General Manager:** Diego Patricio Perez Ochoa.

Manager: Victor Bojorquez.

MONCLOVA ACEREROS
Office Address: Cuauhtemoc #299, Col Ciudad Deportiva, CP 25750, Monclova, Coahuila. **Telephone:** (52) 866-636-2650. **Fax:** (52) 866-636-2688. **E-Mail Address:** contacto@acereros.com.mx. **Website:** acereros.com.mx.

President: Gerardo Benavides Pape. **General Manager:** Miguel Valentin Gamez Mendoza.

Manager: Pat Listach.

MONTERREY SULTANES
Office Address: Estadio de Béisbol Monterrey, en Av. Manuel L. Barragán S/N, Col. Regina, CP. 64290 Monterrey, N.L. **Telephone:** (52) 81-2270-2000. **Fax:** (52) 81-8351-8022. **E-Mail Address:** sultanes@sultanes.com.mx. **Website:** sultanes.com.mx.

President: José Maiz Garcia. **General Manager:** Miguel Flores.

Manager: Roberto Kelly.

OAXACA GUERREROS
Office Address: Calz. Héroes de Chapultepec S.N. esq calle de los Derechos Humanos Col. Centro, Oaxaca de Juárez. **Telephone:** (52) 951-515-5522. **Fax:** (52) 951-515-4966. **E-Mail Address:** contacto@guerreros.mx. **Website:** guerreros.mx.

President: Lorenzo Peón Escalante. **General Manager:** Jaime Brena Núñez.

Manager: Erik Rodriguez.

PUEBLA PERICOS
E-Mail Address: contacto@pericosdepuebla.com. **Website:** pericosdepuebla.com.

President: Jose Miguel Bejos. **General Manager:** Mario Valenzuela.

Manager: Carlos Alberto Gastelum.

QUINTANA ROO TIGRES
Office Address: SM 21, 21, 77500 Cancún, Quintana Roo. **Telephone:** (52) 998-887-3108. **Fax:** (52) 998-887-1313. **E-Mail Address:** medios@tigresqroo.com. **Website:** tigresqroo.com.

President: Fernando Valenzuela Burgos. **General Manager:** Francisco Minjarez Garcia.

Manager: Adam Munoz.

SALTILLO SARAPEROS
Office Address: Blvd. Jesús Valdéz Sánchez y Nazario Ortíz, Cd. Deportiva, Saltillo, Mexico 25280. **Telephone:** (52) 844-416-9455. **Fax:** (52) 844-439-1330. **Website:** saraperos.com.mx.

President: Alvaro Ley Lopez. **General Manager:** Eduardo Valenzuela Guajardo.

Manager: Roberto Vizcarra.

TABASCO OLMECAS
Office Address: Avenida Velodromo de la Ciudad Deportiva S/N, Atasta, 86100 Villahermosa, Tabasco. **Telephone:** (52) 993-352-2787. **Fax:** (52) 993-352-2788. **E-Mail Address:** hola@olmecastasco.mx. **Website:** olmecastabasco.mx.

President: Ángel Solis Carballo. **General Manager:** Felix Zulueta García.

Manager: Pedro Mere.

TIJUANA TOROS

Office Address: Mision de Santo Tomas Rio Eufrates con, Col. Infonavit Capistrano, 22223 Tijuana, B.C., Mexico. **Telephone:** (52) 664-635-5600. **E-Mail Address:** contacto@torosdetijuana.com. **Website:** torosdetijuana.com. **Presidente:** Alberto Ignacio Uribe Maytorena. **Manager:** Omar Vizquel.

YUCATAN LEONES

Office Address: Calle 6 N°315 x 35, Col. Morelos Oriente, Mérida, Yucatán. C.P. 97174. **Telephone:** (52) 999-432-0655. **Fax:** (52) 999-926-3631. **E-Mail Address:** contacto@leones.mx. **Website:** leones.mx.

President: Erick Ernesto Arellano Hernández. **General Manager:** Alejandro Orozco Garcia.

Manager: Roberto Vizcarra.

MEXICAN ACADEMY

Rookie Classification

Mailing Address: Ubicación: Av. El Fundador #100, Col. San Miguel, El Carmen N.L., C.P. 66550. **Telephone:** (81) 8158-7900. **Fax:** (52) 555-395-2454. **E-Mail Address:** pgarza@academia-lmb.com. **Website:** academia-lmb. com.

President: C.P. Plinio Escalante Bolio. **Director General:** Salvador Viera Higuera.

Regular Season: 50 games. **Opening Date:** Not available. **Closing Date:** Not available.

DOMINICAN REPUBLIC

DOMINICAN SUMMER LEAGUE

Member, National Association

Rookie Classification

Mailing Address: Calle Segunda No 64, Reparto Antilla, Santo Domingo, Dominican Republic. **Telephone:** (809) 532-3619. **Website:** dominicansummerleague.com. **E-Mail Address:** ligadeverano@codetel.net.do.

Years League Active: 1985-.

President: Orlando Diaz.

Member Clubs/Division Structure: North—Cubs 1, Dodgers Shoemaker, Indians, Indians/Brewers, Pirates 1, Rangers 1, Rays2, Red Sox 2. **South**—Angels, Cardinals Blue, Mets 1, Nationals, Orioles 2, Phillies Red, Rockies, Twins, Yankees. **Northwest**—Astros, Athletics, Braves, Dodgers Bautista, Marlins, Rays 1, Red Sox 1, Royals 1. **Baseball City**—Blue Jays, D-backs 1, Orioles 1, Padres, Reds, White Sox. **San Pedro de Macoris**—Brewers, Cardinals Red, Cubs 2, D-backs 2, Mets 2, Phillies White, Rangers 2, Tigers 1. **Northeast**—Colorado, Giants, Mariners, Pirates 2, Royals 2, Tigers 2.

Regular Season: 72 games. **Opening Date:** Unavailable. **Closing Date:** Unavailable.

Playoff Format: Six teams qualify for playoffs, including four division winners and two wild-card teams. Teams with two best records receive a bye to the semifinals; four other playoff teams play best-of-three series. Winners advance to best-of-three semifinals. Winners advance to best-of-five championship series.

Roster Limit: 35 active. **Player Eligibility Rule:** No player may have four or more years of prior minor league service. No draft-eligible player from the U.S. or Canada (not including players from Puerto Rico) may participate in the DSL. No age limits apply.

JAPAN

Mailing Address: Mita Bellju Building, 11th Floor, 5-36-7 Shiba, Minato-ku, Tokyo 108-0014. **Telephone:** 03-6400-1189. **Fax:** 03-6400-1190.

Website: npb.or.jp, npb.or.jp/eng

Commissioner: Atsushi Saito.

Executive Secretary: Atsushi Ihara. **Executive Director, Baseball Operations:** Minoru Hata. **Executive Director, NPB Rules & Labor:** Nobuhisa "Nobby" Ito.

Executive Director, Central League Operations: Kazuhide Kinefuchi. **Executive Director, Pacific League Operations:** Kazuo Nakano.

Nippon Series: Best-of-seven series between Central and Pacific League champions, begins Oct 27.

All-Star Series: July 13 at Kyocera Dome; July 14 at Fujisaki Prefectural Baseball Stadium.

Roster Limit: 70 per organization (one major league club, one minor league club). Major league club is permitted to register 28 players at a time, though just 25 may be available for each game.

Roster Limit, Imports: Four in majors (no more than three position players or pitchers); unlimited in minors.

CENTRAL LEAGUE

Regular Season: 143 games.

2020 Opening Date: March 31. **Closing Date:** Oct. 1.

Playoff Format: Second-place team meets third-place team in best-of-three series. Winner meets first-place team in best-of-seven series to determine representative in Japan Series (first-place team has one-game advantage to begin series).

CHUNICHI DRAGONS

Mailing Address: Chunichi Bldg 6F, 4-1-1 Sakae, Naka-ku, Nagoya 460-0008. **Telephone:** 052-261-8811. **Chairman:** Bungo Shirai. **President:** Takao Sasaki. **Field Manager:** Shigekazu Mori.

HANSHIN TIGERS

Mailing Address: 2-33 Koshien-cho, Nishinomiya-shi, Hyogo-ken 663-8152. **Telephone:** 0798-46-1515. **Chairman:** Shinya Sakai. **President:** Keiichiro Yotsufuji. **Field Manager:** Tomoaki Kanemoto.

HIROSHIMA TOYO CARP

Mailing Address: 2-3-1 Minami Kaniya, Minami-ku, Hiroshima 732-8501. **Telephone:** 082-554-1000. **President:** Hajime Matsuda. **General Manager:** Kiyoaki Suzuki. **Field Manager:** Koichi Ogata.

TOKYO YAKULT SWALLOWS

Mailing Address: Seizan Bldg, 4F, 2-12-28 Kita Aoyama, Minato-ku, Tokyo 107-0061. **Telephone:** 03-3405-8960.

Chairman: Sumiya Hori. **President:** Tsuyoshi

INTERNATIONAL LEAGUES

Klnugasa. **Senior Director:** Junji Ogawa. **Field Manager:** Mitsuru Manaka.

YOKOHAMA DENA BAYSTARS
Mailing Address: Kannai Arai Bldg, 7F, 1-8 Onoe-cho, Naka-ku, Yokohama 231-0015. **Telephone:** 045-681-0811.
Chairman: Makoto Haruta. **President:** Shingo Okamura. **General Manager:** Shigeru Takada. **Field Manager:** Alex Ramirez.

YOMIURI GIANTS
Mailing Address: Yomiuri Shimbun Bldg, 26F, 1-7-1 Otemachi, Chiyoda-ku, Tokyo 100-8151. **Telephone:** 03-3246-7733. **Fax:** 03-3246-2726.
Chairman: Kojiro Shiraishi. **President:** Hiroshi Kubo. **General Manager:** Tatsuyoshi Tsutsumi. **Field Manager:** Yoshinobu Takahashi.

PACIFIC LEAGUE
Regular Season: 143 games.
2020 Opening Date: March 31. **Closing Date:** Oct. 5.
Playoff Format: Second-place team meets third-place team in best-of-three series. Winner meets first-place team in best-of-seven series to determine league's representative in Japan Series (first-place team has one-game advantage to begin series).

CHIBA LOTTE MARINES
Mailing Address: 1 Mihama, Mihama-ku, Chiba-shi, Chiba-ken 261-8587. **Telephone:** 03-5682-6341.
Chairman: Takeo Shigemitsu. **President:** Shinya Yamamuro. **Field Manager:** Tsutomu Ito.

FUKUOKA SOFTBANK HAWKS
Mailing Address: Fukuoka Yahuoku Japan Dome, Hawks Town, 2-2-2 Jigyohama, Chuo-ku, Fukuoka 810-0065. **Telephone:** 092-847-1006. **Owner:** Masayoshi Son.
Chairman: Sadaharu Oh. **President:** Yoshimitsu Goto. **Field Manager:** Kimiyasu Kudo.

HOKKAIDO NIPPON HAM FIGHTERS
Mailing Address: 1 Hitsujigaoka, Toyohira-ku, Sapporo 062-8655. **Telephone:** 011-857-3939.
Chairman: Juichi Suezawa. **President:** Kenso Takeda. **General Manager:** Hiroshi Yoshimura. **Field Manager:** Hideki Kuriyama.

ORIX BUFFALOES
Mailing Address: 3-Kita-2-30 Chiyozaki, Nishi-ku, Osaka 550-0023. **Telephone:** 06-6586-0221. **Fax:** 06-6586-0240.
Chairman: Yoshihiko Miyauchi. **President:** Hiroaki Nishina. **General Manager:** Hiroyuki Nagamura. **Field Manager:** Junichi Fukura.

SAITAMA SEIBU LIONS
Mailing Address: 2135 Kami-Yamaguchi, Tokorozawa-shi, Saitama-ken 359-1189. **Telephone:** 04-2924-1155. **Fax:** 04-2928-1919.
President: Hajime Igo. **Field Manager:** Hatsuhiko Tsuji.

TOHOKU RAKUTEN GOLDEN EAGLES
Mailing Address: 2-11-6 Miyagino, Miyagino-ku, Sendai-shi, Miyagi-ken 983-0045. **Telephone:** 022-298-5300. **Fax:** 022-298-5360.
Chairman: Hiroshi Mikitani. **President:** Yozo Tachibana. **Field Manager:** Masataka Nashida.

KOREA

KOREA BASEBALL ORGANIZATION
Mailing Address: 946-16 Dokokdong, Kangnam-gu, Seoul, Korea. **Telephone:** (02) 3460-4600. **Fax:** (02) 3460-4639.
Years League Active: 1982-.
Website: koreabaseball.com.
Commissioner: Koo Bon-Neung. **Secretary General:** Yang Hae-Young.
Member Clubs: Doosan Bears, Hanwha Eagles, Kia Tigers, KT Wiz, LG Twins, Lotte Giants, NC Dinos, Nexen Heroes, Samsung Lions, SK Wyverns.
Regular Season: 128 games. **2020 Opening Date:** March 28.
Playoffs: Third- and fourth-place teams meet in best-of-three series; winner advances to meet second-place team in best-of-five series; winner meets first-place team in best-of-seven Korean Series for league championship.
Roster Limit: 26 active through Sept 1, when rosters expand to 31. **Imports:** Two active.

TAIWAN

CHINESE PROFESSIONAL BASEBALL LEAGUE
Mailing Address: 2F, No 32, Pateh Road, Sec 3, Taipei, Taiwan 10559. **Telephone:** 886-2-2577-6992. **Fax:** 886-2-2577-2606. **Website:** cpbl.com.tw.
Years League Active: 1990-.
Commissioner: Jenn-Tai Hwang. **Deputy Secretary General:** Hueimin Wang. **E-Mail Address:** richard.wang@cpbl.com.tw.
Member Clubs: EDA Rhinos, Chinatrust Brothers, Lamigo Monkeys, Uni-President 7-Eleven Lions.
Regular Season: 120 games. Each team plays 60 games in the first and second halves of the season.
Player Limits: 25 active players. Three foreign players and no more than two foreign players on the field per team at any time.
2020 Opening Date: Not available. **Playoffs:** Half-season winners are eligible for the postseason. If a non-half-season winner team possesses a higher overall winning percentage than any other half-season winner, then this team gains a wild card and will play a best-of-five series against the half-season winner with the lower winner percentage. The winner of the playoff series advances to Taiwan Series (best-of-seven). If the same team clinches both first- and second-half seasons, then that team is awarded one win to start the Taiwan Series.

EUROPE

NETHERLANDS
DUTCH MAJOR LEAGUE

Mailing Address: Koninklijke Nederlandse Baseball en Softball Bond (Royal Dutch Baseball and Softball Association), Postbus 2650, 3430 GB Nieuwegein, Hollanxd.**Telephone:** 31-30-202-0100. **Website:** knbsb.nl

AMERSFOORT
Mailing Address: Postbus 780, 3800 AT Amersfoort. **Telephone:** +31 (0) 33-461-1914. **Website:** bscquick.nl

AMSTERDAM PIRATES
Mailing Address: Herman Bonpad 5, 1067 SN Amsterdam. **Telephone:** +31 (0) 20-616-2151. **Website:** amsterdampirates.nl

DSS
Mailing Address: Rijksstraatweg 206, 2022 DH Haarlem. **Telephone:** +31 (0) 23-527-2678. **Website:** dss-honksoftbal.nl

HAGUE STORKS
Mailing Address: Postbus 53016, 2505 AA 'S-Gravenhage. **Telephone:** +31 (0) 70-323-4151. **Website:** storks.nl

HCAW
Mailing Address: Zanderijweg 4-6l, 1403 XV Bussum. **Telephone:** +31 (0) 35-693-1430. **Website:** hcaw.nl

HOOFDDORP PIONIERS
Mailing Address: Postbus 475, 2130 AL Hoofddorp. **Telephone:** +31 (0) 23-561-3557. **Website:** hoofddorp-pioniers.nl

NEPTUNUS
Mailing Address: Zalm 63, 2986 PD Ridderkerk. **Telephone:** +31 (0) 10-437-5369. **Website:** neptunussport.com

OOSTERHOUT TWINS
Mailing Address: Postbus 4085, 4900 CB Oosterhout NB. **Telephone:** +31 (0) 162-433-760. **Website:** twins-sc.com

ITALY
ITALIAN BASEBALL LEAGUE

Mailing Address: Federazione Italiana Baseball Softball, Viale Tiziano 74, 00196 Roma, Italy. **Telephone:** 39-06-32297201. **FAX:** 39-06-01902684. **Website:** fibs.it
President: Andrea Marcon.

ITALIAN SERIES A1 CLUBS
BOLOGNA
Mailing Address: Stadio Gianni Falchi, Piazzale Atleti Azzurri d'Italia, Bologna. **Telephone:** 39-051-479618.
E-Mail Address: info@fortitudobaseball.it. **Website:** fortitudobaseball.it.
President: Stefano Michelini. **Manager:** Daniele Frignani.

CASTENASO
Mailing Address: Via XXI Ottobre 1944 n.8, Castenaso Bologna 40055. **Telephone:** 39-051-789460.
E-Mail Address: info@castenasobaseball.it **Website:** castenasobaseball.it
President: Bruno Galeotti. **Manager:** Marco Nanni.

GODO
Mailing Address: Viale Rivalona 5, Godo di Russi 48010. **Telephone:** 39-0335-6975175.
E-Mail Address: uffstampa.baseballgodo@gmail.com **Website:** baseball-godo.com
President: Carlo Naldoni. **Manager:** Marco Bortolotti.

NETTUNO
Mailing Address: Via Scipione Borghese, Nettuno 00048. **Telephone:** 39-340-1467939.
Website: facebook.com/Nettuno.Baseball.City
President: Simone Pillisio. **Manager:** Gary Villalobos.

PARMA
Mailing Address: Via Teresa Confalonieri Casati 22, 43125 Parma. **Telephone:** 39-0521-152-3413.
E-Mail Address: info@parmabaseball.it. **Website:** parmabaseball.it.
President: Paolo Zbogar. **Manager:** Gianguido Poma.

REDIPUGLIA
Mailing Address: Via Atleti Azzurri d'Italia 1, Redipuglia 34070. **Telephone:** 39-0481-489050.
E-Mail Address: rangersbc@hotmail.com **Website:** rangersredipuglia.it
President: Salvatore Sechi. **Manager:** Frank Pantoja.

SAN MARINO
Mailing Address: Via Costa del Bello 2,Serravalle, Repubblica di San Marino. **Telephone:** 39-0549-961217.
E-Mail Address: info@sanmarinobaseball.com **Website:** sanmarinobaseball.com.
President: Mauro Fiorini. **Manager:** Mario Chiarini.

WINTER BASEBALL

CARIBBEAN BASEBALL CONFEDERATION
Mailing Address: Frank Feliz Miranda No 1 Naco, Santo Domingo, Dominican Republic. **Telephone:** (809) 381-2643. **Fax:** (809) 565-4654.
Commissioner: Juan Francisco Puello. **Secretary:** Benny Agosto.
Member Countries: Cuba, Colombia, Dominican Republic, Mexico, Nicaragua, Panama, Puerto Rico, Venezuela.
2020 Caribbean Series: Puerto Rico, February.

DOMINICAN LEAGUE
Office Address: Ave. Tiradentes, Ensanche La Fé, Estadio Quisqueya, Santo Domingo, Dominican Republic. **Telephone:** (809) 567-6371. **Fax:** (809) 567-5720. **E-Mail Address:** ligadom@hotmail.com. **Website:** lidom.com.
Years League Active: 1951-.
President: Vitelio Mejía Ortiz. **Vice President:** Winston Llenas Davila.
Member Clubs: Aguilas Cibaenas, Estrellas de Oriente, Gigantes del Cibao, Leones del Escogido, Tigres del Licey, Toros del Este.
Regular Season: 50 games.

Playoff Format: Top four teams meet in 18-game round-robin. Top two teams advance to best-of-nine series for league championship. Winner advances to Caribbean Series.

Roster Limit: 30. **Imports:** 7.

MEXICAN PACIFIC LEAGUE

Mailing Address: Ave. Américas No. 1905, 5to. Piso, Col. Colomos Providencia, Guadalajara, Jalisco. **Telephone:** (52) 662-310-9714. **Fax:** (52) 662-310-9715. **E-Mail Address:** medios@lmp.mx. **Website:** lmp.mx.

Years League Active: 1958-.

President: Omar Canizales Soto. **General Manager:** Christian Veliz Valencia.

Member Clubs: Culiacan Tomateros, Guasave Algodoneros, Hermosillo Naranjeros, Jalisco Charros, Los Mochis Caneros, Mazatlan Venados, Mexicali Aguilas, Monterrey Sultanes, Navojoa Mayos, Obregon Yaquis.

Regular Season: 68 games.

Playoff Format: Six teams advance to best-of-seven quarterfinals. Three winners and losing team with best record advance to best-of-seven semifinals. Winners meet in best-of-seven series for league championship. Winner advances to Caribbean Series.

Roster Limit: 30. **Imports:** 5.

PUERTO RICAN LEAGUE

Office Address: Avenida Munoz Rivera 1056, Edificio First Federal, Suite 501, Rio Piedras, PR 00925. **Mailing Address:** PO Box 191852, San Juan, PR 00019. **Telephone:** (786) 244-1146. **Fax:** (787) 767-3028. **Website:** ligapr.com. **E-mail address:** info@ligapr .com

Years League Active: 1938-2007; 2008-

President: Juan Flores Galarza. **Operations Director:** Carlos J. Berroa Puertas. **Press Director:** Karla Pacheco.

Member Clubs: Caguas Criollos, Carolina Gigantes, Mayaguez Indios, Manati Atenienses, Santurce Cangrejeros.

Regular Season: 40 games.

Playoff Format: Top three teams meet in round robin series, with top two teams advancing to best-of-seven final. Winner advances to Caribbean Series.

Roster Limit: 30. **Imports:** 5.

VENEZUELAN LEAGUE

Mailing Address: Avenida Casanova, Centro Comercial "El Recreo," Torre Sur, Piso 3, Oficinas 6 y 7, Sabana Grande, Caracas, Venezuela. **Telephone:** (58) 212-761-6408. **Fax:** (58) 212-761-7661. **Website:** lvbp.com.

Years League Active: 1946-.

President: Juan Jose Avila. **Vice Presidents:** Esteban Palacios Lozada, Domingo Santander. **General Manager:** Domingo Alvarez.

Member Clubs: Anzoategui Caribes, Aragua Tigres, Caracas Leones, La Guaira Tiburones, Lara Cardenales, Magallanes Navegantes, Margarita Bravos, Zulia Aguilas.

Regular Season: 64 games.

Playoff Format: Top two teams in each division, plus a wild-card team, meet in 16-game round-robin series. Top two finishers meet in best-of-seven series for league championship. Winner advances to Caribbean Series.

Roster Limit: 26. **Imports:** 7.

COLOMBIAN LEAGUE

Office/Mailing Address: Hotel Eslait Cra 53 No. 72-27 2do piso, Baranquilla. **Telephone:** (57) 368-6561. **E-mail Address:** lcpbcolombia@gmail.com. **Website:** lcbp.com. co.

President: Edinson Renteria. **Director, Operations:** Harold Herrera. **Director, Communications:** Gabriel Chavez.

Member Clubs: Barranquilla Caimanes, Cartagena Tigres, Monteria Leones, Sincelejo Toros.

Regular Season: 42 games.

Playoff Format: Top three teams play eight-game round robin. Top two teams meet in best-of-seven finals for league championship.

AUSTRALIA
AUSTRALIAN BASEBALL LEAGUE

Address: Calle 6 Nº315 x 35, Col. Morelos Oriente, Mérida, Yucatán. C.P. 97174. **Telephone:** (52) 999-432-0655. **Fax:** (07) 5510 6855. **E-Mail Address:** abfadmin@ baseball.org.au. **Website:** web.theabl.com.au.

CEO: Cam Vale. **General Manager:** Michael Crooks, Andrew Reynolds.

Teams: Adelaide Bite, Auckland Tuatara, Brisbane Bandits, Canberra Cavalry, Geelong-Korea, Melbourne Aces, Perth Heat, Sydney Blue Sox.

2020 Opening Date: Unavailable. Play usually opens in November with playoffs in February.

Playoff Format: The teams with the best four records qualify for the playoffs. Teams are seeded 1-4, with the top two seeds hosting all three games of the best-of-three semifinal series. Winners advance to a best-of-three championship series.

DOMESTIC LEAGUE
ARIZONA FALL LEAGUE

Mailing Address: Arizona Fall League C/O Salt River Fields - Centerfield Office 7555 North Pima Road Scottsdale, AZ 85258. **Telephone:** (480)-990-1005. **Fax:** (602) 281-7313. **E-Mail Address:** afl@mlb.com. **Website:** mlb.com/arizona-fall-league. **Years League Active:** 1992-.

Operated by: Major League Baseball.

Executive Director: Steve Cobb. **Administrative Supervisor:** Darlene Emert. **Communications:** Paul Jensen.

Teams: Glendale Desert Dogs, Mesa Solar Sox, Peoria Javelinas, Salt River Rafters, Scottsdale Scorpions, Surprise Saguaros.

Regular season: 32 games. **2020 Opening Date:** Unavailable. Play usually opens in mid-October. **Playoff Format:** Division champions meet in one-game championship.

Roster Limit: 35 players per team plus a "taxi squad" of reserve players. Each major-league organization is required to provide seven players. Triple-A and Double-A players are eligible provided they are on Double-A or Triple-A rosters no later than August 15. Each organization is permitted to send two high Class A level players and two players below high Class A. No players with more than one year active or two years total of credited major-league service as of August 31 (including major league disabled list time) are eligible. Each team is allotted 20 pitchers but only 15 are designated "active" each game day.

COLLEGES

COLLEGE ORGANIZATIONS

NATIONAL COLLEGIATE ATHLETIC ASSOCIATION

Mailing Address: 700 W. Washington Street, PO Box 6222, Indianapolis, IN 46206. **Telephone:** (317) 917-6222. **Fax:** (317) 917-6826 (championships), (317) 917-6710 (baseball).

E-mail Addresses: Division I Championship: aholman@ncaa.org (Anthony Holman), rlburhr@ncaa.org (Randy Buhr), ctolliver@ncaa.org (Chad Tolliver), thalpin@ncaa.org (Ty Halpin), jhamilton@ncaa.org (JD Hamilton), kgiles@ncaa.org (Kim Giles). **Division II Championship:** ebreece@ncaa.org (Eric Breece). **Division III:** jpwilliams@ncaa.org (J.P. Williams).

Websites: www.ncaa.org, www.ncaa.com.

President: Dr. Mark Emmert. **Managing director, Division I Championships/Alliances:** Anthony Holman. **Director, Division I Championships/Alliances:** Randy Buhr. **Associate Director, Championships/Alliances:** Chad Tolliver. **Division II Assistant Director, Championships/Alliances:** Eric Breece. **Division III Assistant Director, Championships/Alliances:** J.P. Williams. **Media Contact, Division I Championships, Alliances/College World Series:** J.D. Hamilton. **Playing Rules Contact:** Ty Halpin. **Statistics Contacts:** Jeff Williams (Division I and RPI); Mark Bedics (Division II); Sean Straziscar (Division III).

Chairman, Division I Baseball Committee: Ray Tanner (Director of Athletics, South Carolina).

Division I Baseball Committee: Jeff Altier (Director of Athletics, Stetson); David Blank (Director of Athletics, Elon); Bob Moosburger (Director of Athletics, Bowling Green State); Desiree Reed-Francois (Director of Athletics, UNLV); John Cohen (Director of Athletics, Mississippi State); Joe Karlgaard (Director of Athletics, Rice); Benjamin Shove (Assistant Commissioner, Northeast Conference); James Cole (Director of Athletics, Mercer); Marianne Vydra (Deputy Athletics Director, Oregon State); Kirby Hocutt (Director of Athletics, Texas Tech).

Chairman, Division II Baseball Committee: Sue Willey (Director of Athletics, Indianapolis). **Chairman, Division III Baseball Committee:** Paul F. Murphy (Associate Director of Athletics, Gwynedd Mercy, Pa.).

2021 National Convention: Jan. 13-16 at Washington, D.C.

2020 CHAMPIONSHIP TOURNAMENTS

NCAA DIVISION I
College World Series: Omaha, Neb., June 13-23/24
Super Regionals (8): Campus sites, June 5-8
Regionals (16): Campus sites, May 29-June 1

NCAA DIVISION II
World Series: USA Baseball National Training Complex, Cary, N.C. May 30-June 6.

NCAA DIVISION III
World Series: Veterans Memorial Stadium, Cedar Rapids, Iowa, May 29-June 3

NATIONAL JUNIOR COLLEGE ATHLETIC ASSOCIATION

Mailing Address: 1631 Mesa Ave., Suite B, Colorado Springs, CO 80906. **Telephone:** (719) 590-9788. **Fax:** (719) 590-7324. **E-Mail Address:** rwebster@njcaa.org. **Website:** www.njcaa.org.

Executive Director: Christopher Parker. **Director, Division I Baseball Tournament:** Jamie Hamilton. **Director, Division II Baseball Tournament:** Billy Mayberry. **Director, Division III Baseball Tournament:** Bill Ellis. **Director, Media Relations:** Ricky Webster.

2020 CHAMPIONSHIP TOURNAMENTS

DIVISION I
World Series: Grand Junction, CO, May 23-May 29/30.

DIVISION II
World Series: Enid, OK, May 23-May 29/30.

DIVISION III
World Series: Greeneville, TN, May 23-May 27/28

CALIFORNIA COMMUNITY COLLEGE ATHLETIC ASSOCIATION

Mailing Address: 2017 O St., Sacramento, CA 95811. **Telephone:** (916) 444-1600. **Fax:** (916) 444-2616. **E-Mail Addresses:** ccarter@cccaasports.org, jboggs@cccaasports.org. **Website:** www.cccaasports.org.

Executive Director: Carlyle Carter. **Director, Membership Services:** Jennifer Cardone. **Director, Championships:** George Mategakis. **Buisness Operations Specialist:** Rina Kasim, rkasim@cccaasports.org. **Administrative Assistant:** Rima Trotter, rtrotter@cccaasports.org.

2020 CHAMPIONSHIP TOURNAMENT

State Championship: Pomona, CA, May 6-9.

NORTHWEST ATHLETIC CONFERENCE

Mailing Address: Clark College TGB 121, 1933 Fort Vancouver Way, Vancouver, WA 98663. **Telephone:** (360) 992-2833. **Fax:** (360) 696-6210. **E-Mail Address:** nwaacc@clark.edu. **Website:** www.nwacsports.org.

Executive Director: Marco Azurdia. **Executive Assistant:** Donna Hays. **Sports Information Director:** Tracy Swisher. **Director, Operations:** Alli Young.

2020 CHAMPIONSHIP TOURNAMENT

NWAC Championship: Lower Columbia College, Longview, WA, May 21-25.

AMERICAN BASEBALL COACHES ASSOCIATION

Office Address: 4101 Piedmont Parkway, Suite C, Greensboro, NC 27410. **Telephone:** (336) 821-3140. **Fax:** (336) 886-0000. **E-Mail Address:** abca@abca.org. **Website:** www.abca.org.

Executive Director: Craig Keilitz. **Deputy Executive Director:** Jon Litchfield. **Asst. Executive Director, Trade Show:** Juahn Clark. **Asst. Executive Director, Convention/Marketing:** Zach Haile.

Chairman: Keith Madison. **President:** John Kolasinski (Siena Heights, Mich.).

2020 National Convention: Jan. 7-10 in Washington, D.C.

NCAA DIVISION I CONFERENCES

AMERICA EAST CONFERENCE

Mailing Address: 451 D Street, Suite 702, Boston, MA 02127. **Telephone:** (617) 695-6369. **Fax:** (617) 695-6380. **E-Mail Address:** hager@americaeast.com. **Website:** www.americaeast.com. **Baseball Members (First Year):** Albany (2002), Binghamton (2002), Hartford (1990), Maine (1990), Maryland-Baltimore County (2004), Massachusetts-Lowell (2014), Stony Brook (2002). **Director, Strategic Media/Baseball Contact:** Pete Souris. **2020 Tournament:** Six teams, double-elimination, May 19-24 at LeLacheur Park, Lowell, Mass.

AMERICAN ATHLETIC CONFERENCE

Mailing Address: 15 Park Row West, Providence, RI 02903. **Telephone:** (401) 453-0660. **Fax:** (401) 751-8540. **E-Mail Address:** csullivan@theamerican.org. **Website:** www.theamerican.org. **Baseball Members (First Year):** Central Florida (2014), Cincinnati (2014), Connecticut (2014), East Carolina (2015), Houston (2014), Memphis (2014), South Florida (2014), Tulane (2015), Wichita State (2018). **Director, Communications:** Chuck Sullivan. **2020 Tournament:** Eight teams, double-elimination until the final, May 21-24 at Spectrum Field, Clearwater, Fla.

ATLANTIC COAST CONFERENCE

Mailing Address: 4512 Weybridge Ln., Greensboro, NC 27407. **Telephone:** (336) 851-6062. **Fax:** (336) 854-8797. **E-Mail Address:** sphillips@theacc.org. **Website:** www.theacc.com. **Baseball Members (First Year):** Boston College (2006), Clemson (1954), Duke (1954), Florida State (1992), Georgia Tech (1980), Miami (2005), North Carolina (1954), North Carolina State (1954), Notre Dame (2014), Louisville (2015), Pittsburgh (2014), Virginia (1955), Virginia Tech (2005), Wake Forest (1954). **Associate Director, Communications:** Steve Phillips. **2020 Tournament:** 12 teams, group play followed by single-elimination semifinals and finals. May 19-24 at BB&T Ballpark in Charlotte, N.C.

ATLANTIC SUN CONFERENCE

Mailing Address: 3370 Vineville Ave., Suite 108-B, Macon, GA 31204. **Telephone:** (478) 474-3394. **Fax:** (478) 474-4272. **E-Mail Addresses:** pmccoy@atlanticsun.org. **Website:** www.atlanticsun.org. **Baseball Members:** (First Year): Florida Gulf Coast (2008), Jacksonville (1999), Kennesaw State (2006), Liberty (2019), Lipscomb (2004), New Jersey Tech (2016), North Alabama (2019), North Florida (2006), Stetson (1986). **Director, Sports Information:** Patrick McCoy. **2020 Tournament:** Eight teams, double-elimination. May 20-23 at Swanson Stadium, Fort Myers, Fla.

ATLANTIC 10 CONFERENCE

Mailing Address: 11827 Canon Blvd., Suite 200, Newport News, VA 23606. **Telephone:** (757) 706-3059. **Fax:** (757) 706-3042. **E-Mail Address:** ddickerson@atlantic10.org. **Website:** www.atlantic10.com. **Baseball Members:** (First Year): Davidson (2015), Dayton (1996), Fordham (1996), George Mason (1996), George Washington (1977), La Salle (1996), Massachusetts (1977), Rhode Island (1981), Richmond (2002), St. Bonaventure (1980), Saint Joseph's (1983), Saint Louis (2006), Virginia Commonwealth (2013). **Commissioner:** Bernadette V. McGlade. **Director, Communications:** Drew Dickerson. **2020 Tournament:** Seven teams, double elimination.

May 20-23 at the Diamond, Richmond, Va.

BIG EAST CONFERENCE

Mailing Address: BIG EAST Conference, 655 3rd Avenue, 7th Floor, New York, NY 10017. **Telephone:** (212) 969-3181. **Fax:** (212) 969-2900. **E-Mail Address:** kquinn@bigeast.com. **Website:** www.bigeast.com. **Baseball Members:** (First Year): Butler (2014), Creighton (2014), Georgetown (1985), St. John's (1985), Seton Hall (1985), Villanova (1985), Xavier (2014). **Assistant Commissioner, Olympic Sports/Marketing Communications:** Kristin Quinn. **2020 Tournament:** Four teams, modified double-elimination. May 21-24 at Prasco Park, Mason, Ohio.

BIG SOUTH CONFERENCE

Mailing Address: 7233 Pineville-Matthews Rd., Suite 100, Charlotte, NC 28226. **Telephone:** (704) 341-7990. **Fax:** (704) 341-7991. **E-Mail Address:** brandonm@bigsouth.org. **Website:** www.bigsouthsports.com. **Baseball Members (First Year):** Campbell (2012), Charleston Southern (1983), Gardner-Webb (2009), High Point (1999), Longwood (2013), UNC Asheville (1985), Presbyterian (2009), Radford (1983), South Carolina-Upstate (2019), Winthrop (1983). **Assistant Director, Public Relations/Baseball Contact:** Brandon McGinnis. **2020 Tournament:** Eight teams, double-elimination. May 19-23, at SEGRA Stadium, Fayetteville, N.C.

BIG TEN CONFERENCE

Mailing Address: 5440 Park Place, Rosemont, IL 60018. **Telephone:** (847) 696-1010. **Fax:** (847) 696-1110. **E-Mail Addresses:** kkane@bigten.org. **Website:** www.bigten.org. **Baseball Members (First Year):** Illinois (1896), Indiana (1906), Iowa (1906), Maryland (2015), Michigan (1896), Michigan State (1950), Minnesota (1906), Nebraska (2012), Northwestern (1898), Ohio State (1913), Penn State (1992), Purdue (1906), Rutgers (2015). **2020 Tournament:** Eight teams, double-elimination. May 20-24 at TD Ameritrade Park, Omaha.

BIG 12 CONFERENCE

Mailing Address: 400 E. John Carpenter Freeway, Irving, TX 75062. **Telephone:** (469) 524-1009. **E-Mail Address:** russell@big12sports.com. **Website:** www.big12sports.com. **Baseball Members (First Year):** Baylor (1997), Kansas (1997), Kansas State (1997), Oklahoma (1997), Oklahoma State (1997), Texas Christian (2013), Texas (1997), Texas Tech (1997), West Virginia (2013). **Assistant Director, Media Relations:** Russell Luna. **2020 Tournament:** Eight teams, double-elimination. May 20-24 at Chickasaw Bricktown Ballpark, Oklahoma City.

BIG WEST CONFERENCE

Mailing Address: 2 Corporate Park, Suite 206, Irvine, CA 92606. **Telephone:** (949) 261-2525. **Fax:** (949) 261-2528. **E-Mail Address:** jstcyr@bigwest.org. **Website:** www.bigwest.org. **Baseball Members (First Year):** Cal Poly (1997), UC Davis (2008), UC Irvine (2002), UC Riverside (2002), UC Santa Barbara (1970), Cal State Fullerton (1975), Cal State Northridge (2001), Hawaii (2013), Long Beach State (1970). **Director, Communications:** Julie St. Cyr. **2020 Tournament:** None.

COLONIAL ATHLETIC ASSOCIATION

Mailing Address: 8625 Patterson Ave., Richmond, VA 23229. **Telephone:** (804) 754-1616. **Fax:** (804) 754-1973. **E-Mail Address:** rwashburn@caasports.com. **Website:**

www.caasports.com. **Baseball Members (First Year):** College of Charleston (2014), Delaware (2002), Elon (2015), Hofstra (2002), James Madison (1986), UNC Wilmington (1986), Northeastern (2006), Towson (2002), William & Mary (1986). **Associate Commissioner/Communications:** Rob Washburn. **2020 Tournament:** Six teams, double-elimination. May 20-24 at Brooks Field at UNC Wilmington, Wilmington, NC.

CONFERENCE USA

Mailing Address: 5201 N. O'Connor Blvd., Suite 300, Irving, TX 75039. **Telephone:** (214) 774-1300. **Fax:** (214) 496-0055. **E-Mail Address:** rdanderson@c-usa.org. **Website:** www.conferenceusa.com. **Baseball Members (First Year):** Alabama-Birmingham (1996), Charlotte (2014), Florida Atlantic (2014), Florida International (2014), Louisiana Tech (2006), Marshall (2006), Middle Tennessee State (2014), Old Dominion (2014), Rice (2006), Southern Mississippi (1996), Texas-San Antonio (2014), Western Kentucky (2015). **Assistant Commissioner, Baseball Operations:** Russell Anderson. **2020 Tournament:** Eight teams, double-elimination. May 20-24 at MGM Park, Biloxi, Miss.

HORIZON LEAGUE

Mailing Address: 201 S. Capitol Ave., Suite 500, Indianapolis, IN 46225. **Telephone:** (317) 237-5604. **Fax:** (317) 237-5620. **E-Mail Address:** dgliot@horizonleague.org. **Website:** www.horizonleague.org. **Baseball Members (First Year):** Illinois-Chicago (1994), Northern Kentucky (2016), Oakland (2014), Wright State (1994), Wisconsin-Milwaukee (1994), Youngstown State (2002). **Director, Communications and Digital Media Strategy:** Dan Gliot. **2020 Tournament:** Six teams, modified double-elimination. May 20-23, hosted by No. 1 seed.

IVY LEAGUE

Mailing Address: 228 Alexander Rd., Second Floor, Princeton, NJ 08544. **Telephone:** (609) 258-6426. **Fax:** (609) 258-1690. **E-Mail Address:** trevor@ivyleaguesports.com. **Website:** www ivyleaguesports.com. **Baseball Members (First Year):** Rolfe—Brown (1948), Dartmouth (1930), Harvard (1948), Yale (1930). Gehrig—Columbia (1930), Cornell (1930), Pennsylvania (1930), Princeton (1930). **Assistant Executive Director, Communications/Championships:** Trevor Rutledge-Leverenz. **2020 Tournament:** Best-of-three series between division champions. Team with best Ivy League record hosts. May 16-17.

METRO ATLANTIC ATHLETIC CONFERENCE

Mailing Address: 712 Amboy Ave., Edison, NJ 08837. **Telephone:** (732) 738-5455. **E-Mail Address:** phil.paquette@maac.org. **Website:** www.maacsports.com. **Baseball Members (First Year):** Canisius (1990), Fairfield (1982), Iona (1982), Manhattan (1982), Marist (1998), Monmouth (2014), Niagara (1990), Quinnipiac (2014), Rider (1998), Saint Peter's (1982), Siena (1990). **Director, New Media:** Phil Paquette. **2020 Tournament:** Best-of-three series between division champions. Team with best Ivy League record hosts. May 16-17.

MID-AMERICAN CONFERENCE

Mailing Address: 24 Public Square, 15th Floor, Cleveland, OH 44113. **Telephone:** (216) 566-4622. **Fax:** (216) 858-9622. **E-Mail Address:** jguy@mac-sports.com. **Website:** www.mac-sports.com. **Baseball Members (First Year):** Ball State (1973), Bowling Green State (1952), Central Michigan (1971), Eastern Michigan (1971), Kent State (1951), Miami (1947), Northern Illinois (1997), Ohio (1946), Toledo (1950), Western Michigan (1947). **Assistant Commissioner, Communications and Social Media:** Jeremy Guy. **2020 Tournament:** Eight teams, double-elimination. May 20-24 at Springer Stadium, Avon, Ohio.

MID-EASTERN ATHLETIC CONFERENCE

Mailing Address: 2730 Ellsmere Ave., Norfolk, VA 23513. **Telephone:** (757) 951-2055. **Fax:** (757) 951-2077. **E-Mail Address:** cunninghamj@themeac.com; porterp@themeac.com. **Website:** www.meacsports.com. **Baseball Members (First Year):** Bethune-Cookman (1979), Coppin State (1985), Delaware State (1970), Florida A&M (1979), Maryland Eastern Shore (1970), Norfolk State (1998), North Carolina A&T (1970), North Carolina Central (2012), Savannah State (2012). **Assistant Director, Media Relations:** Jeff Cunningham. **2020 Tournament:** six-teams, double-elimination. May 13-16 at Daytona Stadium, Daytona Beach, Fla.

MISSOURI VALLEY CONFERENCE

Mailing Address: 1818 Chouteau Ave., St. Louis, MO 63103. **Telephone:** (314) 444-4300. **Fax:** (314) 444-4333. **E-Mail Address:** davis@mvc.org. **Website:** mvc-sports.com. **Baseball Members (First Year):** Bradley (1955), Dallas Baptist (2014), Evansville (1994), Illinois State (1980), Indiana State (1976), Missouri State (1990), Southern Illinois (1974), Valparaiso (2019). **Assistant Commissioner, Communications:** Ryan Davis. **2020 Tournament:** Eight-teams, double-elimination. May 19-23 at Richard "Itchy" Jones Stadium, Carbondale, Ill.

MOUNTAIN WEST CONFERENCE

Mailing Address: 10807 New Allegiance Dr., Suite 250, Colorado Springs, CO 80921. **Telephone:** (719) 488-4052. **Fax:** (719) 487-7241. **E-Mail Address:** sbuchanan@themw.com. **Website:** www.themw.com. **Baseball Members (First Year):** Air Force (2000), Fresno State (2013), Nevada (2013), Nevada-Las Vegas (2000), New Mexico (2000), San Diego State (2000), San Jose State (2014). **Director, Strategic Communication:** Stuart Buchanan. **2020 Tournament:** Four teams, double-elimination. May 21-24 at Tony Gwynn Stadium, San Diego, Calif.

NORTHEAST CONFERENCE

Mailing Address: 200 Cottontail Lane, Vantage Court South, Somerset, NJ 08873. **Telephone:** (732) 469-0440. **Fax:** (732) 469-0744. **E-Mail Address:** rventre@northeastconference.org. **Website:** www.northeastconference.org. **Baseball Members (First Year):** Bryant (2010), Central Connecticut State (1999), Fairleigh Dickinson (1981), Long Island -Brooklyn (1981), Mount St. Mary's (1989), Sacred Heart (2000), Wagner (1981). **Director, Communications/Social Media:** Ralph Ventre. **2020 Tournament:** Four teams, double-elimination. May 21-24 at Dodd Stadium, Norwich, Conn.

OHIO VALLEY CONFERENCE

Mailing Address: 215 Centerview Dr., Suite 115, Brentwood, TN 37027. **Telephone:** (615) 371-1698. **Fax:** (615) 891-1682. **E-Mail Address:** kschwartz@ovc.org. **Website:** www.ovcsports.com. **Baseball Members (First Year):** Austin Peay State (1962), Belmont (2013), Eastern Illinois (1996), Eastern Kentucky (1948), Jacksonville State (2003), Morehead State (1948), Murray State (1948), Southeast Missouri State (1991), Southern Illinois-

Edwardsville (2012), Tennessee-Martin (1992), Tennessee Tech (1949). **Assistant Commissioner:** Kyle Schwartz. **2020 Tournament:** Eight teams. May 19-24 at Marion, Ill.

PACIFIC-12 CONFERENCE

Mailing Address: Pac-12 Conference 360 3rd Street, 3rd Floor San Francisco, CA 94107. **Telephone:** (415) 580-4200. **Fax:** (415)549-2828. **E-Mail Address:** jolivero@pac-12.org. **Website:** www.pac-12.com. **Baseball Members (First Year):** Arizona (1979), Arizona State (1979), California (1916), UCLA (1928), Oregon (2009) Oregon State (1916), Southern California (1923), Stanford (1918), Utah (2012), Washington (1916), Washington State (1919). **Public Relations Contact:** Jon Olivero. **2020 Tournament:** None.

PATRIOT LEAGUE

Mailing Address: 3773 Corporate Pkwy., Suite 190, Center Valley, PA 18034. **Telephone:** (610) 289-1950. **Fax:** (610) 289-1951. **E-Mail Address:** rsakamoto@patriot-league.com. **Website:** www.patriotleague.org. **Baseball Members (First Year):** Army (1993), Bucknell (1991), Holy Cross (1991), Lafayette (1991), Lehigh (1991), Navy (1993). **Assistant Commissioner, Communications:** Ryan Sakamoto. **2020 Tournament:** 12 teams, modified single/double-elimination. May 19-24 at Hoover Metropolitan Stadium, Hoover, Ala.

SOUTHEASTERN CONFERENCE

Mailing Address: 2201 Richard Arrington Blvd. N., Birmingham, AL 35203. **Telephone:** (205) 458-3000. **Fax:** (205) 458-3030. **E-Mail Address:** scartell@sec.org. **Website:** www.secsports.com. **Baseball Members (First Year): East Division**—Florida (1933), Georgia (1933), Kentucky (1933), Missouri (2013), South Carolina (1992), Tennessee (1933), Vanderbilt (1933). **West Division**—Alabama (1933), Arkansas (1992), Auburn (1933), Louisiana State (1933), Mississippi (1933), Mississippi State (1933), Texas A&M (2013). **Director, Communications:** Chuck Dunlap. **2020 Tournament:** 12 teams, modified single/double-elimination. May 19-24 at Hoover Metropolitan Stadium, Hoover, Ala.

SOUTHERN CONFERENCE

Mailing Address: 702 N. Pine St., Spartanburg, SC 29303. **Telephone:** (864) 591-5100. **Fax:** (864) 591-3448. **E-Mail Address:** hsimmons@socon.org. **Website:** www.soconsports.com. **Baseball Members (First Year):** The Citadel (1937), East Tennessee State (1979-2005, 2015), Furman (1937), Mercer (2015), UNC Greensboro (1998), Samford (2009), VMI (1925-2003, 2015), Western Carolina (1977), Wofford (1998). **Media Relations Assistant:** Hannah Simmons. **2020 Tournament:** Nine teams, single-game play-in for bottom two seeds, followed by double-elimination bracket play. May 19-24 at Fluor Field, Greenville, S.C.

SOUTHLAND CONFERENCE

Mailing Address: 2600 Network Blvd, Suite 150, Frisco, Texas 75034. **Telephone:** (972) 422-9500. **Fax:** (972) 422-9225. **E-Mail Address:** gstieren@southland.org **Website:** southland.org. **Baseball Members (First Year):** Abilene Christian (2014), Central Arkansas (2007), Houston Baptist (2014), Incarnate Word (2014), Lamar (1999), McNeese State (1973), New Orleans (2014), Nicholls State (1992), Northwestern State (1988), Sam Houston State (1988), Southeastern Louisiana (1998), Stephen F. Austin State

(2006), Texas A&M-Corpus Christi (2007). **Associate Commissioner, Strategic Communications:** George Stieren. **2020 Tournament:** Two four-team brackets, double-elimination. May 20-23 at Whataburger Field, Corpus Christi, Texas.

SOUTHWESTERN ATHLETIC CONFERENCE

Mailing Address: 2101 6th Ave. North, Suite 700, Birmingham, AL 35203. **Telephone:** (205) 251-7573. **Fax:** (205) 297-9820. **E-Mail Address:** a.roberts@swac.org. **Website:** www.swac.org. **Baseball Members (First Year): East Division**—Alabama A&M (2000), Alabama State (1982), Alcorn State (1962), Jackson State (1958), Mississippi Valley State (1968). **West Division**—Arkansas-Pine Bluff (1999), Grambling State (1958), Prairie View A&M (1920), Southern (1934), Texas Southern (1954). **Assistant Commissioner, Communications:** Andrew Roberts. **2020 Tournament:** Eight teams, double-elimination. May 13-17 at Wesley Barrow Stadium, New Orleans, La.

SUMMIT LEAGUE

Mailing Address: 340 W. Butterfield Rd., Suite 3D, Elmhurst, IL 60126. **Telephone:** (630) 516-0661. **Fax:** (630) 516-0673. **E-Mail Address:** powell@thesummitleague.org. **Website:** www.thesummitleague.org. **Baseball Members (First Year):** IPFW (2008), Nebraska-Omaha (2013), North Dakota State (2008), Oral Roberts (1998), South Dakota State (2008), Western Illinois (1984). **Associate Commissioner, Communications:** Ryan Powell. **2020 Tournament:** Four teams, double-elimination. May 20-23 at Omaha, Nebraska.

SUN BELT CONFERENCE

Mailing Address: 1500 Sugar Bowl Dr., New Orleans, LA 70112. **Telephone:** (504) 556-0884. **Fax:** (504) 299-9068. **E-Mail Address:** nunez@sunbeltsports.org. **Website:** www.sunbeltsports.org. **Baseball Members (First Year): East Division**—Appalachian State (2015), Coastal Carolina (2017), Georgia Southern (2015), Georgia State (2014), South Alabama (1976), Troy (2006). **West Division**—Arkansas-Little Rock (1991), Arkansas State (1991), Louisiana-Lafayette (1991), Louisiana-Monroe (2007), Texas-Arlington (2014), Texas State (2014). **Assistant Commissioner, Digital & Creative Services:** Keith Nunez. **2020 Tournament:** Eight teams, double-elimination. May 19-24 at Riverwalk Stadium, Montgomery, Ala.

WESTERN ATHLETIC CONFERENCE

Mailing Address: 9250 East Costilla Ave., Suite 300, Englewood, CO 80112. **Telephone:** (303) 799-9221. **Fax:** (303) 799-3888. **E-Mail Address:** cthompson@wac.org. **Website:** www.wacsports.com. **Baseball Members (First Year):** California Baptist (2019), Cal State Bakersfield (2013), Chicago State (2014), Grand Canyon (2014), New Mexico State (2006), Northern Colorado (2014), Sacramento State (2006), Seattle (2013), Texas-Rio Grande Valley (2014), Utah Valley (2014). **Director, Media Relations:** Chris Thompson. **2020 Tournament:** Six teams, double-elimination, May 20-23/24 at Hohokam Stadium, Mesa, Ariz.

WEST COAST CONFERENCE

Mailing Address: 1111 Bayhill Dr., Suite 405, San Bruno, CA 94066. **Telephone:** (650) 873-8622. **Fax:** (650) 873-7846. **E-Mail Addresses:** rmccrary@westcoast.org. **Website:** www.wccsports.com. **Baseball Members (First Year):** Brigham Young (2012), Gonzaga (1996), Loyola

Marymount (1968), Pacific (2014), Pepperdine (1968), Portland (1996), Saint Mary's (1968), San Diego (1979), San Francisco (1968), Santa Clara (1968). **Assistant Commissioner, Communications:** Ryan McCrary. **2020 Tournament:** Four teams, May 21-23 at Banner Island Ballpark, Stockton, Calif.

NCAA DIVISION I TEAMS

Denotes recruiting coordinator

ABILENE CHRISTIAN WILDCATS.

Conference: Southland. **Mailing Address:** 900 E. Ambler Ave., Abilene, TX 79601. **Website:** www.acusports.com. **Head Coach:** Rick McCarty. **Telephone:** (325) 674-2325. **Baseball SID:** Zach Carlyle. **Telephone:** (325) 674-6171. **Assistant Coaches:** *Blaze Lambert, Craig Parry. **Telephone:** (325) 674-2817. **Home Field:** Crutcher Scott Field. **Seating Capacity:** 4,000. **Outfield Dimension: LF**—330, **CF**—405, **RF**—330.

AIR FORCE FALCONS.

Conference: Mountain West. **Mailing Address:** 2169 Field House Dr., U.S. Air Force Academy, CO 80840. **Website:** www.goairforcefalcons.com. **Head Coach:** Mike Kazlausky (Maj. Retired). **Telephone:** (719) 333-0835. **Baseball SID:** Dan Whitaker. **Telephone:** (719) 333-3950. **Assistant Coaches:** Ryan Forrest, Jimmy Roesinger. **Telephone:** (719) 333-7539. **Home Field:** Falcon Field. **Seating Capacity:** 1,000. **Outfield Dimension: LF**—349, **CF**—400, **RF**—315.

AKRON ZIPS.

Conference: Mid-American. **Mailing Address:** 302 E. Buchtel Ave., Akron, Ohio 44325. **Website:** www.gozips.com. **Head Coach:** Chris Sabo. **Telephone:** N/A. **Baseball SID:** Cathy Bongiovi. **Telephone:** (330) 972-6106. **Assistant Coaches:** *Jordon Banfield, Dan McKinney. **Home Field:** Skeeles Field. **Seating Capacity:** TBD. **Outfield Dimension: LF**—320, **CF**—390, **RF**—310.

ALABAMA CRIMSON TIDE.

Conference: Southeastern. **Mailing Address:** 323 Bryant Drive, Tuscaloosa, AL 35487. **Website:** www.RollTide.com. **Head Coach:** Brad Bohannon. **Telephone:** (205) 348-4029. **Baseball SID:** Alex Thompson. **Telephone:** (205) 348-6084. **Assistant Coaches:** Jason Jackson, *Jerry Zulli. **Telephone:** (205) 348-4029. **Home Field:** Sewell-Thomas Stadium. **Seating Capacity:** 5,867+. **Outfield Dimension: LF**—320, **CF**—390, **RF**—320.

ALABAMA A&M BULLDOGS.

Conference: Southwestern Athletic. **Mailing Address:** 4900 Meridian St., North Normal, **AL 35762 Website:** www.aamusports.com. **Head Coach:** Manny Lora. **Telephone:** (256) 372-7213. **Baseball SID:** Justin Graves. **Telephone:** (256) 372-4005. **Assistant Coaches:** Trennis Grant, Austin Turner. **Telephone:** (256) 372-7213. **Home Field:** Bulldog Baseball Field. **Seating Capacity:** 500. **Outfield Dimension: LF**—330, **CF**—402, **RF**—318.

ALABAMA STATE .

Conference: Southwestern Athletic. **Mailing Address:** 915 S. Jackson St., Montgomery, AL 36106. **Website:** www.bamastatesports.com. **Head Coach:** Jose Vazquez. **Telephone:** (334) 229-5600. **Baseball SID:** Travis Jarome.

Telephone: (334) 229-2601. **Assistant Coaches:** Drew Clark, Matt Crane. **Telephone:** (334) 229-5607. **Home Field:** Wheeler-Watkins Baseball Complex. **Seating Capacity:** 500. **Outfield Dimension: LF**—330, **CF**—400, **RF**—330.

ALABAMA-BIRMINGHAM BLAZERS.

Conference: Conference USA. **Mailing Address:** 1720 2nd Ave. S. Birmingham, AL 35294. **Website:** uabsports.com. **Head Coach:** Brian Shoop. **Telephone:** (205) 934-5181. **Baseball SID:** T.J. Stricklin. **Telephone:** (205) 934-0722. **Assistant Coaches:** Adam Revelette, *Perry Roth. **Telephone:** (205) 934-5181. **Home Field:** JD Young Memorial Field. **Seating Capacity:** 1000. **Outfield Dimension: LF**—330, **CF**—400, **RF**—330.

ALBANY GREAT DANES.

Conference: America East. **Mailing Address:** 1400 Washington Ave. Albany, NY 12222. **Website:** ualbanysports.com. **Head Coach:** Jon Mueller. **Telephone:** (518) 442-3014. **Baseball SID:** Jessica Burg. **Assistant Coaches:** Dave Ames, Jeff Kaier. **Telephone:** (518) 442-3337. **Home Field:** Varsity Field. **Outfield Dimension: LF**—330, **CF**—400, **RF**—330.

ALCORN STATE BRAVES.

Conference: Southwestern Athletic. **Mailing Address:** 1000 ASU Dr. #510 Lorman, MS 39096. **Website:** www.alcornsports.com. **Head Coach:** Bretton Richardson. **Telephone:** (601) 877-4090. **Baseball SID:** Brian Baublitz, Jr. **Telephone:** (601) 877-6501. **Assistant Coaches:** Ryan Fuentes, Kirt Cormier. **Telephone:** (601) 877-6500. **Home Field:** Foster Baseball Field at McGowan Stadium.

APPALACHIAN STATE MOUNTAINEERS.

Conference: Sun Belt. **Mailing Address:** 225 Broyhill Inn Ln. Boone, NC 28607. **Website:** www.appstatesports.com. **Head Coach:** Kermit Smith. **Telephone:** (828) 262-6097. **Baseball SID:** Tyler Hotz. **Telephone:** (865) 803-8022. **Assistant Coaches:** Justin Aspegren, Britt Johnson. **Telephone:** (828) 262-8664. **Home Field:** Beaver Field at Jim and Bettie Smith Stadium. **Seating Capacity:** 1,100. **Outfield Dimension: LF**—335, **CF**—405, **RF**—330.

ARIZONA WILDCATS.

Conference: Pac-12. **Mailing Address:** 1 National Championship Drive, Tucson, AZ, 85721-0096. **Website:** ArizonaWildcats.com. **Head Coach:** Jay Johnson. **Telephone:** (520) 621-4102. **Baseball SID:** Brett Gleason. **Telephone:** (520) 621-0917. **Assistant Coaches:** Dave Lawn, Nate Yeskie. **Telephone:** (520) 626-8859. **Home Field:** Hi Corbett Field. **Seating Capacity:** 9,500. **Outfield Dimension: LF**—366, **CF**—395, **RF**—349. **Press Box Telephone:** (520) 621-4440.

ARIZONA STATE SUN DEVILS.

Conference: Pac-12. **Mailing Address:** 5999 E. Van Buren Phoenix AZ 85008. **Website:** Thesundevils.com. **Head Coach:** Tracy Smith. **Telephone:** N/A. **Baseball SID:** Jeremy Hawkes. **Telephone:** N/A. **Fax:** N/A. **Assistant Coaches:** *Ben Greenspan, Jason Kelly. **Telephone:** (480) 965-3482. **Home Field:** Phoenix Municipal Stadium. **Seating Capacity:** 8,775. **Outfield Dimension: LF**—345, **CF**—410, **RF**—345.

ARKANSAS RAZORBACKS.

Conference: Southeastern. **Mailing Address:** 1255 S. Razorback Rd. Fayetteville, AR 72701. **Website:** arkansasrazorbacks.com. **Head Coach:** Dave Van Horn. **Telephone:** (479) 575-3655. **Baseball SID:** Michael Minshew. **Telephone:** (479) 575-4904. **Assistant Coaches:** Matt Hobbs, *Nate Thompson. **Telephone:** (479) 575-8626. **Home Field:** Baum-Walker Stadium. **Seating Capacity:** 10,737. **Outfield Dimension:** LF—320, CF—400, RF—320.

ARKANSAS STATE RED WOLVES.

Conference: Sun Belt. **Mailing Address:** P.O. Box 1000, State University, AR, 72467. **Website:** www.astatered-wolves.com. **Head Coach:** Tommy Raffo. **Telephone:** (870) 972-2700. **Baseball SID:** Miya Garrett. **Telephone:** (870) 972-2541. **Assistant Coaches:** *Rick Guarno, Rowdy Hardy. **Telephone:** (870) 972-4337. **Home Field:** Kell Field at Tomlinson Stadium. **Seating Capacity:** 1,500. **Outfield Dimension:** LF—330, CF—400, RF—330.

ARKANSAS-LITTLE ROCK TROJANS.

Conference: Sun Belt. **Mailing Address:** 2801 South University Ave. Little Rock, AR 72204. **Website:** www. lrtrojans.com. **Head Coach:** Chris Curry. **Telephone:** (501) 509-2452. **Baseball SID:** Rand Champion. **Telephone:** (501) 569-3167. **Assistant Coaches:** *Noah Sanders, R.D Spiehs. **Telephone:** (501) 351-5264. **Home Field:** Gary Hogan Field. **Seating Capacity:** 2000. **Outfield Dimension:** LF—330, CF—390, RF—305.

ARKANSAS-PINE BLUFF GOLDEN LIONS.

Conference: Southwestern Athletic. **Mailing Address:** 1200 N. University Dr. Pine Bluff, AR 71601. **Website:** www.uapblionsroar.com. **Head Coach:** Carlos James. **Telephone:** (870) 575-8995. **Baseball SID:** Duane Lewis. **Telephone:** (870) 575-7949. **Assistant Coaches:** Roger Mallison, Terrell Brown. **Telephone:** (870) 575-8995. **Home Field:** Torii Hunter Baseball Complex. **Seating Capacity:** 1,500. **Outfield Dimension:** LF—330, CF—400, RF—330.

ARMY BLACK KNIGHTS.

Conference: Patriot League. **Mailing Address:** 639 Howard Rd. West Point, NY 10996. **Website:** www. goarmywestpoint.com. **Head Coach:** Jim Foster. **Telephone:** (845) 938-4938. **Baseball SID:** Nick Lovera. **Telephone:** (845) 938-2351. **Assistant Coaches:** Jamie Pinzino, Logan Parker. **Telephone:** (845) 938-5877. **Home Field:** Johnston Stadium at Doubleday Field. **Seating Capacity:** 880. **Outfield Dimension:** LF—327, CF—400, RF—327.

AUBURN TIGERS.

Conference: Southeastern. **Mailing Address:** 351 South Donahue Drive Auburn, Ala. 36830. **Website:** auburntigers.com. **Head Coach:** Butch Thompson. **Telephone:** (334) 844-4990. **Baseball SID:** George Nunnelley. **Telephone:** (502) 609-9982. **Assistant Coaches:** Gabe Gross, *Karl Nonemaker. **Telephone:** (334) 844-9760. **Home Field:** Plainsman Park. **Seating Capacity:** 4096. **Outfield Dimension:** LF—315, CF—385, RF—331.

AUSTIN PEAY STATE GOVERNORS.

Conference: Ohio Valley. **Mailing Address:** 601 College St. Clarksville, TN 37044. **Website:** www.lets-gopeay.com. **Head Coach:** Travis Janssen. **Telephone:**

(931) 221-6266. **Baseball SID:** Cody Bush. **Telephone:** (931) 221-7561. **Assistant Coaches:** David Weber, Elliott McCummings. **Telephone:** (931) 221-7902. **Home Field:** Raymond C. Hand Park. **Seating Capacity:** 1,000. **Outfield Dimension:** LF—319, CF—392, RF—327.

BALL STATE CARDINALS.

Conference: Mid-American. **Mailing Address:** 2000 W. University Ave. Muncie, IN 47306. **Website:** www.ballstatesports.com. **Head Coach:** Rich Maloney. **Telephone:** (765) 285-1425. **Baseball SID:** . **Telephone:** . **Fax:** . **Assistant Coaches:** Blake Beemer, Larry Scully. **Telephone:** (765) 285-8226. **Home Field:** Ball Diamond at First Merchants Baseball Complex. **Seating Capacity:** 1,500. **Outfield Dimension:** LF—325, CF—394, RF—325.

BAYLOR BEARS.

Conference: Big 12. **Mailing Address:** 1612 S. University Parks Dr., Waco, TX 76706. **Website:** www.bay-lorbears.com. **Head Coach:** Steve Rodriguez. **Telephone:** (254) 710-3029. **Baseball SID:** Rachel Caton. **Telephone:** (254) 710-3784. **Assistant Coaches:** Jon Strauss, *Mike Taylor. **Telephone:** (254) 710-3044. **Home Field:** Baylor Ballpark. **Seating Capacity:** 5000. **Outfield Dimension:** LF—330, CF—400, RF—330. **Press Box Telephone:** (254) 754-5546.

BELMONT BRUINS.

Conference: Ohio Valley. **Mailing Address:** 1900 Belmont Blvd. Nashville, TN 37212-3757. **Website:** www.belmontbruins.com. **Head Coach:** Dave Jarvis. **Telephone:** (615) 460-6166. **Baseball SID:** Grant Cohen. **Telephone:** (615) 460-8023. **Assistant Coaches:** Caleb Longshore, *Aaron Smith. **Telephone:** (615) 460-5586. **Home Field:** E.S. Rose Park. **Seating Capacity:** 750. **Outfield Dimension:** LF—330, CF—400, RF—330.

BETHUNE-COOKMAN WILDCATS.

Conference: Mid-Eastern. **Mailing Address:** 640 Dr. Mary Mcleod Bethune Blvd. Daytona Beach, FL 32114. **Website:** www.bcuathletics.com. **Head Coach:** Jonathan Hernandez. **Telephone:** (386) 481-2224. **Baseball SID:** Dan Ryan. **Telephone:** (386) 481-2240. **Assistant Coaches:** Keith Zuniga. **Telephone:** (386) 481-2241. **Home Field:** Jackie Robinson Ballpark. **Seating Capacity:** 4200. **Outfield Dimension:** LF—317, CF—400, RF—325.

BINGHAMTON BEARCATS.

Conference: America East. **Mailing Address:** 4400 Vestal Parkway East, Binghamton, NY 13902. **Website:** www. bubearcats.com. **Head Coach:** Tim Sinicki. **Telephone:** (607) 777-2525. **Baseball SID:** John Hartrick. **Telephone:** (607) 777-6800. **Assistant Coaches:** Mike Folli, *Ryan Hurba. **Telephone:** (607) 777-5808. **Home Field:** Bearcat Sports Complex. **Seating Capacity:** 500. **Outfield Dimension:** LF—325, CF—390, RF—325.

BOISE STATE BRONCOS.

Conference: Mountain West. **Mailing Address:** Boise State Athletics, 1910 W. University Drive, Boise ID 83725. **Website:** broncosports.com. **Head Coach:** Gary Van Tol. **Telephone:** (509) 389-6787. **Baseball SID:** Craig Lawson. **Telephone:** (208) 426-1515. **Assistant Coaches:** Brock Huntzinger, *Gary Van. **Telephone:** (239) 410-8002. **Home Field:** Memorial Stadium. **Seating Capacity:** 3452. **Outfield Dimension:** LF—330, CF—400, RF—330. **Press Box Telephone:** (509) 432-9063.

COLLEGE

BOSTON COLLEGE EAGLES.

Conference: ACC. **Mailing Address:** 140 Commonwealth Ave., Conte Forum 238, Chestnut Hill, MA 02467. **Website:** BCEagles.com. **Head Coach:** Mike Gambino. **Telephone:** . **Baseball SID:** Brendan Flynn. **Telephone:** . **Fax:** . **Assistant Coaches:** *Greg Sullivan, Alex Trezza. **Telephone:** . **Home Field:** Harrington Athletics Village. **Seating Capacity:** 2500. **Outfield Dimension: LF**—330, **CF**—403, **RF**—330. **Press Box Telephone:** .

BOWLING GREEN STATE EAGLES.

Conference: Mid-American. **Mailing Address:** 1610 Stadium Dr. Bowling Green, OH 43403. **Website:** www.bgsufalcons.com. **Head Coach:** Danny Schmitz. **Telephone:** (419) 372-7065. **Baseball SID:** James Nahikian. **Telephone:** (419) 372-7105. **Assistant Coaches:** Ryan Shay, Kyle Hallock. **Telephone:** (419) 372-7641. **Home Field:** Steller Field at Gary Haas Stadium. **Seating Capacity:** 1,100. **Outfield Dimension: LF**—340, **CF**—400, **RF**—340.

BRADLEY BRAVES.

Conference: Missouri Valley. **Mailing Address:** 1501 W. Bradley Ave. Peoria, IL 61625. **Website:** www.bradley-braves.com. **Head Coach:** Elvis Dominguez. **Telephone:** (309) 677-2684. **Baseball SID:** Bobby Parker. **Telephone:** (309) 677-2624. **Assistant Coaches:** Kyle Trewyn, Andrew Werner. **Telephone:** (309) 677-4583. **Home Field:** Dozer Park. **Seating Capacity:** 7,500. **Outfield Dimension: LF**—310, **CF**—400, **RF**—310.

BRIGHAM YOUNG COUGARS.

Conference: West Coast. **Mailing Address:** 111 MLRP Provo, UT 84602. **Website:** byucougars.com. **Head Coach:** Mike Littlewood. **Telephone:** (801) 422-5049. **Baseball SID:** Jordan Christiansen. **Telephone:** (801) 422-9769. **Assistant Coaches:** *Brent Haring, Trent Pratt. **Telephone:** (801) 422-5064. **Home Field:** Larry H. Miller Field. **Seating Capacity:** 2500. **Outfield Dimension: LF**—330, **CF**—410, **RF**—330.

BROWN BEARS.

Conference: Ivy League. **Mailing Address:** Providence, RI 02912. **Website:** https://brownbears.com. **Head Coach:** Grant Achilles. **Telephone:** (401) 863-3090. **Baseball SID:** Eric Peterson. **Telephone:** (401) 863-7014. **Assistant Coaches:** Jonathan Grosse, *Mike McCormack. **Telephone:** (401) 863-1310. **Home Field:** Attanasio Family Field at Murray Stadium. **Seating Capacity:** 1000. **Outfield Dimension: LF**—343, **CF**—391, **RF**—341.

BRYANT BULLDOGS.

Conference: Northeast. **Mailing Address:** 1150 Douglas Pike Smithfield, RI 02917. **Website:** www.bryantbulldogs.com. **Head Coach:** Ryan Klosterman. **Telephone:** (401) 232-6397. **Baseball SID:** Tristan Hobbes. **Telephone:** (401) 232-6558. **Assistant Coaches:** Ted Hurvul, *Eric Pelletier. **Telephone:** (401) 232-6967. **Home Field:** Conaty Park. **Seating Capacity:** 500. **Outfield Dimension: LF**—330, **CF**—400, **RF**—330. **Press Box Telephone:** (315) 292-8361.

BUCKNELL BISON.

Conference: Patriot League. **Mailing Address:** One Dent Dr. Lewisburg, PA 17837. **Website:** www.bucknellbi-son.com. **Head Coach:** Scott Heather. **Telephone:** (570) 577-3593. **Baseball SID:** Cole Cloonan. **Telephone:** (570) 577-1227. **Assistant Coaches:** Jason Neitz, Chris O'Neill. **Telephone:** (570) 577-1059. **Home Field:** Depew Field. **Seating Capacity:** 1,000. **Outfield Dimension: LF**—330, **CF**—400, **RF**—330.

BUTLER BULLDOGS.

Conference: Big East. **Mailing Address:** 555 W 52nd St., Indianapolis, IN 46208. **Website:** https://butlersports.com. **Head Coach:** David Schrage. **Telephone:** (317) 940-9721. **Baseball SID:** Kit Stetzel. **Telephone:** (317) 940-9994. **Assistant Coaches:** Matt Kennedy, *Ben Norton. **Telephone:** (317) 940-6536. **Home Field:** Bulldog Park. **Seating Capacity:** 500. **Outfield Dimension: LF**—330, **CF**—400, **RF**—325.

CAL BAPTIST LANCERS.

Conference: Western Athletic. **Mailing Address:** 8432 Magnolia Avenue, Riverside, Calif., 92503. **Website:** www.cbulancers.com. **Head Coach:** Gary Adcock. **Telephone:** (951) 343-4382. **Baseball SID:** Andrew Shortall. **Telephone:** (951) 343-4779. **Assistant Coaches:** *Andrew Brasington, Jesse Zepeda. **Telephone:** (951) 552-8477. **Home Field:** Totman Stadium. **Seating Capacity:** 800.

CAL POLY MUSTANGS.

Conference: Big West. **Mailing Address:** 1 Grand Avenue, San Luis Obispo, CA 93407. **Website:** www.gopoly.com. **Head Coach:** Larry Lee. **Telephone:** (805) 756-6367. **Baseball SID:** Eric Burdick. **Telephone:** (805) 756-6550. **Assistant Coaches:** Jake Silverman, *Teddy Warrecker. **Telephone:** (805) 756-1201. **Home Field:** Baggett Stadium. **Seating Capacity:** 3138. **Outfield Dimension: LF**—335, **CF**—385, **RF**—405. **Press Box Telephone:** (805) 756-7456.

CAL STATE BAKERSFIELD ROADRUNNERS.

Conference: Western Athletic. **Mailing Address:** 9001 Stockdale Hwy. 8 GYM Bakersfield, CA 93311. **Website:** www.gorunners.com. **Head Coach:** Jeremy Beard. **Telephone:** (661) 654-2678. **Baseball SID:** Dan Sperl. **Telephone:** (661) 654-6071. **Assistant Coaches:** Ryan Cisterna, Mike Kinkade. **Telephone:** (661) 654-2678. **Home Field:** Hardt Field. **Seating Capacity:** 750. **Outfield Dimension: LF**—325, **CF**—390, **RF**—325.

CAL STATE FULLERTON TITANS.

Conference: Big West. **Mailing Address:** 800 N. State College Blvd. Fullerton, CA 92831. **Website:** fullertontitans.com. **Head Coach:** Rick Vanderhook. **Telephone:** (657) 278-3789. **Baseball SID:** Bryant Freese. **Telephone:** (657) 278-7083. **Assistant Coaches:** *Sergio Brown, Dan Ricabal. **Telephone:** (657) 278-2492. **Home Field:** Goodwin Field. **Seating Capacity:** 3500. **Outfield Dimension: LF**—330, **CF**—400, **RF**—330.

CAL STATE NORTHRIDGE MATADORS.

Conference: Big West. **Mailing Address:** 18111 Nordhoff St., Northridge, CA, 91330. **Website:** www.gomatadors.com. **Head Coach:** Dave Serrano. **Telephone:** . **Baseball SID:** Nick Bocanegra. **Telephone:** (818) 677-7188. **Assistant Coaches:** *Eddie Cornejo, Neil Walton. **Telephone:** N/A. **Home Field:** Matador Field. **Seating Capacity:** 1000. **Outfield Dimension: LF**—325, **CF**—390, **RF**—325.

CALIFORNIA GOLDEN BEARS.

Conference: Pac-12. **Mailing Address:** Haas Pavilion #4422 Berkeley, CA 94720-4422. **Website:** www.calbears.com. **Head Coach:** Michael Neu. **Telephone:** (510) 642-9026. **Baseball SID:** Gerrit Van Genderen. **Telephone:** (510) 642-5363. **Assistant Coaches:** *Noah Jackson, Damon Lessler. **Telephone:** (510) 643-6006. **Home Field:** Evans Diamond. **Seating Capacity:** 2500. **Outfield Dimension:** LF—320, CF—395, RF—320. **Press Box Telephone:** (510) 697-7235.

CAMPBELL FIGHTING CAMELS.

Conference: Big South. **Mailing Address:** 78 Dr. McKoy Rd. Buies Creek, NC 27506. **Website:** www.gocamels.com. **Head Coach:** Justin Haire. **Telephone:** (910) 893-1338. **Baseball SID:** Eric Ortiz. **Telephone:** (910) 893-1529. **Assistant Coaches:** Tyler Robinson, Tyler Shewmaker. **Telephone:** (910) 814-5510. **Home Field:** Jim Perry Stadium. **Seating Capacity:** 700. **Outfield Dimension:** LF—337, CF—395, RF—328.

CANISIUS GOLDEN GRIFFINS.

Conference: Metro Atlantic. **Mailing Address:** 2001 Main Street, Buffalo, N.Y. 14208. **Website:** gogriffs.com. **Head Coach:** Matt Mazurek. **Telephone:** (716) 888-8479. **Baseball SID:** Marshal Filipowicz. **Telephone:** (716) 888-8266. **Assistant Coaches:** *Brandon Bielecki, Blake Urquhart. **Telephone:** (716) 888-8478. **Home Field:** Demske Sports Complex. **Seating Capacity:** 1000. **Outfield Dimension:** LF—325, CF—365, RF—335.

CENTRAL ARKANSAS BEARS.

Conference: Southland. **Mailing Address:** 201 Donaghey Ave. Conway, AR 72035. **Website:** www.ucasports.com. **Head Coach:** Allen Gum. **Telephone:** (501) 499-1707. **Baseball SID:** Steve East. **Telephone:** (501) 450-5743. **Assistant Coaches:** Nick Harlan, Justin Cunningham. **Telephone:** (402) 366-5948. **Home Field:** Bear Stadium. **Seating Capacity:** 1,500. **Outfield Dimension:** LF—330, CF—400, RF—330.

CENTRAL CONNECTICUT STATE CCSU / BLUE DEVILS.

Conference: Northeast. **Mailing Address:** 1615 Stanley Street—New Britain, CT 06050. **Website:** www.ccsubluedevils.com. **Head Coach:** Charlie Hickey. **Telephone:** (860) 832-3074. **Baseball SID:** Jeff Mead. **Telephone:** (860) 832-3057. **Assistant Coaches:** Rob Bono, *Pat Hall. **Telephone:** (860) 832-3579. **Home Field:** CCSU Baseball Field. **Seating Capacity:** 500. **Outfield Dimension:** LF—330, CF—400, RF—310.

CENTRAL FLORIDA KNIGHTS.

Conference: American Athletic. **Mailing Address:** UCF Spectrum Stadium 4465 Knights Victory Way Orlando, FL 32816. **Website:** www.ucfknights.com. **Head Coach:** Greg Lovelady. **Telephone:** . **Baseball SID:** Collin Yeager. **Telephone:** (470) 823-5395. **Assistant Coaches:** Nick Otte, *Ted Tom. **Telephone:** (407) 823-5265. **Home Field:** John Euliano Park. **Seating Capacity:** 3841. **Outfield Dimension:** LF—320, CF—390, RF—320.

CENTRAL MICHIGAN CHIPPEWAS.

Conference: Mid-American. **Mailing Address:** 1200 S Franklin St., Mt. Pleasant, MI 48859. **Website:** www.cmuchippewas.com. **Head Coach:** Jordan Bischel. **Telephone:** (989) 774-4392. **Baseball SID:** Cullen

Maksimowski. **Telephone:** (989) 774-3277. **Assistant Coaches:** Tony Jandron, *Kyle Schroeder. **Telephone:** (989) 774-1484. **Home Field:** Theunissen Stadium. **Seating Capacity:** 2000. **Outfield Dimension:** LF—335, CF—405, RF—335.

CHARLESTON SOUTHERN BUCCANEERS.

Conference: Big South. **Mailing Address:** 9200 University Blvd, Charleston, S.C., 29406. **Website:** www.csusports.com. **Head Coach:** George Schaefer. **Telephone:** (843) 863-7832. **Baseball SID:** Harrison Huntley. **Telephone:** (843) 863-7289. **Assistant Coaches:** Nick Chinners, *George Schaefer. **Telephone:** N/A. **Home Field:** Nielsen Field at CSU Ballpark. **Seating Capacity:** 1000. **Outfield Dimension:** LF—330, CF—400, RF—330. **Press Box Telephone:** (919) 802-0238.

CHARLOTTE 49ERS.

Conference: Conference USA. **Mailing Address:** 9201 University City Blvd. | Charlotte, NC 28223. **Website:** www.charlotte49ers.com. **Head Coach:** Robert Woodard. **Telephone:** (704) 687-1054. **Baseball SID:** Sean Fox. **Telephone:** 704-6871023. **Assistant Coaches:** *Toby Bicknell, Bo Robinson. **Telephone:** (704) 687-0728. **Home Field:** Robert & Mariam Hayes Stadium. **Seating Capacity:** 2500. **Outfield Dimension:** LF—335, CF—390, RF—315.

CHICAGO STATE COUGARS.

Conference: Western Athletic. **Mailing Address:** 9501 S. King Dr. Chicago, IL 60628. **Website:** gocsucougars.com. **Head Coach:** Steve Joslyn. **Telephone:** (773) 995-3637. **Baseball SID:** Andrea Wheeler. **Assistant Coaches:** Dave Harden. **Telephone:** (773) 995-3740. **Home Field:** Cougar Stadium. **Seating Capacity:** 200. **Outfield Dimension:** LF—330, CF—400, RF—330.

CINCINNATI BEARCATS.

Conference: American Athletic. **Mailing Address:** 2751 O'Varsity Way Cincinnati, OH 45221. **Website:** www.gobearcats.com. **Head Coach:** Scott Googins. **Telephone:** (513) 556-0566. **Baseball SID:** Mollie Radzinski. **Telephone:** (513) 556-0667. **Assistant Coaches:** J.D. Heilmann, Kyle Sprague. **Telephone:** (513) 556-0565. **Home Field:** Marge Schott Stadium. **Seating Capacity:** 3,085. **Outfield Dimension:** LF—325, CF—400, RF—325.

CITADEL BULLDOGS.

Conference: Southern. **Mailing Address:** 171 Moultrie St. Charleston, SC 29409. **Website:** www.citadelsports.com. **Head Coach:** Tony Skole. **Baseball SID:** John Brush. **Telephone:** (843) 953-6795. **Assistant Coaches:** Blake Cooper, Zach Lucas. **Home Field:** Joseph P. Riley Park. **Seating Capacity:** 6,000. **Outfield Dimension:** LF—337, CF—398, RF—337.

CLEMSON TIGERS.

Conference: ACC. **Mailing Address:** 100 Perimeter Road; Clemson, SC 29633. **Website:** clemsontigers.com. **Head Coach:** Monte Lee. **Telephone:** (864) 656-1947. **Baseball SID:** Brian Hennessy. **Telephone:** (864) 656-1921. **Assistant Coaches:** *Bradley LeCroy, Andrew See. **Telephone:** (864) 656-1948. **Home Field:** Doug Kingsmore Stadium. **Seating Capacity:** 6272. **Outfield Dimension:** LF—310, CF—390, RF—320.

COASTAL CAROLINA CHANTICLEERS.

Conference: Sun Belt. **Mailing Address:** 132 Chanticleer Drive West. **Website:** www.goccusports.com. **Head Coach:** Gary Gilmore. **Telephone:** (843) 349-2524. **Baseball SID:** Kevin Davis. **Telephone:** (843) 349-2822. **Assistant Coaches:** *Kevin Schnall, Drew Thomas. **Telephone:** (843) 349-2849. **Home Field:** Springs Brooks Stadium. **Seating Capacity:** 5400. **Outfield Dimension:** LF—320, CF—365, RF—320. **Press Box Telephone:** (704) 974-9095.

COLLEGE OF CHARLESTON COUGARS.

Conference: Colonial. **Mailing Address:** 301 Meeting St. Charleston, SC 29401. **Website:** www.cofcsports.com. **Head Coach:** Chad Holbrook. **Telephone:** (843) 953-5961. **Baseball SID:** Whitney Noble. **Telephone:** (843) 953-3683. **Assistant Coaches:** Kevin Nichols, Will Dorton. **Telephone:** (843) 953-7013. **Home Field:** The Ballpark at Patriots Point. **Seating Capacity:** 2,000. **Outfield Dimension:** LF—300, CF—400, RF—330.

COLUMBIA LIONS.

Conference: Ivy League. **Mailing Address:** 505 West 218th Street New York, N.Y. 10034. **Website:** gocolumbialions.com. **Head Coach:** Brett Boretti. **Telephone:** (212) 854-8448. **Baseball SID:** Michael Kowalsky. **Telephone:** (212) 854-7064. **Assistant Coaches:** Erik Supplee, *Dan Tischler. **Telephone:** (212) 854-0105. **Home Field:** Robertson Field at Satow Stadium.

CONNECTICUT HUSKIES.

Conference: American Athletic. **Mailing Address:** 2111 Hillside Rd Storrs, CT 06268. **Website:** www.uconnhuskies.com. **Head Coach:** Jim Penders. **Telephone:** (860) 208-9140. **Baseball SID:** Chris Jones. **Telephone:** (860) 486-4707. **Assistant Coaches:** Jeffrey Hourigan, *Joshua MacDonald. **Telephone:** . **Home Field:** Elliott Ballpark. **Seating Capacity:** . **Outfield Dimension:** LF—330, CF—400, RF—330.

COPPIN STATE EAGLES.

Conference: Mid-Eastern. **Mailing Address:** 2500 West North Avenue Baltimore, MD 21216. **Website:** coppinstatesports.com. **Head Coach:** Sherman Reed, Sr.. **Telephone:** (410) 951-3723. **Baseball SID:** Steve Kramer. **Telephone:** (410) 951-3729. **Assistant Coaches:** *Matthew Greely, Lyndon Watkins. **Telephone:** (410) 951-6941. **Home Field:** Joe Cannon. **Seating Capacity:** 1500. **Outfield Dimension:** LF—325, CF—425, RF—325. **Press Box Telephone:** (410) 222-6652.

CORNELL BIG RED.

Conference: Ivy League. **Mailing Address:** 512 Campus Rd. Ithaca, NY 14853. **Website:** www.cornellbigred.com. **Head Coach:** Dan Pepicelli. **Baseball SID:** Brandon Thomas. **Telephone:** (607) 255-5627. **Assistant Coaches:** Tom Ford, Frank Hager. **Telephone:** (607) 255-6604. **Home Field:** Hoy Field. **Seating Capacity:** 500.

CREIGHTON BLUEJAYS.

Conference: Big East. **Mailing Address:** 2500 California Plaza, Omaha, NE 68178. **Website:** gocreighton.edu. **Head Coach:** Ed Servais. **Telephone:** . **Baseball SID:** Glen Sisk. **Telephone:** (402) 280-2433. **Assistant Coaches:** *Connor Gandossy, Eric Wordekemper. **Telephone:** (402) 280-5545. **Home Field:** TD Ameritrade Park Omaha. **Seating Capacity:** 24000. **Outfield Dimension:** LF—335, CF—408, RF—335.

DALLAS BAPTIST PATRIOTS.

Conference: Missouri Valley. **Mailing Address:** 3000 Mountain Creek Pkwy. Dallas, TX 75211. **Website:** dbu-patriots.com. **Head Coach:** Dan Heefner. **Telephone:** . **Baseball SID:** Reagan Ratcliff. **Telephone:** (214) 333-5942. **Assistant Coaches:** Josh Hopper, *Dan Fitzgerald. **Telephone:** (214) 333-6987. **Home Field:** Horner Ballpark. **Seating Capacity:** 2000. **Outfield Dimension:** LF—330, CF—390, RF—330.

DARTMOUTH BIG GREEN.

Conference: Ivy League. **Mailing Address:** 6083 Alumni Gym, Hanover, NH 03755. **Website:** DartmouthSports.com. **Head Coach:** Bob Whalen. **Telephone:** (603) 646-2477. **Baseball SID:** Rick Bender. **Telephone:** (603) 646-1030. **Assistant Coaches:** *Conor Burke, Blake McFadden. **Telephone:** (603) 646-9775. **Home Field:** Red Rolfe Field at Biondi Park. **Seating Capacity:** 2000. **Outfield Dimension:** LF—324, CF—403, RF—342. **Press Box Telephone:** (603) 646-6937.

DAVIDSON WILDCATS.

Conference: Atlantic 10. **Mailing Address:** 202 Martin Court Dr., Davidson, NC 28035. **Website:** davidsonwildcats.com. **Head Coach:** Rucker Taylor. **Telephone:** (704) 892-2772. **Baseball SID:** Justin Parker. **Telephone:** (704) 894-2931. **Fax:** . **Assistant Coaches:** Parker Bangs, *Ryan Munger. **Telephone:** (704) 894-2002. **Home Field:** Wilson Field. **Seating Capacity:** 1000. **Outfield Dimension:** LF—320, CF—385, RF—330. **Press Box Telephone:** .

DAYTON FLYERS.

Conference: Atlantic 10. **Mailing Address:** University of Dayton, 300 College Park, Dayton, OH 45469. **Website:** www.daytonflyers.com. **Head Coach:** Jayson King. **Telephone:** (603) 381-1279. **Baseball SID:** TBD. **Assistant Coaches:** *Tommy Chase, Travis Ferrick. **Telephone:** (540) 903-4967. **Home Field:** Woerner Field at DP&L Stadium. **Seating Capacity:** 2000. **Outfield Dimension:** LF—330, CF—400, RF—330.

DELAWARE BLUE HENS.

Conference: Colonial. **Mailing Address:** 631 S. College Ave, Newark, DE 19716. **Website:** BlueHens.com. **Head Coach:** Jim Sherman. **Telephone:** (302) 831-8596. **Baseball SID:** Erik Oakley. **Telephone:** (302) 530-0537. **Assistant Coaches:** Dan Hammer, *Juan Pimental. **Telephone:** (302) 831-2723. **Home Field:** Bob Hannah Stadium. **Seating Capacity:** 1500. **Outfield Dimension:** LF—320, CF—400, RF—330.

DELAWARE STATE HORNETS.

Conference: Mid-Eastern. **Mailing Address:** 1200 N. DuPont Highway Dover, DE 19901. **Website:** www.dsuhornets.com. **Head Coach:** J.P. Blandin. **Telephone:** (302) 857-6035. **Baseball SID:** . **Telephone:** . **Fax:** . **Assistant Coaches:** Geoff Kimmel, Matt Domian. **Telephone:** (302) 857-7809. **Home Field:** Soldier Field. **Seating Capacity:** 500. **Outfield Dimension:** LF—320, CF—380, RF—320.

DUKE BLUE DEVILS.

Con-ference: Atlantic Coast. **Mailing Address:** 110 Whitford Drive, Box 90555 Durham, N.C. 27708. **Website:** www.goduke.com. **Head Coach:** Chris Pollard. **Telephone:** (919) 668-0255. **Baseball SID:** Josh Foster.

Telephone: (919) 684-2668. **Assistant Coaches:** Josh Jordan, Dusty Blake. **Telephone:** (919) 698-0932. **Home Field:** Durham Bulls Athletic Park. **Seating Capacity:** 10,000. **Outfield Dimension:** LF—305, CF—400, RF—325.

EAST CAROLINA PIRATES.

Conference: American Athletic. **Mailing Address:** 102 Clark-LeClair Stadium Greenville, NC 27858. **Website:** www.ecupirates.com. **Head Coach:** Cliff Godwin. **Telephone:** (252) 737-1985. **Baseball SID:** Malcolm Gray. **Telephone:** (252) 737-4523. **Assistant Coaches:** Jason Dietrich, *Jeff Palumbo. **Telephone:** (252) 737-1467. **Home Field:** Lewis Field at Clark-LeClair Stadium. **Seating Capacity:** 5600. **Outfield Dimension:** LF—320, CF—390, RF—320.

EAST TENNESSEE STATE BUCCANEERS.

Conference: Southern. **Mailing Address:** 1276 Gilbreath Dr, Johnson City, TN 37614. **Website:** ETSUBucs.com. **Head Coach:** Joe Pennucci. **Telephone:** (423) 439-4496. **Baseball SID:** David Czarlinsky. **Telephone:** (423) 439-8212. **Assistant Coaches:** Ross Oeder. **Telephone:** (423) 439-4485. **Home Field:** Thomas Stadium. **Seating Capacity:** 1000. **Outfield Dimension:** LF—330, CF—400, RF—330.

EASTERN ILLINOIS PANTHERS.

Conference: Ohio Valley. **Mailing Address:** 600 Lincoln Ave. Charleston, IL 61920. **Website:** www.eiupanthers.com. **Head Coach:** Jason Anderson. **Telephone:** (217) 581-6014. **Baseball SID:** Rich Moser. **Telephone:** (217) 581-7480. **Assistant Coaches:** Ryan Cooper, Tim Brown. **Telephone:** (217) 581-6014. **Home Field:** Coaches Stadium. **Seating Capacity:** 500. **Outfield Dimension:** LF—340, CF—390, RF—340.

EASTERN KENTUCKY COLONELS.

Conference: Ohio Valley. **Mailing Address:** 521 Lancaster Ave., 115 Alumni Coliseum, Richmond, KY 40475. **Website:** ekusports.com. **Head Coach:** Edwin Thompson. **Telephone:** (859) 622-2128. **Baseball SID:** Kevin Britton. **Telephone:** (859) 622-2006. **Assistant Coaches:** Shaun Cole, *Julius McDougal. **Telephone:** (859) 622-4996. **Home Field:** Turkey Hughes Field at Earle Combs Stadium. **Seating Capacity:** 1000. **Outfield Dimension:** LF—340, CF—410, RF—330. **Press Box Telephone:** (859) 358-8359.

EASTERN MICHIGAN EAGLES.

Conference: Mid-American. **Mailing Address:** 799 N Hewitt Rd Ypsilanti, MI 48197. **Website:** emueagles.com. **Head Coach:** Eric Roof. **Telephone:** (734) 487-1985. **Baseball SID:** Alex Jewell. **Telephone:** (734) 487-0317. **Assistant Coaches:** *A.J. Achter, Jonathan Roof. **Telephone:** (734) 487-0315. **Home Field:** Oestrike Stadium. **Seating Capacity:** 1,200. **Outfield Dimension:** LF—325, CF—390, RF—325.

ELON PHOENIX.

Conference: Colonial. **Mailing Address:** Bank of America Dr, Elon, NC 27244. **Website:** www.elonphoenix.com. **Head Coach:** Mike Kennedy. **Telephone:** (336) 278-6741. **Baseball SID:** Pierce Yarberry. **Telephone:** (336) 278-6712. **Assistant Coaches:** *Robbie Huffstetler, Vin Redmond. **Telephone:** (336) 278-6742. **Home Field:** Latham Park. **Seating Capacity:** 2000. **Outfield**

Dimension: LF—325, CF—385, RF—325.

EVANSVILLE PURPLE ACES.

Conference: Missouri Valley. **Mailing Address:** 1800 Lincoln Ave. Evansville, IN 47722. **Website:** www.gopurpleaces.com. **Head Coach:** Wes Carroll. **Telephone:** (812) 488-2059. **Baseball SID:** Michael Robertson. **Telephone:** (812) 488-2238. **Fax:** . **Assistant Coaches:** A.J. Gaura, Jake Mahon. **Telephone:** (812) 488-1027. **Home Field:** Braun Stadium. **Seating Capacity:** 1,200. **Outfield Dimension:** LF—330, CF—400, RF—330.

FAIRFIELD STAGS.

Conference: Metro Atlantic. **Mailing Address:** 1076 North Benson Road, Fairfield CT 06824. **Website:** www.fairfieldstags.com. **Head Coach:** Bill Currier. **Telephone:** (203) 254-4000. **Baseball SID:** Ivey Speight. **Telephone:** (203) 254-4000. **Assistant Coaches:** *Brian Fay, Jordan Tabakman. **Telephone:** (203) 254-4000. **Home Field:** Alumni Diamond. **Seating Capacity:** 350. **Outfield Dimension:** LF—330, CF—400, RF—330.

FAIRLEIGH DICKINSON KNIGHTS.

Conference: Northeast. **Mailing Address:** 1130 River Rd Teaneck, NJ 07666. **Website:** www.fduknights.com. **Head Coach:** Rob DiToma. **Telephone:** (201) 692-2245. **Baseball SID:** Bryan Jackson. **Telephone:** (201) 692-2149. **Assistant Coaches:** *Steve Adkins, Ethan Newton. **Telephone:** (201) 692-2245. **Home Field:** Naimoli Family Baseball Complex. **Seating Capacity:** 1500. **Outfield Dimension:** LF—330, CF—365, RF—305.

FLORIDA FLORIDA GATORS.

Conference: Southeastern. **Mailing Address:** 2190 Stadium Rd, Gainesville, FL 32611. **Website:** www.floridagators.com. **Head Coach:** Kevin O'Sullivan. **Telephone:** . **Baseball SID:** Zach Dirlam. **Telephone:** . **Fax:** . **Assistant Coaches:** *Craig Bell, Chuck Jeroloman. **Telephone:** (352) 375-4683 ext. 6199. **Home Field:** Alrfred A. McKethan Stadium. **Seating Capacity:** 5500. **Outfield Dimension:** LF—326, CF—400, RF—321.

FLORIDA A&M RATTLERS.

Conference: Mid-Eastern. **Mailing Address:** 1800 Wahnish Way Tallahassee, FL 32307. **Website:** www.famuathletics.com. **Head Coach:** Jamey Shouppe. **Telephone:** (850) 599-3202. **Baseball SID:** Brian Howard. **Telephone:** (850) 599-3849. **Assistant Coaches:** Bryan Henry, *Jamey Shouppe. **Telephone:** (850) 556-0769. **Home Field:** Moore-Kittles Field. **Seating Capacity:** . **Outfield Dimension:** LF—330, CF—410, RF—330.

FLORIDA ATLANTIC OWLS.

Conference: Conference USA. **Mailing Address:** 777 Glades Road, Boca Raton, Florida, 33431. **Website:** www.fausports.com. **Head Coach:** John McCormack. **Telephone:** (561) 297-1055. **Baseball SID:** Jonathan Fraysure. **Telephone:** (561) 430-7148. **Assistant Coaches:** David Kopp, *Greg Mamula. **Telephone:** (561) 297-3956. **Home Field:** FAU Baseball Stadium. **Seating Capacity:** 1718. **Outfield Dimension:** LF—330, CF—400, RF—330. **Press Box Telephone:** (561) 430-7148.

FLORIDA GULF COAST EAGLES.

Conference: Atlantic Sun. **Mailing Address:** 10501 FGCU Blvd S., Fort Myers, FL 33965. **Website:** www.

fgcuathletics.com. **Head Coach:** Dave Tollett. **Telephone:** (239) 590-7051. **Baseball SID:** Meg Ellis. **Telephone:** (239) 590-1327. **Assistant Coaches:** Matt Reid, *Brandon Romans. **Telephone:** (239) 590-7059. **Home Field:** Swanson Stadium. **Seating Capacity:** 1500. **Outfield Dimension:** LF—325, CF—400, RF—325.

FLORIDA INTERNATIONAL FIU PANTHERS.

Conference: Conference USA. **Mailing Address:** 11491 SW 17th St, Miami, FL 33199. **Website:** www.fiusports.com. **Head Coach:** Mervyl Melendez. **Telephone:** (305) 348-3166. **Baseball SID:** . **Telephone:** (305) 348-2084. **Assistant Coaches:** Wille Collazo, *Dax Norris. **Home Field:** FIU Baseball Stadium. **Seating Capacity:** 2000. **Outfield Dimension:** LF—325, CF—400, RF—325.

FLORIDA STATE SEMINOLES.

Conference: Atlantic Coast. **Mailing Address:** 403 Stadium Dr. Tallahassee FL 32304. **Website:** www.seminoles.com. **Head Coach:** Mike Martin Jr. **Telephone:** (850) 644-9129. **Baseball SID:** Steven McCartney. **Telephone:** . **Fax:** . **Assistant Coaches:** Jim Belanger, *Michael Metcalf. **Telephone:** (850) 644-1072. **Home Field:** Mike Martin Field at Dick Howser Stadium. **Seating Capacity:** 6700. **Outfield Dimension:** LF—340, CF—400, RF—320.

FORDHAM RAMS.

Conference: Atlantic 10. **Mailing Address:** 441 E. Fordham Rd. Bronx, NY 10458. **Website:** www.fordhamsports.com. **Head Coach:** Kevin Leighton. **Telephone:** (718) 817-4292. **Baseball SID:** Scott Kwiatkowski. **Telephone:** (718) 817-4219. **Assistant Coaches:** Elliot Glynn, Pat Porter. **Telephone:** (718) 817-4295. **Home Field:** Houlihan Park. **Seating Capacity:** 500. **Outfield Dimension:** LF—339, CF—390, RF—325.

FRESNO STATE BULLDOGS.

Conference: Mountain West. **Mailing Address:** 1620 E Bulldog Lane, Fresno Ca 93740. **Website:** www.gobulldogs.com. **Head Coach:** Mike Batesole. **Telephone:** (559) 278-2178. **Baseball SID:** Travis Blanshan. **Telephone:** (559) 278-4647. **Assistant Coaches:** Greg Gonzalez, *Ryan Overland. **Home Field:** Beiden Field. **Seating Capacity:** 5500. **Outfield Dimension:** LF—330, CF—400, RF—330.

FURMAN PALADINS.

Conference: Southern. **Mailing Address:** 3300 Pointsett Highway Greenville, SC 29613. **Website:** www.furmanpaladins.com. **Head Coach:** Brett Harker. **Telephone:** (864) 294-2243. **Baseball SID:** Hunter Reid. **Telephone:** (864) 294-2061. **Assistant Coaches:** Taylor Harbin, Kaleb Davis. **Telephone:** (864) 449-1162. **Home Field:** Latham Baseball Stadium. **Seating Capacity:** 2,000. **Outfield Dimension:** LF—330, CF—393, RF—330.

GARDNER-WEBB RUNNIN' BULLDOGS.

Conference: Big South. **Mailing Address:** 110 S. Main Street, Boiling Springs, NC 28017. **Website:** www.gwusports.com. **Head Coach:** Jim Chester. **Telephone:** (704) 406-4421. **Baseball SID:** Ryan Bridges. **Telephone:** (704) 406-3523. **Assistant Coaches:** Wiley Jackson, *Conner Scarborough. **Telephone:** (704) 406-3559. **Home Field:** John Henry Moss Baseball Stadium. **Seating Capacity:** 550. **Outfield Dimension:** LF—340, CF—400, RF—320.

GEORGE MASON PATRIOTS.

Conference: Atlantic 10. **Mailing Address:** 4400 University Dr. Fairfax VA, 22030. **Website:** www.gomason.com. **Head Coach:** Bill Brown. **Telephone:** (703) 993-3282. **Baseball SID:** Steve Kolbe. **Telephone:** (703) 993-3268. **Assistant Coaches:** Shawn Camp, *Brian Pugh. **Telephone:** (703) 993-3591. **Home Field:** Raymond H. "Hap" Spuhler Field. **Seating Capacity:** . **Outfield Dimension:** LF—320, CF—400, RF—320.

GEORGE WASHINGTON COLONIALS.

Conference: Atlantic 10. **Mailing Address:** 600 22nd St. NW Washington, DC 20052. **Website:** www.gwsports.com. **Head Coach:** Gregg Ritchie. **Telephone:** (202) 994-7399. **Baseball SID:** Brian Sereno. **Telephone:** (202) 994-6654. **Assistant Coaches:** Rick Oliveri, Chad Marshall. **Telephone:** (202) 994-5933. **Home Field:** Tucker Field at Barcroft Park. **Seating Capacity:** 500. **Outfield Dimension:** LF—330, CF—380, RF—330.

GEORGETOWN HOYAS.

Conference: Big East. **Mailing Address:** 3700 O St. NW Washington, DC 20057. **Website:** www.guhoyas.com. **Head Coach:** Pete Wilk. **Telephone:** (202) 687-2462. **Baseball SID:** Brendan Thomas. **Telephone:** (202) 687-6783. **Assistant Coaches:** Eric Niesen, Phil Disher. **Telephone:** (202) 687-6406. **Home Field:** Shirley Povich Field. **Seating Capacity:** 1,500. **Outfield Dimension:** LF—330, CF—375, RF—330.

GEORGIA BULLDOGS.

Conference: Southeastern. **Mailing Address:** P.O. Box 1472, Athens, Ga .30603. **Website:** georgiadogs.com. **Head Coach:** Scott Stricklin. **Telephone:** (706) 542-7971. **Baseball SID:** Christopher Lakos. **Telephone:** (706) 542-7994. **Assistant Coaches:** *Scott Daeley, Sean Kenny. **Telephone:** (706) 542-7971. **Home Field:** Foley Field. **Seating Capacity:** 2760. **Outfield Dimension:** LF—350, CF—404, RF—314. **Press Box Telephone:** (706) 542-6161.

GEORGIA SOUTHERN EAGLES.

Conference: Sun Belt. **Mailing Address:** Box 8095 Statesboro, GA 30460. **Website:** www.gseagles.com. **Head Coach:** Rodney Hennon. **Telephone:** (912) 478-7360. **Baseball SID:** Chris Little. **Telephone:** (912) 478-0352. **Assistant Coaches:** B.J. Green, Alan Beck. **Telephone:** (912) 478-1331. **Home Field:** J.I. Clements Stadium. **Seating Capacity:** 3,200. **Outfield Dimension:** LF—335, CF—390, RF—329.

GEORGIA STATE PANTHERS.

Conference: Sun Belt. **Mailing Address:** 755 Hank Aaron Drive, Atlanta, GA, 30315. **Website:** www.georgiastatesports.com. **Head Coach:** Brad Stromdahl. **Telephone:** (404) 290-1743. **Baseball SID:** Allison George. **Telephone:** (404) 413-4032. **Assistant Coaches:** *Daniel Furuto, Matt Taylor. **Telephone:** (404) 374-7477. **Home Field:** GSU Baseball Complex. **Seating Capacity:** 1500. **Outfield Dimension:** LF—330, CF—385, RF—335.

GEORGIA TECH YELLOW JACKETS.

Conference: Atlantic Coast. **Mailing Address:** 150 Bobby Dodd Way, Atlanta, GA 30318. **Website:** www.ramblinwreck.com. **Head Coach:** Danny Hall. **Telephone:** (404) 894-5445. **Baseball SID:** Andrew Clausen. **Telephone:** (404) 894-5445. **Assistant Coaches:** Danny Borrell, *James Ramsey. **Home Field:** Russ Chandler

Stadium. **Seating Capacity:** 3718. **Outfield Dimension: LF**—329, **CF**—390, **RF**—334. **Press Box Telephone:** (404) 894-3167.

GONZAGA BULLDOGS/ ZAGS.

Conference: West Coast. **Mailing Address:** 502 E. Boone, Spokane, WA. **Website:** www.gozags.com. **Head Coach:** Mark Machtolf. **Telephone:** (509) 313-4209. **Baseball SID:** Todd Zeidler. **Telephone:** (509) 313-6373. **Assistant Coaches:** *Danny Evans, Brandon Harmon. **Telephone:** (509) 313-3597. **Home Field:** Patterson Ballpark and Steve Hertz Field. **Seating Capacity:** 2,000. **Outfield Dimension: LF**—320, **CF**—405, **RF**—320.

GRAMBLING STATE TIGERS.

Conference: Southwestern. **Mailing Address:** 403 Main St. Grambling, LA 71245. **Website:** www.gsutigers. com. **Head Coach:** James Cooper. **Telephone:** (318) 274-6566. **Baseball SID:** Habtom Keleta. **Telephone:** (318) 274-6007. **Assistant Coaches:** Davin Pierre, Elliott Jones. **Telephone:** (318) 274-2416. **Home Field:** Wilbert Ellis Field at Ralph Waldo Emerson Jones Park. **Seating Capacity:** 1,100. **Outfield Dimension: LF**—315, **CF**—400, **RF**—350.

GRAND CANYON LOPES.

Conference: Western Athletic. **Mailing Address:** 3300 W Camelback Road, Phoenix, AZ 85017. **Website:** www.gculopes.com. **Head Coach:** Andy Stankiewicz. **Telephone:** (602) 639-6042. **Baseball SID:** Josh Hauser. **Telephone:** (602) 639-8328. **Assistant Coaches:** Blake Hawksworth, *Gregg Wallis. **Telephone:** (602) 639-7106. **Home Field:** Brazell Field at GCU Ballpark. **Seating Capacity:** 4,000. **Outfield Dimension: LF**—320, **CF**—375, **RF**—330.

HARTFORD HAWKS.

Conference: America East. **Mailing Address:** 200 Bloomfield Avenue West Hartford, CT 06117. **Website:** https://www.hartfordhawks.com. **Head Coach:** Justin Blood. **Telephone:** (860) 768-5760. **Baseball SID:** Tyrell Walden-Martin. **Telephone:** (860) 768-4501. **Assistant Coaches:** Associate Head, *Trey Stover. **Telephone:** (860) 768-4656. **Home Field:** Fiondella Field. **Seating Capacity:** 1,000. **Outfield Dimension: LF**—325, **CF**—400, **RF**—325.

HARVARD CRIMSON.

Conference: Ivy League. **Mailing Address:** 65 N. Harvard St. Boston, MA 02163. **Website:** www.gocrimson.com. **Head Coach:** Bill Decker. **Telephone:** (617) 495-2629. **Baseball SID:** Devan Horahan. **Telephone:** (617) 495-2206. **Assistant Coaches:** Bryan Stark, Brad Kirkpatrick. **Telephone:** (617) 496-1435. **Home Field:** O'Donnell Field. **Seating Capacity:** 1,600. **Outfield Dimension: LF**—340, **CF**—415, **RF**—340.

HAWAII RAINBOW WARRIORS.

Conference: Big West. **Mailing Address:** 1337 Lower Campus Rd. Honolulu, HI 96822. **Website:** www.hawaiiathletics.com. **Head Coach:** Mike Trapasso. **Telephone:** (808) 956-6247. **Baseball SID:** Fletcher Like. **Telephone:** (808) 956-4480. **Assistant Coaches:** *Mike Brown, Carl Fraticelli. **Telephone:** (808) 956-6247. **Home Field:** Les Murakami Stadium. **Seating Capacity:** 4,312. **Outfield Dimension: LF**—325, **CF**—385, **RF**—325.

HIGH POINT PANTHERS.

Conference: Big South. **Mailing Address:** 1 University Parkway, High Point, N.C., 27268. **Website:** www. highpointpanthers.com. **Head Coach:** Craig Cozart. **Telephone:** (336) 841-9190. **Baseball SID:** Joe Templin. **Telephone:** (336) 841-4638. **Assistant Coaches:** *Jason Laws, Rick Marlin. **Telephone:** (336) 841-4614. **Home Field:** Williard Stadium. **Seating Capacity:** 550. **Outfield Dimension: LF**—325, **CF**—400, **RF**—330.

HOFSTRA PRIDE.

Conference: Colonial. **Mailing Address:** 230 Hofstra University; PEC Room 233; Hempstead, NY 11549. **Website:** www.gohofstra.com. **Head Coach:** John Russo. **Telephone:** (516) 463-3759. **Baseball SID:** Len Skoros. **Telephone:** (516) 463-4602. **Assistant Coaches:** Blake Nation, *Matt Wessinger. **Telephone:** (516) 463-3800. **Home Field:** University Field. **Seating Capacity:** 600. **Outfield Dimension: LF**—322, **CF**—382, **RF**—337. **Press Box Telephone:** (516) 765-5584.

HOLY CROSS CRUSADERS.

Conference: Patriot. **Mailing Address:** 1 College St. Worcester, MA 01610. **Website:** goholycross.com. **Head Coach:** Greg DiCenzo. **Telephone:** (508) 793-2753. **Baseball SID:** Sarah Kirkpatrick. **Telephone:** (508) 793-2780. **Assistant Coaches:** *George Capen, Ed Kahovec. **Telephone:** (508) 793-2753. **Home Field:** Hanover Insurance Park at Fitton Field. **Seating Capacity:** 3,000. **Outfield Dimension: LF**—332, **CF**—385, **RF**—372.

HOUSTON COUGARS.

Conference: American Athletic. **Mailing Address:** karoger3@central.uh.edu. **Website:** UHCougars.com/ baseball. **Head Coach:** Todd Whitting. **Telephone:** (713) 743-9396. **Baseball SID:** Kyle Rogers. **Telephone:** (713) 743-9407. **Assistant Coaches:** Sammy Esposito, *Terry Rooney. **Telephone:** (713) 743-9396. **Home Field:** Don Sanders Field at Darryl & Lori Schroeder Park. **Seating Capacity:** 3,500. **Outfield Dimension: LF**—330, **CF**—390, **RF**—330.

HOUSTON BAPTIST HUSKIES.

Conference: Southland. **Mailing Address:** 7502 Fondren Rd. Houston, TX 77074. **Website:** www.hbuhuskies.com. **Head Coach:** Jared Moon. **Telephone:** (281) 649-3332. **Baseball SID:** Russ Reneau. **Telephone:** (281) 649-3098. **Assistant Coaches:** Xavier Hernandez, Russell Stockton. **Telephone:** (281) 649-3262. **Home Field:** Husky Field. **Seating Capacity:** 500. **Outfield Dimension: LF**—330, **CF**—406, **RF**—330.

ILLINOIS FIGHTING ILLINI.

Conference: Big Ten. **Mailing Address:** Bielfeldt Athletics Administration Building 1700 S. Fourth Street Champaign, IL 61820. **Website:** www.IlliniBaseball.com. **Head Coach:** Dan Hartleb. **Telephone:** (217) 244-8144. **Baseball SID:** Brett Moore. **Telephone:** (217) 244-2092. **Assistant Coaches:** Mark Allen, *Adam Christ. **Telephone:** (217) 300-2220. **Home Field:** Illinois Field. **Seating Capacity:** 1,785. **Outfield Dimension: LF**—330, **CF**—400, **RF**—330.

ILLINOIS STATE REDBIRDS.

Conference: Missouri Valley. **Mailing Address:** 100 N. University St. Normal, **IL 61761 Website:** www.

GoRedbirds.com. **Head Coach:** Steve Holm. **Telephone:** (309) 438-4458. **Baseball SID:** Mike Williams. **Telephone:** (309) 438-7748. **Assistant Coaches:** TJ Bennett, *Wally Crancer. **Telephone:** (309) 438-3338. **Home Field:** Duffy Bass Field. **Seating Capacity:** 1,000. **Outfield Dimension:** LF—330, CF—400, RF—330.

ILLINOIS-CHICAGO FLAMES.

Conference: Horizon. **Mailing Address:** 839 West Roosevelt Road, Chicago, IL 60608. **Website:** www.uicflames.com. **Head Coach:** Mike Dee. **Telephone:** (312) 996-8645. **Baseball SID:** Dan Wallace. **Telephone:** (312) 355-3139. **Assistant Coaches:** *John Flood, Sean McDermott. **Telephone:** (312) 355-1757. **Home Field:** Les Miller Field at Curtis Granderson Stadium. **Seating Capacity:** 1,800. **Outfield Dimension:** LF—325, CF—400, RF—330.

INCARNATE WORD CARDINALS.

Conference: Southland. **Mailing Address:** 4301 Broadway, CPO 288 San Antonio, TX 78209. **Website:** www.uiwcardinals.com. **Head Coach:** Ryan Shotzberger. **Telephone:** . **Baseball SID:** Alma Solis. **Assistant Coaches:** *Greg Evans, Kyle Winkler. **Home Field:** Sullivan Field. **Seating Capacity:** 2000. **Outfield Dimension:** LF—330, CF—400, RF—330.

INDIANA HOOSIERS.

Conference: Big Ten. **Mailing Address:** Simon Skjodt Assembly Hall | 1001 East 17th Street | Bloomington, IN 47408-1590. **Website:** www.IUHoosiers.com. **Head Coach:** Jeff Mercer. **Telephone:** (812) 855-9155. **Baseball SID:** Scott Burns. **Telephone:** (812) 856-2939. **Assistant Coaches:** *Dan Held, Justin Parker. **Telephone:** (812) 855-9155. **Home Field:** Bart Kaufman Field. **Seating Capacity:** 4,000. **Outfield Dimension:** LF—330, CF—400, RF—340. **Press Box Telephone:** (812) 855-9155.

INDIANA STATE SYCAMORES.

Conference: Missouri Valley. **Mailing Address:** 401 N. 4th Street Terre Haute, IN 47809. **Website:** GoSycamores.com. **Head Coach:** Mitch Hannahs. **Telephone:** (812) 237-4051. **Baseball SID:** Tim McCaughan. **Telephone:** (812) 237-4159. **Assistant Coaches:** *Brian Smiley, Brad Vanderglas. **Telephone:** (812) 237-4090. **Home Field:** Bob Warn Field. **Seating Capacity:** 2,000. **Outfield Dimension:** LF—340, CF—402, RF—340. **Press Box Telephone:** (812) 237-4498.

IONA GAELS.

Conference: Metro Atlantic. **Mailing Address:** Hynes Center, 715 North Ave. New Rochelle, NY 10801. **Website:** www.icgaels.com. **Head Coach:** Paul Panik. **Telephone:** (914) 633-2319. **Baseball SID:** Brian Beyrer. **Telephone:** (914) 637-2726. **Assistant Coaches:** J.T. Genovese. **Telephone:** (914) 633-2319. **Home Field:** City Park.

IOWA HAWKEYES.

Conference: Big Ten. **Mailing Address:** S300 CHA, Iowa City, IA. **Website:** hawkeyesports.com. **Head Coach:** Rick Heller. **Telephone:** (319) 335-9439. **Baseball SID:** James Allan. **Telephone:** (319) 335-6439. **Fax:** . **Assistant Coaches:** Robin Lund, *Marty Sutherland. **Telephone:** (319) 335-9439. **Home Field:** Duane Banks Field. **Seating Capacity:** 3000. **Outfield Dimension:** LF—329, CF—395, RF—329. **Press Box Telephone:** (319) 335-9520.

JACKSON STATE TIGERS.

Conference: Southwestern Athletic. **Mailing Address:** 1400 John R. Lynch St. PB Box 17810 Jackson MS 39217. **Website:** www.gojsutigers.com. **Head Coach:** Omar Johnson. **Telephone:** (601) 979-3930. **Baseball SID:** Dennis Driscoll. **Telephone:** (601) 979-0857. **Assistant Coaches:** Chadwick Hall, *Joel Sanchez. **Telephone:** (601) 979-3928. **Home Field:** Bob Braddy Baseball Field. **Seating Capacity:** . **Outfield Dimension:** LF—325, CF—401, RF—325.

JACKSONVILLE DOLPHINS.

Conference: Atlantic Sun. **Mailing Address:** 2800 University Blvd. N, Jacksonville, FL, 32211. **Website:** www.judolphins.com. **Head Coach:** Chris Hayes. **Telephone:** (904) 256-7476. **Baseball SID:** Scott Manze. **Assistant Coaches:** Jerry Edwards, *Ross Steedley. **Telephone:** (904) 256-7414. **Home Field:** John Sessions Stadium. **Seating Capacity:** 1750. **Outfield Dimension:** LF—340, CF—405, RF—340.

JACKSONVILLE STATE GAMECOCKS.

Conference: Ohio Valley. **Mailing Address:** 700 Pelham Road North, Pete Mathews Coliseum, Jacksonville, AL 36265. **Website:** www.jsugamecocksports.com. **Head Coach:** Jim Case. **Telephone:** (256) 782-5367. **Baseball SID:** Tony Schmidt. **Telephone:** (256) 782-5377. **Assistant Coaches:** *Evan Bush, Mike Murphree. **Telephone:** (256) 782-8141. **Home Field:** Rudy Abbott Field at Jim Case Stadium. **Seating Capacity:** 2020. **Outfield Dimension:** LF—325, CF—390, RF—320.

JAMES MADISON DUKES.

Conference: Colonial. **Mailing Address:** 395 South High Street Harrisonburg, VA 22807. **Website:** www.jmusports.com. **Head Coach:** Marlin Ikenberry. **Telephone:** (540) 568-3932. **Baseball SID:** Aaron Socha. **Telephone:** (540) 568-6155. **Assistant Coaches:** *Alex Guerra, Jimmy Jackson. **Telephone:** (540) 568-6516. **Home Field:** Eagle Field at Veterans Memorial Park. **Seating Capacity:** 3,500. **Outfield Dimension:** LF—330, CF—400, RF—320.

KANSAS JAYHAWKS.

Conference: Big 12. **Mailing Address:** 1651 Naismith Dr. Lawrence, KS 66054. **Website:** www.kuathletics.com. **Head Coach:** Ritch Price. **Telephone:** (785) 864-4196. **Baseball SID:** Brent Beerends. **Assistant Coaches:** Ryan Graves, Ritchie Price. **Telephone:** (785) 864-7908. **Home Field:** Hoglund Ballpark. **Seating Capacity:** 2,200. **Outfield Dimension:** LF—330, CF—395, RF—330.

KANSAS STATE WILDCATS.

Conference: Big 12. **Mailing Address:** 1800 College Ave., Manhattan, KS 66502. **Website:** www.kstatesports.com. **Head Coach:** Pete Hughes. **Telephone:** (785) 340-5274. **Baseball SID:** Christopher Brown. **Telephone:** (785) 532-7976. **Assistant Coaches:** Austin Wates, Buck Taylor. **Telephone:** (785) 473-8158. **Home Field:** Tointon Family Stadium. **Seating Capacity:** 2344. **Outfield Dimension:** LF—325, CF—390, RF—320. **Press Box Telephone:** (785) 532-5801.

KENNESAW STATE OWLS.

Conference: Atlantic Sun. **Mailing Address:** 1000 Chastain Rd Kennesaw GA 30144. **Website:** www.ksuowls.com. **Head Coach:** Mike Sansing. **Telephone:**

(470) 578-6264. **Baseball SID:** Aury St. Germain. **Telephone:** (470) 578-7789. **Assistant Coaches:** *Trey Fowler, Travis McLanahan. **Telephone:** (470) 578-2098. **Home Field:** Stillwell Stadium. **Seating Capacity:** NA. **Outfield Dimension: LF**—330, **CF**—400, **RF**—330.

KENT STATE GOLDEN FLASHES.

Conference: Mid-American. **Mailing Address:** 1025 Risman Drive Kent Ohio 44202. **Website:** KentStateAthletics.com. **Head Coach:** Jeff Duncan. **Telephone:** (330) 672-8432. **Baseball SID:** Dan Griffin. **Telephone:** (330) 672-8468. **Fax:** . **Assistant Coaches:** Mike Birkbeck. **Telephone:** (330) 672-8433. **Home Field:** Schoonover Stadium. **Seating Capacity:** 500. **Outfield Dimension: LF**—330, **CF**—405, **RF**—330. **Press Box Telephone:** (330) 672-8468.

KENTUCKY WILDCATS.

Conference: Southeastern. **Mailing Address:** 1576 College Way, Lexington, KY, 40502. **Website:** www.UKathletics.com. **Head Coach:** Nick Mingione. **Telephone:** (859) 257-8052. **Baseball SID:** Matt May. **Telephone:** (859) 257-8504. **Assistant Coaches:** *Will Coggin, Dan Roszel. **Home Field:** Kentucky Proud Park. **Seating Capacity:** 5,000. **Outfield Dimension: LF**—335, **CF**—400, **RF**—320.

LA SALLE EXPLORERS.

Conference: Atlantic 10. **Mailing Address:** 1900 W. Olney Ave. Philadelphia, PA 19141. **Website:** www.goex-plorers.com. **Head Coach:** David Miller. **Telephone:** (215) 951-5157. **Baseball SID:** Nick Lantz. **Telephone:** (215) 991-2886. **Assistant Coaches:** Andrew Amaro, Bryan Radziewski. **Telephone:** (267) 760-3204. **Home Field:** Hank Da Vincent Field. **Seating Capacity:** 1,000. **Outfield Dimension: LF**—310, **CF**—450, **RF**—310.

LAFAYETTE LEOPARDS.

Conference: Patriot League. **Mailing Address:** 730 High St, Easton, PA 18042. **Website:** www.goleopards.com. **Head Coach:** Joe Kinney. **Telephone:** (610) 330-5476. **Baseball SID:** Hannah Simmons. **Telephone:** (610) 330-5518. **Assistant Coaches:** Ben Flanary, *Tim Reilly. **Telephone:** (610) 330-3212. **Home Field:** Kamine Stadium. **Seating Capacity:** 500. **Outfield Dimension: LF**—332, **CF**—403, **RF**—335.

LAMAR CARDINALS.

Conference: Southland. **Mailing Address:** PO Box 10627, Beaumont, Texas 77710. **Website:** www.lamarcar-dinals.com. **Head Coach:** Will Davis. **Telephone:** (409) 880-8974. **Baseball SID:** Cooper Welch. **Telephone:** (409) 880-7845. **Assistant Coaches:** *Scott Hatten, Sean Snedeker. **Telephone:** (409) 880-8315. **Home Field:** Vincent-Beck Stadium. **Seating Capacity:** 3500. **Outfield Dimension: LF**—325, **CF**—380, **RF**—325.

LEHIGH MOUNTAIN HAWKS.

Conference: Patriot. **Mailing Address:** 641 Taylor Street Bethlehem PA 18015. **Website:** www.lehighsports.com. **Head Coach:** Sean Leary. **Telephone:** (610) 758-4315. **Baseball SID:** Josh Liddick. **Telephone:** (610) 758-5043. **Assistant Coaches:** Dan Gusovsky, *AJ Miller. **Telephone:** (610) 758-4315. **Home Field:** J. David Walker Field at Legacy Park. **Seating Capacity:** 400. **Outfield Dimension: LF**—320, **CF**—400, **RF**—320.

LIBERTY FLAMES.

Conference: Atlantic Sun. **Mailing Address:** 1971 University Blvd., Lynchburg, VA. **Website:** www.liberty-flames.com. **Head Coach:** Scott Jackson. **Telephone:** (434) 582-2305. **Baseball SID:** Ryan Bomberger. **Assistant Coaches:** *Tyler Cannon, Matt Williams. **Home Field:** Worthington Field. **Seating Capacity:** 2500. **Outfield Dimension: LF**—325, **CF**—395, **RF**—325. **Press Box Telephone:** (434) 582-2914.

LIPSCOMB BISONS.

Conference: Atlantic Sun. **Mailing Address:** 1 University Park Dr. Nashville, TN 37204. **Website:** www.lipscombsports.com. **Head Coach:** Jeff Forehand. **Telephone:** (615) 966-5716. **Baseball SID:** . **Telephone:** . **Fax:** . **Assistant Coaches:** Grayson Crawford, Brian Ryman. **Telephone:** (615) 966-5868. **Home Field:** Ken Dugan Field at Stephen L. Marsh. **Seating Capacity:** 750. **Outfield Dimension: LF**—330, **CF**—405, **RF**—330.

LONG BEACH STATE DIRTBAGS.

Conference: Big West. **Mailing Address:** 6300 State University Dr., Long Beach, **CA 90840 Website:** www.longbeachstate.com. **Head Coach:** Eric Valenzuela. **Telephone:** (562) 985-8215. **Baseball SID:** Tyler Hendrickson. **Telephone:** (562) 985-7797. **Assistant Coaches:** *Daniel Costanza, Bryan Peters. **Home Field:** Blair Field. **Seating Capacity:** 3,500. **Outfield Dimension: LF**—330, **CF**—400, **RF**—330.

LONG ISLAND SHARKS.

Conference: Northeast. **Mailing Address:** 1 University Plaza Brooklyn, NY 11201. **Website:** www.liuathletics.com. **Head Coach:** Dan Pirillo. **Telephone:** (516) 299-2939. **Baseball SID:** Tyler Landis. **Telephone:** (516) 299-4156. **Assistant Coaches:** Mike Gaffney, Tom Carty. **Telephone:** (516) 299-2287. **Home Field:** LIU Baseball Stadium. **Outfield Dimension: LF**—330, **CF**—400, **RF**—330.

LONGWOOD LANCERS.

Conference: Big South. **Mailing Address:** 201 High St. Farmville, VA 23909. **Website:** www.longwoodlanc-ers.com. **Head Coach:** Ryan Mau. **Telephone:** (434) 395-2843. **Baseball SID:** Sam Hovan. **Telephone:** (434) 395-2345. **Assistant Coaches:** Daniel Wood, C.J. Rhodes. **Telephone:** (434) 395-2351. **Home Field:** Buddy Bolding Stadium. **Seating Capacity:** 500. **Outfield Dimension: LF**—335, **CF**—400, **RF**—335.

LOUISIANA STATE FIGHTING TIGERS.

Conference: Southeastern. **Mailing Address:** Nicholson Dr. @ N. Stadium Dr. Baton Rouge, LA 70803. **Website:** www.LSUsports.net. **Head Coach:** Paul Mainieri. **Telephone:** (225) 578-4148. **Baseball SID:** Bill Franques. **Telephone:** (225) 578-2527. **Assistant Coaches:** *Nolan Cain, Alan Dunn. **Telephone:** (225) 578-4148. **Home Field:** Alex Box Stadium, Skip Bertman Field. **Seating Capacity:** 10326. **Outfield Dimension: LF**—330, **CF**—405, **RF**—330. **Press Box Telephone:** (225) 578-4149.

LOUISIANA TECH BULLDOGS.

Conference: Conference USA. **Mailing Address:** Thomas Assembly Center ,1650 West Alabama Ruston, LA 71270. **Website:** www.latechsports.com. **Head Coach:**

Lane Burroughs. **Telephone:** (318) 257-5318. **Baseball SID:** Andrew Goodwin. **Telephone:** (318) 257-5305. **Assistant Coaches:** *Mitch Gaspard, Mike Silva. **Home Field:** N/A, due to tornado.

LOUISIANA-LAFAYETTE RAGIN' CAJUNS.

Conference: Sun Belt. **Mailing Address:** 201 Reinhardt Dr, Lafayette, LA 70506. **Website:** www.rag-incajuns.com. **Head Coach:** Matt Deggs. **Telephone:** (337) 482-5191. **Baseball SID:** Tim Wiemann. **Assistant Coaches:** *Jeremy Talbot, Jake Wells. **Telephone:** (337) 482-5189. **Home Field:** M.L 'Tigue' Moore Field at Russo Park. **Seating Capacity:** 6015. **Outfield Dimension:** LF—330, CF—400, RF—330

LOUISIANA-MONROE WARHAWKS.

Conference: Sun Belt. **Mailing Address:** 308 Warhawk Way Monroe, LA 71209. **Website:** www.ulm.edu. **Head Coach:** Michael Federico. **Telephone:** (318) 342-3591. **Baseball SID:** Michael Hammett. **Telephone:** (318) 342-7925. **Assistant Coaches:** *Jake Carlson, Matt Collins. **Telephone:** (318) 342-3598. **Home Field:** Warhawk Field. **Seating Capacity:** 1,800. **Outfield Dimension:** LF—330, CF—400, RF—330.

LOUISVILLE CARDINALS.

Conference: Atlantic Coast. **Mailing Address:** 215 Central Ave., Louisville, KY 40292. **Website:** www.GoCards.com. **Head Coach:** Dan McDonnell. **Telephone:** (502) 852-0103. **Baseball SID:** Stephen Williams. **Telephone:** (502) 852-4857. **Assistant Coaches:** *Eric Snider, Roger Williams. **Telephone:** (502) 852-3929. **Home Field:** Jim Patterson Stadium. **Seating Capacity:** 4000. **Outfield Dimension:** LF—330, CF—402, RF—330.

LOYOLA MARYMOUNT LIONS.

Conference: West Coast. **Mailing Address:** 1 LMU Drive Los Angeles, CA 90045. **Website:** www.lmulions.com. **Head Coach:** Nathan Choate. **Telephone:** (310) 338-2949. **Baseball SID:** Steven Esparza. **Telephone:** (310) 338-7638. **Fax:** . **Assistant Coaches:** *Tony Asaro, Matt Curtis. **Telephone:** (310) 338-4511. **Home Field:** Page Stadium. **Seating Capacity:** 600. **Outfield Dimension:** LF—326, CF—406, RF—321.

MAINE BLACK BEARS.

Conference: America East. **Mailing Address:** 5745 Mahaney Clubhouse, Orono ME, 04469. **Website:** goblackbears.com. **Head Coach:** Nicholas Derba. **Telephone:** (207) 581-1090. **Baseball SID:** Tyler Neville. **Telephone:** (207) 581-4849. **Assistant Coaches:** *Scott Heath, Josh Kieffer. **Home Field:** Mahaney Diamond. **Seating Capacity:** 3,000. **Outfield Dimension:** LF—330, CF—400, RF—330.

MANHATTAN JASPERS.

Conference: Metro Atlantic. **Mailing Address:** 4513 Manhattan College Parkway; Riverdale, NY 10471. **Website:** www.gojaspers.com. **Head Coach:** Mike Cole. **Telephone:** (718) 862-7821. **Baseball SID:** Kevin Ross. **Telephone:** (718) 862-7228. **Assistant Coaches:** *Chris Cody, Bobby Melley. **Telephone:** (718) 862-7218. **Home Field:** Van Cortlandt Park. **Seating Capacity:** . **Outfield Dimension:** LF—, CF—, RF—. **Press Box Telephone:** (716) 969-6126.

MARIST RED FOXES.

Conference: Metro Atlantic. **Mailing Address:** 3399 North Rd. Poughkeepsie, NY 12601. **Website:** www.goredfoxes.com. **Head Coach:** Chris Tracz. **Telephone:** (845) 575-3000 Ext. 2570. **Baseball SID:** Peter Fagan. **Telephone:** (845) 575-3000 Ext. 6047. **Assistant Coaches:** Mike Coss, Andrew Pezzuto*. **Home Field:** McCann Field. **Outfield Dimension:** LF—320, CF—390, RF—320.

MARSHALL THUNDERING HERD.

Conference: Conference USA. **Mailing Address:** 1801 3rd Ave, Huntington, W.Va. 25703. **Website:** www.HerdZone.com. **Head Coach:** Jeff Waggoner. **Telephone:** (304) 696-6454. **Baseball SID:** Cody Linn. **Telephone:** (740) 424-6342. **Fax:** . **Assistant Coaches:** Joe Renner, Brian Karlet. **Telephone:** (304) 696-7146. **Home Field:** Appalachian Power Park. **Seating Capacity:** 4,500. **Outfield Dimension:** LF—330, CF—400, RF—320.

MARYLAND TERRAPINS/TERPS.

Conference: Big Ten. **Mailing Address:** University of Maryland Department of Intercollegiate Athletics, XFINITY Center, 8500 Paint Branch Dr., College Park, MD 20742. **Website:** www.umterps.com. **Head Coach:** Rob Vaughn. **Telephone:** (301) 314-7003. **Baseball SID:** Hunter Dortenzo. **Telephone:** (443) 859-1507. **Assistant Coaches:** Corey Muscara, *Matt Swope. **Telephone:** (301) 314-7003. **Home Field:** Bob "Turtle" Smith Stadium. **Seating Capacity:** 2500. **Outfield Dimension:** LF—320, CF—385, RF—325.

MARYLAND-BALTIMORE COUNTY RETRIEVERS.

Conference: America East. **Mailing Address:** 1000 Hilltop Circle Baltimore, MD 21250. **Website:** www.umbcretrievers.com. **Head Coach:** Liam Bowen. **Baseball SID:** David Castellanos. **Telephone:** (410) 455-2639. **Assistant Coaches:** Ryan Terrill, Mitch Cooksey. **Home Field:** Alumni Field. **Seating Capacity:** 500. **Outfield Dimension:** LF—330, CF—360, RF—340.

MARYLAND-EASTERN SHORE HAWKS.

Conference: Mid-Eastern. **Mailing Address:** WP Hytche Athletic Center 1 Backbone Rd. Princess Anne, MD 21853,. **Website:** https://easternshorehawks.com/sports/baseball. **Head Coach:** Brian Hollamon. **Telephone:** (410) 651-7864. **Baseball SID:** Fatima Butler. **Assistant Coaches:** Chris Bengel, *Ben Kirk. **Telephone:** (410) 621-7014. **Home Field:** Shorebird Stadium. **Seating Capacity:** 6,000. **Outfield Dimension:** LF—309, CF—400, RF—309.

MASSACHUSETTS MINUTEMEN.

Conference: Atlantic 10. **Mailing Address:** 131 Commonwealth Ave. Amherst, MA 01003. **Website:** www.umassathletics.com. **Head Coach:** Matt Reynolds. **Telephone:** (413) 545-3120. **Baseball SID:** Ryan Gallant. **Telephone:** (413) 687-3793. **Assistant Coaches:** *Nate Cole, Mark Royer. **Home Field:** Earl Lorden Field. **Seating Capacity:** 1,000. **Outfield Dimension:** LF—330, CF—405, RF—330.

MASSACHUSETTS-LOWELL RIVER HAWKS.

Conference: America East. **Mailing Address:** 1 University Ave. Lowell, MA 01854. **Website:** www.goriverhawks.com. **Head Coach:** Ken Harring. **Telephone:** (978) 934-2344. **Baseball SID:** Pete Souris. **Telephone:** (978) 934-3771. **Assistant Coaches:** Kevin Barnaby, Brad Cook.

Telephone: (978) 934-2564. **Home Field:** LeLacheur Park. **Seating Capacity:** 5,030. **Outfield Dimension:** LF—337, CF—400, RF—337.

MCNEESE STATE COWBOYS.

Conference: Southland. **Mailing Address:** 700 E. McNeese St Lake Charles, LA 70609. **Website:** www.mcneesesports.com. **Head Coach:** Justin Hill. **Telephone:** (337) 475-5484. **Baseball SID:** Ryan Landry. **Telephone:** (337) 475-5941. **Assistant Coaches:** Jimmy Ricklefsen, *Nick Zaleski. **Telephone:** (337) 475-5903. **Home Field:** Joe Miller Ball Park. **Seating Capacity:** 1500. **Outfield Dimension:** LF—330, CF—400, RF—330.

MEMPHIS TIGERS.

Conference: American Athletic. **Mailing Address:** 570 Normal, Memphis, TN, 38152. **Website:** www.GoTigersGo.com. **Head Coach:** Daron Schoenrock. **Telephone:** (901) 678-5041. **Baseball SID:** John Galatas. **Telephone:** (901) 678-2444. **Assistant Coaches:** *Clay Greene, Russ McNickle. **Telephone:** (901) 678-5041. **Home Field:** Fed Ex Park. **Seating Capacity:** 2,500. **Outfield Dimension:** LF—319, CF—380, RF—320. **Press Box Telephone:** (901) 678-1301.

MERCER BEARS.

Conference: Southern. **Mailing Address:** 1501 Mercer University Dr. Macon, GA 31207. **Website:** www.mercer-bears.com. **Head Coach:** Craig Gibson. **Telephone:** (478) 301-2396. **Baseball SID:** . **Telephone:** . **Fax:** . **Assistant Coaches:** Brent Shade, Willie Stewart. **Telephone:** (478) 301-5210. **Home Field:** OrthoGeorgia Park at Claude Smith Field. **Seating Capacity:** 1,500. **Outfield Dimension:** LF—330, CF—400, RF—320.

MERRIMACK WARRIORS.

Conference: Northeast. **Mailing Address:** 315 Turnpike Street North Andover, MA 01845. **Website:** www.merrimackathletics.com. **Head Coach:** Nick Barese. **Telephone:** (978) 837-5230. **Baseball SID:** Mike Sullivan. **Telephone:** (978) 837-5036. **Assistant Coaches:** Cody Kauffman. **Telephone:** (978) 837-5230.

MIAMI HURRICANES.

Conference: Atlantic Coast. **Mailing Address:** BASEBALL - 6201 San Amaro Drive, Coral Gables, FL 33146 ATHLETICS - 5821 San Amaro Drive, Coral Gables, FL, 33146. **Website:** www.hurricanesports.com. **Head Coach:** Gino DiMare. **Telephone:** (305) 284-4171. **Baseball SID:** David Villavicencio. **Telephone:** (305) 284-3244. **Assistant Coaches:** J.D. Arteaga, *Norberto Lopez. **Telephone:** (305) 284-4171. **Home Field:** Alex Rodriguez Park at Mark Light Field. **Seating Capacity:** 4999. **Outfield Dimension:** LF—330, CF—400, RF—330. **Press Box Telephone:** (305) 284-8192.

MIAMI (OHIO) REDHAWKS.

Conference: Mid-American. **Mailing Address:** 550 E. Withrow St. Oxford, OH 45056. **Website:** www.miamiredhawks.com. **Head Coach:** Danny Hayden. **Telephone:** (513) 529-6631. **Baseball SID:** Mike Roth. **Telephone:** (513) 529-7092. **Assistant Coaches:** Justin Dedman, Matthew Passauer. **Telephone:** (513) 529-7293. **Home Field:** McKie Field at Hayden Park. **Seating Capacity:** 2,000. **Outfield Dimension:** LF—332, CF—400, RF—343.

MICHIGAN WOLVERINES.

Conference: Big Ten. **Mailing Address:** 1114 S. State St. Ann Arbor, MI 48104. **Website:** www.mgoblue.com. **Head Coach:** Erik Bakich. **Telephone:** (734) 615-0010. **Baseball SID:** Kyler Ludlow. **Assistant Coaches:** Chris Fetter, *Nick Schnabel. **Telephone:** (734) 615-0010. **Home Field:** Ray Fisher Stadium, Wilpon Baseball Complex. **Seating Capacity:** 4,000. **Outfield Dimension:** LF—330, CF—400, RF—330.

MICHIGAN STATE SPARTANS.

Conference: Big Ten. **Mailing Address:** 223 Kalamazoo St. Room 212 East Lansing, MI 48911. **Website:** www.msuspartans.com. **Head Coach:** Jake Boss. **Telephone:** (517) 355-4486. **Baseball SID:** Zach Fisher. **Telephone:** (517) 355-2271. **Assistant Coaches:** *Graham Sikes, Mark VanAmeyde. **Telephone:** (517) 355-0259. **Home Field:** McLane Stadium at Kobs Field. **Seating Capacity:** 2,500. **Outfield Dimension:** LF—330, CF—405, RF—310.

MIDDLE TENNESSEE STATE BLUE RAIDERS.

Conference: Conference USA. **Mailing Address:** 1672 Greenland Drive Murfreesboro, TN 37132. **Website:** www.goblueraiders,com. **Head Coach:** Jim Toman. **Telephone:** (615) 898-2961. **Baseball SID:** Brady McBride. **Telephone:** (615) 904-8209. **Assistant Coaches:** *Kyle Bunn, Blake Hunt. **Telephone:** (615) 494-8796. **Home Field:** Reese Smith Jr. Field. **Seating Capacity:** 2600. **Outfield Dimension:** LF—330, CF—390, RF—330. **Press Box Telephone:** (615) 898-2117.

MINNESOTA GOLDEN GOPHERS.

Conference: Big Ten. **Mailing Address:** 516 15th Ave. SE, Gibson-Nagurski Complex, Minneapolis, MN 55455. **Website:** www.gophersports.com. **Head Coach:** John Anderson. **Telephone:** . **Baseball SID:** Sullivan Bortner. **Telephone:** (612) 626-4843. **Assistant Coaches:** *Packy Casey, Ty McDevitt. **Telephone:** (612) 625-3568. **Home Field:** Siebert Field. **Seating Capacity:** 1420. **Outfield Dimension:** LF—330, CF—390, RF—330.

MISSISSIPPI REBELS.

Conference: Southeastern. **Mailing Address:** 908 All-American Drive, University, MS 38677. **Website:** www.OleMissSports.com. **Head Coach:** Mike Bianco. **Telephone:** (662) 915-6643. **Baseball SID:** Alex Sims. **Telephone:** (662) 816-9610. **Assistant Coaches:** Mike Clement, *Carl Lafferty. **Telephone:** (662) 915-6643. **Home Field:** Oxford-University Stadium/Swayze Field. **Seating Capacity:** 11477. **Outfield Dimension:** LF—330, CF—390, RF—330.

MISSISSIPPI STATE BULLDOGS.

Conference: Southeastern. **Mailing Address:** 110 Coliseum Circle, Starkville, MS 39759. **Website:** hailstate.com/baseball. **Head Coach:** Chris Lemonis. **Telephone:** (662) 325-3597. **Baseball SID:** Greg Campbell. **Telephone:** (814) 876-0824. **Assistant Coaches:** Scott Foxhall, *Jake Gautreau. **Telephone:** (662) 325-3597. **Home Field:** Dudy Noble Field. **Seating Capacity:** 15,000+. **Outfield Dimension:** LF—330, CF—400, RF—305. **Press Box Telephone:** (814) 876-0824.

MISSISSIPPI VALLEY STATE DELTA DEVILS.

Conference: Southwest. **Mailing Address:** 14000 Hwy. 82 W. #7246 Itta Bena, MS 38941. **Website:** www.mvsusports.com. **Head Coach:** Aaron Stevens.

Telephone: (662) 254-3834. Baseball SID: Demetrius Howse. Telephone: (662) 220-8165. Assistant Coaches: Terrance Steele. Home Field: Magnolia Field. Seating Capacity: 3,006. Outfield Dimension: LF—315, CF—395, RF—315.

MISSOURI TIGERS.

Conference: Southeastern. Mailing Address: Suite 200, Mizzou Arena, One Champions Drive, Columbia, MO 65211. Website: www.MUTigers.com. Head Coach: Steve Bieser. Telephone: (573) 884-6428. Baseball SID: Andy Oldenburg. Telephone: (573) 882-1645. Assistant Coaches: *Todd Butler, Fred Corral. Telephone: (573) 884-4783. Home Field: Taylor Stadium. Seating Capacity: 3,031. Outfield Dimension: LF—340, CF—400, RF—340.

MISSOURI STATE BEARS.

Conference: Missouri Valley. Mailing Address: 901 S. National Ave., Springfield, MO 65897. Website: missouristatebears.com. Head Coach: Keith Guttin. Telephone: (417) 836-4497. Baseball SID: Eric Doennig. Telephone: (417) 836-4586. Assistant Coaches: Paul Evans, *Matt Lawson. Telephone: (417) 836-4496. Home Field: Hammons Field. Seating Capacity: 8000. Outfield Dimension: LF—315, CF—400, RF—330. Press Box Telephone: (417) 832-3029.

MONMOUTH HAWKS.

Conference: Metro Atlantic. Mailing Address: 400 Cedar Ave. West Long Branch, NJ 07764. Website: www.monmouthhawks.com. Head Coach: Dean Ehehalt. Telephone: (732) 263-5186. Baseball SID: Gary Kowal. Telephone: (732) 263-5557. Assistant Coaches: *Chris Collazo, Josh Epstein. Telephone: (732) 263-5524. Home Field: Monmouth Baseball Field. Seating Capacity: 2,100. Outfield Dimension: LF—325, CF—395, RF—320.

MOREHEAD STATE EAGLES.

Conference: Ohio Valley. Mailing Address: Playforth Pl., Morehead, KY 40351. Website: www.msueagles.com. Head Coach: Mik Aoki. Telephone: (606) 783-2882. Baseball SID: Matt Schabert. Telephone: (606) 783-2556. Assistant Coaches: *Shane Conlon, Rob Youngdahl. Telephone: (606) 783-2882. Home Field: Allen Field. Seating Capacity: 1,000. Outfield Dimension: LF—320, CF—380, RF—315.

MOUNT ST. MARY'S MOUNTAINEERS.

Conference: Northeast. Mailing Address: 16300 Old Emmitsburg Road, Emmitsburg, Md. 21727. Website: www.mountathletics.com. Head Coach: Scott Thomson. Telephone: (301) 447-3806. Baseball SID: Matt McCann. Telephone: (301) 447-5384. Assistant Coaches: *Jeff Gergic, Dan Gerjets. Telephone: (301) 447-3806. Home Field: E.T. Straw Family Stadium. Seating Capacity: 500.

MURRAY STATE RACERS.

Conference: Ohio Valley. Mailing Address: 224 Stewart Stadium Murray, Ky 42071. Website: goracers.com. Head Coach: Dan Skirka. Telephone: (270) 809-4892. Baseball SID: Adam Grossman. Telephone: (270) 809-7044. Assistant Coaches: Tanner Gordon, *Kent Rollins. Telephone: (270) 809-3475. Home Field: Reagan Field. Seating Capacity: 800. Outfield Dimension: LF—330, CF—400, RF—330. Press Box Telephone: (270) 809-5650.

NAVY MIDSHIPMEN.

Conference: Patriot. Mailing Address: 566 Brownson Rd., Annapolis, MD 21402. Website: navysports.com. Head Coach: Paul Kostacopoulos. Telephone: (410) 293-5571. Baseball SID: David Gerhart. Telephone: (410) 293-8787. Assistant Coaches: Bobby Applegate, *Jeff Kane. Telephone: (410) 293-8946. Home Field: Terwilliger Brothers Field at Max Bishop Stadium. Seating Capacity: 1,500. Outfield Dimension: LF—322, CF—397, RF—304.

NEBRASKA CORNHUSKERS.

Conference: Big Ten. Mailing Address: One Memorial Stadium, 800 Stadium Dr., Lincoln, NE 68588. Website: www.huskers.com. Head Coach: Will Bolt. Telephone: (402) 472-2269. Baseball SID: Connor Stange. Telephone: (402) 472-6684. Assistant Coaches: Jeff Christy, Lance Harvell. Telephone: (402) 472-2269. Home Field: Hawks Field at Haymarket Park. Seating Capacity: 8,486. Outfield Dimension: LF—335, CF—395, RF—325.

NEBRASKA-OMAHA MAVERICKS.

Conference: Summit League. Mailing Address: Sapp Fieldhouse, 6001 Dodge St. Omaha, NE 68182. Website: www.omavs.com. Head Coach: Evan Porter. Telephone: (402) 554-2141. Baseball SID: Zack Kirby. Telephone: (615) 300-5854. Assistant Coaches: Brian Strawn, Payton Kinney. Telephone: (402) 554-2141. Home Field: Seymour Smith Park. Seating Capacity: 1,000.

NEVADA WOLF PACK.

Conference: Mountain West. Mailing Address: 1664 North Virginia St. Reno, NV. 89557. Website: www.nevadawolfpack.com. Head Coach: TJ Bruce. Telephone: (775) 682-6978. Baseball SID: Hugh Tomasello. Telephone: (408) 425-9542. Assistant Coaches: *Abe Alvarez, Troy Buckley. Home Field: Peccole Park. Seating Capacity: 3,000. Outfield Dimension: LF—340, CF—401, RF—340.

NEVADA-LAS VEGAS REBELS.

Conference: Mountain West. Mailing Address: 4505 S. Maryland Parkway, Las Vegas, NV 89154. Website: www.UNLVRebels.com. Head Coach: Stan Stolte. Telephone: (702) 895-3499. Baseball SID: Jeff Seals. Telephone: (702) 895-3134. Fax: . Assistant Coaches: Kevin Higgins, *Cory Vanderhook. Telephone: (702) 895-3802. Home Field: Earl E. Wilson Stadium. Seating Capacity: 3000. Outfield Dimension: LF—335, CF—400, RF—335.

NEW MEXICO LOBOS.

Conference: Mountain West. Mailing Address: 1 University of New Mexico, Albuquerque, N.M. 87131. Website: www.golobos.com. Head Coach: Ray Birmingham. Telephone: (505) 925-5720. Baseball SID: Daniel Gallegos. Telephone: (501) 442-2930. Assistant Coaches: *Jon Coyne, Brandon Higelin. Telephone: (505) 925-5720. Home Field: Santa Ana Star Field. Seating Capacity: 1000. Outfield Dimension: LF—338, CF—420, RF—338.

NEW MEXICO STATE AGGIES.

Conference: Western Athletic. Mailing Address: 1815 Wells Street, Las Cruces, NM 88003-8001. Website: www.nmstatesports.com. Head Coach: Mike Kirby. Telephone:

(575) 646-7693. **Baseball SID:** Oliver Grigg. **Telephone:** (575) 646-3269. **Fax:** . **Assistant Coaches:** Michael Pritchard, *Brett Swain. **Telephone:** (575) 646-2739. **Home Field:** Presley Askew Field. **Seating Capacity:** 1,000. **Outfield Dimension: LF**—345, **CF**—400, **RF**—345.

NEW ORLEANS PRIVATEERS.

Conference: Southland. **Mailing Address:** 2000 Lakeshore Dr. **Website:** www.unoprivateers.com. **Head Coach:** Blake Dean. **Telephone:** (504) 280-3879. **Baseball SID:** Kelvin Queliz. **Telephone:** (504) 280-6284. **Assistant Coaches:** AJ Battisto, *Brett Stewart. **Telephone:** (504) 280-7021. **Home Field:** Maestri Field. **Outfield Dimension: LF**—330, **CF**—405, **RF**—330.

NIAGARA PURPLE EAGLES.

Conference: Metro Atlantic. **Mailing Address:** 5795 Lewiston Rd. Niagara University, NY 14109. **Website:** www.purpleeagles.com. **Head Coach:** Rob McCoy. **Telephone:** (716) 286-7361. **Baseball SID:** . **Telephone:** . **Fax:** . **Assistant Coaches:** Matt Spatafora, Stephen Leonetti. **Telephone:** (716) 286-8624. **Home Field:** Bobo Field.

NICHOLLS STATE COLONELS.

Conference: Southland. **Mailing Address:** 906 E 1st St, Thibodaux LA 70301. **Website:** geauxcolonels.com. **Head Coach:** Seth Thibodeaux. **Telephone:** (985) 449-7149. **Baseball SID:** Jay Sullivan. **Telephone:** (985) 448-4282. **Assistant Coaches:** *Zach Butler, Ford Pemberton. **Telephone:** (985) 448-4807. **Home Field:** Ben Meyer Diamond At Ray E. Didier Field. **Seating Capacity:** 2600. **Outfield Dimension: LF**—330, **CF**—405, **RF**—315.

NEW JERSEY TECH HIGHLANDERS.

Conference: Atlantic Sun. **Mailing Address:** 100 Lock St. Newark, NJ 07102. **Website:** www.njithighlanders.com. **Head Coach:** Robbie McClellan. **Telephone:** (973) 596-8396. **Baseball SID:** Myles Rudnick. **Telephone:** (973) 596-8261. **Assistant Coaches:** Anthony Deleo. **Telephone:** (973) 596-8532. **Home Field:** TD Bank Ballpark (Somerset Patriots). **Seating Capacity:** 6100. **Outfield Dimension: LF**—317, **CF**—402, **RF**—315.

NORFOLK STATE SPARTANS.

Conference: Mid-Eastern. **Mailing Address:** 700 Park Ave., Norfolk, VA. **Website:** www.nsuspartans.com. **Head Coach:** Keith Shumate. **Telephone:** (757) 823-8196. **Baseball SID:** Matt Michalec. **Telephone:** (757) 823-2628. **Assistant Coaches:** *Matt Mitchell, Chance Pauley. **Telephone:** (757) 823-8196. **Home Field:** Marty L. Miller Field. **Seating Capacity:** 1500. **Outfield Dimension: LF**—330, **CF**—404, **RF**—318. **Press Box Telephone:** (757) 823-8196.

NORTH ALABAMA LIONS.

Conference: Atlantic Sun. **Mailing Address:** UNA Box 5071 Florence, AL 35632. **Website:** www.roarlions.com. **Head Coach:** Mike Keehn. **Telephone:** (256) 765-4635. **Baseball SID:** Jeff Hodges. **Telephone:** (256) 765-4595. **Assistant Coaches:** Anthony DiCicco, Nick McGregor. **Telephone:** (256) 765-5065. **Home Field:** Lane Field. **Outfield Dimension: LF**—330, **CF**—385, **RF**—320.

NORTH CAROLINA TAR HEELS.

Conference: Atlantic Coast. **Mailing Address:** 100 Ridge Road, Chapel Hill, North Carolina. **Website:** GoHeels.com. **Head Coach:** Mike Fox. **Telephone:** . **Baseball SID:** TJ Scholl. **Telephone:** . **Fax:** . **Assistant Coaches:** *Scott Forbes, Bryant Gaines. **Telephone:** . **Home Field:** Boshamer Stadium. **Seating Capacity:** 5000. **Outfield Dimension: LF**—335, **CF**—400, **RF**—340.

NORTH CAROLINA A&T AGGIES.

Conference: Mid-Eastern. **Mailing Address:** 1601 E. Market St. Greensboro, NC 27411. **Website:** www.ncataggies.com. **Head Coach:** Ben Hall. **Telephone:** (336) 285-4260. **Baseball SID:** Brian Holloway. **Telephone:** (336) 285-3608. **Assistant Coaches:** Jamie Serber, Stefan Jordan. **Telephone:** (336) 285-4272. **Home Field:** War Memorial Stadium. **Seating Capacity:** 2,000. **Outfield Dimension: LF**—327, **CF**—401, **RF**—327.

NORTH CAROLINA CENTRAL EAGLES.

Conference: Mid-Eastern. **Mailing Address:** 1801 Fayetteville St. Durham, NC 27707. **Website:** www.nccueaglepride.com. **Head Coach:** Jim Koerner. **Telephone:** (919) 530-6723. **Baseball SID:** Jonathan Duren. **Telephone:** (919) 530-6892. **Assistant Coaches:** *Neal Henry, Brad Mincey. **Telephone:** (919) 530-5439. **Home Field:** Durham Athletic Park. **Seating Capacity:** 2,000. **Outfield Dimension: LF**—335, **CF**—398, **RF**—290.

NORTH CAROLINA STATE WOLFPACK.

Conference: Atlantic Coast. **Mailing Address:** 1081 Varsity Dr. Raleigh, N.C. 27606. **Website:** www.gopack.com. **Head Coach:** Elliott Avent. **Telephone:** . **Baseball SID:** Lizzie Hattrich. **Telephone:** (919) 760-7767. **Fax:** . **Assistant Coaches:** Clint Chrysler, *Chris Hart. **Telephone:** . **Home Field:** Doak Field. **Seating Capacity:** 3,100. **Outfield Dimension: LF**—320, **CF**—400, **RF**—330.

NORTH DAKOTA STATE BISON.

Conference: Summit. **Mailing Address:** 1300 17th Ave N, Fargo, ND 58102. **Website:** www.gobison.com. **Head Coach:** Tod Brown. **Telephone:** . **Baseball SID:** Ryan Workman. **Telephone:** (701) 231-5591. **Assistant Coaches:** *Tyler Oakes, David Pearson. **Telephone:** (701) 231-7817. **Home Field:** Newman Outdoor Field. **Seating Capacity:** 4,419. **Outfield Dimension: LF**—318, **CF**—408, **RF**—314.

NORTH FLORIDA OSPREYS.

Conference: Atlantic Sun. **Mailing Address:** 1 UNF Drive Jacksonville, Fla.. **Website:** unfospreys.com/. **Head Coach:** Tim Parenton. **Telephone:** (904) 620-1556. **Baseball SID:** Brock Borgeson. **Telephone:** (904) 620-4029. **Assistant Coaches:** *Tommy Boss, Andrew Hannon. **Telephone:** (904) 620-2586. **Home Field:** Harmon Stadium. **Seating Capacity:** 1000. **Outfield Dimension: LF**—325, **CF**—400, **RF**—325.

NORTHEASTERN HUSKIES.

Conference: Colonial. **Mailing Address:** 360 Huntington Ave, 219 Cabot Center, Boston, Mass. 02115. **Website:** www.nuhuskies.com. **Head Coach:** Mike Glavine. **Telephone:** (617) 373-3657. **Baseball SID:** Mike Skovan. **Telephone:** (617) 373-7931. **Fax:** . **Assistant Coaches:** *Kevin Cobb, Nick Puccio. **Telephone:** (617) 373-5256. **Home Field:** Friedman Diamond. **Seating Capacity:** 2400. **Outfield Dimension: LF**—326, **CF**—415, **RF**—342. **Press Box Telephone:** (845) 204-1777.

NORTHERN COLORADO BEARS.

Conference: Western Athletic. **Mailing Address:** 270D Butler-Hancock Athletic Center Greeley, CO 80639. **Website:** www.uncbears.com. **Head Coach:** Carl Iwasaki. **Telephone:** (970) 351-1714. **Baseball SID:** Dylan Morey. **Assistant Coaches:** Pat Jolley, Shane Opitz. **Telephone:** (970) 351-1203. **Home Field:** Jackson Field. **Seating Capacity:** 1,500. **Outfield Dimension:** LF—345, CF—407, RF—356.

NORTHERN ILLINOIS HUSKIES.

Conference: Mid-American. **Mailing Address:** 1525 W. Lincoln Hwy. DeKalb, IL 60115. **Website:** www.niuhuskies.com. **Head Coach:** Mike Kunigonis. **Telephone:** (815) 753-0147. **Baseball SID:** Mike Haase. **Telephone:** (815) 753-1708. **Assistant Coaches:** Andrew Maki, Luke Stewart. **Telephone:** (815) 753-0147. **Home Field:** Ralph McKinzie Field. **Outfield Dimension:** LF—312, CF—395, RF—322.

NORTHERN KENTUCKY NORSE.

Conference: Horizon. **Mailing Address:** 133 BB&T Arena at Northern Kentucky University 500 Nunn Drive Highland Heights, KY 41099. **Website:** www.nkunorse.com. **Head Coach:** Todd Asalon. **Telephone:** (859) 572-6474. **Baseball SID:** Robby Johnson. **Telephone:** (859) 572-7850. **Assistant Coaches:** Dizzy Peyton. **Telephone:** (859) 572-5940. **Home Field:** Bill Aker Baseball Complex. **Seating Capacity:** 500. **Outfield Dimension:** LF—320, CF—395, RF—320.

NORTHWESTERN WILDCATS.

Conference: Big Ten. **Mailing Address:** 1501 Central ave Evanston, IL. **Website:** nusports.com. **Head Coach:** Spencer Allen. **Telephone:** . **Baseball SID:** Amitt Mallik. **Telephone:** . **Fax:** . **Assistant Coaches:** Dusty Napoleon, *Josh Reynolds. **Telephone:** . **Home Field:** Rocky and Berenice Miller Park. **Seating Capacity:** 2,000. **Outfield Dimension:** LF—326, CF—402, RF—310.

NORTHWESTERN STATE DEMONS.

Conference: Southland. **Mailing Address:** 468 Caspari Street, Natchitoches, LA 71497. **Website:** www.NSUDemons.com. **Head Coach:** Bobby Barbier. **Telephone:** (318) 357-5252. **Baseball SID:** Jason Pugh. **Telephone:** (318) 357-6468. **Fax:** . **Assistant Coaches:** *Chris Bertrand, Taylor Dugas. **Telephone:** (318) 357-4134. **Home Field:** Brown-Stroud Field. **Seating Capacity:** 1,200. **Outfield Dimension:** LF—320, CF—400, RF—340. **Press Box Telephone:** (318) 357-4606.

NOTRE DAME FIGHTING IRISH.

Conference: ACC. **Mailing Address:** 113 Joyce Center Notre Dame, IN 46556. **Website:** und.com. **Head Coach:** Link Jarrett. **Telephone:** (574) 631-4840. **Baseball SID:** Matt Paras. **Telephone:** (401) 215-5656. **Assistant Coaches:** Chuck Ristano, *Rich Wallace. **Telephone:** (574) 631-4840. **Home Field:** Frank Eck Stadium. **Seating Capacity:** 3,500. **Outfield Dimension:** LF—325, CF—400, RF—325. **Press Box Telephone:** (401) 215-5656.

OAKLAND GOLDEN GRIZZLIES.

Conference: Horizon. **Mailing Address:** 569 Pioneer Dr. Rochester, MI 48309. **Website:** www.goldengrizzlies.com. **Head Coach:** Colin Kaline. **Telephone:** (248) 370-4059. **Baseball SID:** . **Telephone:** . **Fax:** . **Assistant Coaches:** Justin Karn. **Telephone:** (248) 370-4228. **Home Field:** Oakland Baseball Field. **Seating Capacity:** 500. **Outfield Dimension:** LF—330, CF—380, RF—320.

OHIO BOBCATS.

Conference: Mid-American. **Mailing Address:** 1 Chubb Hall Athens Ohio, 45701. **Website:** www.OhioBobcats.com. **Head Coach:** Rob Smith. **Telephone:** (740) 593-1180. **Baseball SID:** Michael Scholze. **Telephone:** (330) 465-5807. **Assistant Coaches:** Craig Moore. **Telephone:** (740) 593-1954. **Home Field:** Bob Wren Stadium. **Seating Capacity:** 3,000. **Outfield Dimension:** LF—340, CF—405, RF—340.

OHIO STATE BUCKEYES.

Conference: Big Ten. **Mailing Address:** 650 Borror Dr. Columbus, OH 43210. **Website:** ohiostatebuckeyes.com. **Head Coach:** Greg Beals. **Telephone:** (614) 292-1075. **Baseball SID:** Brett Rybak. **Telephone:** (614) 292-1112. **Fax:** . **Assistant Coaches:** *Matt Angle, Dan DeLucia. **Telephone:** (614) 292-1075. **Home Field:** Nick Swisher Field at Bill Davis Stadium. **Seating Capacity:** 4,450. **Outfield Dimension:** LF—330, CF—400, RF—330.

OKLAHOMA SOONERS.

Conference: Big 12. **Mailing Address:** 401 Imhoff Rd, Norman, OK 73072. **Website:** www.soonersports.com. **Head Coach:** Skip Johnson. **Telephone:** . **Baseball SID:** Eric Hollier. **Telephone:** (405) 325-6449. **Fax:** . **Assistant Coaches:** *Clay Overcash, Clay Van Hook. **Telephone:** (405) 325-8354. **Home Field:** L. Dale Mitchell Park. **Seating Capacity:** 3,180. **Outfield Dimension:** LF—335, CF—411, RF—335. **Press Box Telephone:** (405) 325-8363.

OKLAHOMA STATE COWBOYS.

Conference: Big 12. **Mailing Address:** Allie P. Reynolds Stadium, 598 N Duck St, Stillwater, OK 74078. **Website:** www.okstate.com. **Head Coach:** Josh Holliday. **Telephone:** (405) 744-7141. **Baseball SID:** Wade McWhorter. **Telephone:** (405) 744-7853. **Assistant Coaches:** *Marty Lees, Rob Walton. **Home Field:** O'Brate Stadium. **Seating Capacity:** 8,000. **Outfield Dimension:** LF—331, CF—402, RF—325.

OLD DOMINION MONARCHS.

Conference: Conference USA. **Mailing Address:** Jim Jarrett Athletic Administration Building Norfolk, VA 23529-0201. **Website:** www.odusports.com. **Head Coach:** Chris Finwood. **Telephone:** (757) 683-4230. **Baseball SID:** Rebecca Gaona. **Telephone:** (757) 683-3395. **Assistant Coaches:** Mike Marron, *Logan Robbins. **Telephone:** (757) 683-4230. **Home Field:** Bud Metheny Baseball Complex. **Seating Capacity:** 2,500. **Outfield Dimension:** LF—325, CF—395, RF—325.

ORAL ROBERTS GOLDEN EAGLES.

Conference: Summit. **Mailing Address:** 7777 S Lewis Ave Tulsa Ok 74171. **Website:** www.oruathletics.com. **Head Coach:** Ryan Folmar. **Telephone:** (918) 495-7639. **Baseball SID:** Tyler Pounds. **Telephone:** (918) 495-7181. **Assistant Coaches:** Wes Davis, *Ryan Neill. **Telephone:** (918) 495-7206. **Home Field:** J.L. Johnson Stadium.

Seating Capacity: 2,418. **Outfield Dimension: LF**—330, **CF**—400, **RF**—330.

OREGON DUCKS.

Conference: Pac-12. **Mailing Address:** 2727 Leo Harris Parkway. **Website:** www.GoDucks.com. **Head Coach:** Mark Wasikowski. **Telephone:** (541) 346-5235. **Baseball SID:** Todd Miles. **Telephone:** (541) 346-0962. **Assistant Coaches:** Jake Angier, *Jack Marder. **Telephone:** (541) 346-5261. **Home Field:** PK Park. **Seating Capacity:** 4,000. **Outfield Dimension: LF**—333, **CF**—400, **RF**—325.

OREGON STATE BEAVERS.

Conference: Pac-12. **Mailing Address:** 114 Gill Coliseum, Corvallis, OR 97333. **Website:** www.osubeavers.com. **Head Coach:** Mitch Canham. **Telephone:** . **Baseball SID:** Hank Hager. **Telephone:** (541) 737-7472. **Assistant Coaches:** Rich Dorman, Pat Bailey. **Telephone:** (541) 737-0598. **Home Field:** Goss Stadium at Coleman Field. **Seating Capacity:** 3,587. **Outfield Dimension: LF**—335, **CF**—400, **RF**—335.

PACIFIC TIGERS.

Conference: West Coast. **Mailing Address:** 3601 Pacific Avenue, Stockton, CA 95211. **Website:** www.pacifictigers.com. **Head Coach:** Chris Rodriguez. **Telephone:** (209) 946-2163. **Baseball SID:** Chris Fortney. **Telephone:** (209) 946-2479. **Fax:** . **Assistant Coaches:** *Joey Centanni, Garrett DeGallier. **Telephone:** (209) 946-2386. **Home Field:** Klein Family Field. **Seating Capacity:** 3,000. **Outfield Dimension: LF**—317, **CF**—405, **RF**—328.

PENN STATE NITTANY LIONS.

Conference: Big Ten. **Mailing Address:** Medlar Field at Lubrano Park State College, PA 16801. **Website:** gopsusports.com. **Head Coach:** Rob Cooper. **Baseball SID:** Mark Brumbaugh. **Telephone:** (814) 863-1377. **Assistant Coaches:** Sean Moore, *Josh Newman. **Telephone:** (814) 865-8605. **Home Field:** Medlar Field at Lubrano Park. **Seating Capacity:** 5,406. **Outfield Dimension: LF**—325, **CF**—399, **RF**—320. **Press Box Telephone:** (814) 441-9145.

PENNSYLVANIA QUAKERS.

Conference: Ivy League. **Mailing Address:** 235 S. 33rd Street, Philadelphia, Pa. 19104. **Website:** pennathletics.com. **Head Coach:** John Yurkow. **Telephone:** (215) 898-6282. **Baseball SID:** Greg Mays. **Telephone:** (215) 898-6128. **Assistant Coaches:** *Mike Santello, Josh Schwartz. **Telephone:** (215) 746-2325. **Home Field:** Meiklejohn Stadium. **Seating Capacity:** 1000. **Outfield Dimension: LF**—325, **CF**—380, **RF**—330.

PEPPERDINE WAVES.

Conference: West Coast. **Mailing Address:** 24255 Pacific Coast Highway Malibu, CA 90263. **Website:** www.pepperdinewaves.com. **Head Coach:** Rick Hirtensteiner. **Telephone:** (310) 506-4404. **Baseball SID:** Ricky Davis. **Telephone:** (310) 506-4333. **Assistant Coaches:** Danny Worth, Jim Lawler. **Telephone:** (310) 506-4199. **Home Field:** Eddy D. Field Stadium. **Seating Capacity:** 1,800. **Outfield Dimension: LF**—330, **CF**—400, **RF**—330.

PITTSBURGH PANTHERS.

Conference: Atlantic Coast. **Mailing Address:** 3502 Allequippa Street University of Pittsburgh Pittsburgh, PA 15261. **Website:** www.pittsburghpanthers.com. **Head Coach:** Mike Bell. **Telephone:** (412) 648-8556. **Baseball SID:** Korey Blucas. **Assistant Coaches:** *Ty Megahee, Jerry Oakes. **Telephone:** (412) 648-8556. **Home Field:** Charles L. Cost Field. **Seating Capacity:** 900. **Outfield Dimension: LF**—325, **CF**—405, **RF**—330.

PORTLAND PILOTS.

Conference: West Coast. **Mailing Address:** 5000 N. Willamette Blvd. Portland, Oregon 97203. **Website:** www.portlandpilots.com. **Head Coach:** Geoff Loomis. **Telephone:** (503) 943-7707. **Baseball SID:** Adam Linnman. **Telephone:** (503) 943-7731. **Assistant Coaches:** Connor Lambert, *Jake Valentine. **Telephone:** (503) 943-7745. **Home Field:** Joe Etzel Field. **Seating Capacity:** 1050. **Outfield Dimension: LF**—325, **CF**—390, **RF**—325.

PRAIRIE VIEW A&M PANTHERS.

Conference: Southwestern Athletic. **Mailing Address:** PVAMU Athletics Department, P.O. Box 519, MS 1500 Prairie View, TX 77446. **Website:** www.pvpanthers.com. **Head Coach:** Auntwan Riggins. **Telephone:** (936) 261-9121. **Baseball SID:** LaTonia Thirston. **Telephone:** (936) 261-9106. **Assistant Coaches:** Brian White, John Sheehan. **Telephone:** (936) 261-3995. **Home Field:** Tankersley Field. **Seating Capacity:** 512.

PRESBYTERIAN BLUE HOSE.

Conference: Big South. **Mailing Address:** 105 Ashland Ave. **Website:** www.gobluehose.com. **Head Coach:** Elton Pollock. **Telephone:** (864) 833-8236. **Baseball SID:** Greg Hartlage. **Telephone:** (864) 833-8095. **Assistant Coaches:** Blake Miller, *Gil Walker. **Telephone:** (864) 833-7093. **Home Field:** PC Baseball Complex. **Seating Capacity:** 500. **Outfield Dimension: LF**—325, **CF**—400, **RF**—325.

PRINCETON TIGERS.

Conference: Ivy League. **Mailing Address:** Jadwin Gymnasium Princeton, NJ 08544. **Website:** www.goprincetontigers.com. **Head Coach:** Scott Bradley. **Telephone:** (609) 258-5059. **Baseball SID:** . **Telephone:** . **Fax:** . **Assistant Coaches:** Lloyd Brewer, Mike Russo. **Telephone:** (609) 258-5684. **Home Field:** Clarke Field. **Seating Capacity:** 850. **Outfield Dimension: LF**—325, **CF**—400, **RF**—315.

PURDUE BOILERMAKERS.

Conference: Big Ten. **Mailing Address:** Mollenkopf Athletic Center / 1225 Northwestern Ave. / West Lafayette, IN 47907. **Website:** PurdueSports.com. **Head Coach:** Greg Goff. **Telephone:** (765) 494-3998. **Baseball SID:** Ben Turner. **Telephone:** (765) 494-3198. **Fax:** . **Assistant Coaches:** *Cooper Fouts, Chris Marx. **Telephone:** (765) 496-3442. **Home Field:** Alexander Field. **Seating Capacity:** 2000. **Outfield Dimension: LF**—340, **CF**—408, **RF**—330. **Press Box Telephone:** (217) 549-7965.

PURDUE-FORT WAYNE MASTODONS.

Conference: Summit. **Mailing Address:** Fort Wayne, IN. **Website:** www.gomastodons.com. **Head Coach:** Doug Schreiber. **Telephone:** (260) 481-0729. **Baseball SID:** Derrick Sloboda. **Telephone:** (260) 481-0729. **Assistant Coaches:** Ken Jones, *Brent McNeil. **Telephone:** (260) 481-5455.

Home Field: Mastodon Field. Seating Capacity: 250. Outfield Dimension: LF—339, CF—405, RF—339.

QUINNIPIAC BOBCATS.

Conference: Metro Atlantic. Mailing Address: 275 Mount Carmel Ave., Hamden, CT, 06518. Website: www.gobobcats.com. Head Coach: John Delaney. Telephone: (203) 582-6546. Baseball SID: Kevin Noonan. Telephone: (203) 582-5387. Assistant Coaches: *Pat Egan, Corey Keane. Telephone: (203) 582-7774. Home Field: Bobcat Field. Seating Capacity: 1000. Outfield Dimension: LF—340, CF—395, RF—315.

RADFORD HIGHLANDERS.

Conference: Big South. Mailing Address: P.O. Box 6913 Radford, VA 24142. Website: www.radfordathletics.com. Head Coach: Karl Kuhn. Baseball SID: . Telephone: . Fax: . Assistant Coaches: Josh Reavis, Matt Rein. Telephone: (540) 831-6578. Home Field: Williams Field at Carter Memorial Stadium. Seating Capacity: 800. Outfield Dimension: LF—330, CF—400, RF—300.

RHODE ISLAND RAMS.

Conference: Atlantic 10. Mailing Address: 3 Keaney Rd. Website: www.gorhody.com. Head Coach: Raphael Cerrato. Telephone: (401) 874-4550. Baseball SID: Jodi Pontbriand. Telephone: (401) 874-5356. Assistant Coaches: *Sean O'Brien, Kevin Vance. Telephone: (401) 874-4888. Home Field: Bill Beck Field. Seating Capacity: 500. Outfield Dimension: LF—330, CF—400, RF—330.

RICE OWLS.

Conference: Conference USA. Mailing Address: 6100 Main Street; MS 548; Houston, Texas 77004. Website: www.RiceOwls.com. Head Coach: Matt Bragga. Telephone: (713) 348-8864. Baseball SID: john Sullivan. Telephone: (713) 348-5636. Assistant Coaches: *Cory Barton, Paul Janish. Telephone: (713) 348-8862. Home Field: Reckling Park. Seating Capacity: 6,193. Outfield Dimension: LF—335, CF—400, RF—335. Press Box Telephone: (713) 348-4931.

RICHMOND SPIDERS.

Conference: Atlantic 10. Mailing Address: Robins Center, 365 College Road, University of Richmond, VA 23173. Website: www.richmondspiders.com. Head Coach: Tracy Woodson. Telephone: (804) 289-8391. Baseball SID: Dan Wacker. Telephone: . Assistant Coaches: *Nate Mulberg, RJ Thomas. Telephone: (804) 289-8391. Home Field: Pitt Field. Seating Capacity: 600. Outfield Dimension: LF—328, CF—390, RF—328.

RIDER BRONCS.

Conference: Metro Atlantic. Mailing Address: 2083 Lawrenceville Rd Lawrenceville, NJ 08648. Website: gobroncs.com. Head Coach: Dr. Barry Davis. Telephone: . Baseball SID: Steve Cunha. Telephone: (609) 896-5135. Assistant Coaches: *Lee Lipinski, Mike Petrowski. Telephone: (443) 935-1932. Home Field: Sonny Pittaro Field. Seating Capacity: 2,500. Outfield Dimension: LF—330, CF—415, RF—330.

RUTGERS SCARLET KNIGHTS.

Conference: Big Ten. Mailing Address: 83 Rockafeller Road, Piscataway, NJ 08854. Website: ScarletKnights.com. Head Coach: Steve Owens. Telephone: (732) 445-7834.

Baseball SID: Jimmy Gill. Telephone: (732) 445-8103. Assistant Coaches: *Brendan Monaghan, Kyle Pettoruto. Telephone: (732) 445-7882. Home Field: Bainton Field. Seating Capacity: 1,500. Outfield Dimension: LF—329, CF—392, RF—324. Press Box Telephone: (732) 991-9486.

SACRAMENTO STATE HORNETS.

Conference: Western Athletic. Mailing Address: 6000 J St., Sacramento, CA 95691. Website: Hornetsports.com. Head Coach: Reggie Christiansen. Telephone: (916) 278-4036. Baseball SID: Robert Barsanti. Telephone: (916) 278-6896. Assistant Coaches: David Flores, *Tyler LaTorre. Telephone: (916) 278-2018. Home Field: John Smith Field. Seating Capacity: 1,200. Outfield Dimension: LF—330, CF—395, RF—330. Press Box Telephone: (408) 710-7961.

SACRED HEART PIONEERS.

Conference: Northeast. Mailing Address: 5151 Park Ave. Fairfield, CT 06825. Website: www.shubigred.com. Head Coach: Nick Restaino. Telephone: (203) 365-7632. Baseball SID: Chris O'Connor. Telephone: (203) 396-8125. Assistant Coaches: Wayne Mazzoni, T.K. Kiernan. Telephone: (203) 260-4932. Home Field: The Ballpark at Harbor Yard. Seating Capacity: 5,300. Outfield Dimension: LF—325, CF—405, RF—325.

SAINT LOUIS BILLIKENS.

Conference: Atlantic 10. Mailing Address: 3330 Laclede Ave, St. Louis, MO 63103. Website: www.slubillikens.com. Head Coach: Darin Hendrickson. Telephone: (314) 977-3172. Baseball SID: Nick Retting. Telephone: (314) 977-2524. Assistant Coaches: *Evan Pratte, Will Schierholz. Telephone: (314) 779-6768. Home Field: Billiken Sports Center. Seating Capacity: 500. Outfield Dimension: LF—330, CF—403, RF—330.

SAINT MARY'S GAELS.

Conference: West Coast. Mailing Address: 1928 Saint Marys Rd Moraga, CA 94575. Website: https://smcgaels.com/sports/baseball. Head Coach: Greg Moore. Telephone: . Baseball SID: Brian Brownfield. Telephone: (925) 631-4950. Fax: . Assistant Coaches: Riley Goulding, *Jordon Twohig. Telephone: . Home Field: Luis Guisto Field. Seating Capacity: 1,000. Outfield Dimension: LF—330, CF—400, RF—330. Press Box Telephone: (925) 631-4950.

SAM HOUSTON STATE BEARKATS.

Conference: Southland. Mailing Address: 620 Bowers Blvd, Huntsville, TX 77340. Website: www.GoBearkats.com. Head Coach: Jay Sirianni. Telephone: (936) 294-2580. Baseball SID: Ben Rikard. Telephone: (936) 294-1764. Assistant Coaches: *Fuller Smith, Shane Wedd. Telephone: (936) 294-1731. Home Field: Don Sanders Stadium. Seating Capacity: 1,164. Outfield Dimension: LF—330, CF—400, RF—330.

SAMFORD BULLDOGS.

Conference: Southern. Mailing Address: 800 Lakeshore Dr., Birmingham, AL 35229. Website: www.samfordsports.com. Head Coach: Casey Dunn. Telephone: (205) 726-2134. Baseball SID: Joey Mullins. Telephone: (205) 726-2799 . Assistant Coaches: Tony David, *Tyler Shrout. Telephone: (205) 726-4294. Home Field: Joe Lee Griffin Field. Seating Capacity: 1,000.

Outfield Dimension: LF—330, CF—390, RF—335.

SAN DIEGO TOREROS.

Conference: West Coast. Mailing Address: 5998 Alcala Park, San Diego, CA 92110. Website: www.usd-toreros.com. Head Coach: Rich Hill. Telephone: (619) 260-5953. Baseball SID: Rose McPherson. Telephone: (619) 260-4745. Assistant Coaches: *Brock Ungricht, Matt Florer. Home Field: Fowler Park. Seating Capacity: 3,000. Outfield Dimension: LF—312, CF—391, RF—327.

SAN DIEGO STATE AZTECS.

Conference: Mountain West. Mailing Address: 500 Campanile Rd., San Diego, CA 92182. Website: www.goaztecs.com. Head Coach: Mark Martinez. Telephone: (619) 594-6889. Baseball SID: Jim Solien. Telephone: (619) 594-2576. Assistant Coaches: *Joe Oliveira, Sam Peraza. Telephone: (619) 594-6889. Home Field: Tony Gwynn Stadium. Seating Capacity: 3,500. Outfield Dimension: LF—340, CF—405, RF—340.

SAN FRANCISCO DONS.

Conference: West Coast. Mailing Address: 2130 Fulton St., G20, San Francisco, CA 94117. Website: www.usfdons.com. Head Coach: Nino Giarratano. Telephone: (415) 422-2934. Baseball SID: Matt Fontenot. Telephone: (925) 878-5701. Assistant Coaches: Mat Keplinger, *Troy Nakamura. Telephone: (209) 403-6042. Home Field: Benedetti Diamond. Seating Capacity: 1,000. Outfield Dimension: LF—330, CF—420, RF—300.

SAN JOSE STATE SPARTANS.

Conference: Mountain West. Mailing Address: 1393 S. 7th Street, San Jose, CA, 95112. Website: sjsuspartans.com. Head Coach: Brad Sanfilippo. Telephone: (408) 924-1287. Baseball SID: Matt Penland. Telephone: (408) 924-1229. Assistant Coaches: Ross Gusky, *Thomas Walker. Telephone: . Home Field: Excite Ballpark. Seating Capacity: 5,200. Outfield Dimension: LF—320, CF—390, RF—320. Press Box Telephone: (408) 924-7276.

SANTA CLARA BRONCOS.

Conference: West Coast. Mailing Address: 500 El Camino Real, Santa Clara, CA 95053. Website: www.SantaClaraBroncos.com. Head Coach: Rusty Filter. Telephone: (408) 554-4882. Baseball SID: Dean Obara. Telephone: (408) 554-4690. Assistant Coaches: *Jon Karcich, BK Santy. Telephone: (408) 554-4680. Home Field: Stephen Schott Stadium. Seating Capacity: 1,500. Outfield Dimension: LF—340, CF—402, RF—335.

SEATTLE REDHAWKS.

Conference: Western Athletic. Mailing Address: 901 12th Ave., PO Box 222000, Seattle, WA 98122. Website: www.GoSeattleU.com. Head Coach: Donny Harrel. Telephone: (206) 398-4399. Baseball SID: Jason Oliveira. Telephone: (206) 296-2360. Assistant Coaches: Greg Goetz, Wes Long. Telephone: (206) 398-4397. Home Field: Bannerwood Park. Seating Capacity: 1,500. Outfield Dimension: LF—325, CF—400, RF—325.

SETON HALL PIRATES.

Conference: Big East. Mailing Address: 400 South Orange Ave., South Orange, NJ 07079. Website: www.shupirates.com. Head Coach: Rob Sheppard. Telephone: (973) 761-9557. Baseball SID: Peter Long. Telephone: (973) 761-9493. Assistant Coaches: Mark Pappas, Pat Pinkman. Telephone: (973) 275-6437. Home Field: Owen T. Carroll Field. Seating Capacity: 1,000. Outfield Dimension: LF—318, CF—400, RF—325.

SIENA SAINTS.

Conference: Metro Atlantic. Mailing Address: 515 Loudon Rd., Loudonville, NY 12211. Website: www.sienasaints.com. Head Coach: Tony Rossi. Telephone: (518) 786-5044. Baseball SID: Mike Demos. Telephone: (518) 783-2377. Assistant Coaches: *Rob Hardy, Anthony Spataro. Telephone: (518) 782-6875. Home Field: Connors Park. Seating Capacity: 1,000. Outfield Dimension: LF—300, CF—400, RF—325. Press Box Telephone: (336) 675-7374.

SOUTH ALABAMA JAGUARS.

Conference: Sun Belt. Mailing Address: 70 Stadium Blvd., Mobile, AL 36688. Website: www.usajaguars.com. Head Coach: Mark Calvi. Telephone: . Baseball SID: Charlie Nichols. Telephone: (251) 414-8017. Assistant Coaches: Brad Phillips, *Chris Prothro. Telephone: (251) 460-6970. Home Field: Stanky Field. Seating Capacity: 4,000. Outfield Dimension: LF—330, CF—400, RF—330.

SOUTH CAROLINA GAMECOCKS.

Conference: Southeastern. Mailing Address: 431 Williams St., Columbia, SC 29201. Website: www.GamecocksOnline.com. Head Coach: Mark Kingston. Telephone: (803) 777-7808. Baseball SID: Kent Reichert. Telephone: (803) 777-5257. Assistant Coaches: *Trip Couch, Skylar Meade. Telephone: (803) 777-7808. Home Field: Founders Park. Seating Capacity: 8,242. Outfield Dimension: LF—325, CF—400, RF—325. Press Box Telephone: (803) 777-6648.

SOUTH CAROLINA-UPSTATE SPARTANS.

Conference: Big South. Mailing Address: 800 University Way, Spartanburg, SC 29303. Website: www.upstatespartans.com. Head Coach: Mike McGuire. Telephone: (803) 524-2493. Baseball SID: Pat McGuff. Telephone: (513) 827-0959. Assistant Coaches: *Adam Brown, Kane Sweeney. Telephone: (618) 719-1934. Home Field: Harley Park. Seating Capacity: 500. Outfield Dimension: LF—335, CF—402, RF—335.

SOUTH DAKOTA STATE JACKRABBITS.

Conference: Summit. Mailing Address: 2820 Stanley J. Marshall Center, Brookings, SD 57007. Website: www.GoJacks.com. Head Coach: Rob Bishop. Telephone: (605) 690-9851. Baseball SID: Jason Hove. Telephone: (605) 688-4623. Assistant Coaches: Brian Grunzke. Telephone: (605) 592-6501. Home Field: Erv Huether Field. Seating Capacity: 500. Outfield Dimension: LF—325, CF—390, RF—325. Press Box Telephone: (605) 695-1827.

SOUTH FLORIDA BULLS.

Conference: American Athletic. Mailing Address: University of South Florida Athletics Department, 4202 E. Fowler Ave., ATH 100, Tampa, FL 33620. Website: www.gousfbulls.com. Head Coach: Billy Mohl. Telephone: (813) 974-2504. Baseball SID: Thomas Manzello. Telephone: (813) 974-4029. Assistant Coaches: Bo Durac, Alan Kunkel. Telephone: (813) 974-0567. Home Field: US Baseball Stadium. Seating Capacity: 3,211. Outfield Dimension: LF—325, CF—400, RF—330.

SOUTHEAST MISSOURI STATE REDHAWKS.

Conference: Ohio Valley. **Mailing Address:** One University Plaza, Cape Girardeau, MO 63701. **Website:** www.gosoutheast.com. **Head Coach:** Andy Sawyers. **Telephone:** (573) 986-6002. **Baseball SID:** Morgan Harding. **Telephone:** (573) 651-2294. **Assistant Coaches:** Matthew Kinney, *Craig Ringe. **Telephone:** (573) 986-6002. **Home Field:** Capaha Field. **Seating Capacity:** 2,000. **Outfield Dimension: LF**—330, **CF**—400, **RF**—330.

SOUTHEASTERN LOUISIANA LIONS.

Conference: Southland. **Mailing Address:** Southeastern Athletics, 800 Galloway Dr., Hammond, LA 70402. **Website:** www.LionSports.net. **Head Coach:** Matt Riser. **Telephone:** (985) 549-5130. **Baseball SID:** Damon Sunde. **Telephone:** (985) 549-3774. **Assistant Coaches:** Tim Donnelly. **Telephone:** (985) 549-5130. **Home Field:** Pat Kenelly Diamond at Alumni Field. **Seating Capacity:** 2,000. **Outfield Dimension: LF**—330, **CF**—400, **RF**—300.

SOUTHERN JAGUARS.

Conference: Southwestern Athletic. **Mailing Address:** 801 Harding Blvd., Baton Rouge, LA 70813. **Website:** www.gojagsports.com. **Head Coach:** Kerrick Jackson. **Telephone:** (225) 771-2513. **Baseball SID:** Rodney Kirschner. **Telephone:** (225) 771-5609. **Assistant Coaches:** Chris Crenshaw. **Telephone:** (225) 771-3882. **Home Field:** Lee-Hines Stadium. **Seating Capacity:** 2,500. **Outfield Dimension: LF**—360, **CF**—400, **RF**—325.

SOUTHERN CALIFORNIA TROJANS.

Conference: Pac-12. **Mailing Address:** 3501 Watt Way, Los Angeles, CA 90089. **Website:** www.usctrojans.com. **Head Coach:** Jason Gill. **Telephone:** (213) 740-8446. **Baseball SID:** Jacob Breems. **Telephone:** (213) 740-3809. **Assistant Coaches:** *Gabe Alvarez, Ted Silva. **Telephone:** (213) 740-8447. **Home Field:** Dedeaux Field. **Seating Capacity:** 2,500. **Outfield Dimension: LF**—335, **CF**—395, **RF**—335.

SOUTHERN ILLINOIS SALUKIS.

Conference: Missouri Valley. **Mailing Address:** 425 Saluki Dr., Carbondale, IL 62901. **Website:** www.SIUSalukis.com. **Head Coach:** Lance Rhodes. **Telephone:** (618) 453-3794 . **Baseball SID:** John Lock. **Telephone:** (618) 453-7102. **Assistant Coaches:** *Nick Magnifico, Tim Jamieson. **Telephone:** (618) 453-7646. **Home Field:** Itchy Jones Stadium. **Seating Capacity:** 2,000. **Outfield Dimension: LF**—330, **CF**—390, **RF**—330. **Press Box Telephone:** (309) 333-0132.

SOUTHERN ILLINOIS-EDWARDSVILLE COUGARS.

Conference: Ohio Valley. **Mailing Address:** 35 Circle Dr., Edwardsville, IL 62026. **Website:** www.siuecougars.com. **Head Coach:** Sean Lyons. **Telephone:** (618) 650-2032. **Baseball SID:** Joe Pott. **Telephone:** (618) 650-2860. **Assistant Coaches:** P.J. Finigan, Brandon Scott. **Telephone:** (618) 650-2032. **Home Field:** Simmons Complex. **Seating Capacity:** 1,300. **Outfield Dimension: LF**—330, **CF**—390, **RF**—330. ·

SOUTHERN MISSISSIPPI GOLDEN EAGLES.

Conference: Conference USA. **Mailing Address:** 118 College Dr., Box 5161, Hattiesburg, MS 39406. **Website:** www.SouthernMiss.com. **Head Coach:** Scott Berry. **Telephone:** (601) 266-5821. **Baseball SID:** Jack

Duggan. **Telephone:** (601) 266-5947. **Assistant Coaches:** *Travis Creel, Christian Ostrander. **Telephone:** (601) 266-6542. **Home Field:** Pete Taylor Park/Hill Denson Field. **Seating Capacity:** 4,300. **Outfield Dimension: LF**—340, **CF**—400, **RF**—340. **Press Box Telephone:** (601) 266-5684.

ST. BONAVENTURE BONNIES.

Conference: Atlantic-10. **Mailing Address:** Department of Athletics, PO Box G, Reilly Center, St. Bonaventure, NY 14778. **Website:** www.gobonnies.sbu.edu. **Head Coach:** Larry Sudbrook. **Telephone:** (716) 375-2641. **Baseball SID:** Scott Eddy. **Telephone:** (716) 375-4019. **Assistant Coaches:** B.J. Salerno. **Telephone:** (716) 375-2699. **Home Field:** Fred Handler Park. **Seating Capacity:** 500. **Outfield Dimension: LF**—330, **CF**—403, **RF**—330.

ST. JOHN'S RED STORM.

Conference: Big East. **Mailing Address:** 8000 Utopia Parkway, Queens, N.Y. 11439. **Website:** redstormsports.com. **Head Coach:** Mike Hampton. **Telephone:** (718) 990-2332. **Baseball SID:** Andrew O'Connell. **Telephone:** (718) 990-1522. **Assistant Coaches:** George Brown. **Telephone:** (718) 990-7523. **Home Field:** Jack Kaiser Stadium. **Seating Capacity:** 3,500. **Outfield Dimension: LF**—325, **CF**—390, **RF**—325. **Press Box Telephone:** (516) 581-3229.

ST. JOSEPH'S HAWKS.

Conference: Atlantic 10. **Mailing Address:** 5600 City Ave., Philadelphia, PA 19131. **Website:** www.sjuhawks.com. **Head Coach:** Fritz Hamburg. **Telephone:** (610) 660-1718. **Baseball SID:** Joe Greenwich. **Telephone:** (610) 660-1738. **Assistant Coaches:** Ryan Wheeler. **Telephone:** (610) 660-2592. **Home Field:** Smithson Field. **Seating Capacity:** 400. **Outfield Dimension: LF**—325, **CF**—400, **RF**—325.

ST. PETER'S PEACOCKS.

Conference: Metro Atlantic. **Mailing Address:** 2641 Kennedy Blvd., Jersey City, NJ 07306. **Website:** www.saintpeterspeacocks.com. **Head Coach:** Lou Proietti. **Telephone:** (201) 761-7319. **Baseball SID:** Hamilton Cook. **Telephone:** (201) 761-7316. **Assistant Coaches:** *Casey Aubin, Lucas Luopa. **Home Field:** Joseph J. Jaroschak Field. **Seating Capacity:** 500. **Outfield Dimension: LF**—317, **CF**—400, **RF**—307.

STANFORD CARDINAL.

Conference: Pac-12. **Mailing Address:** 641 Campus Dr., Stanford, CA 94305. **Website:** www.gostanford.com. **Head Coach:** David Esquer. **Telephone:** (650) 723-4528. **Baseball SID:** Nick Sako. **Telephone:** (650) 224-0979. **Assistant Coaches:** *Thomas Eager, Tommy Nicholson. **Telephone:** (650) 725-2373. **Home Field:** Klein Field. **Seating Capacity:** 4,000. **Outfield Dimension: LF**—335, **CF**—400, **RF**—335.

STEPHEN F. AUSTIN STATE LUMBERJACKS.

Conference: Southland. **Mailing Address:** SFA Athletics, PO Box 13010, SFA Station, Nacogdoches, TX 75962. **Website:** www.sfajacks.com. **Head Coach:** Johnny Cardenas. **Baseball SID:** Charlie Hurley. **Telephone:** (936) 468-2606. **Assistant Coaches:** Caleb Clowers, *Mike Haynes. **Telephone:** (936) 468-7796. **Home Field:** Jaycees Field. **Seating Capacity:** 1,000. **Outfield Dimension:**

LF—320, **CF**—390, **RF**—320.

STETSON HATTERS.

Conference: Atlantic Sun. **Mailing Address:** 421 N. Woodland Blvd., Unit 8359, DeLand, FL 32723. **Website:** www.gohatters.com. **Head Coach:** Steve Trimper. **Telephone:** (386) 822-8106. **Baseball SID:** Ricky Hazel. **Telephone:** (386) 822-8130. **Assistant Coaches:** *Joe Mercadante, Dave Therneau. **Telephone:** (386) 822-8733. **Home Field:** Melching Field at Conrad Park. **Seating Capacity:** 2,500. **Outfield Dimension:** LF—335, **CF**—403, **RF**—335. **Press Box Telephone:** (386) 736-7360.

STONY BROOK SEAWOLVES.

Conference: America East. **Mailing Address:** 100 Nicolls Rd., Stony Brook, NY 11794. **Website:** stonybrookathletics.com. **Head Coach:** Matt Senk. **Telephone:** (631) 632-9226. **Baseball SID:** Cameron Boon. **Telephone:** (631) 632-7289. **Assistant Coaches:** Tyler Kavanaugh, *Jim Martin. **Telephone:** (631) 632-4755. **Home Field:** Joe Nathan Field. **Seating Capacity:** 1,000. **Outfield Dimension:** LF—330, **CF**—380, **RF**—330.

TENNESSEE VOLUNTEERS.

Conference: Southeastern. **Mailing Address:** 1511 Pat Head Summitt Dr., Knoxville, TN 37996. **Website:** www.UTSports.com. **Head Coach:** Tony Vitello. **Telephone:** (865) 974-2057. **Baseball SID:** Sean Barows. **Telephone:** (865) 974-7478. **Assistant Coaches:** Frank Anderson, *Josh Elander. **Telephone:** (865) 974-2057. **Home Field:** Lindsey Nelson Stadium. **Seating Capacity:** 4283. **Outfield Dimension:** LF—320, **CF**—390, **RF**—320. **Press Box Telephone:** (561) 312-9432.

TENNESSEE TECH GOLDEN EAGLES.

Conference: Ohio Valley. **Mailing Address:** Tennessee Tech Athletics, 1100 McGee Blvd., TTU Box 5057, Cookeville, TN 38505. **Website:** www.ttusports.com. **Head Coach:** Steve Smith. **Telephone:** (931) 372-3925. **Baseball SID:** Michael Lehman. **Telephone:** (931) 372-3088. **Assistant Coaches:** Cooper Farris, *Mitchell Wright. **Telephone:** (931) 372-3853. **Home Field:** Quillen Field at Bush Stadium at the Averitt Express Baseball Complex. **Seating Capacity:** 1,100. **Outfield Dimension:** LF—329, **CF**—405, **RF**—330.

TENNESSEE-MARTIN SKYHAWKS.

Conference: Ohio Valley. **Mailing Address:** 544 University St., Martin, TN 38230. **Website:** www.utmsports.com. **Head Coach:** Ryan Jenkins. **Telephone:** (334) 590-0040. **Baseball SID:** Ryne Rickman. **Telephone:** (731) 881-7632. **Assistant Coaches:** Matt Heath, *Hunter Morris. **Telephone:** (731) 881-3691. **Home Field:** Skyhawk Field. **Seating Capacity:** 500. **Outfield Dimension:** LF—330, **CF**—385, **RF**—330. **Press Box Telephone:** (731) 881-7694.

TEXAS LONGHORNS.

Conference: Big 12. **Mailing Address:** 1300 E Martin Luther King Jr. Blvd., Austin, TX 78702. **Website:** www.TexasSports.com. **Head Coach:** David Pierce. **Telephone:** (512) 471-5732. **Baseball SID:** Kevin Rodriguez. **Telephone:** (512) 471-2078. **Assistant Coaches:** *Sean Allen, Philip Miller. **Telephone:** (512) 471-5732. **Home Field:** UFCU Disch-Falk Field. **Seating Capacity:** 7373. **Outfield Dimension:** LF—340, **CF**—400, **RF**—325.

TEXAS A&M AGGIES.

Conference: Southeastern. **Mailing Address:** 756 Houston Street, College Station, TX 77843. **Website:** www.12thMan.com. **Head Coach:** Rob Childress. **Telephone:** (979) 845-4810. **Baseball SID:** Thomas Dick. **Assistant Coaches:** Chad Caillet, *Justin Seely. **Telephone:** (979) 845-4810. **Home Field:** Olsen Field at Blue Bell Park. **Seating Capacity:** 6,100. **Outfield Dimension:** LF—330-375, **CF**—400, **RF**—375-330. **Press Box Telephone:** (979) 458-3604.

TEXAS A&M-CORPUS CHRISTI.

Conference: Southland. **Mailing Address:** 6300 Ocean Dr., Unit 5719, Corpus Christi, TX 78412. **Website:** www.goislanders.com. **Head Coach:** Scott Malone. **Telephone:** (361) 825-3413. **Baseball SID:** Marshall Fey. **Telephone:** (361) 825-3410. **Assistant Coaches:** Seth LaRue, Marty Smith. **Telephone:** (361) 825-3252. **Home Field:** Chapman Field. **Seating Capacity:** 700. **Outfield Dimension:** LF—330, **CF**—404, **RF**—330.

TEXAS CHRISTIAN HORNED FROGS.

Conference: Big 12. **Mailing Address:** 2900 Stadium Dr., Fort Worth, TX 76129. **Website:** www.gofrogs.com. **Head Coach:** Jim Schlossnagle. **Telephone:** (817) 257-5354. **Baseball SID:** Brandie Davidson. **Telephone:** (817) 257-7479. **Assistant Coaches:** Bill Mosiello, *Kirk Saarloos. **Telephone:** (817) 257-5588. **Home Field:** Lupton Stadium. **Seating Capacity:** 4,500. **Outfield Dimension:** LF—330, **CF**—395, **RF**—330.

TEXAS SOUTHERN.

Conference: Southwestern Athletic. **Mailing Address:** Texas Southern Athletics, 3100 Cleburne St., Houston, TX 77004. **Website:** www.tsusports.com. **Head Coach:** Michael Robertson. **Telephone:** (713) 313-4315. **Baseball SID:** Ryan McGinty. **Telephone:** (713) 313-6829. **Assistant Coaches:** Anthony Dilligard, Aaron Gilbreath. **Telephone:** (713) 313-7993. **Home Field:** MacGregor Park. **Outfield Dimension:** LF—315, **CF**—395, **RF**—315.

TEXAS STATE BOBCATS.

Conference: Sun Belt. **Mailing Address:** Texas State University, Department of Athletics, Darren B Casey Athletic Administration Building, 601 University Dr, San Marcos, TX 78666. **Website:** www.txstatebobcats.com. **Head Coach:** Steven Trout. **Telephone:** (512) 245-3383. **Baseball SID:** Phillip Pongratz. **Telephone:** (512) 245-4692. **Assistant Coaches:** *Josh Blakley, Chade Massengale. **Telephone:** (512) 245-3383. **Home Field:** Bobcat Ballpark. **Seating Capacity:** 2,500. **Outfield Dimension:** LF—330, **CF**—405, **RF**—330. **Press Box Telephone:** (931) 446-4001.

TEXAS TECH RED RAIDERS.

Conference: Big 12. **Mailing Address:** 2901 Drive of Champions Ste. 200, Lubbock, TX 79409. **Website:** www.texastech.com. **Head Coach:** Tim Tadlock. **Telephone:** (806) 834-4646. **Baseball SID:** Ty Parker. **Telephone:** (806) 834-2769. **Assistant Coaches:** Matt Gardner, *J-Bob Thomas. **Telephone:** (806) 834-4583. **Home Field:** Dan Law Field at Rip Griffin Park. **Seating Capacity:** 4,432. **Outfield Dimension:** LF—327, **CF**—402, **RF**—327.

TEXAS-ARLINGTON.

Conference: Sun Belt. **Mailing Address:** Gilstrap Athletic Center, 1309 W. Mitchell St., Arlington, TX 76019. **Website:** www.utamavs.com. **Head Coach:** Darin Thomas. **Telephone:** (817) 272-9744. **Baseball SID:** Ian Applegate. **Telephone:** (817) 272-9610. **Assistant Coaches:** Chad Comer, *Jon Wente. **Telephone:** (817) 272-7170. **Home Field:** Clay Gould Ballpark. **Seating Capacity:** 1,500. **Outfield Dimension:** LF—330, CF—400, RF—330.

TEXAS-SAN ANTONIO ROADRUNNERS.

Conference: Conference USA. **Mailing Address:** One UTSA Circle, San Antonio, TX 78249. **Website:** www.goutsa.com. **Head Coach:** Patrick Hallmark. **Telephone:** (210) 458-4171. **Baseball SID:** Michael High. **Telephone:** (210) 845-9037. **Assistant Coaches:** *Ryan Aguayo, Scott Shepperd. **Home Field:** Roadrunner Field. **Seating Capacity:** 800. **Outfield Dimension:** LF—330, CF—400, RF—330.

TOLEDO ROCKETS.

Conference: Mid-American. **Mailing Address:** 2801 Bancroft St., Toledo, OH 43606. **Website:** www.UTRockets.com. **Head Coach:** Rob Reinstetle. **Telephone:** (419) 530-6263. **Baseball SID:** Chris Cullum. **Telephone:** (419) 530-4913. **Assistant Coaches:** *Nick McIntyre, Tommy Winterstein. **Telephone:** (419) 530-6264. **Home Field:** Scott Park. **Seating Capacity:** 1,000. **Outfield Dimension:** LF—330, CF—400, RF—330. **Press Box Telephone:** (419) 530-3089.

TOWSON TIGERS.

Conference: Colonial. **Mailing Address:** 8000 York Rd., Towson, MD 21252. **Website:** www.towsontigers.com. **Head Coach:** Matt Tyner. **Telephone:** (410) 704-3775. **Baseball SID:** Dave Vatz. **Telephone:** (410) 704-3102. **Assistant Coaches:** Tanner Biagini, *Miles Miller. **Telephone:** (410) 704-3775. **Home Field:** John B. Schuerholz Park. **Seating Capacity:** 500. **Outfield Dimension:** LF—312, CF—424, RF—301.

TROY TROJANS.

Conference: Sun Belt. **Mailing Address:** Tine Davis Fieldhouse, 5000 Veterans Stadium Drive, Troy, AL 36082. **Website:** www.troytrojans.com. **Head Coach:** Mark Smartt. **Telephone:** (334) 670-5945. **Baseball SID:** Andy Stubblefield. **Telephone:** (334) 670-5654. **Assistant Coaches:** *Shane Gierke, Matt Hancock. **Telephone:** . **Home Field:** Riddle-Pace Field. **Seating Capacity:** 2,000. **Outfield Dimension:** LF—340, CF—400, RF—310. **Press Box Telephone:** (334) 670-5701.

TULANE GREEN WAVE.

Conference: American Athletic. **Mailing Address:** 2950 Ben Weiner Dr., New Orleans, LA 70118. **Website:** tulanegreenwave.com. **Head Coach:** Travis Jewett. **Telephone:** (504) 862-8216. **Baseball SID:** Clyde Verdin. **Telephone:** (504) 314-7271. **Assistant Coaches:** Daniel Latham, *Jay Uhlman. **Telephone:** (504) 314-7203. **Home Field:** Greer Field at Turchin Stadium. **Seating Capacity:** 5,000. **Outfield Dimension:** LF—325, CF—400, RF—325. **Press Box Telephone:** (504) 862-8614.

UC DAVIS AGGIES.

Conference: Big West. **Mailing Address:** 1 Shields Ave., Davis, CA 95616. **Website:** www.ucdavisaggies.com. **Head Coach:** Matt Vaughn. **Telephone:** (530) 752-7513. **Baseball SID:** Matt Murphy. **Assistant Coaches:** *Lloyd Acosta, Brett Lindgren. **Telephone:** (530) 752-7513. **Home Field:** Phil Swimley Field. **Seating Capacity:** 3,500. **Outfield Dimension:** LF—330, CF—400, RF—330.

UC IRVINE ANTEATERS.

Conference: Big West. **Mailing Address:** Intercollegiate Athletics Building, Irvine, CA 92697. **Website:** www.ucirvinesports.com. **Head Coach:** Ben Orloff. **Telephone:** (949) 824-6033. **Baseball SID:** Alex Croteau. **Telephone:** (949) 824-5814. **Assistant Coaches:** Daniel Bibona, *J.T. Bloodworth. **Telephone:** (949) 824-1154. **Home Field:** Cicerone Field at Anteater Ballpark. **Seating Capacity:** 3,408. **Outfield Dimension:** LF—335, CF—408, RF—335.

UC RIVERSIDE HIGHLANDERS.

Conference: Big West. **Mailing Address:** 901 University Ave., Riverside, CA 92521. **Website:** www.gohighlanders.com. **Head Coach:** Troy Percival. **Telephone:** (951) 827-5441. **Baseball SID:** Chelsea Pfohl. **Assistant Coaches:** *Justin Johnson, Curtis Smith. **Telephone:** (951) 827-5441. **Home Field:** Riverside Sports Complex. **Seating Capacity:** 2,500. **Outfield Dimension:** LF—330, CF—400, RF—330.

UC SANTA BARBARA GAUCHOS.

Conference: Big West. **Mailing Address:** UCSB Intercollegiate Athletics Department, ICA Building, Santa Barbara, CA 93106. **Website:** www.UCSBGauchos.com. **Head Coach:** Andrew Checketts. **Telephone:** (805) 893-3690. **Baseball SID:** Daniel Moebus-Bowles. **Telephone:** (805) 893-8603. **Assistant Coaches:** *Matt Fonteno. **Telephone:** (805) 893-3690. **Home Field:** Caesar Uyesaka Stadium. **Seating Capacity:** 1,000. **Outfield Dimension:** LF—335, CF—400, RF—335.

UCLA BRUINS.

Conference: Pac-12. **Mailing Address:** J.D. Morgan Center, 325 Westwood Plaza, Los Angeles, CA 90095. **Website:** www.uclabruins.com. **Head Coach:** John Savage. **Telephone:** (310) 794-8210. **Baseball SID:** Andrew Wagner. **Telephone:** (310) 206-7870. **Assistant Coaches:** Rex Peters, *Bryant Ward. **Telephone:** (310) 794-8210. **Home Field:** Jackie Robinson Stadium. **Seating Capacity:** 3,000. **Outfield Dimension:** LF—330, CF—395, RF—330.

UNC ASHEVILLE BULLDOGS.

Conference: Big South. **Mailing Address:** Justice Center, CPO #2600 One University Heights, Asheville, NC 28804. **Website:** uncabulldogs.com. **Head Coach:** Scott Friedholm. **Telephone:** (828) 251-6920. **Baseball SID:** Aaron Cantrell. **Telephone:** (828) 251-6931. **Assistant Coaches:** Chris Bresnahan. **Telephone:** (828) 250-2309. **Home Field:** Greenwood Field. **Seating Capacity:** 600. **Outfield Dimension:** LF—330, CF—390, RF—330. **Press Box Telephone:** (828) 713-5612.

UNC GREENSBORO SPARTANS.

Conference: Southern. **Mailing Address:** 1400 Spring Garden St., Greensboro, NC 27412. **Website:** www.uncg-spartans.com. **Head Coach:** Billy Godwin. **Baseball SID:** Mark Pinkerton. **Telephone:** (757) 812-1926. **Assistant Coaches:** Hunter Allen, *Greg Starbuck. **Home Field:**

UNCG Baseball Stadium. **Seating Capacity:** 3,500. **Outfield Dimension: LF**—340, **CF**—410, **RF**—340.

UNC WILMINGTON SEAHAWKS.

Conference: Colonial. **Mailing Address:** 601 South College Rd., Wilmington, NC. **Website:** www. UNCWSports.com. **Head Coach:** Randy Hood. **Telephone:** (910) 962-3793. **Baseball SID:** Tom Riordan. **Telephone:** (910) 962-4099. **Assistant Coaches:** *Chris Moore, Matt Myers. **Telephone:** (910) 962-7471. **Home Field:** Brooks Field. **Seating Capacity:** 3,500. **Outfield Dimension: LF**—340, **CF**—380, **RF**—340.

UT-RIO GRANDE VALLEY VAQUEROS.

Conference: Western Athletic. **Mailing Address:** 1201 W. University Dr., Edinburg, TX 78539. **Website:** www. GoUTRGV.com. **Head Coach:** Derek Matlock. **Telephone:** (956) 665-2235. **Baseball SID:** Jonah Goldberg. **Telephone:** (956) 665-2240. **Assistant Coaches:** Robert Martinez, *Russell Raley. **Telephone:** (956) 665-2891. **Home Field:** UTRGV Baseball Stadium. **Seating Capacity:** 5,000. **Outfield Dimension: LF**—325, **CF**—410, **RF**—325.

UTAH UTES.

Conference: Pac-12. **Mailing Address:** 1825 E. South Campus Dr., Salt Lake City, Utah, 84112. **Website:** www. UtahUtes.com. **Head Coach:** Bill Kinneberg. **Telephone:** (801) 581-3526. **Baseball SID:** Joseph Feldman. **Telephone:** (801) 231-1329. **Assistant Coaches:** *Jay Brossman, Gary Henderson. **Telephone:** (801) 581-3024. **Home Field:** Smith's Ballpark. **Seating Capacity:** 14,511. **Outfield Dimension: LF**—345, **CF**—420, **RF**—315.

UTAH VALLEY WOLVERINES.

Conference: Western Athletic. **Mailing Address:** Department of Athletics - MS 104, 800 W. University Parkway, Orem, Utah 84058. **Website:** www.gouvu. com. **Head Coach:** Eric Madsen. **Telephone:** (801) 863-6509. **Baseball SID:** James Warnick. **Telephone:** (801) 863-6231. **Assistant Coaches:** David Carter, Joldy Watts. **Telephone:** (801) 863-8647. **Home Field:** UCCU Stadium. **Seating Capacity:** 5,000. **Outfield Dimension: LF**—312, **CF**—408, **RF**—315.

VALPARAISO CRUSADERS.

Conference: Missouri Valley. **Mailing Address:** 2006 Warbler Dr., Valparaiso, IN 46383. **Website:** valpoathletics. com/baseball. **Head Coach:** Brian Schmack. **Telephone:** (219) 464-6117. **Baseball SID:** Brandon Vickrey. **Telephone:** (219) 464-5396. **Assistant Coaches:** Casey Fletcher, *Kory Winter. **Telephone:** (219) 464-5239. **Home Field:** Emory G Bauer Field. **Seating Capacity:** 1,000. **Outfield Dimension: LF**—330, **CF**—400, **RF**—330.

VANDERBILT COMMODORES.

Conference: Southeastern. **Mailing Address:** 2601 Jess Neely Dr., Nashville, TN. 37212. **Website:** www.vucommodores.com. **Head Coach:** Tim Corbin. **Telephone:** (615) 322-3716. **Baseball SID:** Andrew Pate. **Telephone:** (615) 343-6811. **Assistant Coaches:** *Mike Baxter, Scott Brown. **Telephone:** (615) 322-3716. **Home Field:** Hawkins Field. **Seating Capacity:** 3,626. **Outfield Dimension: LF**—310, **CF**—400, **RF**—330.

VILLANOVA WILDCATS.

Conference: Big East. **Mailing Address:** 800 East Lancaster Ave., Jake Nevin Field House, Villanova, PA 19085. **Website:** www.villanova.com. **Head Coach:** Kevin Mulvey. **Telephone:** (610) 519-4529. **Baseball SID:** Davis Dupree. **Telephone:** (610) 519-7579. **Assistant Coaches:** Rob Delaney, *Eddie Brown. **Telephone:** (610) 519-5520. **Home Field:** Villanova Ballpark at Plymouth. **Seating Capacity:** 750. **Outfield Dimension: LF**—330, **CF**—410, **RF**—330.

VIRGINIA CAVALIERS.

Conference: Atlantic Coast. **Mailing Address:** Disharoon Park - **PO Box:** 400839 - Charlottesville, Va., 22904-4839. **Website:** www.virginiasports.com. **Head Coach:** Brian O'Connor. **Telephone:** (434) 243-5114. **Baseball SID:** Scott Fitzgerald. **Telephone:** (434) 924-9878. **Assistant Coaches:** Drew Dickinson, *Kevin McMullan. **Telephone:** (434) 243-5114. **Home Field:** Davenport Field at Disharoon Park. **Seating Capacity:** 5359. **Outfield Dimension: LF**—332, **CF**—404, **RF**—332. **Press Box Telephone:** (908) 246-6818.

VIRGINIA COMMONWEALTH RAMS.

Conference: Atlantic 10. **Mailing Address:** VCU Athletics, Siegel Center, 1200 W. Broad St., Richmond, VA 23284. **Website:** www.vcuathletics.com. **Head Coach:** Shawn Stiffler. **Telephone:** (804) 828-4822. **Baseball SID:** Hannah Jo Riley. **Telephone:** (804) 828-8496. **Assistant Coaches:** Mike McRae. **Telephone:** (804) 828-4821. **Home Field:** The Diamond. **Seating Capacity:** 12,134. **Outfield Dimension: LF**—330, **CF**—402, **RF**—330.

VIRGINIA MILITARY INSTITUTE KEYDETS.

Conference: Southern. **Mailing Address:** 319 Letcher Ave., Lexington, VA 24450. **Website:** www.vmikeydets. org. **Head Coach:** Jonathan Hadra. **Telephone:** (540) 464-7601. **Baseball SID:** Mike Carpenter. **Telephone:** (540) 464-7015. **Assistant Coaches:** *Geoffrey Murphy, Sam Roberts. **Telephone:** (540) 464-7609. **Home Field:** Gray-Minor Stadium. **Seating Capacity:** 1,400. **Outfield Dimension: LF**—,330 **CF**—395, **RF**—330. **Press Box Telephone:** (434) 770-8813.

VIRGINIA TECH HOKIES.

Conference: Atlantic Coast. **Mailing Address:** 25 Beamer Way, Virginia Tech, Blacksburg, VA 24061. **Website:** www.hokiesports.com. **Head Coach:** John Szefc. **Telephone:** (540) 231-5906. **Baseball SID:** Marc Mullen. **Telephone:** (540) 231-1894. **Assistant Coaches:** *Kurt Elbin, Ryan Fecteau. **Telephone:** (540) 231-5906. **Home Field:** English Field at Atlantic Union Bank Park. **Seating Capacity:** 4,000. **Outfield Dimension: LF**—330, **CF**—400, **RF**—330.

WAGNER SEAHAWKS.

Conference: Northeast. **Mailing Address:** Wagner College Athletics, One Campus Rd., Staten Island, NY 10301. **Website:** www.wagnerathletics.com. **Head Coach:** Jim Carone. **Telephone:** (718) 390-3154. **Baseball SID:** Brian Morales. **Telephone:** (718) 390-3215. **Assistant Coaches:** *Craig Noto, Paul Piccolino. **Telephone:** (718) 420-4121. **Home Field:** Richmond County Bank Ballpark. **Seating Capacity:** 7,171. **Outfield Dimension: LF**—320, **CF**—390, **RF**—318.

WAKE FOREST DEMON DEACONS.

Conference: Atlantic Coast. **Mailing Address:** P.O. Box 7346; Winston-Salem, NC 27109. **Website:** GoDeacs.

com. **Head Coach:** Tom Walter. **Telephone:** (336) 758-5570. **Baseball SID:** Jay Garneau. **Telephone:** (336) 758-3229. **Assistant Coaches:** *Bill Cilento, John Hendricks. **Telephone:** (336) 758-4208. **Home Field:** David F. Couch Ballpark. **Seating Capacity:** 3823. **Outfield Dimension:** LF—310, CF—400, RF—300. **Press Box Telephone:** (336) 759-7373.

WASHINGTON HUSKIES.

Conference: Pac-12. **Mailing Address:** Walla Walla Rd, Seattle, WA 98195. **Website:** www.gohuskies.com. **Head Coach:** Lindsay Meggs. **Telephone:** (206) 543-2210. **Baseball SID:** Brian Tom. **Telephone:** (206) 897-1742. **Assistant Coaches:** *Elliott Cribby, Ronnie Prettyman. **Telephone:** (206) 543-2210. **Home Field:** Husky Ballpark. **Seating Capacity:** 2,200. **Outfield Dimension:** LF—327, CF—395, RF—317. **Press Box Telephone:** (206) 897-1742.

WASHINGTON STATE COUGARS.

Conference: Pac-12. **Mailing Address:** Bohler Athletic Complex, Washington State University, Pullman, WA 99163. **Website:** www.wsucougars.com. **Head Coach:** Brian Green. **Telephone:** (509) 335-5785. **Baseball SID:** Bobby Alworth. **Telephone:** (509) 355-5785. **Assistant Coaches:** Anthony Claggett, *Terry Davis. **Telephone:** (509) 335-5785. **Home Field:** Bailey-Brayton Field. **Seating Capacity:** 3,500. **Outfield Dimension:** LF—330, CF—400, RF—330. **Press Box Telephone:** (951) 452-6129.

WEST VIRGINIA MOUNTAINEERS.

Conference: Big 12. **Mailing Address:** 3450 Monongahela Blvd., Morgantown, WV 26505. **Website:** wvusports.com. **Head Coach:** Randy Mazey. **Telephone:** (304) 293-2300. **Baseball SID:** Joe Mitchin. **Telephone:** (304) 293-2821. **Assistant Coaches:** Mark Ginther, *Steve Sabins. **Telephone:** (304) 293-9880. **Home Field:** Monongalia County Ballpark. **Seating Capacity:** 3500. **Outfield Dimension:** LF—325, CF—400, RF—325.

WESTERN CAROLINA CATAMOUNTS.

Conference: Southern. **Mailing Address:** Ramsey Center - Athletics; 92 Catamount Rd., Cullowhee, NC 28723. **Website:** www.CatamountSports.com. **Head Coach:** Bobby Moranda. **Telephone:** (828) 227-2021. **Baseball SID:** Daniel Hooker. **Telephone:** (828) 227-2339. **Assistant Coaches:** *David Garcia, Taylor Sandefur. **Telephone:** (828) 227-2022. **Home Field:** Childress Field at Hennon Stadium. **Seating Capacity:** 1,500. **Outfield Dimension:** LF—325, CF—395, RF—325.

WESTERN ILLINOIS LEATHERNECKS.

Conference: Summit. **Mailing Address:** 1 University Cir, Macomb, IL 61455. **Website:** www.goleathernecks.com. **Head Coach:** Andy Pascoe. **Telephone:** (309) 298-1521. **Baseball SID:** Matthew Hutchison. **Telephone:** (309) 298-1133. **Assistant Coaches:** *Adam McGinnis, Braeden Ward. **Telephone:** (309) 298-1521. **Home Field:** Alfred D. Boyer Stadium. **Seating Capacity:** 502. **Outfield Dimension:** LF—330, CF—400, RF—330. **Press Box Telephone:** (314) 609-5352.

WESTERN KENTUCKY HILLTOPPERS.

Conference: Conference USA. **Mailing Address:** 1000 Champions Ave., Bowling Green, KY 42101. **Website:** wkusports.com. **Head Coach:** John Pawlowski.

Telephone: (270) 745-2277. **Baseball SID:** Matt Keenan. **Telephone:** (270) 745-3756. **Assistant Coaches:** *Adam Pavkovich, Ben Wolgamot. **Telephone:** (270) 745-2274. **Home Field:** Nick Denes Field. **Seating Capacity:** 1,500. **Outfield Dimension:** LF—330, CF—400, RF—330.

WESTERN MICHIGAN BRONCOS.

Conference: Mid-American. **Mailing Address:** 1903 W Michigan Ave., Kalamazoo, MI 49008. **Website:** wmu-broncos.com. **Head Coach:** Billy Gernon. **Telephone:** . **Baseball SID:** Nate Palcowski. **Telephone:** (269) 387-4138. **Assistant Coaches:** Will Nimke, *Adam Piotrowicz. **Telephone:** (269) 276-3208. **Home Field:** Robert J. Bobb Stadium. **Seating Capacity:** 1,500. **Outfield Dimension:** LF—310, CF—395, RF—335.

WICHITA STATE SHOCKERS.

Conference: American Athletic. **Mailing Address:** Wichita State University Dept. of Intercollegiate Athletics, 1845 Fairmount St., Wichita, KS 67260. **Website:** www.goshockers.com. **Head Coach:** Eric Wedge. **Telephone:** (316) 978-3636. **Baseball SID:** Ryan Anderson. **Telephone:** (316) 978-5461. **Assistant Coaches:** Mike Pelfrey, *Mike Sirianni. **Home Field:** Eck Stadium. **Seating Capacity:** 7,851. **Outfield Dimension:** LF—330, CF—390, RF—330.

WILLIAM & MARY TRIBE.

Conference: Colonial. **Mailing Address:** 751 Ukrop Way, Williamsburg, VA 23185. **Website:** www.tribeathletics.com. **Head Coach:** Brian Murphy. **Telephone:** (757) 221-3492. **Baseball SID:** John Moyer. **Telephone:** (757) 221-3344. **Assistant Coaches:** *Brian Casey, Pat McKenna. **Telephone:** (757) 221-3399. **Home Field:** Plumeri Park. **Seating Capacity:** 1,400. **Outfield Dimension:** LF—325, CF—400, RF—325.

WINTHROP EAGLES.

Conference: Big South. **Mailing Address:** 1162 Eden Terrace, Rock HIll , SC 28733. **Website:** www.winthropeagles.com. **Head Coach:** Thomas Riginos. **Telephone:** (864) 903-9796. **Baseball SID:** Brett Rendon. **Telephone:** (803) 367-1649. **Assistant Coaches:** *Austin Hill, Robbie Monday. **Telephone:** (252) 294-4409. **Home Field:** Winthrop Ballpark. **Seating Capacity:** 2000. **Outfield Dimension:** LF—325, CF—390, RF—325.

WISCONSIN-MILWAUKEE PANTHERS.

Conference: Horizon. **Mailing Address:** Milwaukee Athletics, PO Box 413, The Pavillion - Room 150, Milwaukee, WI 53201. **Website:** www.mkepanthers.com. **Head Coach:** Scott Doffek. **Telephone:** (414) 750-4738. **Baseball SID:** Cody Bohl. **Telephone:** (920) 740-3936. **Assistant Coaches:** Cory Bigler, Shaun Wegner. **Telephone:** (414) 265-8346. **Home Field:** Henry Aaron Field. **Seating Capacity:** 500. **Outfield Dimension:** LF—320, CF—390, RF—320.

WOFFORD TERRIERS.

Conference: Southern. **Mailing Address:** 429 N. Church Street, Spartanburg, SC 29303. **Website:** www.woffordterriers.com. **Head Coach:** Todd Interdonato. **Telephone:** (864) 597-4497. **Baseball SID:** Brent Williamson. **Telephone:** (864) 597-4093. **Assistant Coaches:** Seth Cutler-Voltz, *JJ Edwards. **Telephone:** (864) 597-4126. **Home Field:** Russell C. King Field. **Seating Capacity:** 2500. **Outfield Dimension:** LF—325,

CF—395, RF—325. **Press Box Telephone:** (864) 597-4498.

WRIGHT STATE RAIDERS.

Conference: Horizon. **Mailing Address:** 3640 Colonel Glenn Hwy., Dayton, OH 45435. **Website:** www.wsuraiders.com. **Head Coach:** Alex Sogard. **Telephone:** (937) 775-3668. **Baseball SID:** Nick Phillips. **Telephone:** (937) 775-2816. **Assistant Coaches:** *Nate Metzger, Trevin Sinnier. **Telephone:** (937) 775-4188. **Home Field:** Nischwitz Stadium. **Seating Capacity:** 2,000. **Outfield Dimension: LF**—330, **CF**—400, **RF**—330.

XAVIER MUSKETEERS.

Conference: Big East. **Mailing Address:** 3800 Victory Parkway, Cincinnati, OH 45207. **Website:** www.goxavier.com. **Head Coach:** Billy O'Conner. **Telephone:** (513) 745-2890. **Baseball SID:** Hayley Schletker. **Telephone:** (513) 745-3412. **Assistant Coaches:** Brian Furlong, Jake Yacinich. **Telephone:** (513) 745-2891. **Home Field:** Hayden Field. **Seating Capacity:** 500. **Outfield Dimension: LF**—310, **CF**—380, **RF**—310.

YALE BULLDOGS.

Conference: Ivy. **Mailing Address:** Yale Athletic Department, PO Box 28216, New Haven, CT 06520. **Website:** www.yalebulldogs.com. **Head Coach:** John Stuper. **Telephone:** (203) 432-1466. **Baseball SID:** Ernie Bertothy. **Assistant Coaches:** Ray Guarino, *Josh Schulman. **Telephone:** (203) 432-1467. **Home Field:** Yale Field. **Seating Capacity:** 5,000. **Outfield Dimension: LF**—330, **CF**—405, **RF**—335.

YOUNGSTOWN STATE PENGUINS.

Conference: Horizon. **Mailing Address:** Youngstown State University, Athletic Department, One University Plaza, Youngstown, OH 44555. **Website:** www.ysusports.com. **Head Coach:** Dan Bertolini. **Baseball SID:** Drae Smith. **Telephone:** (330) 941-8359. **Assistant Coaches:** Shane Davis, *Eric Smith. **Home Field:** Eastwood Field. **Seating Capacity:** 6,300. **Outfield Dimension: LF**—335, **CF**—405, **RF**—335.

AMATEUR & YOUTH

INTERNATIONAL ORGANIZATIONS

WORLD BASEBALL SOFTBALL CONFEDERATION

Headquarters: Maison du Sport International—54, Avenue de Rhodanie, 1007 Lausanne, Switzerland. **Telephone:** (+41-21) 318-82-40. **Fax:** (41-21) 318-82-41. **Website:** www.wbsc.org. **E-Mail:** office@wbsc.org. **Year Founded:** 1938.

President: Riccardo Fraccari (Italy). **Secretary General:** Beng Choo Low (Japan). **Vice President Baseball:** Willi Kaltschmitt Luján (Guam). **Vice President Softball:** Beatrice Allen (Gambia). **Softball Executive VP:** Craig Cress (USA). **Baseball Executive VP:** Tom Peng (Taiwan). **Treasurer:** Angelo Vicini (San Marino). **Members At-Large:** Ron Finlay (Australia), Paul Seiler (USA). Taeki Utsugi (Japan), Tommy Velázquez (Puerto Rico). **Athlete Representative For Baseball:** Justin Huber (Austrailia). **Athlete Representative For Softball:** María José Soto Gil (Venezuela). **Global Ambassador:** Antonio Castro Soto del Valle (Cuba), Meliton Sanchez Rivas (Panama). **Executive Director:** Michael Schmidt. **Softball Director:** Ron Radigonda. **Assistant to the President:** Giovanni Pantaleoni. **Marketing/Tournament Manager:** Masaru Yokoo, Laurie Gouthro. **Public Relations Officer:** Oscar Lopez, Lori Nolan. **National Federation Relations:** Francesca Fabretto, Brian Glauser, Aki Huang, Amy Park. **Antidoping Officer:** Victor Isola. **Administration/Finance:** Sandrine Pennone, Laetitia Barbey.

CONTINENTAL ASSOCIATIONS

CONFEDERATION PAN AMERICANA DE BEISBOL (COPABE)

Mailing Address: Calle 3, Francisco Filos, Vista Hermosa, Edificio 74, Planta Baja Local No. 1, Panama City, Panama. **Telephone:** (507) 229-8684. **Website:** www.copabe.net. **E-Mail:** copabe@sinfo.net.

Chairman: Eduardo De Bello (Panama). **Secretary General:** Hector Pereyra (Dominican Republic).

AFRICA BASEBALL SOFTBALL ASSOCIATION (ABSA)

Office Address: Paiko Road, Chanchaga, Minna, Niger State, Nigeria.

Mailing Address: P.M.B. 150, Minna, Niger State, Nigeria.

Telephone: (234) 8037188491. **E-mail:** absasecretariat @yahoo.com

President: Sabeur Jlajla. **Vice President Baseball:** Etienne N'Guessan. **Vice President Softball:** Fridah Shiroya. **Secretary General:** Ibrahim N'Diaye. **Treasurer:** Moira Dempsey. **Executive Director:** Lieutenant Colonel (rtd) Friday Ichide. **Deputy Executive Director:** Francoise Kameni-Lele.

BASEBALL FEDERATION OF ASIA

Mailing Address: 9F. -3, No. 288, Sec 6 Civic Blvd.,Xinyi Dist., Taipei City, Taiwan (R.O.C.). **Telephone:** 886-2-27473368. **E-Mail Address:** bfa@baseballasia.org

President: Tom Peng. **Vice Presidents:** Suzuki Yoshinobu, Chen Xu, Hae Young Yang. **Secretary General:** Hua-Wei Lin. **Executive Director:** Richard Lin. **Members At Large:** Allan Mak, Alfonso Martin Eizmendi, Syed Khawar Shah. **Senior Advisor:** Kazuhiro Tawa. **China Baseball Development Executive Director:** Tian Yuan. **West Asia Baseball Development Executive Director:** Syed Khawar Shah.

EUROPEAN BASEBALL CONFEDERATION

Mailing Address: Savska cesta 137, 10 000 Zagreb, Croatia. **Telephone/Fax:** +385 1 561 5227. **E-Mail Address:** office@baseballeurope.com. **Website:** baseball europe.com.

President: Didier Seminet (France). **1st Vice President:** Petr Ditrich (Czech Republic). **2nd Vice President:** Jürgen Elsishans (Germany). **3rd Vice President:** Rainer Husty (Austria). **Secretary General:** Krunoslav Karin (Croatia) **Treasurer:** Rene Laforce (Belgium). **Vocals:** Roderick Balk (Netherlands), Marco Mannucci (Italy), Oleg Boyko (Ukraine).

BASEBALL CONFEDERATION OF OCEANIA

Mailing Address: 48 Partridge Way, Mooroolbark, Victoria 3138, Australia. **Telephone:** +613 9727 1779. **Fax:** 613 9727 5959. **E-Mail Address:** bcosecgeneral@baseball oceania.com.

President: Bob Steffy (Guam). **1st Vice President:** Laurent Cassier (New Caledonia). **2nd Vice President:** Victor Langkilde (American Samoa). **Secretary General:** Chet Gray (Australia). **Executive Committee:** Rose Igitol (CNMI), Temmy Shmull (Palau), Innoke Niubalavu (Fiji).

INTERNATIONAL GOODWILL SERIES, INC.

Mailing Address: 982 Slate Drive, Santa Rosa, CA 95405. **Telephone:** (707) 538-0777. **E-Mail Address:** goodwillseries24@gmail.com. **Website:** www.goodwillseries.org. **President, Goodwill Series, Inc.:** Bob Williams.

ISG BASEBALL

Mailing Address: 3829 S Oakbrook Dr. Greenfield, WI 53228. **Telephone:** 414-704-5467. **E-Mail Address:** isgbaseball14@gmail.com. **Website:** isgbaseball.com. **President:** Tom O'Connell. **Vice President:** Peter Caliendo. **Secretary/Treasurer:** Randy Town. **Board Members:** Jim Jones, John Casey, Ron Maestri, Pat Doyle, John Vodenlich.

NATIONAL ORGANIZATIONS

USA BASEBALL

Mailing Address, Corporate Headquarters: 1030 Swabia Court Suite 201, Durham, NC 27703
Telephone: (919) 474-8721.
Fax: (855) 420-5910.
E-mail Address: info@usabaseball.com.
Website: usabaseball.com.
President: Mike Gaski. **Treasurer:** Jason Dobis.
Board of Directors: Mike Gaski (President), Jason Dobis (Treasurer), Elliot Hopkins (Secretary); **Members:** Veronica Alvarez, Willie Bloomquist, Steve Cloud, John Gall, George Grande, Abraham Key, Chris Marinak, John McHale Jr., Richard Neely.
National Members Organizations: Amateur Athletic Union (AAU); American Amateur Baseball Congress (AABC); American Baseball Coaches Association (ABCA); American Legion Baseball, Babe Ruth Baseball; Dixie Baseball; Little League Baseball; National Amateur Baseball Federation (NABF); National Assocaition of Intercollegiate Athletics (NAIA); National Baseball Congress (NBC); National Collegiate Athletic Association (NCAA); National Federation of State High School Athletic Associations (NFHS); National High School Baseball Coaches Associatin (BCA); National Junior College Athletic Association (NJCAA); Police Athletic League (PAL); PONY Baseball; T-Ball USA; United States Specialty Sports Association (USSSA).
Events: www.usabaseball.com/events/schedule.jsp.

STAFF

Executive Director/CEO: Paul Seiler. **Chief Operating Officer:** David Perkins. **Chief Finance Officer:** Ray Darwin. **Director, Marketing:** Brittany Allen. **Senior Director, Retail:** Carrington Austin. **Graphic Designer:** Taylor Banner. **Director, Coaching Development:** Andrew Bartman. **Assistant Director, Prospect Development Pipeline:** Bailey Beck. **Senior Director Baseball Operations:** Ashley Bratcher. **Senior Director, Player Development:** Scott Brosius. **General Manager, National Teams:** Eric Campbell. **Assistant Director, Youth Programs:** Anthony Cangelosi. **Director, Youth Programs:** Tyler Collins. **Director, Baseball Operations:** Brett Curll. **Assistant Director, Media Relations:** Emily Fedewa. **Director, Travel Services:** Monica Garza. **Assistant Director, Travel Services:** Allison Gupton. **Director, USABat Program:** Russell Hartford. **Assistant Director, SafeSport & Compliance:** Jenny Haskill. **Director, Baseball Operations:** Carter Hicks. **Graphic Designer:** Jenna Hiscock. **Director,**

Prospect Development Pipeline: Jules Johnson. **Director, Creative Services:** Kevin Jones. **Director, Retail Services:** Megan Kane. **Director, Baseball Operations:** Ben Kelley. **Assistant Director, Finance & Accounting:** Alex Kerr. **Director, Baseball Operations:** Charles Lane. **Senior Director, SafeSport & Compliance:** Kyle Lubrano. **Director, Finance & Accounting:** Cicely McLaughlin. **Assistant Director, Prospect Development Pipeline:** Matt Pajak. **Video Producer:** Colin Pelosi. **Assistant Director, Prospect Development Pipeline:** Drew Pomeroy. **Director, Educational Resources:** Lauren Rhyne. **Assistant Director, Baseball Operations:** Ann Claire Robinson. **Assistant Director, Media Relations:** Alec Scercy. **Director, 12U National Team:** Will Schworer. **Director, NTC Operations:** James Vick. **Director, Employment & Recruiting:** Tracey Wiwatowski. **Senior Director, Media Relations:** Brad Young.

BASEBALL CANADA

Mailing Address: 2212 Gladwin Cres., Suite A7, Ottawa, Ontario K1B 5N1. **Telephone:** (613) 748-5606. **Fax:** (613) 748-5767. **E-mail Address:** info@baseball.ca. **Website:** baseball.ca.
Director General: Jim Baba. **Head Coach/Director, National Teams:** Greg Hamilton. **Business/Sport Development Director/Women's National Team Manager:** Andre Lachance. **Program Coordinator:** Kelsey McIntosh. **Media/PR Coordinator:** Adam Morissette. **Administrative Coordinator:** June Sterling. **Administrative Assistant:** Penny Baba.

NATIONAL BASEBALL CONGRESS

Mailing Address: 111 S. Main, Suite 600, Wichita, KS 67202. **Telephone:** (316) 977-9400. **Fax:** (316) 462-4506. **Website:** nbcbaseball.com.
Year Founded: 1931.

ATHLETES IN ACTION

Mailing Address: 651 Taylor Dr., Xenia, OH 45385. **Telephone:** (937) 352-1000. **Fax:** (937) 352-1245. **E-mail Address:** baseball@athletesinaction.org. **Website:** aia-baseball.org. **Director, AIA Baseball:** Chris Beck. **General Manager, Alaska:** Chris Beck. **General Manager, Great Lakes:** Dave Gnau. **General Manager, New York Collegiate League:** Mark Randall. **International Teams Director:** TBD. **Youth Baseball Director:** Chris Beck.

SUMMER COLLEGE LEAGUES

NATIONAL ALLIANCE OF COLLEGE SUMMER BASEBALL

Telephone: (321) 206-9714 **E-Mail Address:** RSitz@ FloridaLeague.com. **Website:** nacsb.org.
Executive Director: Stefano Foggi (Florida League). **Assistant Executive Director:** Bobby Bennett (Sunbelt Baseball League), Jeff Carter (Southern Collegiate Baseball League). **Treasurer:** Jason Woodward (Cal Ripken Collegiate Baseball League). **Director, Public Relations:** Henry Bramwell (Hamptons Collegiate Baseball League).

Compliance Officer: Sean McGrath (New England Collegiate Baseball League).
Member Leagues: Atlantic Collegiate Baseball League, California Collegiate League, Cal Ripken Collegiate Baseball League, Cape Cod Baseball League, Florida Collegiate Summer League, Great Lakes Summer Collegiate League, New England Collegiate Baseball League, New York Collegiate Baseball League, Southern Collegiate Baseball League, Sunbelt Baseball League, Valley Baseball League, Hamptons Collegiate Baseball League.

ALASKA BASEBALL LEAGUE
League Mailing Address: 435 W. 10th Avenue, Ste. B, Anchorage, AK, 99501. 5 teams, 44 league games and approximately 5 non-league games. Season begins play June 5 and ends Aug. 1. **Commissioner:** Jim Posey. **Email:** commissionerposeyabl@gmail.com.

MAT-SU MINERS
General Manager: Pete Christopher.
Mailing Address: P.O. Box 2690 Palmer, AK 99645.
Telephone: 907-746-4914/907-745-6401. **Fax:** 907-746-5068. **E-Mail:** gmminers@gci.net. **Fax:** 907-561-2920. **Website:** matsuminers.org.
Head Coach: Tyler LeBrun, Sunnyslope HS, Phoenix.
Field: Hermon Brothers, Grass, No Lights.

ANCHORAGE BUCS
General Manager: Shawn Maltby
Mailing Address: 435 W. 10th Avenue Suite B, Anchorage, AK 99501. **Office:** 907-561-2827. **Fax:** 907-561-2920. **E-Mail:** shawn@anchoragebucs.com.
Website: anchoragebucs.com
Head Coach: Grant Palmer, El Camino CC (Calif.)
Field: Mulcahy Field -Turf Infield, Grass Outfield, Lights

ANCHORAGE GLACIER PILOTS
General Manager: Mike Hinshaw
Mailing Address: 435 W. 10th Avenue, Suite A, Anchorage, Alaska 99501. **Office:** 907-274-3627.
Fax: 907-274-3628. **E-Mail:** gpilots@alaska.net.
Website: glacierpilots.com.
Head Coach: Jeff Pritchard, Cabrillo CC.
Field: Mulcahy Field -Turf Infield, Grass Outfield, Lights

CHUGIAK-EAGLE RIVER CHINOOKS
General Manager: Chris Beck
Mailing Address: 651 Taylor Drive, Xenia, Ohio 45385. **Office:** 937-352-1000. **Fax:** 937-352-1001.
E-Mail: Chris.beck@athletesinaction.org.
Website: cerchinooks.com.
Head Coach: Ethan Bragg.
Field: Lee Jordan Field-Turf Infield, Grass Outfield, No Lights

PENINSULA OILERS
General Manager: Tory Smith.
Mailing Address: 601 S. Main St., Kenai, Alaska 99611. **Office:** 907-283-7133. **Fax:** 907-283-3390.
E-Mail: tory@oilersbaseball.com.
Website: oilersbaseball.com
Head Coach: Kyle Brown, Southwestern College
Field: Coral Seymour Memorial Park-Grass , No Lights

ATLANTIC COLLEGIATE BASEBALL LEAGUE
Mailing Address: 1760 Joanne Drive, Quakertown, PA 18951.
Telephone: (215) 536-5777. **Fax:** (215) 536-5777.
E-Mail: tbonekemper@verizon.net.
Website: acbl-online.com.
Year Founded: 1967.
Commissioner: Ralph Addonizio.
President: Tom Bonekemper.
Acting Secretary: Mike Kalb. **Vice President:** Angelo Fiore, Doug Cinella. **Treasurer:** Bob Hoffman.

Regular Season: 40 games. **Opening Date:** May 30.
Closing Date: August 4. **All-Star Game:** July 12 at SUNY Cortland vs NYCBL. **Roster Limit:** 28.

ALLENTOWN RAILERS
Mailing Address: Suite 202, 1801 Union Blvd, Allentown, PA 18109. **E-Mail Address:** ddando@lehigh-valleybaseballacademy.com. **Field Manager:** Dylan Dando.

JERSEY PILOTS
Mailing Address: 11 Danemar Drive, Middletown, NJ 07748. **Telephone:** (732) 939-0627. **E-Mail Address:** baseball@jerseypilots.com. **General Manager:** Mike Kalb. **Field Manager:** Fred Orchard.

NEW YORK PHENOMS
General Manager: Rob Bass. **Telephone:** (646) 296-1720. **E-Mail Address:** radbyrob@aol.com. **Field Manager:** Anthony Ferrante. **Field:** College of Staten Island Baseball Complex, Staten Island, NY.

NORTH JERSEY EAGLES
Mailing Address: 12 Wright Way, Oakland NJ 07436.
General Manager: Brian Casey. **Field Manager:** Chris Buser.

OCEAN GULLS
General Manager: Angelo Fiore, afiore@fioreservice group.com. **Telephone:** 904-237-1468. **General Manager:** Joe Mazza. **Email address:** coachmaz7@gmail.com. **Telephone:** 732-803-1290. **Field Manager:** Nick McKee.

QUAKERTOWN BLAZERS
Telephone: (215) 679-5072. **E-Mail Address:** gbonekemper@yahoo.com.
Website: quakertownblazers.com. **General Manager:** George Bonekemper. **Field Manager:** Chris Ray.

TRENTON GENERALS
E-Mail Address: mrolsh@msn.com. **General Manager:** Michael Olshin. **Field Manager:** Kevin Snyder.

CALIFORNIA COLLEGIATE LEAGUE
Mailing Address: 806 W Pedregosa St, Santa Barbara, CA 93101. **Telephone:** (805) 680-1047. **Fax:** (805) 684-8596. **E-Mail Address:** burns@calsummerball.com.
Website: calsummerball.com.
Founded: 1993.
Commissioner: Pat Burns.

ACADEMY BARONS
Address: 901 E. Artesia Blvd, Compton, CA 90221.
Telephone: (424) 209-5727. **Website:** calsummerball.com/academy-barons-roster. **E-Mail Address:** darrell.miller@mlb.com. **Contact:** Natalia Reynoso, director. **Field manager:** Kenny Landreaux.

ARROYO SECO SAINTS
Telephone: (626) 695-6903. **Website:** arroyoseco-saints.com. **E-Mail Address:** amilam@arroyosecobaseball.com. **General Manager:** Aaron Milam/Nicholas Gorman. **Field Manager:** Aaron Milam.

CONEJO OAKS

Address: 1710 N. Moorpark Rd., #106, Thousand Oaks, CA 91360. **Telephone:** 805-304-0126.
Website: calsummerball.com/conejo-oaks-roster/. com. **E-Mail Address:** oaksbaseball@yahoo.com. **Field Manager:** David Soliz. **General Manager:** Randy Riley.

HEALDSBURG PRUNE PACKERS

Address: Rec Park 515 Piper St. Healdsburg, Calif. 95448. **Mailing Address:** PO Box 1543 Healdsburg CA 95448. **Telephone:** 707-280-6693. **Email Address:** JGG21@aol.com. **General Manager/Field Manager:** Joey Gomes.

ORANGE COUNTY RIPTIDE

Address: 14 Calendula Rancho, Santa Margarita, CA 92688. **Telephone:** (949) 228-7676. **Website:** ocriptide. com. **E-Mail Address:** ocriptidebaseball@gmail.com. **Field Manager:** Tyger Pederson. **General Manager:** Moe Geohagen. **Head Coach:** Clemente Bonilla.

SAN LUIS OBISPO BLUES

Address: 3195 McMillan Ave, Ste. B2, San Luis Obispo, CA 93401. **Telephone:** 805-512-9996. **Website:** bluesbaseball.com. **E-Mail Address:** adam@bluesbaseball. com. **General Manager:** Adam Stowe. **Field Manager:** Clay Cederquist.

SANTA BARBARA FORESTERS

Address: 4299 Carpinteria Ave., Suite 201, Carpinteria, CA 93013. **Telephone:** (805) 684-0657. **Website:** sbforesters.org. **E-Mail Address:** pintard@earthlink.net. **General Manager and Field Manager:** Bill Pintard.

SOUTHERN CALIFORNIA SHEPHERDS

Telephone (GM): (562) 686-8262. **Website:** shepherdsbaseball.org. **E-mail Address (GM):** borr@fca. org. **General Manager:** Ben Orr. **Field Manager:** Dan Peters.

VENTURA COUNTY PIRATES

Website: calsummerball.com/ventura-county-pirates-affiliated-team-2018-roster/. **E-Mail Address (GM):** gvranau.pirates@gmail.com. **General Manager:** George Vranau.

CAL RIPKEN COLLEGIATE LEAGUE

Address: 24219 Hawkins Landing Drive, Gaithersburg, MD 20882. **Telephone:** (301) 693-2577. **E-Mail:** jason_d_woodward@mcpsmd.org. **Website:** calripkenleague.org.
Year Founded: 2005.
Commissioner: Jason Woodward. **League President:** Brad Rifkin. **Deputy Commissioner:** Jerry Wargo.
Regular Season: 36 games. **Playoff Format:** Top two teams from each division plus two remaining teams with best records qualify. Teams play best of three series, winners advance to best of three series for league championship. **Roster Limit:** 35 (college-eligible players 22 and under).

ALEXANDRIA ACES

Address: 221 9th Street, S.E. Washington, DC 20003. **Telephone:** (202) 255-1683. **E-Mail:** cberset21@gmail. com. **Website:** alexandriaaces.org. **Chairman/CEO:** Donald Dinan. **General Manager:** TBD. **Head Coach:** Chris Berset. **Ballpark:** Frank Mann Field at Four Mile Run Park.

BALTIMORE DODGERS

Address: 17 Sunrise Court Randallstown, MD 21133. **Telephone:** (443) 834-3500. **Email:** juan.waters@verizon. net. **Website:** baltimoredodgers.org. **President:** Juan Waters. **Head Coach:** Derek Brown. **Ballpark:** Joe Cannon Stadium at Harmans Park.

BETHESDA BIG TRAIN

Address: 6400 Goldsboro Road Suite 220 Bethesda, MD 20817. **Telephone:** 301-229-1854. **Fax:** 301-229-8362. **E-Mail:** faninfo@bigtrain.org. **Website:** bigtrain.org. **General Manager:** David Schneider. **Head Coach:** Sal Colangelo. **Ballpark:** Shirley Povich Field.

D.C. GRAYS

Address: 1800 M Street NW, 500 South Tower, Washington, DC 20036. **Telephone:** (202) 492-6226. **Website:** dcgrays.com. **E-Mail Address:** barbera@acg-consultants.com. **President:** Mike Barbera. **General Manager:** Antonio Scott. **Head Coach:** Reggie Terry. **Ballpark:** Washington Nationals Youth Academy.

GAITHERSBURG GIANTS

Address: 18221A Flower Hill Way, Gaithersburg, MD 20879. **Telephone:** (240) 793-3367. **E-Mail:** gaithersburggiants@gmail.com. **Website:** gaithersburggiants. org. **General Manager:** Matt Cangas. **Head Coach:** Jeff Rabberman. **Ballpark:** Criswell Automotive Field.

FCA BRAVES

Address: 8925 Leesburg Pike, Vienna, VA 22182. **Telephone:** (702) 909-2750. **Fax:** (703) 783-1319. **E-Mail:** fcabraves@gmail.com. **Website:** fcabraves.com. **President/General Manager:** Todd Burger. **Head Coach:** Chris Warren. **Ballpark:** Annandale High School.

SILVER SPRING-TAKOMA T-BOLTS

Address: 906 Glaizewood Court, Takoma Park, MD 20912. **Telephone:** 301-983-1358. **E-Mail:** tboltsbaseball@gmail.com. **Website:** tbolts.org. **General Manager:** Brian Brewer. **Head Coach:** Doug Remer. **Ballpark:** Blair Stadium at Montgomery Blair High School.

CAPE COD BASEBALL LEAGUE

Mailing Address: PO Box 266, Harwich Port, MA 02646. **Telephone:** (508) 432-6909.
E-Mail: info@capecodbaseball.org.
Website: capecodbaseball.org.
Year Founded: 1885.
Commissioner: Eric Zmuda. **President:** Chuck Sturtevant. **Treasurer:** Steve Wilson. **Secretary:** Paula Tufts. **Senior VP:** Bill Bussiere. **VP:** Tom Gay, Paul Logan. **Senior Deputy Commissioner/Umpire-In-Chief:** Sol Yas. **Deputy Commissioner, West:** Mike Carrier. **Deputy Commissioner, East:** Peter Hall. **Director Public Relations:** Ben Brink. **Director Broadcasting:** John Garner. **Director, Communications:** Jim McGonigle. **Division Structure: East**—Brewster, Chatham, Harwich, Orleans, Yarmouth-Dennis. **West**—Bourne, Cotuit, Falmouth, Hyannis, Wareham.
Regular Season: 40 games. **All-Star Game and**

Home Run Contest: July 25. **Playoff Format:** Top four teams in each division qualify for three rounds of best-of-three series.

Roster Limit: 30 (college-eligible players only).

BOURNE BRAVES

Mailing Address: PO Box 895, Monument Beach, MA 02553. **Telephone:** (508) 868-8378. **E-Mail Address:** nnorkevicius@yahoo.com. **Website:** bournebraves.org. **President:** Nicole Norkevicius. **General Manager:** Darin Weeks. **Head Coach:** Harvey Shapiro.

BREWSTER WHITECAPS

Mailing Address: PO Box 2349, Brewster, MA 02631. **Telephone:** (508) 896-8500, ext. 147. **Fax:** (508) 896-9845.

E-Mail Address: ckenney@brewsterwhitecaps.com. **Website:** brewsterwhitecaps.com. **President:** Chris Kenney. **General Manager:** Ned Monthie.

CHATHAM ANGLERS

Mailing Address: PO Box 428, Chatham, MA 02633. **Website:** chathamas.com. **President:** Steve West. **General Manager:** Mike Geylin. **Email:** mgeylin@kgpr.com. **Head Coach:** Tom Holliday.

COTUIT KETTLEERS

Mailing Address: PO Box 411, Cotuit, MA 02635. **Telephone:** (508) 428-3358. **E-Mail Address:** bmurpfcape@aol.com. **Website:** kettleers.org. **President:** Andy Bonacker. **General Manager:** Bruce Murphy. **Head Coach:** Mike Roberts.

FALMOUTH COMMODORES

Mailing Address: PO Box 808 Falmouth, MA 02541. **Telephone:** (508) 566-4988. **Website:** falmouthcommodores.org. **President:** Mark Kasprzyk. **General Manager:** Eric Zmuda. **Head Coach:** Jeff Trundy.

HARWICH MARINERS

Mailing Address: PO Box 201, Harwich Port, MA 02646. **Telephone:** (508) 432-2000. **Fax:** (508) 432-5357. **E-Mail Address:** mehendy@comcast.net. **Website:** harwichmariners.org.

President: Mary Henderson. **General Manager:** Ben Layton. **Head Coach:** Steve Englert.

HYANNIS HARBOR HAWKS

Mailing Address: PO Box 832, West Hyannis Port, MA 02672. **Telephone:** (508) 737-5890. **Fax:** (877) 822-2703. **E-Mail Address:** brpfeifer@aol.com. **Website:** harborhawks.org.

President: Brad Pfeifer. **General Manager:** Tino DiGiovanni. **Head Coach:** Gary Calhoun.

ORLEANS FIREBIRDS

Mailing Address: PO Box 504, Orleans, MA 02653. **Telephone:** (508) 255-0793. **Fax:** (508) 255-2237. **E-Mail Address:** bodonnell15@gmail.com. **Website:** orleansfirebirds.com. **President:** Bob O'Donnell. **General Manager:** Sue Horton. **Head Coach:** Kelly Nicholson.

WAREHAM GATEMEN

Mailing Address: PO Box 287, Wareham, MA 02571. **Telephone:** (508) 748-0287. **Fax:** (508) 880-2602. **E-Mail Address:** alang.gatemen@gmail.com.

Website: gatemen.org. **President:** Tom Gay. **General Manager:** Andrew Lang. **Head Coach:** Jerry Weinstein.

YARMOUTH-DENNIS RED SOX

Mailing Address: PO Box 78 Yarmouth Port, MA 02675. **Telephone:** (508) 889-8721. **E-Mail Address:** sfaucher64@gmail.com. **Website:** ydredsox.org. **President:** James DeMaria. **General Manager:** Steve Faucher. **Head Coach:** Scott Pickler.

CENTRAL VALLEY COLLEGIATE LEAGUE

Mailing Address: P.O. Box 561, Fowler, CA 93625. **E-mail:** j_scot25@hotmail.com, jcederquist@aol.com. **Website:** cvclbaseball.webs.com. **Twitter:** @CVCL1. **Year Founded:** 2013. **President:** Jon Scott. **Regular Season:** 30 games. **2019 Opening Date:** May 31. **Closing Date:** July 26. **All-Star Game:** July 15, Fresno, Calif. **Roster Limit:** 30

BAKERSFIELD BRAVES

Mailing Address: PO Box 20760, Bakersfield, CA, 93390. **Website:** eteamz.com/bakersfieldbraves. **Field Manager:** Bobby Maitia.

CALIFORNIA EXPOS

Mailing Address: P.O. Box 561, Fowler, CA 93625. **E-mail:** exposcv@aol.com. **Website:** calibaseball.com. **Twitter:** @cvexpos. **Field Manager:** Thomas Raymundo.

CALIFORNIA PILOTS

Mailing Address: PO Box 561 Fowler, CA 93625. **E-mail:** valleystormbaseball@aol.com. **Website:** www.calibaseball.com. **Twitter:** @calistorm1. **Field Manager:** Kenny Corona.

CALIFORNIA STORM

Mailing Address: PO Box 561 Fowler, CA 93625. **E-mail:** valleystormbaseball@aol.com. **Website:** calibaseball.com. **Twitter:** @calistorm1. **Field Manager:** Kolton Cabral.

SANTA MARIA PACKERS

Mailing Address: P.O. Box 144, Kingsburg, CA 93631. **E-mail:** j_scot25@hotmail.com. **Website:** cvipers.webs.com. **Twitter:** @SouthcountryV. **Field Manager:** Jon Scott.

SOUTH COUNTY VIPERS

Mailing Address: P.O. Box 144, Kingsburg, CA 93631. **E-mail:** j_scot25@hotmail.com. **Website:** cvipers.webs.com. **Twitter:** @SouthcountryV. **Field Manager:** Jon Scott.

COASTAL PLAIN LEAGUE

Mailing Address: 117 Thomas Mill Road, Holly Springs, NC 27540. **Telephone:** (919) 852-1960. **Email Address:** justins@coastalplain.com. **Website:** coastalplain.com. **Year Founded:** 1997. **Chairman/CEO:** Jerry Petitt. **COO/ Commissioner:** Justin Sellers. **Director of Media & Content Development:** Shelby Hilliard. **Director of Operations & Sponsorships:** Catherine Roth.

Division Structure: East—Florence RedWolves, Holly Springs Salamanders, Morehead City Marlins, Peninsula Pilots, Tri-City Chili Peppers, Wilmington Sharks and Wilson Tobs.

West—Asheboro Copperheads, Forest City Owls, Gastonia Grizzlies, High Point-Thomasville HiToms, Lexington County Blowfish, Macon Bacon, Martinsville Mustangs and Savannah Bananas. **Regular Season:** 52 games (split schedule). **Playoff Format:** Three rounds. **Rd 1/2:** One game. **Rd 3:** Best of three. **Roster Limit:** 32 (college-eligible players and graduated seniors only).

ASHEBORO COPPERHEADS

Mailing Address: PO Box 4036, Asheboro, NC 27204. **Telephone:** (336) 460-7018. **Fax:** (336) 523-1220. **E-Mail Address:** info@teamcopperhead.com. **Website:** team-copperhead.com. **Owners:** Ronnie Pugh, Steve Pugh, Doug Pugh, Mike Pugh. **General Managers:** Keith Ritsche, Dennis Garcia. **Head Coach:** Keith Ritsche

EDENTON STEAMERS

Mailing Address: PO Box 86, Edenton, NC 27932. **Telephone:** (252) 482-4080. **Fax:** (252) 482-1717. **E-Mail Address:** edentonsteamers@hotmail.com. **Website:** edentonsteamers.com. **Owner:** Edenton-Chowan Community Foundation. **General Manager:** Tyler Russell. **Head Coach:** Marshall McDonald.

FAYETTEVILLE SWAMPDOGS

Mailing Address: 2823 Legion Road, Fayetteville, NC 28306. **Telephone:** (910) 426-5900. **E-Mail Address:** info@goswampdogs.com. **Website:** goswampdogs.com. **Owner:** Lew Handelsman. **General Manager:** Jeremy Aagard. **Head Coach:** Matt Hollod

FLORENCE REDWOLVES

Mailing Address: PO Box 809, Florence, SC 29503. **Telephone:** (843) 629-0700. **Fax:** (843) 629-0703. **E-Mail Address:** barbara@florenceredwolves.com. **Website:** florenceredwolves.com. **Owners:** Kevin Barth, Donna Barth. **General Manager:** Barbara Osborne. **Head Coach:** Ryan Vruggink.

FOREST CITY OWLS

Mailing Address: 214 McNair Field Drive, Forest City, NC 28043. **Telephone:** (828) 245-0000. **E-Mail Address:** info@forestcitybaseball.com. **Website:** www.forestcity-baseball.com. **Owners:** Phil & Becky Dangel. **General Manager:** Kiva Fuller. **Head Coach:** Matt Reed.

GASTONIA GRIZZLIES

Mailing Address: 1001 Dr. Martin Luther King Jr. Way, Gastonia, NC 28054. **Telephone:** (704) 866-8622. **Fax:** (704) 864-6122. **E-Mail Address:** jesse@gastoniagrizzlies.com. **Website:** gastoniagrizzlies.com. **Owners:** Matt Perry. **General Manager:** David McDonald. **Head Coach:** Charles Bradley.

HIGH POINT-THOMASVILLE HI-TOMS

Mailing Address: 7003 Ballpark Road, Thomasville, NC 27360. **Telephone:** (336) 472-8667. **Fax:** (336) 472-7198. **E-Mail Address:** info@hitoms.com. **Website:** hitoms.com. **Owner:** Richard Holland. **President:** Greg Suire. **Head Coach:** Mickey Williard.

HOLLY SPRINGS SALAMANDERS

HOLLY SPRINGS SALAMANDERS
Mailing Address: 101 Tennis Court, Holly Springs, NC 27540. **Telephone:** 919-249-7322. **Email Address:** info@salamandersbaseball.com. **Website:** salamandersbaseball.com. **Owner:** Capital Broadcast Company. **General Manager:** Chip Hutchinson. **Head Coach:** Kevin Soine.

LEXINGTON COUNTY BLOWFISH

Mailing Address: 474 Ball Park Road, Lexington, SC 29072. **Telephone:** (803) 254-3474. **E-Mail Address:** info@blowfishbaseball.com. **Website:** goblowfish-baseball.com. **Owner:** Bill & Vicki Shanahan. **Assistant General Manager:** Justin Hall. **Head Coach:** Matt Padgett.

MACON BACON

Mailing Address: 225 Willie Smokey Glover Drive, Macon, GA. **Telephone:** 478-803-1795. **E-Mail Address:** info@maconbaconbaseball.com **Website:** maconbaconbaseball.com. **Owner:** SRO Partners (Jon Spoelstra & Steve DeLay). **President:** Brandon Raphael. **Head Coach:** Jimmy Turk.

MOREHEAD CITY MARLINS

Mailing Address: PO Box 460, New Bern, NC 28563. **Telephone:** (252) 269-9767. **Fax:** (252) 637-2721. **E-Mail Address:** mcmarlins@gmail.com. **Website:** mhcmarlins.com. **General Manager:** Buddy Bengel. **Head Coach:** Jesse Lancaster.

PENINSULA PILOTS

Mailing Address: 1889 W. Pembroke Ave., Hampton, VA 23661. **Telephone:** (757) 245-2222. **Fax:** (757) 245-8030. **E-Mail Address:** info@peninsulapilots.com. **Website:** peninsulapilots.com. **Owner:** Henry Morgan. **General Manager:** Alex Ahl. **Head Coach/Vice President:** Hank Morgan.

SAVANNAH BANANAS

Mailing Address: 1401 E. Victory Drive, Savannah, GA 31404. **Telephone:** 912-712-2482. **E-Mail Address:** jared@thesavannahbananas.com. **Website:** thesavannahbananas.com. **Owner:** Fans First Entertainment (Jesse & Emily Cole). **President:** Jared Orton. **Head Coach:** Tyler Gillum.

WILMINGTON SHARKS

Mailing Address: 2149 Carolina Beach Road, Wilmington, NC 28401. **Telephone:** (910) 343-5621. **Fax:** (910) 343-8932. **E-Mail Address:** media@wilmingtonsharks.com. **Website:** wilmingtonsharks.com. **Owners:**

National Sports Services. **General Manager:** Carson Bowen. **Head Coach:** Russ Burroughs.

WILSON TOBS

Mailing Address: 300 Stadium St. SW., Wilson, NC 27893. **Telephone:** (252) 291-8627. **Fax:** (252) 291-1224. **E-Mail Address:** mike@wilsontobs.com. **Website:** wilsontobs.com. **Owner:** Richard Holland. **President:** Greg Suire. **General Manager:** Mike Bell. **Head Coach:** Bryan Hill.

FLORIDA COLLEGIATE SUMMER LEAGUE

Mailing Address: 250 National Place, Unit #152, Longwood, FL 32750. **Telephone:** (321) 206-9174. **Fax:** (407) 574-7926. **E-Mail Address:** info@floridaleague.com. **Website:** floridaleague.com.

Year Founded: 2004.

President: Stefano Foggi. **League Operations Director:** Phil Chinnery.

Regular Season: 45 games. **2020 Opening Date:** TBD. **All-Star Game:** TBD. **Playoffs Begin:** TBD. **Playoff Format:** Five teams qualify; No. 4 and No. 5 seeds meet in one-game playoff. Remaining four teams play best-of-three series. Winners play best-of-three series for league championship.

Roster Limit: 28 (college-eligible players only). High school grads allowed with MLB approval. Part of the National Alliance of College Summer Baseball.

DELAND SUNS

Operated by the league office. **E-Mail Address:** suns@floridaleague.com. **Head Coach:** Rick Hall.

LEESBURG LIGHTNING

E-Mail Address: lightning@floridaleague.com. **Head Coach:** Rich Billings.

SANFORD RIVER RATS

Operated by the league office. **E-Mail Address:** rats@floridaleague.com. **Head Coach:** Josh Montero.

SEMINOLE COUNTY SCORPIONS

Operated by the league office. **E-Mail Address:** scorpions@floridaleague.com. **Head Coach:** Bob Rikeman.

WINTER GARDEN SQUEEZE

Operated by the league office. **Email Address:** squeeze@floridaleague.com. **Head Coach:** Terry Abbott. **General Manager:** Adam Bates.

WINTER PARK DIAMOND DAWGS

E-Mail Address: dawgs@floridaleague.com. **Head Coach:** Chuck Schall.

FUTURES COLLEGIATE LEAGUE OF NEW ENGLAND

Mailing Address: 46 Chestnut Hill Rd, Chelmsford, MA 01824. **Telephone:** (617) 593-2112. **E-Mail Address:** futuresleague@yahoo.com

Website: thefuturesleague.com.

Year Founded: 2010.

Commissioner: Joe Paolucci.

Teams (Contact): Bristol Blues (www.bristolbluesbaseball.com) (**Brian Rooney:** gm@bristolblues.com); Brockton Rox (**Todd Marlin:** tmarlin@brocktonrox.com); Martha's Vineyard Sharks (**Russ Curran:** russ.curran@mvsharks.com); Nashua Silver Knights (**Rick Muntean:** rick@nashuasilverknights.com); North Shore Navigators (**Bill Terlecky:** navigatorsgm@gmail.com); Pittsfield Suns (**Kristen Huss:** kristen@pittsfieldsuns.com); Worcester Bravehearts (**Dave Peterson:** dave@worcesterbravehearts.com)

Regular Season: 56 games; 28 home, 28 away.

Playoff Format: Six teams qualify. First round consists of two single elimination play-in games (3 seed vs. 6 seed and 4 seed vs 5 seed), two remaining teams play a best of three semifinal round followed by a best-of- three championship round to determine league champion. Extra-inning Games are determined by Home Run Derby!!

Roster Limit: 35. 10 must be from New England or play collegiately at a New England college.

GREAT LAKES SUMMER COLLEGIATE LEAGUE

Mailing Address: PO Box 666, Troy, OH 45373. **Telephone:** (937) 308-1536. **E-Mail:** glsclcommish@gmail.com.

Website: greatlakesleague.org.

Year Founded: 1986.

President: Jim DeSana. **Commissioner:** Deron Brown.

Regular Season: 42 games. **Playoff Format:** Top six teams meet in playoffs. **Roster Limit:** 30 (college-eligible players only).

Teams: (15 Teams)—Cincinnati Steam (Cincinnati, OH); Galion Graders (Galion, OH); Grand Lake Mariners (Celina, OH); Grand River Loggers (Grand Haven, MI); Hamilton Joes (Hamilton, OH); Lake Erie Monarchs (Flat Rock, MI); Licking County Settlers (Newark, OH); Lima Locos (Lima, OH); Lorain County Ironmen (Lorain, OH); Muskegon Clippers (Muskegon, MI); Richmond Jazz (Richmond, IN); Saint Clair Green Giants (Tecumseh, ON); Southern Ohio Copperheads (Athens, OH); Xenia Scouts (Xenia, OH).

METROPOLITAN COLLEGIATE BASEBALL LEAGUE

Mailing Address: 78 Knollwood Drive, Paramus NJ 07652

President: Brian Casey 374-545-1991

Website: metropolitanbaseball.com

Email: mcbl@metropolitanbaseball.com

MIDWEST COLLEGIATE LEAGUE

Mailing Address: 1500 119th Street Whiting IN 46394. **E-Mail Address:** commissioner@midwestcollegiateleague.com. **Website:** midwestcollegiateleague.com.

Year Founded: 2010.

President/Commissioner: Don Popravak.

Regular Season: 52 games. **Playoff Format:** Top four teams meet in best of three series. Winners meet in best of three championship series.

Roster Limit: 30

Teams: Bloomington Bobcats, Crestwood Panthers, DuPage County Hounds, Joliet Admirals, NWI Oilmen, Southland Vikings.

M.I.N.K. LEAGUE

(Missouri, Iowa, Nebraska, Kansas)

Mailing Address: PO Box 367, Nevada, MO 64772. **Telephone:** (417) 667-6159. Fax: (417) 667- 4210.

Email Address: jpost@morrisonpost.com. **Website:** minkleaguebaseball.com

Year Founded: 1995.
Commissioner: Bob Steinkamp. **President**: Jeff Post.
Vice President: Jud Kindle. **Secretary**: Edwina Rains.
Regular season: 44 games.
Playoff Format: The top three teams from each division will qualify for the playoffs. The second and third place finishers in each division will play a "Wild Card" one-game playoff. The winner of those games will play the regular season division winner from each division in a one game playoff. The winner of each division will then play a two out of three series to determine the MINK League Champion. Championship starts on July 25.
Opening day: June 1st. **All-Star Game**: June 26th.

CHILLICOTHE MUDCATS

Mailing Address: 11 E 2nd Street, Chillicothe, MO 64601. **Telephone:** (660) 247-1504. **Fax:** (660) 646-6933. **E-Mail Address:** doughty@greenhills.net. **Website:** chillicothemudcats.com. **General Manager:** Doug Doughty.

CLARINDA A'S

Mailing Address: 225 East Lincoln, Clarinda, IA 51632. **Telephone:** (712) 542-4272. **E-Mail Address:** m.everly@mchsi.com. **Website:** clarindaiowa-as-baseball.org.
General Managers: Ryan Eberly, Rodney J. Eberly. **Head Coach:** Ryan Eberly.

JOPLIN OUTLAWS

Mailing Address: 5860 North Pearl, Joplin, MO 64801. **Telephone:** (417) 825-4218. **E-Mail Address:** merains@mchsi.com. **Website:** joplinoutlaws.com. **President/General Manager:** Mark Rains.

NEVADA GRIFFONS

Mailing Address: PO Box 601, Nevada, MO 64772. **Telephone:** (417) 667-6159. **E-Mail Address:** Ryan.Mansfield@mcckc.edu. **Website:** nevadagriffons.org. **President:** Dan Keller. **General Manager:** Ryan Mansfield. **Head Coach:** Ryan Mansfield.

OZARK GENERALS

Mailing Address: 1336 W Farm Road 182, Springfield, MO 65810. **Telephone:** (417) 832-8830. **Fax:** (417) 877-4625. **E-Mail Address:** rda160@yahoo.com. **Website:** generalsbaseballclub.com. **General Manager/Head Coach:** Rusty Aton.

ST. JOSEPH MUSTANGS

Mailing Address: 2600 SW Parkway, St. Joseph, MO 64503. **Telephone:** (816) 279-7856. **Fax:** (816) 749-4082. **E-Mail Address:** kyturner@stjoemustangs.com. **Website:** stjoemustangs.com. **President:** Dan Gerson. **General Manager:** Ky Turner. **Manager/Director, Player Personnel:** Johnny Coy.

SEDALIA BOMBERS

Mailing Address: 2205 S Grand, Sedalia, MO 65301. **Telephone:** (660) 287-4722. **E-Mail Address:** eric@sedaliabombers.com. **Website:** sedaliabombers.com. **President/General Manager/Head Coach:** Jud Kindle. **Vice President:** Ross Dey.

JEFFERSON CITY RENEGADES

Telephone: 630-781-7247 **E-Mail Address:** jcrenegades@gmail.com. **Website:** jcrenegades.com.

President/General Manager: Steve Dullard. **Head Coach:** Mike DeMilia.

NEW ENGLAND COLLEGIATE LEAGUE

Mailing Address: 122 Mass Moca Way, North Adams, MA 01247. **Telephone:** (413) 652-1031. **Fax:** (413) 473-0012. **E-Mail Address:** smcgrath@necbl.com. **Website:** necbl.com. **Year founded:** 1993. **President:** John DeRosa. **Commissioner:** Sean McGrath. **Deputy Commissioner:** Gregg Hunt. **Secretary:** Max Pinto. **Treasurer:** Tim Porter. **Regular Season:** 44 games. **2020 Opening Date:** June 3. **Closing Date:** Aug. 1. **All-Star Game:** July 19. **Roster Limit:** 33 (college players only).

DANBURY WESTERNERS

Mailing Address: PO Box 3828, Danbury, CT 06813. **Telephone:** (203) 502-9167. **E-Mail Address:** jspitser@msn.com. **Website:** danburywesterners.com. **President:** Jon Pitser. **General Manager:** Chris Nathanson. **Field Manager:** Ian Ratchford.

VALLEY BLUE SOX

Mailing Address: 100 Congress St, Springfield, MA 01104. **Telephone:** 860-305-1684. **E-Mail Address:** hunter@valleybluesox.com. **Website:** valleybluesox.com. **President:** Clark Eckhoff. **General Manager:** Hunter Golden. **Field Manager:** John Raiola.

KEENE SWAMP BATS

Mailing Address: 303 Park Ave., Keene, NH 03431. **Telephone:** 603-731-5240. **E-Mail Address:** swampbatsribby@gmail.com. **Website:** swampbats.com. **President:** Kevin Watterson. **Field Manager:** Unavailable.

WINNIPESAUKEE MUSKRATS

Mailing Address: 97 Ashley Drive, Laconia, NH 03246. **Telephone:** 603-303-7806. **E-Mail Address:** kristian@muskratsbaseball.com. **Website:** winnipesaukeemuskrats.com. **President:** Mike Smith. **General Manager:** Kristian Svindland. **Field Manager:** Mike Miller.

MYSTIC SCHOONERS

Mailing Address: PO Box 432, Mystic, CT 06355. **Telephone:** (860) 608-3287. **E-Mail Address:** dlong@mysticbaseball.org. **Website:** mysticbaseball.org. **Executive Director:** Don Benoit. **General Manager:** Dennis Long. **Field Manager:** Phil Orbe.

NEW BEDFORD BAY SOX

Mailing Address: 309 Princeton St., New Bedford, MA 02740. **Telephone:** 508-985-3052. **E-Mail Address:** tsilveira17@gmail.com. **Website:** nbbaysox.com. **President:** Stephen King. **General Manager:** Tammy Silveira. **Field Manager:** Chris Cabe.

NEWPORT GULLS

Mailing Address: PO Box 777, Newport, RI 02840. **Telephone:** (401) 845-6832. **E-Mail Address:** gm@newportgulls.com. **Website:** newportgulls.com. **President/General Manager:** Chuck Paiva. **Executive VP of Baseball Operations:** Chris Patsos. **Director of Baseball Operations:** Mike Falcone. **Field Manager:** Kevin Winterrowd.

NORTH ADAMS STEEPLECATS

Mailing Address: PO Box 540, North Adams, MA 01247. **Telephone:** 413-896-3153. **E-Mail Address:** matt.tora@steeplecats.org. **Website:** steeplecats.org. **President:** Matt Tora. **General Manager:** Matt Tora. **Field Manager:** Mike Dailey.

OCEAN STATE WAVES

Mailing Address: 875 Kingstown Rd, Wakefield, RI 02879. **Telephone:** (401) 360-2977. **E-Mail Address:** eric@oceanstatewaves.com. **Website:** oceanstatewaves.com. **President/General Manager:** Eric Hirschbein-Bodnar. **Field Manager:** Eric Hirschbein-Bodnar.

PLYMOUTH PILGRIMS

Mailing Address: 111 Camelot Drive, Plymouth, MA 02360. **Telephone:** 617-694-2658.. **E-Mail Address:** KPlant@pilgrimsbaseball.com. **Website:** pilgrims baseball.com. **President:** Peter Plant. **General Manager:** Kevin Plant. **Field Manager:** Greg Zackrison.

SANFORD MARINERS

Field Address: Goodall Park, 38 Roberts Street, Sanford, ME 04073. **Telephone:** (207) 650-1902. **E-Mail:** aizaryk@bridgtonacademy.org. **General Manager:** Aaron Izaryk. **Field Manager:** Cejar Suarez.

VERMONT MOUNTAINEERS

Mailing Address: PO Box 57, East Montpelier, VT 05651. **Telephone:** (802) 272-8728. **E-Mail Address:** gmvtm@comcast.net. **Website:** thevermont mountaineers.com. **General Manager:** Brian Gallagher. **Field Manager:** Charlie Barbieri.

UPPER VALLEY NIGHTHAWKS

Mailing Address: 134 Stevens Road Lebanon, NH 03766. **Telephone:** 864-380-2873 **E-Mail Address:** noah@uppervalleynighthawks.com. **Website:** upper valleybaseball.pointstreaksites.com. **President:** Noah Crane. **General Manager:** Phil Chaput. **Field Manager:** TBA.

NEW YORK COLLEGIATE BASEBALL LEAGUE

Mailing Address: 398 East Dyke St. Wellsville, NY 14895. **Telephone:** (585) 455-2345. **Website:** nycbl.com. **Year founded:** 1978. **President:** Bill McConnell. **Commissioner:** Joe Brown. **Email address:** joebrown.nycbl@gmail.com. **Vice President:** Brian McConnell Jr. **Senior Marketing Director:** Dave Meluni. **Treasurer:** Dennis Duffy. **Secretary:** Steven Ackley. **Franchises: Eastern Division:** Cortland Crush, Onondaga Flames, Rome Generals, Sherrill Silversmiths, Syracuse Spartans, Saratoga Revolution. **Western Division:** Genesee Rapids, Hornell Dodgers, Niagara Power, Olean Oilers, Rochester Ridgemen, Wellsville Nitros. **Playoff Format:** six teams qualify and play a 1 game playoff and then two rounds of best of three series. **Roster Limit:** Unlimited (college-eligible players only).

CORTLAND CRUSH

Mailing Address: 2745 Summer Ridge Rd, LaFayette, NY 13084. **Telephone:** 315-391-8167. **Email Address:** wmmac4@aol.com. **Website:** cortlandcrush.com. **President:** Gary VanGorder. **Field Manager:** Bill McConnell.

GENESEE RAPIDS

Mailing Address: 9726 Rt. 19 Houghton, NY 14474. **Telephone:** 716-969-0688. **Email Address:** rkerr@frontiernet.net. **President:** Ralph Kerr. **Field Manager:** Joe Mesa.

HORNELL DODGERS

Mailing Address: PO Box 235, Hornell, NY 14843. **Telephone:** (607) 661-4173. **Fax:** (607) 661-4173. **E-Mail Address:** gm@hornelldodgers.com. **Website:** hornelldodgers.com. **General Manager:** Paul Welker. **Field Manager:** Justin Oney.

MANSFIELD DESTROYERS

Mailing Address: Mansfield Destroyers, 508 Gaines Street, Elmira, NY 14901. **Telephone:** (570) 335-9575. **E-Mail Address:** info@mansfielddestroyers.com. **President:** Don Lewis. **General Manager:** TBA. **Field Manager:** Brian Hill.

NIAGARA POWER

Mailing Address: P.O. Box 2012, Niagara University, NY 14109. **Telephone:** (716) 286-8653. **E-Mail Address:** ptutka@niagara.edu. **Website:** niagarapowerbase ball.com. **President:** Dr. Patrick Tutka. **Field Manager:** Stu Pederson.

OLEAN OILERS

Mailing Address: 126 N 10th, Olean, NY 14760. **Telephone:** 716-378-0641. **E-Mail Address:** Brian@oconnelllaw.net. **President:** Brian O'Connell. **Field Manager:** Unavailable.

ROCHESTER RIDGEMEN

Mailing Address: 651 Taylor Dr, Xenia, OH 45385. **Telephone:** (937) 352-1225. **E-Mail Addresses:** baseball@athletesinaction.org. **Website:** rochesterridgemen.org. **President:** Jason Jipson. **Field Manager:** John Byington.

ROME GENERALS

Email Address: Romegenerals@gmail.com. **Telephone:** (315) 542-0675. **Website:** rome generals.com. **Baseball Director:** Ray DiBrango. **Field Manager:** Unavailable.

SHERRILL SILVERSMITHS

Mailing Address: 3 VanWoert Ave Unit 12, Oneonta, NY 13820. **Telephone:** (401)-935-1352. **E-Mail Address:** Djduffy316@gmail.com. **Website:** leaguelineup.com/silversmiths. **President:** Dennis Duffy & Mike Sherlock. **Field Manager:** Tim Bailey.

SYRACUSE SALT CATS

Mailing Address: 208 Lakeland Ave, Syracuse, NY 13209. **Telephone:** (315) 727-9220. **Fax:** (315) 488-1750. **E-Mail Address:** mmarti6044@yahoo.com. **Website:** leaguelineup.com/saltcats. **President:** Mike Martinez. **Field Manager:** Mike Martinez.

SYRACUSE SPARTANS

Mailing Address: 208 Lakeland Ave, Syracuse, NY 13209. **Telephone:** (315) 727-9220. **Fax:** (315) 488-1750. **E-Mail Address:** mmarti6044@yahoo.com. **General Manager:** JJ Potrikus. **Field Manager:** Brian Burns.

WELLSVILLE NITROS

Mailing Address: 2848 O'Donnell Rd, Wellsville, NY 14895. **Telephone:** 585-596-9523. **Fax:** 585-593-5260. **E-Mail Address:** nitros04@gmail.com. **Website:** nitrosbaseball.com. **President:** Steven J. Ackley. **Field Manager:** Tucker Hughes.

NORTHWOODS LEAGUE

Office Address: 2900 4th St SW, Rochester, MN 55902. **Telephone:** (507) 536-4579. **Fax:** (507) 536-4597. **E-Mail Address:** info@northwoodsleague.com.

Website: northwoodsleague.com.

Year Founded: 1994.

Chairman: Dick Radatz, Jr. **President:** Gary Hoover. **Vice President, Business Development:** Matt Bomberg. **Vice President, Operations:** Glen Showalter. **Vice President, Licensing/Technology:** Tina Coil. **Vice President, Technology Development:** Greg Goodwin. **Division Structure: East**—Kokomo Jackrabbits, Traverse City, Rockford Rivets, Kalamazoo Growlers, Kenosha Kingfish, Battle Creek Bombers. **West**—Fond du Lac Dock Spiders, Green Bay Booyah, Madison Mallards, Wisconsin Rapids Rafters, Lakeshore Chinooks. **Great Plains Division: East** – Duluth Huskies, Eau Claire Express, Waterloo Bucks, Thunder Bay Border Cats, La Crosse Loggers. **West**—Bismarck Larks, Mankato MoonDogs, Willmar Stingers, St. Cloud Rox, Rochester Honkers. **Regular Season:** 72 games (split schedule). **2020 Opening Date:** TBD. **Closing Date:** TBD. **All-Star Game:** TBD.

Playoff Format: First and second half sub-divisional winners are eligible for the playoffs. The two-playoff eligible teams in each sub-division will compete in a best of three sub-divisional series. The two sub-divisional series winners will play in a one-game divisional championship game. The two divisional game winners will play in a one-game league championship.

Roster Limit: 30 (college-eligible players only).

BATTLE CREEK BOMBERS

Mailing Address: 189 Bridge Street, Battle Creek, MI 49017. **Telephone:** (269) 962-0735. **Fax:** (269) 962-0741. **Email Address:** info@battlecreekbombers.com. **Website:** battlecreekbombers.com. **General Manager:** Tyler Shore. **Field Manager:** Josh Rebandt. **Field:** C.O. Brown Stadium.

BISMARCK LARKS

Mailing Address: 300 N 4th Street, Suite 103, Bismarck, ND 58501. **Telephone:** (701) 557-7600. **Email Address:** info@larksbaseball.com. **Website:** larks baseball.com. **General Manager:** John Bollinger. **Field Manager:** Will Flynt. **Field:** Bismarck Municipal.

DULUTH HUSKIES

Mailing Address: PO Box 16231, Duluth, MN 55816. **Telephone:** (218) 786-9909.

Fax: (218) 786-9001. **E-Mail Address:** huskies@duluth huskies.com. **Website:** duluthhuskies.com. **Owner:** Michael Rosenzweig. **General Manager:** Greg Culver. **Field Manager:** Marcus Pointer. **Field:** Wade Stadium.

EAU CLAIRE EXPRESS

Mailing Address: 108 E Grand Ave, Eau Claire, WI 54701. **Telephone:** (715) 839-7788. **Fax:** (715) 839-7676. **E-Mail Address:** info@eauclaireexpress.com. **Website:** eauclaireexpress.com. **Owner:** Bill Rowlett. **Assistant Managing Director:** Andy Neborak. **General Manager:** Jacob Servais. **Director of Operations/Field Manager:** Dale Varsho. **Field:** Carson Park.

FOND DU LAC DOCK SPIDERS

Mailing Address: 980 E Division St., Fond du Lac, WI 54935. **Telephone:** (920) 907-9833. **Email Address:** info@ dockspiders.com **Website:** dockspiders.com. **President:** Rob Zerjav. **General Manager:** Chris Ward. **Field Manager:** Zac Charbonneau. **Field:** Herr-Baker Field

GREEN BAY BOOYAH

Mailing Address: 2325 Holgrem Way Suite, Green Bay, WI 54303. **Telephone:** (920) 497-7225. **Fax:** (920) 437-3551. **Email Address:** info@booyahbaseball.com. **Website:** booyahbaseball.com. **General Manager:** Sieeria Vieaux. **Field Manager:** TBA. **Field:** Capital Credit Union Park.

KALAMAZOO GROWLERS

Mailing Address: 251 Mills St, Kalamazoo, MI 49048. **Telephone:** (269) 492-9966.

Website: growlersbaseball.com. **General Manager:** Brian Colopy. **Field Manager:** Cody Piechocki. **Field:** Homer Stryker Field.

KENOSHA KINGFISH

Mailing Address: 7817 Sheridan Rd, Kenosha, WI 53143. **Telephone:** (262) 653-0900. **Website:** king fishbaseball.com. **General Manager:** Doug Cole. **Field Manager:** Duffy Dyer. **Field:** Simmons Field.

LA CROSSE LOGGERS

Mailing Address: 1225 Caledonia St, La Crosse, WI 54603. **Telephone:** (608) 796-9553. **Fax:** (608) 796-9032. **E-Mail Address:** info@lacrosseloggers.com. **Website:** lacrosseloggers.com. **Owner:** Dan Kapanke. **General Manager:** Chris Goodell. **Assistant General Manager:** Ben Kapanke. **Field Manager:** Brian Lewis. **Field:** Copeland Park.

LAKESHORE CHINOOKS

Mailing Address: 983 Badger Circle, Grafton, WI 53024. **Telephone:** (262) 618-4659. **Fax:** (262) 618-4362. **E-Mail Address:** info@lakeshorechinooks.com. **Website:** lakeshorechinooks.com. **Owner:** Jim Kacmarcik. **General Manager:** Eric Snodgrass. **Field Manager:** Travis Akre. **Field:** Kapco Park.

MADISON MALLARDS

Mailing Address: 2920 N Sherman Ave, Madison, WI 53704. **Telephone:** (608) 246-4277. **Fax:** (608) 246-4163.

E-Mail Address: info@mallardsbaseball.com. Website: mallardsbaseball.com. Owner: Steve Schmitt. President: Vern Stenman. General Manager: Tyler Isham. Field Manager: Donnie Scott. Field: Warner Park.

MANKATO MOONDOGS

Mailing Address: 1221 Caledonia Street, Mankato, MN 56001. Telephone: (507) 625-7047. Fax: (507) 625-7059. E-Mail Address: office@mankatomoondogs.com. Website: mankatomoondogs.com. General Manager: Austin Link. Field Manager: Matt Wollenzin. Field: Franklin Rogers Park.

ROCHESTER HONKERS

Mailing Address: 307 E Center St, Rochester, MN 55904. Telephone: (507) 289-1170. Fax: (507) 289-1866. E-Mail Address: honkersbaseball@gmail.com. Website: rochesterhonkers.com. General Manager: Jeremy aagard. Field Manager: Deskaeh Bomberry. Field: Mayo Field.

ROCKFORD RIVETS

Mailing Address: 4503 Interstate Blvd., Loves Park, IL 61111. Telephone: 815-240-4159. E-Mail Address: info@rockfordrivets.com Website: rockfordrivets.com. General Manager: Chad Bauer. Field Manager: Josh Keim. Field: Rivets Stadium.

ST. CLOUD ROX

Mailing Address: 5001 8th St N, St. Cloud, MN 56303. Telephone: (320) 240-9798. Fax: (320) 255-5228. E-Mail Address: info@stcloudrox.com. Website: stcloudrox.com. President: Gary Posch. Vice President: Scott Schreiner. General Manager: Mike Johnson. Field Manager: Augie Rodriguez. Field: Joe Faber Field.

ST. CROIX RIVER HOUNDS

Mailing Address: PO Box 10, Hudson, WI 54016. Telephon: (651) 272-7483. E-Mail Address: info@scriverhounds.com. Owners: Klint Klaas, Robb Quinlan, Tom Quinlan, Andy Persby, Kevin McMann, Steve Fleischhacker. President/General Manager: Bill Fanning. Field Manager: TBA.

THUNDER BAY BORDER CATS

Mailing Address: PO Box 29105 Thunder Bay, Ontario P7B 6P9. Telephone: (807) 766-2287. General Manager: Dan Grant. Field Manager: Eric Vasquez. Field: Port Arthur Stadium.

TRAVERSE CITY PIT SPITTERS

E-Mail Address: info@traversecitybaseball.com. General Manager: Mickey Graham. Field Manager: Josh Rebandt.

WATERLOO BUCKS

Mailing Address: PO Box 4124, Waterloo, IA 50704. Telephone: (319) 232-0500. Fax: (319) 232-0700. E-Mail Address: waterloobucks@waterloobucks.com. Website: waterloobucks.com. General Manager: Dan Corbin. Field Manager: Casey Harms. Field: Riverfront Stadium.

WILLMAR STINGERS

Mailing Address: PO Box 201, Willmar, MN, 56201.

Telephone: (320) 222-2010. E-Mail Address: ryan@willmarstingers.com. Website: willmarstingers.com. Owners: Marc Jerzak, Ryan Voz. General Manager: Nick McCallum. Field Manager: Bo Henning. Field: Taunton Stadium.

WISCONSIN RAPIDS RAFTERS

Mailing Address: 521 Lincoln St, Wisconsin Rapids, WI 54494. Telephone: (715) 424-5400. E-Mail Address: info@raftersbaseball.com. Website: raftersbaseball.com. Owner: Vern Stenman. General Manager: Andy Francis. Field Manager: Craig Noto. Field: Witter Field.

WISCONSIN WOODCHUCKS

Mailing Address: 2401 N 3rd St, Wausau, WI 54403. Telephone: (715) 845-5055. Fax: (715) 845-5015. E-Mail Address: info@woodchucks.com. Website: woodchucks. com. Owner: Mark Macdonald. General Manager: Ryan Treu. Field Manager: Ronnie Richardson. Field: Athletic Park.

PACIFIC INTERNATIONAL LEAGUE

Mailing Address: 4400 26th Ave W, Seattle, WA 98199. Telephone: (206) 623-8844. Fax: (206) 623-8361. E-Mail Address: spotter@potterprinting.com. Website: pacifi-cinternationalleague.com.

Year Founded: 1992.

President: Al Oremus. Vice President: Martin Lawrence. Commissioner: Terry Howard. Secretary: Steve Potter. Treasurer: Mark Dow. Member Clubs: Northwest Honkers, Everett Merchants, Seattle Studs, Highline Bears, Redmond Dudes, North Sound Emeralds. Regular Season: 20 league games. Playoff Format: Top team is invited to National Baseball Congress World Series.

Roster Limit: 30; 25 eligible for games (players must be at least 18 years old).

PERFECT GAME COLLEGIATE LEAGUE

Mailing Address: 8 Michaels Lane, Old Brookville, NY 11545. Telephone: (516) 521-0206. Fax: (516) 801-0818. E-Mail Address: valkun@aol.com.

Website: pgcbl.com.

Year Founded: 2010.

President: Jeffrey Kunion.

Director of Communications: Travis Larner

Executive Committee: Bob Ohmann (Newark Pilots), Paul Samulski (Albany Dutchmen). Robbie Nichols (Elmira Pioneers), George Deak (Utica Blue Sox), Kevin Hinchey (Saugerties Stallions)

Teams: East—Albany Dutchmen, Amsterdam Mohawks, Glens Falls Dragons, Mohawk Valley DiamondDawgs, Oneonta Outlaws, Saugerties Stallions, Utica Blue Sox. West—Adirondack Trail Blazers, Elmira Pioneers, Geneva Red Wings, Jamestown Jammers, Newark Pilots, Onondaga Flames

Regular Season: 50. Playoff Format: Top four teams in each division qualify for one-game playoff; next two series are best of three. Roster Limit: 35 (maximum of two graduated high school players per team).

ADIRONDACK TRAIL BLAZERS

President: Bobby Miller. General Manager: Matt Burns. Head Coach: Michael Fauvelle. Telephone: (315) 542-0675. Field: Robert Smith Sports Complex. Email Address: adirondacktrailblazers@rocketmail.com.

ALBANY DUTCHMEN

Mailing Address: PO Box 72, Saratoga Springs, N.Y. 12866. **President:** Paul Samulski. **General Manager:** Jason Brinkman. **E-Mail:** jbrinkma@gmail.com. **Telephone:** 518-210-8383. **Head Coach:** Nick Davey. **Field:** Siena Field.

AMSTERDAM MOHAWKS

Mailing Address: P.O. Box 334, Amsterdam, N.Y., 12010. **President:** Brian Spagnola. **Vice President:** Dave Dittman. **Head Coach:** Keith Griffin. **E-Mail Address:** gm@amsterdammohawks.com. **Telephone:** (518)791-7546. **Field:** Shuttlesworth Park.

ELMIRA PIONEERS

Mailing Address: 546 Luce Street, Elmira, N.Y. 14904. **Owners:** Nellie Franco-Nichols, Donald Lewis, Robbie Nichols. **Head Coach:** Matt Burch. **Telephone:** (607) 734-2690. **E-Mail Address:** donspioneers@gmail.com. **Field:** Dunn Field.

GENEVA RED WINGS

Mailing Address: N/A. **Owners:** Bob Ohmann, Lesilie Ohmann. **Head Coach:** Sean O'Connor. **Email:** info@genevaredwings.com. **Telephone:** (919) 422-4323. **Field:** McDonough Park.

GLENS FALLS DRAGONS

Mailing Address: PO Box 897, Glens Falls, N.Y. 12801. **President:** Ben Bernard. **Head Coach:** Cameron Curler. **Telephone:** (518) 361-5316. **E-Mail Address:** ben bernard1@yahoo.com. **Field:** East Field Stadium.

JAMESTOWN TARP SKUNKS

Owner: Mike Zimmerman. **President:** Dan Kuenzi. **Head Coach:** Anthony Barone. **Telephone:** (716) 720-4465. **E-Mail Address:** dkuenzi@mkesports.com. **Field:** Russell E. Diethrick Jr. Park.

MOHAWK VALLEY DIAMONDDAWGS

Mailing Address: PO Box 902, Little Falls, N.Y. 13365. **Owner:** Travis Heiser. **Head Coach:** Cory Haggerty. **Telephone:** (315) 985-0692. **E-Mail Address:** travis@mydiamonddawgs.com. **Field:** Veterans Memorial Park.

NEWARK PILOTS

Mailing Address: 65 Williams Street, Lyons, N.Y. 14489. **Owner:** Bob Ohmann, Leslie Ohmann. **Head Coach:** Matt Colbert. **Telephone:** (315) 576-6710. **E-Mail Address:** newarkpilots@gmail.com. **Field:** Colburn Park.

ONEONTA OUTLAWS

Mailing Address: 291 Chestnut Street, Oneonta, N.Y., 13280. **Owner:** Gary Laing. **General Manager:** Joe Hughes. **Head Coach:** Joe Hughes. **Telephone:** (607) 432-6326. **E-Mail Address:** joehughes@oneontaoutlaws.com. **Field:** Damaschke Field.

ONONDAGA FLAMES

Mailing Address: 285 Pinehurst Trace Drive, Pinehurst, NC 28374. **Owners:** Wayne Walker & Alyce Lee-Walker. **Head Coach:** Ryan Stevens. **Telephone:** (315) 308-0889. **E-Mail Address:** wayne@onondagaflames.com. **Stadium:** Onondaga Community College Baseball Complex.

SAUGERTIES STALLIONS

Mailing Address: 645 Rte 212, Saugerties, NY 12477. **Owner:** Kevin Hinchey. **Head Coach:** Collin Martin. **Telephone:** (845) 707-0265. **E-Mail Address:** the saugertiesstallions@gmail.com. **Field:** Cantine Field.

UTICA BLUE SOX

Mailing Address: 7179 County Highway 18, West Winfield, N.Y. 13491. **Owner:** George Deak. **General Manager:** George Deak. **Head Coach:** Doug Delett. **Telephone:** (315) 855-5013. **E-Mail Address:** George@globalgraphicsny.com. **Field:** Donovan Stadium at Murnane Field.

WATERTOWN RAPIDS

Mailing Address: PO Box 6250, Watertown, N.Y. 13601. **Owners:** Michael Schell, Paul Velte. **General Manager:** Brandon Noble. **Field Manager:** Dave Anderson. **Telephone:** (315) 836-1545. **E-Mail Address:** rapidsgm@gmail.com. **Field:** Alex T. Duffy Fairgrounds.

PROSPECT LEAGUE

Mailing Address: PO Box 84, Elkville, IL 62932. **Telephone:** (618) 559-1343. **E-Mail Address:** commissioner@prospectleague.com. **Website:** prospectleague.com.

Year Founded: 1963 as Central Illinois Collegiate League; known as Prospect League since 2009.

Commissioner: Dennis Bastien.

Regular Season: 60 games. **2020 Opening Date:** May 28. **Closing Date:** Aug. 2. **All-Star Series:** July 22-23. **Championship Series:** Aug. 4-9. **Roster Limit:** 32.

CHAMPION CITY KINGS

Mailing Address: 1301 Mitchell Blvd., Springfield, OH 45503. **Telephone:** (937) 342-0320. **Fax:** (937) 342-0320. **E-Mail Address:** cckings@gmail.com. **Website:** championcitykings.com. **General Manager:** Ginger Fulton. **Field Manager:** John Jeanes.

CHILLICOTHE PAINTS

Mailing Address: 59 North Paint Street, Chillicothe, OH 45601. **Telephone:** (740) 773-8326. **Fax:** (740) 773-8338. **E-Mail Address:** paints@bright.net. **Website:** chillicothepaints.com. **General Manager:** Bryan Wickline. **Field Manager:** Brian Bigam.

DANVILLE DANS

Mailing Address: 4 Maywood, Danville, IL 61832. **Telephone:** (217) 918-3401. **Fax:** (217) 446-9995. **E-Mail Address:** danvilledans@comcast.net. **Website:** danvilledans.com. **League Director:** Jeanie Cooke. **General Manager:** Jeanie Cooke. **Field Manager:** Eric Coleman.

O'FALLON HOOTS

Telephone: Unavailable. **Email Address:** ofallon@prospectleague.com. **General Manager:** David Schmoll. **Field Manager:** Joe Lincoln. **Stadium:** CarShield Field.

DUPAGE PISTOL SHRIMP

E-Mail Address: info@dupagepistolshrimp.com. **Telephone:** 855-748-2457. **General Manager & Field Manager:** John Jakiemiec. **Field:** BenU Baseball Field (Village of Lisle-Benedictine University Sports Complex).

LAFAYETTE AVIATORS

Mailing Address: PO Box 6494, Lafayette, IN 47904. **Telephone:** (414) 224-9283. **Fax:** (414) 224-9290. **E-Mail Address:** zchartrand@lafayettebaseball.com. **Website:** lafayettebaseball.com. **President:** Sean Churchill. **General Manager:** Zach Chartrand. **League Director:** Dan Kuenzi. **Field Manager:** Brent McNeil.

QUINCY GEMS

Mailing Address: 1400 N. 30th St., Suite 1, Quincy, IL 62301. **Telephone:** (217) 214-7436. **Fax:** (217) 214-7436. **E-Mail Address:** quincygems@yahoo.com. **Website:** quincygems.com. **League Director/General Manager:** Jimmie/Julie Louthan. **Field Manager:** Pat Robles.

SPRINGFIELD SLIDERS

Mailing Address: 1415 North Grand Avenue East, Suite B, Springfield, IL 62702. **Telephone:** (217) 679-3511. **Fax:** (217) 679-3512. **E-Mail Address:** slidersfun@spring fieldsliders.com. **Website:** springfieldsliders.com. **League Director/General Manager:** Todd Miller. **Field Manager:** Chris Holke.

TERRE HAUTE REX

Mailing Address: 111 North 3rd St, Terre Haute, IN 47807. **Telephone:** (812) 478-3817. **Fax:** (812) 232-5353. **E-mail Address:** frontoffice@rexbaseball.com. **Website:** rexbaseball.com. **League Director/General Manager:** Bruce Rosselli. **Field Manager:** Tyler Wampler.

WEST VIRGINIA MINERS

Mailing Address: 476 Ragland Road, Suite 2, Beckley, WV 25801. **Telephone:** (304) 252-7233. **Fax:** (304) 253-1998. **E-mail Address:** wvminers@wvminersbaseball.com. **Website:** wvminersbaseball.com. **President:** Doug Epling. **League Director/General Manager/Field Manager::** Tim Epling.

SOUTHERN COLLEGIATE BASEBALL LEAGUE

Mailing Address: 9723 Northcross Center Court, Huntersville, NC 28078. **Telephone:** (704) 635-7126. **Cell:** (704) 906-7776. **E-mail Address:** hhampton@scbl.org. **Website:** scbl.org.
Year Founded: 1999.
Chairman: Bill Capps, **Commissioner:** Jamie Billings. **President:** Jeff Carter. **Treasurer:** Brenda Templin. **Umpire in Chief:** Gary Swanson.
Regular Season: 42 games. **Playoff Format:** Six-team single-elimination tournament with best of three championship series between final two teams.
Roster Limit: 35 (College-eligible players only).

CHARLOTTE GALAXY

Mailing Address: 7209 East WT Harris Blvd, Suite J #245, Charlotte, NC 28227. **Telephone:** (704) 668-9167. **Email Address:** baseballnbeyond@aol.com. **General Manager:** David "Doc" Booth. **Head Coach:** Addison Rouse.

CONCORD ATHLETICS

Mailing Address: 366 George Lyles Parkway, Suite 125, Concord, NC 28027. **Telephone:** (704) 786-2255. **Email Address:** playconcordathletics@gmail.com.

General Manager: David Darwin. **Head Coach:** Charles Weber

LAKE NORMAN COPPERHEADS

Mailing Address: 16405 Northcross Drive, Suite A Huntersville, NC 28078. **Telephone:** (704) 305-3649. **Email Address:** dshoe@copperheadsports.org. **General Manager:** Derek Shoe. **Head Coach:** Jeremy Johnson.

PIEDMONT PRIDE

Mailing Address: 1524 Summit View Drive, Rock Hill, SC 29732. **Telephone:** (803) 412-7982. **E-Mail Address:** joe@pridebaseball.net. **General Manager:** Logan Hudak. **Head Coach:** Joe Hudak.

CAROLINA VIPERS

Mailing Address: 12104 Copper Way, Suite 200, Charlotte NC 28277. **Telephone:** 980-256-5346. **E-Mail Address:** bnichols@goviperbaseball.com. **President:** Mike Polito. **General Manager:** Blaine Nichols. **Head Coach:** Aaron Bray.

MOORSVILLE SPINNERS

Mailing Address: 2643 N Hwy 16 Denver, NC 28037. **Telephone:** (704) 491-4112. **E-Mail Address:** ploftin@mooresvillespinners.com. **General Manager:** Phillip Loftin. **Head Coach:** Tripp Hamrick.

LINOIRE OILERS

Mailing Address: PO Box 1113 Icard NC 28666. **Telephone** 828-455-1289. **E-Mail Address:** LenoirOilers@gmail.com. **General Manager** Sara Wert. **Head Coach:** Ivan Acuna.

TEXAS COLLEGIATE LEAGUE

Mailing Address: 735 Plaza Blvd, Suite 200, Coppell, TX 75019. **Telephone:** (979) 985-5198. **Fax:** (979) 779-2398. **E-Mail Address:** info@tclbaseball.com.
Website: texascollegeleague.com.
Year Founded: 2004.
President: Uri Geva.
Roster Limit: 30 (College-eligible players only)

ACADIANA CANE CUTTERS

Mailing Address: 221 La Neuville, Youngsville, LA 70592. **Telephone:** (337) 451-6582. **E-Mail Address:** info@canecuttersbaseball.com. **Website:** canecuttersbaseball.com. **Owners:** Richard Chalmers, Sandi Chalmers. **General Manager:** Richard Haifley.

BRAZOS VALLEY BOMBERS

Mailing Address: 405 Mitchell St, Bryan, TX 77801. **Telephone:** (979) 799-7529. **Fax:** (979) 779-2398. **E-Mail Address:** info@bvbombers.com. **Website:** bvbombers.com. **Owners:** Uri Geva. **General Manger:** Chris Clark. **Field Manager:** Curt Dixon.

TEXAS MARSHALS

Mailing Address: 7920 Beltline Rd, 8th Floor Suite 860 Dallas, TX 75254. **Telephone:** (855) 808-7529. **E-Mail Address:** info@texasmarshals.com. **Website:** texas marshals.com. **Owner:** Marc Landry. **General Manager:** Kenderick Moore. **Field Manager:** Brent Lavallee.

TEXARKANA TWINS

Ballpark: George Dobson Field, 4303 N Park Rd, Texarkana, TX 75503. **Telephone:** (903) 294-7529. **Head Coach:** Bill Clay.

VICTORIA GENERALS

Mailing Address: 1307 E Airline Road, Suite H, Victoria, TX 77901. **Telephone:** (361) 485-9522. **Fax:** (361) 485-0936. **E-Mail Address:** info@baseballinvictoria.com, tkyoung@victoriagenerals.com. **Website:** victoria generals.com. **President:** Tracy Young. **VP/General Manager:** Mike Yokum.

VALLEY BASEBALL LEAGUE

Mailing Address: Valley Baseball League, PO Box 1127, New Market, VA 22844. **Telephone:** (540) 810-9194. **Fax:** (540) 435-8453. **E-Mail Addresses:** cbalger@shentel. net. **Website:** valleyleaguebaseball.com. **Year Founded:** 1897. **President:** C. Bruce Alger. **Executive Vice President:** Jay Neal. **Media Relations Director:** John Leonard. **Secretary:** Stacy Locke. **Treasurer:** Ed Yoder. **Regular Season:** 42 games. **Playoff Format:** Eight teams qualify; play three rounds of best of three series. **Roster Limit:** 30 (college-eligible only)

COVINGTON LUMBERJACKS

Mailing Address: PO Box 30, Covington, VA 24426. **Telephone:** (540) 969-9923, (540) 962-1155. **Fax:** (540) 962-7153. **E-Mail Address:** covingtonlumberjacks@valley leaguebaseball.com. **Website:** lumberjacksbase ball.com. **President:** Dizzy Garten. **Head Coach:** Alex Kotheimer.

PURCELLVILLE CANNONS

Mailing Address: P.O. Box 114, Purcellville, VA 20132. **Telephone:** (540) 303-9673. **Fax:** (304) 856-1619. **E-Mail Address:** info@purcellvillecannons.com. **Website:** pur-cellvillecannons.com. **President/Recruiting Coordinator/Head Coach:** Brett Fuller. **General Manager:** Ridge Fuller.

CHARLOTTESVILLE TOM SOX

Mailing Address: P. O. Box 4836, Virginia 22905. **Telephone:** (540)471-0799. **E-Mail:** mpad71@gmail.com. **Website:** TomSox.com. **President/General Manager:** Mike Paduano. **Head Coach:** Kory Koehler.

FRONT ROYAL CARDINALS

Mailing Address: 382 Morgans Ridge Road, Front Royal, VA 22630. **Telephone:** (703) 244-6662, (540) 631-9201. **E-Mail Address:** DonnaSettle@centurylink.net. frontroyalcardinals@valleyleaguebaseball.com. **Website:** valleyleaguebaseball.com. **President:** Donna Settle. **Head Coach:** Zeke Mitchem.

HARRISONBURG TURKS

Mailing Address: 1489 S Main St, Harrisonburg, VA 22801. **Telephone:** (540) 434-5919. **Fax:** (540) 434-5919. **E-Mail Address:** turksbaseball@hotmail.com. **Website:** harrisonburgturks.com. **Operations Manager:** Teresa Wease. **General Manager/Head Coach:** Bob Wease.

NEW MARKET REBELS

Mailing Address: PO Box 902, New Market, VA 22844. **Telephone:** (540) 435-8453. **Fax:** (540) 740-9486. **E-Mail Address:** nmrebels@shentel.net. **Website:** new marketrebels.com. **President/General Manager:** Bruce Alger. **Head Coach:** Arthur E. Stenberg IV.

STAUNTON BRAVES

Mailing Address: PO Box 428, Stuarts Draft, VA 24447. **Telephone:** (540) 886-0987. **Fax:** (540) 886-0905. **E-Mail Address:** sbraves@hotmail.com. **Website:** staunton-bravesbaseball.com. **General Manager:** Steve Cox. **Head Coach:** Lukas Ray.

STRASBURG EXPRESS

Mailing Address: PO Box 417, Strasburg, VA 22657. **Telephone:** (540) 325-5677, (540) 459-4041. **Fax:** (540) 459-3398. **E-Mail Address:** neallaw@shentel.net, strasburgxpress@gmail.com. **Website:** strasburg express.com. **General Manager:** Jay Neal. **Head Coach:** Anthony Goncalves.

WAYNESBORO GENERALS

Mailing Address: 3144 Village Drive, Waynesboro, VA 22980. **Telephone:** (540) 835-6312. **Fax:** (540) 932-2322. **E-Mail Address:** contact@waynesborogenerals.net. **Website:** waynesborogenerals.com. **Chairman:** Kathleen Kellett-Ward. **General Manager:** Tyler Hoffman. **Head Coach:** Zac Cole.

WINCHESTER ROYALS

Mailing Address: PO Box 2485, Winchester, VA 22604. **Telephone:** (540) 974-4104, (540) 664-3978. **Fax:** (540) 662-1434. **E-Mail Addresses:** winchesterroyals@gmail.com, info@winchesterroyals.org. **Website:** winchesterroyals.com. **President:** Donna Turrill. **Operations Director:** Jimmie Shipp. **Coach:** Mike Smith.

WOODSTOCK RIVER BANDITS

Mailing Address: P.O. Box 227, Woodstock, VA 22664. **Telephone:** (540) 481-0525. **Fax:** (540) 459-2093. **E-Mail Address:** woodstockriverbandits@valleyleaguebaseball.com. **Website:** woodstockriverbandits.org. **General Manager:** Robert "porky" Bowman. **Head Coach:** Mike Bocock. **Assistant Head Coach:** Paul Ackerman.

WEST COAST LEAGUE

Mailing Address: PO Box 10771, Portland OR 97296. **Telephone:** 503-233-2490. **E-Mail Address:** info@west coastleague.com. **Website:** westcoastleague.com. **Year Founded:** 2005. **Commissioner:** Rob Neyer. **President:** Tony Bonacci. **Vice President:** Glenn Kirkpatrick. **Secretary:** Jose Oglesby. **Treasurer:** Dan Segel. **Supervisor, Umpires:** Dave Perez. **Division Structure: South**—Bend Elks, Corvallis Knights, Cowlitz Black Bears, Ridgefield Raptors, Walla Walla Sweets. **North**—Bellingham Bells, Kelowna Falcons, Port Angeles

Lefties, Victoria Harbourcats, Wenatchee Applesox, Yakima Valley Pippins. **2020 Opening Date:** June 5. **Closing Date:** August 9. **Playoff Format:** Four-team tournament. **Roster Limit:** 35 (college-eligible players only).

BELLINGHAM BELLS

Mailing Address: 1221 Potter Street, Bellingham, WA 98229. **Telephone:** (360) 527-1035. **E-Mail Address:** stephanie@bellinghambells.com. **Website:** bellinghambells.com. **Owner:** Glenn Kirkpatrick. **General Manager:** Stephanie Morrell. **Head Coach:** Bob Geaslen. **Assistant Coaches:** Jim Clem, Jake Whisler, Boog Leach.

BEND ELKS

Mailing Address: 70 SW Century Dr Suite 100-373 Bend, Oregon 97702. **Telephone:** (541) 312-9259. **Website:** bendelks.com. **Owners:** John and Tami Marick. **Marketing and Sales:** Kelsie Hirko. **General Manager:** Michael Hirko. **Head Coach:** Alan Embree. **Assistant Coaches:** Dylan Jones, Blake Woosley.

CORVALLIS KNIGHTS

Mailing Address: PO Box 1356, Corvallis, OR 97339. **Telephone:** (541) 752-5656. **E-Mail Address:** dan.segel@corvallisknights.com. **Website:** corvallisknights.com. **President:** Dan Segel. **General Manager:** Bre Miller. **Head Coach:** Brooke Knight. **Associate Head Coach/Pitching Coach:** Ed Knaggs. **Assistant Coach:** Youngjin Yoon, Jacob Kopra.

COWLITZ BLACK BEARS

Mailing Address: PO Box 1255, Longview, WA 98632. **Telephone:** (360) 703-3195. **Website:** cowlitzblac kbears.com. **Owner/President:** Tony Bonacci. **General Manager:** Jim Appleby. **Head Coach:** Grady Tweit. **Assistant Coaches:** Jason Mackey, Michael Forgione.

KELOWNA FALCONS

Mailing Address: 201-1014 Glenmore Dr, Kelowna, BC, V1Y 4P2. **Telephone:** (250) 763-4100. **Website:** kelownafalcons.com. **Owner:** Dan Nonis. **General Manager:** Mark Nonis. **Head Coach:** Bryan Donohue.

PORT ANGELES LEFTIES

Mailing Address: PO Box 2204, Port Angeles, WA 98362. **Phone:** (360) 701-1087. **Website:** lefties baseball.com. **E-Mail Address:** matt@leftiesbaseball.com. **Owners:** Matt Acker, Jacob Oppelt, Eric Traut, Connor Traut. **General Manager:** Ryan Hickey. **Head Coach:** Matt Acker. **Assistant Coach:** Earl Smith, Anthony Murillo.

PORTLAND PICKLES

Address: 5308 SE 92nd Ave. Portland, OR 97266. **Phone:** (503)775-3080. **Owners:** Alan Miller, Jon Ryan,

Scott Barchus. **Head Coach:** Justin Barchus. **Hitting Coach:** Mark Magdaleno. **Pitching Coach:** Jim Lawler. **Bench Coach:** Jim Hoppel.

RIDGEFIELD RAPTORS

Owner: Tony Bonacci. **Partner:** Wade Siegel. **E-Mail Address:** info@ridgefieldraptors.com. **General Manager:** Gus Farah. **Head Coach:** Chris Cota.

VICTORIA HARBOURCATS

Mailing Address: 101-1814 Vancouver Street, Victoria, BC, Canada, V8T 5E3. **Telephone:** (778) 265-0327. **Website:** harbourcats.com. **Owners:** Rich Harder, Jim Swanson, Ken Swanson, John Wilson. **Managing Partner:** Jim Swanson. **General Manager:** Brad Norris-Jones. **Head Coach:** Brian McRae. **Assistant Coaches:** Ian Sanderson, Todd Haney, Troy Birtwistle, Jason Leone, Curtis Pelletier.

WALLA WALLA SWEETS

Mailing Address: 109 E Main Street, Walla Walla, WA 99362. **Telephone:** (509) 522-2255. **E-Mail Address:** info@wallawallasweets.com. **Website:** wallawalla sweets.com. **Owner:** Pacific Baseball Ventures, LLC. **President/COO:** Zachary Fraser. **General Manager:** Dan Ferguson. **Head Coach:** Frank Mutz. **Assistant Coaches:** Raul Camacho, Kyle Wilkerson.

WENATCHEE APPLESOX

Mailing Address: 610 N. Mission St. #204, Wenatchee, WA 98801. **Telephone:** (509) 665-6900. **E-Mail Address:** info@applesox.com. **Website:** applesox.com. **Owner/General Manager:** Jose Oglesby. **Owner/Assistant General Manager:** Ken Osborne. **Head Coach:** Ian Sanderson.

YAKIMA VALLEY PIPPINS

Mailing Address: PO Box 2397, Yakima, WA 98907. **Telephone:** (509) 575-4487. **E-Mail Address:** info@pippinsbaseball.com. **Website:** pippinsbaseball.com. **Owner:** Pacific Baseball Ventures, LLC. **President/COO:** Zachary Fraser. **General Manager:** Jeff Garretson. **Head Coach:** Kyle Krustangel. **Pitching Coach:** Cash Ulrich.

HIGH SCHOOL BASEBALL

NATIONAL FEDERATION OF STATE HIGH SCHOOL ASSOCIATIONS

Mailing Address: PO Box 690, Indianapolis, IN 46206. **Telephone:** (317) 972-6900. **Fax:** (317) 822-5700. **E-Mail Address:** baseball@nfhs.org. **Website:** nfhs.org.

Executive Director: Karissa Niehoff. **Chief Operating Officer:** Davis Whitfield. **Director of Sports, Sanctioning and Student Services:** B. Elliot Hopkins. **Director, Publications/Communications:** Bruce Howard.

NATIONAL HIGH SCHOOL BASEBALL COACHES ASSOCIATION

Mailing Address: PO Box 1038, Dublin, OH 43017. **Telephone:** (614) 578-1864. **E-Mail Address:** tsaunders@baseballcoaches.org. **Website:** baseballcoaches.org. **Executive Director:** Tim Saunders (Dublin Coffman HS, Ohio). **Assistant Executive Director:** Ty Whittaker (Eastern Technical HS, Md.). **Associate Executive Director:** Ray Benjamin (St. Charles HS, Ohio). **Associate Exectuive Director:** Paul Twenge (Minnetonka HS, Minn.). Executive Secretary Robert Colburn. **President:** Tony Perkins (Francis Howell HS, Mo.). **1st VP:** Tim Bordenet (Lafayette Central Catholic HS, Ind.). **2nd VP:** Scott Manahan (Bishop Watterson HS, Ohio).

2020 National Convention: Dec. in Scottsdale, Ariz.

NATIONAL TOURNAMENTS

IN-SEASON

INTERNATIONAL PAPER CLASSIC

Mailing Address: 4775 Johnson Rd., Georgetown, SC 29440. **Telephone:** (843) 527-9606. **Fax:** (843) 546-8521. **Website:** ipclassic.com.

Tournament Director: Alicia Johnson.
2020 Tournament: March 5-8.

46TH ANNUAL ANAHEIM LIONS CLUB BASEBALL TOURNAMENT

Mailing Address: 8281 Walker Street, La Palma, CA 90623. **Telephone:** (714) 220-4101x27502. **Fax:** (714) 995-1833. **Email:** Pascal_C@AUHSD.US. **Website:** anaheimlionstourney.com.

Tournament Director: Chris Pascal.
2020 Tournament: March 20-25 (80 teams).

NATIONAL CLASSIC BASEBALL TOURNAMENT

Mailing Address: 1651 Valencia Ave, Placentia, CA 92870. **Telephone:** (714) 993-2838. **Fax:** (714) 993-5350. **E-Mail Address:** mlucas@pylusd.org. **Website:** national-classic.com.

Tournament Director: Matt Lucas.
2020 Tournament: April 6-9.

USA BASEBALL NATIONAL HIGH SCHOOL INVITATIONAL

Mailing Address: 1030 Swabia Ct., Suite 201; Durham, NC 27703. **Telephone:** (919) 474-8721. **Fax:** (919) 474-8822. **Email:** carterhicks@usabaseball.com. **Website:** usabaseball.com.

2020 Tournament: April 1-4 at USA Baseball National Training Complex, Cary, N.C. (16 teams).

POSTSEASON

ALL-STAR GAMES/AWARDS
PERFECT GAME ALL-AMERICAN CLASSIC

Mailing Address: 850 Twixt Town Rd. NE, Cedar Rapids, IA 52402. **Telephone:** (319) 298-2923. Fax (319) 298-2924. **Event Organizer:** Blue Ridge Sports & Entertainment. **VP, Showcases/Scouting:** Greg Sabers.

2020 Game: Aug. 16 at Petco Park, San Diego.

UNDER ARMOUR ALL-AMERICA GAME, POWERED BY BASEBALL FACTORY

Mailing Address: 9212 Berger Rd., Suite 200, Columbia, MD 21046. **Telephone:** (410) 715-5080. **E-mail Address:** jason@factoryathletics.com. **Website:** baseballfactory.com/AllAmerica. **Event Organizers:** Baseball Factory, Team One Baseball.

2020 Game: Summer, TBD.

GATORADE CIRCLE OF CHAMPIONS

(National HS Player of the Year Award)

Mailing Address: The Gatorade Company, 321 N. Clark St., Suite 24-3, Chicago, IL, 60610. **Telephone:** (312) 821-1000. **Website:** gatorade.com.

SHOWCASE EVENTS

AREA CODE BASEBALL GAMES PRESENTED BY NEW BALANCE
Mailing Address: 23954 Madison Street, Torrance, CA 90505. **Telephone:** (310) 791-1142 x 4426. **E-Mail:** baseball@studentsports.com. **Website:** AreaCodeBaseball.com.
Event Organizer: Kirsten Leetch.
2020 Area Code Games: Aug. 6-10 at Blair Field in Long Beach, Calif.

AREA CODE BASEBALL UNDERCLASS GAMES PRESENTED BY NEW BALANCE
Event Organizer: Kirsten Leetch.
2020 Area Code Games: Aug. 11-13 at MLB Youth Academy in Compton, Calif.

ARIZONA FALL CLASSIC
Mailing Address: 9962 W. Villa Hermosa, Peoria, AZ 85383. **Telephone:** (602) 228-1592.
E-mail Address: azfallclassic@gmail.com.
Website: azfallclassic.com.
President: Tracy Heid
Event Director: Trevor Heid,
Information Directors: Tiffini Robinson, Tiana Eves

2020 EVENTS

Four Corner Classic . . . . Peoria, AZ, April 24-26

AZ Freshman
Fall Classic (class of 2024) . . . . Peoria, AZ, May 28-31

AZ Sophomore
Fall Classic (class of 2023) . . . . Peoria, AZ, Sept. 24-27

AZ Senior
Fall Classic (class of 2021) . . . . Peoria, AZ, Oct. 7-11

Senior All Academic Game . . . . .Oct. 8

Junior College All Star Series . . . . TBD

AZ Junior
Fall Classic (class of 2022) . . . . Peoria, AZ , Oct. 1-4

Junior All Academic Tryout & Game . . . . .Oct. 1

Easton Fall Classic . . . . Peoria, AZ, Oct. 22-25

BASEBALL FACTORY
Office Address: 9212 Berger Rd., Suite 200, Columbia, MD 21046. **Telephone:** (800) 641-4487, (410) 715-5080. **Fax:** (410) 715-1975. **E-mail Address:** info@baseballfactory.com. **Website:** baseballfactory.com.
Chief Executive Officer/Founder: Steve Sclafani. **President:** Rob Naddelman. **Chief Program Officer:** Jim Gemler. **Executive VP, Baseball Operations/Chairman, Under Armour All-America Game Selection Committee:** Steve Bernhardt. **Senior VP, Player Development:** Dan Forester. **VP, Tournament Division:** Justin Roswell. **VP, Business Development:** Dave Packer. **Chief Marketing Officer:** Tyler Blyleven. **Director, Marketing & Partnerships:** Catherine Lee. **Executive Director, College Recruiting:** Dan Mooney. **Senior Multimedia Producer:** Brian Johnson. **Senior Director, Web Development:** Wei Xue. **Senior Director, Event Experience:** Ryan Liddle. **Senior Director, Baseball Player Development Events:** Nolan Fuller. **Senior**

Director, Under Armour Baseball Factory National Tryout: Patrick Lawrence.
Executive Player Development Coordinator: Steve Nagler. **Senior Player Development Coordinators:** Adam Darvick, John Perko. **Senior Regional Player Development Coordinators:** Chris Brown, Rob Onolfi. **Regional Player Development Coordinators:** Robert Appleby, Ed Bach, Chris Brown, Josh Eldridge, Corson Fidler, Josh Hippensteel, Jane Lukas, David O'Neil, Julia Rice, Jesse Tome, Patrick Wuebben. **Director of College Recruiting:** Matt Richter.
Director, Athlete & Family Experience: Danielle Lawson. **Director, Social Media/Web Content:** Matt Lund. **Director of Player Development at FDI:** Mike Landis. **Director, Retail & Team Sales:** Lindsey Gutridge & Kevin Heinrich. **Director, Factory Athletics Foundation:** Emma Connor.

Under Armour All-America

Pre-Season Tournament . . . . .Jan. 12-14, Mesa, Ariz. (Sloan Park, Spring Training Home of the Chicago Cubs).
Under Armour
All-America Game . . . . .Summer, TBD

2018 Under Armour Baseball Factory National Tryouts/College PREP Recruiting Program: Year round at various locations across the country. Open to high school players, ages 14–18, with a separate division for middle school players, ages 12–14. **Full schedule:** www.baseballfactory.com/tryouts.

EAST COAST PROFESSIONAL SHOWCASE
Website: www.eastcoastpro.org. **Mailing Address:** Hoover Met Complex, 100 Ben Chapman Dr, Hoover, AL 25244. **E-mail Address:** info@eastcoastpro.org
Tournament Directors: John Castleberry, Rich Sparks, Sean Gibbs, Arthur McConnehead, Lori Bridges.
2020 Showcase: Aug. 1-4, Hoover Met Complex, 100 Ben Chapman Dr., Hoover, AL 35244.

IMPACT BASEBALL
Mailing Address: P.O. Box 47, Sedalia, NC 27342. **E-mail Address:** impactbaseballstaff@gmail.com. **Website:** impactbaseball.com. **Founder/CEO:** Andy Partin. **2020 Events:** Various dates, June-Aug.

NORTHWEST CHAMPIONSHIPS
Mailing Address: 9849 Fox Street, Aumsville, OR 97325. **Telephone:** (503) 302-7117. **E-mail Address:** joshuapwarner@gmail.com. **Website:** baseballnorthwest.com. **Tournament Organizer:** Josh Warner.

2020 EVENTS

Northwest Championships
    Date: August 13-16
    Location: Centralia, Wash.
    Facility: Borst Park Sports Complex
    Grad Classes: 2021-2023

Junior Northwest Championships
    Date: August 6-9
    Location: Centralia, Wash.
    Facility: Borst Park Sports Complex
    Grad Classes: 2024-2025

PERFECT GAME USA

(A Division of Perfect Game USA)
Mailing Address: 850 Twixt Town Rd. NE, Cedar Rapids, IA 52402. **Telephone:** (319) 298-2923. **Fax:** (319) 298-2924. **E-mail Address:** pgba@perfectgame.org. **Website:** perfectgame.org.
Year Founded: 1995.
President: Jerry Ford. **VP, Operations:** Taylor McCollough. **VP, Showcases/Scouting:** Greg Sabers.

PREP BASEBALL REPORT

Mailing Address: 4750 S. Vernon Ave, McCook, IL 60525. **Telephone:** 708-387-0500.
President: Sean Duncan. **Vice President of Operations and Multimedia:** Matt Yarber. **National Crosschecker:** Shooter Hunt. **National Supervisor:** Nathan Rode. **Director of College Scouting:** David Seifert. **Director of National Business Development:** Mark Svoroznak.

PROFESSIONAL BASEBALL INSTRUCTION—BATTERY INVITATIONAL

(for top high school pitchers and catchers)
Mailing Address: 12 Wright Way, Oakland NJ 07436. **Telephone:** (800) 282-4638. **Fax:** (201) 760-8820. **E-mail Address:** info@baseballclinics.com. **Website:** baseballclinics.com/battery invitational/
President: Doug Cinnella.
Director of PR/Marketing: Jim Monaghan.

SELECTFEST BASEBALL

Mailing Address: P.O. Box 852, Morris Plains, NJ 07950. **E-mail Address:** selectfest@selectfestbaseball.org. **Website:** selectfestbaseball.org. **Camp Directors:** Bruce Shatel, Robert Maida. **2020 Showcase:** TBD.

TEAM ONE BASEBALL

(A division of Baseball Factory)
Office Address: 220 Newport Center Drive, 11418, Newport Beach, CA 92660. **Telephone:** (800) 621-5452. **Fax:** (949) 209-1829. **E-Mail Address:** jroswell@teamonebaseball.com. **Website:** teamonebaseball.com.
Executive Director: Justin Roswell. **Chief Program Officer:** Jim Gemler. **Executive VP:** Steve Bernhardt. **Senior VP, Player Development:** Dan Forester.

2020 Under Armour Showcases:
For a full listing of showcases visit www.teamonebaseball.com/showcases.

2020 Under Armour Tournaments:

Under Armour Memorial Day Classic West .....May 22-25
Southern California (Cypress JC/Citrus JC)

Under Armour Memorial Day Classic East......May 22-25
Jupiter, Fla. (Roger Dean Complex)

Under Armour 4th of July Classic ....June 26 –June 29
La Verne, CA (Citrus JC/La Verne)

Under Armour Firecracker Classic.............. July 6-10
Jupiter, FL (Roger Dean Sports Complex)

Under Armour Southwest Championships 16U .... July 17-21
in La Verne, CA (University of La Verne)

Under Armour Southwest Championships 17U .... July 24 – July 28
La Verne, CA (University of La Verne)

Under Armour Fall Classic ....September 25–27
Jupiter, FL (Roger Dean Sports Complex)

Under Armour SoCal Classic Underclass ...October 16–18
La Verne, CA (University of La Verne)

Under Armour SoCal Classic Upperclass ...October 23-25
La Verne, CA (University of La Verne)
For a full listing of tournaments visit:
www.teamonebaseball.com/tournaments.

TOP 96 COLLEGE COACHES CLINICS

Mailing Address: 2639 Connecticut Avenue NW, Suite 250, Washington, DC 20008. **Telephone:** (202) 313-7385. **il Address:** info@top96.com. **Website:** top96.com. **Directors:** Doug Henson, Dave Callum.

YOUTH BASEBALL

ALL AMERICAN AMATEUR BASEBALL ASSOCIATION

Mailing Address: 1101 Flamingo Drive, APT 3106, Altoona, PA 16602.
Cell: (814) 931-8698.
E-Mail Address: aaabaprez@atlanticbb.net.
Website: aaabajohnstown.org
President: Mike Gossner
Executive Director: John Austin
2020 Events: AAABA National Tournament August3-8 in Johnstown PA.

AMATEUR ATHLETIC UNION OF THE UNITED STATES, INC.

Mailing Address: P.O. Box 22409, Lake Buena Vista, FL 32830. **Telephone:** (407) 828-3459. **Fax:** (407) 934-7242. **E-mail Address:** tmeyer@aausports.org. **Website:** aaubaseball.org.
Year Founded: 1982. **Senior Sport Manager, Baseball:** Tim Meyer.

AMERICAN AMATEUR BASEBALL CONGRESS

National Headquarters: 100 West Broadway, Farmington, NM 87401. **Telephone:** (505) 327-3120. **Fax:** (505) 327-3132. **E-mail Address:** info@aabc.us. **Website:** aabc.us.
Year Founded: 1935.
President: Richard Neely.

AMERICAN AMATEUR YOUTH BASEBALL ALLIANCE

Mailing Address: 3851 Iris Lane, Bonne Terre, MO 63628. **Telephone:** (314) 650-0028. **E-mail Address:** info@aayba.com. **Website:** aayba.com.
President, Baseball Operations: Carroll Wood.
President, **Business Operations:** Greg Moore.

AMERICAN LEGION BASEBALL

National Headquarters: American Legion Baseball, 700 N Pennsylvania St., Indianapolis, IN 46204.
Telephone: (317) 630-1213. **Fax:** (317) 630-1369. **E-mail Address:** baseball@legion.org. **Website:** legion.org/baseball.
Year Founded: 1925.
Program Coordinator: Steve Cloud.
2020 World Series (19 and under): Aug. 15-20 at Keeter Stadium, Shelby, N.C. 2019 Regional Tournaments (Aug. 7-11): **Northeast**—Shrewsbury, Mass.; Mid-**Atlantic**—Asheboro, N.C.; **Southeast**—Tampa, Fla..; Mid-**South**—Hastings, Neb.; **Great Lakes**—Charleston, Ill.; **Central Plains**—Sioux Falls, S.D.; **Northwest**—Lewiston, Ida.; **West**—Fairfield, Calif.

BABE RUTH LEAGUE

International Headquarters: 1670 Whitehorse-Mercerville Rd., Hamilton, NJ 08619. **Telephone:** (800) 880-3142. **Fax:** (609) 695-2505. **E-mail Address:** info@baberuthleague.org. **Website:** baberuthleague.org.
Year Founded: 1951.
President/Chief Executive Officer: Steven Tellefsen.

BASEBALL FOR ALL

Mailing Address: 30745 Pacific Coast Hwy #328 Los Angeles, CA 90265. **E-mail Address:** girlsbaseball@baseballforall.com. **Website:** BaseballForAll.com
Providing baseball programming for girls.

CALIFORNIA COMPETITIVE YOUTH BASEBALL

Mailing Address: P.O. Box 338, Placentia, CA 92870.
Telephone: (714) 993-2838. **E-mail Address:** ccybnet@gmail.com. **Website:** ccyb.net.
Tournament Director: Todd Rogers.

COCOA EXPO SPORTS CENTER

Mailing Address: 500 Friday Road, Cocoa, FL 32926.
Telephone: (321) 639-3976. **Fax:** (407) 390-9435. **E-mail Address:** brad@cocoaexpo.com. **Website:** cocoaexpo.com.
Activities: Spring training program, spring & fall leagues, instructional camps, team training camps, youth tournaments.

CONTINENTAL AMATEUR BASEBALL ASSOCIATION

Mailing Address: P.O. Box 1684 Mt. Pleasant, SC 29465. **Telephone:** (843) 860-1568. **E-mail Address:** Diamonddevils@aol.com. **Website:** cababaseball.com.
Year Founded: 1984.
Chief Executive Officer: Larry Redwine. **President/COO:** John Rhodes. **Executive Vice President:** Fran Pell.

COOPERSTOWN BASEBALL WORLD

Mailing Address: P.O. Box 646, Allenwood, NJ 08720.
Telephone: (888) CBW-8750. **Fax:** (888) CBW-8720.
E-mail: cbw@cooperstownbaseballworld.com.
Website: cooperstownbaseballworld.com.
Complex Address: Cooperstown Baseball World, SUNY-Oneonta, Ravine Parkway, Oneonta, NY 13820.
President: Debra Sirianni.
2020 Tournaments (15 Teams Per Week): Open to 12U, 13U, 14U, 15U, 16U

COOPERSTOWN DREAMS PARK

Mailing Address: 330 S. Main St., Salisbury, NC 28144.
Telephone: (704) 630-0050. **Fax:** (704) 630-0737. **E-mail Address:** info@cooperstowndreamspark.com. **Website:** cooperstowndreamspark.com.
Complex Address: 4550 State Highway 28, Milford, NY 13807.
Chief Operating Officer: Mike Walter. Director, **Baseball Operations:** Geoff Davis.
2020 Tournaments: June 6-Aug. 22.

COOPERSTOWN ALL STAR VILLAGE

Mailing Address: P.O. Box 670, Cooperstown, NY 13326. **Telephone:** (800) 327-6790. **Fax:** (607) 432-1076. **E-mail Address:** info@cooperstownallstarvillage.com. **Website:** cooperstownallstarvillage.com.

Team Registrations: Hunter Grace. **Hotel Room Reservations:** Tracie Jones. **Presidents:** Martin and Brenda Patton.

DIXIE YOUTH BASEBALL

Mailing Address: P.O. Box 877, Marshall, TX 75671. **Telephone:** (903) 927-2255. **Fax:** (903) 927-1846. **E-mail Address:** dyb@dixie.org. **Website:** youth.dixie.org.

Year Founded: 1955.
Commissioner: William Wade.

DIXIE BOYS BASEBALL

Mailing Address: P.O. Box 8263, Dothan, AL 36304. **Telephone:** (334) 793-3331. **E-mail Address:** jjones29@sw.rr.com. **Website:** baseball.dixie.org.

Commissioner/Chief Executive Officer: Sandy Jones.

DIZZY DEAN BASEBALL

Mailing Address: P.O. Box 856, Hernando, MS 38632. **Telephone:** (662) 429-4365. **E-mail Address:** danny phillips637@gmail.com. **Website:** dizzydeanbbinc.org.

Year Founded: 1962.
Commissioner: Danny Phillips. **President:** Chris Landry. **VP:** Bobby Dunn. **Secretary:** Joe Chandler. **Treasurer:** Jim Dunn.

HAP DUMONT YOUTH BASEBALL

(A Division of the National Baseball Congress)
E-mail Address: hapdumontbaseball@gmail.com.
Year Founded: 1974.
President: Bruce Pinkall

KC SPORTS TOURNAMENTS

Mailing Address: KC Sports, 6324 N. Chatham Ave., No. 136, Kansas City, MO 64151.
Telephone: (816) 587-4545. **Fax:** (816) 587-4549. **E-mail Address:** info@kcsports.org. **Website:** kcsports.org. **Activities:** USSSA Youth tournaments (ages 6-18).

LITTLE LEAGUE BASEBALL

International Headquarters: 539 US Route 15 Hwy, P.O. Box 3485, Williamsport, PA 17701-0485. **Telephone:** (570) 326-1921. **Fax:** (570) 326-1074. **E-Mail Address:** media@littleleague.org. **Website:** littleleague.org.

Year Founded: 1939.
Chairman: Hugh E. Tanner.
President and Chief Executive Officer: Stephen D. Keener. **Senior Vice President and Chief Financial Officer:** David Houseknecht. **Vice President, Operations:** Patrick Wilson. **Senior Vice President and Chief Marketing Officer:** Liz DiLullo Brown. **Senior Vice President and Chief Legal Officer:** Karl Eckweiler.

NATIONS BASEBALL-ARIZONA

Mailing Address: 20230 Cypress Rosehill Road, Tomball, TX 77377. **Telephone:** (877) 259-1150. **Website:** arizona.nations-baseball.com. **E-Mail:** info@nations-baseball.com.

NATIONAL AMATEUR BASEBALL FEDERATION

Mailing Address: P.O. Box 705, Bowie, MD 20718. **Telephone:** (410) 721-4727. **Fax:** (410) 721-4940.
E-mail Address: nabf1914@aol.com.
Website: nabf.com.
Year Founded: 1914.
Executive Director: Charles Blackburn.

INSTRUCTIONAL SCHOOLS/ PRIVATE CAMPS

ALL-STAR BASEBALL ACADEMY

Mailing Address: 1475 Phoenixville Pike Suite 12, West Chester, PA 19380. **Telephone:** (484) 770-8325. **Fax:** (484) 770-8336. **E-mail Address:** basba@allstarbaseball academy.com. **Website:** allstarbaseballacademy.com. **President/CEO :** Jim Freeman. **Executive Director:** Mike Manning.

AMERICAN BASEBALL FOUNDATION

Mailing Address: 833 Saint Vincent's Drive Suite 205A, Birmingham, AL 35205. **Telephone:** (205) 558-4235. **Fax:** (205) 918-0800. **E-mail Address:** abf@asmi.org. **Website:** americanbaseballfoundation.com. **Executive Director:** David Osinski.

ABC BASEBALL CAMPS

Mailing Address: 3020 ISSQ Pine Lake Road #12, Sammamish, WA 98075. **Telephone:** (800) 222-8152. **Fax:** (888) 751-8989. **E-mail Address:** sandi@abcsportscamps. com. **Website:** collegebaseballcamps.com/abc-baseball-camps/.

CHAMPIONS BASEBALL ACADEMY

Mailing Address: 5994 Linneman Street, Cincinnati, OH 45230. **Telephone:** (513) 831-8873. **Fax:** (513) 247-0040. **E-mail Address:** championsbaseball@ymail.com. **Website:** championsbaseball.net. **Director:** Mike Bricker.

ELEV8 SPORTS INSTITUTE

Mailing Address: 490 Dotterel Road, Delray Beach, FL 33444. **Telephone:** (800) 970-5896. **Fax:** (561) 865-7358. **E-mail Address:** info@elev8si.com. **Website:** elev8sport-sinstitute.com/

FROZEN ROPES TRAINING CENTERS

Mailing Address: 24 Old Black Meadow Rd., Chester, NY 10918. **Telephone:** (845) 469-7331. **Fax:** (845) 469-6742. **E-mail Address:** info@frozenropes.com. **Website:** frozenropes.com.

IMG ACADEMY

Mailing Address: IMG Academy, 5500 34th St. W., Bradenton, FL 34210. **Telephone:** (941) 749-8627. **Fax:** 941-739-7484. **E-mail Address:** colbe.herr@img.com. **Website:** imgacademy.com

MARK CRESSE BASEBALL SCHOOL

Mailing Address: P.O. Box 1596 Newport Beach, CA 92659. **Telephone:** (714) 892-6145. **Fax:** (714) 890-7017. **E-mail Address:** info@markcresse.com. **Website:** markcresse.com.

Owner/Founder: Mark Cresse.

US SPORTS CAMPS/NIKE BASEBALL CAMPS

Mailing Address: 1010 B Street Suite 450, San Rafael, CA 94901. **Telephone:** (800) 645-3226. **Fax:** (415) 479-6061. **E-mail Address:** baseball@ussportscamps.com. **Website:** ussportscamps.com/baseball/.

MOUNTAIN WEST BASEBALL ACADEMY

Mailing Address: 389 West 10000 South, South Jordan, UT 84095. **Telephone:** (801) 561-1700. **E-mail Address:** kent@utahbaseballacademy.com. **Website:** mountainwestbaseball.com. **Director:** Bob Keyes

NORTH CAROLINA BASEBALL ACADEMY

Mailing Address: 1137 Pleasant Ridge Road, Greensboro, NC 27409. **Telephone:** (336) 931-1118. **E-mail Address:** info@ncbaseball.com. **Website:** ncbaseball.com.
Owner/Director: Scott Bankhead.

PENNSYLVANIA DIAMOND BUCKS

Mailing Address: 2320 Whitetail Court, Hellertown, PA 18055. **Telephone:** (610) 838-1219, (610) 442-6998. **E-mail Address:** janciganick@yahoo.com. **Camp Director:** Jan Ciganick. **Head of Instruction:** Chuck Ciganick.

PROFESSIONAL BASEBALL INSTRUCTION

Mailing Address: 1300 Route 17 North, Ramsey Square Shopping Center, Ramsey, NJ 07446. **Telephone:** (800) 282-4638. **Fax:** (201) 760-8820. **E-**mail Address: info@baseballclinics.com. **Website:** baseballclinics.com. **President:** Doug Cinnella.
2020 Batter Invitational Showcase: October 2020

RIPKEN BASEBALL CAMPS

Mailing Address: 873 Long Drive, Averdeen, MD 21209. **Telephone:** (888) 747-5368. **E-mail Address:** information@ripkenbaseball.com. **Website:** ripken baseball.com.

SHO-ME BASEBALL CAMP

Mailing Address: P.O. Box 2270, Branson West, MO 65737. **Telephone:** (417) 338-5838. **Fax:** (417) 338-2610. **E-mail Address:** info@shomebaseball.com. **Website:** shomebaseball.com.

COLLEGE CAMPS

Almost all of the elite college baseball programs have summer/holiday instructional camps. Please consult the college section for listings.

SENIOR BASEBALL

MEN'S SENIOR BASEBALL LEAGUE
(18+, 25+, 35+, 45+, 55+, 65+)

Mailing Address: One Huntington Quadrangle, Suite 3NO7, Melville, NY 11747. **Telephone:** (631) 753-6725. **Fax:** (631) 753-4031.

President: Steve Sigler. **Vice President:** Gary D'Ambrisi.

E-Mail Address: info@msblnational.com.

Website: msblnational.com.

MEN'S ADULT BASEBALL LEAGUE
(18 and Over)

Mailing Address: One Huntington Quadrangle, Suite 3NO7, Melville, NY 11747. **Telephone:** (631) 753-6725. **Fax:** (631) 753-4031.

E-Mail Address: info@msblnational.com. **Website:** msblnational.com.

President: Steve Sigler. **Vice President:** Gary D'Ambrisi.

NATIONAL ADULT BASEBALL ASSOCIATION

Mailing Address: 5944 S. Kipling St., Suite 200, Littleton, CO 80127. **Telephone:** (800) 621-6479. **E-Mail:** nabanational@aol.com. **Website:** dugout.org.

President: Shane Fugita.

NATIONAL AMATEUR BASEBALL FEDERATION

Mailing Address: P.O. Box 705, Bowie, MD 20718. **Telephone:** (410) 721-4727. **Fax:** (410) 721-4940.

Email Address: nabf1914@aol.com.

Website: nabf.com.

Year Founded: 1914.

Executive Director: Charles Blackburn.

ROY HOBBS BASEBALL

Veterans (30 or 35 and Over), Masters (45 and Over), Legends (53 and Over); Classics (60 and Over), Vintage (65 and Over), Timeless (70 and Over), Forever Young (75 and Over).

Mailing Address: 4301-100 Edison Ave., Fort Myers, FL 33916. **Telephone:** (330) 923-3400. **E-Mail Address:** rh_bb@royhobbs.com. **Website:** royhobbs.com.

CEO: Tom Giffen. **President:** Rob Giffen.

DIRECTORIES
- AGENTS
- SERVICES

AGENT DIRECTORY

BALL PLAYERS AGENCY
1985 West Big Beaver Road, Suite 302
Troy, MI 48084
Phone: 877-878-7807
Fax: 248-281-5150
Web: ballplayersagency.com
E-mail: info@ballplayersagency.com
Storm T. Kirschenbaum, Esq. , Alex Hinz,
Esq. , Michael Bonanno , Mark Meisner

SPORTS MANAGEMENT WORLDWIDE
1100 NW Glisan St. Suite 2B
Portland, OR 97209
Phone: 503-445-7105
Fax: 503-445-9392
Web: sportsmanagementworldwide.com
E-mail: info@smww.com
Lynn Lashbrook

VERILL DANA SPORTS LAW GROUP
One Portland Square
Portland, ME 04101
Phone: 207-774-7499
Fax: 207-774-7499
Web: verilldana.com
E-mail: dabramson@verilldana.com
David S. Abramson

SERVICE DIRECTORY

SERVICE DIRECTORY

ACCESSORIES

FRANKLIN SPORTS
17 Campanellli Parkway
Stoughton, MA 02072
Phone: 781-344-1111
Fax: 781-341-0333
E-mail: customerservice@franklinsports.com

MIZUNO
4925 Avalon Ridge Parkway
One Jack Curran Way
Norcross, GA 30071
Phone: 800-966-1211
Fax: 770-448-3234
Web: mizunousa.com

RAWLINGS
510 Maryville University Dr., Suite 110
St. Louis, MO 63141
Phone: 866-678-4327
Web: rawlings.com

WILSON SPORTING GOODS
1 Prudential Plaza
130 East Randolph Street, Suite 600
Chicago, IL 60601
Phone: 800-800-9936
Web: wilson.com
E-mail: askwilson@wilson.com

APPAREL

DEMARINI
6435 NE Croeni Ave.
Hillsboro, OR 97124
Phone: 800-800-9932
Web: demarini.com

BAGS

DEMARINI
6435 NE Croeni Ave.
Hillsboro, OR 97124
Phone: 800-800-9932
Web: demarini.com

DIAMOND SPORTS
PO BOX 55090
Irvine, CA 92619
Phone: 949-409-9300
Fax: 949-409-9301
Web: diamond-sports.com
E-mail: info@diamond-sports.com

FORCE3 PRO GEAR
45 Banner Drive
Milford, CT 06480
Phone: 315-367-2331
Web: Force3progear.com
E-mail: support@force3progear.com

See our ad on the insert!

GERRY COSBY AND COMPANY
11 Pennsylvania Plaza
New York, NY, 10001
Phone: 877-563-6464
Fax: 212-967-0876
Web: cosbysports.com
Email: gcsmsg@cosbysports.com

LOUISVILLE SLUGGER
1 Prudential Plaza
130 East Randolph Plaza, Suite 600
Chicago, IL 60601
Phone: 800-800-9936
Web: slugger.com

MIZUNO
4925 Avalon Ridge Parkway
One Jack Curran Way
Norcross, GA 30071
Phone: 800-966-1211
Web: mizunousa.com

BASEBALLS

WILSON SPORTING GOODS
1 Prudential Plaza
130 East Randolph Street, Suite 600
Chicago, IL 60601
Phone: 800-800-9936
Web: wilson.com
E-mail: askwilson@wilson.com

DIAMOND SPORTS
PO BOX 55090
Irvine, CA 92619
Phone: 949-409-9300
Fax: 949-409-9301
Web: diamond-sports.com
E-mail: info@diamond-sports.com

RAWLINGS
510 Maryville University Dr. Suite 110
St. Louis, MO 63141
Phone: 866-678-4327
Web: rawlings.com

WILSON SPORTING GOODS
1 Prudential Plaza
130 East Randolph Street, Suite 600
Chicago, IL 60601
Phone: 800-800-9936
Web: wilson.com
E-mail: askwilson@wilson.com

BASES

C&H BASEBALL
10615 Technology Terrace #100
Lakewood Ranch, FL 34211
Phone: 941-462-3076
Fax: 941-462-3076
Web: chbaseball.com

See our ad on the inside cover!

BATS

DEMARINI
6435 NE Croeni Ave.
Hillsboro, OR 97124
Phone: 800-800-9932
Web: demarini.com

DIAMOND SPORTS
PO BOX 55090
Irvine, CA 92619
Phone: 949-409-9300
Fax: 949-409-9301
Web: diamond-sports.com
E-mail: info@diamond-sports.com

LOUISVILLE SLUGGER
1 Prudential Plaza
130 East Randolph Plaza, Suite 600
Chicago, IL 60601
Phone: 800-800-9936
Web: slugger.com

MIZUNO
4925 Avalon Ridge Parkway
One Jack Curran Way,
Norcross, GA 30071
Phone: 800-966-1211
Web: mizunousa.com

OLD HICKORY

OLD HICKORY
PO Box 588
White House, TN 37188
Phone: 866-PRO-BATS
Fax: 615-285-0512
Web: oldhickorybats.com
Email: mail@oldhickorybats.com

RAWLINGS
510 Maryville University Dr., Suite 110
St. Louis, MO 63141
Phone: 866-678-4327
Web: rawlings.com

THE WOOD BAT FACTORY
4924 NY0 28
Cooperstown, NY 13326
Phone: 607-282-4431
Web: thewoodbatfactory.com
E-mail: chrissy@thewoodbatfactory.com

BATTING CAGES

BALL FABRICS, INC.
510 West Arizona Ave.
DeLand, FL 32720
Phone: 866-360-1008
Fax: 386-740-7206
Web: www.ballfabrics.com
E-mail: info@ballfabrics.com

C&H BASEBALL
10615 Technology Terrace #100
Lakewood Ranch, FL 34211
Phone: 941-462-3076
Fax: 941-462-3076
Web: chbaseball.com

See our ad on the inside cover!

WEST COAST NETTING
5075 Flightline Drive
Kingman, AZ 86401
Phone: 928-692-1144
Fax: 928-692-1501
Web: westcoastnetting.com
E-mail: info@westcoastnetting.com

BATTING GLOVES

DEMARINI
6435 NE Croeni Ave.
Hillsboro, OR 97124
Phone: 800-800-9932
Web: demarini.com

FRANKLIN SPORTS
17 Campanellli Parkway
Stoughton, MA 02072
Phone: 781-344-1111
Fax: 781-341-0333
Web: franklinsports.com
E-mail: customerservice@franklinsports.com

MIZUNO
4925 Avalon Ridge Parkway
One Jack Curran Way,
Norcross, GA 30071
Phone: 800-966-1211
Web: mizunousa.com

RAWLINGS
510 Maryville University Dr., Suite 110
St. Louis, MO 63141
Phone: 866-678-4327
Web: rawlings.com

CONCESSION OPERATIONS

STADIUM1 SOFTWARE LLC
13479 Polo Trace Drive
Delray Beach, FL 33556
Phone: 561-779-4040
Fax: 561-498-8358
Web: www.stadium1.com
E-mail: ed.mullen@stadium1.com

EMBLEMS

THE EMBLEM SOURCE
4575 Westgrove #500
Addison, TX 75001
Phone: 214-793-7250
Web: theemblemsource.com
E-mail: larry@theemblemsource.com

ENGINEERED BACKSTOP DESIGN BUILD

C&H BASEBALL
10615 Technology Terrace #100
Lakewood Ranch, FL 34211
Phone: 941-462-3076
Fax: 941-462-3076
Web: chbaseball.com

See our ad on the inside cover!

WEST COAST NETTING
5075 Flightline Drive
Kingman, AZ 86401
Phone: 928-692-1144
Fax: 928-692-1501
Web: westcoastnetting.com
E-mail: info@westcoastnetting.com

FIELD COVERS/TARPS

C&H BASEBALL
10615 Technology Terrace #100
Lakewood Ranch, FL 34211
Phone: 941-462-3076
Fax: 941-462-3076
Web: chbaseball.com

See our ad on the inside cover!

FIELD WALL PADDING

C&H BASEBALL
10615 Technology Terrace #100
Lakewood Ranch, FL 34211
Phone: 941-462-3076
Fax: 941-462-3076
Web: chbaseball.com

See our ad on the inside cover!

WEST COAST NETTING
5075 Flightline Drive
Kingman, AZ 86401
Phone: 928-692-1144
Fax: 928-692-1501
Web: westcoastnetting.com
E-mail: info@westcoastnetting.com

FOOD SERVICE

STADIUM1 SOFTWARE LLC
13479 Polo Trace Drive
Delray Beach, FL 33556
Phone: 561-779-4040
Fax: 561-498-8358
Web: www.stadium1.com
E-mail: ed.mullen@stadium1.com

GLOVES

ALL-STAR SPORTING GOODS
17 Leominster Road
Shirley, MA 01464
Phone: 800-777-3810
Web: all-starsports.com
E-mail: weborders@all-starsports.com

See our ad on the insert!

DIAMOND SPORTS
PO BOX 55090
Irvine, CA 92619
Phone: 949-409-9300
Fax: 949-409-9301
Web: diamond-sports.com
E-mail: info@diamond-sports.com

FORCE3 PRO GEAR
45 Banner Drive
Milford, CT 06480
Phone: 315-367-2331
Web: Force3progear.com
E-mail: support@force3progear.com

See our ad on the insert!

LOUISVILLE SLUGGER
1 Prudential Plaza
130 East Randolph Street, Suite 600
Chicago, IL 60601
Phone: 800-800-9935
Web: slugger.com

MIZUNO
4925 Avalon Ridge Parkway
One Jack Curran Way
Norcross, GA 30071
Phone: 800-966-1211
Web: mizunousa.com

RAWLINGS
510 Maryville University Dr., Suite 110
St. Louis, MO 63141
Phone: 866-678-4327
Web: rawlings.com

WILSON SPORTING GOODS
1 Prudential Plaza
130 East Randolph Street, Suite 600
Chicago, IL 60601
Phone: 800-800-9936
Web: wilson.com
E-mail: askwilson@wilson.com

MUSIC/SOUND EFFECTS

SOUND DIRECTOR INC.
2918 SW Royal Way
Gresham, OR 97080
Phone: 503-665-6869
Fax: 503-914-1812
Web: sounddirector.com
E-mail: jj@sounddirector.com

NETTING/POSTS

BALL FABRICS, INC.
510 West Arizona Ave.
DeLand, FL 32720
Phone: 866-360-1008
Fax: 386-740-7206
Web: ballfabrics.com
E-mail: info@ballfabrics.com

C&H BASEBALL
10615 Technology Terrace #100
Lakewood Ranch, FL 34211
Phone: 941-462-3076
Fax: 941-462-3076
Web: chbaseball.com

See our ad on the inside cover!

WEST COAST NETTING, INC
5075 Flightline Dr.
Kingman, AZ 86401
Phone: 928-692-1144
Fax: 928-692-1501
Web: westcoastnetting.com
E-mail: info@westcoastnetting.com

PITCHING MACHINES

ATHLETIC TRAINING EQUIPMENT COMPANY
655 Spice Island Drive
Sparks, NV 89431
Phone: 800-800-9931
Web: atecsports.com

PLAYING FIELD PRODUCTS

C&H BASEBALL
10615 Technology Terrace #100
Lakewood Ranch, FL 34211
Phone: 941-462-3076
Fax: 941-462-3076
Web: chbaseball.com

See our ad on the inside cover!

WEST COAST NETTING, INC
5075 Flightline Dr.
Kingman, AZ 86401
Phone: 928-692-1144
Fax: 928-692-1501
Web: westcoastnetting.com
E-mail: info@westcoastnetting.com

PROTECTIVE EQUIPMENT

ALL-STAR SPORTING GOODS
17 Leominster Road
Shirley, MA 01464
Phone: 800-777-3810
Web: all-starsports.com
E-mail: weborders@all-starsports.com

See our ad on the insert!

C&H BASEBALL
10615 Technology Terrace #100
Lakewood Ranch, FL 34211
Phone: 941-462-3076
Fax: 941-462-3076
Web: chbaseball.com

See our ad on the inside cover!

DIAMOND SPORTS
PO BOX 55090
Irvine, CA 92619
Phone: 949-409-9300
Fax: 949-409-9301
Web: diamond-sports.com
E-mail: info@diamond-sports.com

EVOSHIELD
1 Prudential Plaza
130 East Randolph Street, Suite 600
Chicago, IL 60601
Phone: 800-800-9936
Web: evoshield.com

FORCE3 PRO GEAR
45 Banner Drive
Milford, CT 06480
Phone: 315-367-2331
Web: force3progear.com
E-mail: support@force3progear.com

See our ad on the insert!

MIZUNO
4925 Avalon Ridge Parkway
One Jack Curran Way
Norcross, GA 30071
Phone: 800-966-1211
Web: mizunousa.com

RAWLINGS
510 Maryville University Dr., Suite 110
St. Louis, MO 63141
Phone: 866-678-4327
Web: rawlings.com

WEST COAST NETTING
5075 Flightline Drive
Kingman, AZ 86401
Phone: 928-692-1144
Fax: 928-692-1501
Web: westcoastnetting.com
E-mail: info@westcoastnetting.com

WILSON SPORTING GOODS
1 Prudential Plaza
130 East Randolph Street, Suite 600
Chicago, IL 60601
Phone: 800-800-9936
Web: wilson.com
E-mail: askwilson@wilson.com

RADAR EQUIPMENT

POCKET RADAR, INC.
3535 Industrial Dr., Suite A4
Santa Rosa, CA 95403
Phone: 888-381-2672
Fax: 888-381-2672
Web: pocketradar.com
E-mail: tscaturro@pocketradar.com

STALKER SPORT RADAR
855 E Collins Blvd
Richardson, TX 75081
Phone: 972-398-3780
Web: stalkersportradar.com
E-mail: sales@stalkerradar.com

SCOREBOARD

STALKER SPORT RADAR
855 E Collins Blvd
Richardson, TX 75081
Phone: 972-398-3780
Web: stalkersportradar.com
E-mail: sales@stalkerradar.com

TRAINING EQUIPMENT

ATHLETIC TRAINING EQUIPMENT COMPANY
655 Spice Island Drive
Sparks, NV 89431
Phone: 800-800-9931
Web: atecsports.com

DIAMOND SPORTS
PO BOX 55090
Irvine, CA 92619
Phone: 949-409-9300
Fax: 949-409-9301
Web: www.diamond-sports.com
E-mail: info@diamond-sports.com

LOUISVILLE SLUGGER
1 Prudential Plaza
130 East Randolph Street, Suite 600
Chicago, IL 60601
Phone: 800-800-9935
Web: slugger.com

WEST COAST NETTING, INC
5075 Flightline Dr.
Kingman, AZ 86401
Phone: 928-692-1144
Fax: 928-692-1501
Web: westcoastnetting.com
E-mail: info@westcoastnetting.com

UNIFORMS

FRANKLIN SPORTS
17 Campanellli Parkway
Stoughton, MA 02072
Phone: 781-344-1111
Fax: 781-341-0333
E-mail: customerservice@franklinsports.com

MIZUNO
4925 Avalon Ridge Parkway
One Jack Curran Way,
Norcross, GA 30071
Phone: 800-966-1211
Fax: 770-448-3234
Web: mizunousa.com

WILSON SPORTING GOODS
1 Prudential Plaza
130 East Randolph Street, Suite 600
Chicago, IL 60601
Phone: 800-800-9936
Web: wilson.com
E-mail: askwilson@wilson.com

WINDSCREENS

BALL FABRICS, INC.
510 West Arizona Ave.
DeLand, FL 32720
Phone: 866-360-1008
Fax: 386-740-7206
Web: www.ballfabrics.com
E-mail: info@ballfabrics.com

C&H BASEBALL
10615 Technology Terrace #100
Lakewood Ranch, FL 34211
Phone: 941-462-3076
Fax: 941-462-3076
Web: chbaseball.com

See our ad on the inside cover!

WEST COAST NETTING, INC
5075 Flightline Dr.
Kingman, AZ 86401
Phone: 928-692-1144
Fax: 928-692-1501
Web: westcoastnetting.com
E-mail: info@westcoastnetting.com

INDEX

DAN THORNBERG/EYEEM

MAJOR LEAGUE TEAMS

MINOR LEAGUE TEAMS

BRIAN WESTERHOLT

MINOR LEAGUE TEAMS, CONT.

INDEPENDENT TEAMS

OTHER ORGANIZATIONS

DAVID SCHOFIELD

MIKE JANES/FOUR SEAM IMAGES

OTHER ORGANIZATIONS, CONT.

Patadays